Routledge Handbook of Asian Law

The *Routledge Handbook of Asian Law* is a cutting-edge and comprehensive resource that surveys the interdisciplinary field of Asian law. Written by an international team of experts, the chapters within cover issues as diverse as family law and Islamic courts, decentralisation and the revival of traditional forms of law, and discourses on the rule of law, human rights, commercial law developments and environmental protection.

The volume is divided into five parts, covering:

- Asia in law, the humanities and social sciences;
- The political economy of law in Asia – law in the context of Asian development;
- Asian traditions and their transformations;
- Law, the environment, and access to land and natural resources; and
- People in Asia and their rights.

Offering an overview of the full spectrum of law in Asia, the *Handbook* is an invaluable resource for academics, researchers, lawyers, and graduate and undergraduate students studying this ever-evolving field.

Christoph Antons is Professor of Law at Deakin University, Geelong, Australia. He is also Chief Investigator with the ARC Centre of Excellence for Creative Industries and Innovation, an Affiliated Fellow of the Max Planck Institute for Innovation and Competition, and a Senior Fellow of the Centre for Development Research, University of Bonn, Germany.

Routledge Handbook of Asian Law

Edited by
Christoph Antons

Routledge
Taylor & Francis Group
LONDON AND NEW YORK

First published 2017 by Routledge

2 Park Square, Milton Park, Abingdon, Oxfordshire OX14 4RN
52 Vanderbilt Avenue, New York, NY 10017

Routledge is an imprint of the Taylor & Francis Group, an informa business

First issued in paperback 2019

British Library Cataloguing in Publication Data
A catalogue record for this book is available from the British Library

Library of Congress Cataloging in Publication Data
Names: Antons, Christoph, editor.
Title: Routledge handbook of Asian law / edited by Christoph Antons. Other titles: Handbook of Asian law
Description: Milton Park, Abingdon, Oxon ; New York, NY : Routledge, 2017. | Includes bibliographical references and index.
Identifiers: LCCN 2016022528| ISBN 9780415659406 (hardback) | ISBN 9781315660547 (ebook)
Subjects: LCSH: Law—Asia.
Classification: LCC KNC79 .R68 2017 | DDC 349.5—dc23
LC record available at https://lccn.loc.gov/2016022528

ISBN: 978-0-415-65940-6 (hbk)
ISBN: 978-0-367-37495-2 (pbk)

Typeset in Bembo Std
by Swales & Willis Ltd, Exeter, Devon, UK

Contents

Contributors

Christoph Antons is Professor in the School of Law, Deakin University, Geelong, Australia. He is an Affiliated Research Fellow, Max Planck Institute for Innovation and Competition, Munich, Senior Fellow, Centre for Development Research, University of Bonn, and Chief Investigator, ARC Centre of Excellence for Creative Industries and Innovation. He has published widely on intellectual property law and law and society in Asia.

Rosy Antons-Sutanto holds a PhD in social and cultural anthropology from Leiden University. She has held teaching and visiting research positions in sociology, anthropology, history and art history at Leiden University, Griffith University, La Trobe University and Charles Darwin University. She is currently an Honorary Fellow at the Alfred Deakin Institute for Citizenship and Globalisation at Deakin University, Geelong, Australia.

Vivienne Bath is Professor of Chinese and International Business Law, Director of the Centre for Asian and Pacific Law and Director of Research at the China Studies Centre at the University of Sydney. Her research interests are in international business and investment law, private international law and Chinese law. Representative publications include 'Foreign Investment, the National Interest and National Security: Foreign Direct Investment in Australia and China' (2012) *Sydney Law Review* 34(1): 5–34.

Geoffrey Benjamin is currently a Senior Associate at the Centre for Liberal Arts and Social Sciences (CLASS) of Nanyang Technological University. Benjamin's publications include studies on the languages, societies, cultures, prehistory and musics of the Malay world, as well on issues of general socio-cultural theory. He also co-edited *Tribal Communities in the Malay Word: Historical, Social and Cultural Perspectives* (2002, IIAS/ISEAS). His book *Temiar Religion, 1964–2012: Enchantment, Disenchantment and Re-enchantment in Malaysia's Uplands* (NUS Press) appeared in 2014.

Simon Butt is Professor of Indonesian law at Sydney Law School. He has written several books on Indonesian law, including *Corruption and Law in Indonesia* (2011, Routledge), *The Constitution of Indonesia* (with Tim Lindsey, 2012, Hart), *Climate Change and Forest Governance* (with Rosemary Lyster and Timothy Stephens, 2015, Routledge) and *The Constitutional Court and Democracy in Indonesia* (2015, Martinus Nijhoff). Simon has also worked as a consultant on the Indonesian legal system and has worked on many legal development programmes in Indonesia.

Albert H. Y. Chen is Professor in Constitutional Law, University of Hong Kong. His books include *An Introduction to the Legal System of the People's Republic of China* (4th edn, 2011, LexisNexis), *The World of Jurisprudence* (2nd edn, 2013, Chinese University of Politics and Law Press; in Chinese), and *The World of Constitutional Jurisprudence* (2014, Chinese University of Politics and Law Press; in Chinese). He is co-editor of *Human Rights in Asia* (2006, Routledge), *Administrative Law and Governance in Asia* (2009, Routledge), *Legal Reforms in China and Vietnam* (2010, Routledge) and *Public Law in East Asia* (2013, Routledge), and editor of *Constitutionalism in Asia in the Early Twenty-first Century* (2014, Cambridge University Press).

Dr Philippe Cullet is Professor of International and Environmental Law at SOAS University of London and a Senior Visiting Fellow at the Centre for Policy Research in New Delhi. His main areas of research are environmental law, natural resources and socio-economic rights. His current work focuses on water and sanitation law and policy. His latest book, co-edited with L. Bhullar, is *Sanitation Law and Policy in India: An Introduction to Basic Instruments* (2015, Oxford University Press).

Yves Dezalay is Research Professor Emeritus at the National Center for Scientific Research (CNRS), Paris, France. His research focuses on globalisation, the sociology of law and the legal profession. In addition to the books co-authored with Bryant G. Garth, his works include *Marchand de Droit* (1992, Fayard). He won the International Prize of the Law and Society Association in 2009.

Daniel Fitzpatrick is a Professor at the Australian National University who writes on property and development. In 2007 he won the Hart Article Prize from the UK Socio-Legal Association. He has been a Global Visiting Professor at New York University, a Visiting Professor at the National University of Singapore, and a Distinguished Visitor at the University of Toronto. He was an Australian Research Council Future Fellow from 2012 to 2016.

Bryant G. Garth is Chancellor's Professor at the University of California-Irvine School of Law, where he has been since 2012. He served as Dean of Southwestern Law School (2005–12) and Director of the American Bar Foundation (1990–2004). His scholarship focuses on the legal profession, the sociology of law and globalisation. Books co-authored with Yves Dezalay include *Dealing in Virtue* (1996, University of Chicago Press), *The Internationalization of Palace Wars* (2002, University of Chicago Press) and *Asian Legal Revivals* (2010, University of Chicago Press).

Iza Hussin is a Lecturer in politics and international studies at the University of Cambridge and the Mohamed Noah Fellow at Pembroke College. She is the author of *The Politics of Islamic Law: Local Elites, Colonial Authority and the Making of the Muslim State* (2016, University of Chicago Press), as well as of numerous articles on Islam, colonialism and law's travels. Current research projects include a book on legal circulations in the Indian Ocean arena.

Rajeswari Kanniah is an Honorary Fellow of the School of Law, Deakin University. She holds a doctorate in law, and previously served as Dean of the School of Law in two private universities in Malaysia and as a part-time Lecturer in Law at Heriot Watt University, Malaysia. She has published on intellectual property rights and consumer protection law.

Tim Lindsey is Redmond Barry Distinguished Professor, Malcolm Smith Professor of Asian Law and Director of the Centre for Indonesian Law, Islam and Society at Melbourne Law School. A founder of *The Australian Journal of Asian Law,* his publications include *Indonesia: Law and Society*; *The Indonesian Constitution* (2nd edn, 2008, Federation Press), *Islam, Law and the State in Southeast Asia* (three volumes, 2012, I. B. Tauris) and *Law, Society and Transition in Myanmar* (with Melissa Crouch, 2014, Hart).

Pip Nicholson is Professor of Law and Director of the Asian Law Centre and Associate Director (Vietnam), Melbourne Law School, at the University of Melbourne. Her teaching and research are in dispute resolution, comparative legal studies, law and reform in Asia, and law and society in Asia. She currently holds an ARC grant exploring drugs law and practice in Vietnam. Pip was a barrister and solicitor of the Supreme Court of Victoria (1990–92).

Luke Nottage (BCA, LLB, PhD VUW, LLM *Kyoto*) specialises in arbitration, corporate governance, contract law and consumer product safety law, especially in the Asia-Pacific region. He is Professor of Comparative and Transnational Business Law at Sydney Law School and Co-Director of the Australian Network for Japanese Law. Luke's publications include *Foreign Investment and Dispute Resolution in Asia* (2011, Routledge), ten other books, and more than 100 chapters and refereed articles.

John Ohnesorge is George Young Bascom Professor of Law at the University of Wisconsin Law School, where he teaches administrative law, business organisations, Chinese law, and law and development. He directed Wisconsin's East Asian Legal Studies Center and chaired the Wisconsin China Initiative. He has published extensively on issues related to law, development and East Asia, and is currently writing on the regulation of the Chinese legal profession, and on law and development in Taiwan.

Randall Peerenboom is an Associate Fellow of the Oxford University Centre for Socio-Legal Studies. He has been a consultant to the Asian Development Bank, Ford Foundation, EU–China, UNDP and other international organisations on legal reforms and rule of law in China and Asia, and has served as co-editor-in-chief of *The Hague Journal of Rule of Law.* His many publications focus on law and development, rule of law, human rights and legal theory.

Noer Fauzi Rachman holds a PhD in environmental science, policy and management from the University of California, Berkeley. He is Senior Researcher at the Sajogyo Institute for Indonesian Agrarian Studies and Documentation, Samdhana Institute Fellow. He is a leading scholar-activist in critical agrarian studies and the agrarian reform movement.

Mia Siscawati holds a PhD in anthropology from the University of Washington, Seattle. She is a Lecturer in, and Head of, the Gender Studies Graduate Programme, Graduate Programme in Multidisciplinary Studies, Universitas Indonesia (UI). She also serves as an Associate Researcher at the Center for Anthropological Studies, Faculty of Social and Political Sciences (FISIP), Universitas Indonesia, and as an Associate Lecturer in the graduate programme in anthropology, Department of Anthropology, FISIP, University of Indonesia. She has been focusing her work on the linkages between gender, forest tenure and forest governance, as well as the gendered dimension of forest land use.

Cait Storr is a Sessional Lecturer and PhD candidate at Melbourne Law School, University of Melbourne, Australia. Her research examines issues of law and colonialism in the Pacific region.

David Streckfuss is an Independent Scholar and Honorary Fellow at the University of Wisconsin-Madison who contributes regularly to Asian publications. His book, *Truth on Trial in Thailand: Defamation, Treason, and* Lèse-Majesté, was published by Routledge in 2011. He is presently writing a book on the global experience of *lèse-majesté* through the ages.

Roman Tomasic is Professor of Law at the School of Law and Business School, University of South Australia in Adelaide, and Visiting Professor of Company Law at Durham Law School in the UK. He has published widely on areas of comparative corporate law and insolvency law, with a particular interest in East Asia.

Peter Vandergeest is Professor of Geography at York University, Toronto. His research over the past thirty years has focused on agrarian and environmental transformations in Southeast Asia, with specific attention to resource access, livelihoods, rural livelihoods, territorialisation and state-making. He is currently assessing new approaches to environmental governance in mainland Southeast Asia, with specific attention to new market mechanisms, including sustainability certification, and the involvement of non-state actors in governing access to rural resources.

Jane K. Winn is Charles I. Stone Professor, University of Washington School of Law, Seattle, Washington. Her research focuses on the impact of technological innovation and globalisation on legal institutions in the United States, the European Union, China and India. She received Fulbright research grants for her work in China in 2008 and 2016.

Peter K. Yu is Professor of Law and Co-Director of the Center for Law and Intellectual Property at Texas A&M University School of Law. Born and raised in Hong Kong, he has served as Wenlan Scholar Chair Professor at Zhongnan University of Economics and Law in Wuhan, China, and Visiting Professor of Law at University of Haifa, University of Hong Kong and University of Strasbourg.

Dr Zinian Zhang is a Lecturer in commercial law at University of Leeds, England. His research focuses on corporate reorganisation law. In 2014, he finished his PhD thesis at University of Durham, supervised by Professor Roman Tomasic. Before joining the Leeds Law School early in 2016, Dr Zhang was a post-doc research fellow at Singapore Management University, advised by Professor Tang Hang Wu. Dr Zhang practised law in China for many years before entering academia.

Part I

Asia in law, the humanities and social sciences

1 What is 'Asian law'?

Asia in law, the humanities and social sciences

Christoph Antons

Introduction: The economic and social transformation of Asian countries after World War II

Although there are now many apparent success stories of economic development elsewhere, it was in Asia that countries first achieved the transition from developing to developed country status and broke into the ranks of what had been up to that point an exclusively 'Western' club. Japan, an early role model for the rest of Asia (Allen, 1981; Yamamura and Yasuba, 1987), was soon followed by a further group of countries, often lumped together as 'the Asian tigers'. Precisely who the 'Asian tigers' are and from which regions of Asia they come has changed from time to time. In the late 1980s and early 1990s, there was talk of the 'four Asian tigers with a dragon head', referring to South Korea, Taiwan, Hong Kong and Singapore (Castells, 1992). This led some commentators at the time to infer a connection between Confucianism and economic development (for example Vogel, 1991; Redding, 1993, 1996), which appeared in total contrast to the view of Confucianism as an obstacle to modernity held by early twentieth-century thinkers such as Max Weber (Tu Wei-Ming, 1996) and by modernisation enthusiasts among Asian intellectuals during the same period (Wong, 1996). Soon, however, the 'Asian tigers' were joined by Southeast Asian countries with no Confucian cultures, to which economists referred as 'second-tier newly industrialising economies'.[1] Indonesia, Thailand and Malaysia were included besides Japan, South Korea, Taiwan, Hong Kong and Singapore in the World Bank's influential *East Asian Miracle* study of 1993 (World Bank, 1993). Interestingly, the study did not yet include the most recent examples of Asian economic success, the People's Republic of China (PRC) and India (Peerenboom, 2007; Panagariya, 2008).

The apparent economic success of these countries paralleled diplomatic efforts of countries in 'the region' to spread these economic models more widely and to integrate regional economies. 'Asia Pacific' became the buzzword of recent decades.[2] Initially understood as those Asian countries that actually face the Pacific, it expanded with the formation of the Asia-Pacific Economic Cooperation (APEC) to include countries across the Pacific in North and South America, Australia and New Zealand in the South Pacific, and finally also to Asian countries that were not actually facing the Pacific, such as India and Association of Southeast Asian Nations (ASEAN) member Myanmar. The latest turn in this strategic expansion is the use by regional politicians of the term 'Indo-Pacific region' (Medcalf, 2013). It demonstrates the rising importance of India in economic and strategic terms for those countries that are geographically situated further East.

The emergence of 'Asian law'

Perhaps surprisingly, for a long time the academic discipline of law took little notice of the political and economic changes that were taking place in Asia (Antons, 1995). In comparative law, the laws of Asian countries were seen as belonging to European or US American 'legal families' based on transfers of laws to those countries that had been colonised and on voluntary adoption of European models by countries that were never colonised, such as Japan and Thailand. Where specific 'Asian law' was discussed, it was distinguished from the 'legal families' as 'law in the Far East', 'religious legal systems' (Zweigert and Kötz, 1998), or 'legal tradition' (Glenn, 2007), and the focus was on pre-colonial law transmitted in written form. The unwritten law of communities at the grassroots level had, of course, been of interest to anthropologists (who were often originally trained as lawyers) ever since the discipline had emerged in the nineteenth century.[3] Their writings remained on the margins of mainstream legal study, however, as related largely to 'isolated living' or 'tribal' societies (Donovan and Anderson, 2003: 19–20). After World War II, the governments of young nation states often continued this dismissive attitude towards unwritten, local sources of law.[4] At the same time, the first few decades after independence were often politically tumultuous, and this left little time and few resources for the systematic study of the developing legal systems.

There were exceptions, however, to this relatively low level of interest in the legal systems of Asian countries immediately after World War II. One notable exception was the encounter of the US American occupying forces in Japan with Japanese law and administration. US American lawyers were involved in the drafting of new laws (including of the Constitution), but also reflecting on their experience, once they were back in the United States (Blakemore, 1947). Particularly prominent in Japanese law reform during this period were American lawyers with experience of the civil law system or with knowledge of Japanese language and the legal system. One of them, Alfred Oppler, advocating a gradual approach, explained that '[t]he Japanese would not be able to work an artificially imposed system which differed fundamentally from what they have practised up to the present time' (quoted in Dean, 1997: 78–79, at fn. 95). The American postwar presence in East Asia helped to trigger an academic interest in legal developments in Japan, Korea and China that outlasted the administrative needs of the occupation period. Columbia University, the University of Washington and Harvard University all established courses and (East) Asian Law Programs in the 1950s and 1960s. They have since been followed by many others and the interest in legal developments in Asia has broadened from East Asia to other parts of Asia. Outside of the United States, an early initiative from within the legal profession and the judiciary was the foundation in 1966 of the LAWASIA association, which has now more than 1,500 members from across 50 countries and is publishing its own journal.

Of course, although the situation in Japan at the end of World War II was somewhat exceptional, the encounter between introduced norms and local legal traditions in Asia by that time already had a long tradition. In those countries that had experienced colonisation, various European and neighbouring Asian powers, as well as the Americans, had introduced their laws from the late fifteenth century onwards. Other countries, such as Japan and Thailand, themselves undertook law reform in accordance with Western models after they were forced into unequal treaties exempting the citizens of their treaty partners from local law (Kayaoğlu, 2014; Loos, 2006; Vandergeest, Chapter 15 in this volume). In the case of Japan, the new Japanese laws were subsequently transferred to the Japanese colonies in Korea and Taiwan.

Iza Hussin, in Chapter 2, describes the movement of law across Asia in the nineteenth century. Rather than seeing it as a simple transfer from West to East, she shows how the law changes its character during these travels and sometimes flows back in the opposite direction. Such tracking of law across Asia can help us to better understand its role in Asia's transformation and as a field of Asian studies. There are many similarities between these early movements of law and the current ones described in this volume: the separate domain for religion and custom created in British India and Malaya; the selective adaptation of European legal instruments; the forum shopping across jurisdictions; the conflict between law as a mobile and universal resource and demands for the local and particular in the form of tradition and custom. Hussin convincingly explains that what happened where the law stopped from the metropole to distant sites of Empire is an important, yet overlooked, question in comparative law. The law was translated and rearticulated in critical nodes such as Calcutta and Singapore, and it is this rearticulated law that was ultimately introduced in other parts of the British Empire in Asia. Local projects, rulers and middlemen also played an important role in this rearticulation, which was not the exclusive domain of colonial administrators. Law thereby not only became an instrument of change, but also assured the maintenance and reconstruction of 'tradition'. The current discussions about the removal of the Victorian era Criminal Code provision prohibiting 'gross indecency' between men in Singapore and India serve as example for this reinterpretation of colonial law in a different social context. Asian law, then, in Hussin's definition, 'traces a line of struggle between the general and the particular, and describes a political economy peculiar to each site, in which local actors translate, domesticate and rearticulate law to fit and to reconstruct what is traditional, legitimative and authoritative'.

Lawyers, administrators and university teachers returning from the colonies during the decolonisation movement after World War II also continued to write about and share their experiences (for example Hickling, 2001). In countries that had been colonial powers in the region, legal scholarship related to former Asian colonies continued, although often on a par with academic work on a country's colonies in other parts of the world and/or developing countries more generally and not specifically focused on Asia.[5]

However, the onset of the Cold War and the continuing fragility of the new countries soon led to a militarisation and to new forms of authoritarianism that had little need for refined legal arguments. Legal academics with teaching experience in the colonies often turned to the social sciences in later years.[6] In addition, the US American-led 'law and development' movement of the 1960s in Latin American developing countries was subsequently regarded as a failure and reviewed in a famous self-critique by David Trubek and Marc Galanter (1974). Following this criticism, for a while legal academics shied away to some extent from discussions of law and development for fear of being branded 'legal imperialists' (Gardner, 1980). A notable exception was what Scott Newton (2006: 183) has called a 'distinct (British/Commonwealth, African and Asian) school of the political economy of law', in which he includes people such as Francis Snyder, Anthony Carty, Upendra Baxi, Yash Ghai, Abdullahi An-Naim and, from outside the Commonwealth and the Anglophone world, Boaventura de Sousa Santos. Important exceptions specifically regarding Asia also include the work of comparative law professor M. B. Hooker on Southeast Asia and of political scientist Daniel Lev on Indonesia.

During the 1980s, however, lawyers and social scientists began to take notice of the rapid transformation taking place in Asia. They began to ask questions about the role of law and regulation in these processes. The enlarged concept of the Asia-Pacific meant that research centres and institutes with a comparative regional research focus were no longer confined to the United States and Europe, but also were now founded in Australia,[7] Canada and, of course, in many countries of Asia.[8] The parallel development of Asian studies disciplines means that many younger scholars interested in Asian law today are trained not only in law, but often also in contemporary Asian studies, or social sciences with an Asian focus, and are either native speakers or fluent in languages relevant for their work.[9] Vice versa, there is a growing interest in the various disciplines of Asian studies in regional legal debates and relevant work has been published by economists (Jomo and Wong Sau Ngan, 2008), anthropologists (von Benda-Beckmann, 1979; Dove, 2005; Lucas and Warren, 2003, 2013; Bowen, 2003; McCarthy, 2004), linguists, country and area specialists (Cao, 2004; Burns, 1999; Jacobsen and Bruun, 2000), geographers (Vandergeest and Peluso, 2001a, 2001b), political scientists (Lev, 2000; Jayasuriya, 1999), historians (Steenstrup, 1996; Fasseur, 1994, 2007; Coppel, 1999) and philosophers (Bauer and Bell, 1999).

The promise of multidisciplinary work

Given sufficient elasticity of disciplinary boundaries, the growing interest in so many different disciplines should generate a lively debate. The question about the disciplinary nature of work related to 'Asian law' may, in the future, largely be a question for purists and faculty administrators eager to protect their respective disciplines. The earlier work on Asian legal 'tradition' and that of anthropologists has long been recognised in comparative law (Glenn, 2007; Menski, 2000). As Asian countries become important partners in international trade and educational exchange, they are also increasingly included in comparative studies in the various sub-disciplines of law (for example du Plessis et al., 2014; Heath, 2003; Goldstein and Straus, 2009; Ginsburg and Chen, 2009). On the side of socio-legal studies, the great openness of law and society studies and of Asian studies, both pioneered in the United States, to contributions from many different disciplines and similar approaches in regulatory studies (Gillespie and Peerenboom, 2009) mean that there are now also a number of well-established research fields that are sufficiently broad to accommodate exciting multidisciplinary debates. They can provide an intersection for meetings of academics that are eager to break out of the straightjacket of narrowly defined disciplinary questions.

This book attempts to show a cross-section of such work. Because it appears in an Asian studies series, it allows lawyers with an interest in Asia to approach topical issues without first having to decide into which of the narrow pigeon holes of legal specialisation such work can be placed. It also allows social scientists to examine the legal background of their research questions and to see how it interacts with the detailed knowledge of social context that only they can provide. The remaining part of this introductory chapter will follow the outline of the book and explain the chapters in context.

Law in the context of Asian development

Much of the more recent scholarship on Asian law has been focused on law in the context of Asian development (Jones, 1994; Antons, 1995, 2003b; Jayasuriya, 1999; Gillespie, 1999; Ohnesorge, 2003; Peerenboom, 2006). For those that became interested in such questions during the 1980s, this meant an initial concentration on commercial law and how it was applied in what became seen as the 'Asian model' of capitalism. The Cold War years were not conducive to broader visions of the 'rule of law'. Especially in those countries that were seen as frontline states in the Cold War, and in the real wars that erupted in Korea and Vietnam, many authoritarian and military-backed regimes came to power. They attracted relatively little criticism from Western allies, as long as they were ideologically firm and anti-Communist. They tended to concentrate on massive economic development efforts and law was employed as a tool in this context. The nature of the developmental regimes required some commercial law reform, especially after the paradigm shift in development economics from import substitution to export-led development and the subsequent importance of foreign investment. On the public law side, however, reform efforts were blocked and discussions about human or political rights were nipped in the bud. With constitutional and institutional balancing mechanisms largely absent, law became an instrument in the hands of the rulers. It was mistrusted by foreign investors and trading partners, and it was avoided as far as possible by the population.

The end of the Cold War brought the beginning of what Trubek and Santos (2006) have called the 'second moment' in law and development, with its focus on neoliberal policies and the policy prescriptions of the Washington Consensus. However, analysts soon pointed out that countries were either resisting these policy prescriptions openly or, more frequently, secretly subverting them.[10] Trubek and Santos (2006) conclude with an outlook on the emerging paradigm of a 'third moment', with much more heterogeneous approaches. In the context of Asia, this heterogeneity and complexity is also the result of a much more diverse landscape after the socialist countries of China and Vietnam and the emerging giant of India are included in the discussions.

John Ohnesorge, in Chapter 3, points towards the importance of the experiences of Japan, Korea, Taiwan and China for any hypothesis of how law and legal institutions can function to facilitate development. He stresses the complexity of the task in view of different definitions of development and the usefulness of the developmental history of East Asia in this context. Because of their contrast to established theories of law and development, such theories face an 'East Asia problem' that resembles the 'England problem' of sociologist Max Weber, who struggled with the fact that the country initiating the Industrial Revolution could do so without having what, in his view, was a 'rational' legal system.[11] Ohnesorge examines the divergence of the East Asian experience from mainstream models in the fields of private law, the law of business organisations, and public law and governance. He finds that the experiences of Japan, South Korea and Taiwan differ more in function than form from mainstream law and development models, whereas China challenges such models in terms of both form and function. He sees the importance of the regional experiences for the empirical testing not only of the neoliberal prescriptions of the so-called Washington Consensus, but also of more recent theories regarding the return of state capitalism, the 'new developmental state' or the alternative vision of the BRICS countries (that is, Brazil, Russia, India, China and South Africa). Ultimately, Ohnesorge concludes that mainly two lessons can be drawn from law and development in East Asia: first, industrial policy does not necessarily lead to debilitating rent-seeking and corruption, but close attention has to be paid to local circumstances; and second, openness to foreign direct investment (FDI) does not preclude government screening on industrial policy grounds, although the exact policy mix will depend on the bargaining power of individual countries.

The various fortunes of the 'East Asian model' of development against this backdrop are also the topic of Randall Peerenboom in Chapter 4. He shows the origins of the East Asian model in the questioning of neoliberal orthodoxy by political scientists such as Chalmers Johnson, and how policy prescriptions and models moved from the Washington Consensus, strong in particular after the Asian crisis, to the Beijing

Consensus more recently. However, China's Twelfth Five-Year Plan, with its transition to a consumption-based economy, signals a further shift. Peerenboom sees a post-Washington, post-Beijing Consensus (PWBC) emerging that reflects the current policies of leading developing countries. Examples from the BRICS group serve to show that there are now very heterogeneous approaches that require an emphasis on local context rather than 'one size fits all' models. While the emphasis on process in what Peerenboom regards as the 'new developmental state' paradigm in his view suits the pragmatic, experimental approach of the Chinese, the second part of the chapter shows that, as far as legal developments in China are concerned, there is not much news after all. The *Decision of the Central Committee of the Communist Party of China (CCP) concerning Some Major Issues in Comprehensively Deepening Reform* of 2013 has much to say about the economy and development as 'the key to resolve all of our country's problems', but relatively little about law reform. Peerenboom finds that there are calls for the rule of law and other broad principles, but that they have to be read in conjunction with other statements that emphasise party leadership, stability, democratic centralism and socialism with Chinese characteristics. If anything, the recent crackdown on rights activists and bloggers, and the blocking of foreign websites, in fact points towards further restrictions on freedom of expression.

Peerenboom is critical of this focus on the economy and the question is indeed whether success is solely to be measured in terms of growth in gross domestic product (GDP). Is China more 'successful' than India because of its clearer focus on the economy, or is India more successful than China because of its democratic procedures and structures? Further, if there is now a plurality of locally grown models, then what is the purpose of comparing them? The answer is, of course, that policymakers will continue to make use of 'best practice' studies and will try to learn from the experience of others. The emphasis on local context suggests, however, that they will be well advised to look for their comparisons closer to home. The BRICS group may prove to be too diverse and the countries in it too strong to serve as policy models for smaller or less powerful countries, and their main commonality may in the end lie in geopolitical aims and strategies.

The legal policies of 'Asian developmental states' became increasingly problematic after the end of the Cold War. Freed from strategic considerations, international trading partners began to examine the legal systems of Asian developing countries more comprehensively and to demand reforms not only of commercial laws relevant for their businesses, but also of various fields of public law relevant for the rights of citizens. This 'second moment' in law and development, discussed above, soon brought a focus on the rule of law. Constitutional and political rights are an essential part of the rule of law. Nevertheless, during the emergence of the 'Asian developmental model', little emphasis was placed on them. With the notable exception of India (which was not included in discussions of the Asian model anyway), countries were ruled by totalitarian, authoritarian or semi-authoritarian regimes.[12] Economic development was a priority and it was argued that the economic success justified temporary restrictions of political freedom. It soon became clear, however, that regimes became firmly entrenched and the temporary compromise in favour of economic progress became a permanent structural deficit. Not surprisingly, in situations of economic crisis, as in the Asian Crisis of 1997–98, the compromise quickly unravelled and frustrated citizens took to the streets to demand greater political participation. The resulting democratisation of countries such as South Korea and Indonesia has now created a very diverse political and constitutional landscape in Asia, with some firmly entrenched authoritarian and democratic systems, respectively, and others that seem to swing back and forth between the two.

This very diverse institutional landscape is Albert H. Y. Chen's topic in Chapter 5, in which he surveys the recent developments in the East and Southeast Asian countries. He orders the current Asian constitutions according to regime types and types of constitution into four categories. The first category of 'reasonably consolidated democracies' includes Japan, South Korea and Taiwan. While he finds 'East Asian constitutionalism' a useful reference for the experience of these countries in distinguishing it from 'Asian values' constitutionalism, he thinks that most of the features of this constitutionalism are shared widely among non-Western nations and are not specific to Asia. In the second category, he examines the new or amended constitutions of the Philippines, Thailand and Indonesia, which he regards as 'young, unconsolidated, fragile, unstable or otherwise of poor quality' democracies. Remarkable in these countries to varying degrees are the judicialisation of politics and the politicisation of the judiciary. His primary example is Thailand, and his long list of highly controversial rulings by a politicised judiciary raises the question of whether this example is currently still correctly classified in the same category as countries that have not seen military coups and a succession of constitutions in just a few years. The politicisation of the judiciary was also strong in the Philippines during the Arroyo years, but without the same dramatic consequences as in Thailand. The third category of 'communitarian constitutionalism' is represented by Singapore and Malaysia, which allows for restrictions unknown in Western liberal democracies, based on 'Asian values'. In the final category, Chen critically examines the theory of 'party-state constitutionalism' in China and Vietnam, but in view of contradictions to the text of the PRC Constitution, he doubts that a theory of party-state constitutionalism can fully legitimise the party-state itself. Both of the latter categories of constitutionalism have also strong affinities with the 'thin conceptions of the rule of law' of Peerenboom (2002), with their emphasis on the formal or instrumental aspects of the rule of law. Other analysts, however, still find it more appropriate to distinguish between the rule of law and the 'rule by law' that they see in operation in countries such as China and Vietnam (Chen, 2003, 2007).

Constitutional law was only one field in which a growing judicialisation led to the formation of specialised courts. In areas of business law such as intellectual property, greater specialisation of judges had long been a demand of Western trading partners and the establishment of some of these courts preceded the Asian Crisis of 1997–98.[13] Many more followed during and after the tumultuous crisis period (Antons, 2005; Harding and Nicholson, 2010). Even in the socialist countries characterised by a 'thin conception of the rule of law' or 'rule by law', there was greater emphasis on professionalism, independence and transparency of the judiciary. Pip Nicholson and Cait Storr examine these developments, using the example of Vietnam, in Chapter 6. Vietnam was less affected by the Asian Crisis than some of its ASEAN neighbours and opted for incremental reform of the court system rather than the proliferation of new courts or specialised benches that could be observed elsewhere. Nicholson and Storr see the Vietnamese reform process as a set of dynamics rather than a predictable movement towards an ideal. A number of actors contest the social field of court reform, of which the party-state is the most important. Party leadership creates a tension in the role of the courts, which are neither regarded as instruments of party rule nor as independent from it. The move is therefore towards a 'self-managing' court system. Currently, much of this remains largely on paper, however, because the reform agenda has lacked implementation and international reports suggest that potential users of the system continue to look elsewhere for dispute resolution.

Yet another result of the judicialisation of politics is the changing role of lawyers themselves, examined in Chapter 7 by Yves Dezalay and Bryant G. Garth for South and East

Asia. The authors show how the profession of lawyers expanded in Asia in the context of imperial expansion, and how their status is dependent on the social and legal capital built by colonial powers and, subsequently, by the governments of the newly independent countries. A period of decline during the Cold War, with its many authoritarian regimes, was followed by a comeback of law and lawyers in the context of globalisation beginning in the 1990s. In many ways, India is a special case, because Indian elites took early advantage of the possibility of legal training and lawyers were prominent in the independence movement. A period of decline after independence came to an end when lawyers opposed Indira Ghandi's emergency rule in the 1970s and used public interest litigation to promote good government. In Malaysia, although sharing a similar English colonial legal history, the British developed a division of labour along ethnic lines, with the legal profession drawn largely from migrants from Ceylon, South India and South China. After independence, the New Economic Policy largely continued a division in which the profession was overwhelmingly Indian and Chinese, while positions in government and the judiciary were staffed with the Malay elite. This has prevented a close connection of the Malaysian profession to the state and, accordingly, lawyers have not been able to wield the same political influence as their colleagues in India.

Lawyers were also strong in the Indonesian independence movement, but there were only few trained lawyers after the end of Dutch colonial rule. The role of law and lawyers declined further during the years of the Sukarno and Suharto presidencies. Different from Malaysia, however, the Indonesian elite in the profession did become active in advocating human rights and the rule of law, and has become prominent not only in international business transaction, but also in brokering the domestic legal reform agenda. Activist lawyers were also important in the Korean shift from authoritarianism to reform. Corporate law firms grew considerably after the Asian Crisis, to the extent that legal practice at one of the top firms is now regarded as more desirable than a career as judge or prosecutor. In the Philippines, legal institutions had a promising start after independence. As in the other countries, their reputation declined during the period of the authoritarian Marcos regime, when few lawyers refused to compromise. The situation changed, however, after the assassination of Benito Aquino in 1983. Since then, lawyers have again been influential in the reform movement, although there remains the problem of the links between the legal elite and an entrenched oligarchy.

One of the important strategies of the 'Asian developmental state' was 'picking winners' among domestic corporations able to compete at international level and, especially in many of the young independent nations, to build a domestic entrepreneurial class in a post-colonial economy that had been dominated by foreigners. These aims meant that the drafting of corporations and bankruptcy legislation became heavily politicised, and cross-shareholding and political interference in corporate restructuring were frequently part of the policy toolbox (Antons, 2003a; Halliday and Carruthers, 2007). In the socialist countries, the continuing existence of a large number of state-owned companies has further exacerbated this tendency. Roman Tomasic and Zinian Zhang perfectly illustrate these dynamics in Chapter 8. Although the PRC Enterprise Bankruptcy Law 2006 (EBL) has been heralded as a modern law on corporate rehabilitation using many 'best practices' from abroad, its implementation shows significant deviations from basic principles for political purposes. Because of the poor institutional infrastructure, government support is needed, in particular at the local level. The overarching theme of corporate reorganisation in China is social stability. Courts will not act on petitions without government support for fear that the case could stir social unrest. Further, in the absence of professional insolvency practitioners, they need cooperation from other government agencies, such as tax authorities and the police. Local government, in turn, is evaluated on the basis of its ability to maintain social stability, but is also concerned about the erosion of its tax base and the impact of corporate failures on the local GDP. As a result, corporate reorganisations trigger a bargaining process, with significant deviations from basic legal principles regarding the value distribution in favour of small and individual unsecured creditors, and holders of public securities. This leads the authors to their conclusion that the social stability goal is satisfied at the expense of the rule of law, judicial independence and accountability.

Technological development is another prominent focus in the Asian development model. It has been a cornerstone of discussions about fair terms of trade for many years, reaching back to the intensive discussions about technology transfer of the 1970s and 1980s, and the development by the United Nations Conference on Trade and Development (UNCTAD) of a code of conduct for that matter (UNCTAD and ICTSD, 2005: 3). Intellectual property has been a controversial subject matter in this context. Whereas it was seen as particularly critical in developing countries during the 1970s (Vaitsos, 1976), it has been a favourite topic for bilateral trade negotiations since the 1980s. Bilateral pressure on Asian developing countries to improve their outdated intellectual property systems, often derived from the colonial period, preceded the World Trade Organization (WTO) Agreement on Trade-related Intellectual Property Rights (TRIPS) by many years. During the 1980s, declining terms of trade for raw material dependent developing countries coincided with the increasing interest in intellectual property law in the high-tech economies of the industrialised world to establish the topic firmly on the agenda of international trade negotiations (Antons, 1991).

Peter K. Yu analyses these developments in Chapter 9. He proposes two pairs of analytical tools. The first is the convergence and divergence discussion that has been prominent in comparative law for many years (Watson, 1993; Legrand, 1997). Yu stresses the economic, cultural and social diversity of Asian countries that makes it difficult to achieve consensus on policies related to intellectual property. However, there are nevertheless mainly three drivers of convergence. First, TRIPS has introduced unified standards, but enforcement practices vary greatly.[14] The second driver of convergence is the bilateral pressure exerted via such mechanisms as section 301 of the US Trade and Tariff Act of 1984 and similar procedures in the European Union. Finally, there is the catch-up mentality of leaders oriented towards Asian development. Yu further explains about the 'clusters' emerging in intellectual property policy, ranging from Japan and the Asian component of the BRICS economies, via the 'four little dragons' of Hong Kong, Singapore, South Korea and Taiwan, and what Yu calls the 'middle intellectual property powers' to the least-developed countries (LDCs). The links between these clusters are created by bilateral and regional agreements, and by plurilateral agreements, which Yu terms 'country club agreements', because they are formed by invitation. The first of these plurilateral agreements to have been concluded is the Anti-Counterfeiting Trade Agreement, which seems to be in trouble because, of the signatory states, only Japan has ratified it thus far. The Trans-Pacific Partnership Agreement (TPP) and the Regional Comprehensive Economic Partnership (RCEP) are often seen as competing, because one is sponsored by the United States whereas the other has the backing of China. Yu concludes that it will be interesting to see to what extent Asian countries can cooperate in building a 'normative community' and what sort of intellectual property system they will promote.

The differences in development models are also discussed by Jane K. Winn in Chapter 10. The chapter reminds us that, with the arrival of India and other newcomers to the debate about law and development, the picture has become much more differentiated and generalisations about 'Asian development' frequently made in the 1990s are now much more difficult to make. Winn discusses the development of national electronic payment systems as a central component of e-commerce development strategies and contrasts China's 'state capitalism' approach with that of India's 'entrepreneurial state'. Electronic payment systems illustrate how countries are moving from regulatory competition to governance competition, as national state regulation has to compete with self-regulation by private organisations. The examples of the United States and European Union demonstrate the great difficulties of governance to reign into electronic payment networks by using instruments such as competition law. Winn shows how both China and India have subsidised payment system innovations as part of their respective development strategy, but in very different ways. China very successfully introduced its UnionPay system by copying the business model of Visa and MasterCard, and taking a liberal view of its obligations as member of the WTO – a view that was later successfully challenged by the United States by means of the WTO dispute resolution process. In spite of that decision, Winn believes that global credit card networks are unlikely to enjoy national treatment in China any time soon. India's strategy, on the other hand, aims at providing market infrastructure to fuel competition and new private services, also with the aim of allowing the direct withdrawal of government benefits unaffected by corruption. Introducing so many innovations at the same time is risky, but, if successful, more rewarding in the long run than China's system privileging 'national champions'.

The final chapter in this part of the book on law in the context of Asian development deals with FDI. The attraction of foreign investment became a primary policy goal in the non-socialist East Asian economies most particularly after the paradigm shift in economic policies from industrialisation based on import substitution towards export-led development during the 1970s and 1980s (Haggard, 1990). The embrace of this policy tool has been uneven, however. It was almost unreserved in entrepot trade centres such as Singapore (Rodan, 1989), but accompanied by constant shifts between open door and restrictive policies depending on other revenue sources in resource-rich countries such as Indonesia (Robison and Hadiz, 2004). In Chapter 11, Vivienne Bath and Luke Nottage confirm the ambivalent attitude of many Asian governments towards foreign investment. Legislative frameworks for foreign investment in much of Asia remain relatively restrictive by international standards. This is in spite of the spectacular growth of FDI: North and Southeast Asian countries now account for 24 per cent of the world's FDI inflows and for 20 per cent of its outflows, and the countries of APEC account for 52 per cent of the world's total FDI inflows. Remarkable too is the rise of investment from East Asian countries in particular and the significant increase of intra-Asian investment. The example of China, with its relatively restrictive legal framework, as the region's most attractive FDI destination demonstrates also, however, that the legal framework is but one among many factors in investment decisions.

Bilateral and multilateral initiatives include the non-binding principles developed by APEC, as well as bilateral investment treaties (BITs) and free trade agreements (FTAs). The most exciting developments here are: the creation of the ASEAN economic community by 2015; the negotiation of the TPP with countries from East and Southeast Asia and the Americas; and the negotiation of the Regional Comprehensive Economic Partnership (RCEP), comprising a group often referred to as 'ASEAN+6' (China, Korea, Japan, India, Australia and New Zealand). In the final part of their chapter, Bath and Nottage turn to international arbitration mechanisms. There has been spectacular growth of this field in Asia, and regional arbitration centres in cities such as Singapore, Hong Kong, Beijing and Shanghai are now competing with traditional and long-established centres in Europe and the United States. In this context, the inclusion of investor–state arbitration (ISA) provisions in bilateral and multilateral treaties has been controversial. Civil society groups and academic commentators have expressed concern about ISA provisions as taking away too much power from host countries to act or legislate in the national interest. This is now leading to a backlash against such provisions in countries such as India and Indonesia. Nevertheless, the authors see good prospects for ISA, as more Asian investors file claims and as even LDCs prevail in formal proceedings. In conclusion, they perceive a continuing impact of the tensions between the desire to regionalise and liberalise both trade and investment and economic and political pressures in the domestic arena. As for ISA, its advantages in 'depoliticising' disputes may be recognised, but extensive exceptions and limitations to balance public and private interests are likely.

The revival and/or transformation of Asian traditions

One of the apparent paradoxes accompanying the Asian law reform processes of the past few years is that, at the same time as Western trading partners and parts of the local elites have been pushing for 'modernisation' of a country's legal system largely by referring to models that seem to have worked in the industrialised nations of the West, the same reforms have been accompanied by a resurgence of local traditions and by a discourse about indigenous value systems and national heritage (Antons and Tomasic, 2013). The chapters in Part III of the book discuss these processes, and address important aspects of Asian legal traditions and their relationship with the state legal system. Part of this revival of tradition is the result of decentralisation policies promoted by international financial institutions and funding agencies. The paradigm shift towards decentralisation occurred after centralised modernisation and development policies practised in many countries led to conflicts over resources and the adequate distribution of the gains obtained from relevant projects. In the early 2000s, many developing countries adopted decentralisation and community-based natural resource management as a solution to such problems.[15] Vandergeest and Wittayapak (2010: 3) are critical of what they call the institutionalist approach to decentralisation, which sees politics primarily as an obstacle rather than as constitutive of decentralisation. As the following chapters show, even in countries that officially promote decentralisation policies, their exact extent is in fact heavily contested. Vandergeest and Wittayapak (2010: 4) distinguish between administrative decentralisation and political decentralisation. 'Administrative decentralisation' refers to a transfer of decision-making powers from central to regional or local bureaucracies, which nevertheless remain upwardly accountable to central headquarters. 'Political decentralisation' shifts power and resource rights to authorities who represent, and are downwardly accountable to, local people.

The example of Indonesia shows that this distinction refers to ideal types and that outcomes in reality are often mixed. Indonesia after the end of the Suharto regime, with its centralisation of power and economic opportunities in Indonesia's capital Jakarta, became a primary example of decentralisation and a testing ground for various contested policies. The chapters by Simon Butt and by Noer Fauzi Rachman and Mia Siscawati address aspects of administrative and political decentralisation, respectively. In Chapter 12, Simon Butt explains the new law-making powers of regional and local governments in Indonesia, and offers a detailed analysis of the review process of such legislation by the national government. The main tool of this review process is called the 'clarification' (*klarifikasi*). The whole process is strongly reminiscent of *gyōsei shidō*, the famous administrative guidance used by Japanese bureaucrats (Johnson, 1982). The *klarifikasi* consists of a letter sent to the law-making local government by the Ministry of Home Affairs requesting revision of the local laws, taking into account 'suggestions' of the Ministry. Failure to comply results in the annulment of the regional law.

Under Indonesia's revised Constitution and the Law on Regional Autonomy, the central government retains exclusive jurisdiction in some core subject areas and has concurrent jurisdiction with the local government in other areas. Legislation provides for the basic hierarchy of Indonesian laws and lower ranked laws may not contradict higher ranked ones. The decrees invalidating local laws, however, are not included in this ranking, leading to questions about the formal legality of the process. Statistics suggest that the vast majority of invalidations relate to local laws that impose taxes or levies. Discriminatory by-laws, such as those addressing religious beliefs, have been criticised by government officials, but have not been reviewed, indicating the government's general reluctance to intervene in religious affairs.

Butt identifies the most frequent types of clarification letter as related to revenue-raising in breach of national laws, drafting errors, unlimited or excessive delegation of power, imposition of criminal sanctions without specifying relevant norms, and usurping jurisdiction and contradicting 'higher level' laws. He points out, however, that not only are the local laws flawed, but also many of the clarification letters are vague and lack guidance as to what needs to be improved, and that many of them may simply be ignored. Butt concludes that decentralisation has been a 'mixed bag' for many citizens and that many local governments are now undercutting legal protections established at national level. Central and regional governments may ultimately require the services of an objective arbiter for their ensuing disputes.

While Simon Butt addresses the effects of decentralisation policies on the local administrative branches of the state legal system and points towards the different levels of influence that religious traditions and laws, particularly drawn from Islam, have been able to exert, in Chapter 13, Noer Fauzi Rachman and Mia Siscawati draw attention to the opportunities that decentralisation has created for people on the margins of society trying to revitalise their traditions. The chapter addresses the struggle of those peoples who, since colonial times, have been called 'isolated (living) communities' (*masyarakat terasing*).[16] These were the forest dwellers of the remoter parts of Indonesia. Similar to the indigenous peoples in settler colonies such as Australia, they were not regarded as settled and not given any rights regarding the forested areas that, for many generations, had been their habitat and source of livelihood. During colonial times, but also under the development-oriented governments after independence, they often became the victims of development projects that extended into their areas and pushed them out. Rachman and Siscawati approach their topic as a problem of creating inclusive citizenship, using Hannah Arendt's concept of 'the right to have rights'. They also refer to the work of Vandergeest and Peluso (2001a) on 'political forests', and on the territorialisation of forests and inhabitants in countries such as Thailand (Vandergeest and Peluso, 2001b). In the territorialisation process, the nation-state assumes control of geographical areas presumed to be 'empty' and 'remote', with populations that are regarded as 'unsettled', 'backward' and/or 'uncivilised'. Legally, the process received support from colonial regulations in the nineteenth century, which first introduced state control over forest land and resources, and then demarcated the boundaries of state-controlled and private entitlements.

Finally, the colonial government functionally differentiated between areas opened for production and those reserved for protection.

The developmental Suharto government further differentiated between production forests, protection forests, natural conservation areas and convertible production forests. After the end of Suharto's rule, a new Forestry Law of 1999 recognised only the categories of 'state forest' and 'forest subject to rights'. Forests governed by customary law (*hutan adat*) are recognised as 'located within the territories of customary communities' (*masyarakat hukum adat*). However, the rights of such customary communities depend on state recognition. One of the most interesting developments in the democratising environment of post-Suharto Indonesia has been the establishment of internationally networked organisations that represent the interests of customary communities, such as the Alliance of Indigenous Peoples of the Archipelago (AMAN, *Aliansi Masyarakat Adat Nusantara*). AMAN is part of a wider movement of protests against land, mining, forestry and agrarian concessions that encroach on communal land. In 2012, AMAN and two customary communities submitted a constitutional challenge to the current Forestry Law provisions on communal forests by pointing to the recognition that the revised Indonesian Constitution offered for their traditional rights and cultural identities. The Constitutional Court agreed and revised the Forestry Law in some fundamental aspects by no longer categorically declaring customary forests as state forests, and by putting less stress on the state recognition of a community and on the national interests involved. Rachman and Siscawati end their chapter on a cautious note: while the Constitutional Court has delivered a landmark decision, the future of collective ownership of territories governed by customary law will still depend to a large extent on the political will of Indonesia's leadership and the attitude of the country's elites.

The revival and transformation of tradition is further visible in the importance attached to heritage as a symbol of national and/or local/regional identity, discussed by Christoph Antons in Chapter 14. Focusing on intangible cultural heritage, the chapter shows that heritage is not only symbolically, but also commercially, valuable – used in the tourism industry and marketing of local products and skills, from agriculture and crafts to music, food and traditional medicine. Increasingly, neighbouring countries with similar cultures clash over who is entitled to use and represent the material. This leads to attempts to monopolise cultural expressions and to exclude others by referring to relevant United Nations Educational, Scientific and Cultural Organization (UNESCO) Conventions on cultural property and/or to intellectual property and UNESCO or World Intellectual Property Organization (WIPO) model laws. Frequently, the two become mixed, with governments relying on the cultural property argument to justify their representation of minority cultures and on the intellectual property argument to claim exclusive rights. Community traditions become important for national development programmes and are claimed by governments in fields such as folklore, agriculture and medicine. Once governments are involved as rights holders, their rights can easily clash with those claimed by regional neighbours. The chapter discusses as examples disputes between Indonesia and Malaysia, as well as between Thailand and Cambodia. At the heart of such disputes are often different concepts of space, in which cultures are practised and relevant laws are valid. Different ancient kingdoms are cited to delineate cultural space, while different forms of state law and local law also mean that the law can be relevant for spaces either larger or smaller than the nation-state and its constituting provinces and administrative units. The chapter further shows that such traditions and customs become also important in the conflict over resources. People in the region and the national governments are not always on the same page in this regard: the former may want to restrict the use of culture and the benefits that can be derived therefrom to locals, while the national government may encourage broader use by others and sharing of resources in the national interest.

Law in relation to the environment and access to natural resources

The state's responsibility to protect the environment and to develop equitable solutions for the access to natural resources was not an issue that attracted much attention during the initial period of high-growth Asian development. Centralised development models, an emphasis on industrialisation and on creating jobs in the industrial sector, and the 'top-down' implementation of development projects combined with the lack of democratic mechanisms to leave almost no room for such discussions. The recent efforts at democratisation and decentralisation (although uneven and contested), and a better appreciation of the limits of natural resources, are now creating space for voices to emerge from the margins and from rural and remote areas. The chapters in Part IV of the book provide examples of these new discourses about sustainable development and access to, and distribution of, resources.

In a powerful critique of 'transnational sustainability certification' (TSC), in Chapter 15, Peter Vandergeest discusses the proliferation of various schemes administered by non-governmental organisations (NGOs) to certify forest management, fisheries and aquaculture, examining in detail the schemes for shrimp farming. He compares such certification schemes to the claims of extraterritoriality raised in the nineteenth and early twentieth centuries by imperial powers in Asia. While the imperial claims were based on a portrayal of Asian legal systems as uncivilised, an assessment in which family law played strong role (Loos, 2006), the 'new extraterritoriality' is claimed by private organisations such as the Aquaculture Stewardship Council (ASC) as a supplement to regulation that is regarded as inefficient or inadequately implemented. The problem with this approach, according to Vandergeest, is that 'sustainability enclaves' are created that produce primarily for markets in the global North, and that the schemes have little impact on broader-scale issues of environmental and social justice. The author shows divergent state responses to such TSC. Relevant government agencies in Thailand are seeing 'foreign' certification schemes as a hidden trade barrier. They try to counter the influence of such schemes by developing their own government-run sustainability certification systems. While they are not opposed to the internationalisation of standards, they think that they should be developed by international organisations such as the United Nations Food and Agriculture Organization (FAO), whereby member states can participate in their development. Vietnam is also creating its own certification system based on FAO standards, but has been more welcoming to some TSC schemes, which have been collaborating with state agencies, and which are seen as means to facilitate agrofood exports and enhance the ability of the state to regulate farming. Vandergeest concludes that a more effective way of addressing the concerns than TSC schemes is the direct engagement of state agencies, on the one hand, and relevant social movements, on the other.

The emergence of biotechnology and policy recommendations for increasingly commercialised agricultural sectors of the economy have triggered intensive policy debates everywhere. Such debates have been particularly fierce, however, in 'second generation newly industrialising economies' (Jomo, 2003a) that have ambitions in biotechnological research and in positioning themselves as agricultural exporters, but at the same time still have substantial sectors of smallholder agriculture. The ASEAN countries Indonesia,

Malaysia, Thailand and the Philippines, as well as India, all have this constellation of very diverging interests. Their policies and laws for agricultural innovation and sustainability are analysed by Rajeswari Kanniah and Christoph Antons in Chapter 16. India, in particular, has been a hotbed of discussions regarding the impact of the 'Green Revolution' of the 1960s and 1970s, the question of intellectual property protection for agricultural products and processes after TRIPS, and membership in the 1961 International Convention for the Protection of New Varieties of Plants (UPOV Convention), the international instrument that standardises plant variety protection around the world. Vandana Shiva, one of the most well-known activists arguing against intellectual property rights for seeds, is from India and uses Indian case studies intensively in her writings (Shiva, 1991). The chapter shows how all of these countries had to provide for some form of plant variety protection after TRIPS came into force for developing countries in 2000. Most opted for specialised (*sui generis*) plant variety laws, because the plant variety system, different from patents, still allows farmers to experiment with seeds and to reuse harvested seeds. However, governments have not been very creative in using the flexibilities provided by TRIPS and have largely adopted legislation conforming to the UPOV Convention. Some have now also agreed under bilateral FTAs to ensure that their legislation is in conformity with the 1991 version of the Convention, which is widely regarded as the strongest in protecting breeders and the weakest in safeguarding farmers' rights.

In the context of developing countries, the most frequently contested resources are land and water. In Chapter 17, Daniel Fitzpatrick shows the particularly problematic situation in young post-conflict nations such as Timor-Leste. The country achieved its independence from Indonesia during the turbulent transition of its powerful neighbour to a democratic society. The process was marred by violence, however, and violence erupted again in 2006 during internal power struggles. As a result of the country's history of different colonising and occupying powers, land claims are now based on very diverse legal grounds, ranging from custom over possession to Portuguese title documents and Indonesian title documents to eminent domain. After the 2006 conflicts, however, a new draft law favours recognition of rights based on possession over restitution of title. Yet individual possession as the basis of entitlement to ownership may clash with customary concepts of ancestral domains. Fitzpatrick points out that in a customary system acts of possession, such as construction, settlement and cultivation, have significance only in a context of social status and affiliation with origin groups, rituals, etc. These divergent perceptions may be more relevant in areas of acknowledged customary domains, especially where land is claimed by displaced groups, than in areas cleared under colonial agricultural programmes, where there may be less competition between customary and state based systems of property enforcement. Fitzpatrick concludes that the institutional literature proceeds from assumptions about the effectiveness of formal institutions that are simply not present in emerging nations such as Timor-Leste. There is no consensus as to the meaning of property, so that the institutionalisation of property rules mainly results in rent-seeking opportunities for powerful state-connected actors.

Philippe Cullet's Chapter 18 is the final chapter in this part of the book. India, with its long history of decentralisation, provides an interesting contrast to the contested decentralisation policies elsewhere in Asia, which were discussed in earlier chapters. Decentralised administration – in the case of India, with the states in charge – is to some extent necessary in a field such as water law, which is intimately connected with local environmental conditions. In India, however, it has led to a fragmented coverage of the subject matter. The field is still affected by nineteenth-century colonial legislation regarding water largely as input for productive activities, thereby delaying the shift to more contemporary views of water and its conservation, especially for drinking. A further issue is that regulation leaves either the state or individual landowners in charge of water, and that there are different rules for surface and groundwater. While the Indian courts have recognised a fundamental right to water since the early 1990s and the doctrine that the state holds resources such as water in trust for the public, little has been done to implement these principles in legislation. Individual rights over water are usually connected to property rights in land.

The current regulations are particularly inadequate with regards to groundwater, an area affected by technological change and in which scientific understanding has fundamentally changed since relevant colonial laws were introduced in the mid-nineteenth century. The link to landownership is inequitable for the landless, which account for 40 per cent of India's population. It also creates vested interests and leads to short-term solution for problems that are not easily visible on the surface. Although decentralisation foresees the setting up of 'water user associations', these are dominated by landlords, and they do not include reservation for women, or for the castes or tribes scheduled in the Indian Constitution. Cullet concludes that water law must be the subject of effective democratic legislative processes and should not merely be left to the 'experts'.

Other rights discourses in Asia

The theme of legal pluralism and the revival and/or transformation of tradition returns in Part V of the book on people in Asia and their rights. The title relates to the fact that, in the multi-ethnic societies of many Asian countries, law is often personalised and different laws apply in accordance with an individual's ethnic origins or religion. In some cases, this creates a choice between competing laws and institutions; in other cases, access to the law becomes difficult on ethnic or religious grounds. Tim Lindsey discusses these questions in Chapter 19. Lindsey shows the diversity of approaches towards Islamic courts and the law applied by them in the three Southeast Asian neighbouring countries, including how race and religion as legal classifiers are often conflated in the process. He begins by pointing out that the involvement of the state in the administration of Islamic tradition necessarily changes its content and creates tensions between the divinity of the *Shari'a* and the realities of modern Islamic societies. The historical, political and social context of the three countries explains the different solutions that they have chosen to deal with these tensions. In Indonesia, although numerically the largest Muslim nation in the world, there are significant minorities adhering to other types of faith and Islam is not specifically privileged in the Constitution. The Islamic courts are responsible for family law and inheritance cases, with divorce cases being their main business. They remain subordinated to the secular Supreme Court, which hears final appeals. They apply the national Marriage Law and Islamic law as compiled in national regulations. Lindsey demonstrates this subordination by using the example of the *talak* divorce – that is, the husband's right to divorce a wife by declaring the *talak* formula three times. In Indonesia, it depends on prior permission from the Religious Court and the formula has to be pronounced in court. Also, the courts allow women to obtain a divorce on the grounds of marriage breakdown relying on the implementing regulation of the national Marriage Law, which would be much more difficult to obtain if traditional Islamic principles were applied.

In Malaysia, Islamic courts were traditionally the domain of the different states that make up the Federation of Malaysia, and their traditional rulers were the guardians of Islamic religion and Malay traditions. Significantly, however, and unlike Indonesia, appeals to the secular High Court were abolished in 1988, creating, in effect, a parallel *Syariah* jurisdiction. This creates conflicts in particular with regards to religious freedom and different interpretations of basic rights in different states. The separation from the secular courts has increased the power and influences of the Syariah courts. Unlike those in Indonesia, they also rely heavily on Islamic sources of law. For the example of the *talak*, it means that the courts subsequently ratify a *talak* divorce declared out of court.

The final example comes from Singapore, where Muslims are a significant minority. Here, the authority of the *Syariah* Court is curtailed by giving Muslims a choice between the religious and the secular courts, and by leaving the religious courts outside of the constitutionally guaranteed judicial power structure. Singaporean *Syariah* courts largely apply national legislation and case law, and give relatively little weight to Islamic tradition. Lindsey concludes that the form of Islamic courts in the three states depends rarely on what Muslims want, but rather on what the state finds appropriate to establish.

Earlier chapters in this volume addressed questions of decentralisation and the revival of tradition that followed a paradigm shift in environmental policies towards community-based forest and natural resource management, inspired by the writings of ecologists such as Darrell Addison Posey (2008) and Fikret Berkes (1999). The ecological knowledge at the core of such policies is often associated with indigenous peoples.[17] However, in spite of the widespread usage, the terminology has remained contested, with some governments refusing to recognise the relevance of the concept for their populations or employing the term 'indigenous' in a completely different manner. Social scientists studying the impact of the indigenous movement are equally divided, with some seeing the 'indigenisation' of cultural and intellectual property (Geismar, 2013: ix), while others warn that a broadly framed 'eco-indigenism' could 'undermine the original international agenda of indigenous peoples in relation to settler nations' (Sissons, 2005: 17).

Geoffrey Benjamin analyses the various usages of the terms 'indigenous people' 'indigenousness' and 'indigeneity' in Chapter 20. He identifies at least six different circumstances in which the term is used and regrets the broad application of the terminology, which may become problematic in particular if the terms are having legal implications. The self-identification suggested by, among other international instruments, the UN Declaration on the Rights of Indigenous Peoples to determine which populations are indigenous leaves room for political manipulation. In fact, there is much movement in and out of what Benjamin calls 'tribality'. He proposes a return to the older term 'indigeny' for true, place-linked social circumstances and distinguishes it from 'indigenism' as a self-conscious political stance. In the second part of the chapter, Benjamin contrasts the experiences of six countries in Asia. He shows how, in Malaysia, the rhetoric of indigenism relates to the nation-state construct and has nothing to do with temporal priorities. Similarly, in Indonesia, the term *pribumi* is regularly translated as 'indigenous' and is usually understood as differentiating 'indigenous Indonesians' from those Indonesian citizens whose ancestors arrived from elsewhere. However, as Benjamin's example from West Borneo shows, in some places, the term *pribumi* is also used to create boundaries vis-à-vis migrants from elsewhere in the archipelago. The Philippines has been much discussed as an exception to the widespread reluctance in Asia to recognise indigenous people (Eder and McKenna, 2004), but Benjamin explains that the view is also widespread that indigenous status should rather be accorded to the mainstream lowland-dwelling Filipinos as bringers of civilisation.[18] In Thailand, the political discourse has difficulties accepting anything outside the official national ideology based on language, religion and Thai indigenousness. In India, the local term *adivāsi* applies to approximately 8 per cent of the population.

The Constitution provides for 'scheduled castes' and 'scheduled tribes', but these categories are not normally understood in the sense of being 'indigenous peoples'. Benjamin concludes that the terminology is ambiguous and that this is problematic when it comes to formal judicial deliberations over political, cultural and land rights. Truly indigenous concerns have difficulties in getting a fair hearing in such settings. The author warns that, without better differentiation, indigenist arguments may actually work against the interests of true place-linked indigenes.

A further important rights discourse in Asia relates to freedom of expression and freedom of the press. Especially journalists, but also academics and Internet bloggers, often become targets for authorities that interpret criticism as overstepping the mark and constituting defamation of leading politicians or, even worse, subversion of national interests (Coronel, 2001; Gan, Gomez and Johannen, 2004; Rodan, 2004). The danger of defamation applies to journalism worldwide, of course, but it is worse in those countries in which the independence of the courts is not firmly established. Freedom of expression is also often curtailed for reasons of religion and/or morality, or to save face, or to enforce what is regarded as appropriate behaviour. A variety of laws, including cyber and sedition laws, is used for such purposes (Antons, 2008; Cochrane, 2014a, 2014b; Berthelsen, 2014). In an increasingly nervous political atmosphere in Thailand in recent years, the frequent use of the country's strict *lèse-majesté* provisions has stirred considerable controversy (Fuller, 2013). In Chapter 21, David Streckfuss examines the use of *lèse-majesté* laws in pre-war Japan and present-day Thailand. He shows the foundation of Japan's national ideology during the Meiji period, with the components of emperor, religion, national polity (*kokutai*) and law. *Lèse-majesté* provisions were included in the Japanese Criminal Code from 1882 onwards, with the circle of persons objected to insult and disrespect widened in a revision in 1907.

In Thailand, *lèse-majesté* charges were included in the country's first modern Criminal Code in 1908 and first strengthened in 1927, then temporarily weakened after the overthrow of the absolute monarchy in 1932. With the revitalisation of the monarchy, a further extended *lèse-majesté* article appeared in the Criminal Code of 1957 and penalties were further increased in 1976. Streckfuss compares different cases of *lèse-majesté* in Japan depending on whether they apply to the elite (severe consequences, but not officially prosecuted), to the people (vague interpretation and reach into the private realm) or to liberal intellectuals (prosecuted under milder laws limiting free speech in Imperial Japanese society). The final type related to the concept of *kokutai* and a revision of the Peace Preservation Law led to the high point of *lèse-majesté* in Japan, as the country geared up for war, with the number of prosecutions peaking in 1937. In Thailand, cases dropped after a democratic movement led to Thailand's most democratic Constitution in 1997, but increased by 1,500 per cent between 2005 and 2010 following another military coup in 2006. Streckfuss concludes that the rise in *lèse-majesté* cases in pre-war Japan and in present-day Thailand is a sign of crisis, with one faction of society imposing orthodoxy in an overly zealous fashion irrespective of the potentially severe consequences for society as a whole.

While Benjamin, in his chapter on 'indigenousness', examines one important debate concerned with relationships between ethnic groups, in Chapter 22 – the final chapter of the book – Antons-Sutanto and Antons turn to another debate that has been a persistent issue in many countries, namely, the integration of what sociologist Wertheim (1959) termed the 'foreign trading minorities'. This issue recently came to the fore again during the Indonesian election campaign, when it was alleged that President Joko Widodo was of Chinese descent (*Jakarta Post*, 2014), which, prior to constitutional reforms in the first decade of the new millennium, would have prevented him from becoming president. The authors show in this chapter how categories of 'race' and 'ethnicity' were constructed by the colonial authorities in the Netherlands East Indies to assign economic roles in the colonial economy to each of the constructed groups. In the colonial legal system, 'foreign Orientals' with important roles as middlemen in trade, such as Chinese, Indians and Arabs, were, from the mid-nineteenth century onwards, given different access to civil and commercial law from that of Indonesian 'natives', who – with the exception of the elite – largely remained confined to working in agriculture.

The chapter shows how the meaning of these ethnic labels and classifications changed over time – in the case of 'foreign Orientals', from everyone (including Indonesians) outside Dutch enclaves in the early colonial period to 'foreign Asians' from other countries that were applying laws considered as not of equal standard with those derived from Europe. A detailed discussion of the example of the locally born *Peranakan* Chinese, often with roots in Indonesia going back many generations, shows that many of these minorities were in fact legally classified as 'foreign'. As with the term 'foreign Orientals', the meaning of the term *Peranakan* also changed, from being a reference to locally born Muslims of Chinese descent to designating locally born people of foreign descent in general, such as Indonesian Chinese, Indians and Arabs. In the case of the *Peranakan* Chinese, as they became increasingly associated with Chinese newcomers (*Totok*) in the late colonial period, they were therefore seen as retaining similarly strong ties to China. The code of the Qing dynasty was regarded as their customary law, although they already had their own local customary rules (*adat istiadat*), just like other Indonesian communities. This association with China also led to discriminative laws and regulations, especially after the purges of Communists and their sympathisers carried out by the military-backed government of President Suharto during the second half of the 1960s. After the end of Suharto's rule in 1998, successive governments have been progressively dismantling this discriminative framework. Significant issues remain, however, and the invalidation of relevant laws will ultimately have to concern the courts. The authors conclude that laws employing ethnic and racial categorisations impact in a negative manner on the entire population, and should be abolished rather than reformed.

Conclusion

Asian law, as a field of academic debate, has come a long way since economic success in the region triggered its emergence as a specialised field of research. A lively debate in many different countries and across several disciplines increasingly goes beyond the instrumental and utilitarian considerations that were driving legal research in the colonial period and during the occupation immediately after World War II. As influences on Asian law making can be traced to many countries, analysts from the region frequently collaborate with commentators from such source countries and regions of legal transfers. The contributions in this book offer examples of such work. Perhaps the most striking difference to earlier work on Asia, mostly in comparative law and anthropology of law, is the increasingly interdisciplinary and multidisciplinary nature of the work, which is no longer confined to technical and dogmatic legal arguments, but puts developments into the social, economic and political contexts of the countries concerned. More recently, in the context of decentralisation policies and policies promoting community-based natural resource management, there has also been a renewed interest in local laws and customary laws, and their interaction with state laws.

This interaction used to be discussed mainly in the anthropology literature, but is now becoming relevant for legal research in fields such as environmental law, land law, intellectual property law and comparative law more generally.

The much greater understanding of the local context reveals the limited reach of many state laws in both post-colonial societies and those that were never colonised, but which imported their laws from elsewhere for other reasons. Reform of such imported laws has been slow and they can still sometimes include discriminative provisions that should be unacceptable to independent countries. In ethnically very diverse countries, this is sometimes related to the fact that different sections of the population find their interests best represented by different types of law, so that the finding of workable compromises becomes difficult. Another difficulty in some countries is that while many of the imported laws are still present, the language of the colonising power is no longer spoken and accessing original sources can be difficult, even for specialised academics. This access problem can be perceived to some extent for laws that originated from Spain, Portugal and the Netherlands. Not surprisingly, therefore, imported laws have long become localised. Besides specifically local influences, they often merge influences from a variety of countries that are seen as having advanced legislation in particular fields and whose laws serve as models for others.

It is debatable whether all of this is sufficient to see Asian law as requiring a distinct form of legal research, or whether the field is better placed as a subset of comparative law, law and society research, regulatory studies, postcolonial studies, or similar fields that cross disciplinary and geographic boundaries. However, as the examples in this collection show, it can also be an exciting topic for the interdisciplinary field of Asian studies, because it can bring together legal scholars from, or with an interest in, Asia and academics from the different disciplines of the humanities and social sciences that are normally included in Asian studies (Antons, 1998). The insights about the local contexts that such research is able to generate can be of tremendous benefit for technical experts, governments and NGOs involved in law reform, as well as for the debate in civil society in Asian countries about such reform, and the establishment of such ideals as democracy and the rule of law.

Notes

1 See the contributions in Jomo (2003b).
2 For a critical examination of the concept, see the contributions in Dirlik (1993).
3 See, for the examples of Maine, Bachofen and Gluckman, the survey in Donovan and Anderson (2003: 14–20).
4 For the ambivalent attitudes of Indonesian governments, see Lev (2000: 27–28; 126–127); for East Timor, see Fitzpatrick, Chapter 17 in this volume.
5 Examples are the research and teaching programmes of the Law Department of the School of Oriental and African Studies (SOAS) at the University of London in the UK and the Van Vollenhoven Institute for Law, Governance and Development at Leiden University in the Netherlands.
6 On Ernst Utrecht, see McFarlane (1993); see also Wertheim (1959).
7 The Asian Law Centre at the University of Melbourne commenced activities in 1985. On the development of teaching and research of Asian law in Australia, see Smith (1996).
8 For example, the Asian Law Institute (ASLI) at the National University of Singapore, established in 2003 with thirteen founding members as a network of law schools from all over Asia.
9 See, e.g., the contributions in Taylor (1996) and Lindsey (2008).
10 See the contributions in Antons and Gessner (2007); Gillespie and Peerenboom (2009).

11 See also Jones (1994); Antons (2001: 206–207).
12 For the terminology, see Chen, Chapter 5 in this volume.
13 On the establishment of the Intellectual Property and International Trade Court in Thailand, see Aryanuntaka (1999) and Morgan (2000).
14 See also the contributions in Antons (2011).
15 See the contributions in Wittayapak and Vandergeest (2010); Brosius, Lowenhaupt Tsing and Zerner (2005).
16 See also Persoon (2009).
17 See the contributions in Ellen, Parkes and Bicker (2000); Graber, Kuprecht and Lai (2012).
18 See also Kramer (2006).

References

Allen, G. C. (1981) *A Short Economic History of Japan*, 4th edn, Houndmills: Macmillan Press.

Antons, C. (1991) 'Intellectual Property Law in ASEAN Countries: A Survey', *European Intellectual Property Review*, 13(3): 202–209.

Antons, C. (1995) 'Analysing Asian Law: The Need for a General Concept', *Law in Context*, 13(1): 106–123.

Antons, C. (1998) 'Asian Studies and Law: A Difficult Encounter?', *IIAS Newsletter* #15, 3.

Antons, C. (2001) 'Law and Development Thinking after the Asian Crisis of 1997', *Forum of International Development*, 20(12): 205–232.

Antons, C. (2003a) 'Japan as a Model? Comparing Law and Development in Japan, Singapore and Indonesia', in C. Antons (ed.) *Law and Development in East and Southeast Asia*, London/New York: Routledge Curzon, 216–248.

Antons, C. (ed.) (2003b) *Law and Development in East and Southeast Asia*, London/New York: Routledge Curzon.

Antons, C. (2005) 'Specialised Intellectual Property Courts in Southeast Asia', in A. Kur, S. Luginbühl and E. Waage (eds) '. . .und sie bewegt sich doch!' *Patent Law on the Move*, Cologne/Berlin/Munich: Carl Heymanns, 287–299.

Antons, C. (2008) 'National Bans for YouTube: The Debate in Thailand in Comparison with India, Turkey and Germany', *Computer Law Review International*, 9(1): 1–6.

Antons, C. (ed.) (2011) *The Enforcement of Intellectual Property Rights: Comparative Perspectives from the Asia-Pacific Region*, Alphen aan den Rijn: Kluwer Law International.

Antons, C., and Gessner, V. (2007) *Globalisation and Resistance: Law Reform in Asia since the Crisis*, Oxford/Portland, OR: Hart.

Antons, C., and Tomasic, R. (2013) 'Introduction: Law Reform and Legal Change in East Asia', in C. Antons and R. Tomasic (eds) *Law and Society in East Asia*, Aldershot/Burlington, VT: Ashgate, xi–xxxiii.

Aryanuntaka, V. (1999) 'TRIPS and the Specialised Intellectual Property Court in Thailand', *International Review of Industrial Property and Copyright Law*, 30(4): 360–376.

Bauer, J. R., and Bell, D. A. (eds) (1999) *The East Asian Challenge for Human Rights*, Cambridge: Cambridge University Press.

Berkes, F. (1999) *Sacred Ecology: Traditional Ecological Knowledge and Resource Management*, Philadelphia, PA/London: Taylor & Francis.

Berthelsen, J. (2014) 'Sedition Axe Falls on Malaysian Press', *Asia Sentinel*, 6 September.

Blakemore, T. L. (1947) 'Post-war Developments in Japanese Law', *Wisconsin Law Review*, July: 632–653.

Bowen, J. (2003) *Islam, Law and Equality in Indonesia: An Anthropology of Public Reasoning*, Cambridge: Cambridge University Press.

Burns, P. J. (1999) *The Leiden Legacy: Concepts of Law in Indonesia*, Jakarta: PT Pradnya Paramita.

Brosius, J. P., Lowenhaupt Tsing, A., and Zerner, C. (eds) (2005) *Communities and Conservation: Histories and Politics of Community-based Natural Resource Management*, Lanham, MD/Plymouth: Altamira Press.

Cao, D. (2004) *Chinese Law: A Language Perspective*, Aldershot: Ashgate.
Castells, M. (1992) 'Four Asian Tigers with a Dragon Head: A Comparative Analysis of State, Economy and Society in the Asian Pacific Rim', in R. P. Appelbaum and J. Henderson (eds) *States and Development in the Asian Pacific Rim*, Newbury Park, CA/London/New Delhi: Sage, 33–70.
Chen, J. (2003) 'Policy as Law and Law as Policy: The Role of Law in China's Development Strategy', in C. Antons (ed) *Law and Development in East and Southeast Asia*, London/New York: Routledge Curzon, 251–270.
Chen, J. (2007) 'Role/Rule of Law in China Reconsidered', in C. Antons and V. Gessner (eds) *Globalisation and Resistance: Law Reform in Asia since the Crisis*, Oxford/Portland, OR: Hart, 179–207.
Cochrane, J. (2014a) 'Defamation Law Reminds Critics of Indonesia's Past', *The New York Times*, 22 September.
Cochrane, J. (2014b) 'Embrace of Atheism Put an Indonesian in Prison', *The New York Times*, 3 May.
Coppel, C. (1999) 'The Indonesian Chinese as "Foreign Orientals" in Indonesia', in T. Lindsey (ed.) *Indonesia: Law and Society*, Sydney: Federation Press, 33–41.
Coronel, S. S. (ed.) (2001) *The Right to Know: Access to Information in Southeast Asia*, Quezon City: The Philippine Center for Investigative Journalism.
Dean, M. (1997) *Japanese Legal System: Text and Materials*, London: Cavendish.
Dirlik, A. (ed.) (1993) *What Is In a Rim? Critical Perspectives on the Pacific Region Idea*, Boulder, CO/ Oxford: Westview Press.
Donovan, J. M., and Anderson, H. E., III (2003) *Anthropology and Law*, New York/Oxford: Berghahn Books.
Dove, M. R. (2005) 'Use of Global Legal Mechanisms to Conserve Local Biogenetic Resources: Problems and Prospects', in M. R. Dove, P. E. Sajise and A. A, Doolittle (eds) *Conserving Nature in Culture: Case Studies from Southeast Asia*, New Haven, CT: Yale University Southeast Asian Studies, 279–305.
du Plessis, J. J., Hargovan, A., Bagaric, M., and Harris, J. (2014) *Principles of Contemporary Corporate Governance*, 3rd edn, Melbourne: Cambridge University Press.
Eder, J. F., and McKenna, T. M. (2004) 'Minorities in the Philippines: Ancestral Lands and Autonomy in Theory and Practice', in C. R. Duncan (ed.) *Civilizing the Margins: Southeast Asian Government Policies for the Development of Minorities*, Ithaca, NY/London: Cornell University Press, 56–85.
Ellen, R., Parkes, P., and Bicker, A. (eds) (2000) *Indigenous Environmental Knowledge and its Transformations: Critical Anthropological Perspectives*, London/New York: Routledge.
Fasseur, C. (1994) 'Cornerstone and Stumbling Block: Racial Classification and the Late Colonial State in Indonesia', in R. Cribb (ed.) *The Late Colonial State in Indonesia: Political and Economic Foundations of the Netherlands Indies 1880–1942*, Leiden: KITLV Press, 31–56.
Fasseur, C. (2007) 'Colonial Dilemma: Van Vollenhoven and the Struggle between *Adat* Law and Western Law in Indonesia', in J. Davidson and D. Henley (eds) *The Revival of Tradition in Indonesian Politics*, London/New York: Routledge, 50–67.
Fuller, T. (2013) 'In Thailand, a Broader Definition of Insulting Royalty', *The New York Times*, 17 January.
Gan, S., Gomez, J., and Johannen, U. (eds) (2004) *Asian Cyberactivism: Freedom of Expression and Media Censorship*, Bangkok: Friedrich Naumann Foundation.
Gardner, J. (1980) *Legal Imperialism: American Lawyers and Foreign Aid in Latin America*, Madison, WI/London: University of Wisconsin Press.
Geismar, H. (2013) *Treasured Possessions: Indigenous Interventions into Cultural and Intellectual Property*, Durham, NC/London: Duke University Press.
Gillespie, J. (1999) 'Law and Development in "the Market Place" ': An East Asian Perspective', in K. Jayasuriya (ed.) *Law, Capitalism and Power in Asia*, London/New York: Routledge, 118–150.
Gillespie, J., and Peerenboom, R. (eds) (2009) *Regulation in Asia: Pushing back on Globalization*, London/New York: Routledge.

Ginsburg, T., and Chen, A. H. Y. (eds) (2009) *Administrative Law and Governance in Asia: Comparative Perspectives*, London/New York: Routledge.

Glenn, H. P. (2007) *Legal Traditions of the World: Sustainable Diversity in Law*, 3rd edn, Oxford/New York: Oxford University Press.

Goldstein, P., and Straus, J. (eds) (2009) *Intellectual Property in Asia: Law, Economics, History and Politics*, Berlin/Heidelberg: Springer.

Graber, C. B., Kuprecht, K., and Lai, J. C. (eds) (2012) *International Trade in Indigenous Cultural Heritage: Legal and Policy Issues*, Cheltenham /Northampton, MA: Edward Elgar.

Haggard, S. (1990) *Pathways from the Periphery: The Politics of Growth in the Newly Industrializing Countries*, Ithaca, NY/London: Cornell University Press.

Halliday, T. C., and Carruthers, B. G. (2007) 'Foiling the Financial Hegemons: Limits to the Globalization of Corporate Insolvency Regimes in Indonesia, Korea and China', in C. Antons and V. Gessner (eds) *Globalisation and Resistance: Law Reform in Asia since the Crisis*, Oxford/Portland, OR: Hart, 255–301.

Harding, A., and Nicholson, P. (eds) (2010) *New Courts in Asia*, London/New York: Routledge.

Heath, C. (ed.) (2003) *Intellectual Property Law in Asia*, London: Kluwer Law International.

Hickling, R. H. (2001) *Malaysian Law: An Introduction to the Concept of Law in Malaysia*, Subang Jaya: Pelanduk.

Jacobsen, M., and Bruun, O. (eds) (2000) *Human Rights and Asian Values: Contesting National Identities and Cultural Representations in Asia*, London/New York: Routledge Curzon.

Jakarta Post (2014) 'PDI-P Reports Jokowi's Fake Obituary to Police', 17 May.

Jayasuriya, K. (ed.) (1999) *Law, Capitalism and Power in Asia: The Rule of Law and Legal Institutions*, London/New York: Routledge.

Johnson, C. (1982) *MITI and the Japanese Miracle: The Growth of Industrial Policy, 1925–1975*, Stanford, CA: Stanford University Press.

Jomo, K. S. (2003a) 'Introduction: Southeast Asia's Ersatz Miracle', in K. S. Jomo (ed.) *Southeast Asian Paper Tigers? From Miracle to Debacle and beyond*, London/New York: Routledge Curzon, 1–18.

Jomo, K. S. (2003b) *Southeast Asian Paper Tigers? From Miracle to Debacle and beyond*, London/New York: Routledge Curzon.

Jomo, K. S., and Wong Sau Ngan (eds) (2008) *Law, Institutions and Malaysian Economic Development*, Singapore: NUS Press.

Jones, C. A. G. (1994) 'Capitalism, Globalization and Rule of Law: An Alternative Trajectory of Legal Change in China', *Social and Legal Studies*, 3(2): 195–221.

Kayaoğlu, T. (2014) *Legal Imperialism: Sovereignty and Extraterritoriality in Japan, the Ottoman Empire, and China*, Cambridge: Cambridge University Press.

Kramer, P. A. (2006) *The Blood of Government: Race, Empire, the United States and the Philippines*, Manila: Ateneo de Manila University Press.

Legrand, P. (1997) 'The Impossibility of "Legal Transplants" ', *Maastricht Journal of European and Comparative Law*, 4(2): 111–124.

Lev, D. S. (2000) *Legal Evolution and Political Authority in Indonesia: Selected Essays*, The Hague/Cambridge, MA: Kluwer Law International.

Lindsey, T. (ed.) (2008) *Indonesia: Law and Society*, 2nd edn, Sydney: Federation Press.

Loos, T. (2006) *Subject Siam: Family, Law, and Colonial Modernity in Thailand*, Chiang Mai: Silkworm Books.

Lucas, A., and Warren, C. (2003) 'The State, the People and Their Mediators: The Struggle over Agrarian Law Reform in Post-New Order Indonesia', *Indonesia*, 76: 87–126.

Lucas, A., and Warren, C. (eds) (2013) *Land for the People: The State and Agrarian Conflict in Indonesia*, Athens, OH: Ohio University Press.

McCarthy, J. F. (2004) 'Changing to Gray: Decentralization and the Emergence of Volatile Socio-Legal Configurations in Central Kalimantan, Indonesia', *World Development*, 32(7): 1199–1223.

McFarlane, B. (1993) 'Review of M. Howard and T. Wheelwright (eds), *The Struggle for Development: Essays in Honour of Ernst Utrecht*', *Journal of Contemporary Asia*, 23(2): 284–286.

Medcalf, R. (2013) 'The Indo-Pacific: What's In a Name? *The American Interest* 9(2): 60–65.
Menski, W. (2000) *Comparative Law in a Global Context: The Legal Systems of Asia and Africa*, London: Platinum.
Morgan, A. (2000) 'TRIPS to Thailand: The Act for the Establishment of and Procedure for Intellectual Property and International Trade Court', *Fordham International Law Journal*, 23(3): 795–847.
Newton, S. (2006) 'The Dialectics of Law and Development', in D. M. Trubek and A. Santos (eds) *The New Law and Economic Development: A Critical Appraisal*, Cambridge: Cambridge University Press, 174–202.
Ohnesorge, J. K. M. (2003) 'The Rule of Law, Economic Development, and the Developmental States of Northeast Asia', in C. Antons (ed.) *Law and Development in East and Southeast Asia*, London/New York: Routledge Curzon, 91–127.
Panagariya, A. (2008) *India: The Emerging Giant*, Oxford/New York: Oxford University Press.
Peerenboom, R. (2002) 'Varieties of Rule of Law: An Introduction and Provisional Conclusion', in R. Peerenboom (ed.) *Asian Discourses of Rule of Law: Theories and Implementation of Rule of Law in Twelve Asian Countries, France and the US*, London/New York: Routledge Curzon, 1–55.
Peerenboom, R. (2006) 'What Have We Learned about Law and Development? Describing, Predicting and Assessing Legal Reforms in China', *Michigan Journal of International Law*, 27: 823–871.
Peerenboom, R. (2007) *China Modernises: Threat to the West or Model for the Rest?*, Oxford/New York: Oxford University Press.
Persoon, G. A. (2009) ' "Being Indigenous" in Indonesia and the Philippines', in C. Antons (ed.) *Traditional Knowledge, Traditional Cultural Expressions and Intellectual Property Law in the Asia-Pacific Region*, Alphen aan den Rijn: Kluwer Law International, 195–216.
Posey, D. A. (2008) 'Indigenous Management of Tropical Forest Ecosystems: The Case of the Kayapó Indian of the Brazilian Amazon', in M. R. Dove and C. Carpenter (eds) *Environmental Anthropology: A Historical Reader*, Malden, MA/Oxford/Melbourne: Blackwell, 89–101.
Redding, S. G. (1993) *The Spirit of Chinese Capitalism*, Berlin/New York: Walter de Gruyter.
Redding, S. G. (1996) 'Societal Transformation and the Contribution of Authority Relations and Cooperation Norms in Overseas Chinese Business', in Tu Wei-Ming (ed.) *Confucian Traditions in East Asian Modernity: Moral Education and Economic Culture in Japan and the Four Mini-Dragons*, Cambridge, MA/London: Harvard University Press, 310–327.
Robison, R., and Hadiz, V. R. (2004) *Reorganising Power in Indonesia: The Politics of Oligarchy in an Age of Markets*, London: Routledge Curzon.
Rodan, G. (1989) *The Political Economy of Singapore's Industrialization: National State and International Capital*, Basingstoke: Macmillan.
Rodan, G. (2004) *Transparency and Authoritarian Rule in Southeast Asia: Singapore and Malaysia*, London/New York: Routledge.
Shiva, V. (1991) *The Violence of the Green Revolution: Third World Agriculture, Ecology and Politics*, London/New York/Penang: Zed Books.
Sissons, J. (2005) *First Peoples: Indigenous Cultures and their Futures*, London: Reaktion Books.
Smith, M. (1996) 'Australian Perspectives on Asian Law: Directions for the Next Decade', in V. Taylor (ed.) *Asian Laws through Australian Eyes*, Sydney: LBC Information Services, 3–16.
Steenstrup, C. (1996) *A History of Law in Japan until 1868*, 2nd edn, Leiden: Brill.
Taylor, V. (ed.) (1996) *Asian Laws through Australian Eyes*, Sydney: LBC Information Services.
Trubek, D. M., and Galanter, M. (1974) 'Scholars in Self-estrangement: Some Reflections on the Crisis in Law and Development Studies in the United States', *Wisconsin Law Review*, 4: 1062–1102.
Trubek, D. M., and Santos, A. (2006) 'Introduction: The Third Moment in Law and Development Theory and the Emergence of a New Critical Practice', in D. M. Trubek and A. Santos (eds) *The New Law and Economic Development*, Cambridge: Cambridge University Press, 1–18.
Tu Wei-Ming (1996) 'Introduction', in Tu Wei-Ming (ed.) *Confucian Tradition in East Asian Modernity*, Cambridge, MA/London: Harvard University Press, 1–10.

UNCTAD and ICTSD (2005) *Resource Book on TRIPS and Development*, Cambridge: Cambridge University Press.

Vaitsos, C. V. (1976) 'The Revision of the International Patent System: Legal Considerations for a Third World Position', *World Development*, 4(2): 85–102.

Vandergeest, P., and Peluso, N. L. (2001a) 'Genealogies of the Political Forest and Customary Rights in Indonesia, Malaysia and Thailand', *The Journal of Asian Studies*, 60(3): 761–812.

Vandergeest, P., and Peluso, N. L. (2001b) 'Territorialization and State Power in Thailand', in N. Blomley, D. Delaney and R. T. Ford (eds) *The Legal Geographies Reader*, Oxford/Malden, MA: Blackwell, 177–186.

Vandergeest, P., and Wittayapak, C. (2010) 'Decentralisation and Politics', in C. Wittayapak and P. Vandergeest (eds) *The Politics of Decentralisation: Natural Resource Management in Asia*, Chiang Mai: Mekong Press, 1–20.

Vogel, E. F. (1991) *The Four Little Dragons: The Spread of Industrialization in East Asia*, Cambridge, MA/London: Harvard University Press.

von Benda-Beckmann, F. (1979) *Property in Social Continuity: Continuity and Change in the Maintenance of Property Relationships through Time in Minangkabau, West Sumatra*, The Hague: Martinus Nijhoff.

Watson, A. (1993) *Legal Transplants: An Approach to Comparative Law*, 2nd edn, Athens, GA: University of Georgia Press.

Wertheim, W. F. (1959) *Indonesian Society in Transition: A Study of Social Change*, The Hague: W. van Hoeve.

Wittayapak, C., and Vandergeest, P. (2010) *The Politics of Decentralization: Natural Resource Management in Asia*, Chiang Mai: Mekong Press.

Wong, J. (1996) 'Promoting Confucianism for Socioeconomic Development: The Singapore Experience', in Tu Wei-Ming (ed.) *Confucian Tradition in East Asian Modernity*, Cambridge, MA/London: Harvard University Press, 277–293.

World Bank (1993) *The East Asian Miracle: Economic Growth and Public Policy*, Oxford: Oxford University Press.

Yamamura, K., and Yasuba, Y. (eds) (1987) *The Political Economy of Japan, Vol. 1: The Domestic Transformation*, Stanford, CA: Stanford University Press.

Zweigert, K., and Kötz, H. (1998) *An Introduction to Comparative Law*, 3rd edn, Oxford/New York: Clarendon Press.

2 Law; networks; mobility

Nineteenth-century provocations

Iza Hussin

A collective of scholars seeking to produce a handbook of Asian law in the early years of the twentieth century might have found themselves in much the same position as we do, a century later, asking some of the same questions: amidst the global, cosmopolitan and international, where should one start to seek out 'Asian law'? At a time when law's promises seem so reliably to have been followed by its limitations, what continuities and ruptures matter most for understanding a period of rapid transformation in law, its institutions and its politics? How might we balance the work of charting law's infinite variety with mapping its internal consistencies and prevailing tendencies? This chapter uses questions that arise from charting the movement of law across Asia in the nineteenth century as provocations for contemporary research: first, what does an exploration of law's movements reveal about Asia's politics, polities and political economies? Second, how do these politics vary across time and space, and why? Third, what might an exploration of Asian law in movement reveal about law itself and how might it advance a critical agenda for Asian or comparative law?[1]

As at the end of the twentieth century, in the last decades of the nineteenth, faith in law as an instrument of policy was in its ascendance, evident in large-scale efforts at legal reform and consolidation such as the Indian Penal Code (1862), the Ottoman Civil Code (1877), the Meiji Constitution (1890), the Johor Constitution (1895) and the Constitution of the Malolos Congress (1899). The location and timing of these legal transformations raise critical questions about the geography and chronology of 'Asian law' in the nineteenth century that continue to require answers today: what were the routes and networks that made Calcutta, Constantinople, Tokyo, Johor and Manila significant ports of call for law? The first of the nineteenth-century provocations for our current project is that *the study of law's mobility reveals underlying topologies of people, ideas and commodities.* In nineteenth-century Asia, these included colonialism, imperialism, trade and family, and the study of law across Asia continues to require attention to law's multiple genealogies in the region. Similar questions about the topology of law in the twentieth century might reveal the importance of both old and new ports of call for Asian law: Singapore, Beijing, Delhi, Washington, DC, and Brussels, and the currents of people, ideas and commodities that run among these nodes.

An analytic focus on these genealogies of law may also make evident the continuing importance of networks across Asia for the movement and translation of law, comprising travelling legal professionals, diplomats, entrepreneurs, diaspora and labourers, and the actors at each port who worked to domesticate law for local use and for the furtherance of their own interests. The second provocation, therefore, is that *the study of law's networks across Asia reveals the articulation of the mobile with the local.* In the nineteenth century, colonial officials, indigenous rulers, members of diasporic families and merchant houses all balanced their cosmopolitanism with local knowledge and contacts. These local articulations continue to be important because, in addition to the insight they provide into the work that must be done to maintain law's legibility, authority and efficacy across time and space, they condition law's politics and its potential at every site. As the travels of criminal and constitutional law in the nineteenth century and beyond show, the mere diffusion of a legal text or code is ultimately far less impactful for the life of the law than the meanings and institutional implications it takes on upon arrival.

Efforts at legal reform and transformation across Asia in the nineteenth century also marked a heightened consciousness that law should reflect the indigenous and particular at the same time as it appealed to the global and universal – a consciousness that continues to dominate today in law's politics. This concern raises the third of our analytic provocations: that the study of law across the Asian arena makes possible a deeper understanding of the systematic and institutional elements of law that enable and impel its movement. In other words, *tracking law across Asia reveals the processes by which law itself travels* – that it is dependent on multiple and competing claims to authority and sovereignty, that the ambiguity of language and the work of translation play critical roles in law's mobility, and that institutional path dependencies condition law's limits and its logic in each case. As we seek answers in this volume to questions of law's impact on development, its entanglements in tradition and transformation, its promises of rights, order and access, hence we may also contribute to deeper understanding of law itself, of its role in defining and transforming Asia, and of its potential as a field of Asian studies.

Mobility: People, ideas and commodities

The careers of British colonial officials, which regularly began in one site of empire and progressed within a hierarchy of posts that included Ireland, India, Malaya, Egypt and Africa, provide one kind of trajectory along which people, ideas and economic interests moved across large swathes of distance and time. The spread of common law systems throughout the British Empire and beyond, to sites never officially colonised by the British, was effected by men such as Evelyn Baring, Lord Cromer (1841–1917), who went to India as private secretary for Lord Northbrook, Viceroy of India in 1872, and then served as Imperial Proconsul in Egypt between 1883 and 1907, during which time he put into action lessons learned in India (Owen, 2005).[2] These lessons included the need for law to achieve economic liberalisation alongside social reform, in a formula that may ring familiar today: low taxation, free trade and *laissez-faire* economic policies, the stabilisation of contract and property, anti-corruption and the regularisation of government, the alleviation of poverty and the maintenance of social order (Mowat, 1973: 113). The prioritisation of economic policies facilitated imperial economic interests while maintaining a sense of non-interference in local institutions.[3]

Colonial law was neither a uniform nor neutral vehicle for the transplantation of law: colonial officials and local elites not only adapted law for local use and institutionalisation, but interpreted the meanings and application of these laws based on assumptions about local contexts and mores. The overall pattern of change was towards the extension of state authority over new domains and the strengthening of state sovereignty vis-à-vis local power-holders. The pattern of colonial-era rule of law calls into question whether it is possible to change the structure of a legal system and not its political dynamics, whether it is possible to 'reform' only Islamic law and not affect the scope of state law, and whether a mixed system can really be understood as simply the sum of its parts (Hussin, 2012). In the case of British law, in both the settler colonies and territories under direct and indirect rule, the process by which law moved was iterated, contingent and contentious, and creative of new power arrangements. In British India and Malaya, for example, colonial legal reforms helped to carve out a separate domain for religion and custom, into which a new politics of Hindu and Muslim identity would emerge with increasing valency in the nineteenth and twentieth centuries (Hussin, 2016).

The British were, of course, but one of a number of imperial players in the region and, in fact, the experience of travel, trade and politics in Asia in the period of colonialism and imperialism was more often than not conditioned by imperial competition and nested sovereignty. For both the Ottoman and the Meiji Empires, legal reforms modelled on European systems were undertaken for the purposes of internal consolidation and external recognition (*New York Times*, 1890; Collier, 1994; Aydin, 2006; Hussin, 2014a; Kazuhiro, 2007). The Ottoman Empire served as a powerful symbolic and political counterpoint to European powers at the doorstep of Muslim rulers in Aceh and Johor (Reid, 2005); the Meiji and Ottoman regimes provided important object lessons for monarchs contemplating legal reforms, such as Chulalongkorn (who rejected an 1885 proposal for a constitution along Japanese lines) and Abu Bakar (who proposed an Ottoman-style civil code for Johor in 1893 and a constitution in 1895). The chronology and geography of legal reform across Asia in the nineteenth century reveals a circuit of legal ideas and institutions conditioned by imperial competition, by inter-Asian exchange and mobility, and marking a common concern among Asian monarchs to consolidate their power and their succession through the selective adaptation of European legal instruments (Hussin, 2014a).

Beyond the level of statecraft, other types of mobility persisted and flourished, aided by new communications technologies and imperial consolidation. Trading diaspora such as the Hadhrami Arabs, circuits of Muslim pilgrims, teachers and texts, and multi-generational families connected by land and estates across the Indian Ocean all depended upon, and generated, law – whether in the form of legal agents and experts whose stock in trade was translating among legal orders (Freitag, 2003; Ho, 2004; Gilsenan, 2011), in shared contractual lexicons of trust and exchange (Bishara, 2014), or in the negotiation of colonial and personal law systems (Stephens, 2014). In other cases, mobility itself might be instigated by legal opportunity, such as when litigants went forum-shopping across the courts of various jurisdictions to achieve more favourable verdicts (Sharafi, 2010), or to flee the jurisdiction of unfavourable laws.

These flows of law accompanied flows of people and commodities, but operated in accordance to multiple logics and chronologies: while estates and inheritances followed the pace of births and deaths, the conflicts sparked by litigants' claims based upon marriage and lineage, contracts, promissory notes and certificates of manumission were dependent upon markets, labour and migration. Law travelled in many and diverse trajectories, therefore: some aimed at colonial extraction and administration, and others at imperial consolidation and domestic order; some at legibility and continuity across generations, and others at targeted opportunities for profit and advantage.

Networks: The articulation of mobile and local

Tracing the movement of law across Asia in the nineteenth century makes clear that law depended upon existing networks of agents, institutions and interests, and that European empires played important, but not monopolistic, roles in this traffic. Attention to law's itineraries also helps to highlight another matter that tends to have been overlooked in the literature on legal transmission and transplant (Watson, 1993; Legrand, 1997; Kennedy, 2003; Twining, 2004; Westbrook, 2006): where the law stopped on the way from the metropole to distant sites of empire. At critical nodes across Asia such as Calcutta and Singapore, British law was translated, domesticated, rearticulated and repackaged for onward transport, and here we will briefly discuss processes by which criminal and constitutional law underwent transformation as they travelled through India in particular (Metcalf, 2007).

The Indian Penal Code was brought to Singapore, Sri Lanka, Malaysia, Brunei and Burma, and remains the core of criminal law in these states (Hussin, 2012: 25–26 *passim*). Yet the movement of law from England to India to other sites of empire had important effects on the law itself and continues to be significant for the criminal law of post-British colonies. The development of the Indian Penal Code is perhaps the definitive example of the manner in which law travelled from England to India and the transformation it underwent on the way. The 1862 Indian Penal Code was put into place in India as a result of debates in England over the criminal justice system – debates that did not result in a criminal code in England, but which stimulated the desire to put British justice into effect in India. The Code attempted to create in India a rule of law that could be only an ideal in England (Skuy, 1998). The English law reform movement was led by utilitarians such as Bentham and Mill, and the Indian Penal Code shows their influence in both its form and its content, but also the influence of a growing unease over criminality in England and the perceived inability of the justice system to stem the tide of crime. The myth of origins runs deep and continues to affect Indian law: even though the Indian Penal Code did not draw exclusively from English law and even though its drafter, Thomas Babington Macauley (1800–59), inserted new elements based on supposed 'Indian' realities such as criminal castes, *thuggee* (ritual murder) and *dacoity* (banditry) (Singha, 1993), English law is still a referent for Indian judges.

The Indian Penal Code formed the basis of criminal law in Singapore, Malaya, Egypt and other states, where it is still in effect and where judges still refer to Indian case law. The aims of the Code were understood by colonial reformers to be 'modern' and to be particularly suited to native, non-European populations: the commission appointed to draft a penal code in Egypt in 1919 looked to the Indian Penal Code 'to bring them into harmony with modern ideas', since it was a criminal law that 'has for many years been successfully applied to races . . . that in character and habits closely resemble those inhabiting Egypt, and it has already been adopted in a modified form by the Sudan' (Alexander, 1919: 244). The codification, regularisation and enforcement of criminal law was itself an innovation wherever the Indian Penal Code was instituted, but particular substantive provisions of the Code (such as those arbitrating sexual morality, gender and family life) placed new domains of life into the jurisdiction of the state, with consequences reaching into the contemporary period.

In the area of constitutional law, too, India has played a critical role throughout Asia. To cite another case of travelling law, albeit briefly, the Indian Constitution has been a model for constitutions throughout the Commonwealth, in the absence of a written British constitution. The constitutional documents drawn up in Whitehall in the post-war era were aimed at a number of goals, among them the development of parliamentary style democracies based on the British ideal, the securing of rights for minority Anglo settlers in regimes now under local elite control and the sense of a legacy passed on to the Commonwealth at the end of Empire (Dale, 1993). In addition, the Indian Constitution took on elements from the United States, such as guarantees of civil liberties.

Constitutional conventions and intermediate instruments provided the basis for modifications to fit each context. In Malaysia, for example, the legacy of nineteenth-century reforms of law reorganised local elite hierarchies and resources (such as land), and formed the basis for constitutional modifications that privileged Malay ethnic identity in the newly independent Malaysia. Other elements of the Indian Constitution were imported wholesale, but to different effect; among the most important of these differences were the ways in which constitutional issues were elaborated by the courts. In India, constitutional issues were brought to the courts and hotly contested in the initial years of its promulgation; in Malaysia, there was much less contest in the courts over constitutional provisions (Sheridan, 1964). As a result, constitutional debates in Malaysia continue to cite earlier Indian cases; as the courts in Malaysia and India take on new constitutional issues, it will be a matter of some interest whether these constitutional traditions diverge or continue to draw from each other. Here, the work of judges, lawyers and activists in framing issues and their interpretations has been of signal importance (Moustafa, 2013).

These travels of law through India illustrate that there are multiple factors that might cause the law to move: metropolitan desires for reform that were thwarted domestically, but found in the colonies a laboratory for social and political experimentation; the entrepreneurialism of local rulers, judges, lawyers and litigants; and the sense that legal reform carried with it social and political progress and modernisation. While law offered itself as a mobile and universal resource, it also generated a demand for the local and particular, some of which demands were met with new colonial imaginaries of tradition and custom, some met with strategic articulations of local context and circumstances, and others elaborated through contest and arbitration into local legal institutions and logics. Local articulations of mobile law matter a great deal for what law can do and what its limits are seen to be. In the late nineteenth century, legal reforms that introduced penal codes, civil codes and constitutions in the Ottoman Empire, India, Malaya and Japan did not merely import texts wholesale, but were projects of selection, negotiation and interpretation. In these local projects, rulers, diplomats, scribes and translators, lawyers, judges and middlemen played critical arbitrating and interpretive roles, and the work these actors undertook in law's travels makes clear how dependent the law itself is on iteration, repetition, translation and maintenance for its continued authority and legibility (Hussin, 2014b).

How law travels: Competition; ambiguity; institutionalisation

In 1895, the Sultan of Johor put into place what seems to have been Southeast Asia's first constitution, to which moment we can trace the origins of modern constitutional monarchy in the Malay Peninsula and components of the language of the Federal Constitution of Malaysia on issues critical to the contemporary politics of Islam, ethnicity, the state religion, the position of the sovereign and the privileges of the monarch. The Sultan's motivations appear largely to have been for the security of his succession and its sovereignty from direct British control. Thus the adoption of the Constitution combined an awareness of the precarity of his position with the potential that law held for consolidating his authority, his legitimacy and the image of his state – as modern, as civilised along European lines, and as representative of his people and his constituencies. Two years earlier, the Sultan had adopted the *Mecelle*, the civil code of the Ottoman Empire, placing the Constitution within the context of legal reforms that also positioned Johor as a Muslim state, and linking Johor to the symbolic and Islamic authority of the Ottoman state.

Both of these legal moves were made possible by a careful and iterated process of translation and interpretation among multiple languages – Arabic, Malay and English – and law's ambiguity facilitated its mobility (Hussin, 2014b).

These reforms, like those undertaken in Constantinople and Japan a few decades earlier, represented concerns common to Asian states in the late nineteenth century – that is, to facilitate internal consolidation through legal instruments and state institutions selectively adopted from European models. Monarchs such as Abu Bakar undertook extensive world travels and were themselves part of a cosmopolitan elite well known within both European and Asian diplomatic circles (Nakahara, 1994; Hussin, 2014a). Court advisers frequently travelled both regionally and globally, carrying comparative lessons from one court to another, and relying upon the same legal firms, lawyers and business advisers. European legal advisers were consulted across a range of possible models in the making of the Meiji Constitution, the Prussian inflections of which in turn became one possible future for Asian states contemplating legal reform, such as Siam and Johor. Certainly, by the end of the nineteenth century, rulers and rising elites in Asia would have had a number of referents for both the potential of law as an instrument of regime consolidation and its pitfalls. When contemplating a constitution for Johor, Sultan Abu Bakar and his advisers would have been well aware of King Chulalongkorn's decision to reject an 1885 proposal for constitutional monarchy for Siam, put forward by Siamese elites in Europe; likewise, he would have borne witness to the suspension of the Tanzimat Constitution by Sultan Abdulhamid II in 1878.[4]

Rather than understanding legal adoptions in terms of legal transplant or diffusion, therefore, it may be productive to see the patterns of legal adoption and adaptation as outcomes of repeated and manifold struggles between the mobile and the local, each of these mapping an ongoing demarcation between the general and particular elements of law and legal institutionalisation. Asian states such as Japan, Turkey and Johor, rather than entering a modern era with their acceptance of European law, were themselves involved in the making of a critical and increasingly global understanding of what it meant to be modern and/or European, as part of the project of state-building in the nineteenth century. European empires and rising states were also deeply invested in the success and extension of these models, the contours of which were just beginning to emerge as part of a global lexicon of comparative legal scholarship and policy.

The pressing realities of the state-building project included a world of nested, rather than absolute, sovereignties, and of carefully balanced domestic and imperial constituencies. Here, again, law's travels depended upon the success of its translation across institutional and political vernaculars – that is, the ability of legal reforms to be seen as building upon key foundations of regime legitimacy, such as Islam, imperial stability or divine kingship. Law's mobility, far from being only an instrument of change, was very often a component of the maintenance and reconstruction of 'tradition'; hence the path-dependencies of law were part of its onward trajectories and critical to its legitimations.

Ongoing concerns: New ports of call; new ambiguities

In this new era of faith in law, looking back to the nineteenth century allows a few questions to remain in focus: who are the Cromers, Kitcheners and Wingates of twenty-first-century rule of law? What baggage (economic, political, social and ideological) travels with them? And what networks facilitate the contemporary travels of law? Who are their local counterparts, what domestications of rule of law have they created, and upon what assumptions about local life and society have these been based? The role of the United States, international organisations and non-governmental players has increased dramatically, and new models for rule of law have become prominent. Even though agencies such as the World Bank, International Monetary Fund (IMF) and US Agency for International Development (USAID) may begin with policies of non-interference, as did the British in some colonial states, what interventions has the project of rule of law required? How have local elites negotiated these projects, and the opportunities and the challenges they present? The colonial project of legal reform resulted in new local hierarchies, new definitions of state, society and subject, and unintended consequences in the realms of ethnicity, religion, public and private: how far does this history allow us to see into the future of current rule-of-law projects? This last question takes us to new ports of call in the circulation of rule of law: just as India played an important role for the extension of British rule of law, we now look to Singapore for the trajectories of contemporary rule of law (Hussin, 2012).

While Singapore's legal system owes much to India, there are marked differences in the handling of law and legal instruments, for example between the handling of criminal law and that of family law. The British attempt to domesticate the Penal Code for India involved inserting elements of 'Indian' criminality, as defined by the British – dacoity, thuggery – into a reformed code that could not be implemented in the United Kingdom. The Code stopped in Calcutta on its way to Cairo and Singapore, dispersing Indian Penal Code provisions through criminal law in post-colonial Singapore and Malaysia. In the post-colonial legatees of British India, as well as in Singapore and Malaysia, an autonomous sphere of law was constructed for Islam and Hinduism, defined by a reliance on ancient/classical texts and limited in its scope to matters of family law and religious observance. These localisations not only secured the support and legitimacy of some local elites, but also reinforced Victorian-era British ideals of family, patriarchy and a private domestic sphere (Hussin, 2016).

These localisations and domestications continue to have important consequences. In Singapore, for example, attempts to remove section 377A (which prohibits 'gross indecency' between men) from the Penal Code were met with objections from the ruling government on the grounds that the law expressed local cultural sensitivities that would be offended by the decriminalisation of sex between men. Local advocates and scholars have argued that the 'local sensitivities' of section 377A to which the government refers are Victorian strictures, rather than the cultural views of either the Chinese majority or minority ethnic communities. This argument seems borne out by the preponderance of evangelical Christian objections to the abolition of section 377A and the human-rights-based arguments of pro-abolitionists, in the face of largely silent Chinese (Confucianist/Taoist), Indian (Hindu/Christian) or even Malay (Muslim) groups. Defending the decision to maintain section 377A on the law books, Prime Minister Lee Hsien Loong argued that Singapore was 'a conservative society' and that he wished to keep it so (BBC News, 2007).[5] British colonial law written for the Indian Penal Code has therefore been used in Singapore to reconstitute a social vision: that of a 'conservative' society. Rule of law in Singapore, despite its role as a translatable model, had turned out to remain a profoundly local instrument (Tan, 1989). The model of Singaporean rule of law has its share of proponents and detractors, but if we see Singapore, by virtue of its economic successes and political stability, as an important new clearing house for developing legal systems in Asia – in China and Cambodia, for example – this raises troubling questions about rule of law.

Singapore is significant as a port of call for rule of law because of its economic success, its social stability and its growing influence on countries in Asia, as well as elsewhere, which wish to replicate this success. As in the case of India in the colonial and immediate post-colonial period, where law stops in its travels is significant for what law becomes. A World Bank report on judicial reform in Singapore has praised its efforts at 'modernisation' and characterised its strategies as 'Using Leadership', 'Refining Models of Justice and Expanding Alternatives', 'Increasing Access', 'Improving Court Administration Capacity', 'Improving Human Resource Management', 'Emphasising Performance and Results', 'Leveraging Technology' and 'Building Bridges' (Malik, 2007). While the report itself is quite clear that it takes a 'managerial' view of the question of reform, it is also clear that Singapore is explicitly a model for other countries to follow.

Here is where the vagueness of rule-of-law concepts becomes more than a frustration for scholars and rather a problem for the realisation of rule of law itself (Santos, 2006): what does rule of law, as exemplified by Singaporean legal reform, imply for the states which wish to emulate it? As this chapter has shown, the terms 'common law' or mixed legal system are not up to the task of specifying rule of law. Tracing the path of legal travel, its personnel and their interests, worldviews and assumptions goes some way towards clarifying the complexities of rule-of-law circulations. Being aware of transformations in law as it stops at particular ports of call adds another layer of understanding. Even so, the case of Singaporean rule of law illustrates the fundamental problem of this capacious concept: what exactly does the term 'rule of law' contain? And when one kind of rule of law – for example market-friendly legal reforms or judicial efficiency – takes precedence in state policies over another – such as political freedoms or constitutional robustness – how should scholars evaluate the project as a whole?

Definitive answers are few, but this chapter has attempted to trace possible trajectories for analysis, based on a methodology attuned to law's circulation through networks of agents, ideas and commodities, seeking out continuities and patterns across the Asian arena, and through the supposed ruptures wrought by state-building and modernisation. As law moves from one site to another, it traces a line of struggle between the general and particular, and describes a political economy peculiar to each site, in which local actors translate, domesticate and rearticulate law to fit and to reconstruct what is traditional, legitimate and authoritative. Law's ability to move depends upon its ability to articulate with local institutions and meanings, even as its appeal resides in its ambiguity and multiplicity. Historically, these ambiguities have often lent themselves to projects of state consolidation, in the area of constitutional and criminal law, as we have discussed above, but state elites in Asia have long been keenly aware of the potential of law for disruption, as well as for stabilisation. Long-standing networks and circulations of families, of trade and labour, and of information and ideas have served to limit the ability of states to control the movement of law or its outcomes, and continue to provide a large measure of law's itinerancy, as well as its horizons.

Notes

1 Portions of this chapter were previously published as a working paper (Hussin, 2012: 18–32).

2 Similarly, Kitchener (1850–1916), who was Proconsul in Egypt shortly after Cromer (1911–14), was before then Commander-in-Chief in India (1902), having also served as Commander-in-Chief of the Egyptian Army (1892), in Sudan (1898) and in the Boer War (1900). Reginald Wingate, who took the post of High Commissioner in Egypt shortly after Kitchener's departure (1916–19), began in the India Service and was posted to Egypt in 1883, where he became commander of Military Intelligence in 1889.

3 The literature on the extent and nature of colonial interference and transformation in local institutions is complex and indicates that interference was not only wide-ranging, but also long-lasting (Merry, 2000; Benton, 2002; Mamdani, 1996).

4 The Tanzimat reforms of the nineteenth century were undertaken to modernise and consolidate the Ottoman state, and introduced a number of channels for elite and popular representation. The Ottoman Constitution of 1876 was drafted by the Young Ottomans and adopted by Sultan Abdulhamid II; in 1878, he suspended the Constitution and dissolved Parliament – a state of affairs that continued until the Young Turk revolution of 1908, which reinstated the 1876 Constitution.

5 In contrast, India's courts have declared portions of section 377 unconstitutional: *Naz Foundation v Government of NCT of Delhi* (Delhi High Court 2009), a verdict overturned in 2013 at the Supreme Court level.

References

Alexander, G. (1919) 'The Egyptian Draft Penal Code, 1919', *Journal of Comparative Legislation and International Law*, 1(3): 244–247.

Aydin, C. (2006) 'Between Reverse Orientalism and the Global Left: Islamic Critiques of the West in Modern Turkey', *Comparative Studies of South Asia, Africa and the Middle East*, 26(3): 446–461.

BBC News (2007) 'Singapore Retains Its Gay Sex Ban', 23 October, available online at http://news.bbc.co.uk/2/hi/asia-pacific/7059300.stm [accessed 18 July 2016].

Benton, L. (2002) *Law and Colonial Cultures: Legal Regimes in World History, 1400–1900*, Cambridge: Cambridge University Press.

Bishara, F. (2014) 'Paper Routes: Inscribing Islamic Law across the Nineteenth-century Western Indian Ocean', *Law and History Review*, 32(4): 797–820.

Collier, J. (1994) 'Intertwined Histories: Islamic Law and Western Imperialism', *Law and Society Review*, 28(2): 395–408.

Dale, W. (1993) 'The Making and Remaking of Commonwealth Constitutions', *The International and Comparative Law Quarterly*, 42(1): 67–83.

Freitag, U. (2003) *Indian Ocean Migrants and State Formation in Hadhramaut: Reforming the Homeland*, Leiden: Brill.

Gilsenan, M. (2011) 'Translating Colonial Fortunes: Dilemmas of Inheritance in Muslim and English Laws across a Nineteenth-century Diaspora', *Comparative Studies of South Asia, Africa and the Middle East*, 31(2): 355–371.

Ho, E. (2004) 'Empire through Diasporic Eyes: The View from the Other Boat', *Comparative Studies of Society and History*, 46(2): 210–246.

Hussin, I. (2012) 'Circulations of Law: Colonial Precedents, Contemporary Questions', *Oñati Socio-legal Series*, 2(7): 18–32.

Hussin, I. (2014a) 'Circulations of Law: Cosmopolitan Elites, Global Repertoires, Local Vernaculars', *Law and History Review*, 32(4): 773–795.

Hussin, I. (2014b) 'Misreading and Mobility in Constitutional Texts: A Nineteenth-century Case', *Indiana Journal of Global Legal Studies*, 21(1): Article 6.

Hussin, I. (2016) *The Politics of Islamic Law: Local Elites, Colonial Authority and the Making of the Muslim State in India, Malaya and Egypt*, Chicago, IL: University of Chicago Press.

Kazuhiro, T. (2007) *The Meiji Constitution: The Japanese Experience of the West and the Shaping of the Modern State*, trans. D. Noble, Tokyo: International House of Japan.

Kennedy, D. (2003) 'Two Globalizations of Law and Legal Thought: 1850–1968', *Suffolk University Law Review*, 36(3): 637–648.

Legrand, P. (1997) 'The Impossibility of "Legal Transplants" ', 4 *Maastricht Journal of European & Comparative Law* 111.

Malik, W. (2007) *Judiciary-led Reforms in Singapore: Framework, Strategies, and Lessons*, Washington, DC: World Bank.

Mamdani, M. (1996) *Citizen and Subject: Contemporary Africa and the Legacy of Late Colonialism*, Princeton, NJ: Princeton University Press.

Merry, S. E. (2000) *Colonising Hawaii: The Cultural Power of Law,* Princeton, NJ: Princeton University Press.

Metcalf, T. (2007) *Imperial Connections: India in the Indian Ocean Arena, 1860–1920,* Berkeley, CA: University of California Press.

Moustafa, T. (2013) 'Liberal Rights v. Islamic Law? The Construction of a Binary in Malaysian Politics', *Law and Society Review,* 47(4): 771–802.

Mowat, R. C. (1973) 'From Liberalism to Imperialism: The Case of Egypt 1875–1887', *The Historical Journal,* 16(1): 109–124.

Nakahara, M. (1994) 'Modern Japan in Asia: Meiji Japan in the Eyes of the Maharaja Abu Bakar', 16 *Waseda Journal of Asian Studies* 15.

New York Times (1890) 'Old and Modern Japan: The Birth of Constitutional Government', 13 February.

Owen, R. (2005) *Lord Cromer: Victorian Imperialist, Edwardian Proconsul,* Oxford: Oxford University Press.

Reid, A. (2005) 'The Ottomans in Southeast Asia', Asia Research Institute Working Paper No. 36, Singapore: National University of Singapore, available online at http://www.ari.nus.edu.sg/wps/wps05_036.pdf [accessed 18 July 2016].

Santos, A. (2006) 'The World Bank's Uses of the "Rule of Law" Promise in Economic Development', in D. M. Trubek and A. Santos (eds) *The New Law and Economic Development: A Critical Appraisal,* Cambridge: Cambridge University Press, 253–300.

Sharafi, M. (2010) 'The Marital Patchwork of Colonial South Asia: Forum Shopping from Britain to Baroda', *Law and History Review,* 28(4): 979–1009.

Sheridan, L. A. (1964) 'Constitutional Problems of Malaysia', *The International and Comparative Law Quarterly,* 13(4): 1349–1367.

Singha, R. (1993) 'Providential Circumstances: The Thuggee Campaign of the 1830s and Legal Innovation', *Modern Asian Studies,* 27(1): 83–146.

Skuy, D. (1998) 'Macaulay and the Indian Penal Code of 1862: The Myth of the Inherent Superiority and Modernity of the English Legal System Compared to India's Legal System in the Nineteenth Century', *Modern Asian Studies,* 32(3): 513–557.

Stephens, J. (2014) ' "An Uncertain Inheritance": The Imperial Travels of Legal Migrants, from British India to Ottoman Iraq', *Law and History Review,* 32(4): 749–772.

Tan, K. (1989). 'The Evolution of Singapore's Modern Constitution: Developments from 1945 to the Present Day', *Singapore Academy of Law Journal,* 1: 1–28.

Twining, W. (2004) 'Diffusion of Law: A Global Perspective', *Journal of Legal Pluralism,* 36(49): 1–45.

Watson, A. (1993) *Legal Transplants: An Approach to Comparative Law,* Athens, GA: University of Georgia Press.

Westbrook, D. (2006) 'Theorizing the Diffusion of Law: Conceptual Difficulties, Unstable Imaginations, and the Effort to Think Gracefully Nonetheless', *Harvard International Law Journal,* 47(2): 489–506.

Part II

The political economy of law in Asia: Law in the context of Asian development

3 East Asia and the study of law and development

John Ohnesorge

Introduction

From a comparative perspective, one of the most noteworthy aspects of East Asia[1] over the past five or six decades has been the region's rapid development, which is true whether one defines 'development' in economic terms alone or takes a broader view. Growth rates in Japan, South Korea, Taiwan and, more recently, China have been outstanding over sustained periods, as has been these societies' performance on many broader measures of well-being (World Bank, 1993). For scholars interested in understanding how law and legal institutions interact with social processes of development, East Asia therefore provides a rich arena for research, not only to deepen understanding of fundamental theoretical issues, but also perhaps to provide practical guidance to today's developing countries as they seek to structure their own legal systems to facilitate development. As this chapter will demonstrate, the East Asian experience challenges many claims and assumptions found in the mainstream law and development field. This was true of the East Asian 'miracle' economies of Japan, South Korea and Taiwan, but the challenges posed by China's development path are even more fundamental.

This chapter will first discuss how specific areas of law functioned during high-growth episodes in East Asia, highlighting areas of general agreement, as well as areas in which views conflict. This will include comparisons of these findings with claims or assumptions within the broader law and development literature. The remainder of the chapter will explore to what extent the East Asian experience with law and development might be generalisable, aiming to provide the basis for an alternative model or at least to provide guidance in specific areas.

Law and development, as a field, has been organised around the basic question of how law and legal institutions can function to facilitate development,[2] and thus should be thought of as a socio-legal enterprise focused on a specific set of questions within the broader socio-legal tradition. Although this basic orientation of the field sounds straightforward, the reality is in fact complex. Even within a narrow definition of development, there exists substantial room for diversity of approaches and emphases. For example, even one who defines development purely in terms of economic growth will still confront long-standing debates in economics over whether the best way in which to maximise growth is through limiting the role of the state and expanding private enterprise and the market – a view now described as 'neoliberalism' or associated with the so-called Washington Consensus – or through state-orchestrated industrial policy. Either path will have implications for the role of law in that society, but those implications will be substantially different. Adding to the complexity is the fact that development itself can be defined in different ways and adjusting the definition of development often requires shifts in the legal institutions or fields of law that must be studied. To take a current example, the popular tendency to incorporate environmental concerns into the definition of development (the 'sustainable development' movement) will require that environmental law be part of the law and development inquiry for anyone who adopts the broadened definition. Broadening the definition of development beyond economic growth to include concerns such as environmental sustainability, wealth distribution, or social development thus greatly increases the complexity of the task by fragmenting the ends to which law and legal institutions are expected to contribute, while a range of potential means also remains available.

In the face of such complexity, law and development research should maintain an empirical emphasis, and an inductive approach to theory building (Ohnesorge, 2007a) and the developmental history of history of East Asia in the era post World War II provides a rich laboratory for this kind of work. Not only have the societies of East Asia experienced long stretches of rapid economic growth, but they have also demonstrated many other characteristics of development more broadly defined, including transitions to democracy (South Korea and Taiwan), rising literacy rates, longer life expectancies and technological advancement, among other things. Moreover, despite their generally positive trajectories, each of the societies has faced significant policy challenges – some originating internally and some resulting from external shocks – which have pushed them to adjust their legal or regulatory arrangements in response. Such episodes of policy shift involving substantial legal system adjustment create valuable natural experiments in law and social change that can help to improve law and development, and socio-legal studies more broadly. Finally, despite important similarities, each of the societies of East Asia is truly unique from the others in important ways, and this pattern of discrete differences within broad similarities can help to facilitate the scholarly enterprise of seeking to identify which legal institutions or attributes are actually most important to development.

Using the East Asian law and development experience to generate and/or test ideas about law and development has an important corrective effect because, simply put, East Asian societies have experienced rapid development while conforming loosely, if at all, to mainstream law and development orthodoxies (Ohnesorge, 2003b). Just as Max Weber faced his famous 'England problem' – that is, the fact that the Industrial Revolution and nineteenth-century capitalism were led by a country that did not conform to some of his important claims – so today the dominant theories about law and development face an 'East Asia problem' (Ohnesorge, 2007a). This East Asia problem is troubling not simply because influential theories are developed in seeming isolation from knowledge of East Asia, which could result from methodological issues (deduction vs induction), or could stem from the fact that people who develop general ideas about law and development do not necessarily study East Asia. More troubling is the fact that there seems to be a real reluctance to test general theories or claims, however constructed, against the empirical reality of the region. This is not to claim that the history of law and development in the region could be reduced to a single agreed-upon empirical reality, a claim that would be belied by noted disagreements in some areas. But there are substantial areas of agreement about how law and legal institutions *functioned* in the region, even if there is debate over why they functioned in that way, and, provided that they are used with care, such areas of agreement do provide a legitimate basis against which general theories can be tested. A number of scholars have done this in different ways, and the following section will highlight some of their findings and conclusions.

Law and legal institutions in East Asia's high-growth episodes

In spite of the potential complexity arising from differing ends and contested means, the law and development literature tends to focus on a fairly standard set of concerns about legal systems and how they operate. Different themes have been emphasised by different writers and in various historical periods, but that standard set of concerns typically includes doctrines and institutions in both private and public law. Private law concerns include the clarity and effectiveness of private property and contract rights, the availability of the judiciary to fairly and efficiently adjudicate economic disputes between private actors, and the effectiveness of corporate law in facilitating business activities. The public law side focuses on both the effectiveness of regulatory tools to implement public policy initiatives and on the ability of public law, administrative or constitutional, to constrain state actors.[3] Especially in the regulatory arena, there is an overlap between legal and policy concerns, although the institutions of private law also reflect policy choices. The following discussion follows this basic framework in presenting an overview of how law and legal institutions functioned in specific fields during East Asia's high-growth episodes, and how those realities challenge mainstream law and development thinking. The pattern that emerges from this exercise is that post-war Japan, South Korea and Taiwan diverged from mainstream thinking more in function than in form, while China's continuing episode of rapid development challenges mainstream claims in terms of both form and function.

Private law in East Asian development

With respect to the basic law of private economic activity – primarily property and contract – East Asia divides into two distinct groups. On the one hand are Japan, South Korea and Taiwan, in which, as a doctrinal matter, property and contract law were relatively clear, developed and comprehensive during rapid growth, being derived primarily from European civil and commercial law of the late nineteenth and early twentieth centuries. These societies also had courts, government agencies and legal professions organised along recognisably Western lines, each combining European and US influences in its own unique way. The fact that such legal infrastructure was in place during these societies' high-growth episodes tends to confirm mainstream thinking, which, echoing Max Weber, has long posited a positive relationship between economic development and legal systems that support market activity by enforcing private property and contract rights (Trubek, 1972). The fact that these legal systems were of civil law origin is noteworthy, however, as a corrective to currently popular claims for the economic superiority of the common law over the civil law espoused by the legal origins/LLSV school – so-called after authors Rafael La Porta, Florencio Lopez-de-Silanes, Andrei Shleifer and Robert Vishny – which has gained institutional voice through the World Bank's 'Doing Business' project.[4]

More noteworthy than the black-letter law and the formal institutional arrangements were the ways in which East Asia's laws and institutions functioned in practice, which deviated significantly from standard assumptions. In comparison to the developed West, it was often said that business in the region was done on the basis of relatively short written contracts and that business litigation was relatively rare. The relative lack of formality and comprehensiveness in contracting behaviour has been discussed in cultural terms, but might also be explained by structural factors such as a prevalence of long-term relationships in the region's economies. With respect to litigation rates, the relative rarity of litigation could have been based on structural features of the legal regimes, such as few licensed lawyers, a lack of civil discovery, rules against contingency fees, or 'loser pays' systems for legal fees (Ohnesorge, 2007c). Other explanations focused on traditional cultural norms against litigation and in favour of compromise or mediation, and a healthy debate over the motives of East Asia's 'reluctant litigant' has taken place in the academic literature (Ginsburg and Hoetker, 2004). Whatever the cause, however, the outstanding feature of the systems from a law and development perspective was the lack of resort to formal legality and dispute settlement rather than the doctrines of substantive law. The extent to which the East Asian experience confirms or contradicts mainstream law and development claims is thus complex. It does not contradict the general Weberian notion, popularised recently in the new institutional economics of Douglass North and others, that legal infrastructure is of fundamental importance to the operation of market economies, but it would contradict strong claims for the importance of particular black-letter rules, or functional claims for the importance of highly contractualised business relations, or of easy resort to litigation to solve disputes.

In contrast to the experiences of Japan, Korea and Taiwan, China constitutes a much more radical challenge to mainstream notions in that it presents an example of rapid economic development taking place without even a solid foundation of private law on the books, let alone in functioning reality. China's rapid growth began in the 1980s, at about the same time as the country began its efforts to build a legal system appropriate to a market economy. Over the subsequent thirty years, economic development seems to have preceded developments in the private law system, not vice versa (Clarke, 2003b; Clarke, Murrell and Whiting, 2006). What was true of Chinese private law was also true of the institutions involved in the functioning of private law, such as the judiciary, government agencies and the legal profession. In China, these institutions all began their modern development in the 1980s, as the country abandoned Stalinist economic management, and have subsequently developed contemporaneously with the economy, not ahead of it. In this respect, China's experience of law and development offers a more extreme challenge to prevailing assumptions than do the experiences of China's East Asian neighbours. China's experience shows that a political commitment to support private enterprise that is sufficiently clear and stable may not need to manifest itself in the form of well-articulated law, strong courts and an independent legal profession, as much as some argue otherwise. Keeping private rights somewhat nebulous and out of the hands of independent courts clearly supports the Chinese government's effort to retain flexibility in dealing with the private sector, and, at least so far, this does not appear to have significantly hindered economic development.

Business organisation law

The law of business organisational forms is also clearly important for development in which the private sector is expected to play a major role, and the history of this area of law in East Asia largely parallels the history of property and contract law.[5] During their rapid-growth eras, Japan, Korea and Taiwan all had on their books modern statutes creating a typical range of business structures, from simple agency relationships, through partnerships, to publicly traded corporations, as well as regulation of the sale of securities. As with property and contract law, these statutes reflected a mix of European and American influences, and what was noteworthy was partly the legal doctrine itself, but perhaps more importantly how the legally constituted organisations operated in their local contexts. Business organisations operated differently in each of the three societies in important ways, but in each case successfully enough to support robust private sectors and rapid economic development.

With respect to corporations, where most of the attention has been focused, Korea and Taiwan were characterised by high levels of concentrated share ownership among founders and their families, while Japan was not (Claessens, Djankov and Lang, 1999). But whereas Korea's large business groups (*chaebol*), such as Samsung, LG or Hyundai, developed into enormous, hierarchically organised conglomerates operating in many areas of the economy (Kang, 1996), Taiwan's family-dominated business groups were more loosely organised and less hierarchical (Claessens et al., 1999; Chi-Nien Chung, 2003). Japan's major private corporate groups (*keiretsu*) have been more similar to Korea's *chaebol* than to Taiwan's business groups, although with financial institutions to some extent replacing the founder and their family members as long-term, stable shareholders.[6] Importantly from a law and development perspective, in none of these economies did financial markets play a dominant role in financing corporate growth, with bank lending playing a comparatively larger role. The 'varieties of capitalism' literature would classify these as bank-centred, as opposed to market-centred, financial systems, despite other important differences noted above.[7] The fact that these economies developed so successfully with bank-centred financial systems tends to undermine central claims of the legal origins/LLSV school, which builds its claim for the superiority of the common law on a claim that deep, liquid financial markets are important for development and that common law systems are better for such markets (Ohnesorge, 2009). East Asia's experience shows that bank-centred financial systems operating within civilian legal frameworks are perfectly capable of supporting rapid private sector development, so even if the common law tradition is more hospitable to advanced financial systems, this does not mean that the common law is in general superior for economic development.

Also noteworthy from a law and development perspective was the weakness in East Asia of litigation as a mechanism by which shareholders could influence management or protect themselves from the actions of dominant shareholders. That was as true in Taiwan and Korea, where corporations tended to be dominated by founder/controlling shareholders, as in Japan, where shares were more widely dispersed. This is how East Asia's generally observed propensity against litigation manifested itself in the specific setting of corporate governance and it tends to undermine the claims of the World Bank's influential Doing Business group, whose system for grading legal systems places great weight on legal protections for minority shareholders.[8] Since the 1990s, legal rules and institutions have been adjusted in East Asia precisely to encourage shareholder litigation as a way in which to improve corporate governance (Ohnesorge, 2007c), but this came after those countries' rapid-growth episodes were long over. Although the mainstream view is now that weak minority shareholder protections are detrimental, the successes of East Asia's corporations suggest that protecting minority shareholders is less important than creating an incentive structure conducive to entrepreneurship, risk taking and long-term vision (Ohnesorge, 2009).

Turning to China, the story of corporate law there again provides a very interesting contrast with the rest of East Asia. As with areas of private law, such as property and contract, the law of business organisation in China was not in place prior to rapid development, but has instead been evolving along with economic development since roughly 1980, when China abandoned Soviet economic organisation in favour of a largely market-oriented model – albeit one in which enterprise ownership by various arms of the state remains pervasive. As the government has made policy choices in favour of specific economic activities, it has developed the legal forms necessary to carry them out, often on a provisional or local basis. For example, when China decided in the late 1970s to open the country to foreign direct investment (FDI) in manufacturing, there existed no law of business organisation under which appropriate legal entities could be created. China could have put foreign investment on hold pending the creation of a generally applicable statutory structure of organisational forms for conducting private enterprise. That, however, might have been a fraught process in a country eschewing 'shock therapy' and instead transitioning gradually out of a Soviet economy, while also still ruled by a Chinese Communist Party claiming to adhere to socialism. In what became the pattern for Chinese law reform, the government deferred the larger legislative project, creating instead a regime of business and tax law designed specifically for the FDI sector (Gelatt, 1989). It was not until 1994, well into China's high-growth episode, that the generally applicable Company Law became effective, after stock markets had been created in Shenzhen and Shanghai on which shares of Chinese corporations were being traded (Green, 2003: 12). Even now, the actual ownership and control structure of many Chinese business entities remains highly idiosyncratic, because ownership by governmental units, national and local, remains much more common, and much more opaque, than in a typical economy and because the Communist Party still appoints the leaders of many state-owned enterprises as part of its cadre system (Clarke, 2003a).

Public law and governance: Economic regulation and administrative law

With respect to regulation and administrative law, the experience of East Asia as compared with that of other parts of the world has been most noteworthy in two respects. First, in terms of substantive policies, governments in the region have engaged in industrial policies involving economic interventions well beyond the prescriptions of most modern economists.[9] Secondly, in terms of public law, procedure and process, executive branch authorities in the region were able to implement these policies with relative freedom from the strictures of public law and judicial review that constrain government action in many other societies, and which tend to inform mainstream law and development thinking. In keeping with the pattern identified above, Chinese performance has been the most extreme on both metrics, thus presenting the greatest challenge to orthodox views. This section will first discuss the legal environment within which East Asia's developmental policies were carried out, then focus on the substance of those policies.

Treating administrative law as a set of legally formulated constraints on executive action, East Asia during high growth was noteworthy for the fact that administrative legality operated primarily internally, within bureaucracies, rather than though external legal checks enforced by the courts. Legal scholars, perhaps especially those trained in the United States, too often think of legal control of administrative action as being external and judicial almost as a matter of definition, and this type of thinking is common where the mainstream law and development literature discusses the role of public law. However, as Japan scholar Richard Boyd (2003: 175) made clear many years ago in discussing Japanese industrial policy, a full understanding of the relationship between law and bureaucratic action in East Asia requires study of internal, as well as external legal, checks:

'The officials in question are overwhelmingly lawyers, . . . [who] have on their desks volumes of their industry laws, plastic bound in flexible covers so as to withstand constant use and reference.' At the same time, however, Boyd (2003: 176–177) highlighted the fact that the legal documents to which the law-trained officials constantly referred maximised administrative discretion both by their expansive scope and by the vagueness of their language and that judicial review was, in practical terms, unavailable. Thus although Japan's economic bureaucracy operated according to a type of internal administrative legality, it was nonetheless relatively unconstrained by externally operating administrative law in the way that is typically prescribed in the law and development literature. Japan was a democracy with a well-established legal culture at the time its economic bureaucracy enjoyed this high level of legal autonomy, and there are varying views concerning how and why this occurred (Ginsburg, 2001). In authoritarian Korea and Taiwan, the courts were naturally weaker and the economic bureaucracy, like the rest of the executive branch, was even less constrained by law. Whatever its origins, this oddly legalistic, yet legally unconstrained, bureaucracy nevertheless helped to shepherd East Asia's economies through decades of rapid growth and has earned the praise of generations of development scholars searching empirically for the institutional bases of the region's success.

Another important attribute of public authority during East Asia's rapid-development eras was that executive authorities in the region were comparatively unified, rather than fragmented by the creation of quasi-independent regulatory authorities. From a law and development perspective, this is important because it has been common since the 1990s for development assistance programmes to encourage developing countries to adopt the independent agency model for certain governance functions (Dubash and Morgan, 2012). Centralisation and coordination were especially prominent in pre-democratisation Korea and Taiwan, where it was very clear that bureaucracies reported to the single chief executive, but this was also true in Japan when compared to other established democracies, perhaps owing to the fact of Liberal Democratic Party dominance and a strong bureaucratic tradition (Ohnesorge, forthcoming).

Turning from the legal and institutional environment for regulation to the substantive policy choices that governments made, the overall thrust of the region's policies during rapid growth can perhaps be captured in the term 'pro-growth interventionism'. Governments were interventionist in that they used legal tools to intervene across broad swathes of their economies, so in no sense could these be described as free-market economies. As has been discussed by many development scholars, they implemented a host of industrial policy measures affecting the flow of goods, capital and technology across their borders in order to foster export-led development, and the serious debates have been over whether such industrial policies were effective or in keeping with international obligations, not whether or not they existed. This interventionism was exercised in a general pro-growth policy environment, however, which can be seen in the ways in which other areas of law and regulation operated. While, in the United States and Europe, interventionist industrial policy is often championed by the political Left and is thus associated with Left-leaning regulation in other areas, in East Asia, other regulatory interventions seemed to be minimised in order to maximise economic growth. Enforcement in areas such as environmental law, consumer protection law, competition law, intellectual property law, anti-discrimination law and labour law, among others, was not non-existent, but by the same token it was rarely aggressive by international standards and appeared to be subordinated to a more fundamental concern for economic growth led by a thriving private sector.

Applying this analysis to the role of public and regulatory law in China's current era of high-speed growth, one again can see the basic dynamics of the East Asian experience being played out in an even more extreme form. In terms of administrative law and legal controls on bureaucratic action, China's courts appear at least as impotent as those in pre-democratic Korea or Taiwan and face the additional burden that separation of powers is not necessarily even accepted at the theoretical level within the official Marxist legal ideology. With respect to law operating internally to constrain bureaucratic action, as described in Boyd's discussion of Japan's industrial policy bureaucracy, observers provide a description of China's bureaucrats wielding a similarly impressive set of regulatory documents, but being even less legally constrained in practice owing to the broad wording of the documents, continuing difficulties in establishing a clear and exclusive hierarchy of legal norms, and an open subservience of the courts to political will. The more complex nature of China's regulatory norm structure may be related to another difference, which is that regulatory authority in China appears much more fragmented than was the case in the rest of East Asia during rapid development (US Chamber of Commerce, 2014).[10] This apparent fragmentation may have resulted from the fact that China built so many of its institutional structures during the 1990s and, for that reason, may have been more influenced than its neighbours by the global trend toward the independent regulatory commission model (Dubash and Morgan, 2012). While this might count as an exception to the general pattern of China displaying in more extreme form what was already visible in East Asia, the practical reality is that the Communist Party's continuing monopoly on power means that even where authority appears fragmented, such agencies, like the courts, cannot ultimately implement the law independently, while the Party itself remains above the ordinary legal system. In terms of substance, too, China displays the pattern of 'pro-growth interventionism' observed in the context of East Asian development, although arguably with even greater intervention, on the one hand, and an even greater pro-growth regulatory bias, on the other. Although China appears to be growing increasingly serious about environmental and consumer protection, perhaps diminishing to some extent its pro-growth policy bias, it appears increasingly open about pursuing an interventionist industrial policy (Dubash and Morgan, 2012), albeit perhaps one with a diminished bias towards growth.

Conclusion: East Asia, law and development, and today's developing countries

Although drawing on both legal and economic theory, law and development is an inherently action-oriented field. Descriptively and analytically, it explores what legal rules and institutions have been put in place historically that have seemed conducive to development, and why governments and development institutions have adopted the approaches they have. Another major strand of the field is less theoretical and more prescriptive, trying to determine what governments and aid institutions should do to reform national legal systems for development purposes. Knowledge of East Asia's experiences with law and development could contribute substantially to both endeavours, to inform retrospective analysis and theory building, but to also guide current and future law and development initiatives.

As earlier sections of this chapter have shown, there has long been a disconnect between the realities of law and legal institutions during East Asia's rapid-development episodes and the assumptions and prescriptions found in the literature and practices of mainstream law and development. This incongruity has been demonstrated even more dramatically during China's current rapid-growth phase, which has taken place despite the underdevelopment of its private and corporate law regimes, and the weakness of its courts and its legal constraints on bureaucratic action. This disconnect between mainstream law and development thinking and the East Asian experience is unfortunate, because it means that theory is being developed without careful consideration of obviously important evidence and that the theory so developed is also not being tested against what should be an important body of evidence. The tendency is not new, however, and has been noted by several scholars of Asian law who have ventured into the law and development literature. Over twenty years ago, Frank Upham (1994) pointed out inconsistencies between Japan's experience and claims of the World Bank and Peruvian economist Hernando de Soto (1990), suggesting that the legal informality that many observers say characterised Japanese law during that country's high-growth period undercuts claims by de Soto and World Bank General Counsel Ibrahim Shihata that legal formality is necessarily important for economic growth in developing economies. Not incidentally, Upham presented these views in commenting on a paper by Taiwan scholar Jane Kaufmann Winn (1994), which itself documented a high level of informality in commercial law in Taiwan during that economy's high-growth period. Over a decade ago, several essays in the volume *Law and Development in East and Southeast Asia* (Antons, 2003; for example Boyd, 2003) explored similar themes and scholars such as Don Clarke (2003a, 2003b) voiced similar objections based on China's experience. The East Asian experience has been useful in this way as a corrective to claims about law and development often described as 'neoliberal' – that is, calling for a limited role for the state and for the role of law to be limited primarily to creating market frameworks based on secure private property and contract rights. This is not to say that the East Asian experience proves that the World Bank's rule-of-law efforts, or the theorising of Douglass North or the legal origins/LLSV scholars, are without merit, but it is now abundantly clear that those approaches, so influential in the 1990s and 2000s, describe at best the role that law might play in *one* path to development. Attention to the East Asian experience with law and development is put to its best use not as a way in which to prove that neoliberal approaches cannot work, but as a way in which to show that effective governments have deviated from such prescriptions quite significantly – even radically, in the case of China – and yet still achieved outstanding development outcomes.

In the last decade, a new use for knowledge of East Asian law and development has arisen, which is to test ideas and assumptions not of neoliberalism, but of its critics, many of who are calling for a return to state-centric development models. In 2012, *The Economist* prominently proclaimed the return of state capitalism; scholars are seeking to define and justify interventionist industrial policies of a so-called new developmental state (Trubek et al., 2013; Ohnesorge, 2007b); the BRICS countries (Brazil, Russia, India, China and South Africa) have just taken another major step toward the creation of an alternative global development bank, promising that it will impose fewer market-oriented disciplines upon its clients (that is, it will be less neoliberal) than existing institutions such as the World Bank and the International Monetary Fund (IMF) (Leahy and Harding, 2014). Because of East Asia's perceived success with industrial policy and a more state-centric development path, the region's experience plays a central role in the intellectual underpinnings of this movement, making it even more important that scholars and policymakers consider what lessons they might learn from how law and legal institutions functioned in the region during rapid development (Ohnesorge, 2007b).

The following are some of the many lessons that might be drawn from this exercise. First, East Asia shows that activist industrial policy need not degenerate into debilitating rent seeking and corruption, as a strong version of neoliberalism might suggest (Ohnesorge, 1999). This is an important affirmation of the possibility of successful industrial policy interventions, which, at least on the rhetorical level, are often dismissed as impossible. On the other hand, East Asia's experience does not guarantee that corruption and rent seeking will not follow government interventions, because corruption has been, and remains, a serious issue in the region.[11] If the social, political or other characteristics of a particular developing country make successful implementation of industrial programmes especially improbably, then the East Asian experience ought to be heavily discounted. It is no coincidence that the earliest efforts to analyse East Asian industrial policy quickly focused on the characteristics of the state apparatus and the economic policy bureaucracy, identifying 'hardness', or relative autonomy from social and political forces, as key to their success. The extent to which a bureaucracy is insulated from outside forces and allowed to exercise its developmental expertise depends to a great extent upon how the legal system operates, especially in the fields of administrative and constitutional law. As noted previously, those areas of law played quite restrained roles during East Asia's high-growth periods, so any country seeking to replicate East Asian industrial policy must ask whether it can, or even wishes to, replicate those conditions. The East Asian experience might be most useful as a source of ideas for designing industrial policy institutions to keep rent seeking and corruption to manageable levels, keeping in mind that some aspects of the East Asian experience may not be replicable, or desirable, today.

A second lesson that East Asia teaches is that openness to FDI and a heavy focus on exports do not necessarily require a capital-importing country to adopt a free-market approach, with no government screening or guidance on industrial policy grounds. All of East Asia engaged in bureaucratic screening of FDI, but in substance China has so far been far more open than its East Asian neighbours, in which FDI played quite a small role during rapid development. On the other hand, East Asian countries have enjoyed particular traits or circumstances that likely helped to make this possible, so their experience may not be generalisable. Japan, South Korea and Taiwan were important allies of the United States and Europe during the Cold War, when they engaged in their most aggressive industrial policy measures, and many believe that this helped to moderate foreign pressures to open their economies. China does not enjoy the same geopolitical advantage, but the enormous size of its internal market and its enormous pool of low-cost labour likely help investors to overcome concerns that they might have about government intervention and a highly imperfect legal system. The fact that East Asian countries have been able to engage in certain kinds of screening practices while still attracting sufficient FDI therefore does not disprove the common perception of a global competition for FDI, in which openness and regulatory simplicity are one metric upon which countries compete. A developing country today that wishes to emulate the East Asian approach to managing foreign investment for industrial policy purposes will need to consider carefully where it stands in the competition and whether it will benefit most from openness or from policy-driven selectivity.

Although there are certainly other lessons to be learned from close study of the East Asian experience of law and development, perhaps the most important to those exploring the contours of a new developmental state, as well as to those espousing neoliberal approaches to development, is humility in the face of substantial uncertainty. Critics of law and development activities often say that developing countries *should* be given room to develop their own policies free from top-down, one-size-fits-all solutions imposed from the outside, but the fact is that the ways in which law functions in developing economies inevitably *will* vary with each country's specific historical, political and economic circumstances. Paying careful attention to law's role in East Asian development might do no more than reduce the high level of uncertainty that will exist in any actual exercise in law and development, but even that would be a most worthy accomplishment.

Notes

1 'East Asia' here refers to Japan, the Republic of Korea ('South Korea'), the Republic of China ('Taiwan'), and the People's Republic of China ('China').
2 This chapter follows David Trubek and Alvaro Santos (2006: 3–5) in understanding the field of law and development as combining legal and economic theory with the practices of national and international institutions engaged in legal technical assistance.
3 Public, especially constitutional, law is thus used in part to further goals associated primarily with private law.
4 For a brief introduction to that approach in the specific context of China's legal and economic development, see Ohnesorge (2003a). See also Ohnesorge (2009). For further discussion of this approach in the context of business organisation law, see nn. 5–8 and accompanying text.
5 This section draws on Ohnesorge (2009).
6 For a detailed explication of Japanese enterprise types, see Imai (1994: 117–140).
7 For a helpful discussion of bank versus market-centred financial systems discussing Japan in comparative perspective, see Vitols (2001).
8 Information on the Doing Business project can be found online at http://www.doingbusiness.org [accessed 18 July 2016]. The main Doing Business metric relevant to corporate law, 'Protecting Investors' (http://www.doingbusiness.org/data/exploretopics/protecting-investors/), draws heavily on the LLSV/legal origins approach.
9 The literature on the industrial policies of the East Asian 'developmental state' is enormous.
10 For example, authority for implementing China's Anti-Monopoly Law is divided among at least three bodies – the National Development and Reform Commission (NDRC), the Ministry of Commerce (MOFCOM), and the State Administration for Industry and Commerce (SAIC) – none of which operates independently within China's party-state political system (US Chamber of Commerce, 2014).
11 Corruption arguably follows the general pattern identified in this chapter, with China displaying in extreme form a characteristic already seen in South Korea and Taiwan, and to a lesser extent in Japan.

References

Antons, C. (2003) *Law and Development in East and Southeast Asia*, London/New York: Routledge Curzon.

Boyd, R. (2003) 'The Rule of Law or Law as Instrument of Rule? Law and the Economic Development of Japan with Particular Regard to Industrial Policy', in C. Antons (ed.) *Law and Development in East and Southeast Asia*, London/New York: Routledge Curzon, 154–196.

Chi-Nien Chung (2003) 'Managerial Structure of Business Groups in Taiwan: The Inner Circle System and its Social Organization', *The Developing Economies*, 41(1): 37–64.

Claessens, S., Djankov, S., and Lang, L. (1999) 'Who Controls East Asian Corporations?', World Bank Policy Research Working Paper No. 2045, Washington, DC: World Bank.

Clarke, D. C. (2003a) 'Corporate Governance in China: An Overview', *China Economic Review*, 14(4): 494–507.

Clarke, D. C. (2003b) 'Economic Development and the Rights Hypothesis: The China Problem', *The American Journal of Comparative Law*, 51(1): 89–112.

Clarke, D. C., Murrell, P., and Whiting, S. (2006) 'The Role of Law in China's Economic Development', The George Washington University Law School Public Law and Legal Theory Working Paper No. 187, Washington, DC: George Washington University Law School.

de Soto, H. (1990) *The Other Path: The Invisible Revolution in the Third World*, New York: Harper & Row.

Dubash, N., and Morgan, B. (2012) 'Understanding the Rise of the Regulatory State of the South', *Regulation & Governance*, 6(3): 261–281.

The Economist (2012) 'The Rise of State Capitalism', 21 January.

Gelatt, T. A. (1989) 'China's New Cooperative Joint Venture Law', *Syracuse Journal of International Law and Commerce,* 15(2): 187–201.

Ginsburg, T. (2001) 'Dismantling the Developmental State? Administrative Procedure Reform in Japan and Korea', *American Journal of Comparative Law*, 49(4): 585–625.

Ginsburg, T., and Hoetker, G. (2004) 'The Unreluctant Litigant? An Empirical Analysis of Japan's Turn to Litigation', *Journal of Legal Studies*, 35(1): 31–59.

Green, S. P. (2003) *China's Stockmarket: A Guide to its Progress, Players and Prospects*, London: Bloomberg.

Imai, K. (1994) 'Enterprise Groups', in K. Imai and R. Komiyam (eds) *Business Enterprise in Japan: Views of Leading Japanese Economists*, Cambridge, MA: MIT Press, 117–140.

Kang, M. (1996) *Korean Business Conglomerate: Chaebol Then and Now*, Korea Research Monograph 21, Berkeley, CA: Institute of East Asian Studies.

Leahy, J., and Harding, R. (2014) 'Shanghai Leads Race for BRICS Bank HQ', *Financial Times*, 2 July, available online at https://next.ft.com/content/aea32354-00eb-11e4-b94d-00144feab7de [accessed 18 July 2016].

Ohnesorge, J. K. M. (1999) ' "Ratch"eting up the Anti-Corruption Drive: Could a Look at Recent History Cure a Case of Theory-Determinism?' *Connecticut Journal of International Law*, 14: 467–473.

Ohnesorge, J. K. M. (2003a) 'China's Economic Transition and the New Legal Origins Literature', *China Economic Review,* 14(4): 485–493.

Ohnesorge, J. K. M. (2003b) 'The Rule of Law, Economic Development, and the Developmental States of Northeast Asia', in C. Antons (ed.) *Law and Development in East and Southeast Asia,* London/New York: Routledge Curzon, 91–127.

Ohnesorge, J. K. M. (2007a) 'Developing Development Theory: Law and Development Orthodoxies and the Northeast Asian Experience', *University of Pennsylvania Journal of International Economic Law*, 28(2): 219–308.

Ohnesorge, J. K. M. (2007b) 'Northeast Asia's Developmental States and the Problem of Rights: Challenges for a New Developmental State?', in T. Groppi, V. Piergigli and A. Rinella (eds) *Asian Constitutionalism in Transition: A Comparative Perspective*, Rome: Giuffre Editore, 305–319.

Ohnesorge, J. K. M. (2007c) 'Politics, Ideology, and Legal System Reform in Northeast Asia', in C. Antons and V. Gessner (eds) *Globalisation and Resistance: Law Reform in Asia since the Crisis*, Oxford/Portland, OR: Hart, 105–130.

Ohnesorge, J. K. M. (2009) 'Legal Origins and the Tasks of Corporate Law in Economic Development: A Preliminary Exploration', *Brigham Young University Law Review*, 6: 1619–1634.

Ohnesorge, J. K. M. (forthcoming) 'The Regulatory State in East Asia', in F. Bignami and D. Zaring (eds) *Comparative Law and Regulation: Understanding the Global Regulatory Process*, Cheltenham: Edward Elgar.

Trubek, D. M. (1972) 'Max Weber on Law and the Rise of Capitalism', *Wisconsin Law Review*, 3: 720–753.

Trubek, D. M., and Santos, A. (2006) *The New Law And Economic Development: A Critical Appraisal*, Cambridge/New York: Cambridge University Press.

Trubek, D. M., Garcia. H., Coutinho, D., and Santos, A. (2013) *'Law and the New Developmental State': The Brazilian Experience in Latin American Context*, Cambridge: Cambridge University Press.

Upham, F. K. (1994) 'Speculations on Legal Informality: On Winn's Relational Practices and the Marginalisation of Law', *Law & Society Review*, 28(2): 233–242.

US Chamber of Commerce (2014) *Competing Interests in China's Competition Law Enforcement: China's Anti-Monopoly Law Application and the Role of Industrial Policy*, Washington, DC: USCC.

Vitols, S. (2001) 'The Origins of Bank-based and Market-based Financial Systems: Germany, Japan, and the United States', Social Science Research Center Berlin, Discussion paper FS I 01–302, Berlin: SSRC.

Winn, J. K. (1994) 'Relational Practices and the Marginalisation of Law: Informal Financial Practices of Small Business in Taiwan', *Law & Society Review*, 28(2): 193–232.

World Bank (1993) *The East Asian Miracle: Economic Growth and Public Policy*, New York: Oxford University Press.

4 A new China model for the era post global financial crisis

Legal dimensions

Randall Peerenboom

Introduction

The Washington Consensus, which dominated the development world for over two decades, has been called into question on both theoretical and empirical grounds (Peerenboom and Bugaric, 2014). Those countries that adhered most closely to it have failed to achieve sustained growth, while the East Asian 'tigers' that rejected it and followed their own development path achieved remarkable growth. Many attributed the success of the early East Asian tigers to the East Asian model and the more recent success of China to the China model or Beijing Consensus (Johnson, 1982; Woo-Cumings, 1999).[1] However, the lost decade in Japan, the global financial crisis and growing concerns that China may be caught in the dreaded 'middle-income trap' have called into question the viability of the East Asian model and its more specific China variants (Eichengreen, Park and Shin, 2011).

The shortcomings of the Washington Consensus and Beijing Consensus have led to attempts to develop new theories and approaches to development, variously referred to as the 'new development state' (Trubek, 2008), 'state capitalism' (Ramanujam et al., 2012), 'liberal neo-developmentalism' (Ban, 2013: 299), 'new structural economics' (Lin, 2011), the post Washington Consensus (Birdsall and Fukuyama, 2012: 49), or the 'post Washington, post Beijing Consensus' (PWBC). This chapter delineates the main features of this new paradigm, the PWBC, and assesses both its potential and limits for guiding development policies in China in the era post global financial crisis. It goes on to discuss growing concerns with the East Asian model and its Chinese variants, then summarises the salient features of the emerging PWBC. The chapter next assesses the implications of the PWBC for the China model, and considers to what extent the Decision of the Central Committee of the Communist Party of China (CCP) concerning Some Major Issues in Comprehensively Deepening Reform addresses the challenges and provides a new model of development.[2] It then focuses on the implications for legal reforms in light of the Decision and draws conclusions.

The East Asian model, its progeny and their problems

The East Asian model and its Chinese variants have been defined in different ways. In general, think-tank commentators, big-picture pundits and journalists prefer more parsimonious versions, which offer more rhetorical bang for the buck and are easier to weave into dramatic storylines that make big claims (Ramo, 2004).[3] The most stripped-down version of the China model attributes China's success to only two factors, authoritarianism and markets, without explaining why other authoritarian regimes with market economies have not enjoyed such high growth rates (Halper, 2010).

Economists tend to prefer to present lists of elements and not to pay a great deal of attention to how the elements fit together nor to discuss which elements are necessary or sufficient.[4] In explaining the success of East Asian tigers, for example, the World Bank cited a laundry list of factors.[5] The strategy seemed to be motivated in part by political considerations within the Bank, where the dominant view remained that Asian countries succeeded by following generally applicable neoclassical economic principles, in contrast to the view among area and country specialists both within and outside the Bank that, in fact, much of the success of Asian countries resulted from the interventionist policies of the developmental state that sought to protect infant industries, favoured investment over consumption and resisted advice to liberalise the financial sector (Terry, 2002).

Political scientists and legal scholars for their part tend to prefer versions that go beyond economics to consider as well the political, legal and social context in which the economy operates and in which development takes place (Peerenboom, 2007; Pan, 2009). There have always been sceptics who question the value and viability of the East Asian model and its progeny. Some economists, such as Paul Krugman (1994), argued that the East Asian 'miracle' was no such thing, but simply the result of shifting from labour-intensive agriculture towards more productive manufacturing and services. Other sceptics conceded that there was considerable deviation from neoclassical economic principles and Washington Consensus policies, but questioned whether an interventionist developmental state was the reason for success (Chang, 2009). The Asian financial crisis led many commentators, including Alan Greenspan, to declare with undisguised glee that the East Asian model was a failure. However, the East Asian model bounced back into favour as a result of the subsequent recovery of East Asian countries, more careful analysis that showed that the economies most affected were those that had not followed that model, but which had adopted the early financial liberalisation policies advocated by the Washington Consensus, and, most importantly, the rapid rise of China.

Nevertheless, despite the return to high growth rates in East Asia, the rise of China and the relative success of East Asian countries in weathering the global financial crisis so far, sceptics continue to argue that the East Asian model is neither unique nor sustainable. Michael Pettis (2013), for instance, has argued that the China model is nothing special and that it too will fail, as was the case in Germany in the 1930s, the Soviet Union in the 1950s and 1960s, Brazil in the 1960s and 1970s, and Japan in the 1990s. Are all examples of state-led investment models that relied on massive subsidies for manufacturing and investment to generate rapid growth by building up infrastructure and manufacturing capacity and promoting real estate development (Pettis, 2013).

Critics also contend that the global financial crisis has exposed the shortcomings of the East Asian model (Pettis, 2013; Dumas and Choyleva, 2011; Zhang, 2012). The argument, in a nutshell, is that Beijing has encouraged investment and boosted growth rates by subsidising energy costs for manufacturers, suppressing wages, tolerating environmental degradation and engaging in financial repression (maintaining artificially low interest rates that allow banks to provide cheap financing to real estate developers and manufacturers, combined with few investment alternatives for household depositors). The government has also promoted exports by maintaining a weak currency. As a result, China ran large current account surpluses, which meant that other countries, by definition, had to run deficits. The global financial crisis followed, with the real estate bubble in the United States and Europe fuelled by excess liquidity and the availability of cheap credit from China buying US treasuries and Eurobonds. The global economy must now rebalance. China therefore has no choice but to adjust its economic model because (a) other countries are no longer able or willing to import as much, as consumers recover from the crisis by reducing debt and saving more, and (b) investment-driven growth is increasingly inefficient.

A 2012 World Bank report, written with significant participation from Development Research Center of the State Council, emphasised that China is now in danger of extended periods of slower growth, because wages have increased and China has reached the limits of gains from the exploitation of foreign technologies. To avoid the 'middle-income trap', new growth drivers are required, including 'increased efficiency in input use, higher human capital investments, increased innovation and a shift to high-value services' (World Bank and Development Research Center of the State Council, PRC, 2012: 11). The report lays out six strategic directions for China's future:

- completing the transition to a market economy;
- accelerating the pace of open innovation;
- going 'green' to transform environmental stresses into green growth as a driver for development;
- expanding opportunities and services such as health, education and access to jobs for all people;
- modernising and strengthening its domestic fiscal system; and
- seeking mutually beneficial relations with the world by connecting China's structural reforms to the changing international economy.

In sum, there is now a growing consensus that the East Asian model and its state-investment-led, export-oriented variants work well during the catch-up phase under favourable global conditions, but do not work at higher stages of development. As early as 2007, Premier Wen Jiabao acknowledged that there were structural problems to the China model that caused 'unsteady, unbalanced, uncoordinated and unsustainable growth' (Yang, 2010). Accordingly, the Twelfth Five-Year Plan highlighted the need for a transition from state-led investment to a more consumption-based economy. Unfortunately, while there is general agreement about the need to rebalance the economy, there are deep disagreements about how this is to be done and how fast to proceed (Freeman and Wen, 2011).[6] What is clear, however, is that the change in economic model has significant political, legal and social ramifications, and will entail a new role for China's government and society:

> It is imperative that China adjusts its development strategy as it embarks on its next phase of economic growth. At its core, this adjustment requires changing the role of government and its relations with the market, the private sector, and society at large. While the government needs to withdraw from direct involvement in production, distribution, and resource allocation, it will need to focus greater attention on designing and implementing the policy and regulatory framework that empowers others to participate in economic decision making so that the desired outcome of rapid, inclusive, and sustainable growth is achieved. To play this role, the government will need to transform itself into a lean, clean, transparent, and highly efficient modern government that operates under the rule of law. In redefining its role, the government will need to accelerate reforms in the state-owned sector and combine it with further development of the private sector. It will also need to advance reforms in factor markets (capital, land, and labor) to help strengthen the foundations of a market economy and promote greater competition and innovation. At the same

> time, society's role will need to change significantly, with the middle class becoming a major force in promoting harmonious development through greater participation of the people in the development process.
>
> (World Bank and Development Research Center of the State Council, PRC, 2012: 18)

Whereas, in the neoliberal-driven Washington Consensus approach, the problem was an invisible hand and too little government intervention, in China, the problem has been too visible a hand and too much government intervention. This suggests that there may be some convergence on a PWBC.

The emerging post Washington, post Beijing consensus (PWBC)

The emerging PWBC draws on both the successes and failures of developing countries over the last several decades. It takes into consideration changes in the international economic order, including the more restrictive space for domestic policymakers in light of the World Trade Organization (WTO), while emphasising that the BRICS countries (Brazil, Russia, India, China and South Africa) and other emerging powers in particular have the capacity not only to resist policies, but also to push for new rules in line with their interests (Shaffer and Sutton, 2014: 59; Santos, 2013: 167). The PWBC is still being debated, and it is unclear to what extent the PWBC will receive backing from developed countries and international financial institutions. Nevertheless, the PWBC reflects the current policies, practices and thinking of a significant group of developing countries.

Whereas the Washington Consensus, like most development advice, was heavy on the content and substance of reforms and light on the process and methodology of reform, laying out the end state, but not shedding much light on how to get there, the PWBC emphasises the process of reform, the importance of second-best solutions, the need for experimentation and the diversity of possible end-states. Accordingly, developing states must be more proactive in setting, controlling and implementing the development agenda. In the PWBC, the Washington Consensus 'one size fits all' model gives way to a plurality of different models, each suitable for a particular country or a group of countries at a particular level of development. These alternative models of development are not 'temporary detours' on the road to global homogeneity, but alternatives suitable for different cultural and socio-economic foundations in developing countries (Kupchan, 2012).

As a result, developing countries cannot simply imitate international best practices, but need 'second-best' solutions and institutions that take into account context-specific market and government failures that cannot be removed in short order. Developing economies should be encouraged to experiment with various forms of institutional configurations most likely to advance and promote their development. Successful states will need to be pragmatic, willing to experiment and able to assess the results non-ideologically. Much of the success of China can be attributed to the approach of 'feeling the stones as you cross the river' – that is, the multi-stage methodology comprising (a) theoretical and empirical analysis of the problem, followed by debate over various policy options, with input from non-government experts, academics and, increasingly, citizens, (b) semi-controlled testing of various policy options in different localities, (c) close monitoring of results, (d) local benchmarking or the identifying of the best results for the particular circumstances of China, and then (e) the ramping up to national scale of promising experiments, often with policies that acknowledge and accommodate local differences and provide local officials the discretion and incentives with which to adapt national policies.

Moreover, rather than conceiving of development models as static and based on a set of enduring principles, the PWBC views models as dynamic and iterative, calling for constant adjustment and adaptation in light of changing international and domestic circumstances. Accordingly, successful states will also need to be more flexible, more adaptive, more responsive and less top-down. They will also need to be less obsessed with producing formal rules, many of which are never implemented, and to pay more attention to informal institutions. Many new developmental states 'have low scores in terms of the formalization of their rules, yet have grown relatively fast over a sustained period' (Wade, 2010; 157; Gillespie, 2014: 108).

Most fundamentally, there is no development without indigenously created developmental strategies by developing countries themselves. The PWBC represents a clear shift in the development agenda. For the last four decades, the development agenda was generated primarily in the developed world for implementation primarily in the developing world. Yet many of the most pressing problems are political economy obstacles that require local knowledge of who benefits and loses from reform, with, ultimately, a political solution. The World Bank and other international donors are not well positioned to address these types of local political contest, in some cases because of limited mandates, in other cases because of the lack of local knowledge and other financial and institutional limitations. Accordingly, ready-made models of legal texts, political institutions or economic policies must yield to a more dialogical approach based on context-specific discussions between the donors and the recipients of developmental aid. Although the developed world and international institutions will remain important sources for development advice and financial aid, the specific articulation of appropriate development models will have to be done in-country.

Central to the PWBC is a new role for the state between the invisible hand of the neoliberal Washington Consensus and the too-heavy hand of the old development state of the East Asia model – a middle way that acknowledges the need to avoid relying too heavily on either government or markets, with the specific contours determined by the local context. What is required now is a smart state with a light touch, able to address deficiencies in the market and adopt a long-term perspective that facilitates sustainable growth. Intervening less directly in the economy, the new development state is charged with: fostering the process of learning, innovation and research; promoting entrepreneurships and new product development; coordinating projects and providing information, especially in projects with multiple inputs and long-term payoffs; and encouraging extensive collaboration and communication between public and private sectors in order to address coordination problems that discourage private investment in new industries and technologies (Trubek, 2013). For instance, Brazil introduced a new policy programme called *Brasil Maior* ('Greater Brazil'), with the motto 'innovate to compete, compete to grow' (Trubek, Coutinho and Schapiro, 2012: 281). One of the distinguishing features is the complex governance structure that brings together representatives of ministries and agencies, and links them to the private sector through a variety of coordination devices and supporting institutions such as the Council of Economic and Social Development, the National Council of Industrial Development and the Brazilian Agency for Industrial Development.

For the state to carry out these functions requires effective public sectors, with capable and autonomous bureaucrats, who are capable of managing and coordinating sophisticated policies, as found at central levels in China (Kennedy and

Stiglitz, 2013: 455) and, more recently, in Brazil. Brazil has increased the level of professionalism of the bureaucracy, decreased the influence of political patronage by means of a constitutionally mandated system of open exams, enhanced internal coordination in the bureaucracy, promoted public–private collaboration and developed better methods for defining policy mandates (Trubek et al., 2012: 303). Unlike in Central and Eastern European (CEE) countries, where building effective public sectors was largely neglected until accession negotiations with the European Union, the PWBC emphasises the state's capacity 'to coordinate agents, stabilize their confidence in the states' behavior and establish national development as an urgent overarching project' (Wade, 2010: 157).

In contrast with earlier East Asian developmental states, among the key features of the new development state are: a more even balance of power between the state and business; an activist, public-service-oriented mindset among public officials; the creation of bifurcated political and economic administrative structures; and an absence of significant discretionary power of budget resources for the public officials who are coordinating with private firms (Wade, 2010: 158–159).

The PWBC also emphasises enlightened and humane social policies that provide for more equitable and sustainable growth, rather than a single-minded focus on aggregate gross domestic product (GDP). The new development state is willing to sacrifice efficiency for equity, within limits. As Cornel Ban (2013: 298) notes: 'Brazil's steady increases in the minimum wage, industrial policies targeted at high employment sectors and the use of state-owned firms to expand welfare and employment programs better fit a neo-developmentalist policy regime.'

Socio-economic issues are particularly problematic in middle-income countries because citizen demands rise exponentially, yet the government lacks the resources to meet all legitimate demands and institutions are still relatively weak compared to institutions in rich countries. Rather than relying solely on the judiciary to resolve these controversial disputes, the more successful countries have experimented with political, administrative and public–private mechanisms. Judiciaries, for their part, have mitigated the risks of overreaching by carefully selecting remedies, adopting a cautious and collaborative dialogic approach that facilitates discussion between different state and non-state actors (Brinks and Forbath, 2014; Rodríguez-Garavito, 2014), and developing enforcement alliances with other government branches, administrative agencies and private sector organisations (van Rooij and McCallister, 2014).

In terms of more specific policies, the PWBC draws on the 'lessons learned' from the last several decades of development projects and their critiques, but treats them as rules of thumb that must be adapted to a country's level of development and particular conditions. With that caveat in mind, the successful East Asian tigers and, more recently, the BRICS, despite having followed diverse economic paths, share some broad similarities.[7] All have adopted a pragmatic approach to reforms, with governments following some aspects of the Washington Consensus and rejecting or modifying others – although how they did so depended on particular circumstances, including competing ideas and ideologies, local interest groups, elite and mass politics, geography and geopolitics. In particular, they adopted most of the basic macroeconomic principles of the Washington Consensus for the domestic economy.[8] However, they rejected or modified the neoliberal aspects that would greatly reduce the role of the state through rapid deregulation and privatisation (except in Russia),[9] with the state also more active in reducing poverty and in ensuring minimal material standards to compete in a more competitive global economy.[10] They also modified the prescribed Washington Consensus relationship between the domestic and global economy by gradually exposing the domestic economy to international competition, while offering some protection to key sectors and some support to infant industries.

Although the PWBC allows for protection of infant industry,[11] targeting of particular industries and support for national champions,[12] including polices that require foreign investors to transfer technology and source locally where possible, the goal is to create globally competitive export industries and to increase the share of medium and high value-added products and services (Ban, 2013: 310). Thus, as countries make the transition from low- to middle- to high-income countries, there is less need for such policies, and companies face increased competition from domestic and foreign firms.

In general, the new development states tend to impose capital controls and to rely more on domestic financing to avoid exchange rate fluctuations and the all-too-frequent financial crises that have plagued those countries that have followed the Washington Consensus. They have also sought to promote exports (through management of the exchange rate, export credits from newly developed import–export banks, and support for infant industries and national champions) and to control while still being open to imports, thus running surpluses and building up foreign exchange reserves as further protection against financial crises. Major banks are often state-owned or state-controlled and are treated as policy banks, particularly during times of economic crisis. This has allowed new development states to soften the blow of the global financial crisis by pumping money into the economy, thus maintaining relatively high growth rates and levels of employment, albeit at a cost of weakening the banks and arguably misallocating funds to economically inefficient projects (Birdsall, 2011: 12).

Implications of the PWBC for the China model

The good news for China is that much of the PWBC is derived from the experiences of China and other successful East Asian countries. Most notably, the emphasis on the process of reform reflects the pragmatic, experimental approach of the China model. For example, China has been insistent on charting its own development path, resistant to conditionalities tied to outside funding from international financial institutions and careful to adapt international best practices to local circumstances.

In terms of substance, China and other successful East Asian countries have exemplified the general policy of following the Washington Consensus regarding macroeconomic policies for the domestic economy, rejecting rapid privatisation and extreme neoliberalism, and gradually exposing domestic firms to international competition, while subsidising infant industries and promoting national champions. China has also maintained capital account currency controls, used the central banks and major state-owned banks as policy banks to stimulate the economy during times of crisis or slowdown, and stockpiled unprecedented foreign reserves.

Nevertheless, the PWBC highlights three major areas for change. First, China's state-investment, export-oriented economic model appears to have run its course. There now needs to be a transition towards a more consumption-based growth model, with greater reliance on services and more emphasis on innovation in the manufacturing sector. Although China has made considerable progress in approaching the technological frontier in many sectors, Chinese firms now need to take the final step and close the remaining gap, becoming international leaders in the global marketplace.

Secondly, the role of the state must change. The state must become more efficient and govern with a lighter hand. The state must grant greater authority and autonomy to the civil and business sectors, and promote public-private modes of governance. To be fair, China has engaged in significant administrative reforms over the last thirty years and the civil service, in general, compares favourably to those of other countries at a similar level of development. Nevertheless, China falls far short of the performance standards of high-income countries on rule-of-law and good governance measures, and much remains to be done.

Thirdly, the PWBC highlights the interrelationships between economic reforms and political, legal and social reforms as countries reach the middle-income stage. For the last three decades, the emphasis in China has been on economic reforms, with political, legal and social changes following at a more measured pace. Critics contend that the gap between political-legal reforms and economic reforms is creating a bottleneck for economic growth and leading to social instability. Many were hoping that the 2013 Decision would announce a bold reform agenda that embraced not only major new economic reforms, but significant political and legal reforms as well.

The decision in light of the PWBC

The 2013 Decision as a whole is an impressive document, particularly in light of the political context. Although pundits have repeatedly and incorrectly predicted the downfall of the CCP for decades (Chang, 2001), there was a widespread feeling that major reforms were urgently needed. Despite the seeming consensus about the need for deep and comprehensive reforms, the Hu-Wen administration failed to act aggressively and proactively enough to major challenges. The delay in rebalancing the economy allowed interest groups to grow wealthier and more powerful, making the task all the more difficult for the Xi administration. Although steps were taken to improve governance and strengthen the legal system, the political-legal system became more concerned with social stability under Zhou Yongkang[13] and the judiciary, more populist under Supreme People's Court (SPC) President Wang.

The weak response of the Hu-Wen regime led to considerable speculation as to whether the Party really understood the urgent need for reforms, and whether it had the political will and capacity to push through contested reforms. The fears that the Party was out of touch and out of control rose dramatically when the first public announcement after the Plenum was the disjointed, inconsistent and rambling Communiqué.[14] Investors reacted negatively, and stock markets in Hong Kong and China fell sharply (Zweig, 2013). However, the subsequent release of Xi Jinping's Explanation and the detailed Decision restored confidence in the market, resolving the issues of whether the Party leaders understood the urgency of reforms and what was needed to put China on a path towards more sustainable growth (Kroeber, 2013).

Although there are still many doubts about whether the Party will be able to implement the ambitious economic agenda, the Decision does provide a comprehensive roadmap for reforms, set forth in six substantive sections on the economy, politics, culture, society, the environment, and national defence and the military.

In assessing the Decision, the first point to bear in mind is that the main focus is economic reforms: it is primarily a roadmap for economic reforms. Indeed, this is explicitly acknowledged by Xi in his Explanation and stated in the Decision:

> In comprehensively deepening reform, we must base ourselves on the reality that our country will remain in the preliminary stage of socialism for a long time, persist in the predominant strategic judgment that development is still the key to resolve all of our country's problems, and put economic construction at the center. . . . Economic structural reform is the focus of deepening reform. The core issues are dealing with the relationship between the government and the market well, ensuring that the market has a decisive function in resource allocation, and giving better rein to the function of government.
>
> (Xi, 2013)

Although the Decision addresses a number of areas, the vast majority of the document deals with economic issues. The economic section contains six parts, with twenty-one subsections; in contrast, there are three parts for politics, including one for legal reforms, with just four subsections, two parts for society, and one each for culture, ecological civilisation and national defence. A full third of the operative subsections deal with economic issues and many of the issues discussed in other sections, such as social welfare programmes, rural property rights and the environment, are also essentially economic issues.

Towards a consumption-based economy

The Decision clearly addresses the main issue of the need for a new model that is more dependent on markets and consumption and less dependent on state-led investment and exports. The major theoretical breakthrough is the announcement that the market would now play a decisive role – as opposed to a basic or fundamental role – in resource allocation. Previously, China had deregulated product markets, but the government had continued to intervene in the allocation of key inputs such as capital, energy and land natural resources, and to control prices. There is also to be increased competition, including greater market access for private companies and foreign investment enterprises. Would-be entrepreneurs will need fewer approvals to establish a company and registered capital requirements will be eliminated.

The Decision outlines a wide range of financial reforms that would allow for more private banks, would increase avenues to raise capital and would expand the bond markets. Notably, there are also signs that the capital account will be opened, that the renminbi (RMB) will become freely convertible and that interest rates will be liberalised.

In terms of socio-economic reforms, the Decision promises increased efforts to address income inequality, mainly by making sure that the rich pay taxes, but also though increasing minimum wages and redistribution from wealthier to poorer regions. There is also some hint of future land reforms, including the right of farmers to sell their land, and further restrictions on government takings of land without adequate compensation. The Decision signals that there will be further reforms to the household registration (*hukou*) system as part of a broader effort to increase urbanisation and address China's looming ageing crisis. In addition, the Decision highlights the need to improve the social security, welfare and medical care systems, as well as to provide more government-subsidised low-income and affordable housing.

Role of the state: Smaller, smarter state

The Decision also clearly endorses a new role of the state consistent with the smaller, smarter state of the PWBC. The government is now charged with five main duties or functions: maintaining macro-economic stability; regulating and supervising the markets; strengthening public services; promoting sustainable development (including environmental protection); and supervising society.

The lighter hand is reflected in the reduction of the number of approvals to do business, the streamlining of the approval process to make it less burdensome and the decentralising of power to local governments. The emphasis is on more efficient administrative agencies and more public-service-oriented civil servants.

Reforms of the still significant state-owned enterprise (SOE) sector focused less on further privatisation and more on increased competition and regulations. For instance, SOEs will have to pay 30 per cent of post-tax profits as dividends for social security system. The entity in charge of supervising state-owned assets will also focus more on returns to capital rather than the aggregate value of assets or aggregate profits.

In keeping with the notion of a smarter state, the government will play a role in stimulating research and development (R&D) and innovation. There will be increased reliance on public–private collaboration, but with the market and the private sector playing a more prominent role. The Decision also emphasises that the goal is to commercialise R&D.

The government's hand is still evident in the emphasis on industrial policy, the promotion of national champions and the extension of infant industry protection in favoured sectors. The scope, however, is more narrowly defined as key areas relating to national security or key areas of the national economy, including forward-looking strategic industries.

Relationship between economic and political-legal reforms

In comparison to the economic reform agenda, the political, legal and social reform agendas are more modest in scope and less ambitious in nature. The Decision calls for a larger role for civil society and more public participation as part of an expansion of 'consultative democracy', but all clearly under the leadership of the CCP and within the existing institutional framework. The major areas of institutional innovation are in the creation of a central-level 'small group' to oversee the comprehensive reform agenda, the establishment of a new state security commission and reforms that provide more vertical controls over the Party discipline system to overcome local protectionism of corrupt officials. There is no doubt that Xi has orchestrated an aggressive anti-corruption campaign, although it remains unclear whether the goal is to rid the Party and government of corruption or only to eliminate those who oppose Xi and his agenda.

The implications of the decision for legal reforms

The Decision's section on legal reforms mainly sets forth a series of broad principles or political slogans that have been circulating and debated for many years, along with a mixed bag of technical reforms touching on a seemingly random set of issues that have been previously discussed or were already being implemented. There is no major theoretical or ideological breakthrough, in contrast to economic reforms in which Xi highlighted the change in policy to the market playing a 'decisive' role in allocating resources as the centrepiece of the eighteenth Party Congress.

The Decision's calls for rule of law, respect for the Constitution, the protection of human rights, judicial independence, and a fair and efficient judiciary are, of course, nothing new. The problem has been in reaching a consensus on what these grand, but vague, ideals are supposed to mean in practice and then translating them into concrete legal reforms. Nor does the Decision or the Explanation provide any hint of how the basic conflicts discussed above that have undermined reform efforts in the past are to be resolved.

For instance, the Decision once again reiterates the need to safeguard the authority of the Constitution, but it says nothing about how to resolve the tension between the leading role of the Party and the Constitution. While it recommends further development of mechanisms and procedures for constitutional interpretation and supervision, there is no suggestion that a constitutional court will be established; rather, the intention seems to be to improve the current mechanism whereby a subcommittee of the National People's Congress (NPC) reviews the constitutionality of laws and regulations. Nor is there any suggestion that the Constitution will be made directly justiciable. Thus, although the Decision reiterates that no organisation or individual may exceed the authority of the Constitution and the law, and declares that all acts violating the Constitution and the law must be punished, it is hard to see how this is to be accomplished through existing institutions and what, if anything, has changed.

The Decision is somewhat more forthcoming about specific measures to enhance judicial independence. Most notably, the Decision calls for more centralised management of the judiciary in terms of funding for the courts and judicial appointments, and also raises more tentatively the possibility of a system whereby jurisdiction is not tied to an administrative region. This could perhaps mean having courts in other provinces hear certain types of case or the establishment of regional courts. Centralised funding and regional courts have been proposed as a way of overcoming local protectionism for decades. There have been some efforts to centralise funding in recent years, but the courts at the local level remain dependent to a considerable extent on local government funding. These proposals would be significant reforms if they were to be carried out. However, it is not clear whether funding will be provided by the central or provincial governments or, more importantly, whether funding will be adequate. There is also the worry that local courts will then become more beholden to provincial governments. Nor is it clear how appointments will be handled and whether Party organisations will continue to have a role in the process.

In addition, the Decision recommends reforming the way in which cases are heard, including requiring judges who decide the case to hear the case, and more authority for the presiding judges and collegiate panel. This implies a more limited role for adjudicative committees (committees of senior judges that review major or controversial cases). However, the Decision stops short of abolishing adjudicative committees and does not offer any details as to how to reconcile the need for those who decide the case to hear the case with the role of adjudicative committees.

The Decision also emphasises the need to sort out the relationship between higher and lower courts, which presumably refers in part to eliminating or restricting the practice of *qingshi*, whereby lower court judges seek advice from higher courts about legal issues that have arisen in the cases they are hearing – another practice that restricted judicial independence and mitigated the value of appeal. But the Decision does not call for changes to the current system for assessing performance where reversals on appeal are counted against a judge. Without changes to the incentive structure, judges are likely to continue to seek guidance from higher courts.

The Decision mentions the need to strengthen supervision of the judiciary, including by expanding the people's assessor system, increasing public participation in the judiciary, ensuring that trials are open to the public, requiring judges to fully articulate the reasons for their decisions in their judgments and making judgments more accessible to the public. However, social supervision is a double-edged sword, with judges expressing concerns that populist pressures from the public have encroached upon judicial independence and led to results at odds with law (Liebman, 2011).

All of these reforms, if implemented, would enhance the independence and authority of the judiciary, and would be positive steps forward.[15] However, it bears noting that they enhance the independence and authority of the judiciary against state organs, including local government officials, the police and prosecutors, as well as private actors, including politically powerful business interests. They do not address the relation of the judiciary to Party organs such as the Political-Legal Committee, or entail greater independence and authority over politically sensitive cases involving national security or challenges to the authority of the Party from human rights activists and 'dissidents'.[16] Nothing in the Decision suggests that the outcome would be any different in future cases involving the likes of Bo Xilai, Liu Xiaobo[17] or Xu Zhiyong.[18] Indeed, the establishment of the National Security Commission, along with the continued emphasis on stability, suggests that the recent attempts to reform the Political-Legal Committee system by increasing professional and transparency, and limiting its power and ability to intervene in ongoing cases, have more to do with making sure that the Xi regime retains control over the coercive state institutions in the wake of Bo Xilai and Zhou Yongkang than with any major rebalancing of state organs such that the judiciary has more authority or independence to decide issues that threaten the ruling regime.

Moreover, the general principles set out in the section on legal reforms must be read in light of the document as a whole and the broader political context. Thus the calls for the rule of law, respect for the Constitution, the protection of human rights and so on must be read in conjunction with the other paragraphs that express ideas that have served to undermine efforts to strengthen the rule of law, the status of the Constitution and the protection of human rights, such as the leading role of the Party, the need to maintain stability, the mass line, democratic centralism, and the emphasis on ideology and socialism with Chinese characteristics.

The future of legal reforms will depend on how the Decision is interpreted and implemented, and how the major areas of contention are resolved. Everyone – whether on the Right or the Left, or anywhere in between – will be able to find some support for their views in the Decision. Not surprisingly, the battles over how to interpret the Decision have already begun, with prominent jurists, such as Politburo member and head of the Political-Legal Committee Meng Zhianzhu, and law professors, such as Jiang Ping and Zhang Qianfan, weighing in with their views (Meng, 2013).[19]

Perhaps most importantly, in assessing the future direction of legal reforms, the broad principles set out in the Decision should also be read in light of actual practice. Contrary to the hopes of liberals that the new administration would embark on ambitious political reforms, or at least adopt a kinder, gentler approach to dissent, Xi has tolerated, if not overseen, a further restriction on the already-limited spheres of freedom of assembly and expression, and cracked down on rights activists advocating constitutionalism – that is, a more robust role for civil society and greater transparency.[20] New regulations have been passed to stop the spread of 'rumours' on the Internet, leading to the arrests of prominent bloggers and the closure of many popular blogs, including the blog of well-known legal scholar He Weifang (Global Voices, 2014). Legal activists and human rights lawyers are regularly subject to surveillance and harassment by authorities, or increasingly prosecuted for the vague offence of 'gathering a crowd to disrupt public order' (*South China Morning Post*, 2013). Despite the public exposures of the incredible family fortunes of the CCP leadership, including relatives of Wen Jiabao, Bo Xilai and Xi himself,[21] the almost-daily accounts of government officials absconding with millions of dollars and Xi's own promise to crack down on corruption, efforts to require the public disclosure of the assets of government officials and Party leaders have failed to produce a significant change in policies; rather, the government retaliated against Bloomberg and the *New York Times* by blocking their websites, then refusing to renew their journalists' visas, until US Vice President Biden personally intervened (Lynch, 2013; Wan, 2014).

Apart from reiterating general principles, the Decision contains a hodge-podge of technical reforms only loosely tied to subsections that themselves lack coherence or any obvious relationship to other subsections. Again, most of the reforms are not new. Some involve partially completed reforms that have been ongoing for years. These include: addressing legal inconsistency by improving the file-and-review system; improving the enforcement of judgments; improving the quality of legislation, and opening up the legislative process to public participation through notice and comment provisions and more hearings; strengthening the professional qualifications of judges and the ethical standards of lawyers; expanding legal aid and public legal education campaigns; resolving overlapping jurisdictional conflicts and reducing bureaucratic protectionism; and reining in administrative discretion and holding government officials accountable for their actions.

In addition, there are a number of criminal law reforms that could be significant. Most notably, the Decision calls for the elimination of re-education through labour. The Decision reiterates that torture and forced confessions are not allowed, and calls for strict implementation of rules excluding tainted evidence. This is consistent with long-term trends in criminal law reforms, although, in practice, torture, coercion and the reliance on tainted evidence are still major issues. The Decision also calls for further reductions in the number of crimes subject to capital punishment, but the list of crimes subject to capital punishment is likely to continue to be much longer than reformers would hope and to include non-violent crimes.

In sum, the Decision provides a much bolder, more comprehensive and more detailed agenda for economic reforms than for legal reforms. Nonetheless, the Decision highlighted a number of problematic areas that affect the operation of the judiciary and impact the legal reform process, but which are beyond the power of the courts to resolve by themselves, including the ongoing problems with corruption and the limits of transparency, the problems dealing with socio-economic issues and the need to create a more robust social security system, environmental issues, rural–urban inequality and ethnic tensions. Even if legal reformers within the SPC were able to agree among themselves as to what was needed, they would need to work with other Party organisations and state actors to address many of these issues, and they would encounter considerable opposition along the way, as they have in the past.

In many ways, the Decision is as notable for what it did *not* include as for what it did. A number of significant reforms were not addressed.

A more ambitious agenda would arguably have included some or all of the following:

- the creation of a constitutional court;
- the ratification of the 1966 International Covenant on Civil and Political Rights (ICCPR);

- the elimination of not only re-education through labour, but also all forms of administrative detention, as well as the abolishment of black jails, *shuanggui*, the misuse of mental institutions for detention purposes and other forms of illegal detention;
- increasing the autonomy and authority of the legal profession by making the Bar self-governing and eliminating the supervisory role of the Ministry of Justice, and changing the way in which cases alleging misbehaviour by criminal defence lawyers are handled to better protect them against trumped-up charges;
- the elimination of adjudicative committees, or limiting of their role to internal court management and policymaking, and elimination, or at least major reformation, of the Political-Legal Committee system such that it plays only a general policymaking role;
- a firm financial commitment by the central government that all courts will be adequately funded and need not rely on local government funding for anything, with the central government stepping in if provincial funding is inadequate;
- major changes to the appointment process for judges that make it more open and transparent, and more determined by the judiciary and the Bar, with the PNC role reduced to one of review and approval, and no role for Party organisations;
- the enhancement of the authority of the judiciary by allowing courts the power to strike down abstract Acts and legislation that is inconsistent with higher level legislation (which power could be tied to the level of court, so that lower courts would be able to strike down only lower level normative documents); and
- the encouragement of class action suits by changing standing rules, creating new financing mechanisms allowing lawyers to charge contingency fees and revising the performance criteria for judges, so that they are evaluated simply on the number of cases they handle each year, but receive more credit for handling complex cases.

The point is not to argue that the Decision should necessarily have endorsed these changes, nor is it meant as a comprehensive list of essential reforms; rather, the point is to illustrate some of the types of issue that were not addressed, and to highlight some of the challenges that legal reformers face and the nature of the legal reform process. For instance, few, if any, of these reforms are within the power of the SPC or the judiciary alone to decide. They deal with the relationship of the courts to other state and Party actors. Moreover, all are complex, multifaceted issues. It is not simply a matter of changing one thing; they all involve a number of changes in rules, practices, and institutional and social culture that are necessary complements to make them work. For instance, now that re-education through labour is eliminated, we can expect police and prosecutors to rely on other forms of administrative detention, new forms of detention such as community correction centres or even less-regulated forms of detention, such as black jails (Dui Hua Foundation, 2013a). Similarly, creating a constitutional court would require intense detailed discussions and negotiations about how members would be selected, what powers the court would have and so on. There is tremendous institutional variation on such issues among constitutional courts. These issues also illustrate the ongoing, iterative nature of legal reforms. Again taking the example of constitutional courts, whatever their initial powers, constitutional courts evolve over time, often through informal conventions rather than formal constitutional amendments or amendments to the organic laws governing them. It was by no means a foregone conclusion, for example, that the US Supreme Court would emerge with the broad powers of constitutional review that it currently enjoys.

All of these factors help to explain why the 'rule of law' is so difficult to achieve (or, more accurately, since rule of law is an ideal, to more fully realise) in any country. There is no single game-changer that will suddenly fix all of the problems and make a legal system leap into the top rank of rule-of-law charts when it has been muddling along in the middle ranks.

Conclusion

The 2013 Decision continues the two-track approach to reforms, prioritising economic reforms over political, legal and social reforms, despite all the talk of the need for a coordinated and integrated approach to development. Liberals hoping once again that the new leadership would aggressively pursue political reform have been disappointed. But they were forewarned and should not have been surprised by the two-track approach or the continued emphasis on stability at the expense of personal liberties.

Prioritising economic reforms is not necessarily bad. The global economy remains weak. Europe has yet to emerge from the numerous crises spawned by the global financial crisis and its own structural flaws, and some economists still predict that Greece and other debtor countries will be forced to exit the eurozone. The risk of increased trade protectionism and the threat of a trade war remain, with China still facing international criticism over exchange rates, the lack of financial liberalisation, government subsidies for SOEs and infant industries, and policies that discriminate against foreign companies in favour of national champions. Perhaps most importantly, rebalancing the Chinese economy will require overcoming many powerful interests at a time when the line between the political and economic spheres has become blurred, if not vanished, as result of the decision to allow capitalists into the Party and the increased concentration of wealth within China.

One general lesson for middle-income country governments is that, at the end of the day, to use a popular phrase from American political campaigns, 'it's the economy, stupid'. What separates middle- and high-income countries is wealth. The only way in which middle-income countries are ever going to join the ranks of high-income countries is by growing the economy. There is, after all, a reason that so much of the development literature is by economists.

Nevertheless, it is *not only* the economy. Middle-income countries must strive for sustainable, high-quality growth. They must also strengthen governance institutions, build up social welfare systems and meet the demands of citizens for a higher quality of life.

If the Xi administration is successful at rebalancing the economy towards consumption, it will have laid the groundwork for more rapid and fundamental political, legal and social reforms in its second term. The people will be better off, having benefited from higher interest rates and the end of financial repression. Growth will be more equitable. There will be fewer environmental problems and more resources available for prevention and clean-up. Spending on education, job training, health care and pensions will have increased. There will be more subsidised low-income housing. Illegal land takings will have decreased and compensation increased. State oligopolies will face more competition, bringing down prices and improving the quality of services. The 'have-nots' will have gained relative to the 'haves'. The Xi administration will enjoy broad support and have the political capital to take on political reforms without fear – or at least lower risk – that the process will undermine the Party in the way that *perestroika* led to the breakup of the Soviet Union. Whether that will happen remains to be seen.

Notes

1 By 2009, there were more than 3,000 articles available on the Internet discussing the China model and related concepts (Fewsmith, 2011).

2 Decision of the Chinese Communist Party Central Committee on Several Major Questions about Deepening Reform, Passed at the Third Plenum of the Eighteenth Central Committee of the Chinese Communist Party, 12 November 2013, Chinese version available online at http://news.xinhuanet.com/politics/2013-11/15/c_118164235.htm [accessed 18 July 2016]. For an English translation, see online at http://chinacopyrightandmedia.wordpress.com/2013/11/15/ccp-central-committee-resolution-concerning-some-major-issues-in-comprehensively-deepening-reform/ [accessed 18 July 2016]. For further background on the drafting of the Decision and its main contents, see Xi Jinping (2013).

3 To the extent that pundits and journalists do get into the details, they are often wrong, leading to a series of articles by earnest academics pointing out that, in fact, Japan, South Korea and the other earlier East Asian tigers did not conform to the principles set out by the World Bank in *The East Asian Miracle* (World Bank, 1993), or that the alleged Beijing Consensus was more of a statement of the development path that Beijing was hoping to follow rather than the path it actually followed (Ohnesorge, 2007; Kennedy, 2010).

4 In holding an online debate on whether China offers a better development model than 'the West' – which resulted in 53 per cent disagreeing and 47 per cent agreeing – *The Economist* (2011) noted disagreement about what the China model consists of, but listed as key ingredients a 'managed exchange rate, state control over key industries including the banking system, preference for diktat rather than democratic debate, heavy state investment in infrastructure and strong support for the export sector'.

5 Among the factors cited were: sound macroeconomic management, including fiscal discipline and control of inflation; high levels of private domestic investment, domestic savings and investment in education; agricultural policies that increased productivity; promotion of exports; flexible labour markets; limited price distortions; openness to foreign technology; a demographic transition from high to low birth rates; politically insulated and reasonably compensated technocratic leaders; a business-friendly environment; and selective state interventions subject to strict performance criteria – although the Bank was ambivalent at best about the positive value of state interventions that deviated from 'the neoclassical' model (World Bank, 1993).

6 In China, this is often portrayed as a debate between the New Left and those on the Right. Although useful as a first cut, there are widely divergent views within these broad categories.

7 How much of the PWBC is really new depends on the starting point. The approach summarised in this paragraph reflects the East Asia model (Peerenboom, 2007: 32). In this regard, the PWBC is more post Washington Consensus than post East Asia model. However, the value of the PWBC more generally is that it reflects recent concerns about the limitations of the East Asia model, China model or Beijing Consensus.

8 As Fourcade (2013: 257) argues, the Washington Consensus commitment to macroeconomic prudence has been 'naturalized into policy common sense'.

9 Russia privatised rapidly, with largely negative results, but not in the manner prescribed by the Washington Consensus or international advisers (Rutland, 2013).

10 For example, state-owned enterprises (SOEs) play a key role in so-called strategic sectors of the economy (banks, oil, electricity) in both China and Brazil (Ban, 2013: 313–314).

11 Proponents of infant industry protection are divided as to whether to promote industries or firms that already have a comparative competitive advantage, or to promote companies in newer industries (just) beyond the current technology frontier (Lin and Chang, 2009).

12 While China, Brazil and Russia have invested heavily in state-owned national champions through government-controlled banks, the governance structures vary from direct control and appointment of executives to control via majority or minority shareholder stakes (Ramanujam et al., 2012).

13 Zhou was a Politburo member and the head of public security and the Political-Legal Committee. He was an ally of Bo Xilai, the mayor of Chongqing who attempted to circumvent the Party process for selecting leaders in his quest for a Politburo position, and who was subsequently expelled from the Party and sentenced to life imprisonment for corruption and abuse of power (Forsythe, 2015).

14 Communiqué of the Third Plenum of the Eighteenth CPC Central Committee, Chinese version available online at http://news.xinhuanet.com/politics/2013-11/12/c_118113455.htm [accessed 18 July 2016].

15 Such reforms would require complementary changes in many sectors. There are also many additional steps that could be taken within the existing political framework (Fu and Peerenboom, 2010).

16 Some measures have been taken to reduce intervention by Party committees and political-legal committees in ongoing cases (Dui Hua Foundation, 2013b; Zhai, 2013). There are also proposals to prevent political-legal committees from intervening in cases other than those involving national security and foreign affairs.

17 Liu Xiaobo is a public intellectual and co-author of *Charter'08*, a political manifesto calling for democracy, human rights and the end of CCP dominance, which was modelled on *Charter'77*, a petition written in 1977 by Czech intellectuals and artists that helped to undermine the Soviet Union in Eastern Europe. After being convicted for endangering state security, Liu Xiaobo was awarded the Nobel Peace Prize (China Human Rights Defenders, 2009).

18 Xu Zhiyong was a prominent legal-scholar-cum-activist who founded the New Citizen Movement, which sought, among other things, a requirement that government officials disclose their assets and the assets of their family members (Hayashi, 2013; An, 2013).

19 See also *Legal Evening News* (2013).

20 See Buckley (2013); Jacobs (2013). See also the open letter to judges presiding over civil rights trials in China, alleging more than 100 arrests of citizens for exercising their basic rights (China Change, 2013).

21 The *New York Times* reported that relatives of Wen Jiabao had accumulated wealth of US$2.7 billion, while Bo's relatives had more than $126 million of assets, many of them held abroad (Barboza, 2012). While the *New York Times* and Bloomberg received the Long Island University 2012 George Polk Awards in Journalism for their efforts, their websites were blocked in China (Long Island University, 2013).

References

An, B. (2013) 'Anti-graft Body Pushes Officials to Disclose Assets', *China Daily*, 3 December, available online at http://usa.chinadaily.com.cn/china/2013-12/03/content_17146640.htm [accessed 15 May 2015].

Ban, C. (2013) 'Brazil's Liberal Neo-developmentalism: New Paradigm or Edited Orthodoxy?', *Review of International Political Economy*, 20(2): 298–331.

Barboza, D. (2012) 'Billions in Hidden Riches for Family of Chinese Leader', *New York Times*, 25 October.

Birdsall, N. (2011) 'The Global Financial Crisis: The Beginning of the End of the "Development" Agenda', in N. Birdsall and F. Fukuyama (eds) *New Ideas on Development after the Financial Crisis*, Baltimore, MD: John Hopkins University Press, 1–28.

Birdsall, N., and Fukuyama, F. (2012) 'The Post-Washington Consensus', *Foreign Affairs*, March/April, available online at https://www.foreignaffairs.com/articles/2011-02-16/post-washington-consensus [accessed 15 May 2015].

Brinks, D. M., and Forbath, W. (2014) 'The Role of Courts and Constitutions in the New Politics of Welfare in Latin America', in R. Peerenboom and T. Ginsburg (eds) *Law and Development of Middle-income Countries: Avoiding the Middle-income Trap*, New York: Cambridge University Press, 221–245.

Buckley, C. (2013) 'China Takes Aim at Western Ideas', *New York Times*, 19 August, available online at http://www.nytimes.com/2013/08/20/world/asia/chinas-new-leadership-takes-hard-line-in-secret-memo.html?hp&_r=0 [accessed 15 May 2015].

Chang, D. (2009) *Capitalist Development in Korea: Labor, Capital, and the Myth of the Developmental State*, London/New York: Routledge.

Chang, G. G. (2001) *The Coming Collapse of China*, New York: Random House.

China Change (2013) 'Align Your Loyalty with the Constitution and the Law: An Open Letter to Judges Who Will Be Presiding over the Civil Rights Trials in China', 7 January, available online at https://chinachange.org/2014/01/07/align-your-loyalty-with-the-constitution-and-the-law-an-open-letter-to-judges-who-will-be-presiding-over-the-civil-rights-trials-in-china/ [accessed 18 July 2016].

China Human Rights Defenders (2009) 'China Human Rights Briefing, 3–9 August 2009', 11 August, formerly available online at http://chrdnet.com/2009/08/china-human-rights-briefing-august-3-9-2009/ [accessed 15 May 2015].

Dui Hua Foundation (2013a) 'Community Correction Expands as RTL Contracts', *Human Rights Journal*, 19 December, available online at http://www.duihuahrjournal.org/2013/12/community-correction-expands-as-rtl.html [accessed 15 May 2015].

Dui Hua Foundation (2013b) 'Political-legal Committee Issues Rules to Prevent Injustice', *Human Rights Journal*, 22 October, available online at http://www.duihuahrjournal.org/2013/10/politico-legal-committee-issues-rules.html [accessed 15 May 2015].

Dumas, C., and Choyleva, D. (2011) *The American Phoenix – and Why China and Europe Will Struggle after the Coming Slump*, London: Profile Books.

The Economist (2011) 'China Model', 13 August, formerly available online at http://www.economist.com/debate/overview/179 [accessed 15 May 2015].

Eichengreen, B., Park, D., and Shin, K. (2011) 'When Fast-growing Economies Slow Down: International Evidence and Implications for China', NBER Working Paper No. 16919, available online at http://www.nber.org/papers/w16919 [accessed 15 May 2015].

Fewsmith, J. (2011) 'Debating the China Model', *China Leadership Monitor*, 21 September, formerly available online at http://www.hoover.org/publications/china-leadership-monitor/article/93636 [accessed 15 May 2015].

Forsythe, M. (2015) 'Zhou Yongkang, Ex-Security Chief in China, Gets Life in Prison for Graft', *New York Times*, 11 June.

Fourcade, M. (2013) 'The Material and Symbolic Construction of the BRICS: Reflections Inspired by the *RIPE* Special Issue', *Review of Political Economy*, 20(2): 256–267.

Freeman, C. W., and Wen, J. Y. (2011) *China's New Leftists and the China Model Debate after the Financial Crisis*, Washington, DC: Center for Strategic and International Studies, available online at http://csis.org/files/publication/110728_Freeman_ChinaNewLeftists_Web.pdf [accessed 15 May 2015].

Fu, Y., and Peerenboom, R. (2010) 'A New Analytical Framework for Understanding and Promoting Judicial Independence in China', in R. Peerenboom (ed.) *Judicial Independence in China*, Cambridge: Cambridge University Press, 95–132.

Gillespie, J. (2014) 'Growing Wealth in East Asian MICs with Transnational Production Regimes', in R. Peerenboom and T. Ginsburg (eds) *Law and Development in the Middle-income Countries: Avoiding the Middle-income Trap*, New York: Cambridge, 108–128.

Global Voices (2014) 'Censorship, Prosecution Drive Exodus of Opinion Leaders from China's Sina Weibo', 6 January, available online at http://globalvoicesonline.org/2014/01/06/censorship-prosecution-drive-exodus-of-opinion-leaders-from-chinas-sina-weibo/ [accessed 18 July 2016].

Halper, S. (2010) *The Beijing Consensus: How China's Authoritarian Model Will Dominate the Twenty-first Century*, New York: Basic Books.

Hayashi, N. (2013) 'Activist Arrested as China Stifles Calls for Asset Transparency', *The Asahi Shimbun*, 10 May, formerly available online at http://ajw.asahi.com/article/asia/china/AJ201305100089 [accessed 15 May 2015].

Jacobs, A. (2013) 'Chinese Professor Who Advocated Free Speech Is Fired', *New York Times*, 10 December, available online at http://www.nytimes.com/2013/12/11/world/asia/chinese-professor-who-advocated-free-speech-is-fired.html [accessed 15 May 2015].

Johnson, C. (1982) *MITI and the Japanese Miracle: The Growth of Industrial Policy, 1925–1975*, Stanford, CA: Stanford University Press.

Kennedy, D., and Stiglitz, J. E. (2013) 'Institutional Foundations for the Chinese Market Economy: The State', in *Law and Economics with Chinese Characteristics: Institutions for Promoting Development in the Twenty-first Century*, Oxford: Oxford University Press, 455–465.

Kennedy, S. (2010) 'The Myth of the Beijing Consensus', *Journal of Contemporary China*, 19(65): 461–477.

Kroeber, A.R. (2013) 'Xi Jinping's Ambitious Agenda for Economic Reform in China', *Brookings*, 17 November, available online at http://www.brookings.edu/research/opinions/2013/11/17-xi-jinping-economic-agenda-kroeber [accessed 15 May 2015].

Krugman, P. (1994) 'The Myth of Asia's Miracle', *Foreign Affairs*, 73(6): 62–78.

Kupchan, C. A. (2012) *No One's World: The West, the Rising Rest, and the Coming Global Turn*, Oxford: Oxford University Press.

Legal Evening News (2013) 22 November, formerly available online at http://www.fawan.com.cn/html/2013-11/22/content_464997.htm [accessed 15 May 2015].

Liebman, B. L. (2011) 'A Populist Threat to China's Courts?', in M. E. Gallagher and M. Y. K. Woo (eds) *Chinese Justice: Civil Dispute Resolution in Post-reform China*, Cambridge: Cambridge University Press, 109–138.

Lin, J. Y. (2011) 'New Structural Economics: A Framework for Rethinking Development', *The World Bank Research Observer*, 26(2): 193–221.

Lin, J., and Chang, H. (2009) 'Should Industrial Policy in Developing Countries Conform to Comparative Advantage or Defy It? A Debate between Justin Lin and Ha-Joon Chang', *Development Policy Review*, 27(5): 483–502.

Long Island University (2013) 'Liu Announces George Polk Awards in Journalism', Press release, 18 February, available online at http://www.liu.edu/About/News/Univ-Ctr-PR/2013/February/UC_PR-Feb18 [accessed 18 July 2016].

Lynch, E. (2013) 'The Widening Gyre: The Changed Power Dynamics of Journalist Visas', *China Law and Policy*, 23 December, available online at http://chinalawandpolicy.com/2013/12/23/the-widening-gyre-the-changed-power-dynamics-of-journalists-visas/ [accessed 15 May 2015].

Meng, J. (2013) '*Shenhua Sifa Tizhi Gaige* [Deepen judicial system reform]', 25 November, available online at http://politics.people.com.cn/n/2013/1125/c1001-23640310.html [accessed 15 May 2015].

Ohnesorge, J. K. M. (2007) 'Developing Development Theory: Law and Development Orthodoxies and the Northeast Asian Experience', *University of Pennsylvania Journal of International Economic Law*, 28(2): 220–306.

Pan, W. (ed.) (2009) *Zhongguomoshi: jiedurenmingongheguo 60 nian* [*The China Model: Understanding 60 Years of the People's Republic of China*], Beijing: Central Translation Press.

Peerenboom, R. (2007) *China Modernises: Threat to the West or Model for the Rest?*, Oxford: Oxford University Press.

Peerenboom, R., and Bugaric, B. (2014) 'Development after the Global Financial Crisis: The Emerging Post Washington, Post Beijing Consensus', available online at http://ssrn.com/abstract=2277427 [accessed 15 May 2015].

Pettis, M. (2013) *The Great Rebalancing: Trade, Conflict and the Perilous Road ahead for the World Economy*, Princeton, NJ: Princeton University Press.

Ramanujam, N., Verna, M., Betts, J., Charamba, K., and Moore, M. (2012) *Rule of Law and Economic Development: A Comparative Analysis of Approaches to Economic Development across the BRIC Countries*, Rule of Law and Economic Development Research Group Report, Montreal: ROLED, available online at https://www.mcgill.ca/roled/files/roled/mcgill_roled_report_2012.pdf [accessed 15 May 2015].

Ramo, J. C. (2004) *The Beijing Consensus: Notes on the New Physics of Chinese Power*, London: The Foreign Policy Centre, available online at http://fpc.org.uk/fsblob/244.pdf [accessed 15 May 2015].

Rodríguez-Garavito, C. (2014) 'The Judicialisation of Health Care: Symptoms, Diagnosis, and Prescriptions', in R. Peerenboom and T. Ginsburg (eds) *Law and Development of Middle-income Countries: Avoiding the Middle-income Trap*, New York: Cambridge University Press, 246–269.

Rutland, P. (2013) 'Neoliberalism and the Russian Transition', *Review of International Political Economy*, 20(2): 332–362.

Santos, A. (2013) 'Carving out Policy Autonomy for Developing Countries in the World Trade Organization: The Experience of Brazil and Mexico', in D. M. Trubek, H. A. Garcia, D. R. Coutinho and A. Santos (eds) *Law and the New Developmental State: The Brazilian Experience in Latin American Context*, New York: Cambridge University Press, 167–245.

Shaffer, G., and Sutton, C. (2014) 'The Rise of Middle-income Countries in the International Trading System', in R Peerenboom and T. Ginsburg (eds) *Law and Development of Middle-income Countries: Avoiding the Middle-income Trap*, New York: Cambridge University Press, 59–83.

South China Morning Post (2013) 'Citizens Movement Leader Xu Zhiyong Arrested', 23 August, available online at http://www.scmp.com/news/china/article/1298888/citizens-movement-leader-xu-zhiyong-arrested [accessed 15 May 2015].

Terry, E. (2002) *How Asia Got Rich: Japan, China and the Asian Miracle*, Armonk, NY: M. E. Sharpe.

Trubek, D. M. (2008) 'Developmental States and the Legal Order: Towards a New Political Economy of Development and Law', University of Wisconsin Legal Studies Research Paper No. 1075, available online at http://papers.ssrn.com/sol3/papers.cfm?abstract_id=1349163 [accessed 15 May 2015].

Trubek, D. M. (2013) 'Law, State and the New Developmentalism: An Introduction', in D. M. Trubek, H. A. Garcia, D. R. Coutinho and A. Santos (eds) *Law and the New Developmental State: The Brazilian Experience in Latin American Context*, Cambridge: Cambridge University Press, 3–27.

Trubek, D. M, Coutinho, D. R., and Schapiro, M. G. (2012) 'Toward a New Law and Development: New State Activism in Brazil and the Challenge for Legal Institutions', *The World Bank Legal Review*, 4: 281–314.

van Rooij, B., and McCallister, L. (2014) 'Environmental Challenges in MICs: A Comparison of Enforcement in Brazil and China', in R Peerenboom and T. Ginsburg (eds) *Law and Development of Middle-income Countries: Avoiding the Middle-income Trap*, New York: Cambridge University Press, 288–308.

Wade, R. (2010) 'After the Crisis: Industrial Policy and the Developmental State in Low-income Countries', *Global Policy*, 1(2): 150–161.

Wan, W. (2014) 'China Renews Western Journalists' Visas after Month-long Standoff', *Washington Post*, 9 January, available online at http://www.washingtonpost.com/world/china-renews-western-journalists-visas-after-months-long-standoff/2014/01/09/fde67b9c-792c-11e3-8963-b4b654bcc9b2_story.html [accessed 15 May 2015].

Woo-Cumings, M. (ed.) (1999) *The Developmental State*, Ithaca, NY: Cornell University Press.

World Bank (1993) *The East Asian Miracle: Economic Growth and Public Policy*, New York: Oxford University Press.

World Bank and the Development Research Center of the State Council, PRC (2012) *China 2030: Building a Modern, Harmonious, and Creative Society*, 27 February, available online at http://www.worldbank.org/en/news/2012/02/27/china-2030-executive-summary [accessed 15 May 2015].

Xi, J. (2013) 'An Explanation of the Chinese Communist Party Central Committee Decision on Several Major Questions about Deepening Reform', Speech during Third Plenum of the Eighteenth Central Committee of the Chinese Communist Party, 12 November, Chinese version available online at http://news.xinhuanet.com/politics/2013-11/15/c_118164294.htm and English version available online at http://chinacopyrightandmedia.wordpress.com/2013/11/19/

explanation-concerning-the-ccp-central-committee-resolution-concerning-some-major-issues-in-comprehensively-deepening-reform/ [accessed 15 May 2015].

Yang, Y. (2010) 'The End of the Beijing Consensus? Can China's Model of Authoritarian Growth Survive?', *Foreign Affairs*, 2 February, available online at http://www.foreignaffairs.com/articles/65947/the-end-of-the-beijing-consensus [accessed 15 May 2015].

Zhai, K. (2013) 'Communist Party Committees Are Meddling Less in Courtrooms: Judges', *South China Morning Post*, 12 December, available online at http://www.scmp.com/news/china/article/1378830/party-committees-are-meddling-less-courtrooms-judges [accessed 15 May 2015].

Zhang, M. (2012) 'The Transition of China's Development Model', Policy Brief, Research Center for International Finance, Institute of World Economics and Politics, Chinese Academy of Social Sciences, 31 October, formerly available online at http://en.iwep.org.cn/news/518514.htm [accessed 15 May 2015].

Zweig, D. (2013) *Breaking the Bureaucratic Blocks to China's Development: Comments on the Third Plenum of the 18th Central Committee*, Asia Pacific Foundation of Canada Research Reports, 19 December, available online at http://www.asiapacific.ca/sites/default/files/filefield/researchreport_david_zweig_0.pdf [accessed 15 May 2015].

5 Constitutions, constitutional practice and constitutionalism in East Asia

Albert H. Y. Chen

The constitutions and constitutional practice of states in East and Southeast Asia (hereafter 'East Asia') provide worthwhile case studies for scholars of comparative constitutional law, constitutional theory and politics. This chapter seeks to provide a conceptual framework for such comparative studies and discusses some key components of the existing literature on this subject. It is hoped that the chapter can serve as a point of departure or guide for further research into the topic. Given space limitations, the treatment in this chapter is necessarily selective and incomplete, in terms of both the countries and the literature included in the discussion.

East Asia is a region characterised by great ethnic, cultural, religious and linguistic diversities, different levels of economic development and large variations in the types of political regime that have existed or are now prevalent. This is highly relevant to the study of Asian constitutionalism, because constitutional law is bound up with history and politics. All states in East Asia have adopted written constitutions in modern times, but the nature, purposes and functions of these constitutions vary according to the nature and character of the political regimes in which they exist. This chapter will therefore begin with a discussion of the types of regime that have existed in modern East Asia, before proceeding to investigate the relationship between constitutions and regime types.

Political regimes in the contemporary world may be classified as democratic, non-democratic (or authoritarian) and hybrid regimes (which have both democratic and authoritarian elements). It is easy to recognise political systems in East Asia that resemble Western liberal democracies as democratic regimes. Such cases include post-war Japan, and South Korea and Taiwan after they embarked on democratisation in the 1980s. Non-democratic regimes in the modern world (Brooker, 2000) and in contemporary Asia are those in which political power is concentrated in one single party (as in the People's Republic of China and Vietnam), one single strongman (as in North Korea), or the military (as in Thailand, for various periods since royal absolutism was replaced with constitutional monarchy in 1932, and in Myanmar for significant periods). Hybrid regimes (Diamond, 2002) constitute a more complex category. Because the phenomenon of hybrid regimes has been significant in modern East Asia, we will investigate it further by examining some key ideas relating to hybrid regimes.

Political scientists have pointed out that the boundary between democratic and non-democratic political systems is often 'blurred and imperfect' (Diamond, Linz and Lipset, 1990: 7). There exist regimes that may be described as a 'half-way house' between democracy and authoritarianism (Case, 1996); they inhabit the 'vast gray zone that occupies the space between authoritarianism . . . and consolidated democracy' (Ottaway, 2003: 6). These are what may be called 'hybrid' regimes (Diamond, 2002), alternatively known as 'semi-democratic' (Case, 1996) or 'semi-authoritarian' regimes (Ottaway, 2003). Scholars have researched the 'grades of distinction among less than democratic systems' (Diamond et al., 1990: 7). For example, in their authoritative work on politics in developing countries, Diamond and his colleagues (1990: 7–8) identified several species of hybrid regimes, which may be summarised as follows.

The first type is called 'semi-democracy'. Competing political parties and elections exist in such a political system, but the elections held are not completely free and fair elections; restrictions exist on political parties' activities, and civil and political liberties are limited. As a result, the 'electoral outcomes, while competitive, still deviate significantly from popular preferences' and 'some political orientations and interests are unable to organize and express themselves' (Diamond et al., 1990: 7–8). Furthermore, in a semi-democracy, the 'effective power of elected officials' may be 'limited'.

A second type of hybrid regimes is the 'hegemonic party system'. As in semi-democracy, opposition political parties are allowed to exist and elections are held. However, there are 'pervasive electoral malpractices' and 'frequent state coercion' against the opposition. As a result, the opposition is 'denied . . . any real chance to compete for power' (Diamond et al., 1990: 7–8). This means that the existing power holders are able to perpetuate their monopoly of political power and to pass it to others within the same 'hegemonic party system'.

Diamond and colleagues (1990: 7–8) also formulated a third category, which they called the 'pseudo democracy'. In their classification scheme, this is a 'subset of authoritarian regimes'. Authoritarian regimes are those in which little 'pluralism' is permitted, there are few or no civil and political freedoms, and 'most forms of political organization and competition' are banned. It is recognised that authoritarian regimes vary in terms of the space available for 'independent and critical political expression and organisation', whereas in the 'totalitarian' regime, there is no such space at all. In the case of the pseudo democracy, 'the existence of formally democratic political institutions, such as multiparty electoral competition, masks . . . the reality of authoritarian domination' Diamond and colleagues (1990: 7–8). In this theory, the difference between the pseudo democracy and hegemonic party system seems to be a matter of degree. The former is 'less institutionalised', 'more personalised, coercive, and unstable' (Diamond et al., 1990: 8).

The concepts of semi-democracy and hegemonic party system discussed above may be usefully compared with that of 'semi-authoritarianism', as formulated by Ottaway (2003), who considered Egypt under Mubarak and Venezuela under Chávez to be typical examples of this type of regime, and that of 'semi-democracy' as formulated by Case (1996, 2002), who applied it to the study of politics in Singapore and Malaysia. According to Ottaway (2003: 3), the key feature of semi-authoritarianism is that although there exist opposition political parties and elections, there is 'little real competition for power', because there are 'mechanisms that effectively prevent the transfer of power through elections from the hands of the incumbent leaders or party to a new political elite or organisation' (Ottaway, 2003: 15). Ottaway (2003: 134) points out that semi-authoritarianism usually relies on 'power networks independent of the formal democratic processes and institutions'. The latter are often weak and manipulated by the rulers (Ottaway, 2003: 16–17). There is thus a 'discrepancy between the way in which power is generated and allocated in practice and the way in which it ought to be generated and allocated according to the formal institutional framework' (Ottaway, 2003: 16).

Ottaway (2003: 3) stresses that the semi-authoritarian systems that she describes in her book are not 'imperfect democracies struggling toward improvement and consolidation';

rather, the countries concerned are 'semi-authoritarian by design, not by default: They are successful semi-authoritarian regimes rather than failed democracies' (Ottaway, 2003: 9). This converges with Case's (1996: 438) assessment of what he calls 'semi-democracy', whereby the rulers 'borrow cunningly some features of democracy in order substantially to avoid it'. According to Case (1996: 439), semi-democracy is characterised by 'electoral contestation' without 'liberal participation'. Restrictions on civil liberties and on the opposition's activities are such that the opposition would not be able to win power in an election, which is no more than a 'visible outlet for social grievances' (Case, 1996: 439). Case (1996: 437) argues that, as a 'distinct regime form', semi-democracy can be stable. Developing this theory of semi-democracy in the mid-1990s, he considered Singapore and Malaysia to be typical examples, as contrasted with the Philippines and Thailand, which in his view were unstable, low-quality or unconsolidated democracies (which are more democratic than semi-democracy), although he classified Thailand in the 1980s as a semi-democracy (Case, 1996: 437; Case, 2002: 26–28).

On the basis of the above discussion, it may be observed that the key distinction between a hybrid regime and a full democracy is that, in the former case, although different political parties are allowed to exist and regular elections are held, the possibility of different political parties taking turns to form the government after winning a general election is largely or completely ruled out in practice. The monopoly of power by the ruling elite, or the practical impossibility of transfer of power to a different political party or group, is secured by restrictions on civil and political liberties, persecution of and coercion against opposition politicians (for example by means of repressive laws or selective enforcement of the law), informal power networks (including those based on a culture of patrimonialism, patronage and clientelism), and practices inconsistent with free and fair elections (including vote buying, rigging the election), among other things. On the other hand, the difference between a hybrid regime and a completely authoritarian one is that, in the latter case, there exist minimal or no civil and political liberties (including freedom of the press), little or no space for political and social pluralism (such as political parties other than the ruling party and civil society organisations outside the control of the regime), and elections (if they exist) are merely those in which there are no candidates who are not from or approved by the ruling party.

These differences between democratic, authoritarian and hybrid regimes have important implications for their constitutions, constitutional practice and constitutionalism. We now proceed to review some existing classifications of constitutions and then seek to correlate them with these types of regime. Two schemes of classification of constitutions will be considered here: that developed by Loewenstein (1957) and that developed by Sartori (1962).

Loewenstein (1957) proposes an 'ontological' approach to the classification of constitutions, which focuses on the degree to which political practice conforms or relates to the norms set out in the constitution. In his theory, there are three types of constitution: 'normative', 'nominal' and 'semantic'. A constitution is normative if it is 'faithfully observed by all concerned' and is effective in 'governing the dynamics of the power process' (Loewenstein, 1957: 148–149). A constitution is said to be nominal if it is 'not lived up to in practice' – because of, for example, unfavourable 'socioeconomic conditions', but it serves an 'educational' purpose and function, 'with the goal, in the near or distant future, of becoming fully normative' (Loewenstein, 1957: 148–149). According to Loewenstein (1957: 151), this type of constitution is often found in 'states where western democratic constitutionalism has been implanted into a colonial or feudal-agrarian social order'.

The semantic constitution, which, in Lowenstein's view, was exemplified by that of the former Soviet Union, does provide information about the political and legal systems, but is no more than an instrument of political control and 'the formalisation of the existing location of political power'; 'The peaceful, non-revolutionary change in the location of political power is impossible' (Loewenstein, 1957: 149–150).

Sartori (1962) also developed a threefold classification of constitutions, but the terms he used and their meanings are slightly different from those of Loewenstein. In Sartori's theory, the three types of constitution are the '*garantiste*', the 'nominal' and the 'facade (or fake)'. The *garantiste* constitution secures civil liberties, restricts arbitrary power and ensures a limited government (Sartori, 1962: 854–855). It is therefore equivalent to Loewenstein's normative constitution. Likewise, Satori's nominal constitution is, as Satori himself acknowledges, the same as Loewenstein's semantic constitution: it is a 'collection of rules which organize but do not restrain the exercise of political power' (Sartori, 1962: 861). The main discrepancy between Satori's scheme and Loewenstein's lies in Sartori's concept of the facade constitution, which 'give[s] us no reliable information about the real governmental process' and is 'basically a disguise' (Sartori, 1962: 861). Facade constitutions 'take the appearance of "true constitutions" ', but 'are disregarded (at least in their essential *garantiste* features)'; 'As far as the techniques of liberty and the rights of the power addressees are concerned, they are a dead letter' (Sartori, 1962: 861). Sartori considered his concept of the facade constitution to be different from Loewenstein's nominal constitution, which (in Loewenstein's view) is intended to become fully normative at some future point in time. Sartori (1962: 861) also pointed out that there is 'often a considerable overlapping between nominal and façade constitutions', thus giving rise to 'a "mixed type" (partly nominal and partly fake) of pseudo-constitution'.

We can now map the types of constitution on to the types of regime as follows (see Table 5.1). Democratic regimes that are governed by liberal-democratic constitutions have normative or *garantiste* constitutions. Such constitutions may also operate to varying degrees in democracies that are fragile, unstable, unconsolidated or of poor quality. On the other hand, transitional or new democratic regimes that have enacted liberal-democratic constitutions and are aspiring towards the full practice of democracy may have nominal constitutions in Loewenstein's sense. Authoritarian and hybrid regimes that have constitutions that are textually liberal-democratic are likely to have what Sartori calls a facade constitution or pseudo-constitution. Authoritarian or totalitarian regimes of the Marxist-Leninist type, in which the leadership of the Communist Party is prescribed by the constitution, which also rejects multi-party competitive elections, may be said to have semantic constitutions (in Loewenstein's sense) or nominal constitutions (in Sartori's sense).

Table 5.1 Relationship between regime types and nature of constitution

Types of regime	*Types of constitution*
Democratic	Normative (Loewenstein, 1957) or Garantiste (Sartori, 1962)
Transitional (towards democracy)	Nominal (Loewenstein)
Hybrid	Facade (Sartori) or Pseudo-constitution (Sartori)
Authoritarian	Facade (Sartori) or Pseudo-constitution (Sartori)
Authoritarian (communist)	Semantic (Loewenstein) or Nominal (Sartori)
Totalitarian (communist)	Semantic (Loewenstein) or Nominal (Sartori)

We now turn to examine the constitutional practice of East Asian states with different types of regime. The survey here is by no means comprehensive or exhaustive; we will consider countries whose constitutionalism has figured more prominently in the existing literature. The following four groups of states and the species of constitutionalism that is practised by them will be discussed:

(a) the relatively well-developed democracies of Japan, South Korea and Taiwan (hereafter called 'Category I Cases'), which, together with Singapore and Hong Kong, represent the East Asian political entities with the highest level of economic development;
(b) the new, fragile, unstable or low-quality democracies of the Philippines, Thailand and Indonesia ('Category II Cases');
(c) the semi-democracies of Singapore and Malaysia ('Category III Cases'); and
(d) the authoritarian states of the People's Republic of China (PRC) and Vietnam ('Category IV Cases'), which may be distinguished from the totalitarian state of North Korea.

Category I cases: Japan, South Korea and Taiwan

Japan was the first East Asian state to adopt a Western-style constitution: the Meiji Constitution of 1889. Since the end of World War II, Japan has developed into the wealthiest nation in East Asia and a stronghold of liberal democracy in the region. In the post-war era, Taiwan and South Korea, together with Hong Kong and Singapore, achieved rapid economic growth as the 'four little dragons' of East Asia. Whereas both South Korea and Taiwan had experienced authoritarian strongman rule under Park and the Chiangs, respectively, democratisation in both states has made good progress since the late 1980s, and both South Korea and Taiwan today may be regarded as reasonably consolidated democracies. Indeed, if the turnover of ruling parties is to be used as an important measure of democracy, in their relatively short lives as democracy thus far South Korea and Taiwan have perhaps surpassed Japan, where the Liberal Democratic Party has been long dominant.

The constitutions and constitutional practice of these Category I cases have been studied systematically by Yeh and Chang (2011) in their definitive article on 'The Emergence of East Asian Constitutionalism', which will therefore be used here as our point of departure in the present study. Yeh and Chang (2011: 805) point out that Japan, South Korea and Taiwan are 'vibrant constitutional democracies' today. They discuss the historical and social contexts in which liberal democracy has evolved in these states in the post-war period, including rapid economic growth, political pluralism and development of civil society, modernising social changes, and relative ethnic homogeneity. They then identify what they believe to be four features common to the constitutional practice of these states (Yeh and Chang, 2011: 816–833): (a) an 'instrumental approach' to constitutions as part of the project of modernisation and state-building; (b) 'continuity', in terms of the text and institutions of the constitution, which has been maintained as 'incremental' constitutional changes took place; (c) 'a reactive and cautious style of judicial review'; and (d) the recognition of 'a wide range of rights responsive to social and political progress', including both civil and political rights and social and economic rights. Yeh and Chang (2011: 833) then argue that these four features define what they call 'East Asian constitutionalism', which they consider to be a 'distinctive form' (Yeh and Chang, 2011: 805) of constitutionalism or 'a distinct constitutional model' (Yeh and Chang, 2011: 834) that can be compared and contrasted with Western constitutionalism, 'transitional constitutionalism', as in Eastern Europe, and 'Asian values' constitutionalism (Yeh and Chang, 2011: 834–838).

In this author's opinion, 'East Asian constitutionalism' is indeed a useful term that can conveniently be used to refer to the collective and similar constitutional experience of Japan, South Korea and Taiwan, which can be distinguished from that of the Category II, III and IV cases to be discussed later in the chapter. However, in my opinion, what justifies the grouping of these three states within one category is that, compared to the other three categories of states, Category I cases are more successful and mature in their practice of the normative constitution (in Loewenstein's sense) or the *garantiste* constitution (in Sartori's sense), which may be correlated with the fact that, unlike the other three categories of states, Category I cases are well-developed, consolidated or relatively mature liberal democracies – a fact noted by Yeh and Chang when they describe the sociopolitical context of the emergence of East Asian constitutionalism. In these Category I cases, the liberal-democratic constitutions are fully effective and do regulate the behaviour of political actors. Free elections are regularly held in which there is fair competition for political power among political parties with different platforms. There exist healthy legal systems that afford protection for human rights and civil liberties. The rule of law both empowers and constrains administrative authorities, which are capable of enforcing the law efficiently and are largely free of corruption. Separation of powers and judicial independence are well established, and the constitutionality and legality of legislative and executive actions are often subject to judicial review. Freedom of the press and civil society flourish. The practice of democracy is stable, and competition for power in accordance with constitutional and electoral law is 'the only game in town'. These are all features of a normative constitution that is successfully at work.

As regards the four features of East Asian constitutionalism identified by Yeh and Chang (2011), I have doubts as to whether any of them or their combination together is unique to the three East Asian states and thus contributes to constitute a distinctive form of constitutionalism. Let us examine the four features one by one. First, Yeh and Chang (2011) stress that East Asian constitutionalism is characterised by an instrumental approach to the constitution in the sense that the constitution was adopted by modernising elites for purposes such as nation-building rather than as an act of 'We the People' in a revolutionary or constitutional moment for the protection of their rights and limitation of state power. However, a broader view of the emergence of constitutions in the non-Western world would suggest that the phenomenon that Yeh and Chang identify was in fact common in the late nineteenth and early twentieth centuries among non-Western states whose survival was threatened by the expansion of the West, and states that emerged towards the end of the age of colonialism and imperialism, which used their newly promulgated constitutions to assert their newfound national identity and to legimitise their newly established political systems (Chen, 2014). Such constitutions are often 'politically enabling documents' (Brown, 2007: 49, 67). Referring to the invention of the modern constitution in the West and the subsequent widespread adoption of constitutions all over the world, Grimm (2012: 104) has pointed out that 'once invented the constitution could be instrumentalized for purposes other than the original ones, adopted only in part or even as a mere form'.

Secondly, it seems that the constitutional continuity discussed by Yeh and Chang (2011) is only a question of degree. The constitutional histories of different countries display varying degrees of constitutional continuity or discontinuity and it is by no means clear or obvious that the East Asian states exhibit a high degree of continuity in this regard that distinguishes them from other countries in the world. For example, the degree of constitutional continuity in East Asia cannot be said to be high when compared to older democracies in the West, such as the UK, the United States, Canada and Australia, or some other states in Asia, such as India, Malaysia and Singapore. Even among the three East Asian states themselves, it would appear that Japan differs considerably from South Korea and Taiwan. As Yeh and Chang (2011) point out in their article, the Japanese Constitution of 1946 has not experienced even a single amendment (although there have been calls to amend it – particularly the famous article 9 on pacifism), even though constitutional reforms (such as electoral reforms) have been introduced by statute. On the other hand, South Korea's first Constitution of 1948 has been amended eight times in the course of a fairly tumultuous constitutional history (Chen, 2010: 867–871), culminating in the 1987 Constitution of the 'Sixth Republic', which established the subsequently famous and successful Constitutional Court. Since democratisation began in the late 1980s, the Constitution of the Republic of China that has been in force in Taiwan has undergone seven major amendments (the last being in 2005), in addition to the repeal in 1991 of its 'Temporary Provisions' of 1948.

Thirdly, we turn to what Yeh and Chang (2011) describe as the 'reactive and cautious style' of constitutional adjudication in East Asia. Their article provides useful data on the records of constitutional review by the Supreme Court of Japan and the constitutional courts of South Korea and Taiwan. It is well known that the Japanese Supreme Court is conservative and has made rulings of unconstitutionality in only eight cases over six decades. On the other hand, as Yeh and Chang point out, the constitutional courts in both South Korea and Taiwan have ruled against legislative or governmental acts in roughly a third of cases in the last two decades. Indeed, these constitutional courts have established themselves as respectable guardians of constitutional rights and have made a significant contribution to reforming the repressive laws of the previous authoritarian eras in the two states, and to adjudicating difficult issues of political and social conflicts that emerged in the course of democratisation.

Yeh and Chang (2011: 823) argue that the three courts of Japan, South Korea and Taiwan 'share an underlying attitude: they are reactive and cautious'. They are 'reactive – rather than proactive – to social and political demands and constrained largely by social and political circumstances'; 'They are "cautious" because they did not rule directly against the majoritarian preferences of the public', and they seek to provide 'more space for political dialogue and deliberation' (Yeh and Chang, 2011: 836). In my opinion, being reactive and cautious (and politically prudent) are probably the traits of successful constitutional or supreme courts engaged in constitutional adjudication all over the world. Furthermore, the Constitutional Court of South Korea and the post-1987 Constitutional Court of Taiwan (which dated back to the 1946 Constitution) can be said to have engaged in a significant degree of judicial activism, as contrasted with the judicial restraint of the Japanese Supreme Court. It is therefore doubtful whether all three courts should fall under the same rubric of being 'reactive and cautious' in their approach to constitutional adjudication.

Finally, as regards the willingness to recognise a wide range of rights, including civil and political rights, as well as social and economic rights, this again can hardly be said to be a defining feature of constitutional adjudication in East Asia. Indeed, progressive constitutional and supreme courts all over the world share such willingness; hence the trends of the globalisation of constitutional law (Tushnet, 2009) and the increasing judicialisation of constitutional rights and of governance as a global phenomenon (Ginsburg and Chen, 2009). However, Yeh and Chang (2011: 838) do have a good point in drawing a distinction between East Asian constitutionalism and what they call 'Asian values' constitutionalism, in the sense that the former is more liberal in prioritising individuals' rights, whereas the latter emphasises collective or communitarian values. We shall visit 'communitarian constitutionalism' in a later section of this chapter.

Category II cases: The Philippines, Thailand and Indonesia

We now turn to Category II cases, where democracy exists, but is young, unconsolidated, fragile, unstable or otherwise of poor quality. These states operate a normative constitution to varying degrees, but the normative constitution may break down from time to time as a result of coups (as in Thailand frequently and most recently in 2014), states of emergency or martial law, popular uprisings (including what have been known in the Philippines as 'People Power' events – in 1986, when Marcos was ousted, and again in 1998, when Estrada was ousted – and which also occurred in Indonesia in 1998, leading to Suharto's downfall), or civil unrest or serious confrontations (as in Thailand since 2006). The operation of a normative constitution may also suffer from the 'poor quality' of the democracy. Because the 'quality' of the democracy that exists today in the three Southeast Asian states discussed under this Category II leaves much to be desired, the concept of the quality of democracy needs to be elaborated upon here.

According to Morlino, Dressel and Pelizzo (2011),[1] the quality of democracy in a particular country may be assessed by reference to a multidimensional framework, in which the three main dimensions are, respectively, (a) procedural, (b) content-based and (c) outcome-based. Some of the dimensions may be further subdivided. The quality of democracy in each dimension or sub-dimension may be evaluated on the basis of a number of indicators. With regard to the procedural dimension of democracy, the sub-dimensions include the rule of law (the indicators of which include respect for physical integrity, government effectiveness and level of corruption), electoral accountability (indicators of which include press freedom and voters' electoral self-determination), inter-institutional accountability (indicators of which include the parliament's oversight capacity and effectiveness of constraints on executive powers), political participation (an indicator of which is the voter turnout rate) and political competition (indicators of which include the number of political parties and the difference in the numbers of parliamentary seats held by the largest and second largest parties).

Morlino's second dimension of democracy – the 'content-based' dimension – is an assessment of the degree of freedom and of equality that exists in the country concerned.

As regards the third dimension – the 'outcome-based' dimension – this addresses mainly the perceived legitimacy of, or degree of popular satisfaction with, the regime.

It may therefore be seen that whereas some of the dimensions and sub-dimensions of democracy relate directly to democracy, understood as political participation and electoral competition, others are more relevant to constitutionalism, understood as the rule of law, separation of powers, checks and balances, and constitutional protection of human rights. The latter would include what Morlino (2011) calls the 'rule of law, inter-institutional accountability, freedom and equality'. The inclusion of elements of constitutionalism in the assessment of the quality of democracy shows that there is a close relationship between constitutionalism – particularly the practice of the 'normative constitution' in

Loewenstein's sense – and democracy, and that a democracy of low quality is likely to be a country where the constitution is not fully normative, or is a nominal constitution in Loewenstein's sense.

Compared to Category I cases above, Category II cases are less wealthy economically and less well developed or well established in terms of their democracy, and thus have democracy of a weaker quality. It has been pointed out that whereas democratisation in South Korea and Taiwan may be understood as a 'negotiated trans-placement' or 'state-modulated transformation' (Case, 2002: 25, 247, 250) characterised by negotiation between government and opposition (in South Korea in 1987) or liberalisation initiated by the regime itself (in Taiwan in 1987), the 'modal form of transition' and of democratisation in Southeast Asia seems to be a kind of 'opposition-led replacement' that was more of a bottom-up process led by civil society protests (Case, 2002: 25, 247–250) (as in the Philippines in 1986, Thailand in 1973 and 1992, and Indonesia in 1998). In all three Category II cases, new constitutions were drafted or existing constitutions were substantially amended to mark the transition from authoritarianism or hybrid regime to democracy, with strenuous efforts in constitutional engineering for the purpose of constructing a more perfect democratic political system with strong constitutional guarantees of citizens' rights and high aspirations towards social justice, elaborate mechanisms of separation of powers and checks and balances, and a powerful judicial machinery to safeguard the integrity and supremacy of the constitution. Thus the empowerment of the Supreme Court of the Philippines by the 1987 Constitution (Ciencia, 2012) and the establishment of new constitutional courts in Thailand and Indonesia by Thailand's 1997 Constitution and Indonesia's constitutional amendment of 2001, respectively (Harding and Leyland, 2008; Harding and Nicholson, 2010). This in turn gave rise to the phenomenon of the judicialisation of politics (Dressel, 2012a) and, in the cases of the Philippines and Thailand, even the politicisation of the judiciary, as will be discussed later.

Let us first consider Indonesia's transition from Suharto's strongman rule to democracy, the constitutional foundation for which was laid by a series of constitutional amendments adopted by the Indonesia's People's Consultative Assembly between 1999 and 2002. Given the country's complex ethnic and cultural cleavages, the sudden collapse of Suharto's regime in 1998 amidst the Asian financial crisis and mass protests, the fragmented political configuration of the country at the time, the long-standing role of the military in Indonesia's politics, the weakness of the legal system, and the political subordination and corruption of the judiciary, Indonesia was not, as of the turn of the twenty-first century, a likely candidate for successful transition to constitutional democracy. Yet this most populous and Muslim nation of Southeast Asia succeeded against all the odds and achieved a democratising transition the relative smoothness of which went beyond expectations. Horowitz (2013: 8–10) points out that the process of constitutional renovation that took place in Indonesia was unconventional in the sense that it did not follow the 'standard operating procedures' or 'rules . . . of democratic constitution making' usually advocated by international experts. Instead, the process was managed by the political elites and involved minimal public participation; a national election was conducted before constitutional reform took place; there was no constituent assembly specially elected for the purpose of constitution making; and the constitutional reform was achieved in an 'incremental' and 'gradualist' manner in the course of four years. Yet, according to Horowitz (2013), the success of Indonesia's democratisation was largely attributable to this particular process chosen by the political elites at the time.

Another interesting feature of Indonesia's constitutional reform was the creation of a constitutional court, which was in some respects (particularly as regards the manner of selection of its justices) closely modelled on the reputable and successful Constitutional Court of South Korea (Hendrianto, 2010).[2] It seems that the historically contingent and politicised event of the impeachment of President Wahid in 2001 contributed to the Assembly's decision to establish a constitutional court in Indonesia that could render a fair and impartial decision in any future case of impeachment (Hendrianto, 2010: 162; Harding and Leyland, 2008: 125).[3] Since its establishment in 2003, the Indonesian Constitutional Court has maintained a good record in independent and active review of laws that were challenged before it, and in the performance of other functions, such as adjudication of disputes arising from elections (Harding and Leyland, 2008; Hendrianto, 2010).

We now turn to the case of the Philippines. Compared to other Southeast Asian states, the Philippines has had a longer experience of the practice of constitutional democracy, because one of the expressed aims of American colonial rule in the Philippines had been to prepare the Filipinos for democracy and self-government (Nadeau, 2008). Democracy was practised in the Philippines after it acquired its independence in 1946 until Marcos declared martial law in 1972. The 'People Power' revolution of 1986 that toppled Marcos was a watershed event in Southeast Asian democratisation and ushered in the 1987 Constitution, which was carefully designed to guard against any recurrence of authoritarianism, dictatorship or abuse of human rights, and to stipulate social and economic policies that were considered just and progressive. The power of the judiciary, led by the Supreme Court as the constitutional guardian, was considerably strengthened by the new Constitution (Ciencia, 2012).

It has been argued that the enhancement of the Court's authority by the 1987 Constitution has actually contributed to the judicialisation of politics in the Philippines, which was a gradual process that reached a climax during the presidency of Arroyo in the first decade of the twenty-first century (Ciencia, 2012). In my opinion, such judicialisation was largely a result of the operation of a normative constitution in circumstances of fierce political struggles, in which political and social actors used litigation as a means of advancing their interests and claims. The concepts of judicialisation of politics and the related one of politicisation of the judiciary are indeed useful for the purpose of studying comparative constitutional law. East Asian countries with constitutional courts or tribunals (Taiwan, South Korea, Mongolia, Cambodia, Thailand, Indonesia, Myanmar) or supreme courts actively involved in constitutional adjudication of political controversies (such as the Philippines) provide interesting case studies in this regard (Dressel, 2012a).

The judicialisation of politics may be understood as the increasingly active role of the constitutional or supreme court in making crucial decisions in the domain of what Hirschl (2008) calls 'mega-politics' (including fundamental moral and policy issues, electoral outcomes and issues of regime change, collective identity and nation-building). As regards the politicisation of the judiciary (Ciencia, 2012: 118, 128–129), this would occur when public perceptions of the judiciary (particularly the constitutional or supreme court) are such that it is not considered to be fair and impartial in its decision making, but is partisan and has been co-opted or captured by one among several competing political forces or groups. The judicialisation of politics may or may not be accompanied by the politicisation of the judiciary.[4] However, the more powerful the court is and the greater the degree of judicialisation of politics, the greater is the incentive on the part of political actors to 'capture' the court by ensuring that it is staffed by their allies.

In the case of the Philippines, the politicisation of the judiciary was evidenced by the facts that, by 2009, the number of Supreme Court justices appointed by President Arroyo was so significant that it was perceived as an 'Arroyo Court' (Ciencia, 2012: 129); this court decided in favour of Arroyo and her government in 'the most politically sensitive cases' (Ciencia, 2012: 130); Arroyo's 'midnight' appointment of Corona as chief justice just before she was due to vacate her presidency was upheld by the Supreme Court although it was apparently in violation of a constitutional prohibition against the president's exercise of general powers of appointment near the time of a presidential election (Ciencia, 2012: 130). The subsequent impeachment of Corona by the Senate in 2012 (Bonoan et al., 2012) was partly a reaction against such a politicised appointment.

Finally, we turn to Thailand, which, since 2006, has been the most constitutionally unstable state in East Asia, and also a site where constitutionalism and constitutional adjudication is put to the most severe test. After experiencing many cycles of constitution making, election, conflict, coup and constitutional reordering in the six decades since royal absolutism was replaced by constitutional monarchy in 1932 (during which a total of fourteen constitutions had come and gone), Thailand in the mid-1990s experienced democratic participation in the making of a new constitution – the 'People's Constitution' (Kuhonta, 2008) – that was intended to put an end to the vicious cycles of the past and to introduce in Thailand, once and for all, a genuine constitutional order that was democratic and progressive, and which would minimise bureaucratic domination, politicians' corruption and the instability of coalition governments. The 1997 Constitution, in its broad declaration of rights, and its elaborate design of electoral systems and mechanisms of checks and balances, such as the new 'watchdog' (Harding and Leyland, 2008: 132, 136) or 'guardian' agencies of the Constitutional Court, Administrative Court and independent commissions on elections and anti-corruption (Ginsburg, 2009: 83–84), was a codification of the world's most advanced constitutional jurisprudence and has been described as a 'post-political' constitution (Ginsburg, 2009). The tragedy is that it was one of the instances in the world's modern constitutional history in which the ambitions, hopes and ideals of constitution makers were particularly high, and yet the consequences and end results were particularly disappointing and disastrous.

It has been argued that the text and institutions of the 1997 Constitution actually contributed to Thaksin's autocratic rule, which ended in the coup of 2006 (Kuhonta, 2008). In my opinion, there is insufficient evidence in support of this thesis and the 1997 Constitution could have worked well if the person elected to power under it had been a different person. In other words, the fateful path taken by Thailand was more a result of the individual's agency than a result of institutional design and constitutional rules. On the other hand, the establishment of a constitutional court by the 1997 Constitution, which lives an 'afterlife' (Ginsburg, 2009) in the current 2007 Constitution, did inaugurate a new era of judicialisation of politics in Thailand. Such judicialisation was subsequently accompanied by politicisation of the judiciary; indeed, the degree of judicialisation of politics in Thailand since 2006 has become extremely high by world standards.

The Constitutional Court under the 1997 Constitution, the Constitutional Tribunal under the interim 2006 Constitution promulgated after the coup and the new Constitutional Court established by the 2007 Constitution have each rendered the boldest decisions at the highest level of 'mega-politics', including decisions on the survival of an existing government or political party, and the validity of national electoral outcomes and of constitutional amendments. In May 2006, in the midst of popular protests against Thaksin and shortly after King Bhumibol intervened[5] by meeting the judges of the

Constitutional, Supreme and Administrative Courts, and encouraging them to take action to resolve the current constitutional crisis (Ginsburg, 2009: 98; Harding, 2010: 121), the Constitutional Court invalidated the result of the general election held on 2 April 2006 – the 'snap election' (Harding, 2010: 121) that had been called (and won) by Thaksin and boycotted by the Opposition.

After the coup of 19 September 2006, the Constitutional Tribunal that replaced the Constitutional Court decided in May 2007, on the basis of findings of electoral misconduct, to dissolve Thaksin's political party (*Thai Rak Thai*) and to ban its leaders from running in elections in the next five years (Harding and Leyland, 2008: 122; Ginsburg, 2009: 100). In December 2007, the first general election was held under the 2007 Constitution (adopted by a referendum in August 2007 and retaining most of the institutional innovations of the 1997 Constitution) and was won by pro-Thaksin forces. In September 2008, the new Constitutional Court held that Prime Minister Samak had violated the law by hosting a cooking programme on television; he was thus forced to resign. In December 2008, in the midst of large-scale demonstrations against the pro-Thaksin government, the Court disbanded the ruling pro-Thaksin coalition on the ground of electoral fraud; Prime Minister Somchai, as Samak's successor, was forced to step down (Harding and Leyland, 2008: 133). A new government led by the anti-Thaksin Democratic Party then came to power. In May 2010, a violent crackdown on pro-Thaksin demonstrators occurred.

In July 2011, the second general election held under the 2007 Constitution again resulted in the victory of pro-Thaksin forces, and his sister, Yingluck Shinawatra, became prime minister. Under the new government, Thai society continued to be polarised between pro- and anti-Thaksin forces, culminating in anti-government protests that engulfed Bangkok in late 2013 and early 2014. In the meantime, the Constitutional Court made several controversial decisions on issues of mega-politics (Harding, Leelapatana and Tongsakulrungruang, 2013). In July 2012, it held that, in the absence of a referendum, the government and National Assembly could not proceed to enact an entirely new constitution and could only proceed to amend the existing Constitution piecemeal, article by article.[6] In November 2013, a Bill introduced by the government to amend the constitutional provisions on the composition of the Senate (by providing for a wholly elected Senate to replace the existing one, which was half-elected) and passed by the National Assembly was struck down by the Court as unconstitutional.[7] After Yingluck called the national election of 2 February 2014 in order to resolve the political crisis caused by large-scale demonstrations – an election that was boycotted by the Opposition, which also obstructed the conduct of the election – the Court annulled the election result on technical grounds (Ginsburg, 2014). Finally, on 7 May 2014, the Court found Yingluck and nine Cabinet ministers to be guilty of abuse of power in the making of a personnel decision, and dismissed them from their offices with immediate effect. Yingluck thus became the third prime minister dismissed by the Constitutional Court since 2008. The caretaker government established after Yingluck's fall from power was toppled by the military coup of 22 May 2014, suspending once again Thailand's fragile constitutional democracy.

It is clear from the above that Thailand has, since 2006, become an extreme case of the judicialisation of politics and, given that the major judicial decisions documented were all against Thaksin and his allies or supporters, the perception of the politicisation of the judiciary cannot be avoided. Actually, the 2007 Constitution has aggravated these trends by giving the judiciary prominent roles in the selection of that half of Senate members who are not popularly elected and of members of the independent 'watchdog' agencies. In modern Thai history, the Thai judiciary has generally been respected and trusted by the people (Harding and Leyland, 2008: 126). The recent trend of its politicisation is therefore regrettable and sad.

It may be observed that the judicialisation of politics in Thailand was the inevitable and combined result of the constitutionalisation of politics by the 1997 Constitution and its successors (which charged the Constitutional Court with the mission to police and enforce constitutional rules governing matters such as elections, political behaviour and constitutional change), and the intensity and continuity of the political conflict between pro- and anti-Thaksin factions in Thai society. Had Thai society been less divided between two strongly opposing camps, the position of the Constitutional Court as the guardian of the constitution would not have been so difficult. The Thai case thus illustrates the inherent limitations of constitutional democracy in socio-political circumstances in which the key institutions of constitutional democracy, such as free and fair elections, civil and political liberties, and a constitutional court intended to be independent and impartial, are inadequate in coping with, regulating and containing the deep divisions in a society torn by conflicting values, interests and political convictions.

Category III cases: Singapore and Malaysia

With no turnover in the ruling party or ruling coalition, despite periodic elections, in more than half a century, considerable restrictions on civil liberties – sometimes justified by the discourse of 'Asian values' – for the purpose of upholding political stability and social harmony in a multi-ethnic society in pursuit of rapid economic development, strict national security and public order laws, and a very limited judicial role in constitutional adjudication, Singapore and Malaysia are often regarded as semi-democracies rather than full democracies. Despite the gains made by the Opposition in Malaysia in the 2008 election and the Opposition winning half of the votes (although not a parliamentary majority) in the 2013 election, which seem to suggest that Malaysia is probably reaching what Ramraj (2010) calls a 'constitutional tipping point',[8] we will discuss both Malaysia and Singapore here under the heading 'Category III', with particular reference to Thio's (2012) concept of communitarian constitutionalism.

Thio (2012) points out that, in so far as constitutionalism means restraint on arbitrary power and government limited by the rule of law, it embraces varieties and trajectories other than liberal constitutionalism and can be found in 'illiberal polities'. Thio discusses in particular two species of non-liberal constitutionalism: 'theocratic constitutionalism', such as 'Islamic constitutionalism' in Iran, and 'communitarian constitutionalism', as exemplified in Southeast Asia by Singapore and Malaysia. Unlike liberal constitutionalism, which requires the state to be morally neutral and privileges the individual's autonomy and the judicial enforcement of individuals' rights, communitarian constitutionalism allows the state to be paternalistic, to uphold communitarian and cultural values, and to take actions to promote the common good, including the pursuit of economic growth and the maintenance of public order and religious harmony in a multiracial and multicultural society. Thus, in Singapore and Malaysia, free speech may be restricted to a greater extent than in Western liberal democracies (Thio, 2012: 138, 147). In the case of Malaysia, where the Constitution itself defines Malays as Muslims, the judicial enforcement (in the famous *Lina Joy* case[9]) of restrictions on the freedom of religious conversion and on apostasy on the part of Malays is considered to be justified (Thio, 2012: 141–142).

Communitarian constitutionalism, at least in the context of Southeast Asia, seems to be associated with the 'Asian values' discourse, which asserts that liberal Western notions of human rights are not necessarily universally valid and applicable, and that Asian culture does not balance individuals' liberties and the collective interest in exactly the same manner as in the West (Chen, 2006: 492, 507–511). Such an 'Asian values' thesis was probably more persuasive in the 1970s than in the 2010s, given the spectacular advance of liberal constitutionalism in the last three decades in Taiwan, South Korea, the Philippines, Thailand and Indonesia. Today, the sphere of influence of communitarian constitutionalism seems to be shrinking in Asia, except that this species of constitutionalism has an affinity with the emerging constitutionalism in the Communist-Party-dominated polities of China and Vietnam. To these, we now turn.

Category IV cases: The PRC and Vietnam

One of the distinctive features of East Asia from the perspective of comparative constitutional law is that, despite the global decline of Communism after the collapse of the former Soviet Union, significant parts of East Asia today – China, North Korea, Vietnam and Laos – are still ruled by Communist parties that monopolise political power and do not permit the multi-party elections that take place in the Category I, II and III Cases discussed above. Among these four states, China and Vietnam may be regarded as belonging to one subcategory, because both have successfully pursued market-oriented economic reforms since the 1980s, opened up their societies to Western influences and moved from totalitarianism to some form of authoritarianism. For our present purposes, it is particularly noteworthy that both China and Vietnam have, in recent decades, introduced rather similar constitutional revisions and legal reforms, including constitutional recognition of socialist legality or rule of law, human rights and private property rights, and the construction of a socialist legal system in which detailed laws would govern all domains of economic and social activities, state organs and officials are required to exercise their powers in accordance with the law, and systems of courts, procuratorates, lawyers and legal education were built up for the purpose of operating the legal system effectively (Gillespie and Chen, 2010).

Despite bold calls for liberal-democratic constitutional reforms by small numbers of intellectuals, such as the 'Charter 08' of 2008 in China, led by Liu Xiaobo, who was convicted and jailed as a result, but also awarded a Nobel Peace Prize in 2010 (Béja et al., 2012), and 'Petition 72' in Vietnam in 2013 (Bui, 2013a), the regimes in both countries have firmly resisted any political reform that might weaken or threaten the Communist Party's monopoly of state power. Although human rights are now enshrined in the constitutions of both countries (and Vietnam's new Constitution of 2013 has placed increased emphasis on human rights and on the role of the courts in securing justice and human rights), the courts have no role to play in constitutional adjudication in their legal systems. Moreover, although a provision on the establishment of a constitutional tribunal was included in an earlier draft, the final version of the Vietnamese Constitution adopted on 28 November 2013 does not include this provision (Bui, 2013b). According to the classification schemes developed by Loewenstein (1957) and Sartori (1962) discussed above, the constitutions of the PRC and Vietnam are 'semantic constitutions' (Loewenstein's term) or 'nominal constitutions' (Sartori's term) in the sense that they reflect the allocation of power (including the supreme leadership of the Communist Party), but do not effectively constrain its exercise. However, given the two regimes' normative commitment to the rule of law and reasonable records in making laws and developing legal institutions in the last three decades,[10] it may be doubted whether the concepts of 'semantic' or 'nominal' constitutions are completely adequate in describing and analysing the nature and character of constitutional practice or constitutionalism (if any) in contemporary China and Vietnam. In this regard, Backer's (2009) theory of 'party–state constitutionalism', which was developed in the course of his study of PRC constitutional practice, but is arguably equally applicable to Vietnam given the similar political-legal trends in the two countries, deserves to be considered here.

As in the case of Thio's (2012) theory mentioned above, Backer (2009: 103) adopts a broad understanding of constitutionalism that is not limited to liberal constitutionalism: 'Constitutionalism is grounded on the fundamental postulate of rule of law', which 'avoid[s] tyranny or despotism by grounding state action in law and by limiting the reach of such lawful state action on the basis of values reflecting the values of the political collective'. Depending on the content of the 'legitimating value system' in the state concerned, constitutionalism may take the form of 'nationalist constitutionalism', 'transnational constitutionalism', 'theocratic constitutionalism', 'natural law constitutionalism', etc.; '[T]hey all share equally in the commitment to the fundamental values of a constitutional order – a rule of law based governance structure grounded in limits on state power and popular accountability based on law' (Backer, 2009: 104–105).

In studying the Constitution and constitutional practice of the PRC, Backer (2009: 108) takes as his point of departure the idea that the Communist Party of China (CCP) is constitutionally entrenched as the 'party in power'. Thus, unlike political parties in liberal-democratic systems, the CCP is not merely one among several political parties, but is an integral and vital part of the state's constitutional, political and legal systems. In Backer's view, the real constitution of the PRC includes not only the Constitution of the PRC state, but also the constitution of the CCP.[11] In so far as the CCP promotes the rule of law, subordinates itself to the rule of law and engages in 'self-discipline' (Backer, 2009: 152) for this purpose, and in so far as there is some form of 'separation of powers' (Backer, 2009: 141) between the CCP, which Backer (2009: 148) considers to be the source of the values and fundamental policies that guide the government, and the state organs, which engage in concrete administrative tasks, constitutionalism can be said to be practised in China. This may be called 'state–party constitutionalism', a kind of 'constitutionalism with Chinese characteristics' (Backer, 2009: 111). Backer (2009: 110) admits that, in this kind of constitutionalism, not all citizens have 'political citizenship' and exercise political rights, although all of them have 'economic and social citizenship' and exercise economic and social rights. Political citizenship in China, according to Backer's theory, is confined to members of the CCP, whose membership is open to everyone who subscribes to its values and visions (Backer, 2009: 151). The CCP as an updated version of the Leninist 'vanguard' party (Backer, 2009: 143, 150) represents the interest of the Chinese people, acts as their 'proxy' and in a 'fiduciary capacity' (Backer, 2009: 109), and discharges 'pedagogical and tutelage responsibilities' (Backer, 2009: 150).

Backer's analysis is useful for the purpose of studying the evolution of a Communist-Party-dominated political system that abandons totalitarianism, withdraws itself from the control of many sectors of the economy and society, concedes a large space for private life and private pursuits, seeks to regulate itself by the rule of law and recognises that citizens' rights should be afforded legal protection. The state–party constitutionalism theorised by Backer shares some of the features of the communitarian constitutionalism discussed above – particularly the adherence to the rule of law and legal restrictions on civil liberties – but differs from communitarian constitutionalism in that it does not permit any space for opposition political parties and multi-party elections. Without such space, it may be questioned whether Backer's portrayal of the role of the 'party in power' under 'state–party constitutionalism' is too idealised and too distant from the reality that, despite the fact that the CCP has 85 million members today, its power is actually exercised by a small elite of Party leaders who are subject to little electoral accountability. The de facto lack of political citizenship on the part of the great majority of Chinese citizens as recognised by Backer also contradicts the text of the PRC Constitution itself, according to which all citizens have equal political rights. It is therefore doubtful whether this theory of state–party constitutionalism can fully legitimise the state–party itself.

Conclusion

It may be seen from the above that East Asia has been, and remains, a great laboratory for diverse constitutional projects. The study in this chapter is based on the premise that there is a close relationship between regime types and the nature and character of constitutional practice in the states concerned. It has discussed four categories of East Asian cases, which differ from one another in terms of the political systems and constitutional practices that exist today. It should be borne in mind that the present-day constitutional situations in these countries can be fully understood and explained only in the light of their constitutional history and the dynamics of their constitutional development, which are not covered in this chapter. Such a historical study would reveal that the constitutional landscape of most of the countries studied in this chapter has changed beyond recognition in the last three decades, with most of the originally authoritarian or hybrid regimes being transformed into vibrant liberal constitutional democracies. This has been the case in Taiwan, South Korea, the Philippines, Thailand and Indonesia. Even in Communist China and Vietnam, legal reforms have made such progress in the last three decades that previous theorisations of constitutions and of the lack of constitutionalism in Communist one-party states may have become out of date. Constitutions and constitutionalism, although originating from Western modernity, have thus been transplanted to Asian soils and grown up considerably. The constitutional future of this part of the world promises to be an exciting and challenging one.

Notes

1 For further details, see Morlino (2011).
2 For the Korean Constitutional Court, see Ginsburg (2010). For a discussion of Asian constitutional courts generally, see Ginsburg (2008).
3 See generally Ginsburg's (2003) 'insurance theory', which seeks to understand and explain the decisions of political elites at the time that a constitutional settlement is made by opposing camps to establish a constitutional court, with reference to their calculations regarding what might happen if they lose power in future and how a constitutional court might offer them some protection in such circumstances.
4 See, in this regard, Dressel's (2012b: 6–7) four-category typology of judicial politics: 'Working from the two dimensions of de facto judicial independence and engagement in mega-politics, we can build a matrix that illustrates a typology of ideal judicial pattern types, ranging from judicial restraint and judicial muteness to judicial activism and politicization of the judiciary.'

5 In doing so, exercising a residual power, which, according to Ginsburg's (2009) study, exists under Thailand's unwritten constitution, which operates side by side with, and is even more enduring than, the formal written Constitution.

6 Article 291 of Thailand's 2007 Constitution, which governs constitutional amendment, does not provide for a referendum and allows the Constitution to be amended by a simple majority of the National Assembly, i.e. the collective membership of its two Houses (the House of Representatives and the Senate). However, the article prohibits any amendment that 'has the effect of changing the democratic regime of government with the King as Head of State or changing the form of State'.

7 The main legal basis for the Court's decision was article 68 of the Constitution of 2007, which prohibits any act 'to overthrow the democratic regime of government with the King as Head of State under this Constitution or to acquire the power to rule the country by any means which is not in accordance with the modes provided in this Constitution'.

8 It is also noteworthy that, in Singapore's 2011 general election, the ruling party (the People's Action Party) won only 60 per cent of the popular votes, although this also meant that it won the overwhelming majority of parliamentary seats.

9 *Lina Joy v Majlis Agama Islam Wilayah Persekutuan* [2004] 2 MLJ 119, [2007] 3 CLJ 557. Lina Joy is a Malay Muslim woman who converted to Christianity. She applied to the courts to delete from her identity card the reference to Islam as her religion. She wanted to marry a Christian man, but, under Malaysian law, she could not do so if she was Muslim. The Federal Court rejected her application on the ground that the change in the identity card that she sought could not be made in the absence of a certificate or declaration from the *Syariah* court that she had apostatised.

10 See particularly Peerenboom's (2002: 130–141) discussion on 'specifying the minimum conditions for rule of law' and how to distinguish between rule *of* law and mere rule *by* law.

11 Jiang Shigong, Professor of Law at Peking University, shares Backer's views on the Chinese Constitution: see Jiang (2010, 2014a, 2014b).

References

Backer, L. C. (2009) 'The Party as Polity, the Communist Party, and the Chinese Constitutional State: A Theory of State–Party Constitutionalism', *Journal of Chinese and Comparative Law*, 16(1): 101–168.

Béja, J.-P., Fu, H., and Pils, E. (eds) (2012) *Liu Xiaobo, Charter 08, and the Challenges of Political Reform in China*, Hong Kong: Hong Kong University Press.

Bonoan, C., Ciencia, A., and Dressel, B. (2012) '"Thrilla" in Manila: The Impeachment of a Chief Justice', I-CONnect: Blog of the *International Journal of Constitutional Law and Constitution Making*, 10 March, available online at http://www.iconnectblog.com/2012/03/thrilla-in-manila-the-impeachment-of-a-chief-justice/ [accessed 18 July 2016].

Brooker, P. (2000) *Non-democratic Regimes*, London: Macmillan.

Brown, N. J. (2007) 'Regimes Reinventing Themselves: Constitutional Development in the Arab World', in S. A. Arjomand (ed.) *Constitutionalism and Political Reconstruction*, Leiden: Brill, 47–68.

Bui Ngoc Son (2013a) 'Petition 72: The Struggle for Constitutional Reforms in Vietnam', I-CONnect: Blog of the *International Journal of Constitutional Law and Constitution Making*, 28 March, available online at http://www.iconnectblog.com/2013/03/petition-72-the-struggle-for-constitutional-reforms-in-vietnam/ [accessed 18 July 2016].

Bui Ngoc Son (2013b) 'Vietnam's New Constitution': A Charter for Comprehensive Renovation?', ConstitutionNet, 12 December, available online at http://www.constitutionnet.org/news/vietnams-new-constitution-charter-comprehensive-renovation [accessed 21 April 2014].

Case, W. F. (1996) 'Can the "Halfway House" Stand? Semi-democracy and Elite Theory in Three Southeast Asian Countries', *Comparative Politics*, 28(4): 437–464.

Case, W. F. (2002) *Politics in Southeast Asia*, Richmond, VA: Curzon.

Chen, A. H. Y. (2006) 'Conclusion: Comparative Reflections on Human Rights in Asia', in R. Peerenboom, C. J. Petersen and A. H. Y. Chen (eds) *Human Rights in Asia*, London: Routledge, 487–516.

Chen, A. H. Y. (2010) 'Pathways of Western Liberal Constitutional Development in Asia: A Comparative Study of Five Major Nations', *International Journal of Constitutional Law*, 8(4): 849–884.

Chen, A. H. Y. (2014) 'The Achievement of Constitutionalism in Asia: Moving beyond "Constitutions without Constitutionalism" ', in A. H. Y. Chen (ed.) *Constitutionalism in Asia in the Early Twenty-first Century*, Cambridge: Cambridge University Press, 1–31.

Ciencia Jr, A. N. (2012), 'From Judicialization of Politicisation of the Judiciary: The Philippine Case', in B. Dressel (ed.) *The Judicialisation of Politics in Asia*, Abingdon: Routledge, 117–138.

Diamond, L. (2002) 'Thinking about Hybrid Regimes', *Journal of Democracy*, 13(2): 21–35.

Diamond, L., Linz, J. J., and Lipset, S. M. (eds) (1990) *Politics in Developing Countries*, Boulder, CO: Lynne Rienner.

Dressel, B. (ed.) (2012a) *The Judicialisation of Politics in Asia*, Abingdon: Routledge.

Dressel, B. (2012b) 'The Judicialization of Politics in Asia: Towards a Framework of Analysis', in B. Dressel (ed.) *The Judicialisation of Politics in Asia*, Abingdon: Routledge, 1–14.

Gillespie, J., and Chen, A. H. Y. (eds) (2010) *Legal Reforms in China and Vietnam*, London: Routledge.

Ginsburg, T. (2003) *Judicial Review in New Democracies: Constitutional Courts in Asian Cases*, Cambridge: Cambridge University Press.

Ginsburg, T. (2008) 'Constitutional Courts in East Asia: Understanding Variation', *Journal of Comparative Law*, 3(2): 80–99.

Ginsburg, T. (2009) 'Constitutional Afterlife: The Continuing Impact of Thailand's Post-political Constitution', *International Journal of Constitutional Law*, 7(1): 83–105; reprinted in A. H. Y. Chen and T. Ginsburg (eds) (2013) *Public Law in East Asia*, Farnham: Ashgate, 289–312.

Ginsburg, T. (2010) 'The Constitutional Court and Judicialization of Korean Politics', in A. Harding and P. Nicholson (eds) *New Courts in Asia*, London: Routledge, 145–157.

Ginsburg, T. (2014) 'Perverse Ruling from Thai Constitutional Court Extends Political Crisis', I-CONnect: Blog of the *International Journal of Constitutional Law and Constitution Making*, 21 March, available online at http://www.iconnectblog.com/2014/03/perverse-ruling-from-thai-constitutional-court-extends-political-crisis/ [accessed 18 July 2016].

Ginsburg, T., and Chen, A. H. Y. (eds) (2009) *Administrative Law and Governance in Asia*, Abingdon: Routledge.

Grimm, D. (2012) 'Types of Constitutions', in M. Rosenfeld and A. Sajó (eds) *Oxford Handbook of Comparative Constitutional Law*, Oxford: Oxford University Press, 98–132.

Harding, A. (2010) 'The Constitutional Court of Thailand, 1998–2006: A Turbulent Innovation', in A. Harding and P. Nicholson (eds) *New Courts in Asia*, London: Routledge, 121–144.

Harding, A., and Leyland, P. (2008) 'The Constitutional Courts of Thailand and Indonesia: Two Case Studies from South East Asia', *Journal of Comparative Law*, 3(2): 118–137.

Harding, A., and Nicholson, P. (2010) *New Courts in Asia*, London: Routledge.

Harding, A., Leelapatana, R., and Tongsakulrungruang, K. (2013) 'Thailand Update: The Search for Perfect Paper Continues', I-CONnect: Blog of the *International Journal of Constitutional Law and Constitution Making*, 2 December, available online at http://www.iconnectblog.com/2013/12/thailand-update-the-search-for-perfect-paper-continues/ [accessed 18 July 2016].

Hendrianto (2010) 'Institutional Choice and the New Indonesian Constitutional Court', in A. Harding and P. Nicholson (eds) *New Courts in Asia*, London: Routledge, 158–177.

Hirschl, R. (2008) 'The Judicialisation of Mega-Politics and the Rise of Political Courts', *Annual Review of Political Science*, 11: 93–118.

Horowitz, D. L. (2013) *Constitutional Change and Democracy in Indonesia*, New York: Cambridge University Press.

Jiang Shigong (2010) 'Written and Unwritten Constitutions: A New Approach to the Study of Constitutional Government in China', *Modern China*, 36(1): 12–46.

Jiang Shigong (2014a) 'Chinese-style Constitutionalism: On Backer's Chinese Party–State Constitutionalism', *Modern China*, 40(2): 133–167.

Jiang Shigong (2014b) 'How to Explore the Chinese Path to Constitutionalism? A Response to Larry Catá Backer', *Modern China*, 40(2): 196–213.

Kuhonta, E. M. (2008) 'The Paradox of Thailand's 1997 "People's Constitution": Be Careful What You Wish for', *Asian Survey*, 48(3): 373–392.

Loewenstein, K. (1957) *Political Power and the Governmental Process*, Chicago, IL: University of Chicago Press.

Morlino, L. (2011) *Changes for Democracy: Actors, Structures, Processes*, Oxford: Oxford University Press.

Morlino, L., Dressel, B., and Pelizzo, R. (2011) 'The Quality of Democracy in Asia-Pacific: Issues and Findings', *International Political Science Review*, 32(5): 491–511.

Nadeau, K. M. (2008) *The History of the Philippines*, Westport, CT: Greenwood.

Ottaway, M. (2003) *Democracy Challenged: The Rise of Semi-authoritarianism*, Washington, DC: Carnegie Endowment for International Peace.

Peerenboom, R. (2002) *China's Long March toward Rule of Law*, Cambridge: Cambridge University Press.

Ramraj, V. V. (2010) 'Constitutional Tipping Points: Sustainable Constitutionalism in Theory and Practice', *Transnational Legal Theory*, 1(2): 191–220.

Sartori, G. (1962) 'Constitutionalism: A Preliminary Discussion', *American Political Science Review*, 56(4): 853–864.

Thio, L.-A. (2012) 'Constitutionalism in Illiberal Polities', in M. Rosenfeld and A. Sajó (eds) *Oxford Handbook of Comparative Constitutional Law*, Oxford: Oxford University Press, 133–152.

Tushnet, M. (2009) 'The Inevitable Globalization of Constitutional Law', *Virginia Journal of International Law*, 49(4): 985–1006.

Yeh, J. R., and Chang W. C. (2011) 'The Emergence of East Asian Constitutionalism: Features in Comparison', *American Journal of Comparative Law*, 59(3): 805–839.

6 The Vietnamese courts and reform dynamics

Pip Nicholson and Cait Storr

Introduction

The Vietnamese courts have undergone a period of significant change in the contemporary period, taken here to commence with the adoption of the 'renovation', or *đổi mới*, policy adopted in 1986 by the Communist Party of Vietnam ('the Party'). *Đổi mới* sought to shift the country from the system of collectivised agriculture and industry envisaged during the 1960s and 1970s toward a 'socialist-oriented market economy'. In terms of the impact on courts, this post-1986 period can be viewed as a series of broadly stated reform agendas. Speaking generally, these reforms have sought to increase the efficiency, consistency and transparency of court processes, both judicial and administrative, and to increase access to the courts. Arguably, the policies using the language of court independence have also strived to ensure independence from influence over individual case decisions, rather than any independence from Party-state guidance.

However, it is overly simplistic to characterise these reform processes as a singular progressive movement away from a socialist system and toward a Western-style system based on the rule of law, as the notion of court 'independence' might suggest from a Western perspective.[1] This chapter argues, on the basis of an analysis of the role and dynamics of current actors in the field of Vietnamese court reform, that the last twenty-five-year period in Vietnamese court history is better characterised as a movement toward building a 'self-managing' court system under Party leadership. More particularly, the chapter suggests this movement does not fall neatly into broad historical dichotomies of 'Soviet versus Western' or 'socialist versus rule of law' systems; rather, the Vietnamese court system itself reflects the particular set of historical, political and cultural influences at play in contemporary Vietnam, which are varied and nuanced. To continue to characterise the processes of court reform in Vietnam as a residual struggle between alternative economic systems is retrogressive, and overlooks the local complexity and nuance of the Vietnamese court system and its many stakeholders.

This discussion of the court reform field in Vietnam is structured in three parts. First, a historical interpretation of the field is offered. This is followed by an introduction to the current actors and an analysis of actors' approaches to, and the dynamics evident within, the court reform space. It is suggested that the Party-state, while fostering support for some limited public debate about court reform, has ultimately remained constraining of public discussion on the issue and strongly in favour of retaining the status quo while it remains unable to agree internally on major reforms.

A note on method

Comparative law practice has moved to embrace the insights of socio-legal studies and legal anthropology, and now insists that it is crucial in any engagement with a 'foreign' legal system to identify the methodological assumptions informing that engagement (Biddulph and Nicholson, 2008: 10–21; Riles, 2006).[2] This sensitivity is especially important when examining histories of 'legal transfer' or 'legal transplants' (Zürn, Nollkaemper and Peerenboom, 2012; Berkowitz, Pistor and Richard, 2003; Gillespie, 2006: 17–26; Nicholson, 2007: 22–30). An exclusive focus on legal institutions and formal legal documentation can miss the significant ways in which the social, economic and cultural environment influences the implementation and expression of the law. This consideration of the reform dynamics at play in the Vietnamese courts over the last twenty-five-year period takes as its methodological point of reference the work of sociologist Pierre Bourdieu – particularly Bourdieu's metaphor of the social field (Bourdieu, 1987).[3] In Bourdieu's figuring, a social field is shaped by the relationship between actors within that field and the contestations between them for the resources within the field, whether economic, social, political, cultural or legal (Bourdieu and Wacquant, 1992: 104). This is the key assumption informing this discussion's approach to the field of reform within the Vietnamese courts as a set of dynamics rather than an easily identifiable or predictable movement toward a clearly stated ideal. This approach also enables analysis of the 'conversion dynamics' impacting Western or foreign ambitions for Vietnamese court reform (Zürn et al., 2012: 1–3).

The field and its history

The contemporary complexity of court reform dynamics reflects the complexity of Vietnam's recent history. Vietnam experienced a protracted period of civil war between 1945 and 1975, during the period of international relations history known as the Cold War. Although later Western histories of 'the Vietnam War' focus on the period of US military engagement from the south of Vietnam with the Communist North, the existence of a North and South Vietnam – and the way in which this has influenced court development – can be understood only by looking further back into Vietnamese history to the period(s) before and during French colonialism. The contemporary court system reflects aspects of a number of recent historical periods, each of which will be considered briefly in turn, starting with the French colonial period, which began in 1864 and ended officially as late as 1954.

Before the arrival of the French, Vietnam was ruled by imperial dynasties, each of which placed a different emphasis on the roles of law and Confucianism (Nicholson, 2007: 201–211). Before the mid-nineteenth century, what is now Vietnam was a series of distinct regions with contested and shifting borders, with varying Chinese and Vietnamese influence. The Chinese ceased direct control of the region in AD 939, but systems of tribute existed at various times in the 850 years before the arrival of the French. Over this time, the Viet peoples extended their influence south, conquering the Cham peoples and the Khmer. Various legal codes and local administrative practices circulated within and across these regions, with moral tenets drawn from Taoist, Confucian and animist traditions (Nicholson, 2007: 202–205, 218–219).

France obtained a treaty with the imperial Court in Hue in 1875 granting it sovereignty over a region of southern Vietnam then labelled Cochinchina (Osborne, 1969;

Nicholson, 2007: 211–218, 219–222). However, France held protectorates over only the central Annam region and northern Tonkin region. The French colonial period officially ended in 1954 with their decisive defeat at the battle of Dien Bien Phu, although French rule had been briefly interrupted by Japanese de facto occupation between 1941 and 1945.[4] Following the retreat of the Japanese from Vietnam in 1945, Ho Chi Minh declared the independence of the Democratic Republic of Vietnam (DVRN) in the north, with the support of the Soviet Union, and civil war began with the then-named Republic of Vietnam in the south. The official bifurcation of Vietnam occurred after the 1954 defeat of the French colonial regime in the south, by then propped up with support from the United States and its allies. The bloody conflict that followed between 1954 and 1975 in Vietnam has since become emblematic of the manner in which Cold War competition between capitalist and Communist powers was played out by 'proxy' in decolonising countries.

It would be erroneous, however, to assume that the period of civil war equated to a period of lawlessness in Vietnam. Throughout the period 1945–59, Ho Chi Minh and his supporters were simultaneously waging war and commencing the construction of a new state founded on socialist principles (Nicholson, 2007: 37). This period saw the construction of two distinct legal systems in North and South Vietnam, each built on politically alternative legacies of Soviet influence in the North, and French then North American influence in the South. Neither system developed as a simple, clean transplant; the reception and expression of each system on the ground in Vietnam was affected by pre-existing landscape of legal codes and customs in each region.

In the South, a court system based on the French Civil Code was operative until 1975, complete with professional training in law schools based on French-inspired formal sources of law (Nicholson and Low, 2013: 9). In the North, a system of people's courts subject to a central authority was introduced in 1959, based on the Soviet legal system. The 1959 Constitution introduced the Supreme People's Court (SPC), which remains the highest court in the hierarchy, and formalised the relationship between the judiciary and the procuracy. A package of laws was introduced between 1959 and 1961, including the Decree Stipulating Obligations of the Powers of the Supreme People's Court, the Law on the Organisation of the People's Courts, and the Decree of Reorganisation of the People's Courts of Appeal. The structure created by this package of laws created a civil hierarchy running from local justice committees to district people's courts, to provincial people's courts, and up to the SPC. Military and criminal jurisdictions were created, also feeding up to the SPC (Nicholson, 2007: 104–105).

In the development of this court system, law was cast as a tool for popular justice and initially also as a mechanism whereby those perceived as traitors to the new regime could be punished. The Soviet system figured law as a political instrument of the state, rather than a protective instrument of the individual, as commonly figured in democratic systems. Ho Chi Minh himself had criticised the excesses of the ostensibly democratic French colonial legal system as effectively maintaining inequality between the colonisers and the local Vietnamese population. This perspective resonated with the wider Communist critique of law in capitalist societies as a tool of the bourgeoisie. However, this is not to say that law was regarded as out of place in the new state structure; rather, law was figured as a tool of the Party to be used to implement Party policy, itself seen as the expression of the people's will (Nicholson, 2007: 41). Unlike the early days of the Russian Revolution, the rhetoric about law 'withering' was absent in Vietnam. The Vietnamese state structure was described by Ho Chi Minh in 1951 as a form of 'democratic centralism'. The package of laws introduced from 1959 explicitly connected the courts with the political and social life of the newly formed DVRN, and charged them with the responsibility of assisting the construction of the socialist state and with the unification of the country. The emphasis of the Soviet-inspired courts in the North was thus on achieving popular justice rather than on achieving consistency and technical coherence across legal decision making. Vietnamese legal functionaries were encouraged by the Party-state to apply moral, rather than technical legal, reasoning in order to give effect to the ideals of the revolution (Le Kim Que, 1974: 99).

Following the defeat of the US-led allies in 1975, a long-divided Vietnam was unified into one state, with the establishment of the Socialist Republic of Vietnam. During the unification period from 1975 to 1986, the Soviet-styled system of the North – itself just over twenty years old and established during the long civil war – was officially exported to the South.

In 1986, the Party-state began a concerted process of reform to shift Vietnam from a socialist agrarian structure toward a socialist-oriented market economy. The period from 1986 is known broadly as the period of *đổi mới*, or 'renovation'. At its Seventh National Congress in 1991, the Party announced that it would introduce a socialist law-based state under Party leadership (Gillespie, 2004). With respect to the court system, the fundamental development that occurred over this period was this affirmation of a law-based state. This precipitated a shift away from instrumentalist use of the courts by the Party and towards an insistence on 'judicial independence' within the Party-state structure. As indicated above, the Party introduced a new Constitution in 1992 based on this reconceptualisation of the Vietnamese state, which had been approved at the Communist Party's Seventh National Congress in 1991. The reforms introduced a socialist law-based state (*nhà nước pháp quyền*) (Gillespie, 2004; Nicholson, 2007: 243–247).[5] The new Constitution formalised the *đổi mới* period and provided the basis for the extraordinarily prolific period of law making that followed (Nicholson, 2007: 241). Not only was article 2 introduced, which asserts that state power is unitary and subject to law, but article 4 asserted that all Party functionaries were also bound by law. Chapter X, dealing with courts, was also amended, to remove the reference to socialist legality within the chapter and to establish that judges should be appointed and not elected (Nicholson, 1999: 317). Providing the courts with a clear constitutional basis allowed for the possibility of a gradual separation of the court administrative system from the Ministry of Justice and from local Party structures, although this possibility has only partially and unevenly been expressed to date – a matter discussed further below.

As indicated above, changes to the court system during the *đổi mới* period were part of a broader shift toward a socialist-oriented market economy, a profound policy change that envisaged an increase in private-sector activity, a decrease in state-owned enterprise and a reduction of state management of the Vietnamese economy (Nicholson and Low, 2013: 9). This at least partly mirrored a corresponding shift in both the Soviet Union and China. In Vietnam, a raft of legislation was introduced over this period to encourage the marketisation of the economy, including the introduction of a Foreign Investment Law and a Commercial Code. Over the same period, Vietnam's Labour and Penal Codes were also redrafted (Nicholson, 2007: 241). However, it should be noted that neither the 1992 Constitution nor the *đổi mới* period at large introduced any significant institutional restructuring of the Vietnamese state itself. Whilst article 2 promotes a particular understanding of the rule of law – in that the state is to be subject to law – and article 4 provides that the Party is also legally bound, the 1992 Constitution maintains a conception of unitary state power under Party rule. The architecture of the court system set up through the 1959 Law on the Organisation of the People's Courts was not renovated in any significant way at this time (and has not been since, despite calls for renovation in the Party policy documents of 2002 and 2005, as discussed below).[6] Instead, there was a new emphasis on the formalisation of *đổi mới* policy in legislation and on the promulgation of that legislation across Vietnam.

Thus, over the latter half of the twentieth century in Vietnam, a gradual movement away from Soviet-inspired courts designed to deliver popular justice and toward a court system expected to deliver legal, rather than populist, judgments is clearly discernible. However, as noted above, caution should be exercised in inferring a clear ideological intentionality to this movement. More particularly, the movement over this period from a populist to a legal spirit in the court system should not be read as a unidirectional movement toward the institutional separation of legal and political institutions in Vietnam.

Identifying current actors

Examining the range of actors operating within the field of court reform today reveals the tensions at play within the Party-state 'court reform agenda'. After identifying the actors, this chapter will offer an interpretation of the exchange dynamics and tensions between stakeholders, including observations on where the Party-state court reform agenda has been implemented and where reform dynamics fall short of the expectations of other stakeholders in the field.

Party-state

The Party-state is the pre-eminent actor in the field of court reform, and its policy and practice in the field is formative: it both drives and constrains reform agenda. The classic formulation of the contemporary Vietnamese state is three-pronged, positing a Party that 'leads', a state that 'manages' (through the government, including the ministers and the National Assembly) and mass organisations (primarily the Fatherland Front) that 'represent' (Nicholson, 2007: 245). Within this framework, the basic touchstone for understanding the position of the courts is the 1992 Constitution, as amended in 2013. Article 103 provides for judicial independence, stating that: 'The trials of the judges and assessors are independent and shall only obey the law; the interference into the trials of the judges and assessors by bodies, organizations, and individuals is strictly prohibited.' The preceding article 102 introduced the concept of 'judicial power', while leaving it undefined.

The 2013 amendments that took effect from 1 January 2014 specifically include a prohibition on 'interference'. That said, Party leadership is constitutionally intact and it is unlikely that 'guidance from the Party' would constitute interference as such. Article 4 of the Constitution, as amended, retains the entrenched role of the Party as leader of the people and state (article 103). In addition, article 103 and its statement of court independence must be read with article 2, which provides that: 'State power is unity with delegation of power to, and co-ordination among State bodies in exercising legislative, executive and judicial rights.' Together, these articles work to position the courts' relationship with the state in a profoundly different way from the mode of relationship common in Western constitutions, which habitually posit at least some form of separation of powers between an executive, parliament and judiciary.[7] The independence of Vietnamese courts, as reflected in the Constitution, is thus better characterised as a form of internal autonomy or self-management, which is ultimately subject to the power and constitutionally enshrined leadership of the Party-state (Nicholson, 2007: 241–273).

However, a singular emphasis on constitutional structure misses the depth and complexity of the factors influencing the reform agenda and practices of the Vietnamese court system. There have been several significant reform policies issued by the Communist Party of Vietnam over the last twelve years. In 2000, the Party began introducing a new series of policies and laws, which, when read together, both restated its authority over the Vietnamese courts and concurrently called for courts to judge cases independently. Within this call for greater court independence was an emphasis on greater technical competence, access and transparency within the judiciary, and within the court administrative system in general. In 2002, the Politburo of the Party issued a Resolution entitled 'On Forthcoming Principal Judiciary Tasks' (known as 'Resolution 8'), which contained a significant critique of the shortcomings of the legal system and called for reform of various legal institutions, including both the courts and the procuracy.[8] Whilst Resolution 8 again restated the Party's leadership over all court-related institutions, it also called for those institutions to follow and implement all legislative, executive and judicial instructions. This dual insistence on Party leadership and on policy-based initiative creates a tension in the role of the courts, which are figured neither as purely instrumental to Party rule nor clearly independent from it (Nicholson, 2007: 249). In order to make sense of this tension from a Western perspective, it is perhaps better to approach Vietnamese courts as more akin to the Western concept of the tribunal (Nicholson, 2007: 31–32).

Following Resolution 8, the National Assembly issued the new Law on the Organisation of People's Courts (LOOPC) in April 2002. The unifying policy shift in the 2002 Law was toward increased internal management by the courts of personnel and resources, areas previously reserved to the Ministry of Justice within the procuracy. It stipulated a significant set of reforms that focused on the capacity and training of court personnel, on the one hand, and on the normalisation of court funding across the country with stronger reference to court need, on the other. Key provisions included: section 37, which provided that judges must have a Bachelor of Laws degree, have attended adjudication training and have legal experience (an insistence on qualification absent from pre-*đổi mới* Soviet courts); section 44, which provided that the Standing Committee of the National Assembly would determine court budgets on the advice of the Chief Justice of the Supreme People's Court; and section 46, which explicitly recognised the need to develop stronger information technology to assist court work.

The Party's focus on court reform continued, with further statements made in 2005 on legal reform in Resolution 48/NQ-TW of the CPV, 'On the Strategy for Development and Improvement of Vietnam's Legal System to the Year 2010 and Direction for the Period 2020' (24 May 2005) ('Resolution 48'), and on judicial reform in Resolution 49/NQ-TW of the CPV, 'Judicial Reform Strategy to 2020' (2 June 2005) ('Resolution 49'). These Resolutions are notable for the ambitious ideological scope they articulate. Resolution 49, for example, stated its intention as '(t)o overhaul judicial procedures to make them more democratic, equal, open, transparent and consistent as well as more accessible'. Resolution 49 also proposed that courts be reorganised along jurisdictional lines, rather than reflecting the regional political units of the country (Resolution 49, section 2.1). The supposed intention of this architectural change was to sever, or at least decrease, the connection between local political institutions and local courts, as a means of increasing the internal independence of the courts.

However, as with the earlier 1992 reform agenda, the sweeping scope of the policy reforms announced between 2002 and 2005 was accompanied by only slow efforts toward implementation and existing ambiguities were retained. In 2015, the 2014 Law on the Organisation of People's Courts took effect, introducing the much-debated new level of court, the High Court. This freed the Supreme People's Court to be an appeal court. Article 2 of the 2014 Law also provided the first definition of the new 'judicial power' introduced in article 102 of the 2013 Constitution. Nevertheless, the Party has not followed a clear reform trajectory. As such, the meaning in practice of its broad statements on court reform remains largely untested, particularly the scope and authority vested in the grant of judicial power. Certainly, some movement toward reform is evident. For example, judges are, on the whole, increasingly better qualified and better paid, although the degree to which judges report greater independence from local party structures differs greatly across the country (UNDP, 2013). In addition, the number of cases arriving in Vietnamese courts steadily increased over the late 2000s, which suggests increased promulgation of legislation to the Vietnamese people and easier access to the court system – although, again, there is uneven growth across different jurisdictions (Nicholson, 2014: 536–539). This type of data is now available as a result of the proliferation of empirical studies on the court system in Vietnam, much of it funded by aid donors and most notably the United Nations Development Program (UNDP). The UNDP, under the banner of its Access to Justice programme, has carried out data-collecting fieldwork across the local and district court systems by surveying judges and, most recently, by surveying court users (Nguyen Hung Quang, 2007; UNDP, 2013, 2014). Whether the availability of this burgeoning body of data will assist in the translation of the Party's stated reform agenda remains to be seen.

Other actors

Who, then, are the other relevant actors within the field of court reform? For the purposes of defining what shape the 'court reform agenda' in Vietnam is taking, a number of sets of actors have been identified though empirical and socio-legal study as contributing to the shape of reform. These include: the range of bilateral aid donors addressing themselves to challenges within the Vietnamese court system; the UNDP; the judiciary, in its hierarchy of three levels and its regional differences; the legal profession; critical activists; and, albeit to a minor extent, court users.

Donors Foreign aid, both bilateral and multilateral, has a particular history in Vietnam, a state that did not exist as such prior to the arrival of colonial interests in the mid-nineteenth century. More specifically, particular foreign aid programmes will, whether directly or indirectly, inflect the assumed relationship between law, development and the market at play in the donor's general approach to its role in foreign relations. Arguably, this claim remains valid whether contemplating Western-funded aid or, for example, aid from Japan (Nicholson and Low, 2013: 1–2; Nicholson and Pitt, 2009). For the purposes of this chapter, key donors in the field of court reform divide roughly along at least two lines. First, it is possible to distinguish between institutional/multilateral donors – such as the UNDP, World Bank and the Asian Development Bank – and bilateral donors, including Canada, the United States, Denmark, Australia and Japan. Secondly, it is possible to distinguish between donors seeking to implement 'rule of law' projects versus donors seeking to implement more technically oriented assistance projects (Nicholson and Low, 2013: 42–43).

The operative difference between technical aid and rule-of-law-directed aid lies in the degree to which aid projects seek to import external socio-political or ideological principles and practices into Vietnamese court principles and practice. On the one hand, rule-of-law projects are generally characterised as focusing on the effective transplant of Western-inspired notions of the rule of law (Nicholson and Low, 2013: 3). Following Tamanaha, Sage and Woolcock (2012: 1), the 'rule of law' is defined here as the notion that 'government officials and citizens are bound by and generally abide by the rule of law'. This chapter will not enter the debates over the definition of 'rule of law' except to note that the phrase attracts variant definitions, with some definitions privileging formal expression of the principle (the 'thin' definition) and others, habitual popular observance (the 'thick' definition) (Peerenboom, 2004: 114–138; Kleinfeld, 2006: 31).

Examples of aid initiatives in Vietnam informed by a rule-of-law agenda include projects that take as their focus the publication of judgments. Several bilateral agencies have been involved in such projects. More particularly, the United States' STAR project enabled the publication of limited cassational judgments drawn from 2003 and 2004, and 2005 and 2006 (Supreme People's Court, 2004). The Danish International Development Agency (Danida) also worked with the SPC to mainstream case publication. Examples of aid initiatives in the same space that demonstrate a tighter focus on technical assistance include the Japan International Cooperation Agency (JICA) working with the SPC to develop teaching and manuals on how to draft judgments. These technically focused projects are viewed locally as less interventionist, because they ostensibly concern themselves with improving the implementation of Vietnamese policy into practice. Other examples of technical assistance projects include information technology (IT) initiatives and constructing physical infrastructure, such as the new Judicial Training School supported by the Korea International Cooperation Agency (KOICA).

In assessing the court-oriented reform dynamics in Vietnam, it is important to appreciate that aid donors and official actors within the field, such as ministerial personnel, do not necessarily, or even largely, share a vision for court-oriented reform. Ideological tensions between donors and local officials or bureaucrats – and between donors and donors – can and do arise. Furthermore, the attitude with which aid is received by different local actors seems to diverge significantly, depending at least in part on the ideological intentions of the relevant donor and its modes of project implementation. Japan – which, through JICA, focuses specifically on rendering technical assistance and improving technical performance over the long term – is not seen within Vietnam to be running a rule-of-law agenda.[9] But, at the risk of undue generalisation, JICA seems on the whole to be better received in Vietnam than other donors or projects with a rule-of-law focus, which also tend to run initiatives of a shorter time frame on the ground (Nicholson and Low, 2013: 27–29).

Local legal experts Beyond the Party and the donor sector, local stakeholders are a diverse category and better understood as disaggregated. The term 'legal expert' (*chuyên gia pháp lý*) in Vietnam refers both to those who are legally trained and to those who work in the legal sector. Broadly speaking, it includes members of the judiciary (some legally trained and some not), local employees in donor agencies (again, both lawyers and untrained legal experts), legal professionals and court users. Within each of these groups circulate many divergent views on the structural and ideological aspects of reform (Nicholson and Low, 2013: 2–3).

First, the existence of divergent views on reform is particularly evident in the judiciary. Vietnamese judges form a diverse demographic across a set of key variables, including level of qualification, status in the three-tier hierarchy of district, provincial and Supreme courts, regional location and relationship to local Party structures. This diversity plays a significant role in both the regional expression and the depth of implementation of the Party's reform agenda (UNDP, 2014).

Secondly, the legal profession in Vietnam is a comparatively loose and marginal influence on court reform, although instances of legal activism from the profession are growing (discussed further below). Activism within the profession has largely focused around the need for independent decision making within the judiciary, free from the 'relational' influence that attends the closeness of some judges with the local Party structure and individuals within it. However, there are also activist groups operating within the Party-state structure or sanctioned by it; therefore it cannot be said that all legal activism in Vietnam openly agitates for greater court independence in the Western rule-of-law sense. This latter group often seeks incremental change, although it may well aspire to more fundamental reforms. This is also true of local Vietnamese working within donor groups: some foster and support radical changes, while others are much more attuned to the Party-state's incremental change agenda.

Court users Finally, court users themselves remain largely unexamined actors within the field of Vietnamese court reform. There are nevertheless indications that court users are increasing their calls for a corruption-free system of judicial decision making in which the laws, rules and administrative practices relevant to their disputes are easily accessible.

Through their respective ideological intentions and practical expectations, these diverse local and international actors produce diverging ambitions for the Vietnamese court reform agenda. It therefore makes more sense to conceive of the field of court reform as a set of interactive and contingent dynamics, rather than a clear movement away from a Soviet-based socialist and towards a Western-based democratic system. When viewed from the local historical perspective, the 'reform agenda' dissolves into a range of distinct reform agendas that are not amenable to such neat characterisation.

Court reform dynamics

As we have seen, there has been some movement within the Party-state towards implementation of court reform over the last twenty years, but it is better characterised as cautious incrementalism rather than a decisive shift. Over the same period, the end of the Cold War occasioned renewed interest in international development circles on the social and economic role of legal systems in post-Cold War states. In many respects, the bilateral and multilateral aid programmes introduced have become more ambitious over this time, seeking not only to export funds to assist recipient states in catering to the basic needs of their populations, but also to export cultural, social, political and economic influence (Van Rooij and Nicholson, 2013). This is particularly so of Western aid programmes, most of which explicitly or implicitly deploy concepts of liberal economic development, human rights and democracy in the design and delivery of aid to their nominated recipient countries (Nicholson and Hinderling, 2013: 274; Nicholson and Pitt, 2009). In terms of legal development, emphasis on the rule of law has become a primary driver of aid funding to countries such as Vietnam. In assessing court reform dynamics from the post-*đổi mới* period onward, it thus becomes particularly important to keep an eye to the diversity of actors affecting the reform agenda.

Adding further complexity to the trajectory of court reform, in January 2013 the Party-state embarked on a renewed legal reform project by releasing a new draft Constitution to the public. The revised version was drafted by the new Constitutional Amendment Committee. On the release of the draft, a three-month period of public consultation was announced, indicating that, as with previous constitutional amendments, the Party sought to invite public participation on the final draft, to be presented to the National Assembly for adoption in October 2013.

In the context of the Party-state's seeming willingness to consult, three identifiable groups have advocated for legal reform in contemporary Vietnam. The first is a loose cluster of professional activists and bloggers, who use the Internet and social media to express concerns with the current legal system both within Vietnam and to the international community. Central issues raised by legal activists are the influence of local Party officials on judicial decision making and, more controversially, the harsh treatment of dissidents by the Party-state. Prominent activist bloggers who have fallen foul of the Party-state include Cù Huy Hà Vũ, a Vietnamese legal academic and prominent government critic who was jailed for seven years in April 2011 for spreading anti-state propaganda via the Internet (Timberlake, 2011). Other key concerns raised by bloggers include the question of associational rights, a source of conflict that has deepened between the Party-state and the unions, professional associations and non-governmental organisations (NGOs) in the context of strengthening industry and trade activity in post-*đổi mới* Vietnam (Sidel, 2009: 157).

Reasons for the recent rise in informal modes of activism such as blogging are not entirely transparent to the external observer. However, a number of parallel phenomena can be noted.

1 As commented above, on the domestic level the Party-state has, in recent times, invited open consultation and participation in the constitutional reform process.
2 Technology is steadily improving in Vietnam, assisting the dissemination of the immense body of Vietnamese legislation that has been released since the LOOPC reforms of 2002.
3 On the regional level, this rise in advocacy and activism parallels a similar increase in public awareness in China and elsewhere (such as Singapore and, most recently, Myanmar) around matters of law and social justice (Sidel, 2008: 167).
4 On the international level, global discourse on constitutionalism has increased significantly over the last decade (Ginsburg and Dixon, 2011), a discourse more easily available to Vietnamese legal activists and advocates via the Internet.
5 As Sidel (2008: 169) suggests, there may be a growing understanding within Vietnam that whilst the legal system seems to serve institutional and economic needs reasonably well, it frequently fails to provide basic services or ensure access to justice to the general population (UNDP, 2013).

The second group are scholars and some politicians/leaders who have argued generally for greater rights recognition, eliminating corruption and, at times, fundamental reform. By way of illustration, there has been a burgeoning scholarship in Vietnam about rights violations, such as the proposed limitation on the right to own motorbikes, by both media and scholars (Bui Ngoc Son, 2014). This commentary provokes reflection, at least among the elite, about the appropriate limitation of rights in a socialist democracy and the role of legal institutions in the protection of those rights. By way of example, the Minister for Justice clearly articulated the benefits of a Constitutional Council in 2012 in a speech to the National Assembly.[10]

The third group advocating for reform in the contemporary moment is a group of seventy-two senior scholars from legal and other disciplines, whose formation responded directly to the release of the draft Constitution in January 2013. The group – led by Dr Nguyen Dinh Loc, a senior constitutional law scholar and former Minister of Justice – submitted a petition to the Constitutional Amendment Committee on 4 February 2013 and has come to be known collectively as 'Petition 72'.[11] This petition echoed similar calls for reform from within the profession made during the 2001–02 period.[12] The 2013 petition called for a broad sweep of changes to the Constitution and also for an extension to the period of consultation, in order to allow full public ventilation of the proposed draft. The submission of the petition to the Party-state by the former Minister for Justice was covered by state-owned media, another seeming gesture from the Party-state towards opening space for public dialogue on legal reform.

However, this seeming relaxation of Party-state control of public discourse on law reform was largely undermined in the latter part of 2013. A number of repressive actions suggested that the Party itself is not necessarily settled on a course of reform, although allowing consultation and public debate, particularly in respect of such bedrock issues as judicial independence. While state-owned media covered the submission by Petition 72 and the collective call for reform, the Party-state formally responded only a few days later on 7 February 2013 with a rejection of the petition's key premises, a warning against publication of the group's alternative draft and a refusal to extend the public consultation period (Bui Ngoc Son, 2013). On 2 October 2013, Le Quoc Quan, a lawyer and blogger who advocates for the protection of human rights and religious freedoms within Vietnam, was jailed for thirty months on charges of tax evasion (BBC News, 2013). The final Constitution released in late October 2013 did not fundamentally address the matters raised by activist groups or Petition 72 during the consultation period, although some concessions were made (Bui Ngoc Son and Nicholson, forthcoming).

As noted above, donor presence within the contemporary field of court reform is prominent, yet not uniformly well received. Although it is overly simplistic to divide donors into categories of West and East, the ubiquity of rule-of-law discourse within the development frameworks of Western donors calls for some distinction. Further, local accounts of donor participation in the process of court reform suggest that recipient attitudes have changed over time. Survey evidence indicates that, from 1990 to 1995, the SPC was uncertain about its relationship with donors and remained cautiously open to their contributions (Nicholson and Low, 2013: 26). During this period, the UNDP and associated groups developed a working relationship with the SPC (Nicholson and Low, 2013: 26). The next ten years saw a significant rise in donor activity, with the courts themselves seeking technical assistance with the expansion of Vietnam's body of legislation, a shared and largely politically uncontroversial goal. However, since 2005, dissonance between donor and Vietnamese concepts of court independence has become increasingly evident. There is limited agreement both between donors and Vietnamese officials, and sometimes between donors themselves, on the goals of development assistance to the courts (Nicholson and Low, 2013: 26). It is in this environment of ambivalence and division on reform trajectories that the Japanese emphasis on technical assistance has proven more palatable for those the receiving end of donor aid – even as Japan develops its own nascent discourse on what the 'rule of law' might require in the Vietnamese context (Nicholson and Hinderling, 2013: 274).

In order to provide a fuller account of the contemporary field of court reform, it is important to note the silences in the debate. Individual views on court reform from within the Vietnamese judiciary – often a prominent source of contribution to such debates in Western rule-of-law jurisdictions – are largely missing. Judges are public servants and Party members, whose ultimate duty is to the Party-state. It is therefore unusual to hear individual voices of opinion from within the judiciary on questions of legal reform (although retired judges are not infrequently among those contributing robust calls for reform).

In the absence of access to individual perspectives, a sense of the general institutional position can be gleaned from official court reports and from donor-funded research collected via anonymous surveys.[13] From these materials, it is clear that there are judges active in reform around the key issues of transparency, more consistent processes and enabling access to the courts (Anonymous, 2012). There are also judges active in promoting discussions about the ways in which the court system might be freed from Party leadership and judges who caution against fundamental change that loses sight of 'socialist or popular' justice. Overall, it appears that, at the current time, the status quo is stable, particularly in Party circles, where decisions to make change are made, although there are voices for reform within the Party also.

The position of the Vietnamese people themselves on court reform is the hardest to gauge from an external perspective. Recent research tends to caution against overestimating the effects of improvements in technology and increased publication of Vietnamese legislation, for example it is hard to read from available data any improvement in public awareness of operative laws or in public use of the legal system (UNDP, 2013). Although overall case numbers have appreciably increased since 2002, this rise in application is almost exclusively in the new economic jurisdiction. Jurisdictions of more general application (criminal and civil law) have shown rises comparable to population growth only; applications brought in the administrative and labour jurisdictions have remained notably low in the post-2002 era (Nicholson, 2014: 539).The UNDP's report on the Justice Index suggests that the court system's habitual failure to assure basic legal rights limits public confidence and leads many to prefer informal modes of dispute resolution (UNDP, 2013: 15–16).

Conclusion

An historical use of the concept of the field allows better apprehension of the multiplicity of experience of court systems across Vietnam. Different regions across the North and South have experienced different series of development and intervention, and this is reflected in the contemporary era through, for example, divergent administrative practices within courts and differing levels of relationship between judges and the local Party apparatus. Arguably, the American-influenced South (1954–75), which has had an appreciably shorter exposure to socialism, is more open to change.

In assessing the dynamics of contemporary Vietnamese court reform, the court formally occupies a position of little power within the Party-state structure, but with some power and growing autonomy to resolve individual disputes. Put another way, the Vietnamese court system is neither independent in the Western rule-of-law sense of acting as a constitutional counterbalance on the decision-making power of the Party-state nor does it function as a mere rubber stamp on ad hoc exertions of Party-state power. In the constitutional structure of Vietnam today, the Party 'assumes leadership of the state and society', and is at the same time bound to 'operate within the framework of the Constitution and the law' (article 4). The principles underpinning this system might therefore best be characterised as socialist legality and democratic centralism (Nicholson and Nguyen Hung Quang, forthcoming), and it can be said that the Party-state is slowly working to give expression to these principles through court reform (Nicholson, 2007: 242).

However, understanding this structural architecture and the formal policy operating within it is only one aspect of any such assessment of the contemporary reform agenda in Vietnam. The Party-state is not an entirely homogenous entity. Debates continue even within the Party as to what might constitute the ideal Vietnamese legal system and the Constitution itself is subject to this dynamism. Consideration of court reform as a field within which various actors compete for resources allows for an appreciation of the sets of dynamics that circulate unresolved in the field, creating tensions and debates that continue unabated into the contemporary era.

The current field is populated by a broad range of agitants for legal reform, which includes reform of the court sector. As noted above, the profession has been active on matters of legal reform through support for Petition 72, and through individual and collective activism around rights reform and constitutional change. In addition, many lawyers are actively engaged in strengthening legal institutions, whether working as facilitators in donor offices, in private practice or as advisers to the government drawn from the private sector. There are also different views within government about the advisability of bedrock legal institutional reforms. It is widely alleged, for example, that many within the Ministry of Justice espouse the construction of an independent properly resourced and supported judiciary. The involvement of former Justice Minister Nguyen Dinh Loc with Petition 72 adds credibility to this perception of the Ministry. Moreover, the fact that, while he held office, the most recently retired Minister of Justice argued during the constitutional consultation for a constitutional council in Vietnam also supports this view. There are also academics exploring legal reform in their writing. Most lawyers advance technical reforms to eliminate influence, promote transparency and ensure better access to courts, and a smaller group is deeply committed to fundamental reform; some are activists and some are working within the system, although many calls for fundamental reform eschew a major role for the courts.

This chapter has suggested that, rather than indicating the development of a Western-style rule-of-law system in which the legal and political spheres of the state are independent, the last twenty-five-year period in Vietnamese court history has seen the Party-state endorse reforms for the construction of a 'self-managing' court system under Party leadership, while failing to give effect to reforms it has embraced. Over the same period, other actors have advocated for more fundamental reforms, some targeting courts and others suggesting the need to work around perceived court weaknesses. Such advocacy, whether activist and thus risking Party-state disapproval or operative within the established Party-state boundaries, does not currently have widespread political support within Vietnam. Nevertheless, there is clear political support for achieving a more transparent, accessible, technically competent court system free from influence from individuals and entities, while retaining the Communist Party of Vietnam as the leader of courts.

Notes

1 In the context of China, Randall Peerenboom (2014) makes the same point.
2 Compare with Zweigert and Kötz (1998: 17).
3 For a more recent exploration of the applicability of this approach, see Biddulph (2007, 2008).

4 For a deeper examination of French colonialism in the region, see Osborne (1969). On the influence of French colonialism on legal development, see Hooker (1978).
5 See also article 4 of the 1992 Constitution, as amended in 2013.
6 Resolution 08/NQ-TW of the CPV, 'On Justice Reform' (2 January 2008); Resolution 49/NQ-TW of the CPV, 'Judicial Reform Strategy to 2020' (2 June 2005); Resolution 48/NQ-TW of the CPV, 'On the Strategy for Development and Improvement of Vietnam's Legal System to the Year 2010 and Direction for the Period 2020' (24 May 2005).
7 For a general statement on socialist constitutional principles, see Osakwe (1977).
8 Resolution 08/NQ-TW of the CPV, 'On Justice Reform' (2 January 2008). See also Nicholson (2007: 248).
9 Interviews by Nicholson in Vietnam with thirty local and international legal professionals conducted over the period 2008–13.
10 See online at http://duthaoonline.quochoi.vn/DuThao/Lists/DT_DUTHAO_NGHIQUYET/View_Detail.aspx?ItemID=32&TabIndex=4&YKienID=890 [accessed 28 March 2013].
11 A summary of the petition can be found in Bui Ngoc Son (2013).
12 In 2002, a group of twenty-one critics petitioned the National Assembly to establish a constitutional court (Sidel, 2008: 51).
13 Examples include UNDP (2007, 2014). See also, more generally, the Court's own annual reports to the National Assembly, including Supreme People's Court (2008, 2010).

References

Anonymous (2012) *Report on Understanding of Vietnamese Judges' and Court Staff's Understanding of Donor-Court Cooperation*, Copy on file with author.

BBC News (2013) 'Vietnam Dissident Le Quoc Quan Jailed for Tax Evasion', 2 October, available online at http://www.bbc.co.uk/news/world-asia-24361701 [accessed 19 July 2016].

Berkowitz, D., Pistor, K., and Richard, J. (2003) 'Economic Development, Legality, and the Transplant Effect', *European Economic Review*, 47(1): 165–195.

Biddulph, S. (2007) *Legal Reform and Administrative Detention Powers in China*, Cambridge: Cambridge University Press.

Biddulph, S. (2008) 'The Field of Crime Control and Social Order: Prospects for Criminal Procedure Reform in China', in P. Nicholson and S. Biddulph (eds) *Examining Practice, Interrogating Theory: Comparative Legal Studies in Asia*, The Hague: Martinus Nijhoff, 110–115.

Biddulph, S., and Nicholson, P. (2008) 'Expanding the Circle: Comparative Legal Studies in Transition', in P. Nicholson and S. Biddulph (eds) *Examining Practice, Interrogating Theory: Comparative Legal Studies in Asia*, The Hague: Martinus Nijhoff, 10–21.

Bourdieu, P. (1987) 'The Force of Law: Towards a Sociology of the Juridical Field', *Hastings Law Journal*, 38: 814–854.

Bourdieu, P., and Wacquant, L. (1992) *An Invitation to Reflective Sociology*, Chicago, IL: University of Chicago Press.

Bui Ngoc Son (2013) 'Petition 72: The Struggle for Constitutional Reforms in Vietnam', I-CONnect: Blog of the *International Journal of Constitutional Law*, 28 March, available online at http://www.iconnectblog.com/2013/03/petition-72-the-struggle-for-constitutional-reforms-in-vietnam/ [accessed 13 February 2014].

Bui Ngoc Son (2014) 'The Discourse of Constitutional Review in Vietnam', *Journal of Comparative Law*, 9(2): 191–221.

Bui Ngoc Son and Nicholson, P. (forthcoming) 'Activism and Popular Constitutionalism in Contemporary Vietnam', *Law & Social Inquiry*.

Gillespie, J. (2004) 'Concepts of Law in Vietnam: Transforming Statist Socialism', in R. Peerenboom (ed.) *Asian Discourses on the Rule of Law*, London: Routledge, 146–182.

Gillespie, J. (2006) *Transplanting Commercial Law Reform: Developing a 'Rule of Law' in Vietnam*, Aldershot: Ashgate.

Ginsburg, T., and Dixon, R. (eds) (2011) *Comparative Constitutional Law*, Cheltenham: Edward Elgar.

Hooker, M. B. (1978) *A Concise Legal History of South-East Asia*, Oxford: Clarendon Press.

Kleinfeld, R. (2006) 'Competing Definitions of the Rule of Law', in T. Carothers (ed.) *Promoting the Rule of Law Abroad: In Search of Knowledge*, Washington, DC: Carnegie Endowment for International Peace, 31–73.

Le Kim Que (1974) 'The People's Courts', in *An Outline of the Institutions of the Democratic Republic of Vietnam*, Hanoi: Gioi.

Nguyen Hung Quang (2007) *Report on the Survey of Needs of District People's Courts Nationwide*, Hanoi: Judicial Publishing House.

Nicholson, P. (1999) 'Vietnamese Institutions in Comparative Perspective', in K. Jayasuriya (ed.) *Law, Capitalism and Power*, London: Routledge, 300–329.

Nicholson, P. (2007) *Borrowing Court Systems: The Experience of Socialist Vietnam*, The Hague: Martinus Nijhoff.

Nicholson, P. (2014) 'Renovating Courts: The Role of Courts in Contemporary Vietnam', in Jiunn-rong Yeh and Wen-Chen Chang (eds) *Asian Courts in Context*, Cambridge: Cambridge University Press, 528–565.

Nicholson, P., and Hinderling, S. (2013) 'Japanese Aid in Comparative Perspective', *Hague Journal on the Rule of Law*, 5(2): 274–309.

Nicholson, P., and Low, S. (2013) 'Local Accounts of Rule of Law Aid: Implications for Donors', *Hague Journal on the Rule of Law*, 5(1): 1–43.

Nicholson, P., and Nguyen Hung Quang (forthcoming) 'Asia-Pacific Judiciaries: Independence, Impartiality, and Integrity in Vietnam', in H. P. Lee (ed.) *Asia Pacific Judiciaries*, Cambridge: Cambridge University Press.

Nicholson, P., and Pitt, S. (2009) 'Vietnamese Legal Reform: The Discourses of Aid?', in P. Bergling, J. Ederlof and V. Taylor (eds) *Rule of Law Promotion: Global Perspectives, Local Applications*, Uppsala: Iustus Forlag, 287–315.

Osakwe, C. (1977) 'The Common Law of Constitutions of the Communist-Party States', *Review of Socialist Law*, 3(1): 155–217.

Osborne, M. (1969) *The French Presence in Cochinchina and Cambodia*, Ithaca, NY: Cornell University Press.

Peerenboom, R. (2004) 'Competing Conceptions of Rule of Law in China', in R. Peerenboom (ed.) *Asian Discourse of Rule of Law: Theories and Implementation of Rule of Law in Twelve Asian Countries, France and the US*, London: Routledge, 113–145.

Peerenboom, R. (2014) 'The Future of Legal Reforms in China: A Critical Appraisal of the Decision on Comprehensively Deepening Reform', available online at http://ssrn.com/abstract=2379161 [accessed 2 February 2013].

Riles, A. (2006) 'Comparative Law and Socio-Legal Studies', in M. Reimann and R. Zimmermann (eds) *The Oxford Handbook of Comparative Law*, Oxford: Oxford University Press, 775–814.

Sidel, M. (2008) *Law and Society in Vietnam: The Transition for Socialism in Comparative Perspective*, Cambridge: Cambridge University Press.

Sidel, M. (2009) *The Constitution of Vietnam: A Contextual Analysis*, Oxford: Hart.

Supreme People's Court (2004) Quyết Định Giám Đốc Thẩm Của Hội Đồng Thẩm Phán Tòa Án Nhân Dân Tối Cao 2003–2004, Quyển 1 va 2 [*Cassational Review Decisions of the Supreme People's Court Justice Council 2003–2004, Volumes I and 2*], Hanoi: Supreme People's Court.

Supreme People's Court (2008) Báo cáo Tổng kết Công tác năm 2007 và Phương hướng Nhiệm vụ Công tác năm 2008 của Ngành Tòa án Nhân dân [*Report on the Performance of People's Courts in 2007 and Their Task Orientations in 2008*], Hanoi: Supreme People's Court.

Supreme People's Court (2010) Báo cáo Tổng kết Công tác năm 2009 và Phương hướng Nhiệm vụ Công tác năm 2010 của Ngành Tòa án Nhân dân [*Report on the Performance of People's Courts in 2009 and Their Task Orientations in 2010*], Hanoi: Supreme People's Court.

Tamanaha, B. Z., Sage, C., and Woolcock, M. (eds) (2012) *Legal Pluralism and Development: Scholars and Practitioners in Dialogue*, Cambridge: Cambridge University Press.

Timberlake, I. (2011) 'Prominent Vietnam Dissident Jailed for Seven Years', Mysinchew.com, 4 April, available online at http://www.mysinchew.com/node/55578 [accessed 19 July 2016].

United Nations Development Program (UNDP) (2007) Report on the Survey of Needs of District People's Courts Nationwide. Hanoi: Justice Publishing House.

United Nations Development Program (UNDP) (2013) Justice Index: Assessment of Distributive Justice and Equality from a Citizen-Based Survey in 2012, available online at http://www.vn.undp.org/content/vietnam/en/home/library/democratic_governance/justice_index_report.html [accessed 19 July 2016].

United Nations Development Program (UNDP) (2014) Report on the Survey of the Reality of Local Court Governance in Vietnam, available online at http://www.vn.undp.org/content/vietnam/en/home/library/democratic_governance/reality_of_local_court_governance_in_viet_nam.html [accessed 19 July 2016].

Van Rooij, B., and Nicholson, P. (2013) 'Inflationary Trends in Law and Development and Development', *Duke Journal of Comparative & International Law*, 24(2): 297–348.

Zürn, M., Nollkaemper, A., and Peerenboom, R. (eds) (2012) *Rule of Law Dynamics in an Era of International and Transnational Governance*, Cambridge: Cambridge University Press.

Zweigert, K., and Kötz, H. (1998) *An Introduction to Comparative Law*, Oxford: Clarendon Press.

7 The role of lawyers in South and East Asia

Yves Dezalay and Bryant G. Garth

Scholarship on the legal profession in Asia usually focuses on how lawyers in Asia 'measure up' to global standards. A common assumption is that factors associated with globalisation, increasing economic exchange and technological improvements bring a convergence toward organisational structures and practices. The local legal profession changes in order to compete better in global markets, which require globally adept lawyers. This chapter will look at factors of convergence, but the structure of the legal profession in any given context is a product of a mix of local and global influences. We can, however, point towards practices and reforms that are consistent with gradual convergence.

There are US- and British-style corporate law firms in all of the major capitals in global markets, legal non-government organisations (NGOs) play a far greater role than in the past and the structure of legal education has changed in many Asian countries to emulate what are deemed to be the virtues of the US model of legal education – among other things, graduate rather than undergraduate law degrees, full-time professors and clinical legal education. One line of research suggests that law-trained individuals are gaining more places in political power. A recent article by a China expert makes the case that in China, in particular, as happened earlier in Taiwan, top political leaders increasingly have been trained in the law and social sciences rather than in engineering, as had been the case (Li, 2013). The potential convergence fits the scholarly agenda of those who tend to believe that lawyers are more or less natural political liberals (for example Feeley, Halliday and Karpik, 2008). It is also consistent with the idea that globalisation, as experienced in the past several decades, is essentially a universalisation of US values and approaches – either because of their universal appeal (Friedman, 2007) or because of US hegemonic influence and pressure. Either way, the movements within law reflect a strong imperial dimension, which in fact has always been central to legal developments and the legal profession outside of Europe.

Lawyers, as a distinctive profession, came to Asia with, or in reaction and adjustment to, European empires. The British, for example, brought law and the lawyers to their colonies in Hong Kong, India, Malaysia and Singapore. The Dutch brought lawyers to Indonesia and the Spanish, and later the United States, brought lawyers to the Philippines. The Japanese and Chinese developed their own law schools and lawyers under the pressure of the European empires, and the Japanese then took their version of lawyers to Korea as part of the Japanese empire. Lawyers are not therefore indigenous to Asia, or indeed anywhere outside of Europe. Global and imperial processes quite clearly have played a major and enduring role in structuring legal professions, and the legacy and continuing influence of imperial and global processes helps to account for the place and role of lawyers in particular Asian countries today.

This phenomenon, however, does not mean that local and indigenous factors were or are unimportant. The local structures of power, including existing local roles that could be built upon, were central to determining who lawyers were and what their social position became in particular settings. Further, whatever constituted law and lawyers in a particular setting was part of a mutual process of co-optation. The imperial powers sought to gain local participation and both local and international legitimacy for their empires by co-opting local elites to govern under the banner of law; local elites in turn co-opted the imperial rulers and their institutions, including law, to strengthen their own local positions (Benton, 2001).

The comparative study of law and the legal profession in Asia must therefore contend with past and current imperial practices, as well as local factors that together generate path-dependent histories. This chapter will not try to cover all of Asia and, for the most part, it will leave out the two biggest economies, China and Japan. This chapter is largely based on qualitative work by the authors (Dezalay and Garth, 2010) and that research did not cover those two countries in any detail. The focus here will nevertheless cover countries that represent a variety of contrasting pathways in Asia. The chapter will cover two different countries from the British Empire, India and Malaysia; Indonesia from the Dutch empire, Korea from the Japanese empire and the Philippines from the US empire.

Asian lawyers can be studied comparatively in a variety of ways. One is to assemble quantitative demographic data on the number of lawyers, how many work in the government and private sectors, how many are judges and prosecutors, and the composition of the lawyers in terms of gender and ethnicity, and to explain the processes and requirements for admission to the profession in terms of training and credentials in the different settings. Lawyers are studied in this way as an occupational or professional category. Those data, however, are of interest here only if they relate to a basic set of theoretical and practical concerns that crucially define what lawyers represent in any given country. The central question is the evolving position of law and lawyers in the governance of the state and the economy.

It is also useful to distinguish the discussion in this chapter from the classic 'Asian question' of whether – especially in countries linked to Confucian values such as China, Japan and Korea – the rule of law is replacing personal relations (in China, *guangxi*). The more there is rule by law, from this perspective, the less there is reliance on personal and familial relationships. At one level, the dichotomy between rule of law and personal relations makes perfect sense: law may constrain personalistic behaviour. From the Bourdieusian perspective, which informed the research on which this chapter is based, however, the relationship between social capital and legal capital is conceived differently: they are not only competing, but also complementary. The strength of law and lawyers comes – perhaps paradoxically – from the social capital that is embedded in the law in a particular setting.

The strongest position of law is that in which sufficient power is embedded in the law and lawyers to lead those with power to trust that law will not shake up the status quo too much. Even if relatively autonomous, the law in this manner serves what could be called an 'establishment' – not necessarily a fixed set of people – of local power relationships and the relative autonomy provides legitimacy for that establishment. As Kantorowicz (1997) noted in his classic work, the process is one by which holders of state power give up a portion of that power in order to make their power legitimate and more secure. The local version of this phenomenon is very similar to the way in which law was used imperially. Colonial governance, purportedly under law, made the foreign domination appear more rule-based and legitimate; at the same time, colonial law did not challenge colonialism and foreign rule. And the foreign-derived legitimacy of law could also serve to strengthen and provide legitimacy to local elites.

With the exception of South Korea, which will be explained below, there is a kind of ideal progression that helps to organise comparative work in Asia on the legal profession. First is what can be defined as the investment of the imperial power in law and lawyers in a given colony. The strength of that investment is important in determining the extent to which social capital is embedded in legal capital – shaping the power of law and lawyers. The second is the period of independence for the colonies after World War II and, typically, individuals with legal training played a central role in the movements for independence – gaining considerable local prestige and power because of that role. Third is a relative decline, especially in the 1960s and 1970s, because lawyers are seen as the enemies of development – too close to the propertied elite, and too resistant to social and economic change – and because authoritarian states, often advised by Western-trained economists, put a relatively low value on law. The Cold War also meant that the United States, despite its power and influence, did not focus on building the rule of law among its Cold War allies such as Indonesia, South Korea and the Philippines. Finally, there is a period during which law and lawyers makes what can be called a comeback, which not coincidentally coincides with the end of the Cold War and the rise of US-style globalisation.

India and the comeback of the elite Bar

Elite lawyers in India are of great importance in the governance of the economy and the state. But out of a population of more than 1.2 million lawyers (up from 72,000 in 1952), with 900 law colleges producing about 80,000 law graduates a year, only a relatively few count in terms of high-level participation and influence (Galanter and Robinson, 2013: 5). Less than 1 per cent are either High Court or Supreme Court advocates, and the group termed the 'grand advocates', according to Galanter and Robinson (2013: 7), numbers only about 150. There are also now relatively large corporate law firms, a number of which have ties to the colonial past, but many of which have been more recently created, with the number rising tremendously since the opening of the Indian economy in 1991 (Krishnan, 2013). As a percentage of Indian lawyers, again, the numbers are still very small and recruitment into those firms comes from a very small number of elite law schools (Gingerich and Robinson, 2014).

The strength of law and lawyers – and the attractiveness of law as a profession for talented and well-connected individuals – stems in large part from the colonial history of India. In the eighteenth century, as the British Empire was questioned at home for corruption and exploitation in India and elsewhere under the administration of the British East India Company, the rationale for empire moved away from trade towards the idea of 'civilising' India (Pitts, 2005). Part of the process involved forming, in Thomas Babington Macaulay's famous words, 'a class who may be interpreters between us and the millions whom we govern; a class of persons, Indian in blood and colour, but English in taste, in opinions, in morals, and in intellect' (Ferguson, 2004: 189). With the termination of the governance of the British East India Company in favour of the Indian Raj (1857), the importance of law further increased.

Indian elites, including Brahmins from Madras especially and Parsis from Bombay (Sharafi, 2014), took early advantage of the opportunity to gain training in law at the Inns of Court in London. They became extremely prosperous through litigation – especially protecting the huge private Indian land holdings in the nineteenth and twentieth centuries.

The Indian advocates also replicated the British system of apprenticeship with a senior advocate, which in practice meant that family ties were essential to entry into the upper reaches of the profession. Many of the leading practitioners took their profits and became the core of the Congress Party as it began to push for independence. Among the famous names of advocates becoming leaders in the drive for independence are Motilal Nehru and his son Jawarharlal Nehru, and Mohatma Gandhi.

The essential point is that, for almost 200 years, the British invested in the legal system and the law in India, and an important sector of the Indian elite in turn did likewise. Accordingly, coupled with the legacy of leadership toward independence, the legal profession had very high status at the time of separation from Britain. It is notable that both the British and the Indians considered the legal system to be the one undeniable positive legacy of the British Empire, and the legal elite in India was embedded in politics, in business, among the landowning class and among the leading families.

Nevertheless, in the decades following independence, the prestige of law and lawyers began to plummet as elite Indian lawyers used their power to fight the moderate socialist agenda of Jawarharlal Nehru, who charged lawyers with 'purloining the constitution'. By the 1960s, law had lost prestige, compared especially to engineering, fostered by the Indian Institutes of Technology. Law, from the perspective of the Ford Foundation, which had sought to find ways in which to strengthen legal education and the profession in India (Krishnan, 2004), was 'a second rate profession' (Dezalay and Garth, 2010: 150). The legitimacy of a largely conservative, family-dominated profession was questioned, culminating in Indira Gandhi's declaration of a state of emergency to get around legal resistance to change – with the backing of her allied Supreme Court – in 1975.

The leaders of the Bar responded to the emergency by reasserting the value of law, while the Supreme Court, at the same time, reinvigorated its reputation by turning against Indira Gandhi and then developing a form of public interest law on behalf of good government. The legal elite also at that point took advantage of the interest within the United States and elsewhere in public interest law and human rights. The retooling and re-legitimation of the legal profession led by the elite Bar Council took place with the help of the Ford Foundation, which encouraged and ultimately helped to fund public interest litigation within the elite Bar and, of particular importance, gave a grant to establish the first National Law School of India, located in Bangalore. The Law School, the first graduates of which finished in 1992, was meant to feed the public interest movement, but, more importantly, was also to provide an avenue to attract ambitious and smart students into law (Gingerich and Robinson, 2014: 11). As it turned out, the Law School was tremendously successful – in part because of the opening of the economy in 1991. The first class immediately went into corporate law firms, which, as noted above, had been growing rapidly. At time of writing, there are seventeen national law schools in India and there are also notable private law schools, led by the Jindal Global Law School, established in 2009. These relatively elite law schools have graduating classes that are generally under 100, which graduates compete for the corporate law jobs. The schools also self-consciously imitate many characteristics of US law teaching and scholarship. The traditional or legacy law schools, such as the Delhi law faculty, do not generally feed the corporate sector, nor do the hundreds of other new law schools, and there are still large lecture classes and low-prestige professors.

The revival of the Indian legal elite has restored the prominence and prestige of lawyers, who participate very actively in the growing Indian economy and – in part, through public interest litigation – in promoting good government of the state. Contrasting a more social justice approach in the aftermath of the Emergency, Manoj Mate (2014: 420) shows that the activism of justices in the post-1990 era was motivated by 'emerging consensus of political, professional, and intellectual support for the neo-liberal economic reform policies of liberalization, privatization, and development advanced by successive governments'. It is well aligned, he notes, with elite public opinion. The elite Bar is also thriving with globalisation, even branching into such transnational areas as trade law (Shaffer, Nedumpara and Sinha, 2014). The leading trade advocate, Krishnan Venugopal, not surprisingly, is the Harvard-trained son of one of the giants of the Supreme Court Bar in India. India is thriving with globalisation and also producing law graduates of a very high level. Because of the very closed and familial nature of the elite Bar, most go into the corporate law firms. But the leading firms also remain family-dominated, exemplified by the firm Amarchand Mangaldas comprising more than 500 lawyers (Nath, 2010). Jayath Krishnan (2013) shows, therefore, that there are rapidly growing numbers of 'peel-off' corporate firms whereby lawyers seek to set up their own firms to make sure that they get their share of the profits. The family dominance also helps to explain the attractions of outsourcing, providing legal services for law firms in the United States and elsewhere.

India has its own particular structure of hierarchy, but the combination of strong colonial investment, the reinvestment in the 1980s in education and public interest law, the opening of the economy and close connections to US philanthropy in the Cold War period have allowed Indian elite lawyers to access economic rewards and influence.

Malaysia and the political marginalisation of the corporate Bar

Malaysia shares the legacy of the British Empire with India and, indeed, shared history with Singapore as part of Malaya through independence in 1957, until formal separation in 1965. And, as reported by Daniel Lev (1998: 147), law was afforded a prominent place after independence, in part because the political elite, many of whom were lawyers, united in promoting law as the safest political medium for ethnic relations. The first three Malaysian prime ministers were legally trained abroad in England. There are therefore strong parallels to the Indian history and those who moved toward independence shared a respect for the English-bestowed legal system in the same way as did the leaders in India.

The major difference historically, however, is that the strategy of co-optation in India gave way to a strategy of divide, conquer and co-opt in Malaysia – all along ethnic lines. This approach was a response to riots in 1867 that made the British fear coalitions across ethnic lines against the British. Accordingly, the British cultivated the sultans and the traditional Malay aristocracy, educated them abroad and gave them privileged places in the colonial bureaucracy. The Malay peasant population, however, was excluded and prevented even from education in English. The professional class was then imported, largely from Ceylon, South India and South China. Until 1962, all lawyers in Malaya were educated in Britain. First Indians, then Chinese, paid for their education abroad, returning to join the expatriate practitioners. The local elite lawyers, very limited in number at the time of independence, were found in law firms oriented abroad and originally staffed with expatriates. The three traditional corporate law firms – known as the 'S firms' – are Shearn Delamore, established in 1905, Shook Lin & Bok, established in 1918, and Skrine, which can be traced to firms of a different name early in the twentieth century, and remain dominated by ethnic Indians and Chinese. These firms have also provided a disproportionate percentage of the leadership of the Malaysian Bar.

After independence, the division of labour more or less continued even though legal education was now available first in Singapore (1959) and then at the University of Malaya (1976). The Malay elite governed the state and staffed the judiciary, while the advocates were overwhelmingly ethnic Indian and Chinese. This arrangement worked very well, according to scholarly accounts, until Prime Minister Mahathir Mohamad, the first non-law-trained and non-English-trained prime minister, came to power. He was trained as a physician and came from the ordinary middle classes. His particular mandate was economic development through the Malay population, the New Economic Policy, and the policy favouring the local Malays, the *Bumiputra*. One early consequence of the *Bumiputra*, however, was that a high percentage of spots in the law schools were reserved for Malay nationals, who began to swell the ranks of the profession. The number of lawyers rose from 300 in 1960 to 1,700 in 1975. There were 15,000 in 2013, including thirty firms of more than thirty lawyers. The Bar prospered and did not rock the boat until the mid-to-late 1980s, when Mahathir began to assert his power and take charge of the courts.

In order to understand the position of law and lawyers in Malaysia today, it is important to account both for the leadership of the elite Malaysian Bar in challenging excessive executive power and emergency powers and, despite strong Bar leadership, the failure of that activity to have any real impact. As Harding and Whiting (2012: 261) point out:

> There is plentiful evidence that Malaysian lawyers, as individuals and through their professional association, have positioned themselves at the forefront of the struggle for civil and political liberties and a moderate state in post-colonial Malaysia. Moreover they appear to have done so quite self-consciously.

Yet, even after Mahathir's regime ended, a basic human rights agenda and moderation of the emergency measures such as preventive detention have not been implemented (Whiting, 2013). There has been no effective legal resistance akin to what happened in India after the Emergency. The reason is that the value of Malaysian legal capital is not very high at home.

While considerable social capital was embedded in the Indian Bar (family capital, state capital and business, not to mention Brahmin and other high-caste equivalents), the S firms of Malaysia have only two sources of power: legal capital, as such, and strong relationships with foreign clients – and indeed foreign lawyers as well. Elite Malaysian lawyers are global leaders in issues related to democracy and human rights. But they are not closely tied to the Malaysian state nor to local economic power. And while the Bar is reported to be unified (Harding and Whiting, 2012), there are differences between the S firms and the new *Bumiputra* firms, such as Zaid Ibrahim and Co., the largest firm at time of writing, which suggest the S firms still are associated more with the anti-authoritarian impulse of the profession in Malaysia. The government still keeps social peace with emergency powers analogous to those that the British used before independence. Finally, it is notable too that Malaysia was not one of the key stakes in the Cold War. Unlike the other countries discussed in this chapter, it was not the recipient of massive aid from the United States and its philanthropic foundations, and there were no extensive programmes of educational exchange with the United States. The lack of strong connection in the Cold War helps to differentiate Malaysia from the other countries discussed in this chapter.

Indonesia and corporate lawyers as social activists

The legal profession remains relatively small in Indonesia, with reportedly only 22,000 lawyers, despite there now being 200 law faculties – only twenty-seven of which are state-owned. As elsewhere, the elite of the profession is seen in the corporate law firms of Jakarta, whose lawyers are well embedded in the Indonesian economy, but also at this point in governance of the state through participation in influential NGOs.

The colonial investment in the law and lawyers was especially weak compared to the British investment in India and Malaysia. The Dutch East Indies Company was oriented toward trade and the Dutch themselves were ambivalent about empire, which meant that there was little focus on governance for most of the period of Dutch rule. Only at the turn of the twentieth century did the Dutch, in response to domestic criticism, develop the so-called Ethical Policy of building and co-opting indigenous leaders and investing more in law. The first steps to educate the Indonesians in Dutch law came in 1909 and only in 1924 did the first law faculty open in what is now Jakarta. The legal training was self-consciously limited to the Javanese elite – the traditional local aristocracy – and designed for positions in the colonial bureaucracy: '[T]he traditional elite was to be modernized, not expanded' (Lev, 1972: 256). There were also strong traditions among the Javanese elite against involvement in trade or commerce (Lev, 1972: 262). There were accordingly very few private Indonesian advocates at the time of independence – only about 350 generally, including 150 located on Java (Lev, 1976) – and they predominantly represented the Dutch. Nevertheless, these private advocates, as Daniel Lev's work demonstrates, were among the central leaders in Indonesia's move for independence – five of the eight leading founders of the Indonesian National Party (Lev, 1972: 276).

The position of law and lawyers was still not very strong at the time of independence after World War II. The departure of the Dutch shrank the legal profession considerably, and the local advocates were cut off from their clientele and source of legitimacy. Under Sukarno's Leftist agenda, the role of the lawyers declined further – to the extent that the legal profession 'basically collapsed' (Dezalay and Garth, 2010: 119). The courts were weakened and a hoped-for 'comeback' of lawyers with the coup that ultimately brought Suharto to power did not materialise. The gradual replacement of the 'Javanese old boys network' in the courts continued as well (Pompe, 2005: 389). After a brief period, Suharto allied with the military and Berkeley-trained economists (the 'Berkeley mafia') in the name of economic development. Indonesia was a key country in the Cold War, and the US policy after the Cuban Revolution shifted away from law and became more inclined to support authoritarian governments. The Ford Foundation, second only to its focus on India, took initiatives in Indonesia to work with and build a 'modernising elite' – with some, but relatively little, investment initially in law and lawyers.

The legal profession grew under Suharto, with some 13,000 new law graduates every year by 1992 (Reksodiputro, 2003), but most lawyers had very little in common with the small group of law-trained descendants of the Dutch-trained elite. During the Suharto regime, the small elite, organised in 1964 as Perkumpulan Advokat Indonesia (PERADIN), already began to define themselves as custodians of the rule of law. A key figure was Yap Thiam Hien, a key figure in human rights globally and in Indonesia (Lev, 2012). After the coup and the disappointment of this group in the policies of Suharto, a number of these individuals teamed up with American lawyers to start corporate law firms aimed to serve the US investment that came with the shift to Suharto and the Berkeley economists – by now favouring opening up Indonesia to foreign investment. The corporate Bar in Indonesia as it exists today built on these initial law firms, including what is now Mochtar, Karuwin & Komar; Ali Budiardjo, Nugroho, Reksodiputro and the law offices of Professor S. Gautama & Associates.

These same Indonesian founders, in addition, maintained their inherited ambivalence about devoting themselves fully to trade and commerce. One of the key figures, Adnan Buyung Nasution, even established a corporate law firm in order to fund the human-rights-oriented Lembaga Bantuan Hukum (LBH) (legal aid institute) opened in 1970 (with Yap as one of its co-founders). The idea to start a law firm to fund the LBH, furthermore, came from one of the leading economics professors and advisers to Suharto (Dezalay and Garth, 2010: 220). The leading lawyers at other corporate law firms similarly developed their own NGOs along with their law firms. By the 1980s, the LBH gained funding from the Ford Foundation and the US Agency for International Development (USAID), and developed a strong international profile. The LBH and offshoot organisations were able to survive under Suharto's repressive regime in part because they came from the same milieu as the economists in power – the descendants of the Javanese elite – and because that pedigree made them seem less of a threat to the government. They did not claim a mass base, were not expressly political and were linked to relatively moderate foreign funders (Davis, 2007).

The LBH attracted the most ambitious and well-connected law graduates, who went on to create the leading 'civil society' organisations active during and after the period in Indonesia that led to Suharto's resignation in 1998. They also, according to Indonesian observers, attracted those who became the 'power lawyers' in Indonesia, by creating a 'prestige credential', 'excellent training for litigation', a way in which to 'say no' to corruption and a way in which to draw on excellent media ties (Dezalay and Garth, 2010: 224). The NGO world populated by LBH alumni became a key to the success of these corporate lawyer social entrepreneurs in gaining a central role not only in the business transactions central to Indonesian economic life, but also in brokering reform agendas designed to give Indonesia more credibility internationally in terms of its political governance. The new elite path goes through and connects the NGOs and the law firms, putting elite lawyers in a relatively strong position today.

South Korea and the coming together of human rights pioneers and corporate lawyers

The legal profession in South Korea was established mainly through Japan. The Chosun dynasty in Korea declared 'fourteen reforms' in 1895 – directed against feudalism – under the pressure of the Japanese, who began to absorb Korea into the emerging Japanese empire. The Legal Training Institute was set up following the Japanese pattern that year (Kim, 2011). Under pressure from the West, the Japanese had already borrowed from Prussia the idea of a legal profession serving a strong state with a relatively marginal role for private lawyers. Law in Japan was above all a branch of public administration (Feeley and Miyazawa, 2007:160) and the same approach was taken in Korea. Partly to co-opt Korean moves for independence, the Japanese expanded legal education in the 1920s along the Japanese model. By 1942, there were some 230 private lawyers (from among the more than 5,200 individuals who attempted the Bar exam). At the time of independence from Japan following World War II, the South Koreans increased the number of faculties of law, but there was a shortage of professors because of the departure of the Japanese. And, despite that departure, Japanese influence remained strong, since virtually all of the law professors had been educated in Japan and most of the legal materials were translated from Japanese.

At the time of independence, therefore, unlike any of the other countries discussed in this chapter, the legal profession had no reputation for leadership and independence, and indeed was strongly identified with the defeated Japanese. Further, the model of the state left little place for private lawyers in the state or the economy. The typical career pattern for one who passed the Bar exam was public prosecutor or judge, before moving into the lucrative private practice positions in litigation.

During most of the Cold War period, the very small private Bar prospered from representation in litigation and did not invest in politics. Only 100 individuals passed the Bar exam per year, roughly 2 per cent, with those who failed to pass the exam typically working in banks and corporations. Because of the very close relationship to the United States in the Cold War, corporate law firms emerged in Seoul already in the 1950s – established by Koreans with law degrees from the United States. Law firms such as Lee & Kim and Kim & Chang prospered by serving the US corporations that entered when the military regime began to open markets in the 1960s. As in Indonesia, the US-trained economists allied with the authoritarian government and the United States in favour of allowing foreign investment. The prosperity of the corporate law firms, however, was dependent on the foreign clientele, and it was consistent with a lack of influence of law and lawyers in the South Korean economy or state.

The close relationship between South Korea and the United States promoted considerable educational exchange, but the US efforts to build a 'modernising elite' in South Korea for the most part did not address lawyers. The transformation in the position of law and lawyers began with a few heroic criminal defence lawyers who sought to defend targets of the Park regime in the 1960s (Kim, 2007: 60–61). They also began to link up to the international human rights movement in the 1970s, even though the US government provided little support at that time. These lawyers had little success initially, but they built up the credibility of lawyers who already had considerable prestige in South Korean society. By the 1980s, especially after the government increased the numbers passing the Bar exam from 100 to 200, there was 'a major force of human rights lawyers' in South Korea (Kim, 2007: 63). Accordingly, after mass demonstrations in 1986 led toward democratisation, activist lawyers had considerable prestige. They organised under the name of Minbyun, with more than fifty lawyers initially and more than 500 today (Ginsburg, 2007: 52; Kim, 2011). The group included Roh Moo-hyun, who became the president of South Korea from 2003 to 2005.

These activist lawyers have played a major role in Korean politics. According to Ginsburg (2007: 54), the 'activist lawyers have *become* the establishment'. Kim (2011: 231) notes that 'some members [of Minbyun] became high-ranking bureaucrats' and he names a Minister of Justice, the Chief Director of the National Intelligence Service, ex-Korean CIA, the Chair of the Reform Commission of the National Tax Service and others, noting too that many different political parties are represented. The small, but expanded, legal profession in Korea also moved from anti-authoritarianism into activism by means of NGOs with expanded reform agendas. The leaders of the most prominent of these organisations began in the struggles for democracy, fortified with Leftist ideology, but they converted into more US-style NGOs or public interest firms. The two pivotal organisations in the development of civil society in Korea are the Citizen's Coalition for Economic Justice (CCEJ), founded in 1989, and the People's Solidarity for Participatory Democracy (PSPD), established in 1994.

The role and importance of the corporate law firms has also increased steadily, even though in the 1970s 'corporate law practice in Korea was restricted within a small boundary that mainly covered international business transactions' (Lee, 2007: 231). The demand for these services serving mainly foreign clients long exceeded the supply. And the domestic demand grew considerably after the Asian financial crisis in 1997. Before 1997, Kim & Chang was the only law firm with more than 100 lawyers; in three or four years, the top four firms all exceeded 100 (Lee, 2007: 234). Structural adjustment and deregulation increased domestic competition and, importantly, led the huge *chaebols* to begin to rely more on domestic corporate lawyers. The success of the corporate law firms, coupled with democratisation, has led the top law graduates increasingly to begin their careers at the firms rather than as prosecutors or judges. The number of Korean lawyers is augmented by the so-called foreign legal consultants. According to Kim (2011: 225), citing the Korean Ministry of Justice, 'the number of foreign lawyers was 55 between 1992 and 1993 but increased suddenly to 119 in 1999, two years after the Korean financial crisis'. Most were US citizens. There is also a large and uncounted group of Korean citizens who have passed a US Bar exam and returned to Korea as legal consultants – 'Eighty percent of foreign lawyers in Korea are estimated to be Korean American Lawyers' (Kim, 2011: 225) – many of whom are, in fact, Korean citizens. Many Koreans obtain Juris Doctor (JD) degrees in the United States and even more receive Master of Laws (LLM) degrees. The Korean-American lawyers help to integrate the corporate law firms into the international market in legal services. Finally, the trend toward the importance of a more US-style profession with corporate law firms and NGOs complementing each other has been reinforced by reforms in legal education. Reforms enacted in 2009 – following similar Japanese reforms in 2004 – have moved legal education away from the undergraduate model towards the JD modelled on the United States. The idea, still not realised, is that the Bar examination will also be relaxed for these graduates, allowing the Bar to expand – particularly in corporate law.

As in Indonesia, the South Korean reform agenda has moved very closely toward the US agenda even if, of course, it has been pursued in a very different context. Lawyers are moving with relative ease back and forth into politics, corporate law and public interest law, and the situation in South Korea has been aided by transformations in the role of the courts, including the Constitutional Court, created in 1987. There was a very inauspicious beginning and little investment in the law by the Japanese colonisers, but the relative prestige of the legal profession, the rise of a corporate Bar, the rise of an activist Bar, and the strong links through the Cold War and after to the United States through educational and other exchange have elevated law and lawyers in South Korea today.

The Philippines and the power of a profession embedded in a local oligarchy

The Philippines provides a particularly revealing counterpoint to India, since the United States, as a colonial power, placed a comparable emphasis on the mission of 'civilising' the locals through law. There had been considerable opposition to the Spanish–American war in the United States and the military occupation of the Philippines late in the nineteenth century required a legitimating rationale that could defuse the opposition. President McKinley and his Secretary of War, Eliju Root, a well-known Wall Street lawyer, enlisted the help of Judge William Howard Taft – at the time, the presiding judge of the Sixth Circuit Court of Appeals and dean of the Law School of the University of Cincinnati. Taft accepted the position to lead the effort to build a new government in the

Philippines because it was, in his words, 'a national obligation, indeed a "sacred duty," to create a government adapted to the needs of the Filipinos, one that would help to develop them into a self-governing people' (Minger, 1975: 2). Taft led 'the effort of the United States to transplant its values and institutions in the Philippines' (Karnow, 1989: 170).

Along with this idealism came a strategy of winning over the Philippines by befriending the elite – the *ilustrados,* the 'rich intelligentsia' emerging under Spanish colonialism (Karnow, 1989: 15). The Philippine elites had been given a role in local governance under Spanish colonial rule and they used elections to maintain their power. Taft sought to turn them into 'statesmen lawyers' akin to those identified with the Wall Street elite. They were to be the delegated leaders of the Philippines during colonial rule and the leaders of the independent Philippines promised by the Americans and finally realised after World War II.

The descendants of the leading families used a legal education for careers in business, government and law, which accordingly stayed very closely connected. The oligarchic leaders were also closely connected to the Roman Catholic Church and to the United States. The most connected and talented students obtained graduate law degrees from Harvard, Yale and the University of Michigan in particular. The legacy of the US colonial relationship was a strong role for lawyers and at least the trappings of law, but the state that was produced was far from what legal idealists linked to reform in the Philippines had hoped. Those who gained power typically used that power mainly to reward their friends and punish their enemies.

Still, the earlier legacy of investment in legal capital remained very evident in the 1960s and, indeed, the legal institutions of the Philippines were considered relatively strong despite the essentially oligarchic rule. The character and eminence of the Supreme Court judges made the Supreme Court, according to a book written in 1964, 'the most important legitimising institution' in the Philippines (cited in Del Carmen, 1973: 1051). In 1957, George Malcolm, the American who served first as dean of the University of the Philippines Faculty of Law and then as a justice on the Supreme Court for nearly thirty years (1917–45), stated that 'for the first fifty years of the twentieth century, no national region could lay claim to jurists who outranked the Filipino Justices in the same period in character, probity, and erudition' (Malcolm, 1957: 147). They were schooled in the role of the US Supreme Court, as Malcolm also noted. Law schools were highly stratified, with the elite represented by the University of the Philippines School of Law, established by the United States to train future leaders, and the Ateneo de Manila School of Law, the leading Catholic School.

The decline of law and the reputation of the legal profession occurred in a different way in the Philippines than in the other countries. Ferdinand Marcos came into power in 1965 well armed with arguments that would appeal to US reformist critics and the business constituency at home. He denounced the oligarchy, called for land reform, and built an initial administration with legal and technocratic legitimacy. Marcos himself graduated from the University of Philippines School of Law and led the nation in the performance on the Bar exam. He surrounded himself with notables with a legitimacy that counted abroad. The background of one of his most prominent lawyer allies, Juan Ponce Enrile, a leading senator, is a particularly striking example. A graduate of Harvard Law School as well as the University of the Philippines, Ponce Enrile was a corporate lawyer from 1954 to 1966 with the law firm Ponce Enrile, Siguion Reyna, Montecillo & Belo. His father, Don Alfonso Ponce Enrile, was a famous trial lawyer and, in 1936, the first Philippine partner of a US-led firm. The credibility of Harvard and the law were thus well represented in the early career of Marcos. Marcos, in short, was not outside the mainstream in the Philippines until he took advantage of the Cold War to declare martial law in 1972 as a means of continuing in power. At that point, Marcos, as with respect to his counterparts in India, Indonesia, Malaysia and South Korea, took on law and legal institutions while enhancing his own power. He also took advantage of the change in US domestic politics favouring those who could be counted as allies in the Cold War. As in Indonesia and South Korea, at that point the military regimes looked more appealing as the key to a modernisation consistent with Cold War containment of the Left.

Legal institutions were therefore demeaned under Marcos after martial law. The reputation of the Supreme Court and the judiciary declined over the period of the Marcos regime. The judicial branch became one of the least respected among governmental institutions in the Philippines. Because of the US colonial legacy, lawyers were everywhere in the Marcos administration and its policies, but that presence did not mean support for legal institutions. Marcos was able not only to continue, but even to enhance the pattern of using law and other weapons to enrich himself and his cronies through politics and state power.

The corporate law firms close to Marcos thrived. Around the time Marcos came to power, there were two major corporate firms – Sycip Salazar and Ponce Enrile, Siguion Reyna, Montecillo & Belo. Both had US expatriate origins and served mainly foreign clients The Ponce Enrile firm had about forty lawyers in the early 1970s. ACCRA, the key firm for Marcos, was formed in 1972 – just around the time of Marcos' declaration of martial law. The lawyers who started the firm were partners in the Sycip Salazar firm. From the outset, ACCRA lawyers became closely involved in the economic activities of Marcos and his circle – organising questionable businesses, for example (Manapat, 1991).

Furthermore, at the time of martial law in the Philippines, there was no real principled opposition from among the elite lawyers. According to Jovito Salonga (2001: 246), an elite lawyer and an opponent of Marcos, 'we were only a handful among pre-martial law politicians who refused to compromise with Marcos'. There was some activity, supported in part by groups such as the Ford Foundation, which helped to set up NGOs concerned with legal rights. But the overwhelming story was a decline in the prestige of the law and lawyers under Marcos – seen also in a growing number of more radical groups organising and fighting against Marcos. The situation changed only with the assassination of Benigno Aquino in 1983. Domestic protest increased, and the legal elites and allies in the Roman Catholic Church mobilised – with greater cover now that the international community had turned against Marcos.

The legal elite, including Salonga, took advantage of their social capital to commandeer the resistance to Marcos in the name of a Third Way between the Left and the Right. They reinvented themselves as defenders of democracy against authoritarianism, staved off more radical movements and regained their position of strength in the field of state power. As in India, but even more so, the social capital embedded in the law provided strong resources to fuel a retooling and a comeback for lawyers.

The elite leaders of the resistance to Marcos are now prominent politicians with strong constituencies abroad. They succeeded in toppling the Marcos government, but only after the United States finally turned on Marcos when Aquino was assassinated. But when the elite lawyers came to power, they also helped to maintain the position of their friends and fraternity brothers who had committed themselves to Marcos and received handsome rewards for that commitment. A number of them became prominent senators in the Philippines. The corporate lawyers closest to Marcos similarly maintained their strong position as power brokers in the field of state power and also as respected counsel to multinationals. In 2008, *The Legal 500* stated that: 'The same full-service players maintain their positions at the top end of the market. SyCip Salazar Hernandez & Gatmaitan and Angara Abello Concepcion Regala & Cruz (ACCRALAW) remain at the top of the tree, with over 100 lawyers apiece.'[1]

At the same time, however, the elite movement against Marcos led to some change as the legal profession refurbished its image and credibility. There are now numerous activist NGOs staffed with lawyers. The Ford Foundation even celebrated the development of strategies of 'legal empowerment' pioneered in the Philippines. The legal system is more open and more reformist than it was in the past. Nonetheless, the groups favoured with funding by the Ford Foundation and the Asia Foundation, among others, are led by the elite graduates of the top law schools – those tied into the web of relationships that comprise the Philippine oligarchy today. The political leaders continue to come from the same families who reap essentially the same rewards.

The colonial legacy and the successful comeback of lawyers means that the position of law and lawyers remains very strong in the Philippines, both in the state and in the economy, and closely connected to international NGOs and international law firms. At the same time, however, the profession in the Philippines is closely linked to an interconnected oligarchy that has been entrenched since before independence.

Conclusion

The role of lawyers in Asia today depends on local and global processes. This chapter sought to account briefly for the position of law and lawyers in the governance of a set of Asian countries. All of the countries have relatively thriving corporate law firms linked to foreign trade and investment, and the growth of these firms is one reflection of what can be seen as a converging trend within different legal professions. But there is a large difference between corporate law firms operating more or less as foreign enclaves serving mainly foreign commerce, which was the origin of all of these corporate law firms, and the position of lawyers involved in the governance of the state, as well as the economy. For somewhat different reasons, elite lawyers in South Korea and Indonesia have moved from an inauspicious beginning to important places in state governance and important roles within the domestic economy, as well as among foreign investors. In India and the Philippines, there was a revival of what, from colonial history, was a strong role in domestic governance. Finally, Malaysia, despite a relatively propitious history (compared to Korea and Indonesia, at least), today looks more isolated from the state and the domestic economy than it was at the time of independence. Other countries in Asia with different histories and local contexts, such as Japan and China in particular, are linked into global trade and commerce, and also have been growing their corporate law firm sector in prestige and number – fuelled by reforms in legal education designed to promote more corporate lawyers. But it remains for researchers to determine whether there is any trend toward the kind of convergence found in, for example, South Korea and Indonesia, towards a meaningfully strong role for law and lawyers in the domestic economy and state.

Note

1 *The Legal 500* is available online at http://www.legal500.com/c/philippines [accessed 19 July 2016].

References

Benton, L. (2001) *Law and Colonial Cultures: Legal Regimes in World History, 1400–1900*, New York: Cambridge University Press.

Davis, B. (2007) *Advocacy NGOs, Transnationalism and Political Space: An Indonesian Case Study*, Sydney: University of Sydney.

Del Carmen, R. V. (1973) 'Constitutionalism and the Supreme Court in a Changing Philippine Polity', *Asian Survey*, 13(11): 1050–1061.

Dezalay, Y., and Garth, B.G. (2010) *Asian Legal Revivals: Lawyers in the Shadow of Empire*, Chicago, IL: University of Chicago Press.

Feeley, M., and Miyazawa, S. (2007) 'The State, Civil Society, and the Legal Complex in Modern Japan: Continuity and Change', in T. Halliday, L. Karpik and M. Feeley (eds) *Fighting for Political Freedom: Comparative Studies of the Legal Complex and Political Change*, Portland, OR/Oxford: Hart, 151–193.

Feeley, M., Halliday, T., and Karpik, L. (eds) (2008) *Fighting for Political Freedom: Comparative Studies of the Legal Complex and Political Change*, Oxford/Portland, OR: Hart.

Ferguson, N. (2004) *Empire: The Rise and Demise of the British World Order and the Lessons for Global Power*, New York: Basic Books.

Friedman, T. (2007) *The World is Flat: A Brief History of the 21st Century*, New York: Picador.

Galanter, M., and Robinson, N. (2013) 'India's Grand Advocates: A Legal Elite Flourishing in the Era of Globalisation', HLS Program on the Legal Profession Research Paper No. 2013–5, available online at http://ssrn.com/abstract=2348699 [accessed 19 July 2016].

Gingerich, J., and Robinson, N. (2014) 'Responding to the Market: The Impact of the Rise of Corporate Law Firms on Elite Legal Education in India', HLS Program on the Legal Profession Research Paper No. 2014–11, available online at http://papers.ssrn.com/sol3/papers.cfm?abstract_id=2398506 [accessed 19 July 2016].

Ginsburg, T. (2007) 'Law and the Liberal Transformation of the Northeast Asian Legal Complex in Korea and Taiwan', in M. Feeley, T. Halliday and L. Karpik (eds) *Fighting for Political Freedom: Comparative Studies of the Legal Complex and Political Change*, Oxford: Hart, 43–64.

Harding, A., and Whiting, A. (2012) 'Custodian of Civil Liberties and Justice in Malaysia: The Malaysian Bar and the Moderate State', in T. C. Halliday, L. Karpik and M. M. Feeley (eds) *Fates of Political Liberalism in the British Post-Colony: The Politics of the Legal Complex*, New York: Cambridge University Press, 247–305.

Kantorowicz, E. H. (1997) *The King's Two Bodies: A Study in Mediaeval Political Theology*, Princeton, NJ: Princeton University Press.

Karnow, S. (1989) *In Our Image: America's Empire in the Philippines*, New York: Random House.

Kim, J.-W. (2007) 'Legal Profession and Legal Culture during Korea's Transition to Democracy and a Market Economy', in W. Alford (ed.) *Raising the Bar: The Emerging Legal Profession in East Asia*, Cambridge, MA: Harvard University Press, 47–80.

Kim, S.-H. (2011) 'The Democratization and Internationalization of Korean Legal Field', in Y. Dezalay and B. G. Garth (eds) *Globalization and the Rule of Law*, New York: Routledge, 217–238.

Krishnan, J. K. (2004) 'Professor Kingsfield Goes to Delhi: American Academics, the Ford Foundation, and the Development of Legal Education in India', *American Journal of Legal History*, 46(4): 447–499.

Krishnan, J. K. (2013) 'Peel-off Lawyers: Legal Professionals in India's Corporate Law Firm Sector,' *Socio-Legal Review*, 9(1): 1–59.

Lee, K.-W. (2007) 'Corporate Lawyers in Korea: An Analysis of the "Big 4" Law Firms in Seoul', in D.-K. Choi (ed.) *Korea and Japan: Judicial System in Transformation in the Globalizing World*, Seoul: Seoul National University Press, 219–250.

Lev, D. (1972) 'Judicial Institutions and Legal Culture in Indonesia', in C. Holt (ed.) *Culture and Politics in Indonesia*, Ithaca, NY/London: Cornell University Press, 246–318.

Lev, D. (1976) 'Origins of the Indonesian Advocacy', *Indonesia*, 21: 135–169.

Lev, D. (1998) 'Lawyers' Causes in Indonesia and Malaysia', in A. Sarat and S. Scheingold (eds.) *Cause Lawyering: Political Commitments and Professional Responsibilities*, New York: Oxford University Press, 349–430.

Lev, D. (2012) *No Concessions: The Life of Yap Thiem Hien*, Seattle, WA: University of Washington Press.

Li, C. (2013) 'The Rise of the Legal Profession in the Chinese Leadership', *China Leadership Monitor*, 42(2): 1–26.

Malcolm, G. A. (1957) *American Colonial Careerist: Half a Century of Official Life and Personal Experience in the Philippines and Puerto Rico*, Boston, MA: Christopher.

Manapat, R. (1991) *Some Are Smarter than Others: The History of Marcos' Crony Capitalism*, New York: Aletheia.

Mate, M. (2014) 'Elite Institutionalism and Judicial Assertiveness in the Supreme Court of India', *Temple International and Comparative Law Journal*, 28: 361–429.

Minger, R. E. (1975) *William Howard Taft and United States Foreign Policy: The Apprenticeship Years, 1900–1908*, Urbana, IL: University of Illinois Press.

Nath, S. (2010) 'India's Biggest in Law, Amarchand Mangaldas', *Forbes India*, 26 July, available online at http://forbesindia.com/article/boardroom/indias-biggest-in-law-amarchand-mangaldas/15382/1 [accessed 19 July 2016].

Pitts, J. (2005) *A Turn to Empire: The Rise of Imperial Liberalism in Britain and France*, Princeton, NJ: Princeton University Press.

Pompe, S. (2005) *The Indonesian Supreme Court: A Study of Institutional Collapse*, Ithaca, NY: Cornell Southeast Asia Program.

Reksodiputro, M. (2003) 'Challenges to Legal Education in Indonesia', available online at http://www.aseanlawassociation.org/docs/w3_indo.pdf [accessed 19 July 2016].

Salonga, J. R. (2001) *A Journey of Struggle and Hope: The Memoir of Jovito R. Salonga*, Quezon City: University of the Philippines Center for Leadership, Citizenship, and Democracy/Regina.

Shaffer, G., Nedumpara, J., and Sinha, A. (2014) 'Indian Trade Lawyers and the Building of State Trade-related Legal Capacity', University of Minnesota Law School Legal Studies Research Paper No. 14–08, available online at http://ssrn.com/abstract=2390673 [accessed 19 July 2016].

Sharafi, M. (2014) *Law and Identity in Colonial South Asia: Parsi Legal Culture, 1772–1947*, Cambridge: Cambridge University Press.

Whiting, A. (2013) 'Emerging from Emergency Rule? Malaysian Law "Reform"', *Australian Journal of Asian Law*, 14(2): 1–55.

8 The political determinants of corporate reorganisation in China

Roman Tomasic and Zinian Zhang

Introduction

This chapter examines the political factors that have influenced the management of court-supervised corporate reorganisations in the People's Republic of China (PRC) following the passage of the PRC Enterprise Bankruptcy Law 2006 (EBL 2006). It follows a wider body of research that has pointed towards the political determinants affecting the way in which corporate governance is structured in different countries, including China.[1] Examples of political considerations affecting the implementation of the EBL 2006 are discussed. China's new bankruptcy law has been hailed as representing 'a large step forward in clarifying and strengthening' the rights of creditors (Peerenboom and He, 2009: 13). To some degree, this is true. The Law has sought to move away from the largely political and administrative mechanisms for dealing with corporate insolvency, and to make much greater use of the courts. However, China's law reforms seeking to support the rapidly developing market economy have taken place in an environment in which the state remains a dominant player in markets and in shaping and implementing legal reforms.

Professors Peerenboom and He (2009: 13) have reminded us that '[w]hile the government's role has been diminished, there are still various opportunities for the government to intervene to pursue non-economic policy goals such as social stability'. This problem is especially evident in regard to corporate reorganisations, in which local protectionism remains a powerful factor. Indeed, the eminent China scholar Jerome Cohen (2001: 403) has described local protectionism as 'the greatest weakness in China's judicial system'.[2] This problem continues to be felt in the way in which corporate reorganisation has taken place in China since 2006.

With regard to the handling of commercial disputes in China generally, it has been suggested that local protectionism may be decreasing in some major urban areas, such as in Guangdong; as a result of successful reform efforts, this has led some to note that, in urban areas in this region, 'the direct influence of major political forces on the courts has decreased' (He, 2009: 453). Whilst this may be so in regard to routine contractual disputes between commercial parties, the picture may not be as clear-cut in regard to company law and corporate insolvency matters, especially where well-connected corporate entities are involved. Professor He (2009: 427) has noted that 'big companies and SOEs were infrequent users of the courts' and that, '[w]hen there are major and significant disputes affecting the interests of large companies, local officials may not even allow a court to take on the dispute: they will straighten everything out using political channels'. He did, however, point out that there is still a paucity of detailed empirical evidence in regard to such matters (He, 2009: 421). This chapter will seek to fill this gap to some degree.

Some other detailed research has already pointed to difficulties that arise in the handling of company law cases involving public companies in China. In a study of the company law cases dealt with by the Shanghai People's Courts between 1992 and 2008, Professor Howson (2010b: 143) reported that these company law cases illustrated that the courts acted primarily as administrative units and that, in conformity with bureaucratic instructions, the courts often simply gave priority to 'national social and economic policy over and above more specific mandates (and rights) set forth in the Company Law'.

In passing, Howson (2010b: 143–144) also noted that Shanghai courts were hesitant to accept or allow company dissolution or liquidation pleadings and rarely considered cases involving public companies or joint stock companies. A number of reasons can be given for this failure of leading Chinese courts to consider cases involving public companies, one of which has been suggested to be the reluctance of shareholders to bring actions. Howson (2010b: 145) has argued that there are a number of other more important explanations for the lack of public company cases in Shanghai courts, including that these courts '(i) voluntarily avoid taking such cases, and (ii) are specifically directed not to take such cases'. Exploring why this may be so, Professor Howson (2010b: 146–147) offered the following explanations:

> One rationale [for judicial inaction] dictates that courts be told to decline or voluntarily refuse listed company cases for fear of large plaintiff groups, and the attendant perceived threat of social instability or impact on the 'super-value' in Chinese administrative-political culture: social harmony . . . A second rationale can also be perceived, albeit more subtly, in the Shanghai court system's consistent bias in favour of stability (including . . . business entity preservation at all costs) over values that might be held high in corporate law . . . A third, largely unspoken rationale perhaps informing the rejectionist stance toward public company cases is twofold: (i) that such firms involve what were state-owned assets . . . , and (ii) that the promoters, controlling shareholders, and directors, officers, and supervisory board members and other insiders are tied to superior political power, whether the state, the party, or the military. There is evidence that the courts will avoid cases concerning state-owned assets.[3]

Donald Clarke and Nicholas Howson (2012: 279) painted a similar picture in regard to the absence of minority shareholder derivative claims under company law brought by shareholders against companies limited by shares or publicly listed companies in China; this is despite the existence of legal rights in the new PRC Company Law 2005 permitting the bringing of such legal proceedings.

In spite of the difficulties in enforcing corporate laws in practice, China's stated commitment to integrate into the global legal community is clear. This is reflected in its recent enactment of the rescue-oriented EBL 2006, which responded to the global wave of rescue-centred bankruptcy law reforms (Booth, 2008). In the EBL 2006, the area of corporate reorganisation is given some priority, being located before chapters on the use of compromises and liquidation (Zou, 2007: 50–51). The EBL 2006 sought to adopt many corporate reorganisation 'best practices' from abroad and has been acclaimed by some as a modern law on corporate rehabilitation (Falke, 2007). But this is not to say that it does not have some serious shortcomings.

The EBL 2006 has not been implemented to the extent that some foreign observers might have expected.[4] The predicaments encountered during the making of this Law might have signalled future difficulties in its enforcement. After over a decade of slow bankruptcy law reform debates, it was clear that there was considerable reluctance in many quarters in China to enact such a wide-ranging law.[5] Halliday and Carruthers (2007: 284) have discussed the lead-up to the enactment of the EBL 2006, and have noted that this reluctance continued despite the urgings of international experts and multilateral bodies, such as the Asian Development Bank and the World Bank:

> [T]he Chinese government resisted the urgings of the World Bank for rapid enactment [of a new bankruptcy law] and repeatedly delayed putting the [draft Enterprise Bankruptcy] bill before the Standing Committee of the National People's Congress (NPC) until 2003. It moved stop-and-start through successive readings until enactment suddenly took place in August 2006 . . . The twelve-year marathon demonstrated simultaneously the overwhelming influence of domestic issues and the comparative weakness of international influence.

Reviewing the politics of law making in China after the Asian financial crisis, Halliday and Carruthers (2009: 407) pointed towards the limited capacity of multilateral financial institutions such as the World Bank to place direct leverage on China (in contrast to Indonesia and Korea) and noted that this meant that they 'had to be satisfied with the passage of a comprehensive bankruptcy law in 2006 that deviated from global norms in its insistence on preserving many "Chinese characteristics" '. One of these characteristics was China's retention of power exercised by administrative agencies over bankruptcy cases. This was a consequence of Chinese fears 'that law may not have the capacity to cope with market demands or public imperatives' (Halliday and Carruthers, 2009: 407). This reflected a focus on 'domestic concerns while symbolically expressing adherence to the broad contours of global standards' (Halliday and Carruthers, 2009: 408).

The passage of the 2006 legislation had been delayed by resistance from state agencies that were determined to preserve their powers over state-owned enterprises (SOEs), as well as by the 'loose coalition of SOE managers, provincial leaders, and senior [State Economic and Trade Commission] SETC administrators [who] viewed the diminution of the SETC's leading role with anxiety' (Halliday and Carruthers, 2007: 284). There was also ideologically based opposition to the idea of introducing a capitalist instrument, such as a new bankruptcy law, into China. Halliday and Carruthers (2009: 285) insightfully observed that:

> It is no surprise that the final road-block to enactment came in the form of a struggle between factions that supported the priority of workers versus those who favoured secured creditors and banks. Most fundamentally, to implement the ADB and World Bank reports [proposing bankruptcy law reform in China] presupposed institutions China does not yet have (such as a comprehensive welfare safety net for unemployed workers) and entailed political risks (such as large-scale economic disaster and social unrest) that the Party will not tolerate.[6]

The problem of dealing with the 'implementation gap' created by the enactment of the EBL 2006 has remained a significant one for China.[7] In 2009, Halliday and Carruthers tentatively predicted a major implementation gap that would arise as a result of the bringing into force of the EBL 2006:

> Although the novelty of China's bankruptcy law does not permit any analysis of implementation, the severe limitations of [China's] implementing institutions, together with the government's continued administrative controls, suggest that national and local politics will open up a substantial implementation gap that varies significantly across China.
> (Halliday and Carruthers, 2009: 409)

This prediction was to prove quite prescient. Before the EBL 2006 came into effect in June 2007, it was somewhat optimistically expected that there would be a proliferation of corporate reorganisations following its passage (Li, 2002: 58). This hope was based on the theory that the new rescue Law sought to effectively preserve the going-concern value of troubled companies (Wang, 1996: 91) as well as to curb destructive corporate liquidations (Wang, 2002: 83). But, as with other recent Western-influenced legislation enacted in China (Economy, 2007: 51), the EBL 2006 was not well enforced or implemented during the first few years after its enactment (Tomasic and Zhang, 2012); notably, only a small number of large companies were allowed to file for reorganisation in China under the Law.

Furthermore, it soon became clear that there would continue to be heavy government intervention in corporate reorganisations in China, although in theory these cases were to be managed through court-supervised judicial processes. In many such corporate reorganisations, political interests came to prevail over compliance with basic legal rules. It is appropriate to ask why local governments were so keen to intervene in corporate reorganisations and what their expectations were. Geographic factors should also be kept in mind, because Chinese companies are effectively tied to the place where they are domiciled; thus section 3 of the EBL 2006 provides that: 'Jurisdiction in a bankruptcy case shall lie with a people's court of the place where the debtor is domiciled.' This nexus gives significant power to local courts in dealing with corporate reorganisations in China and creates a major concern for creditors dealing with a well-connected local company, because local protectionism remains 'the biggest concern of most commercial litigants' (Peerenboom and He, 2009: 23).

The level of protectionism is probably greater in less-developed rural areas than in urban areas. But legal disputes involving key SOEs or key industrial sectors may still be of significant interest to both national and provincial governments, especially where government policies seek to protect domestic companies or industries (Peerenboom and He, 2009: 23).

This chapter discusses the impact of these factors on corporate reorganisations and it does so by drawing upon publicly available information, such as relevant newspaper reports regarding these reorganisations. In addition, one of the authors conducted some twenty face-to-face interviews in Zhejiang Province with lawyers, judges, accountants, creditors and government officials who had participated in corporate rescue cases.

The remainder of this chapter is organised as follows. First, the chapter describes the legal context of China's corporate rescue legislation. This is followed by a discussion of government roles in allowing the commencement of corporate reorganisation procedures. Thereafter, there is a discussion of political considerations affecting value distribution in corporate reorganisations. Finally, the chapter concludes by discussing the likely impact of the political dimensions of corporate reorganisation upon the future development of China's corporate reorganisation regime.

An overview of China's corporate reorganisation regime

Under the EBL 2006, three main bankruptcy procedures were created to cope with corporate bankruptcy. Chapter 8 of this Law deals with reorganisation and seeks to facilitate the rescue of financially troubled companies (Baird, 1998: 580), and Chapter 9 focuses on compromise, and is intended to assist renegotiations between a debtor and its creditors, whilst Chapter 10 governs liquidation and is designed as a conventional mechanism to sell assets of bankrupt companies either piecemeal or as a going concern. Zou (2007: 50–51) argued that the order of these three chapters suggests that China's lawmakers were willing to see more corporate reorganisations; for this purpose, many pro-rescue mechanisms were included in the EBL 2006.

To encourage the use of the new corporate reorganisation procedure under the EBL 2006, companies in danger of bankruptcy or likely to become bankrupt are permitted to file reorganisation petitions – that is, a company that seeks to use a bankruptcy reorganisation procedure in court has the opportunity to avoid bankruptcy (Li, 2005: 15). The Law provides an early opportunity for the rescue of troubled businesses. More importantly, contrary to the old PRC Enterprise Bankruptcy Law of 1986 (for Trial Implementation) (EBL 1986) (Tomasic and Wang, 2006), the EBL 2006 abolished the need to obtain government permission as a precondition to commencing a court-supervised corporate bankruptcy procedure, which meant that a corporate reorganisation petition could now be directly filed by companies without first asking for government approval.

So as to provide a breathing space for troubled companies entering into the corporate reorganisation procedure, the Law stays all claims of creditors, including secured creditors (Wang, 2005b: 40). Thus the new corporate reorganisation regime could be used by beleaguered companies to keep aggressive creditors at bay. This, in turn, creates a legal shelter for companies in difficulty, allowing them to be better rehabilitated (Woodward, 2008: 146).

To build a market-driven corporate bankruptcy system, the EBL 2006 included for the first time rules to facilitate the emergence of a body of insolvency practitioners in China. Under sections 13 and 24, at the time that a corporate bankruptcy petition is accepted, the court is required to appoint a qualified insolvency practitioner as the administrator to take control of the company's assets and to manage the company's affairs (Wang, 2005a: 8). This reform sought to abolish the practice of appointing government-organised liquidation committees as administrators, as occurred under the old EBL 1986; these committees had long been criticised as lacking competence and accountability (Wang, 2005b: 39; Wang, 2005a: 8).

On the basis that corporate reorganisation is rehabilitating companies in distress rather than liquidating their assets, section 73 of the EBL 2006 now permits the debtor being reorganised to recover control from the administrator, adopting the debtor-in-possession approach found in the United States (Li, 2006: 19). However, this procedure is slightly different from its US counterpart: China's debtor-in-possession approach has a court-appointed administrator remaining as a monitor overseeing the rescue process (Parry, 2009: 50).

Moreover, because a viable corporate reorganisation requires firm-specific knowledge and information possessed by the debtor, with certain limits, the EBL 2006 has relaxed the absolute priority principle to motivate a debtor to engage in the corporate rescue. This principle normally gives priority to creditors over shareholders. Section 87 stipulates that deviating from the absolute priority principle could occur with the consent of creditors; this means that the debtor, especially its shareholder-managers, could bargain to share the company value even if creditors were not paid in full (Blum and Kaplan, 1974).

Finally, to improve efficiency and to promote rescue outcomes, section 87 provides that a 'cram-down' can be requested to confirm a plan of reorganisation that has not been accepted by one or more impaired parties, if the plan can meet the prescribed statutory standards (Zou, 2012: 28–29; Wang, 2007: 61).

Overall, a cutting-edge legal framework for corporate reorganisation has been established in China with the promulgation of the EBL 2006 (Rapisardi and Zhao, 2010; Shi, 2007). However, as noted earlier, the greater challenges lie in its enforcement, especially given China's legal development and poor infrastructure (Peerenboom, 2002; Lubman, 2000; Naughton, 2007, 2010). The next section sheds light on the political determinants regarding entry into formal corporate reorganisation procedures in China.

Finding government support to initiate a corporate reorganisation

In theory, under the EBL 2006, it seems to be easy to commence a corporate reorganisation process in the courts. In practice, however, it is almost impossible for a company to trigger this procedure in the absence of government support. From research looking at cases over the first three-and-a-half years of the effort to implement the EBL 2006 (between June 2007 and November 2010), only ninety-two reported corporate reorganisation cases (which were opened to rescue 120 companies) could be found in China as a whole (Zhang, 2013: ch. 5). As Figure 8.1 shows, forty-eight cases (52 per cent) were concentrated in three economically well-developed provinces (Guangdong, Zhejiang and Jiangsu), with other provinces having relatively smaller numbers: Shaanxi and Henan had five reorganisation cases each, while Beijing had four, with Shanghai having only three cases.[8]

It should nevertheless be emphasised that the social and economic impact of these reorganisations cannot be measured merely by their number, because nearly all of them involved the rescue of large companies; in particular, twenty-nine out of all ninety-two reorganisations (31.52 per cent) sought to rescue publicly traded companies (Zhang, 2013: ch. 5).

In reality, courts have required government support before being able to accept corporate reorganisation petitions. Without government support, courts simply ignore corporate reorganisation petitions, although this appears to be unlawful (Wang, 2010: 26). Two reasons could help to explain why government support has been needed. First, government support could exempt the court from being negatively assessed under China's social stability assessment systems. These assessment systems are complex and political in nature, but largely unwritten (Minzner, 2011); all state agencies, including courts, are required to meet the social stability targets set up by the government (Li, 2012a). Discussing such systems is outside the scope of this chapter, but, put simply, according to one of the key criteria of these systems, the court (and especially its president and the judge in charge) will be negatively assessed, and may even be disciplined if there is a social stability incident that takes place and is related to the court's business (Yu, 2012).

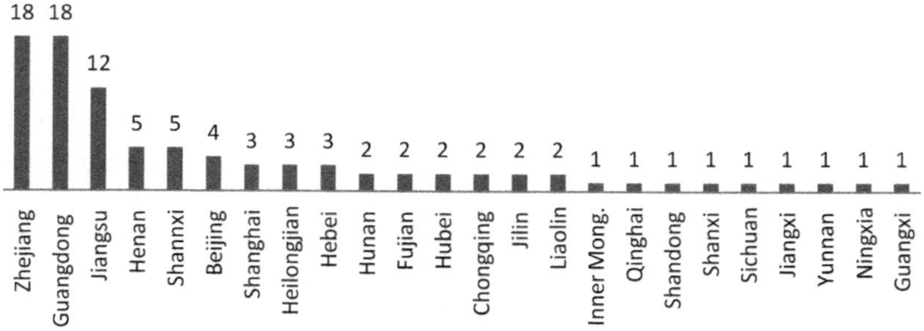

Figure 8.1 Number of corporate reorganisations by province in China, June 2007–November 2010

Source: Data collected by Zhang.

A 'social stability incident' is, in effect, a euphemism for a protest or group petition made by a number of people (Lum, 2006). In response to these assessment systems, since 2000, most of China's courts have sought to avoid cases that would involve a large number of individuals (Gan, 2004). A corporate reorganisation case may trigger such concerns because it always has many disgruntled individual parties who are either employees or creditors. Empirical evidence suggests that the fear of a negative assessment by the social stability assessment systems would be the court's most serious concern when a corporate reorganisation petition is presented (Gödel and Ong, 2012: 43). The court would simply remain silent if there were a corporate rescue petition: the petition would not even be registered by the court at the first stage, let alone formally dismissed afterwards under section 12 of the EBL 2006. Most insolvency-related practitioners and officials interviewed by the author confirmed that the new corporate bankruptcy law is generally unavailable in practice, mainly because courts do not accept bankruptcy petitions, whether corporate reorganisations or liquidation filings.

Things would be very different if courts were instructed by local government to accept a reorganisation case. In such circumstances, the government steps in and the court would be protected by the provision of a political shield, because it would be the government rather than the court that would take responsibility for social stability issues. Such a practice has now been formalised in China. In 2012, the China Supreme People's Court issued a judicial notice urging courts to obtain local government support regarding social stability issues before accepting a corporate reorganisation petition regarding a publicly traded company (Supreme People's Court, 2012). By implication, in the case of reorganisation petitions for other types of company, courts usually react in the same way (Tang and Shi, 2011: 105). So one of the de facto preconditions for judicial initiation of a corporate reorganisation procedure is that the court must first obtain government support in regard of potential social stability concerns.

Second, many of those interviewed by Zhang indicated that the courts need to secure government support to gain assistance or cooperation from other government agencies so as to facilitate the corporate reorganisation process. Without the involvement of local government, the court will usually be too weak to persuade government agencies to provide administrative and regulatory services. In substance, however, it can be argued that the lack of cooperation from some government agencies is partly attributable to the oversimplification of the EBL 2006 (Xi, 2013: 3), and partly a result of the less-developed state of the rule of law in China.

Two typical illustrations can help to explain this pattern. The first of these was the 2009 *Reorganisation of Tianting Paper Co. Ltd.*[9] When Tianting entered into the reorganisation procedure, it continued trading so as to maintain confidence of both its employees and suppliers – but the local tax authority stopped providing Tianting with tax-approved receipts on the grounds that the company had an unpaid tax liability that had accrued prior to its bankruptcy. Without tax-approved receipts, the company could not continue its business operations, because, in China's business environment, the company had to issue tax-approved receipts to its customers before they could collect payment. This then created a deadlock. The local tax authority's refusal was lawful under China's tax regulations,[10] because the tax authority could restrict and even cease providing tax-approved receipts if a company were to fall behind in its tax payments. A key problem is that the EBL 2006 is so skeletal in nature that it has no mechanism for coping with such a conflict, which could be anticipated in advance. The oversimplified EBL 2006 lies at the core of this deadlock, because the Law is not synchronised with the tax law.

However, in the *Tianting* case, an interim committee was established by local government to support the company reorganisation, the local government was able to apply pressure so that the tax authority conceded, and by circumventing the tax law, the tax authority resumed the supply of these receipts. In the absence of local government involvement, the Tianting rescue might not have proceeded, since it was highly unlikely that the local court could have persuaded or pressured the tax authority to provide the necessary exemption.

Thus, on the face of it, whilst the court might complain that it is difficult to obtain administrative services from the tax authority, in substance it is the oversimplification of the EBL 2006 that has left gaps that have impeded the rescue process by creating too many obstacles. A similar lack of statutory synchronisation of the EBL 2006 with other laws also arises with the PRC banking and public utility laws (Wang and Yi, 2009: 23).

An illustration of the underdeveloped state of the rule of law in China can be found in the 2009 *Reorganisation of Dadi Paper Co. Ltd.*[11] In the *Dadi* case, the judge, who was subsequently interviewed by Zhang, noted that the local police played a critical role in investigating the company's assets, which were spread over many provinces in China. The police department took part in the Dadi corporate rescue because it was ordered to do so by the local government. In principle, however, investigating the company's assets should be undertaken by the lawyer administrator; in this case, the lawyer was largely denied access to the company's property records possessed by government agencies such as the Land Registration Authority. The judge stated that the whole reorganisation process of Dadi would have been impossible if the local police had not been involved: without the aid of the police service, the administrator would not have known of, and could not have verified, the existence and whereabouts of the company's assets.

The *Dadi* case raises two serious concerns regarding the rule of law in China. First, some laws are simply not respected by authorities. Under section 35 of China's Lawyer Law 2007, lawyers are given rights and privileges of access to, and the right to obtain copies of, the company's property records held by government. But this does not occur in practice. As a result, government agencies will not be held accountable when they breach the law by denying a lawyer's rights (Wang and Guo, 2010: 4), as happened in the *Dadi* case. Secondly, some laws are often abused by public authorities. In the *Dadi* case, police involvement led to controversies over issues of legality. Police officers used their criminal investigation powers to intervene in the reorganisation process, even though this process was commercial in nature. It was legally inappropriate for the police to be involved in corporate reorganisations in this way.

Thus, to a large extent, the need for government support arises in corporate reorganisations because the EBL 2006 lacked sufficiently detailed rules and because China's rule of law is not as well developed as it might be. Faced with these difficulties, it is not surprising that most courts have therefore shunned corporate reorganisations.

We can now turn to examine government incentives for helping to initiate corporate reorganisations. From the perspective of government, it is easy to exploit corporate rescue laws so as to pursue governmental agendas. The corporate reorganisation regime may even give government a new tool with which to tackle political and economic problems. By and large, government control and financing of courts hearing corporate reorganisations had a number of goals (Li S., 2012). First, a concern for maintaining social stability has forced governments to intervene in business failures. As noted above, the social stability assessment system applies not only to courts, but also to local government. If a court becomes embroiled with a social stability incident, the court will be negatively evaluated by government, but the local government is also, in turn, assessed by the government at a superior level (Minzner, 2009). This is because of the existence of multilevel, hierarchical evaluation systems. The court can avoid criticism by remaining silent when a petition is likely to be social-stability sensitive, but the local government has nowhere to escape if such an incident arises in, or originates from, its area of responsibility.

In general, the threat to social stability has taken two forms in corporate reorganisation cases. First, this threat was occasioned by unpaid employees. In most cases, when the company was financially distressed, it delayed paying wages; if employees lost patience – and particularly if they lost confidence – they would collectively petition local government in the belief that section 85 of China's Labour Law 1994 requires the government to ensure that employers honour employment contracts, including wage payments.

In the province of Zhejiang, for example, it was found that group petitions by unpaid angry employees were received in at least eleven out of twenty corporate reorganisations (55 per cent). In this way, business failure escalated into a political event. Local government was therefore forced to intervene in dealing with the company's economic distress, since its own political interests were under threat owing to the social stability assessment system. In such circumstances, local governments have sought to buy peace by preventing employees from continuing group petitions or from petitioning a superior government – effected by means of the government paying employees on behalf of the company. This has happened in most corporate reorganisations in China.

For example, in the 2009 *Reorganisation of Jingwoniu Manufacture Co. Ltd, Guangdong*,[12] the local Qingxi Township government paid employees accrued unpaid wages of ¥7 million (about £700,000) (Chu, 2009). And in the 2009 *Reorganisation of Xingxing Artefacts Co. Ltd*,[13] the local Haichang District government spent ¥24 million (about £2.4 million) to satisfy aggrieved employees (Kang and Chen, 2009). Although such a practice has been widely criticised by academics as being counterproductive (Tsinghua University, 2010), this approach has been sanctioned by the China Supreme People's Court. In the judicial notice issued in 2009, the China Supreme People's Court ordered that, in corporate reorganisation cases, courts should rely on local government to meet unpaid wages of employees so as to prevent them from causing social instability.[14]

After the commencement of a corporate reorganisation procedure, local government would take the place of employees, claiming that it had paid the company's debts owed to employees. Usually, these debts would be fully reimbursed, because, under section 113 of the EBL 2006, employee claims are regarded as priority claims and so should be paid even before tax arrears are paid. Before paying employees, local governments would usually have consulted the local court, which would assess the situation so as to ensure that the payment to employees would be fully recovered if a formal bankruptcy process were to begin.

A second form of social stability threat arises in the violent seizure by creditors of a company's assets. Unlike employees, it was rare for creditors to collectively petition the government to claim defaulted debts. Creditors understand that the government was not duty-bound to force debtors to pay their debts; as a result, they have no cause to pressure the government to take action. Instead, creditors who were dissatisfied by available legal remedies would be likely to seize the debtor company's assets by themselves. In the province of Zhejiang, it was found that violent seizure of the company's assets by creditors took place in at least four out of twenty corporate reorganisations (20 per cent). The violent seizure of company assets was usually seen as a sign of social chaos, which might lead to destructive social consequences. This danger was a major concern for governments, at both the local level and above (Tong and Lei, 2010: 497).

One typical example of this fear arose in the 2008 *Reorganisation of Kehong Steel Manufacture Co. Ltd, Jiangsu.*[15] When Kehong's business operations ceased because of its sudden illiquidity, several hundred creditors surrounded the company's compound on the morning of 8 October 2008 and were infuriated when told that Kehong's boss had absconded abroad some days before the crisis. Some creditors attempted to enter the company's premises to seize property. Shortly afterwards, the local Changshu government deployed the police force and took over the company's compound. The Changshu government understood that this situation might easily escalate into social unrest if Kehong's crisis were allowed to get out of control.

After preventing a violent seizure of Kehong's assets, the local government organised meetings with the main creditors so as to discuss the fate of the company. One month later, supported by the Changshu government, Kehong entered into the corporate reorganisation procedure in the local Changshu Lower People's Court (Ding, 2009). Thus, because of the social stability assessment system, the local government feels obliged to intervene in a company's crisis and, if properly advised, will arrange the local court to begin a formal corporate reorganisation procedure.

Apart from the goal of maintaining social stability, local governments would also support a corporate reorganisation case in order to stabilise the local economy, as well as to protect its tax base. Because the health of the local economy is reflected in the annual growth of the gross domestic product (GDP), this can be both politically and economically important for local government. At present, the GDP figure is still one of the key elements in assessing China's local government performance and in determining the promotion of local government leaders (Landry, 2008: 162). As a result, rescuing a large local company was also politically significant to local government in the light of the likely impact that the company had on GDP figures.

For example, when the Hualun Group Co. Ltd[16] was financially distressed in 2009, the local Fuyang County government did not treat such business failure lightly. As one of the three largest companies in the county, Hualun's annual turnover was about ¥2.1 billion (approximately £210 million), contributing about 5 per cent of the county's annual GDP (in 2009, Fuyang County's GDP was ¥37 billion). Therefore, it was not surprising that the Fuyang County government formed an ad hoc crisis committee chaired by its mayor and supported the local Fuyan Lower People's Court to rescue this failing company (Ying and Wu, 2009).

Maintaining the local GDP figure was also important so as to stabilise the local tax base. This motivation appeared to be more visible in some economically less-developed areas in China. Local governments would give more consideration to the tax base when deciding whether to support local courts in the rescue of a large, local company. For example, in the 2009 *Reorganisation of Tianting*, referred to above, Tianting was the only company that had contributed over ¥10 million in tax (about £1 million) during the previous seven consecutive years in the comparatively less-developed Pujiang County in East China. Losing Tianting would have meant the local Pujiang County government losing its largest taxpayer (Pujiang Lower People's Court, 2009).

To sum up, by commencing a corporate reorganisation procedure, the courts have required government support, so as to have a political shield to prevent them from being scapegoated; such government support would also be essential in tackling the legal gaps that remained unfilled in the bankruptcy law and in coping with the less-developed rule of law in China. From the local government's point of view, supporting a local company's reorganisation served the maintenance of social stability, as well as the stabilisation of the local economy.

The converse is also true: if a company's failure had not led to social stability concerns for local government, and if the company were not strategically vital for the local GDP and revenue, it would be highly unlikely that this company would be able to access the formal corporate reorganisation process. It is therefore clear that many corporate reorganisations in China's courts were, in effect, initiated by local government. Because a corporate reorganisation procedure was usually entered because of political concerns, political concerns would be likely to influence how assets of the company were distributed in the rescue procedure. The next section will look more closely at this issue.

Political considerations affecting value distributions in reorganisations

The application of the EBL 2006 allows for some flexibility in regard to corporate reorganisations; this flexibility is provided by two fundamental value distribution norms – the *pari passu* rule and the absolute priority principle – which serve as default rules in regard to reorganisations (Mokal, 2001; Han, 2002; LoPucki and Whitford, 1990). This means that the distribution of the company's value may be subject to negotiation between the parties; if no agreement is reached, the *pari passu* and the absolute priority principle must apply.

The pari passu *principle*

In the absence of sufficient assets to pay all creditors in full, the *pari passu* rule calls for the payment of creditors of the debtor company to be made in proportion to the respective size of its claim. The application of the *pari passu* principle (Tomasic, 1998) can be perceived in sixty-nine corporate reorganisations among those studied: it was found that this principle was applied in fifty-one cases (73.91 per cent); deviations from this rule occurred in the remaining eighteen reorganisations (26.09 per cent). At first, many deviations from the *pari passu* principle were made in favour of small unsecured creditors in an effort to obtain their support for reorganisation plans. This strategy was commercially motivated: the amount of a small creditor's claim may be insignificant in regard to the passage of a reorganisation plan, but the number of such claims often matters. This is because section 84 of the EBL 2006 stipulates that a reorganisation plan is deemed accepted by each class of impaired parties only if more than half of impaired parties who vote to accept the plan represent at least two-thirds of claims in the class.

For example, the 2008 *Reorganisation of Beishen Pharmaceuticals Co. Ltd*[17] provides an excellent illustration of the operation of this principle. The company had 226 unsecured creditors, 112 of which had a claim of less than ¥50,000. Nearly half of the unsecured creditors were small creditors. To gain the support of these small creditors, the Beishen reorganisation plan provided for the full payment of each unsecured claim of up to ¥50,000; a 50.04 per cent payment was made to claims above ¥50,000. In fact, the first ¥50,000 in unsecured claims combined amounted to only ¥7 million, representing less than 1 per cent of the total ¥1,187 million in unsecured debts. Not surprisingly, the reorganisation plan was endorsed by 204 of the 211 unsecured creditors voting on the plan (96.68 per cent) and it is likely that all small creditors voted in favour of the plan.[18]

However, a limit upon deviations from the *pari passu* principle is that such a plan must be accepted by the disadvantaged parties (under section 87 of the EBL 2006). If this does not occur, the reorganisation plan cannot be confirmed by the court. In the case of *Beishen*, large unsecured creditors voted for the plan. In other cases, however, it was found that large creditors voted against a reorganisation plan that contained a deviation from the *pari passu* principle, yet the court still confirmed the plan. This took place, for example, in the 2007 *Reorganisation of Chuangzhou Chemical Co. Ltd,*[19] even though the court's confirmation of the plan was a breach of section 87.

Paying unsecured creditors at a higher rate can result in many uncertainties. Although the amount paid to small creditors might constitute only a tiny proportion of unsecured claims, it still deviates from the basic principle of fairness in corporate reorganisations (Tomasic, 1998). Such a practice was likely to be occasioned by the vaguely worded section 82 of the EBL 2006. According to the priority order for payments made in bankruptcy proceedings, section 82 divides those who can vote on a reorganisation plan into four classes of creditors: secured, employees, taxation and unsecured creditors. But there is a second paragraph in section 82, which provides that 'a class of small unsecured creditors can be separately established at the discretion of the court to vote on the reorganisation plan, if necessary'. This gives rise to two ambiguities – namely, how small claims are to be quantified and whether small creditors are to be paid differently from larger creditors.

In the *Beishen* case, unsecured creditors holding less than ¥50,000 in claims were defined as small; in the *Chuangzhou Chemical* case, an amount of ¥500,000 was used to separate unsecured creditors. Because there was a tenfold difference between these classifications of small creditors, this threshold is somewhat unclear. This has created a lack of legal certainty and predictability, and as a result might produce disputes. Moreover, it must be asked whether small unsecured creditors should, or could, be paid at a higher level, as has happened from time to time. Section 82 does not clarify this issue, leading to the emergence of two different views of this matter in academic circles in China.

One interpretation of section 82 has been that it cannot be interpreted to refer to the legislature's intent to offer a higher recovery rate to small creditors, because the *pari passu* principle should apply to all unsecured creditors, whether a class comprising small unsecured creditors is created or not (Wang, 2012: 19). A second view has been that, for the sake of efficiency, small creditors should be paid in full rather than only at a higher recovery rate (Wang, 2006: 136; Tang, 2005: 35). Arguably, both views are not totally wrong, but they have to be understood in the statutory context. As noted earlier, the EBL 2006 treated the *pari passu* principle as a default norm. This means that, in the case of any deviation from this principle, the consent of all disadvantaged unsecured creditors must be obtained. More specifically, such consent cannot be assumed merely by looking at whether a class of unsecured creditors has voted for a plan (Wang, 2012: 19); the required consent should be unanimous.

But this raises two practical issues. The first is that if there is a deviation from this principle, the fact that a class of unsecured creditors votes in favour of the reorganisation plan does not demonstrate that this class has agreed to the deviation, because the issue of the deviation is usually not separated and singled out in a vote. The second issue is that all disadvantaged unsecured creditors must have unanimously voted in favour of the deviation (Tomasic, 1998). These technical details should be addressed and enforced.

To some extent, the confusion attributed to section 82 of the EBL 2006 appears to be the result of an incomplete legal transplantation from Chapter 11 of the US Bankruptcy Code. Section 1122(b) of the US Bankruptcy Code 1978 states that: '[A] plan may designate a separate class of claims consisting only of every unsecured claim that is less than or reduced to an amount that the court approves as reasonable and necessary for administrative convenience.' So, under Chapter 11, it is clear that the objective of designating a class of small creditors arises for administrative convenience rather than to offer a higher recovery rate. When borrowing from the US Chapter 11, China's lawmakers may have created confusion by forgetting to add the goal of setting up a class of unsecured creditors.

Thus, in general, this first type of deviation from the *pari passu* principle in China's corporate reorganisations was allowed by the EBL 2006 only if certain statutory conditions were met. But the second type of deviating from *pari passu* seemed to have gone too far.

Some deviations from the *pari passu* principle have been politically motivated. The beneficiaries of this second type of deviation have been individual unsecured creditors who were seen as social stability troublemakers. Under the influence of government, the courts relaxed the *pari passu* principle so as to prevent them from protesting by paying them in full. The maintenance of social stability clearly outweighed the *pari passu* norm.

The first such case involved the 2009 *Reorganisation of Zhonggu Sugar Co. Ltd, Guangdong*,[20] a company which had about 300,000 sugar farmer creditors. After being told that Zhonggu was bankrupt, many farmer creditors sought to express their grievances and formed a group that then petitioned the local Zhanjiang government. This action was that which the local government had feared. To alleviate the tension, the Zhanjiang Intermediate People's Court supervising the case decided that the sugar farmers' debts, of about ¥24 million, should be paid in full, whereas other unsecured creditors recovered only 28.3 per cent of their claims. Interestingly, the judges in charge knew that the case raised legality concerns when farmer creditors were paid in full, whilst other unsecured creditors were not. To hide this inconsistency, the buyer of the company was asked to pay farmer creditors in full outside the reorganisation plan. Thus, on the one hand, the political problem was solved – farmer creditors were placated and judges were praised by local government for being politically wise; on the other hand, under the Zhonggu reorganisation plan, there was no written evidence of the improper deviation from the *pari passu* principle that could hold the court and the judges accountable in the future (Feng et al., 2010).

The second such case involving a deviation from this legal principle took place in the 2008 *Reorganisation of Qingtai Trust Co. Ltd, Qinghai*.[21] In contrast to the large number of sugar farmer creditors in the *Zhonggu* case, Qingtai had only ninety-four individual unsecured creditors, but on average each of these had a claim of about ¥350,000 (roughly £35,000). Before Qingtai was brought into the reorganisation procedure, these individual creditors had repeatedly protested before the local Qinghai Provincial government; this was probably because Qingtai was a state-owned finance company. Under political pressure based on concerns for social stability, the Qingtai reorganisation plan arranged for full payment to be made to these individual unsecured creditors who held ¥33 million in claims; while the institutional unsecured creditors who held a total of ¥818 million in claims were paid only 10 per cent of their pre-bankruptcy claims (Sun, 2008).

Moreover, some deviations from *pari passu* have been hidden or disguised, because they could not be identified simply by reading the reorganisation plans; hence some unsecured claims were treated as preferential debts. This can also be seen as politically motivated because the beneficiaries were employees who had become unsecured creditors not because the company owed them wages or pension contributions, but because the company had borrowed from them. The literature indicated that some of China's companies, the majority of which were state-owned or collectively owned companies, borrowed from their employees after the 1990s. In many such cases, it was compulsory for employees to allow this borrowing to occur; although China's central government sought to ban such borrowing from 1993, this decree was not well enforced (Qi and Liu, 1996). In a legal sense, the employees who made loans to their companies were unsecured creditors, but they were more likely to be treated differently if they applied political leverage through social protest.

In the cases of *Tianting* and *Zhonggu*, mentioned above, employees who had lent to their companies collectively petitioned local governments when their companies' reorganisation procedures commenced. These employees understood that they were likely to face a sharp 'haircut' if they were treated as unsecured creditors in the forthcoming value distribution under the *pari passu* principle. The employees in the *Tianting* case protested by collectively sitting outside the local Pujiang County government buildings, holding a banner that proclaimed 'protecting our debts' (Chen, 2011). In both the *Tianting* and *Zhonggu* cases, these protestors were rewarded: the employees' unsecured claims were elevated into preferential debts, which meant that they were paid in full. Shortly afterwards, a prominent lawyer in China argued that such an approach was short-sighted and counter-productive, because it placed short-term political expediency ahead of a commitment to the rule of law (Wu, 2013).

In sum, when applying the *pari passu* principle in China's corporate reorganisations, political considerations have been relevant in handling the claims of those individual creditors who had pressured local government by using group petitioning or protests. But it should be noted that the *pari passu* principle was strictly applied in other reorganisations in China.

The absolute priority principle

The absolute priority principle provided that creditors would be given priority over shareholders in the handling of bankruptcy claims. Examining the application of the absolute priority principle, sixty-two out of all eighty-seven corporate reorganisations studied (71.26 per cent) were found to have publicly available information in regard to this matter. It was found that the deviation from this principle took place in thirty-three of these cases (53.23 per cent) – a surprisingly high percentage. This meant that, in these cases, holders of equity joined in receipt of the distributions that were made, even though creditors were not first paid in full. Unlike deviations from the *pari passu* principle, most of the deviations from the absolute priority principle occurred for political reasons.

In reorganisations of publicly traded companies, it was the norm, rather than the exception, to depart from the absolute priority principle when making distributions of assets. In particular, twenty-seven out of all thirty-three such deviations occurred in publicly traded company reorganisations. As argued earlier, under section 87 of the EBL 2006, the absolute priority principle is a default rule; however, two months before the promulgation of the EBL 2006, Mr Song Xiaoming, a member of the China Supreme People's Court, gave a speech in which he stated that, in cases of publicly traded company reorganisations, some equity in new companies must be reserved for former medium and small shareholders (who were public securities holders) in order to maintain social stability regardless of whether these companies were insolvent (Song, 2006).

Several key points made in Judge Song's speech should be noted. First, Song's statement should be seen as a decree from the China Supreme People's Court. In practice, although this kind of statement will not directly appear in court judgments, its spirit will bind all judges in China. Second, the purpose of this kind of decree was to prevent holders of public securities from causing social instability. The number of holders of public securities in a publicly traded company is a serious political issue in China. Unlike stock exchanges in more developed countries where the majority of investors are usually institutions, the vast majority of investors in China's stock exchanges are members of the general public (Yuan, Zhen and Hu, 1999). Most of these companies have more than 10,000 individual shareholders. For example, Guangxia Co. Ltd. Ningxia, a publicly traded company, had more than 65,500 general public shareholders who were spread across China when it entered reorganisation in 2010 (Zhang and Zhao, 2012).[22] If these individual shareholders had been unhappy and taken action as a group by petitioning Beijing's central government against the strict application of the absolute priority principle in the reorganisation, it would have been seen as a national event that was destructive of social stability in China. This was something to be prevented and Judge Song's speech was probably aimed at doing this. Third, because only general public shareholders are given special protection, this means that institutional and controlling shareholders are not in a position to benefit in this way.

In theory, however, Judge Song's speech would have been in conflict with the EBL 2006. The EBL 2006 set up a precondition for any such deviation, which Song's speech removed. In reality, Song's statement was used to justify deviations from the absolute priority principle in publicly traded company reorganisations – and this strategy has been widely relied upon in many reorganisation cases in China.

Deviations of this kind in publicly traded company reorganisations have taken two forms. The first sought to ensure that the equity of the company was kept intact, which meant that the reorganisation was undertaken entirely at the expense of unsecured creditors. For example, in the 2007 *Reorganisation of Haina Tech Co. Ltd, Zhejiang*,[23] unsecured creditors recovered 25.35 per cent of their claims, but shareholders did not make any economic sacrifices as a result of the application of the absolute priority under its reorganisation plan.[24]

The second, and perhaps more common, form of deviation arose where shareholders joined unsecured creditors to share the costs of the reorganisation. In such situations, all shareholders forfeited a percentage of their equity to the administrator, who then sold it in order to increase recoveries for unsecured creditors. A typical example of this was the 2008 *Reorganisation of Changling Group Co. Ltd, Shaanxi*.[25] In the *Changling* case, under its plan of reorganisation, the general public shareholders each surrendered 10 per cent of their equity; the largest shareholder (the local government) conceded 80 per cent of its equity and the remaining shareholders contributed 50 per cent of their shares. After selling the forfeited equity, the administrator was able to make an 18 per cent payment to unsecured creditors, who otherwise would not have received any payment (Changling Group Co. Ltd, 2009).

Ironically, even in this situation, deviations in favour of general public shareholders have not appeared to serve the goal of maintaining social stability very well. In some cases, individual investors still protested, arguing that they should not have to bear any reorganisation costs at all, because the controlling shareholders had abused their positions and they should therefore have shouldered all costs. For example, during the 2011 *Reorganisation of Guangxia Co. Ltd, Ningxia*, on 12 December 2011 disgruntled general public shareholders assembled in Beijing, protesting and blocking the entrance of the China Securities Regulatory Commission (Li, 2012b). This strategy is not always effective as the general public shareholders sometimes also want to receive just treatment as well.

Two main concerns were raised by these routine deviations. First, Song's speech seems to have been misused. As noted above, under this decree, general public shareholders of publicly traded companies are given special protection, but other categories of shareholders are not. Yet the practice of reorganisations has also led other shareholders to take advantage of this decree by retaining their equity in full or in part. For instance, in the *Haina* case, as noted above, all shareholders, including the general public and institutional investors, relied upon this judicial statement and retained their equity intact.

Secondly, using this statement to justify deviation was not entirely unlawful, because the absolute priority principle is a default rule; departures from it have to be agreed upon by disadvantaged parties through voting processes. This means that if creditors, especially unsecured creditors, vote against a plan of reorganisation that contains such a deviation, the court cannot confirm such a plan. Unfortunately, the use of the cram-down confirmation procedure occurred in eight out of twenty-nine deviations (27.59 per cent) among the cases studied, even though this means of enforcing agreement was arguably unlawful (Wang, 2012: 18).

Leaving aside deviations made for the benefit of public securities holders, most deviations have also occurred to protect the interests of the state. In particular, in thirty out of thirty-three deviations (90.90 per cent), the company had at least one SOE among its shareholders. This meant that the absolute priority rule was modified to serve state interests. In the 2010 deviation case involving Jinhua Co. Ltd. Liaoning,[26] for example, 55.89 per cent of the company's equity was owned by a local SOE, Jinhua Holding Co. Ltd. To overcome the objections of creditors against such deviations, ten out of thirty deviations (33 per cent) used the 'cram-down' procedure to forcibly confirm reorganisation plans (Jinhua Co. Ltd. Liaoning, 2010).

Apart from these thirty deviations (which were made either to comfort general public shareholders or to serve the state's interests), the remaining three deviations appeared to be commercially motivated. In these three deviation cases (*Dadi* in Zhejiang, *Xingxing* in Fujian and *Jingwoniu* in Guangdong), the reorganisation had to rely on the former equity managers because there were no ready buyers of the company. To induce the equity managers to restructure their companies, creditors agreed to set aside the absolute priority rule by retaining the former's ownership of the company, as a result of which creditors could recover more than they would have in a company liquidation. In sum, most of the deviations from the absolute priority rule in China's existing corporate reorganisations were heavily influenced by political considerations.

Conclusion

By examining China's much-heralded corporate reorganisation law in action, this chapter has sought to show that political considerations have played a major role in shaping corporate reorganisation practice in China. Three main points could be made in conclusion. First, in choosing between providing judicial services on corporate reorganisation under the EBL 2006 and meeting the requirements of China's social stability assessment system, most Chinese courts have had to be realistic and have had to prioritise the latter. This has shown that local courts in China have been very weak, in a political sense.[27] Most courts superficially satisfy the requirements of the social stability assessment system by deliberately refusing corporate reorganisation petitions. Obviously, this suggests a lack of judicial accountability (Gewirtz, 2002), because it has been argued that it is wrong for courts to remain silent when a corporate reorganisation petition is lodged (Wang, 2010: 26).[28]

Second, it should be noted that most of China's existing corporate reorganisations were, in effect, initiated and used by governments in pursuit of political ends. This is in contrast to the usual Western assumption that formal corporate reorganisation systems were primarily created to serve business purposes. This emphasises the dominance of the state in China's legal and economic systems.[29] In such a system, government has often triggered the formal corporate reorganisation procedures so as to tackle social stability problems caused by business failures. Also, because the local GDP and tax base are firmly associated with local government leaders' political promotions, local governments have had more incentive to order or support local courts to reorganise troubled large local companies. This was especially reflected in the fact that the continuity of companies in reorganisation was always a preferred option for local government, as a result of which all corporate reorganisation plans were confirmed by courts regardless of whether or not they conformed to the EBL 2006 (Liu and Chi, 2011: 89).

Third, in regard to government expectations from corporate reorganisations, it is clear that both political and economic interests are highlighted. To allay social stability concerns, people who voiced their concerns most loudly and who might pose potential social stability threats were simply paid more, or even in full, during a reorganisation; most deviations from the *pari passu* and absolute priority principles were made in this way (Phan, 2005). As a result, the social stability goal was largely satisfied, even though it may have produced only short-term stability and even though, in the long run, it may have damaged the rule of law in China. As far as economic interests are concerned, governments have exploited the corporate reorganisation procedure so as to protect state interests. This was clearly demonstrated in reorganisations of publicly traded companies, in which the absolute priority principle was relaxed in the interests of state-owned companies that were shareholders. Additionally, governments expected large companies to continue to exist because local government needed them to produce GDP and to generate taxes. Again, this was achieved by confirming reorganisation plans at any costs.

Enforcing the corporate reorganisation law in China is difficult, but failing to enforce this law may be worse. In planning for the future of China's corporate reorganisation regime, considerations may need to be given to the following matters.

1 The corporate rescue law should be better synchronised with other related statutes, which are mainly concerned with business regulation. The first several years' implementation of the EBL 2006 has provided a chance to expose these inconsistencies.
2 Existing corporate reorganisations have given rise to concerns over the lack of judicial independence, as well as judicial accountability, of most Chinese courts hearing reorganisation cases. Perhaps an informal or voluntary corporate reorganisation regime without court involvement should be established.[30]
3 Given the weak position of courts in China, the entire corporate bankruptcy system could be improved if a government agency were to be established to supervise future corporate bankruptcy procedures, including corporate reorganisations (Li, 2010).

Notes

1 See generally Roe (2003); Shi (2007).
2 See also Cohen (2001).
3 See Howson (2010a) for a more detailed report on this body of research.

4 See, e.g., the papers delivered at the Organisation for Economic Co-operation and Development (OECD) Fifth Forum for Asian Insolvency Reform (FAIR), held in Beijing on 27–28 April 2006, shortly before the enactment of the PRC Enterprise Bankruptcy Law 2006, available online at http://www.oecd.org/daf/ca/corporategovernanceprinciples/5thforumforasianinsolvencyreformfairbeijingchina27-28april2006.htm [accessed 3 January 2014].

5 See generally Shi (2007); Tomasic and Wang (2006).

6 For a further discussion of the process of making and implementing the PRC Enterprise Bankruptcy Law 2006, see further Halliday and Carruthers (2009: 321–327, 406–414).

7 See generally Halliday (2007).

8 See further Tomasic and Zhang (2012: 312).

9 *Reorganisation of Tianting Paper Co. Ltd*, Pujiang Lower People's Court, Zhejiang, 1 September 2009.

10 China State Administration of Taxation, 'Unpaid Taxation Regulation' (Beijing China, 7 June 2004).

11 *Reorganisation of Dadi Paper Co. Ltd*, Fuyang Lower People's Court, Zhejiang, 1 June 2009.

12 *Reorganisation of Jingwoniu Manufacture Co. Ltd*, Guangong, Dongguan Intermediate People's Court, Guangdong, 28 May 2008.

13 *Reorganisation of Xingxing Artefacts Co. Ltd*, Haichang Lower People's Court, Xiamen, Fujian, 27 February 2009.

14 Supreme People's Court, *Notice on Corporate Bankruptcy Affairs*, 12 June 2009.

15 *Reorganisation of Kehong Steel Manufacture Co. Ltd*, Changshu Lower People's Court, Jiangsu, 18 November 2008.

16 *Reorganisation of Hualun Group Co. Ltd*, Fuyang Lower People's Court, Zhejiang, 1 June 2009.

17 *Reorganisation of Beishen Pharmaceuticals Co. Ltd*, Beihai Intermediate People's Court, Guangxi, 27 November 2008.

18 Administrator of Beishen Pharmaceuticals Co. Ltd, *Public Notice on Voting of the Reorganisation Plan*, Beihai Guangxi China, 23 February 2009.

19 *Reorganisation of Chuangzhou Chemical Co. Ltd*, Chuangzhou Intermediate People's Court, Hebei, 16 November 2007. See also *Securities Daily* (2008).

20 *Reorganisation of Zhonggu Sugar Co. Ltd*, Zhanjiang Intermediate People's Court, Guangdong, 22 December 2009.

21 *Reorganisation of Qingtai Trust Co. Ltd*, Qinghai Supreme People's Court, 10 September 2009.

22 *Reorganisation of Guangxia Co. Ltd*, Yinchuan Intermediate People's Court, Ningxia, 16 September 2010.

23 *Reorganisation of Haina Tech Co. Ltd*, Hangzhou Intermediate People's Court, Zhejiang, 14 September 2007.

24 Administrator of Haina Tech Co. Ltd, *The Reorganisation Plan of Haina Tech Co. Ltd. Zhejiang*, Hangzhou Zhejiang China, 24 October 2007.

25 *Reorganisation of Changling Group Co. Ltd*, Baoji Intermediate People's Court, Shaanxi, 15 May 2008.

26 *Reorganisation of Jinhua Co. Ltd*, Huludao Intermediate People's Court, Liaoning, 19 March 2010.

27 It is not our purpose here to get into a debate about the nature of judicial independence, a notoriously slippery subject. See further the discussion on this matter in Peerenboom (2010).

28 It is interesting to note that the problem of political meddling in court affairs has become a matter of concern to the Supreme People's Court in China. See, e.g., *The Economist* (2013: 34). Also, the Third Plenum of the Eighteenth Chinese Communist Party Congress held in November 2013 also pledged to introduce judicial reforms that would seek to protect the independence of local courts from the influence of local government (Meng and Zhai, 2013). It is too early to know how these promised reforms will be implemented. However, the proposed removal of local courts from the direct political supervision of local government could enhance the independence of local courts in corporate reorganisation cases. But courts would still be subject to political decisions at higher levels of government, as well as those made by the Communist Party.

29 See generally Huang (2008); Lin (2010); McNally (2008); Oi (1995).

30 In Australia, for example, such a non-judicial system of corporate reorganisation exists in the form of the system of voluntary administration under Part 5.3A of the Corporations Act 2001. But such a voluntary system is unlikely to be used in mainland China for a number of reasons, including the underdeveloped state of the insolvency practitioner profession in China. Such a profession does, however, exist in Hong Kong.

References

Baird, D. G. (1998) 'Bankruptcy's Uncontested Axioms', *Yale Law Journal*, 108(3): 573–599.

Blum, W. J., and Kaplan, S. A. (1974) 'The Absolute Priority Doctrine in Corporate Reorganisations', *University of Chicago Law Review*, 41: 651–684.

Booth, C. D. (2008) 'The 2006 PRC Enterprise Bankruptcy Law: The Wait is Finally Over', *Singapore Academy of Law Journal*, 20(Special Issue): 275–315.

Changling Group Co. Ltd (2009) *Annual Report 2008*, Shaanxi China: Changling Group Co. Ltd.

Chen, D. (2011) 'Petitions in Pujiang County Declined by 57 per cent during the Past Seven Years', *The Legal Daily*, 9 May, available online at http://www.legaldaily.com.cn/fxy/content/2011-05/09/content_2646580.htm?node=21409 [accessed 25 December 2013].

Chu, B. (2009) 'Corporate Reorganisation of Jingwoniu', *Dongguan Daily*, 22 May, available online at http://epaper.timedg.com/html/2009-05/22/content_292372.htm [accessed 20 July 2016].

Clarke, D. C., and Howson, N. C. (2012) 'Pathway to Minority Shareholder Protection: Derivative Actions in the People's Republic of China', in D. W. Puchniak, H. Baum and M. E. Chow (eds) *The Derivative Action in Asia: A Comparative and Functional Approach*, Cambridge: Cambridge University Press, 243–295.

Cohen, J. A. (2001) 'Settling Business Disputes with China', in R. P. Appelbaum, W. L. F. Felstiner and V. Gessner (eds) *Rules and Networks: The Legal Culture of Global Business Transactions*, Oxford: Hart, 403–420.

Ding, G. (2009) 'The Odyssey of the Largest Corporate Reorganisation Case in China', *Legal Daily*, 16 September, available online at http://www.legaldaily.com.cn/0801/2009-09/16/content_1154229.htm [accessed 21 December 2013].

The Economist (2013) 'Court Orders', 7 December, available online at http://www.economist.com/news/china/21591210-it-turns-out-torturing-people-confessions-isnt-all-right-after-all-court-orders [accessed 19 July 2016].

Economy, E. C. (2007) 'The Great Leap Backward? The Costs of China's Environmental Crisis', *Foreign Affairs*, 86(5): 38–59.

Falke, M. (2007) 'China's New Law on Enterprise Bankruptcy: A Story with a Happy End?', *International Insolvency Review*, 16(1): 63–74.

Feng, F., Zhong Zhong, Jingrong Liang, Ruozhu Li, Jiangzhong Ling and Juan He (2010) 'The Reorganisation of Zhonggu Sugar Has Been Completed', *Zhanjiang Evening News*, 16 September, available online at http://www.chinainsol.org/show.aspx?id=2053&cid=13 [accessed on 1 July 2010].

Gan, B. (2004) 'Guangxi Supreme People's Court Clarifies Thirteen Categories of Cases as Politically Sensitive', *China Youth Daily*, 24 August, available online at http://www.people.com.cn/BIG5/shehui/8217/34282/34284/2734628.html [accessed 20 July 2016].

Gewirtz, P. (2002) 'Independence and Accountability of Courts', *Global Law Review*, 1: 7–16.

Gödel, C., and Ong, L. H. (2012) *Social Unrest in China*, London: Europe China Research and Advice Network.

Halliday, T. C. (2007) 'Lawmaking and Institution Building in Asian Insolvency Reforms: Between Global Norms and National Circumstances', in OECD (ed.) *Asian Insolvency Systems: Closing the Implementation Gap*, Paris: OECD, 17–49.

Halliday, T. C., and Carruthers, B. G. (2007) 'Foiling the Financial Hegemons: Limits to the Globalisation of Corporate Insolvency Regimes in Indonesia, Korea and China', in C. Antons and V. Gessner (eds) *Globalisation and Resistance: Law Reform in Asia since the Crisis*, Oxford: Hart, 255–301.

Halliday, T. C., and Carruthers, B. G. (2009) *Bankrupt: Global Lawmaking and Systemic Financial Crisis*, Stanford, CA: Stanford University Press.

Han, C. (2002) 'Exceptions from *Pari Passu* for Public Policy', *China Legal Science*, 3: 26–40.

He, X. (2009) 'Enforcing Commercial Judgments in the Pearl River Delta of China', *American Journal of Comparative Law*, 57(2): 419–455.

Howson, N. C. (2010a) 'Corporate Law in the Shanghai People's Courts, 1992–2008: Judicial Autonomy in a Contemporary Authoritarian State', *East Asia Law Review*, 5: 303–442.

Howson, N. C. (2010b) 'Judicial Independence and the Company Law in the Shanghai Courts', in R. Peerenboom (ed.) *Judicial Independence in China: Lessons for Global Rule of Law Promotion*, Cambridge: Cambridge University Press, 134–153.

Huang, Y. (2008) *Capitalism with Chinese Characteristics: Entrepreneurship and the State*, Cambridge: Cambridge University Press.

Jinhua Co. Ltd. Liaoning (2010), *Annual Report 2009*, Huludao Liaoning China: Jinhua Co. Ltd.

Kang, Q., and Chen, H. (2009) 'Xingxing Was Bankrupt and Its Boss Absconded to the US', *Strait Urban News*, 7 January, available online at http://news.letfind.com.cn/news/2009-1/43821.html [accessed 28 August 2013].

Landry, P. F. (2008) *Decentralized Authoritarianism in China*, Cambridge: Cambridge University Press.

Li, G. (2012a) 'Assessment of Local Government's Maintaining Stability at the Initial Stage: A Case of T County', *Comparative Economics & Social Systems*, 1: 122–131.

Li, M. (2012b) 'China Securities Regulatory Commission's Gate Was Blocked by Guangxia Shareholders', 12 December, available online at http://t.hexun.com/wdqhgtq/12576158_d.html [accessed 26 December 2013].

Li, S. (2002) 'Problems of Enacting the New Enterprise Bankruptcy Law in China', *China Licensed Accountants*, 7: 55–58.

Li, S. (2005) 'Drafting of New Bankruptcy Law and Credit Culture and Credit System of China', *The Jurists*, 2: 12–17.

Li, S. (2006) 'Some Issues on New Bankruptcy Law', *China Law Express*, 6: 17–19.

Li, S. (2010) 'Establishing Two Government Agencies to Facilitate Corporate Bankruptcies', *National Think Tank*, 1: 30–34.

Li, S. (2012) 'Amendment of China's Corporate Reorganisation Regime', *Capital Markets*, 4: 28–29.

Lin, J. Y. (2010) 'The China Miracle Demystified', Presentation at The Econometric Society World Congress, Shanghai, China, 19 August.

Liu, M., and Chi, W. (2011) 'Confirmation of Corporate Reorganisation Plans', *Journal of Law Application*, 10: 81–89.

LoPucki, L. M., and Whitford, W. C. (1990) 'Bargaining over Equity's Share in the Bankruptcy Reorganisation of Large, Publicly Held Companies', *University of Pennsylvania Law Review*, 139: 125–196.

Lubman, S. (2000) 'Bird in a Cage: Chinese Law Reform after Twenty Years', *Northwestern Journal of International Law & Business*, 20: 383–424.

Lum, T. (2006) 'Social Unrest in China', Congressional Research Service Reports and Issue Briefs, available online at http://digitalcommons.ilr.cornell.edu/cgi/viewcontent.cgi?article=1018&context=crs [accessed 19 July 2016].

McNally, C. A. (2008) 'Introduction: The China Impact', in C. A. McNally (ed.) *China's Emergent Political Economy: Capitalism in the Dragon's Lair*, London: Routledge, 3–16.

Meng, A., and Zhai, K. (2013) 'Communist Party Pledges to Improve Judicial Independence, Transparency – to a Point', *South China Morning Post*, 15 November.

Minzner, C. F. (2009) 'Riots and Cover-ups: Counterproductive Control of Local Agents in China', *University of Pennsylvania Journal of International Law*, 31(1): 53–123.

Minzner, C. F. (2011) 'China's Turn against Law', *The American Journal of Comparative Law*, 59(4): 935–984.

Mokal, R. J. (2001) 'Priority as Pathology: The *Pari Passu* Myth', *Cambridge Law Journal*, 60(3): 579–619.

Naughton, B. (2007) *The Chinese Economy: Transitions and Growth*, Cambridge, MA: The MIT Press.

Naughton, B. (2010) 'China's Distinctive System: Can it Be a Model for Others?', *Journal of Contemporary China*, 19(65): 437–460.

Oi, J. (1995) 'The Role of the Local State in China's Transitional Economy', *The China Quarterly*, 144: 1132–1149.

Parry, R. (2009) 'Is UK Insolvency Law Failing Struggling Companies?', *Nottingham Law Journal*, 18(2): 42–52.

Peerenboom, R. (2002) *China's Long March toward Rule of Law*, Cambridge: Cambridge University Press.

Peerenboom, R. (2010) 'Judicial Independence in China: Common Myths and Unfounded Assumptions', in R. Peerenboom (ed.) *Judicial Independence in China: Lessons for Global Rule of Law Promotion*, Cambridge: Cambridge University Press, 69–94.

Peerenboom, R., and He, X. (2009) 'Dispute Resolution in China: Patterns, Causes and Prognosis', *East Asia Law Review*, 4(1): 1–61.

Phan, P. N. (2005) 'Clinical Legal Education in China: In Pursuit of a Culture of Law and a Mission of Social Justice', *Yale Human Rights & Development Law Journal*, 8: 117–152.

Pujiang Lower People's Court (2009) *Report on Handling* Tianting Reorganisation *Affairs*, Pujiang Zhejiang China: Pujiang LPC.

Qi, Z., and Liu, M. (1996) 'Employee Lending in Corporate Bankruptcy', *Journal of Central Leadership Institute of Politics and Law*, 6: 46–48.

Rapisardi, J. J., and Zhao, B. (2010) 'A Legal Analysis and Practical Application of the PRC Enterprise Bankruptcy Law', *Business Law International*, 11: 49–63.

Roe, M. J. (2003) *Political Determinants of Corporate Governance: Political Context, Corporate Impact*, Oxford: Oxford University Press.

Securities Daily (2008) 'Most Classes of Impaired Parties Votes for the Chuangzhou Chemical Co. Ltd. Reorganisation Plan', 2 January, available online at http://zqrb.ccstock.cn/html/2008-01/02/content_8177.htm [accessed 24 December 2013].

Shi, J. (2007) 'Twelve Years for One Sword: Does 2006 Bankruptcy Law Symbolize a Market Economy in China?', *West-Norton Journal of Bankruptcy Law and Practice*, 17: 745–777.

Song, X. (2006) 'The Court's Role in the Proceedings of Enterprise Bankruptcy and Restructuring and the Problems that Need to be Solved', Paper presented after the Fifth Forum for Asian Insolvency Reform (FAIR), Beijing, China, 27–28 April, available online at http://www.oecd.org/china/38184314.pdf [accessed 02 October 2012].

Sun, M. (2008) 'A Fresh Start of Qingtai Trust', *The 21st Economic News*, 2 August, available online at http://trust.jrj.com.cn/2008/08/000003894024.shtml [accessed 25 December 2013].

Supreme People's Court (2012) 'Issues of Handling Corporate Reorganisation of Publicly Traded Companies', 29 October, available online at http://www.csrc.gov.cn/pub/newsite/flb/flfg/sfjs_8249/201312/t20131205_239353.html [accessed 20 July 2016].

Tang, H., and Shi, Y. (2011) 'Private Company Reorganisation', *Journal of Rule of Law*, 12: 102–107.

Tang, W. (2005) 'Suggestions on the New Corporate Reorganisation Regime', *The Jurists*, 2: 33–37.

Tomasic, R. (1998) 'Insolvency Law Principles and the Draft Bankruptcy Law of the People's Republic of China', *Australian Journal of Corporate Law*, 9: 211–233.

Tomasic, R., and Wang, M. (2006) 'The Long March towards China's New Bankruptcy Law' in R. Tomasic (ed.) *Insolvency Law in East Asia*, Hampshire: Ashgate, 93–124.

Tomasic, R., and Zhang, Z. (2012) 'From Global Convergence in China's Enterprise Bankruptcy Law 2006 to Divergence in Implementation', *Journal of Corporate Law Studies*, 12(2): 295–332.

Tong, Y., and Lei, S. (2010) 'Large-scale Mass Incidents and Government Responses in China', *International Journal of China Studies*, 1(2): 487–508.

Tsinghua University (2010) 'Long-term Social Stability and Freedom of Expression', Tsinghua University Social Development Conference, Beijing, April.

Wang, L. (2002) 'Several Issues of Amending China's Bankruptcy Law', *China Legal Science*, 5: 78–93.
Wang, L. (2005a) 'Problems of Amending the Bankruptcy Law', *Legal Science*, 3: 3–15.
Wang, S. (2006) 'Examination of China's Corporate Reorganisation Regime', *Modern Law Science*, 28: 131–138.
Wang, S. (2007) 'Tests in Confirming Corporate Reorganisation Plans', *Journal of Business Economics*, 183: 57–63.
Wang, W. (1996) 'Corporate Reorganisation', *Chinese Journal of Law*, 18: 81–99.
Wang, X. (2005b) 'The New Bankruptcy Law', *Journal of Capital Normal University (Social Sciences Edition)*, 4: 34–41.
Wang, X. (2010) 'Bankruptcy Tests and Enforcement', *Tianjin Legal Science*, 1: 16–27.
Wang, X. (2012) 'Theories and Practices of Corporate Reorganisation', *Journal of Law Application*, 11: 10–19.
Wang, X., and Guo, D. (2010) 'Roles of Bankruptcy Administrators', *Politics and Law*, 9: 2–9.
Wang, X., and Yi, Z. (2009) 'Roles of the Bankruptcy Law in the Global Financial Crisis', *Chinese Lawyer*, 8: 20–23.
Woodward, W. J., Jr (2008) '"Control" in Reorganisation Law and Practice in China and the United States: An Essay on the Study of Contrast', *Temple International & Comparative Law Journal*, 22: 141–160.
Wu, Z. (2013) 'An Analysis of Employee Lending in Corporate Bankruptcy', *China Liquidation*, 27 January, available online at http://www.chinaqingsuan.com/news/detail/3634/page/3 [accessed 25 December 2013].
Xi, X. (2013) 'Problems of Handling Corporate Bankruptcy', *Journal of Law Application*, 2: 3–4.
Ying, Y., and Wu, Z. (2009) 'Hualun is Troubled with Back-street Loans and Jinding is Embroiled', *Shanghai Stock News*, 19 May, B3.
Yu, J. (2012) 'Maintaining Social Stability: Problems and Perspectives', *Exploration and Free Views*, 9: 3–6.
Yuan, G., Zhen, J., and Hu, Z. (1999) 'A Case Study of the Financing Propensity and Ability of China's Quoted Corporations', *Management World*, 3: 150–157.
Zhang, Z. (2013) 'Corporate Reorganisation under PRC Enterprise Bankruptcy Law 2006: The Relevance of Anglo-American Models for China', Unpublished thesis, Durham University.
Zhang, B., and Zhao, J. (2012) 'Difficulties of Reorganising Guangxia', *Caixing Net*, 20 February, available online at http://finance.qq.com/a/20120220/000260.htm [accessed 12 July 2013].
Zou, H. (2007) 'China's Corporate Rehabilitation System: Theories and Application', *Journal of China University of Political Science and Law*, 25: 48–62.
Zou, H. (2012) 'Uncertainties of Cram-downs', *Journal of Law Application*, 11: 24–29.

9 Clusters and links in Asian intellectual property law[1]

Peter K. Yu

Introduction

Three decades ago, the development of intellectual property laws in Asia did not garner much attention from policymakers, commentators and the media. If attention was paid, it was often devoted to the massive piracy and counterfeiting problems within the region. Be it China or South Korea or Thailand, Asian countries were criticised for being the hotbeds of intellectual property problems, with ramifications going beyond the continent. Even Japan was accused of imitation and piracy in the early days of its effort to climb up the technological ladder.

Today, however, growing attention has been paid to the progress that Asian countries have made in the intellectual property arena. In 2015, for instance, three countries in the region – Japan, China and South Korea – were among the top five countries filing patent applications through the Patent Cooperation Treaty (PCT) under the auspices of the World Intellectual Property Organization (WIPO) (WIPO, 2016b). Together, they made up for over 40 per cent of the total PCT applications filed. Out of the top ten corporate applicants, more than half of them (Huawei Technologies, ZTE Corporation, Samsung Electronics, Mitsubishi Electric, LG Electronics and Sony Corporation) were from the region. In that year, China and Japan also ranked seventh and eighth, respectively, in terms of international trademark applications filed under the Madrid system (WIPO, 2016a). In addition, India has been a key driver in the Asian economy, with growing technological proficiency and noticeable success in pharmaceuticals, software and information technology (IT) services.

These developments are interesting, because they resonate with the ongoing discussion about the rise of Asia. The last time policymakers, commentators and the media paid this much attention to Asia was more than two decades ago, amidst the rise of Japan and other newly industrialised economies. The recent developments are also interesting, because they show how China, India, South Korea and other Asian countries have greatly improved their competitiveness and technological capabilities. Although massive piracy and counterfeiting problems remain in the region, these countries have now played a much better intellectual property game. Some of them are even threatening to compete with the West on its home turf.

Given the growing interest in intellectual property developments in Asia, it is worthwhile to explore whether these developments are unique. More importantly for our purposes, how should we conduct research to answer this question? How can we develop a deeper understanding of these developments and put them in the right perspective? Do such developments reveal the wrongheadedness of those culture-based criticisms made by policymakers and commentators in the 1980s and the 1990s? Or do they actually prove their correctness in arguing for a greater use of external pressure to induce Asian countries to adopt higher intellectual property standards?

Although the scope and length of this chapter do not allow us to explore these questions in detail, it is important to keep in mind that intellectual property developments in Asia are dynamic, distinct and diverse. There are also significant complexities both within the region and within each individual country. To advance research and understanding in this area, this chapter underscores the insights provided by two pairs of analytical concepts. The first pair covers divergences and convergences. It aims to shed light on the similarities and differences in intellectual property regimes in Asia. It also explains why intellectual property laws have developed as they have.

The second pair concerns clusters and links. Instead of asking why similarities and differences exist, countries are clustered together to provide a more systematic and meaningful comparison. Through a discussion of links, this chapter also reminds us that clusters do not stand alone; rather, they interact with each other and with intellectual property regimes outside Asia.

Taken together, these two pairs of analytical concepts serve an additional goal. They reflect the duality – or the yin and yang – inherent in Asian societies, as well as the highly uneven development both within Asia and inside each Asian country. Although observers have been understandably uncomfortable with this duality, there is no easy way to discuss intellectual property developments in Asia without also mentioning their complexities.

Divergences

Although literature often lumps Asian countries together, these countries are more different than similar. As Simon Tay (2010: 19) declares: 'The region has no single, strong, and enduring history of unity and accepted commonality, whether in polity, culture, language, or religion.' Likewise, David Llewelyn (2010: xiv–xv) reminds us:

> The term 'Asia' was originally a Western concept to describe the eastern part of the land mass of Eurasia separated from Europe by the Ural Mountains – or, as the ancient Greeks would have said, 'everything east of Greece.' It incorporates a number of regions and peoples from vastly varied civilisations. It is likely that the peoples of ancient Asia themselves, such as the Chinese, Indians, Japanese, Persians and Arabs, did not conceive the idea of Asia because they did not view themselves collectively in the way Europeans did.

For analytical convenience, the UN Statistics Division (2013) divided Asia into five different macro sub-regions: Central Asia, Eastern Asia, Southern Asia, South-eastern Asia and Western Asia. These regions, some of which will be used throughout the chapter, cover many different countries, histories, languages, cultures, philosophies, religions, and political and economic systems. Even if we limit our focus to only Eastern, Southern and South-eastern Asia, sub-regions in Asia that have similarities and frequent interactions, it remains difficult to compare the developments in these different sub-regions, not to mention those in each individual country.

Historically, the colonisation efforts of European imperialist powers have deeply affected Asian countries. For example, the Opium War (1839–42) led to an influx of foreign ideas and institutions that shook the foundation of traditional Chinese culture.

The arrival of the British East India Company and its counterparts in continental Europe resulted in the transplant of laws, policies, practices and institutions that were different from those in other parts of Asia.

Moreover, not all Asian countries have been colonised nor were the former Asian colonies colonised to the same extent. For instance, India, Malaysia and Singapore were British colonies, and the Dutch East Indies and French Indochina belonged to the Netherlands and France, respectively. The Philippines was once a Spanish colony, but was later ceded to the United States. China was merely a semi-colony, with foreigners having control and special rights in different parts of the country. Meanwhile, Thailand remained an independent country throughout the colonisation era, acting only as a buffer state. In the early twentieth century, Korea and Taiwan became colonies of another Asian country, Japan. Thus, in Simon Tay's (1996: 747) view, any discussion of homogenous values in Asia 'underestimates . . . the historical ruptures of colonization'.

Culturally, countries in Asia have also been very different. Although commentators have widely noted how Confucianism has militated against intellectual property reforms in Asia (Alford, 1995: 19–29; Gadbaw, 1988: 275; Yu, 2001: 16–21), Confucianism forms the cultural basis of only a small number of countries in Eastern Asia. Islam, for example, is important to countries such as Indonesia, Malaysia and Pakistan. Hinduism is very important to South Asia, covering places such as Bangladesh, India and Nepal. Buddhism is also very important to countries in South-eastern Asia, such as Cambodia, Laos, Myanmar, Thailand and Sri Lanka. Indeed, as David Kang (2010: 52) observes, 'the states of Southeast Asia experienced twin cultural influences, from India and from China'. Meanwhile, George Coedès (1996) titled his book tracing India's influence on Southeast Asian culture *The Indianized States of Southeast Asia.*

Even in China, Confucianism is only one among the three dominant philosophies in traditional Chinese society. Buddhism and Daoism (which drew on the teachings of Laozi and Zhuangzi) had, and continue to have, a very significant influence (Yu, 2012a: 6). Also present in the Chinese territory are many minority cultures and beliefs, including the Zhuang, Hui, Uygur, Yi, Tibetan, Miao, Manchu, Mongol and Buyei (Wang, 1999: 176). Even if we focus on Confucian influences in Asia alone, countries embraced Confucianism for different reasons and to varying extents. As Professor Kang (2010: 26) observes:

> In Korea, Vietnam, and Japan, the debate about how to organize government and society occurred between warriors and scholars, with the Confucian literati winning in Korea and Vietnam and the warriors ultimately winning in Japan. Although Chinese ideas were deeply embedded from the founding of these states, just as significantly, Chinese ideas were grafted onto vibrant indigenous cultures, and the two coexisted – sometimes uncomfortably – resulting in only partial Sinicization.

Economically, the developments in Asia have been highly diverse and uneven (Assafa, 2010: 3; Beeson, 2009: 4; Ghai, 1995: 54–55). As shown in World Bank and WIPO data, the Global Competitiveness Index and the Global Innovation Index, considerable variations have existed in technological developments and innovation capabilities in Asian countries (Yu, 2006b: 364; Yu, 2014b: 92–95). Because economic development heavily influences the state of intellectual property protection and enforcement, the wide diversity of regional developments virtually guarantees the non-existence of any established consensus on intellectual property law and policy in Asia.

Finally, the geopolitical rivalries, tensions and conflicts within Asia have deeply complicated developments in the region, including developments in the areas of intellectual property and international trade. Lacking a regional hegemon, Asia is filled with developments spearheaded by three different leaders: China, India and Japan. If one includes the important role that the United States has played in the region, one will find the picture even more complicated. Certainly, similarities can be found between China and India, and between Japan and the United States, in light of their similar stages of development. Nevertheless, these similarities do not undercut the impact of geographical rivalries and the regional leaders' continued disagreement over how intellectual property standards are to be harmonised.

Thus, when all of these factors are taken into consideration, it is quite clear that developments in Asia have not been homogenous. In the intellectual property area, for instance, Professor Llewelyn (2010: 117) observes:

> Countries around Asia feature in every different category of [intellectual property] development: from the advanced relying on its own innovation and creativity (Japan), to those moving – at varying speeds – from imitator to innovator (China, India, Taiwan and South Korea); those aiming to use in the development of their own Invisible Gold the technology and know-how introduced by foreign investors (Singapore, Indonesia, Malaysia and Thailand); to the newly industrialising countries . . . still highly dependent on foreign technology and assistance (Vietnam, Cambodia and Laos).

Convergences

Notwithstanding the presence of diverse historical, cultural, economic and technological conditions in Asia, intellectual property laws and policies in the region share some common characteristics. These characteristics do not owe their origin to any distinct values, approaches or practices in Asia; rather, they were the result of three sets of converging forces.

The primary driver of convergence of intellectual property laws in Asia is the World Trade Organization (WTO), which was established in April 1994. Except for Bhutan, Iran and Timor-Leste, all countries in Eastern, Southern and South-eastern Asia (under UN classification) are members of this trading body. As a result, they abide by the Agreement on Trade-Related Aspects of Intellectual Property Rights (TRIPS). Indeed, countries such as China and Vietnam had to strengthen their intellectual property regimes and go through a strenuous accession process before they could finally join the WTO – in December 2001 and January 2007, respectively.

The WTO separates countries into four different groups: developed, developing, transition and least-developed. Although these distinctions were important in the first decade of the WTO, they have recently become less important, thanks to the expiration of the transition periods for developing and transition countries on 1 January 2000. Even Article 70, which allowed WTO members to delay the introduction of patent protection for pharmaceutical and agricultural chemical products, expired on 1 January 2005. Thus, except for those Asian countries that have been deemed least developed, which will be discussed further below, the same TRIPS standards apply to all Asian countries.

Using a one-size-fits-all – or, more precisely, super-size-fits-all – approach, Part II of TRIPS stipulates the high minimum standards of intellectual property protection in a wide variety of areas. These areas include copyrights, patents, trademarks, geographical indications, industrial designs, plant variety protection, integrated circuit topographies and protection of undisclosed information (such as trade secrets and clinical trial data). Part III further delineates the standards of intellectual property enforcement, including civil, administrative and criminal procedures and remedies, as well as border control measures.

In addition, Article 64 requires WTO members to settle all TRIPS-related disputes through the mandatory dispute settlement process. Since its inception, this process has been used by powerful developed countries as a major weapon to induce Asian trading partners to bring their laws into conformity with the high TRIPS standards (Yu, 2011a: 333–337). In the past two decades, the European Union and the United States have filed TRIPS complaints against Japan, Pakistan, India, Indonesia and China.

Thus far, the main differences between intellectual property regimes in Asia are not in the laws themselves, but in the area of enforcement. The problem of lax enforcement can be largely attributed to the weak intellectual property enforcement mechanisms built into TRIPS, which commentators have referred to as the Agreement's 'Achilles' heel' (Reichman and Lange, 1998; Yu, 2011d). During the TRIPS negotiations, developed and developing countries failed to agree to adopt high standards of intellectual property enforcement (Yu, 2011d: 483–504). As a result, what is on the books in Asia is not always the same as what is in action.

To complicate matters, the effective enforcement of intellectual property rights requires economic and human resources (Yu, 2010: 2–6). As I have noted elsewhere, such enforcement also relies on the existence of an 'enabling environment' that provides the preconditions needed for successful intellectual property law reforms (Yu, 2007a: 213–216). Among these preconditions are a consciousness of legal rights, a respect for the rule of law, an effective and independent judiciary, a well-functioning innovation and competition system, a sufficiently developed basic infrastructure, established business practices and a critical mass of local stakeholders. Given the varying 'levels of economic development and organization, political practices and structures of government' in Asia (Beeson, 2009: 4), it is understandable why the levels of intellectual property enforcement vary significantly across the region.

The second converging force concerns the external pressures that powerful trading partners outside the region exerted on Asian countries. Cases in point are those concerning the section 301 actions taken by the Office of the US Trade Representative and the suspension, or threats of suspension, of Generalised System or Scheme of Preferences (GSP) benefits by both the European Union and the United States. Given the considerable support of these governments, multinational intellectual property industries have also been very successful in pressuring Asian countries to strengthen intellectual property laws and institutions.

Consider, for example, the section 301 process, which has obtained notoriety in the region. This process requires the USTR to identify foreign countries that provide inadequate intellectual property protection to US intellectual property goods or those denying these goods fair or equitable market access. Although WTO members were prohibited from taking retaliatory measures before exhausting all actions permissible under WTO rules, the USTR has successfully used the section 301 process to induce its less powerful trading partners in Asia to transplant laws and institutions from the United States.

Thus far, the USTR has placed quite a number of Asian countries on the section 301 watch list or priority watch list. While China, India, Indonesia, Pakistan and Thailand are the perennial occupants of the priority watch list, Brunei Darussalam, Malaysia, the Philippines, South Korea, Taiwan and Vietnam have been placed on either the watch list or the priority watch list since 2001. South Korea and Taiwan got off the list in 2009, and Brunei Darussalam, Malaysia and the Philippines have since followed suit.

The section 301 process is particularly problematic for Asian countries, because the USTR can take actions even when these countries abide by WTO standards. The US Trade Act of 1974 specifically stipulates that actions can be taken 'notwithstanding the fact that [the country] may be in compliance with the specific obligations of [TRIPS]'. In the past decade, for instance, the USTR has taken into consideration a country's compliance with non-WTO treaties. As it noted in the *2005 National Trade Estimate Report on Foreign Trade Barriers*, 'the United States considers the WIPO treaties to reflect many key international norms for providing copyright protection over the Internet' (Office of the US Trade Representative, 2005: 96).

Unlike the first two converging forces, which are exogenous, the last one is endogenous. It is derived from the catch-up mentality found in most Asian leaders. Whether on their own, or through persuasion or education, these leaders increasingly see the establishment of a well-functioning intellectual property regime as an important tool for economic development, growth and integration. In their view, such a regime would help to create jobs, generate tax revenues, bring in foreign investment, facilitate transfer of technology and promote the development of indigenous industries (Yu, 2000: 193–194).

Following World War II and the subsequent decolonisation movement, many Asian countries were in search of economic models that would allow them to develop their comparative advantage and to catch up with their neighbours. Although many of these countries began as manufacturing centres, producing garments, toys, plastic products and light electronics, they quickly realised the need to foster strength and development in the high-tech area. Among those that successfully transformed their economies in this direction were Japan and the four newly industrialised economies (Hong Kong, Singapore, South Korea and Taiwan).

The late Chalmers Johnson (1982) and other commentators attributed such transformation to the 'Asian developmental state' model – a model of economic development driven by state-led macroeconomic reforms and policy interventions. Although this model has been widely touted as a formula for economic success for Japan and other newly industrialised economies, leading to the so-called East Asian miracle (Chang, 2006; World Bank, 1993), it has also been blamed for the Asian financial crisis in 1997 (Beeson, 2007: 141–142). From an intellectual property standpoint, however, the impact of the developmental state model is less certain. While this model, along with the Asian leaders' eagerness to catch up with the developed world, could help to accelerate intellectual property reforms, such a model could also stifle these reforms should the leaders consider stronger intellectual property protection to be a major impediment to their catch-up efforts (Yu, 2000: 189–190).

Regardless, Asian countries have continued to diversify and move into high-tech areas in the past decade, and their leaders have increasingly seen the importance and benefits of having a well-functioning intellectual property regime in place. In earlier works, I showed how countries have historically crossed over from a pirate nation to a nation respectful of intellectual property rights (Yu, 2009b: 10–15; Yu, 2012c: 529–543). Within Asia, such a crossover has already taken place in Japan, Singapore, South Korea and Taiwan. At the time of writing, large middle-income countries in Asia, such as China and India, are also poised to follow the lead of these once-developing economies. With more Asian countries seeing the benefit of stronger protection, intellectual property laws in the region are likely to converge even more in the future.

In sum, although vast historical, cultural, economic and technological differences exist in Asia, the establishment of the WTO and TRIPS, the increased external demands for higher standards and the gradual internal push for accelerated intellectual property reforms have resulted in greater convergence of intellectual property laws in Asia. As a result, intellectual property regimes in Asia have both similarities and differences.

Clusters

The paired concepts of divergences and convergences mentioned in the previous section have provided important insight into why differences and similarities exist in intellectual property regimes in Asia. This section now takes a different focus and separates these regimes into six crudely defined clusters. By bringing similarly situated regimes together, a cluster-based analysis will foster a more systematic and meaningful comparison.

Japan

Out of all Asian countries, Japan has the strongest and most sophisticated economy. In Mark Beeson's (2007: 106) view, this country is 'especially important as an exemplar of a highly successful *Asian* state'. Although China overtook Japan to become the world's second largest economy on an aggregate basis in 2010, Japan still dominates China dramatically on a per capita basis. With a gross domestic product (GDP) per capita of US$32,477.22 in 2015, Japan is one of the world's richest countries. By contrast, with a GDP per capita of only $7,924.65, China is still classified as a middle-income country – and, until recently, only a lower middle-income country. Indeed, China's GDP per capita remains lower than that of Malaysia, not to mention Japan, Singapore and South Korea.

In the area of intellectual property protection, Japan has improved considerably in the past two decades. In the early 1980s, Japan was widely criticised for its limited intellectual property protection, in part to explain away the United States' large trade deficit with the country (Ryan, 1995: 16–17; Watal, 2001: 24). By the time of the TRIPS negotiations, Japan slowly assumed the role of a key trilateral partner with the United States and the (then) European Community – thanks in no small part to the push by local and foreign intellectual property industries (Matthews, 2002; Sell, 2003: 96–120).

China and India: The Asian BRICs

Unlike Japan, China arrived much later in both the economic and intellectual property scenes. Acceding to the WTO in only December 2001, it is the new kid on the block. Nevertheless, China has successfully established itself as a dominant Asian economic power. Today, it is the world's largest exporter and second largest economy and trading nation (Bergsten et al., 2009: 9). It is also one of the world's largest recipients of foreign direct investment (FDI) with capital inflows of about US$50 billion, behind only the United States and the United Kingdom (Chow, 2007: 198). As Oded Shenkar (2005: 2–3) observes, Chinese factories now:

> make 70 percent of the world's toys, 60 percent of its bicycles, half its shoes, and one-third of its luggage. . . . [China also] builds half of the world's microwave ovens, one-third of its television sets and air conditioners, a quarter of its washers, and one-fifth of its refrigerators.

In the intellectual property area, China's developments have also been quite impressive, especially in major cities and coastal areas (Yu, 2006a: 975–999; Yu, 2007a: 185–188). Today, the country is among the top three in terms of patent applications filed through the PCT. In 2015, the number of PCT applications increased to 29,846, moving China to the third spot, behind only the United States and Japan (WIPO, 2016b). Among all of the corporate applicants, Huawei Technologies and ZTE Corporation had the first and third largest number of PCT applications, respectively.

Since 1994, the Chinese Patent Office, which later became the State Intellectual Property Office (SIPO), has been recognised as an international searching authority for PCT purposes. In Peter Drahos' (2010: 233) view, such recognition has made China 'a player in the top tier of patent offices that will dominate the emerging system of global patent administration'. It is therefore no surprise that, since 2007, SIPO has met with the European Patent Office, the Japanese Patent Office, the Korean Intellectual Property Office and the US Patent and Trademark Office to discuss measures to 'improve the efficiency of their examination systems and to harmonize their office systems' (Drahos, 2010: 236).

While piracy and counterfeiting problems remain, China has proactively shifted its economic focus from the imitation model to a new innovation model (Li, 2010; Yu, 2012c: 529–532). In June 2008, the State Council adopted the National Intellectual Property Strategy, which aimed to strengthen the country's indigenous innovative capacities. This strategy strongly indicates the Chinese leaders' growing understanding of the important role that intellectual property protection can play in driving a country's economy (Yu, 2011e: 1123).

Like China, India has had very impressive economic and technological developments. Thus far, it has yet to compete effectively against China, in part because of its poor infrastructure, bureaucratic red tape and failure to attract a substantial amount of FDI (BusinessWeek, 2006b: 49; BusinessWeek, 2006c: 27). However, India, which already has the world's second largest population, is catching up fast and possesses strengths that China may not have. These strengths include a younger workforce with a good command of English, higher population growth, superior capital efficiency, strong investment growth potential and a large amount of entrepreneurship (BusinessWeek, 2006b, 2006c). Some commentators have even predicted that India will overtake China economically in the second half of this century (BusinessWeek, 2006a: 14; BusinessWeek, 2006c).

Within the intellectual property area, India has also garnered significant attention. The strength of its software industry speaks for itself (Athreye, 2006). Its generic pharmaceutical industry, which features such companies as Ranbaxy and Dr. Reddy's Laboratories, is also considered one of the most important and sophisticated in the world (Chaudhuri, 2005: 180–221). Because India 'makes more than a fifth of the world's generic drugs' (Nath, 2008: 110) and 85 per cent of generic HIV/AIDS antiretrovirals in sub-Saharan Africa (Chien, 2007), commentators have noted the significant impact that a reduced supply of Indian generic drugs will have on the global access to essential medicines in the developing world (Shadlen, 2013: 36; Yu, 2008: 388–389).

In December 2007, India finally had its Patent Office designated as an international searching authority for PCT purposes. Since October 2013, the Indian Patent Office has begun operating as such an authority. In the future, India is likely to join China, Japan and South Korea as a world leader in PCT applications.

As if these accomplishments were not enough, India, along with Brazil, has for decades been the undisputed leader of the developing world in international intellectual property negotiations (Yu, 2008: 350–351). Before the arrival of TRIPS, India demanded the revision of both the Berne Convention for the Protection of Literary and Artistic Works and the Paris Convention for the Protection of Industrial Property, the two leading international intellectual property conventions (Yu, 2008: 351). The goodwill and leadership that it developed during this early period continue even today. Although it remains unclear whether 'India and Brazil are prepared to provide the general leadership on intellectual property issues that they once did' (Drahos, 2002: 765), India is likely to continue to feature prominently in regional and international intellectual property debates (Yu, 2008: 351).

In recent years, China and India have been discussed together in the context of high-growth middle-income countries. Jim O'Neill (2001, 2011: 69–79), Goldman Sachs's then-chief global economist, and his associates discussed them in the context of the 'BRIC countries' (Brazil, Russia, India and China) – and later 'growth markets'. The 'BRIC' terminology has since been generalised to cover other emerging middle-income countries such as South Africa (Yu, 2008: 346). Pete Engardio (2006), the former Asia correspondent for *BusinessWeek*, also coined the term 'Chindia' to denote the importance of China and India. In addition, Asian leaders, especially those in South-eastern Asia, increasingly linked the two countries together in their discussions of the region's future development. As Singapore's Senior Minister Goh Chok Tong (2005) declared:

> I like to think of new Asia as a mega jumbo jet that is being constructed. Northeast Asia, comprising China, Japan and South Korea, forms one wing with a powerful engine. India, the second wing, will also have a powerful engine. The southeast Asian countries form the fuselage. Even if we lack a powerful engine for growth among the 10 countries, we will be lifted by the two wings.

'Four little dragons'

Outside these three powerful Asian countries, Hong Kong, Singapore, South Korea and Taiwan are in a league of their own. Commentators have called these newly industrialised economies the 'four little dragons' or the 'four Asian tigers'.

Consider South Korea, for example. The country already has a highly successful home electronics industry that produces many innovative products. Today, South Korea has the fifth largest volume of patent applications through the PCT (WIPO, 2016b). Samsung and LG Electronics – both household names in the West – are among the top fifteen corporate applicants. Based on 2007 figures, Park Ji-hyun (2009: 275) found South Korea to have 'the highest number of resident patent applications filed per billion dollars of GDP and per million dollars of R&D [research and development] expenditures'.

Moreover, the Korean Intellectual Property Office (KIPO) has been very active in recent years. As one of the 'Asian trilaterals', the KIPO regularly engages in policy dialogues with its counterparts in China and Japan (Drahos, 2010: 233). In addition, the KIPO now 'has superhighway arrangements in place with the Japanese Patent Office . . . and the [US Patent and Trademark Office], and it is also moving into a superhighway arrangement with the Danish [Patent Office]' (Drahos, 2010: 239). Such arrangements streamline and accelerate the process for examining corresponding applications filed in participating patent offices.

In June 2007, South Korea signed a free trade agreement (FTA) with the United States, which came into effect three years later following the conclusion of several new agreements. Included in the US–Korea FTA is an extensive intellectual property chapter that seeks to align South Korea's intellectual property standards with those of the United States. The agreement also includes side confirmation letters, focusing on limitations on Internet service provider (ISP) liability and online piracy prevention.

Like South Korea, Singapore has entered into a FTA with the United States. More importantly, it is one of the first Asian countries to do so and its agreement precedes the US–Korea FTA by more than half a decade. Singapore's emphasis on the development of a knowledge-based economy is understandable. Being a small, but highly urbanised, city-state that focuses primarily on foreign investment, high-tech exports and a reliance on service industries (Beeson, 2007: 165; Llewelyn, 2010: 157; Ng-Loy, 2009: 235, 240), intellectual property rights have played a very important role in the country's economic development.

While Singapore has a high GDP per capita and very high levels of intellectual property protection and enforcement, it is also a founding member of the Association of Southeast Asian Nations (ASEAN), a regional group that includes some of the weakest economies in South-eastern Asia. If this city-state asserts greater leadership within the group, it is likely to play a very important role in the development of intellectual property law and policy in Asia.

Other middle intellectual property powers

In addition to Singapore, ASEAN also includes a number of middle-income countries that could have strong potential to shape intellectual property developments in Asia. In a study on what I coined the 'middle intellectual property powers', I analysed ten countries that are outside the Organisation for Economic Co-operation and Development (OECD) and which have a gross national income (GNI) per capita of less than US$15,000 and some of the world's highest volumes of high-tech exports (Yu, 2014b). Among those Asian countries included in this study were Indonesia, Thailand, Malaysia, the Philippines and Thailand (in addition to China and India). The study further noted that other highly populous Asian countries, such as Bangladesh, Pakistan and Vietnam, could make a strong case for inclusion in the group.

This study resonates with the studies conducted by Goldman Sachs analysts. Following their pioneering work on the 'BRIC countries', Jim O'Neill and his associates conducted a study in 2005 on the so-called N-11 ('Next Eleven') countries. This study sought to determine which countries are likely to follow the trajectory of the BRIC countries. Included in Asia were Bangladesh, Iran, Indonesia, Pakistan, the Philippines, South Korea and Vietnam (O'Neill et al., 2005: 7–8). According to the study, these large developing countries, like the BRIC countries, have the potential to pose considerable challenge to today's major developed economies.

Least-developed countries

Although ASEAN includes some important middle intellectual property powers, it also features three least-developed countries (LDCs). Indeed, its membership reflects the significant variations in economic and technological developments in Asia. As far as economic development is concerned, Cambodia, Laos and Myanmar, the three new ASEAN members, are considered LDCs, similarly to Afghanistan, Bangladesh, Bhutan, Nepal and Timor-Leste.

For the purposes of the WTO and TRIPS, LDCs are defined based on the criteria the UN General Assembly established in 1971. At the time of writing, the income threshold is US$1,035, based on a three-year average estimate of GNI per capita for the period 2011–13, using the World Bank Atlas method (UNOHRLLS, undated). Although only four countries (Botswana, Cape Verde, Maldives and Samoa) have ever graduated from this group, countries can do so by achieving a certain average GNI per capita. In the 2015 triennial review, for instance, the Committee for Development Policy of the UN Economic and Social Council recommended Angola for graduation after it had 'met the criteria for graduation for the second consecutive time' (UNOHRLLS, undated).

Under TRIPS, LDCs have the maximum amount of policy space in implementing intellectual property protection and enforcement standards. When the Agreement entered into force in 1995, it granted to LDCs a ten-year transition period. This period has since been extended to 1 January 2033, regardless of whether the extension-seeking country has already met or exceeded the TRIPS requirements.

The rest

The last group of countries includes the remaining countries in Asia. The intellectual property developments in these countries are likely to fall between the middle intellectual property powers and LDCs. This section does not analyse them in greater detail because these countries will neither receive the special and differential treatment of LDCs nor play as prominent a role in international intellectual property negotiations as the middle intellectual property powers.

Links

Although intellectual property regimes in Asia can be crudely classified into clusters, these clusters are not isolated from each other; rather, they remain deeply influenced by the interactions among themselves, as well as between these clusters and those intellectual property regimes outside Asia. The most important interactions, on which this section will focus, derive from two different types of trade agreement. The first type is bilateral and regional agreements, which are negotiated both within and outside the region; the second is plurilateral agreements, which are sometimes also called 'minilateral' or 'mega-regional' agreements. The negotiation of the latter usually includes both Asian and non-Asian countries.

Bilateral and regional agreements

Commentators have widely discussed the importance of bilateral and regional trade agreements, such as FTAs and economic partnership agreements (EPAs) for the European Union and FTAs for the United States. Examples of bilateral agreements involving Asian countries are the US–Singapore FTA, the US–Korea FTA and the EU–Korea FTA. Also under negotiation, or in the process of being signed, are those FTAs that the European Union seeks to establish with ASEAN, India, Indonesia, Malaysia, the Philippines, Singapore, Thailand and Vietnam.

Consider US FTAs, for instance. Since the early 2000s, the United States has used bilateral and regional trade agreements widely to transplant US intellectual property laws into the soil of its less powerful trading partners. As section 2102(a)(4) of the US Trade Act of 2002 explicitly states:

> . . . The principal negotiating objectives of the United States regarding trade-related intellectual property are—
>
> (A) to further promote adequate and effective protection of intellectual property rights, including through—
>
> (i) [. . .]
> (ii) ensuring that the provisions of any multilateral or bilateral trade agreement governing intellectual property rights that is entered into by the United States reflect a standard of protection similar to that found in United States law;
> [. . .]

Among the provisions included in the US FTAs were those calling for the extension of the copyright and patent terms, restrictions on the parallel importation of pharmaceuticals, the establishment of a data exclusivity regime to protect clinical trial data submitted during the regulatory approval process, the linkage of the registration of pharmaceutical products to their patent status and the requirement that patents be granted for 'new uses', or second indications, of known compounds (Yu, 2007b: 866–870).

From the standpoint of the United States' trading partners, however, the transplant of US intellectual property laws has been rather controversial and unpopular. Because these laws often provide protections in excess of the levels required under TRIPS and, to some extent, also the WIPO-administered intellectual property treaties (such as the WIPO Copyright Treaty and the WIPO Performances and Phonograms Treaty), the 'TRIPS-plus' intellectual property provisions in US FTAs threaten to ignore the trading partners' local needs, national interests, technological capabilities, institutional capacities and public health conditions.

Thus far, the European Union and the United States have been leaders in negotiating bilateral and regional trade agreements. Nevertheless, Asian countries such as China, India and Japan have followed suit (Matsushita, 2008; Urata, 2007; Wang, 2010; Yu, 2011b). The agreements negotiated by China and India are particularly important. Initiated by countries having very different levels of development, these agreements may have terms that are very different from those found in agreements negotiated by the European Union and the United States (Yu, 2011b: 986–1002).

Since the mid-2000s, China has negotiated FTAs with Chile, Pakistan, New Zealand, Singapore, Peru, Costa Rica, Iceland, Switzerland, South Korea and Australia (Gao, 2008; Lanteigne, 2010; Wang, 2010; Yu, 2011b). With the ten ASEAN members, China also established a set of regional agreements culminating in the formation of the ASEAN–China Free Trade Area (Wang, 2009; Yu, 2011b: 1007–1009). These agreements not only include an 'early harvest programme', which provides for the early opening of the Chinese market for specific goods and services (Yu, 2011b: 996–997), but also feature memoranda of understanding on cooperation in the fields of intellectual property and of standards, technical regulations and conformity assessment.

Similarly, India has been actively establishing bilateral and regional agreements with its trading partners, including Bhutan, Sri Lanka and ASEAN members (Hsu, 2010: 266–268; Wang, 2010: 356–358). India is also currently negotiating an EPA with the European Union, a trading bloc with comparable size and strength to the United States. As if these negotiations were not enough, India was instrumental in the development of the India–Brazil–South Africa (IBSA) Dialogue Forum, which features trilateral cooperation among Brazil, India and South Africa. India is also one of the five key participants of the BRICS Summit, along with Brazil, China, Russia and South Africa.

Although the bilateral and regional trade agreements negotiated by China – and likely India – have not yet included many intellectual property provisions, the picture has been slowly changing. A case in point is the China–Switzerland FTA, which has a far longer and more detailed intellectual property chapter than any other FTA China has signed. Included are provisions on copyright and related rights, trademarks, patents, genetic resources and traditional knowledge, plant variety protection, undisclosed information, industrial designs and geographical indications. Although most of the provisions correspond to the protection levels already required under TRIPS, this chapter includes detailed provisions on the disclosure of origin or source of genetic resources – provisions not found in TRIPS (Yu, 2015). The China–Switzerland FTA also offers language concerning the efforts needed to establish a mutually supportive relationship between TRIPS and the Convention on Biological Diversity.

In addition to China and India, ASEAN members have also been active in developing common positions in the intellectual property area. One such effort is the 1995 ASEAN Framework Agreement on Intellectual Property Cooperation (Weerawit, 2003). Developed out of efforts to strengthen protection for sound recordings, this agreement aims to 'promote cooperation in the field of intellectual property among government agencies as well as among the private sectors and professional bodies of ASEAN'. It calls on the participating members to explore the possibility of setting up regional patent and trademark systems within ASEAN. It also facilitates 'consultations on the development of their intellectual property regimes with a view to creating ASEAN standards and practices which are consistent with international standards'.

Plurilateral agreements

While countries both within and outside Asia are busy negotiating bilateral and regional trade agreements, the United States – and, to a lesser extent, the European Union – introduced a new form of norm-setting activity. Based on what other commentators and I have described as the 'country club' approach to international norm-setting (Gervais, 2012; Yu, 2014a), these countries teamed up with likeminded countries in both the developed and developing worlds to increase obligations concerning the protection and enforcement of intellectual property rights.

A leading example is the Anti-Counterfeiting Trade Agreement (ACTA), which was negotiated by Australia, Canada, the European Union, Japan, Morocco, Mexico, New Zealand, Singapore, South Korea, Switzerland and the United States. This agreement aimed to set a new and higher benchmark for international intellectual property protection and enforcement among likeminded countries (Yu, 2011c: 980–983). More importantly for our discussion, this agreement originated from a proposal from Japan, advanced by Prime Minister Junichiro Koizumi at the June 2005 G-8 meeting in Gleneagles, Scotland (Yu, 2011c: 980–983).

After three years and eleven rounds of formal negotiations, this highly controversial plurilateral agreement was finally adopted on 15 April 2011. Out of the eleven negotiating parties, all but Switzerland and five members of the European Union (Cyprus, Estonia, Germany, the Netherlands and Slovakia) have since signed the agreement. Thus far, Japan is the only country to have ratified this agreement. Because Article 40.1 states that ACTA will not enter into force until six parties have deposited their instruments of ratification, it remains unclear if and when this agreement will enter into force.

While the United States was busy negotiating ACTA, it also began the negotiation of another equally controversial plurilateral agreement known as the Trans-Pacific Partnership (TPP) Agreement. This agreement began as a quadrilateral agreement called the Trans-Pacific Strategic Economic Partnership Agreement, more commonly known as the 'P4' or 'Pacific 4'. As Meredith Lewis (2009: 403–404) recounts:

> [The negotiations were initially] launched by Chile, New Zealand and Singapore at the APEC [Asia-Pacific Economic Cooperation] leaders' summit in 2002. These original negotiations contemplated an agreement amongst the three participating countries, to be known as the Pacific Three Closer Economic Partnership . . . However, Brunei attended a number of rounds as an observer, and ultimately joined the Agreement as a 'founding member'. The Agreement was signed by New Zealand, Chile and Singapore on July 18, 2005 and by Brunei on August 2, 2005, following the conclusion of negotiations in June 2005.

In March 2010, shortly before the eighth round of the ACTA negotiations in Wellington, New Zealand, negotiations began among Australia, Peru, Vietnam, the United States and the P4 members for an expanded agreement. Since then, Malaysia, Mexico, Canada and Japan have joined the negotiations.

After nearly six years of formal negotiations, the TPP Agreement was finally signed in Auckland, New Zealand, on 4 February 2016. The final Agreement contains thirty chapters, including an intellectual property chapter. Similar to those found in existing US FTAs, the TPP intellectual property chapter covers a wide variety of areas, including cooperation, trademarks, country names, geographical indications, patents and undisclosed test data, industrial designs, copyright and related rights, enforcement and ISPs.

Interestingly, the TPP is not the only plurilateral agreement involving Asian countries. Like the European Union and the United States, these countries have embraced the new 'country club' approach to international norm-setting. In November 2012, ASEAN and its neighbours launched the negotiation of the Regional Comprehensive Economic Partnership (RCEP). Building on past trade and non-trade discussions under the ASEAN+6 framework (ASEAN, Australia, China, India, Japan, New Zealand and South Korea), this partnership covers not only the two most economically powerful BRIC countries (China and India), but also two other major Asian economies (Japan and South Korea), as well as seven of the TPP partners (Australia, Brunei Darussalam, Japan, Malaysia, New Zealand, Singapore and Vietnam).

At the time of writing, thirteen rounds of the RCEP negotiations have already been held. Although it remains to be seen what standards this partnership will eventually include, the final RCEP Agreement, like the TPP Agreement, is likely to contain an intellectual property chapter. Nonetheless, the standards included in this chapter may be somewhat different, considering that both China and India have been left out of the TPP negotiations (Yu, 2014c: 1132–1163). Also excluded were other major Asian countries, such as Indonesia, the Philippines, South Korea and Thailand.

Once the RCEP Agreement is completed, it will be worth exploring whether the Agreement's terms will conflict with those of the TPP Agreement. If the terms are indeed conflicting, they will lead to inconsistencies, tensions or even conflicts over trade and regulatory standards, thereby precipitating what I have described as the 'battle of the

FTAs' (Yu, 2011b: 1018–1027). If the terms are complementary, however, they may pave the way for the much-discussed Free Trade Area of the Asia-Pacific, which is being developed under the auspices of the APEC Forum (Morrison and Pedrosa, 2007).

It is also worth recalling that the RCEP negotiations have involved more than half of the TPP partners (Australia, Brunei Darussalam, Japan, Malaysia, New Zealand, Singapore and Vietnam). Because many of these countries are unlikely to have the ability, resources and sustained interest in actively developing two rather similar trade pacts in the same region, at some point they will have to decide whether they want to focus on one or the other (Lewis, 2012: 231; Lewis, 2013: 369–370). It is therefore no surprise that '[a]n analyst with the Asian Development Bank has predicted that ASEAN+6 and the TPP will ultimately merge together' (Lewis, 2012: 235).

Conclusion

The intellectual property developments in Asia are dynamic, distinct and diverse. These developments have also been highly uneven, not to mention rapidly changing. Because what we see today consists mostly of works in progress, it would be difficult to use the same methodologies and approaches to analyse these developments. It would also be misguided, if not foolhardy, to treat these developments as if they originate from a homogenous region (Beeson, 2007: 116).

To complicate the analysis even further, the internal developments within each individual country, especially large developing countries such as China, India and Indonesia, have been pluralistic and at times contradictory. As I have noted elsewhere, the economic and technological developments in the major cities in China, such as Beijing, Shanghai and Guangzhou, and the coastal regions far exceed those in the inner and rural areas (Yu, 2007a: 203). Likewise, Fareed Zakaria (2008: 133) observes that 'India might have several Silicon Valleys, but it also has three Nigerias within it – that is, more than 300 million people living on less than a dollar a day'.

To address these complexities and complications, and to enhance our understanding of the multifaceted intellectual property developments in Asia, this chapter introduces two pairs of analytical concepts. The first pair, divergences and convergences, reminds us of the diverging historical, cultural, economic and technological conditions in Asia. It also highlights the external pressure and the internal push that eventually result in greater convergence of intellectual property laws in the region.

The second pair, clusters and links, enables us to systematically compare the different intellectual property regimes in Asia. Instead of asking why these systems are similar or different, a cluster-based analysis helps us to separate similarly situated regimes into more manageable groups. The concept of links also helps us to develop a better appreciation of the interactions among these clusters, as well as between these clusters and intellectual property regimes outside Asia.

In the future, Asian countries are likely to play a bigger and more active role in international intellectual property negotiations. Among the ongoing issues that are likely to be on the Asian intellectual property policy agenda are the enforcement of intellectual property rights, the protection of genetic resources, traditional knowledge and traditional cultural expressions, the protection of geographical indications, access to essential medicines, and standards concerning the Internet and new communications technologies (Yu, 2012b: 379–388). In addition, Asian countries are likely to play very important roles in shaping new or emerging norms concerning global climate change, the promotion of alternative innovation models (including utility models), the special and differential treatment for developing countries, solutions to address uneven economic and technological developments, and abuse of rights and restraints on trade (Yu, 2012b: 388–397).

To a large extent, it will be interesting to see whether Asian countries can work together with each other to shape global intellectual property norms. If they managed to create an Asia-based alliance, that alliance could provide in the intellectual property field what Simon Tay (2010: 150–158) described as the 'Asia's normative community'. The development of such a community is important, because a coherent normative or common policy agenda will help the community to achieve a more powerful voice, greater political leverage and more desirable bargaining outcomes (Yu, 2008: 370; Yu, 2009a). The shared regional norms will also help to bind the members together, notwithstanding the divergences and clustering discussed in this chapter.

It remains to be seen whether Asian countries, especially China and India, will want the same global intellectual property system enshrined in TRIPS and the WIPO treaties once they become economically and technologically developed. As I suggested in the inaugural issue of the *WIPO Journal*, '[t]here is a good chance that they may want or need something rather different' (Yu, 2009b: 15). Regardless of how international intellectual property negotiations will play out in the future, there is no denying that intellectual property developments in Asia will deserve more policy and scholarly attention. Hopefully, the analytical tools provided in this chapter will not only deepen our understanding of these complex developments, but also make research in this challenging area more systematic and manageable.

Note

1 This chapter draws on research from the author's earlier articles in the *Drake Law Review Discourse*, the *Fordham International Law Journal*, the *Marquette Intellectual Property Law Review* and a book chapter published by Cambridge University Press. The author is grateful to Brooke Yang for excellent research and editorial assistance.

References

Alford, W. P. (1995) *To Steal a Book Is an Elegant Offense: Intellectual Property Law in Chinese Civilization*, Stanford, CA: Stanford University Press.

Assafa, E. (2010) *Intellectual Property in Asian Emerging Economies*, Burlington, VT: Ashgate.

Athreye, S. S. (2006) 'The Indian Software Industry', in A. Arora and A. Gambardella (eds) *From Underdogs to Tigers: The Rise and Growth of the Software Industry in Brazil, China, India, Ireland, and Israel*, Oxford: Oxford University Press, 7–40.

Beeson, M. (2007) *Regionalism and Globalization in East Asia: Politics, Security and Economic Development*, New York: Palgrave Macmillan.

Beeson, M. (2009) *Institutions of the Asia-Pacific: ASEAN, APEC and Beyond*, London: Routledge.

Bergsten, C. F., Freeman, C., Lardy, N. R., and Mitchell, D. J. (2009) *China's Rise: Challenges and Opportunities*, Washington, DC: Peterson Institute for International Economics.

BusinessWeek (2006a) 'The Rise of Chindia', in P. Engardio (ed.) *CHINDIA: How China and India Are Revolutionizing Global Business*, New York: McGraw-Hill, 13–34.

BusinessWeek (2006b) 'The Rise of India', in P. Engardio (ed.) *CHINDIA: How China and India Are Revolutionizing Global Business*, New York: McGraw-Hill, 45–55.

BusinessWeek (2006c) 'Why India May Be Destined to Overtake China', in P. Engardio (ed.) *CHINDIA: How China and India Are Revolutionizing Global Business*, New York: McGraw-Hill, 27–31.

Chang, H.-J. (2006) *The East Asian Development Experience: The Miracle, the Crisis and the Future*, London: Zed Books.

Chaudhuri, S. (2005) *The WTO and India's Pharmaceuticals Industry: Patent Protection, TRIPS, and Developing Countries*, New Delhi: Oxford University Press.

Chien, C. (2007) 'HIV/AIDS Drugs for Sub-Saharan Africa: How Do Brand and Generic Supply Compare?', *PLOS ONE*, 2: e278.

Chow, D. (2007) 'The Role of Intellectual Property in Promoting International Trade and Foreign Direct Investment', in P. K. Yu (ed.) *Intellectual Property and Information Wealth: Issues and Practices in the Digital Age, Vol. 4*, Westport, CT: Praeger, 187–200.

Coedès, G. (1996) *The Indianized States of Southeast Asia*, ed. W. F. Vella, trans. S. Brown Cowing, Honolulu: East-West Center Press.

Drahos, P. (2002) 'Developing Countries and International Intellectual Property Standard-Setting', *Journal of World Intellectual Property*, 5(5): 765–789.

Drahos, P. (2010) *The Global Governance of Knowledge: Patent Offices and Their Clients*, Cambridge: Cambridge University Press.

Engardio, P. (2006) 'Introduction', in P. Engardio (ed.) *CHINDIA: How China and India Are Revolutionizing Global Business*, New York: McGraw-Hill, 1–12.

Gadbaw, R. M. (1988) 'Republic of Korea', in R. M. Gadbaw and T. J. Richards (eds) *Intellectual Property Rights: Global Consensus, Global Conflict?* Boulder, CO: Westview Press, 272–310.

Gao, H. (2008) 'The RTA Strategy of China: A Critical Visit', in R. Buckley, V. Io Lo and L. Boulle (eds) *Challenges to Multilateral Trade: The Impact of Bilateral, Preferential and Regional Agreements*, Alphen aan den Rijn: Kluwer Law International, 53–64.

Gervais, D. (2012) 'Country Clubs, Empiricism, Blogs and Innovation: The Future of International Intellectual Property Norm Making in the Wake of ACTA', in M. Burri and T. Cottier (eds) *Trade Governance in the Digital Age*, Cambridge: Cambridge University Press, 323–343.

Ghai, Y. (1995) 'Asian Perspectives on Human Rights', in J. T. H. Tang (ed.) *Human Rights and International Relations in the Asia-Pacific Region*, London: Pinter, 54–67.

Goh, C. T. (2005) Keynote Address by Senior Minister GOH Chok Tong of the Republic of Singapore at the Singapore Conference, London, 15 March, available online at http://www.mfa.gov.sg/content/mfa/overseasmission/pretoria/press_statements_speeches/2005/200503/press_200503_01.html [accessed 1 August 2016].

Hsu, L. (2010) 'China, India and Dispute Settlement in the WTO and RTAs', in M. Sornarajah and J. Wang (eds) *China, India and the International Economic Order*, Cambridge: Cambridge University Press, 250–276.

Johnson, C. (1982) *MITI and the Japanese Miracle: The Growth of Industrial Policy, 1925–1975*, Stanford, CA: Stanford University Press.

Kang, D. C. (2010) *East Asia before the West: Five Centuries of Trade and Tribute*, New York: Columbia University Press.

Lanteigne, M. (2010) 'Northern Exposure: Cross-regionalism and the China–Iceland Preferential Trade Negotiations', *China Quarterly*, 202: 362–380.

Lewis, M. K. (2009) 'Expanding the P-4 Trade Agreement into a Broader Trans-Pacific Partnership: Implications, Risks and Opportunities', *Asian Journal of the WTO and International Health Law and Policy*, 4(2): 401–422.

Lewis, M. K. (2012) 'Achieving a Free Trade Area of the Asia-Pacific: Does the TPP Present the Most Attractive Path?', in C. L. Lim, D. K. Elms and P. Low (eds) *The Trans-Pacific Partnership: A Quest for a Twenty-first Century Trade Agreement*, Cambridge: Cambridge University Press, 223–241.

Lewis, M. K. (2013) 'The TPP and the RCEP (ASEAN+6) as Potential Paths toward Deeper Asian Economic Integration', *Asian Journal of WTO and International Health Law & Policy*, 8(2): 359–378.

Li, Y. (2010) *Imitation to Innovation in China: The Role of Patents in Biotechnology and Pharmaceutical Industries*, Cheltenham: Edward Elgar.

Llewelyn, D. (2010) *Invisible Gold in Asia: Creating Wealth through Intellectual Property*, Singapore: Marshall Cavendish Business.

Matsushita, M. (2008) 'Japanese Policies toward East Asian Free Trade Agreements: Policy and Legal Perspectives', in R. Buckley, V. Io Lo and L. Boulle (eds) *Challenges to Multilateral Trade: The Impact of Bilateral, Preferential and Regional Agreements*, Alphen aan den Rijn: Kluwer Law International, 41–51.

Matthews, D. (2002) *Globalising Intellectual Property Rights: The TRIPS Agreement*, London: Routledge.

Morrison, C. E., and Pedrosa, E. (eds) (2007) *An APEC Trade Agenda? The Political Economy of a Free Trade Area of the Asia-Pacific*, Singapore: Institute of Southeast Asian Studies.

Nath, K. (2008) *India's Century*, New York: McGraw-Hill.

Ng-Loy, W. L. (2009) 'Singapore', in P. Goldstein and J. Straus (eds) *Intellectual Property in Asia: Law, Economics, History and Politics*, Berlin: Springer, 233–257.

Office of the US Trade Representative (2005) *2005 National Trade Estimate Report on Foreign Trade Barriers*, Washington, DC: Office of the US Trade Representative.

O'Neill, J. (2001) 'Building Better Global Economic BRICs', Goldman Sachs Global Economics Paper No. 66, available online at http://www.goldmansachs.com/our-thinking/archive/archive-pdfs/build-better-brics.pdf [accessed 1 August 2016].

O'Neill, J. (2011) *The Growth Map: Economic Opportunity in the BRICs and Beyond*, New York: Portfolio.

O'Neill, J., Wilson, D., Purushothaman, R., and Stupnytska, A. (2005) 'How Solid Are the BRICs?', Goldman Sachs Global Economics Paper No. 134, available online at http://www.goldmansachs.com/our-thinking/archive/archive-pdfs/how-solid.pdf [accessed 1 August 2016].

Park, J.-H. (2009) 'South Korea', in P. Goldstein and J. Straus (eds) *Intellectual Property in Asia: Law, Economics, History and Politics*, Berlin: Springer, 259–280.

Reichman, J. H., and Lange, D. (1998) 'Bargaining around the TRIPS Agreement: The Case for Ongoing Public–Private Initiatives to Facilitate Worldwide Intellectual Property Transactions', *Duke Journal of Comparative and International Law*, 9(1): 11–68.

Ryan, M. P. (1995) *Playing by the Rules: American Trade Power and Diplomacy in the Pacific*, Washington, DC: Georgetown University Press.

Sell, S. K. (2003) *Private Power, Public Law*, Cambridge: Cambridge University Press.

Shadlen, K. C. (2013) 'Is AIDS Treatment Sustainable?', in O. Aginam, J. Harrington and P. K. Yu (eds) *The Global Governance of HIV/AIDS: Intellectual Property and Access to Essential Medicines*, Cheltenham: Edward Elgar, 29–56.

Shenkar, O. (2005) *The Chinese Century: The Rising Chinese Economy and Its Impact on the Global Economy, the Balance of Power, and Your Job*, Upper Saddle River, NJ: Wharton School.

Tay, S. S. C. (1996) 'Human Rights, Culture, and the Singapore Example', *McGill Law Journal*, 41(4): 743–780.

Tay, S. S. C. (2010) *Asia Alone: The Dangerous Post-crisis Divide from America*, Singapore: Wiley.

UN Office of the High Representative for the Least Developed Countries, Landlocked Developing Countries and Small Island Developing States (UNOHRLLS) (undated) 'Criteria for Identification and Graduation of LDCs', available online at http://unohrlls.org/about-ldcs/criteria-for-ldcs/ [accessed 1 August 2016].

UN Statistics Division (2013) 'Composition of Macro Geographical (Continental) Regions, Geographical Sub-Regions, and Selected Economic and Other Groupings', available online at http://unstats.un.org/unsd/methods/m49/m49regin.htm [accessed 1 August 2016].

Urata, S. (2007) 'Japan's FTA Strategy and Free Trade Area of Asia-Pacific', in C. E. Morrison and E. Pedrosa (eds) *An APEC Trade Agenda? The Political Economy of a Free Trade Area of the Asia-Pacific*, Singapore: Institute of Southeast Asian Studies, 99–126.

Wang, J. C. F. (1999) *Contemporary Chinese Politics: An Introduction*, 6th edn, Englewood Cliffs, NJ: Prentice-Hall.

Wang, J. (2009) 'Association of Southeast Asian Nations–China Free Trade Agreement', in S. Lester and B. Mercurio (eds) *Bilateral and Regional Trade Agreements: Case Studies*, Cambridge: Cambridge University Press, 192–225.

Wang, J. (2010) 'The Role of China and India in Asian Regionalism', in M. Sornarajah and J. Wang (eds) *China, India and the International Economic Order*, Cambridge: Cambridge University Press, 333–386.

Watal, J. (2001) *Intellectual Property Rights in the WTO and Developing Countries*, The Hague: Kluwer Law International.

Weerawit, W. (2003) 'The Harmonisation of Intellectual Property Rights in ASEAN', in C. Heath (ed.) *Intellectual Property Law in Asia*, London: Kluwer Law International, 247–266.

World Bank (1993) *The East Asian Miracle: Economic Growth and Public Policy*, Oxford: Oxford University Press.

World Intellectual Property Organization (WIPO) (2016a) 'Who Filed the Most Madrid Trademark Applications in 2015?', available online at http://www.wipo.int/export/sites/www/ipstats/en/docs/infographics_madrid_2015.pdf [accessed 1 August 2016].

World Intellectual Property Organization (WIPO) (2016b) 'Who Filed the Most PCT Patent Applications in 2015?', available online at http://www.wipo.int/export/sites/www/ipstats/en/docs/infographics_pct_2015.pdf [accessed 1 August 2016].

Yu, P. K. (2000) 'From Pirates to Partners: Protecting Intellectual Property in China in the Twenty-first Century', *American University Law Review*, 50(1): 131–243.

Yu, P. K. (2001) 'Piracy, Prejudice, and Perspectives: An Attempt to Use Shakespeare to Reconfigure the U.S.–China Intellectual Property Debate', *Boston University International Law Journal*, 19(1): 1–87.

Yu, P. K. (2006a) 'From Pirates to Partners (Episode II): Protecting Intellectual Property in Post-WTO China', *American University Law Review*, 55(4): 901–1000.

Yu, P. K. (2006b) 'TRIPS and Its Discontents', *Marquette Intellectual Property Law Review*, 10(2): 369–410.

Yu, P. K. (2007a) 'Intellectual Property, Economic Development, and the China Puzzle', in D. J. Gervais (ed.) *Intellectual Property, Trade and Development: Strategies to Optimize Economic Development in a TRIPS Plus Era*, Oxford: Oxford University Press, 173–220.

Yu, P. K. (2007b) 'The International Enclosure Movement', *Indiana Law Journal*, 82(4): 827–907.

Yu, P. K. (2008) 'Access to Medicines, BRICS Alliances, and Collective Action', *American Journal of Law and Medicine*, 34(2): 345–394.

Yu, P. K. (2009a) 'Building Intellectual Property Coalitions for Development', in J. de Beer (ed.) *Implementing the World Intellectual Property Organization's Development Agenda*, Waterloo, ON: Wilfred Laurier University Press, 79–99.

Yu, P. K. (2009b) 'The Global Intellectual Property Order and Its Undetermined Future', *WIPO Journal*, 1(1): 1–15.

Yu, P. K. (2010) 'Enforcement, Economics and Estimates', *WIPO Journal*, 2(1): 1–19.

Yu, P. K. (2011a) 'Are Developing Countries Playing a Better TRIPS Game?', *UCLA Journal of International Law and Foreign Affairs*, 16(2): 311–342.

Yu, P. K. (2011b) 'Sinic Trade Agreements', *U.C. Davis Law Review*, 44(3): 953–1028.

Yu, P. K. (2011c) 'Six Secret (and Now Open) Fears of ACTA', *SMU Law Review*, 64(3): 975–1094.

Yu, P. K. (2011d) 'TRIPS and Its Achilles' Heel', *Journal of Intellectual Property Law*, 18(2): 479–531.

Yu, P. K. (2011e) 'The TRIPS Enforcement Dispute', *Nebraska Law Review*, 89(4): 1046–1131.

Yu, P. K. (2012a) 'The Confucian Challenge to Intellectual Property Reforms', *WIPO Journal*, 4(1): 1–9.

Yu, P. K. (2012b) 'Intellectual Property and Asian Values', *Marquette Intellectual Property Law Review*, 16(2): 329–399.

Yu, P. K. (2012c) 'The Rise and Decline of the Intellectual Property Powers', *Campbell Law Review*, 34(3): 525–578.

Yu, P. K. (2014a) 'The ACTA/TPP Country Clubs', in D. Beldiman (ed.) *Access to Information and Knowledge: 21st Century Challenges in Intellectual Property and Knowledge Governance*, Cheltenham: Edward Elgar, 258–283.

Yu, P. K. (2014b) 'The Middle Intellectual Property Powers', in R. Peerenboom and T. Ginsburg (eds) *Law and Development in Middle-income Countries: Avoiding the Middle-income Trap*, Cambridge: Cambridge University Press, 84–107.

Yu, P. K. (2014c) 'TPP and Trans-Pacific Perplexities', *Fordham International Law Journal*, 37(4): 1129–1181.

Yu, P. K. (2015) 'Sinic Trade Agreements and China's Global Intellectual Property Strategy', in C. Antons and R. M. Hilty (eds) *Intellectual Property and Free Trade Agreements in the Asia-Pacific Region*, Heidelberg: Springer, 247–283.

Zakaria, F. (2008) *The Post-American World*, New York: W.W. Norton.

10 Innovation governance competition

Comparing India's and China's electronic commerce development strategies

Jane K. Winn

Introduction

After India experienced a broad economic revival in the 2000s, it became fashionable for globalisation pundits to use China and India as case studies to compare the relative merits of their competing economic development models (Eichengreen, Gupta and Kumar, 2010). This chapter continues that debate by comparing Chinese and Indian strategies for using electronic commerce (e-commerce) as an economic development strategy, with particular reference to the promotion of electronic payment systems. Decades of rapid innovation in payments technology, combined with increased recognition of the role of financial inclusion and transaction costs in development theory, have brought the operation of national payment systems from the margins to the core of national economic development strategies in countries such as China and India.

Payment systems were once a sleepy backwater not only of development strategies but even within the business of banking and the regulation of financial markets. In modern market economies, a banking licence issued by a national bank regulator normally covers two primary lines of business: financial intermediation between savers and borrowers, and payment services. Most of the revenue and most of the risk associated with running a bank traditionally arose out of the lending branch of banking business. By contrast, payment services were often perceived by bank management as little more than a necessary cost of doing business rather than a strategically important undertaking. As banks have found themselves increasingly disintermediated from their core lending and savings markets by more nimble competitors, however, revenues from payment services have become a lifeline that bank management can no longer afford to take for granted.

Many different countries around the world are witnessing a tidal wave of technological and business process innovations in payment systems, which in turn pose major challenges for national regulators charged with maintaining the safety and soundness of banking systems and protecting consumers. In advanced market economies such as the United States and most European Union member states, incumbent service providers such as banks have struggled to update their ageing legacy computer systems to compete with nimble start-up payment service providers using newer technologies, while regulators have struggled to update laws written with paper or mainframe computers in mind. Regulators in some developing countries, most notably Kenya, have embraced the 'creative destruction' of innovation by authorising the launch of new payment services outside the banking system (Buku et al., 2013). By contrast, regulators in China and India have chosen to work with regulated financial intermediaries to achieve their payment system reform strategies. Although regulators in both India and China have embraced payment system reform as a development strategy, their national strategies differ widely from almost every other perspective.

In 2002, China's retail payment systems were still fragmented and underdeveloped, but by 2012 China's new UnionPay card network had already overtaken MasterCard to become the second largest card network in the world, second only to Visa (Wu, 2012). The People's Republic of China (PRC) government was able to capitalise on its tight control over China's domestic financial services markets to achieve this phenomenal feat of purposive innovation in less than a decade. China's bank regulators and oligopoly of state-owned banks accomplished this by adapting the business models of Visa and MasterCard to accommodate China's unique form of 'state capitalism', by deploying existing payment card technologies already in widespread use outside of China and by leveraging their control over China's domestic payment market to roll out a new global payment network in record time. By the time a World Trade Organization (WTO) panel ruled in 2013 that China could not continue to use a de facto monopoly over domestic payment card network to subsidise the growth of its global network, China UnionPay had already established itself as a formidable competitor to Visa and MasterCard in global payment markets (WTO, 2012).

The government of India is taking a radically different approach by subsidising the development of an open, interoperable, public platform for new payment services, and creating a level playing field between incumbents and start-up service providers to promote competition. While both India and China may share a commitment to modernising their payment systems to reduce transaction costs, financial inclusion is a much more urgent public policy goal in India than it is in China, because of India's much higher rates of absolute poverty. The government of India is combining payment system reform with the rollout of Aadhaar, a new electronic national identity system, in an effort to increase the efficiency of its benefit programmes designed to aid India's poor and to reduce corruption in their administration. India's payment system reforms incorporate sophisticated public–private partnerships, such as the creation of the National Payment Council of India as a new self-regulatory organisation, and the use of open standards to increase consumer welfare by promoting competition in the Indian market for payment services. India's reform strategies are both more complex and more inclusive than China's, and will require the widespread adoption of new technologies in order to succeed. As a result, it is not yet clear whether India's efforts will ultimately enjoy the same success as China's.

These differences in national payment system modernisation strategies reflect not only the overall level of development of domestic electronic payment systems, but also much broader, deeper differences in national cultures of regulation and innovation. China's national payment system modernisation programme reflects its economic culture of strong Communist Party control over both the 'commanding heights' and the innovation vanguard of China's economy (McGregor, 2012). As with many of China's other economic development initiatives, its strategy of promoting China UnionPay to compete with Visa and MasterCard in global markets has been executed decisively, although with an apparent disregard for the subtleties of international trade law. India's national payment system modernisation programme reflects India's economic culture of democratic pluralism and technocratic nationalism. Just as India's ambitious attempt to bring democracy to the developing world is continuously fraught with peril, its attempt to prove that economic development strategy can simultaneously be open, efficient and innovative is also fraught with peril.

Networks, platforms and governance competition

Global payment networks such as Visa and MasterCard enter local markets not only as vendors of payment services, but also as private self-regulatory organisations that can leverage their global market power to challenge the authority of local regulators. The primary objective of China and India's payment system modernisation policies may have been domestic economic development, but their policies also serve to keep the power of global payment networks in check in their domestic markets for payment services. To understand how the operator of something as basic as a payment system could mount a credible challenge to the authority of different national regulators around the world, it is necessary to consider the political economy of global information and communication (ICT) networks and the rise of global governance institutions as competitors to national governments.

Networks and platforms

Networks, such as telecommunications networks, the Internet, or payment card networks, become more valuable to each individual user of the network as the total number of users increases.[1] If users of the network are not required to make any additional payment in exchange for enjoying the benefits that come from more users joining the network, then that benefit is a positive 'externality' – that is, a value not reflected in market prices. The strong positive externalities associated with ICT networks are often referred to as 'network effects'. Consumers have strong incentives to converge on a single ICT network because that will usually maximise the value of the network effects that they enjoy. The anti-competitive effect of individual consumers' preferences for access to the network with the largest number of other participants is exacerbated by conditions in producer markets for digital goods and services. Production of many forms of mass-market digital goods and services is characterised by very high initial development costs, combined with marginal costs of production at zero or close to zero. This characteristic of the production of digital goods and services tends to create high barriers to entry into networked markets, further reducing users' options for switching to a new network. If a networked market is characterised by strong network effects and high barriers to entry are also controlled by a single network operator, then that operator may be able to act as the de facto regulator of activity within the network (Winn, 2009: 191).

Once a network is established, users may become 'locked in' to that network if they face significant barriers to migration to a new network. These barriers are often caused by collective action problems: no individual user wants to switch to a new network unless certain that all other users will do the same. Just as free access to other network users is normally a positive externality, the difficulty of shifting from an old technology to a new one, or from an old network to a new one, may be a negative externality if market prices for network services do not reflect that cost. If lock-in occurs, then users of a network may find themselves stuck using an outdated or otherwise less desirable network even though a superior alternative is available, merely as a result of the difficulty in organising the migration of a large group of users from the old to the new. In a similar manner, it is often difficult to launch an ICT network for the first time. Payment systems, whether based on paper or electronic record-keeping systems, can be thought of as 'networks' in the sense that their value to individual users increases as the total number of users of the payment system increases and it is often very difficult to launch a new payment system, or migrate an established payment system to a new technology architecture, because of lock-in problems.

The technical interoperability required to access ICT networks can be achieved in a wide variety of ways, including proprietary technologies that operate as de facto standards, such as the Microsoft Windows operating system or open, public *de jure* standards developed under the auspices of public international organisations such as International Organization for Standardization (ISO) or the International Telecommunications Union (ITU). One of the primary governance tasks of ICT network operators is the development of the technical standards that define the scope of their networks by making different computer systems interoperable. While compliance with traditional industrial product and process standards (for example the US 'Energy Star' product standard for efficient appliances, or the 'Dolphin-free' process standard for canned tuna) may be very difficult to monitor, compliance with ICT network standards is often very simple: interoperability, and hence access to the network, is impossible without compliance with the relevant standards (such as the IEEE 802.11 Wi-Fi standard).

ICT networks may also operate as 'multi-sided platforms' (Rochet and Tirole, 2003; Evans, Hagiu and Schmalensee, 2006). A simple model of a 'multi-sided platform' is a 'two-sided market' – that is, a market that cannot be sustained unless two very different groups participate in the market, each on very different terms and conditions. Traditional newspaper publishing is an example of a two-sided market, with readers being one 'side', advertisers being the other 'side' and the newspaper publisher acting as the 'platform operator'. Although two-sided, or multi-sided, markets exist apart from ICT networks, it is rare for a commercial ICT networks not to operate as multi-sided platforms.[2]

In order for such a two-sided market to operate successfully, the platform operator must devise a pricing strategy that maximises the commitment of both sides to the success of the platform. Newspapers traditionally charged advertisers high prices for access to readers and used those advertising revenues to subsidise readers. A successful platform pricing strategy normally imposes high prices on the side that is most committed to the success of the platform and uses low or subsidised prices to attract less committed users. Much of the growth of global card payment networks has been financed by high fees imposed on merchants that accept card payments. Although these fees are bitterly resented by the merchants who pay them, they fuel the growth of payment card networks by providing an important revenue source for banks issuing cards and processing card payments, and subsidise incentives given to consumers to make payments with cards.

From regulatory competition to governance competition

'Regulatory competition' refers to competition among different sovereigns for mobile economic resources such as labour and capital by offering different regulatory regimes to attract them (Tiebout, 1956). 'Race to the bottom' regulatory competition strategies generally involve regulatory regimes that externalise the costs of attracting mobile economic resources onto someone other than the owner of the resource either inside or outside of a sovereign's territory. For example, using weak labour and environmental protection laws to attract foreign investment may externalise some production costs onto workers and citizens affected by pollution within that country, while allowing foreign investors to enjoy increased profits as a result of lower nominal production costs. 'Race to the top', or the 'California effect', is the opposite strategy: a sovereign with market power can require producers to internalise more production costs than other sovereigns do. California used this strategy successfully when it required the use of catalytic converters on all cars sold in California. When other sovereigns followed California's example, then producers that had adapted to the stricter California standard had a competitive advantage over producers that had not yet done so. Regulatory competition strategies become more complex when traditional territorial sovereigns compete with private regulators whose scope of authority is ambiguous and whose regulatory tools are different (Eberlein et al., 2013).

The rise of global markets both determines and reflects the rise of global governance institutions whose jurisdiction is defined by the scope of their activities, rather than geography, and which are accountable to their stakeholders, rather than to citizens of a territory (Büthe and Mattli, 2011; Peters et al., 2009). However, not all private regulators were spawned by globalisation: law and medicine have operated as independent self-regulating professions for centuries in the West, while modern institutions of industrial self-regulation arose in the late nineteenth century (Russell, 2014). The notion of multi-stakeholder governance institutions as a collaborative effort among nation-states, intergovernmental organisations, the private sector and non-governmental organisations (NGOs) first emerged in the environmental arena following the 1992 Rio Convention (Koechlin and Calland, 2009). Bigman (2007: 150) has described governance as dealing 'with processes and systems by which an organisation or society operates. Frequently a government is established to administer these processes or systems.' As the frequency with which the term 'governance' is used has increased, it comes as no surprise that its scope has become increasingly vague and contested. In response to the subsequent proliferation of meanings of the term 'governance', later commentators have tried to impose order on the chaos. To focus on comparative empirical studies of governance, Hufty (2011: 403–424) has proposed defining governance as 'a category of social facts, namely the processes of interaction and decision-making among the actors involved in a collective problem that lead to the creation, reinforcement, or reproduction of social norms and institutions'.

As a result of globalisation, regulatory competition increasingly takes place in the form of 'governance competition' among governments and private regulators based in global markets outside a government's national borders. The authority of global governance institutions may be based more on the de facto ability to achieve results than *de jure* legitimacy within any national legal order. Self-regulatory organisations that are also successful global ICT network platform operators may be able to leverage considerable market power to support their governance strategies whenever there are strong network effects associated with their networks (Winn, 2008). The power of ICT network operators is often further enhanced by the migration of almost every possible form of administration from paper-based record-keeping systems to electronic record systems linked by computers and the increasing dependence of almost every kind of management system on ICT networks to function at all.

The global payment card networks are governance institutions that, in tandem with the formal political and legal systems maintained by nation-states, mediate political conflict and exercise regulatory powers over markets defined by global ICT networks. Such ICT network governance institutions respond to the demands of their stakeholders, while governments respond to the demands of their citizens. As governance institutions, they may regulate behaviour within their networks in much the same way a nation-state does, although their writ extends only over the economic 'ecosystem' defined by their networks instead of the territory of a nation-state. In the case of global payment card networks such as Visa and MasterCard, they maintain the boundaries of their ecosystems through a combination of the symbolic exercise of authority, in the form of 'brand management', and by requiring every participant in the system to acknowledge their 'constitution', in the form of system rules through a binding contractual undertaking. Disputes among card network stakeholders rarely spill over into public litigation, but are normally enforced through private alternative dispute resolution processes.

National regulators respond to the challenges to their authority posed by global ICT network operators in different ways that often reflect their national culture (Winn, 2009). One common way in which to distinguish national regulatory cultures is by classifying legal systems as members of the common law or civil law legal 'families' or 'traditions'. In the 'varieties of capitalism' approach, political scientists Hall and Soskice (2001) suggest that national regulatory cultures can be classified as either 'liberal market economies' (LMEs), which includes most common law countries, and others identified as 'coordinated market economies' (CMEs), which includes many leading civil law countries. The most noteworthy LMEs include the United States, the United Kingdom, Canada, Australia and New Zealand, while Germany, France and Japan are noteworthy examples of CMEs. Hall and Soskice (2001) noticed that LMEs are more likely to use indirect market incentives to achieve their goals, while CMEs are more likely to use direct government action. The culture of independent professions and industry self-regulation also tends to be stronger in LMEs than in CMEs.

Countries within the LME/common law tradition tend to defer to competitive market outcomes and to try to minimise direct involvement of government in private economic activity, while countries within the CME/civil law tradition are more likely to support invasive public oversight of markets, so it should not be surprising to find that their responses to the rise of private regulation by network platform operators might differ. In fact, Visa and MasterCard first achieved their status as de facto private regulators within the United States, an environment more tolerant of private regulation than Europe or developing countries, as well as the largest national economy in the world. After Visa and MasterCard expanded into global markets, and resisted efforts by regulators in both the United States and Europe to accommodate greater competition and to lower the fees they charge retailers, regulators in Europe responded by imposing strict price controls on payment card services to offset the lack of competition among networks. By contrast, regulators in China and India sidestepped the problems faced by regulators in advanced market economies, because they intervened directly in domestic markets to establish alternative card payment systems before Visa and MasterCard had a chance to penetrate local markets deeply.

Card network regulation in the United States and European Union

Industry self-regulation of payment systems in the United States dates back to at least 1853, with the founding of the New York Clearing House, which is now known simply as The Clearing House and still plays an important role in American payment systems in the twenty-first century (The Clearing House, 2014). Widespread use of cheques as a medium of payment in the nineteenth and twentieth centuries, combined with a highly decentralised, fragmented banking system, made cooperation among American banks essential to maintaining any semblance of a national payment system.[3] The development of the American retail payment card industry in the 1960s was a natural extension of this tradition of industry self-regulation.

The first successful national credit card brand was BankAmericard, which was launched by Bank of America in California and then distributed nationwide by other banks through licensing agreements. Many banks felt deeply ambivalent about relying on a product carrying a competitor's brand, which soon led to the formation of the MasterCharge consortium to challenge the dominance of BankAmericard. In response, Bank of America turned its card network over to its licensees and its name was changed to Visa, while MasterCharge later changed its name to MasterCard. Unbridled competition among banks when the American credit card market was being established prompted Congress to impose strong consumer protection laws on the credit card industry in 1970.[4]

A fundamental breakthrough in the business model of payment card networks that contributed enormously to the ultimate triumph of Visa and MasterCard was the development of multilateral interchange fees. These fees are paid by merchants in the form of a discount from the face value of a card transaction, for example 3 per cent. The bank that deals directly with the merchant collects the interchange fee and then splits it with the bank that issued the card. This sharing of interchange fees gave banks an incentive to promote card use among their depositors, as well as among retailers. When the only payment cards were credit cards, merchants did not object to paying an interchange fee, because it was, in effect, the cost of outsourcing the management of their in-house store charge accounts to banks. Merchant objections to multilateral interchange fees arose when Visa and MasterCard began promoting the use of debit cards as a substitute for payments by cash or cheque. In retail sectors with narrow profit margins, the difference between the service charges that they paid to banks to process cash and cheque deposits and multilateral exchange fees could be the difference between profit and loss for some merchants. Even though merchants have paid most of the costs of operating the card payment networks, until very recently Visa and MasterCard did not recognise merchants as full 'stakeholders' in their bank-centric governance processes.[5]

With regard to the challenges posed by global card networks as de facto private regulators, however, regulators in advanced market economies on both sides of the Atlantic have been trying for decades, with negligible success, to neutralise the market power of the network operators with competition law and policy. The failure of competition enforcement actions to curb the power of global card networks has been compounded by the lack of viable competitors in retail payment markets in the United States and Europe. In Europe, the Commission of the European Union has repeatedly taken enforcement actions against Visa and MasterCard in an effort to force them to reduce the interchange fees they charge merchants, with limited success.[6] Repeated European Commission efforts to persuade European banks to launch a European competitor to Visa or MasterCard have been equally unsuccessful, perhaps because Visa and MasterCard are among the most profitable services offered by European banks. In 2013, the Commission finally changed course, and proposed a new regulation that would simply cap the fees that Visa and MasterCard could charge in Europe.[7]

In the United States, antitrust enforcement actions against the credit card networks have been led primarily by retail merchants angry about the high level of fees that Visa and MasterCard require them to pay for access to their networks. Walmart launched a coalition of retailers, which started suing the card networks for antitrust violations in 1996 and continued the litigation almost without interruption up to 2014. Even though American retail merchants have twice won multibillion-dollar judgments against the card networks and the card networks were required to make some changes in their policies as a result,[8] many retail merchants were still dissatisfied. In 2010, lobbying by American retailers to enact legislation to curb the power of the payment networks produced the 'Durbin Amendment' to the Dodd–Frank Act of 1989, which overhauled regulation of American financial services following the global financial crisis.[9] Although the Durbin Amendment was clearly intended to impose punitive restrictions on card fees, the Federal Reserve

Board softened the impact of the legislation when it drafted regulations to implement it – an interpretation that was upheld in the face of a challenge by the retail merchants.[10] Walmart and other retailers finally responded to the failure of either litigation or political lobbying to force the card networks to change their basic business model by organising a competing retail payment platform. In 2012, the Merchant Customer Exchange, a new mobile payment platform that the retailers would own and operate, was launched, although by 2014 it had still not commenced operations.

Lock-in is one reason why the payment card networks in the United States and Europe have not faced any serious competition, notwithstanding regulators' and retailers' frustration with their pricing policies. Payment card networks were originally launched in the 1960s; by the 1980s, they had become ubiquitous payment mechanisms in the United States and Europe, so that any new payment mechanism launched to compete with them would not only have to meet the needs of bank, merchant and consumer stakeholders, but also have to overcome all of the current stakeholders' lock-in to the card networks. Although mobile payments have had a revolutionary impact in many developing countries (*The Economist*, 2009), they have had relatively little impact in advanced market economies locked in to payment card network technologies.

Although the global payment card networks had established operations in both India and China by the 1980s, by the 2000s they had still not become ubiquitous payment mechanisms. The lack of a dominant payment card network in either country gave regulators a chance to act as entrepreneurs and to sponsor the development of home-grown competitors to Visa and MasterCard. Mazzucato (2013) has argued that entrepreneurship is a function often played quite successfully by national governments, even though the conventional wisdom (at least in advanced market economies) is that national governments are clumsy, bureaucratic and capable of shifting risks only between private parties, or of redistributing the costs of externalities. In both China and India, national governments have subsidised payment system innovations as part of a larger economic development strategy to promote efficiency and financial inclusion. By 2014, the China UnionPay network had already established itself as the number two global payment network after Visa, overtaking MasterCard.

China: State capitalism

Following the victory of the Communist Party of China (CCP) in 1949 and the founding of the People's Republic of China (PRC), private commercial banks were merged into a single Soviet-style 'monobank' designed to support central economic planning. Only the Bank of China remained in operation to provide essential commercial banking services to the PRC government (He and Sappideen, 2008). As China gradually emerged from the Great Proletariat Cultural Revolution in the late 1970s, a handful of commercial banks were once again established in China. These banks are now known as the 'big four' state-owned commercial banks: Bank of China, Industrial and Commercial Bank of China, China Construction Bank and Agricultural Bank of China. During the 1980s, intra-bank fund transfers across different provinces of China and interbank clearing and settlement systems were paper-based and labour-intensive. Although credit cards were accepted in a small number of international businesses catering to foreign tourists, they were not available for Chinese citizens and the card-processing infrastructure was rudimentary. (The author personally remembers seeing half a dozen different card readers for each of the major international card networks attached to each cash register when making purchases in the government Friendship Stores in the 1980s.) In 1989, development of the 'Electronic Interbank System' began; in 1991, it commenced operation among banks in China's largest cities (Carnegie Mellon Institute for eCommerce, 2004).

Although China was one of the founding members of the General Agreement on Trade and Tariffs (GATT) in 1948, it withdrew following the Communist victory in 1948 and faced considerable obstacles when it tried to rejoin, beginning in the 1980s. China's re-entry was slowed not merely by the launching of the Uruguay Round in 1986, which eventually led to the creation of the WTO in 1995, but also by the reluctance of existing members to have to compete directly with China without protective tariffs. As a result, China was forced to make broader and deeper concessions to existing WTO members than any developing country had ever been asked to make as a condition to entry. While the motivation of existing members in demanding the concessions is obvious, it was less obvious why the CCP would agree to them. Commentators have speculated that China's commitment to joining the WTO reflected a desire by the 'reform and opening' faction within the CCP to make the policy of market reforms as close to irreversible as possible, and a recognition on the part of China's economic planners that access to global markets was essential to achieving China's long-term economic development goals (Lardy, 2001). China's membership of the WTO finally took effect on 11 December 2001.

During the 1990s, the PRC government launched several 'golden projects' to promote the development of its information infrastructure and to modernise the delivery of government services. These included: the Golden Bridge Project, focused on developing a commercial Internet service; the Golden Customs project, focused on linking customs service computers; the Golden Tax Project, focused on using ICT to increase compliance with tax laws; the Golden Shield Project, better known as the Great Firewall of China; and the Golden Card Project, focused on developing a national credit card network (Zhang and Wang, 1995). The Electronic Interbank System was replaced in 2001 by the China National Advanced Payment System (CNAPS), which contained a high-value wire transfer system and a low-value bulk payment processing system.

Around the same time that CNAPS was being launched, China's economic planners and bank regulators became interested in modernising its card payment system. In 2002, China UnionPay was launched as a joint venture of China's domestic banks and, in 2004, the network began processing transactions (People's Bank of China, 2008). With the support of China's central bank regulator, the People's Bank of China (PBOC), China UnionPay cards were integrated into the framework of domestic retail banking services, triggering rapid growth in the number of cards issued, the number of retail merchants accepting card payments and the total volume of domestic payment card transactions in the Chinese domestic market.

Around the time that the PBOC began vigorously promoting China UnionPay card use within the domestic PRC, China's relationship with the WTO subtly began to change. China's early commitment to overhauling its economic laws and opening its domestic market to international competition faded, and a new policy of promoting 'national champions' took over (*The Economist*, 2011). Before China's admission to the WTO, 'state-owned enterprise' (SOE) in China was synonymous with aging relics of post-1949 industrialisation used to warehouse unproductive surplus labour. During the 1990s, those uncompetitive SOEs were closed down or sold off, while competitive SOEs were retained or, in the case of China UnionPay, created as part of the PRC's portfolio of investments.

During its infancy, China UnionPay was sheltered from international competition in China's domestic market for card payment services. Visa and MasterCard initially did not object to this apparent violation of China's WTO market-access obligations, because they had the impression that they would be allowed to provide cross-border transaction processing for Chinese bank cards. 'Dual-currency' cards bearing both China UnionPay and either Visa or MasterCard logos were issued by Chinese banks, with the Visa and MasterCard functions designed to be used only outside of China. Before too long, however, it became obvious that China UnionPay intended to launch its own competing global card network and to process as many of its own cross-border transactions as possible, without the assistance of Visa and MasterCard. While Visa's and MasterCard's complaints in China produced no results, the two organisations began lobbying the US government to initiate a WTO dispute proceeding against China for giving the state-owned card network a de facto monopoly in China's domestic market.

In 2010, the United States initiated a WTO proceeding against China, under the General Agreement on Trade in Services (GATS), to challenge China UnionPay's domestic monopoly in China as a violation of China's GATS obligations. Although China had committed to open its financial services markets to foreign competition when it joined the WTO, China claimed that China UnionPay's monopoly over card-clearing and settlement services in the Chinese domestic economy was outside the scope of that commitment. In most countries, card-clearing and settlement services are provided by the central bank or by non-profit private service organisations operating under the close control of the central bank, so China's argument that clearing and settlement services were not covered by its commitment to permit competition in financial services was compelling. The problem with the Chinese position was that China UnionPay was operating as a for-profit joint venture of the state-owned banks under China's system of 'state capitalism', not as a government agency or non-profit utility. As a result, the United States argued that China UnionPay should be grouped with other for-profit financial services for GATS purposes and not covered by an exception for regulators providing financial services market oversight functions. The panel ruled in China's favour on the issue of monopolisation, noting that dual-brand cards bearing Visa and MasterCard logos had been issued in China. However, the panel found that China had failed to honour its 'national treatment' obligation to treat foreign and domestic enterprises equally within those markets that it had agreed to open to foreign competition. China chose not to appeal the panel ruling, and entered into negotiations with the United States to make changes to domestic market policies to level the playing field between foreign and domestic card networks in order to achieve national treatment. A year after the WTO opinion was issued, however, Chinese regulators shut down an attempt by MasterCard to partner with a Chinese payment service provider to issue cards without the China UnionPay logo, indicating that the global card networks are unlikely to enjoy national treatment in China any time soon.

India: Entrepreneurial state

While China has successfully used a 'state capitalism' model to develop its national card payment network, but ran into conflict with the United States over its WTO obligations as a result, India has used a more complex 'entrepreneurial state' model to promote the development of inclusive financial services markets and competition, while developing its national card payment network. India's embrace of openness and competition in the electronic payments arena is a surprising development in light of the Indian government's frequent ambivalence about free markets since its policy of economic liberalisation was launched in 1992 (Panagariya, 2008). However, the government is affirming its Gandhian roots by operating a platform on which for-profit payment services will compete as a public institution.

Governments concerned about anti-competitive behaviour by private ICT network operators may respond by promoting 'open' standards. If this strategy is successful, consumers enjoy the positive effects of a single network without any of the downsides of dealing with a monopoly service provider. However, it is much more difficult to coordinate production based on open standards rather than on closed, proprietary technologies. So the adoption of open standards by governments may slow down the development of the market, as compared to allowing private enterprises driven by profit motives to construct the network and recapture their development costs by charging whatever the market will bear. In addition, it is easier for closed, proprietary networks to guarantee the level of services delivered to end-users, while open, standards-based networks tend to have more technical problems: Apple's iPhone, for example, delivers premium service at a high price using a closed system, while Google's Android phone delivers a low-cost service with uneven performance as an open system. And while Visa, MasterCard and China UnionPay, the three largest global payment networks, have all pursued the closed proprietary network model, India is working to create an open, standards-based platform.

In 1996, India's central bank, the Reserve Bank of India (RBI) established the Institute for Development and Research in Banking Technology (IDRBT) in Hyderabad to provide technical support for modernising the ICT infrastructure of the Indian banking and payment systems. It launched its first national electronic funds transfer system in the 1990s and, in 2005, substantially improved it with the launch of the National Electronic Fund Transfer (NEFT) system. In 2005, the RBI spun off governance of payment services in India to the National Payments Corporation of India (NPCI), a public–private partnership designed to promote responsible industry self-regulation under the watchful eye of the RBI. The goal of the NPCI is for one member of every household in India to have a bank account by 2016 and to provide modern payment services to all of India's citizens by 2020. Given that more than 50 per cent of India's population in 2014 was still excluded from the formal financial sector and that over half of adults in some states are illiterate rural farm workers, these are extremely ambitious goals.

Payment system modernisation is merely one element of a much larger government strategy to use ICT to achieve economic development in India. One of the challenges of operating a modern electronic payment system in India is compliance with anti-money-laundering 'know your customer' requirements in a country where illiteracy is high and no official record is created of the births of many citizens in rural areas. The government launched the Unique Identification Authority of India (UIDAI) in 2009, to create twelve-digit 'Aadhaar numbers' for Indian citizens registered on a digital national identity system that maintains accurate records of all citizens. Once the Aadhaar system is fully operational, it will dramatically lower the costs of complying with anti-money-laundering compliance obligations, such as the 'know your customer' requirement, which in turn will help India to achieve its financial inclusion goals. By 2014, 700 million Aadhaar numbers had already been issued.

Since its inception, however, the Aadhaar system has been dogged by controversy. Some critics alleged it would serve only to fuel discrimination in a society still profoundly divided along caste and ethnic lines, while others pointed out the injustice of conditioning access to benefits on enrolment, thus subjecting only the poor to surveillance. Supporters argued that it would reduce the burden of corruption on India's poor by allowing undocumented citizens from rural communities to access their benefits outside of the villages in which someone can personally vouch for their identities. Aadhaar supporters also believe it offers the only hope of reducing 'leakage' in government benefit programmes caused by corruption, which siphons off many benefits before they ever reach the poor. As the controversy mounted, however, Congress Party support for Aadhaar faded and the pace of enrolments began to drop. The Supreme Court of India waded into the controversy, first in September 2013, by declaring that local governments could not condition access to public services upon use of an Aadhaar number, and then again in March 2014, to support UIDAI's right to refuse to turn over Aadhaar information to law enforcement without the consent of the citizen being identified. After the Bharatiya Janata Party swept to power in May 2014, the new Prime Minister Narendra Modi threw his weight behind Aadhaar by announcing that the new target date for 'universal enrolment' would be moved forward to June 2015 (Tewari, 2014). In 2011, the NPCI announced the launch of the national RuPay card. This was only one of many payment services that the NPCI was helping to develop. In 2006, the RBI and IDRBT founded the Mobile Payment Forum of India (MPFI) to work with the hundreds of Indian banks and dozens of Indian mobile network operators to build an open platform for mobile payments to promote interoperability and competition in the market for mobile payments. In 2010, an open, standards-based Immediate Payment System delivered via mobile phone messages was launched. Poor, rural citizens in India are entitled to a variety of direct cash benefits and, to migrate the payment of those benefits to ICT networks, a system of portable 'micro-ATMs' was developed: representatives of banks with 'no frills' bank accounts for each rural citizen visit villages with a handheld card reader and cash, permitting the immediate withdrawal of 100 per cent of central government benefit payments in the village without any 'shrinkage' from corruption in intermediate layers of government. Because this system is incorporated into the RuPay card system, the use of biometric authentication is being abandoned in favour of international standard 'chip and PIN' authentication, allowing the rural poor access to any RuPay-enabled ATM or point-of-sale terminal in India.

In August 2014, Prime Minister Narendra Modi provided pivotal support for the success of the RuPay card network when he announced that the government would pay interchange to the banks that provide support for its programme to use RuPay cards as the distribution channel for benefit transfers to the poor (Mehta, 2014). In 2015, RuPay was to be launched as an international card payment system to compete against Visa, MasterCard and China UnionPay. Both China UnionPay and RuPay card networks work with the Discover card network to reach consumers in foreign markets. Discover is an American card network long dwarfed by Visa and MasterCard. It has recently begun to emerge from their shadows with a strategy of partnering with foreign card networks, including those of Japan and Korea, as well as China and India.

The government of India is acting as an entrepreneurial state by providing market infrastructure as public goods to fuel the development of new private services and to promote competition. The payment system modernisation commitment to open standards is just one element of a broader commitment by the government to using open standards as an economic development tool (Government of India et al., 2014). As with any public or private entrepreneurial undertaking, the ambitious programme of payment system modernisation taking place in India is risky. Unlike its Chinese counterparts, who largely cloned mature technologies and business models that had succeeded in other markets, the RBI is reinventing the governance framework for payments at the same time as it is reengineering ICT infrastructure used to deliver payment services. Attempting simultaneous innovations on so many levels at once, of course, magnifies the entrepreneurial risks the Indian government is taking. If the government wins its gamble on building an open, inclusive, transparent ICT architecture, it could finally start to make some significant progress on its financial inclusion and anti-corruption. But there is no guarantee that the gamble will pay off.

Conclusion

In the 1990s, credit cards were not yet a significant part of the national payment systems of either China or India, but the central banks of both countries were actively promoting the development of national electronic payment systems generally. In the 2000s, the central banks of both China and India elevated the strategic importance of payment card networks within their national payment systems and launched strategies to build national payment card networks. In the 2010s, both China and India were reaping the benefits of their investments in payment system modernisation as a development strategy. The success of these national payment card networks may also permit regulators in China and India to avoid the prolonged struggles now being fought by regulators in the United States and Europe to ensure that the national operations of the global card networks are compatible with their national economic policies.

One of the great ironies that emerges from any careful comparison of Chinese and Indian strategies for economic development is the contrast between official ideology and practice on the ground in both countries. Although China is ostensibly socialist, much of its economy is now capitalist, and the CCP is the leading capitalist. Although India has ostensibly committed to market reforms, support for socialist economic policies remains strong owing to the combination of democratic political institutions and persistent widespread poverty. A comparison of payment system modernisation strategies reveals a further contrast: China has seized the 'low hanging fruit' of payment system reform as a development strategy by copying the basic business model of Visa and MasterCard, so it is enjoying a quick return on its investment, but is unlikely to enjoy the longer-term benefits of an innovation 'ecosystem' surrounding payments innovation, because of China UnionPay's privileged and closed status in China.

By contrast, the depth, breadth and originality of India's ambitions are little short of breath-taking and, in contrast with the deplorable dysfunction that prevails in other areas of the Indian economy, they may even succeed. India is attempting to build an open, inclusive, transparent information economy within which both global multinationals and illiterate rural farmers can participate fully. Execution of the government of India's strategy will be slower and riskier than China's execution of its strategy, because there are so many more variables in play, but the potential payoff for India could be a national innovation ecosystem that could restore its place at the vanguard of world politics.

Notes

1 This basic relationship is often referred to as 'Metcalfe's Law', which predicts that the value of a network increases exponentially as the number of users increases, even though it really is only a rough heuristic that indicates what the value of a network might be rather than a law and it is unclear whether it can be attributed to Robert Metcalfe, the inventor of Ethernet network technology (Shapiro and Varian, 1999; 184).

2 A simple non-ICT network example of a two-sided market is 'ladies night' at a bar, where the price that male customers pay for their drinks is set high enough to subsidise drinks consumed by female customers.

3 The system of private regulation had many problems, however, and in 1913 the Federal Reserve System was established in part to guarantee the smooth operation of the national system of cheque clearing.

4 The Truth in Lending Act of 1968 and Regulation Z, 12 CFR 226, were revised in 1970 to protect consumers from liability for charges on unsolicited credit cards and to establish a procedure to permit consumers to dispute charges to their accounts. See generally Guseva (2008: ch. 1).

5 'But you do need to start calling on merchants as if they're clients which is not something we had done in any kind of strategic way. Our conversations with merchants historically were much more around acceptance and upon rate. The conversations we have today again they are in the early stages because there's years of hostility built up amongst some of the merchants and ourselves as well as some of the issuers. And the conversation now is much more the same conversation we would have with an issuer' (Charles Scharf, CEO, Visa Inc., 10 February 2014).

6 Commission Decision of 19 December 2007 relating to a proceeding under Article 81 of the EC Treaty and Article 53 of the EEA Agreement (Case COMP/34.579 – MasterCard, Case COMP/36.518 – EuroCommerce, Case COMP/38.580 – Commercial Cards), *OJ* C 264/8, 6 November 2009; Case T-111/08 *MasterCard v. Commission*, General Court (Seventh Chamber), 24 May 2012.

7 European Commission (2013) Proposal for a Regulation of the European Parliament and of the Council on interchange fees for card-based payment transactions, COM(2013)/0550 final – 2013/0265 (COD), Brussels.

8 *Wal-Mart Stores, Inc. v. Visa USA Inc.*, 396 F.3d 96 (2d Cir. NY 2005); *In re Payment Card Interchange Fee & Merch. Disc. Antitrust Litig.*, 2013 US Dist. LEXIS 179340 (EDNY 13 December 2013).

9 The Durbin Amendment was codified at 15 USCS 1693o-2 (2010).

10 *NACS [National Association of Convenience Stores] v. Federal Reserve Board System*, 2014 US App. LEXIS 5299 (D.C. Cir. 2014).

References

Bigman, D. (2007) *Globalization and the Least Developed Countries: Potentials and Pitfalls*, Oxfordshire: CABI.

Buku, M. W., Merideth, M. W., Safaricom and M-Pesa (2013) 'Kenya: Financial Inclusion and Financial Integrity', *Washington Journal of Law, Technology & Arts*, 8(3): 375–400.

Büthe, T., and Mattli, W. (2011) *The New Global Rulers: The Privatization of Regulation in the World Economy*, Princeton, NJ: Princeton University Press.

Carnegie Mellon Institute for eCommerce (2004) *Payment Systems in China*, available online at http://euro.ecom.cmu.edu/resources/elibrary/epay/ChinasPaymentSystems.pdf [accessed 1 August 2016].

The Clearing House (2014) 'A Look Back', available online at https://www.theclearinghouse.org/about-tch/a-look-back [accessed 19 August 2014].

Eberlein, B., Abbott, K. W., Black, J., Meidinger, E., and Wood, S. (2013) 'Transnational Business Governance Interactions: Conceptualization and Framework for Analysis', *Regulation & Governance*, 8(1): 1–21.

The Economist (2009) 'The Power of Mobile Money', 24 September, available online at http://www.economist.com/node/14505519 [accessed 19 July 2016].

The Economist (2011) 'China's Economy and the WTO: All Change', 10 December, available online at http://www.economist.com/node/21541448 [accessed 19 July 2016].

Eichengreen, B., Gupta, P., and Kumar, R. (eds) (2010) *Emerging Giants: China and India*, Oxford: Oxford University Press.

Evans, D. S., Hagiu, A., and Schmalensee, R. (2006) *Invisible Engines: How Software Platforms Drive Innovation and Transform Industries*, Cambridge, MA: MIT Press.

Government of India, Ministry of Communications & IT and Department of Electronics & Information Technology (2014) 'Standards & Policies', available online at http://deity.gov.in/content/standards-policies [accessed 20 August 2014].

Guseva, A. (2008) *Into the Red: The Birth of the Credit Card Market in Post-Communist Russia*, Stanford, CA: Stanford University Press.

Hall, P. A., and Soskice, D. (2001) 'An Introduction to Varieties of Capitalism', in P. A. Hall, and D. Soskice (eds) *Varieties of Capitalism: The Institutional Foundations of Comparative Advantage*, Oxford: Oxford University Press, 1–68.

He, L.-L., and Sappideen, R. (2008) 'The Payment System in China', *Journal of International Banking Law and Regulation*, 23(3): 168–174.

Hufty, M. (2011) 'Investigating Policy Processes: The Governance Analytical Framework', in U. Wiesmann and H. Hurni (eds) *Research for Sustainable Development: Foundations, Experiences, and Perspectives*, Bern: Geographica Bernensia, 403–424.

Koechlin, L., and Calland, R. (2009) 'Standard Setting at the Cutting Edge: An Evidence-based Typology for Multi-stakeholder Initiatives', in A. Peters, L. Koechlin, T. Förster and G. Fenner Zinkernagel (eds) *Non-state Actors as Standard Setters*, Cambridge: Cambridge University Press, 84–112.

Lardy, N. J. (2001) *Issues in China's WTO Accession*, Washington, DC: Brookings Institution.

Mazzucato, M. (2013) *The Entrepreneurial State: Debunking Public vs Private Sector Myths*, London: Anthem Press.

McGregor, J. (2012) *No Ancient Wisdom, No Followers: The Challenges of Chinese Authoritarian Capitalism*, Westport, CT: Prospecta Press.

Mehta, S. (2014) 'Narendra Modi Government to Pay Banks Fee for Pursuing Financial Inclusion Plan', *The Economic Times*, 15 August, available online at http://articles.economictimes.indiatimes.com/2014-08-15/news/52845858_1_financial-inclusion-plan-government-owned-banks-5-banks [accessed 2 October 2014].

Panagariya, A. (2008) *India: The Emerging Giant*, Oxford University Press.

People's Bank of China, Payment and Settlement Department (2008) *China Payment System Development Report*, Beijing: China Financial & Economic.

Peters, A., Koechlin, L., Förster, T., and Fenner Zinkernagel, G. (eds) (2009) *Non-state Actors as Standard Setters*, Cambridge: Cambridge University Press.

Rochet, J.-C., and Tirole, J. (2003) 'Platform Competition in Two-sided Markets', Journal of the European Economic Association, 1(4): 990–1029.

Russell, A. (2014) *Open Standards and the Digital Age: History, Ideology, and Networks*, Cambridge: Cambridge University Press.

Scharf, C. (2014) 'Visa Inc.', Presentation at KBW Cards, Payments & Financial Technology Conference, New York, 10 February.

Shapiro, C., and Varian, H. (1999) *Information Rules*, Cambridge, MA: Harvard Business School Press.

Tewari, R. (2014) 'PM Modi Orders Aadhaar Cards for Al by June 2015', *The Indian Express*, 2 October, available online at http://indianexpress.com/article/india/india-others/pm-modi-orders-aadhaar-cards-for-all-by-june-2015/ [accessed 2 October 2014].

Tiebout, C. M. (1956) 'A Pure Theory of Local Expenditures', *Journal of Political Economy*, 64(5): 416–424.

Winn, J. K. (2008) 'Technical Standards as Data Protection Regulation', in S. Gutwirth and Y. Poullet (eds) *Reinventing Data Protection*, Dordrecht: Springer, 191–206.

Winn, J. K. (2009) 'Globalization and Standards: The Logic of Two-level Games', *Journal of Law and Policy for the Information Society*, 5(2): 185–218.

World Trade Organization (WTO) (2012) *Report of the Panel: China – Certain Measures Affecting Electronic Payment Services*, WT/DS413/R, 16 July, available online at https://www.wto.org/english/tratop_e/dispu_e/cases_e/ds413_e.htm [accessed 19 July 2016].

Wu, Z. (2012) 'UnionPay: Visa and MasterCard's Tough Chinese Rival', *BusinessWeek*, 20 December, available online at http://www.businessweek.com/articles/2012-12-20/unionpay-visa-and-mastercards-tough-chinese-rival [accessed 20 August 2014].

Zhang, J. X., and Wang, Y. (1995) *The Emerging Market of China's Computer Industry*, Westport, CT: Praeger.

11 Foreign investment law

Asian investment and the growth of regional investment agreements

Vivienne Bath and Luke Nottage#

Introduction: Investment trends in and out of Asia

Foreign direct investment (FDI) plays an increasingly important part in the economies of the Asian region.[1] Over the last twenty-five years, there has been a marked increase in FDI into and out of East, Southeast and South Asia (see Table 11.1). Investment into these parts of Asia was relatively low in 1993 (US$54 billion), but had increased sevenfold by 2013 to $384 billion. Outbound investment increased from $44 billion to more than $430 billion during this period. While China and Hong Kong account for a substantial amount of the increase, and the ability of countries in the region to attract and to make investments varies considerably, the overall trend has been towards growth across the three sub-regions. Outbound investment has also increased considerably, although again much of the growth is attributable to North Asia. In 2012, North and Southeast Asia accounted for 24 per cent of the world's total FDI inflows and 20 per cent of outflows (UNCTAD, 2013). Using a different measure, in 2013, inflows to the twenty-one economies in the Asia Pacific Economic Cooperation (APEC) group – including Canada, the United States, Mexico, Peru, Australia and Russia – constituted 54 per cent of the world's total FDI inflows (UNCTAD, 2014b). Intra-Asian investment has also increased significantly (ASEAN, 2013b).

The legal and regulatory approaches taken to FDI across the Asian region reflect the diversity in the legal systems of the many countries of the region. These come from a variety of legal traditions (Taylor and Pryles, 2006), including the common law (Singapore, Hong Kong, Malaysia, India and Pakistan) and the civil law (including Japan, Korea, Indonesia and Taiwan), and countries with a socialist history (such as China and Vietnam). In addition, the degree to which Asian nations are open to and encourage FDI varies considerably. At one end of the spectrum, Singapore and Hong Kong have traditionally taken a very open approach to foreign investment of all kinds (World Bank, 2014). However, other countries in the region (such as China, Myanmar, Indonesia, India, and even Japan and Korea) are considered by the Organisation for Economic Co-operation and Development (OECD, 2013) to maintain relatively high levels of regulatory restrictiveness in relation to FDI, notwithstanding moves at a domestic level and within the region towards the liberalisation of FDI regulation. In its 2014 *Report on East Asia and the Pacific*, the World Bank noted that East Asian countries, particularly ASEAN countries, impose more legal restrictions on FDI than any other sub-region. It also noted that East Asian countries are, in practice, very restrictive in relation to FDI in services.

Notwithstanding this, the overall regional trend in both domestic legislation and regional initiatives has been towards the promotion of FDI, through investment encouragement measures such as incentives and relaxation of restrictions on investment. Countries such

Table 11.1 Inbound and outbound investment, 1993–2013 (East, South and Southeast Asia)

	Inbound			*Outbound*		
	1993	*2003*	*2013*	*1993*	*2003*	*2013*
East Asia (China, Hong Kong, Macao, Korea (DPR), ROK, Mongolia) [developing economies]	36,206	80,271	221,058	26,181	26,377	236,141
China	27,515	53,505	123,911	4,400	2,855	101,000
Hong Kong	6,930	18,601	76,633	17,713	12,828	91,530
East Asia – Japan	210	6,324	2,304	13,913	28,800	135,749
South Asia (Afghanistan, Bangladesh, Bhutan, India, Iran, Maldives, Nepal, Pakistan, Sri Lanka)	1,354	8,419	35,561	-61	1,586	2,393
Southeast Asia (Brunei Darussalam, Cambodia, Indonesia, Lao PDR, Malaysia, Myanmar, Philippines, Singapore, Thailand, Timor-Leste, Vietnam)	16,585	29,788	125,455	4,307	5,618	56,374
Totals	**54,355**	**124,802**	**384,378**	**44,340**	**62,381**	**430,657**

Source: UNCTADStat (2014)

Note: US dollars at current prices and current exchange rates in millions

as India, Korea and Japan have taken major steps, especially over the last decade, to liberalise their FDI regimes and to encourage inbound investment (OECD, 2009; Nicolas, Thomsen and Bang, 2013). Cambodia has revised its investment regime to facilitate foreign investment and is now considered by the World Bank (2014) to have the most open FDI regime in the Association of Southeast Asian Nations (ASEAN). Myanmar has undertaken an investment review with the OECD (OECD, 2014). In 2013, the Pakistan government approved a new investment policy designed to remove regulatory restrictions on foreign investment (Kundi, 2013).

As detailed below, moves towards unilateral reform of FDI regulation by individual states have been supported and encouraged both by regional initiatives providing a framework for the reform and gradual liberalisation of investment regulation, and by the negotiation by Asian states of a range of bilateral and multilateral treaties dealing with investment, including regional free trade agreements (FTAs) aimed at liberalising and encouraging intra-regional trade and investment. ASEAN is an outstanding example of ambitious agreements, with its objective of establishing an economic community within Southeast Asia by the end of 2015. Other regional initiatives, such as the Regional Comprehensive Economic Partnership (RCEP, or the 'ASEAN+6' FTA)[2] and the expanded Trans-Pacific Partnership (TPP),[3] also have the potential to have a major effect on the liberalisation of investment rules inside their respective areas.

It is not possible in one chapter to give a thorough analysis of investment law and dispute settlement across the diverse Asian region. This chapter provides an overview of regulatory developments affecting FDI, both national and international, and the important issue of investment dispute settlement. It therefore looks at a number of different systems of national regulation, at APEC's efforts to encourage unilateral liberalisation of FDI regulation, at bilateral and multilateral initiatives, as well as their effect on the standardisation and liberalisation of FDI regulation, and at the issue of investment disputes and their resolution in the region.

National regulation of FDI: Examples within the region

Mainland China (without taking into account Taiwan, or the Special Administrative Regions of Hong Kong and Macao) is the major success story of the region in terms of its ability to attract FDI. In 2013 alone, it attracted almost US$124 billion in inbound FDI (UNCTADstat, 2014). Notwithstanding this, FDI in China has been tightly regulated since the first foreign investment law was enacted, the Chinese–Foreign Equity Joint Venture Law of 1979. The basic structure of inbound FDI regulation in China is based on three premises (Bath, 2011).

1 Foreign investors must invest through a foreign investment enterprise structure (joint venture, wholly foreign owned enterprise or partnership) set up under Chinese law, which is a Chinese enterprise or entity.
2 The establishment and any subsequent modification of the entity are subject to government approval.
3 Investment can be made only in industries and sectors permitted by regulations.

Since 1979, however, and particularly since China's accession in 2001 to the World Trade Organization (WTO), the sectors available for investment have been widened considerably, local governments have obtained more autonomy to approve major projects, and other steps have been taken to facilitate and expedite the investment process.

It is clear from the amount of inbound FDI that the regulatory structure has not deterred foreign investors from seeking access to the Chinese market. Despite this, China is currently ranked by the OECD as the most restrictive of the fifty-five countries surveyed in the 2014 FDI Regulatory Restrictiveness Index (OECD, 2013). However, recent steps taken by the Chinese government – particularly by establishing a 'negative list' approach to investment in the newly established Shanghai Free Trade Zone in 2013[4] and, in 2014, issuing regulations replacing the need to obtain prior government approval for most projects with an obligation to register new investments[5] – potentially herald substantial liberalisation of the Chinese FDI regime.

In 2013, FDI in India was approximately US$28.2 billion (UNCTADstat, 2014). India has taken a compromise position in regulating FDI. Investment is prohibited in certain industries, such as gambling, real estate development and the agricultural sector; in most other cases, however, investments can be made without central government approval, pursuant to what is described as the 'automatic route'. In sectors not covered by the automatic route, central government approval is required, pursuant to the 'government route', although investment is not permitted at all in sectors such as gambling, atomic energy and cigarette manufacturing (Government of India Ministry of Commerce and Industry, 2014).[6] Investments must be made in the form of equity shares or preference shares, or debentures that are fully and mandatorily convertible at a predetermined price (Reserve Bank of India, 2014). India has engaged in a relatively continuous policy of opening up the economy to foreign participation (Palit, 2009), although foreign investment in some areas – particularly retail – are highly controversial. Changes in 2013, for example, moved a number of items (such as investment in courier services, test marketing and commodity exchanges) from the government route to the automatic route and lifted investment caps in other areas (such as asset reconstruction and telecom services). Despite these reforms, the OECD ranks India as very restrictive in terms of regulation of FDI (after China, Myanmar, Saudi Arabia, Indonesia and Jordan) and well above the OECD average (OECD, 2013).

Japan, although a highly developed country, has surprisingly small amounts of FDI, attracting only US$1.7 billion in 2012 and a slight increase to US$2.3 billion in 2013 (UNCTADstat, 2014). The reasons are no longer related to restrictive FDI laws or practices per se, and the government has actively encouraged and achieved significant increases in inbound FDI over the last decade (Hamamoto and Nottage, 2013). Japan does not screen most investments, instead requiring post-investment reporting. However, investment in certain sectors, such as regulated industry sectors and sectors such as agriculture, can be made only after prior notification. Japan also imposes restrictions on a range of sectors, including agriculture and fisheries, the oil sector, energy and infrastructure (APEC, 2011).

At the other end of the spectrum, Hong Kong has a very liberal approach to foreign investment. Inbound FDI in 2013 was approximately US$76.6 billion.[7] There is no formal approval procedure for foreign investors and there are very few restrictions directed specifically at limiting the ability of foreign investors to acquire interests in companies in Hong Kong, with the exception of limitations on investment in telecommunications and media (Liu, Berry and Tam, 2012).

Bilateral and multilateral initiatives: Non-binding and treaty-based

There are various economic groupings and non-binding initiatives in the Asian region that seek to have an impact on the FDI regimes of Asian states. APEC is particularly active in the area of non-binding regional initiatives. APEC is a group of twenty-one economies around the Pacific Rim, which describes itself as 'the premier Asia-Pacific economic forum' (APEC, 2014a). One of its important goals is the liberalisation of trade and investment. In 1993, the members established the APEC Trade and Investment Framework, followed in 1994 by the APEC Economic Leaders' Declaration of Common Resolve (the Bogor Principles), which outlined an agenda for trade and investment liberalisation in the Asia-Pacific by reducing trade and investment barriers (APEC, 1994b). Non-binding Investment Principles were endorsed in November 1994 (APEC, 1994a). These Principles encourage APEC members to aspire to transparency, non-discrimination between investors and 'national treatment' of investors (subject to exceptions in domestic law), maintaining appropriate health, safety and environmental regulations, and minimising performance requirements. They also contain principles relating to compensation for expropriation, repatriation and convertibility, dispute settlement, entry and exit of personnel, and minimisation of barriers to capital export, as well as standards of investor behaviour.

The 1994 Principles were followed in 1995 by the Osaka Action Agenda (APEC, 1995), Annex II of which sets out principles for individual and collective action by member economies. These were subsequently amplified by the 1997 Menu of Options (APEC, 2013) and the 2002 Transparency Standards on Investment (APEC, 2007). Individual economies present individual action plans on a biennial basis, recording the actions taken to meet the Bogor Principle goals (APEC, 2014c).

Importantly, the member economies are not bound to implement the Principles or any recommendations from APEC, which are specifically expressed to be non-binding. Individual members of APEC are, however, provided with advice and support by APEC, and encouraged to adhere to the Principles through the process of regular reviews by APEC and reports, which are published on the APEC website summarising progress overall in relation to the aims to which APEC members have committed. For example, the report of August 2012 (APEC, 2012: 1), while finding some progress in lifting sectoral restrictions, raising screening levels for investment, increased transparency and simplification of procedures, also notes that sectoral restrictions remained common for areas deemed strategic. Reports by individual members describe the progress that the members have made in meeting the goals. Thus the Korean report in 2012 highlighted the small number of areas in which FDI was restricted, the abolition of the minimum capital requirement, changes to broadcasting rules, the publication of information on FDI rules on an annual basis and the number of bilateral investment treaties (BITs) entered into by Korea (APEC, 2012).

APEC members also support the creation of a regional economic area for trade and investment incorporating all APEC members, the Free Trade Area of the Asia-Pacific (FTAAP). In the short term, this should be achieved by a 'two-track' approach involving both a trans-Pacific track (through the TPP) and an East Asian track (through RCEP), with the latter still under negotiation (Scollay, 2012; APEC, 2014b).

Many Asian states, including both members and non-members of APEC, have also engaged to encourage and promote FDI by entering into bilateral or multilateral BITs, double tax agreements and regional FTAs (APEC, 2012) – all of which, in contrast to APEC Principles, bind the respective parties under international law. This includes the ASEAN states, which are bound by the ASEAN treaties (discussed below), but which also have bilateral treaties with each other, as well as with non-ASEAN states.

China is the clear leader in Asia in terms of the number of the BITs that it has signed (130 as at 16 September 2014), but nations such as India (eighty-four BITs) and Indonesia (sixty-three), as well as smaller trading nations such as Sri Lanka (twenty-eight) have also entered into numerous BITs to encourage investment (UNCTAD, 2014a).

While the content of BITs varies, a survey of investment and trade agreements entered into by APEC economies in 2008 (UNCTAD, 2008) found that there was a high degree of consistency among the APEC states in relation to the inclusion of certain core elements: national and most-favoured nation (MFN) treatment for established investments; 'fair and equitable treatment' of investments; guarantees of prompt, adequate and effective compensation for expropriation and of free transfers; and consent to state–state and investor–state dispute settlement. On the other hand, the survey also found that there were some significant variations in wording and content of provisions relating to investment-related capital transfers, key personnel and dispute settlement mechanisms (notably investor–state arbitration, detailed below). Particularly significantly for investment liberalisation, there were marked differences in the willingness of states to agree to the grant of MFN and national treatment for the pre-establishment phase of investments, and in the restriction of performance requirements.

The survey concludes that most of these agreements were focused on protecting investment by limiting the host country's discretion to regulate and that they were only indirectly focussed on the promotion of investment. Significantly, although the agreements are moderately liberalising, particularly when compared to the other areas of the world, much more could be done. In particular, the report concludes that the treaties did not satisfy the liberalisation requirements set out in the Non-Binding Principles and other APEC documents (UNCTAD, 2008).

In addition to BITs, many Asian states have also been relatively enthusiastic participants in negotiating FTAs. These may provide for significant commitments in relation to the liberalisation of trade and often include an investment chapter providing for investment protection and, on occasion, committing to investment liberalisation. Commitments in FTAs in relation to the liberalisation of investment are, however, generally less substantial than the commitments made in connection with trade (Bath and Nottage, 2015). The 2009 Agreement on Investment of the Framework Agreement on Comprehensive Economic Cooperation between China and the Association of Southeast Asian Nations, for example, does not include substantial commitments in relation to liberalisation of market access. There are some indications that this position in relation to investment market access may be beginning to change, both within ASEAN (as discussed below) and for other Asian nations. In particular, China has indicated in its BIT negotiations with the United States that it is prepared to negotiate on the basis that the treaty would cover all stages of investment and sectors, including pre-establishment – a major change in Chinese policy in relation to investment (Bourassa, 2013). Similarly, in the recent Australia–Korea FTA, both Australia and Korea agreed to provide improved terms in relation to investors, particularly in relation to the establishment of investments (DFAT, 2014b).

However, ASEAN economies have generally opted for a tighter legal structure in relation to trade and investment. In 1987, the governments of Brunei Darussalam, Indonesia, Malaysia, Philippines, Singapore and Thailand entered into the ASEAN Agreement for the Promotion and Protection of Investments (IGA) (ASEAN, 1987), followed by the launch of the ASEAN Free Trade Area in 1992 (with the aim of providing free movement of goods, services and investment) and the 1998 Framework Agreement on the ASEAN Investment Area (AIA) (ASEAN, 1998), which aimed to achieve liberalisation of investment policy and the establishment of a regional investment zone (Desierto, 2013). In 2008, the ASEAN states agreed on a new ASEAN Charter, which set out an ambitious plan, with a Blueprint, to create by 2015 three distinct ASEAN communities, including an economic community (ASEAN, 2008, 2016). In addition, the Blueprint set a target of not less than 70 per cent foreign (ASEAN) participation in services, whereby ASEAN investors should be permitted to own up to 70 per cent of the shares in service companies (Chirathivat and Srisangnam, 2013).

In addition, the IGA and AIA were replaced in 2012 when the 2009 ASEAN Comprehensive Investment Agreement (ACIA) finally came into force (ASEAN, 2009; Bath and Nottage, 2015). The ACIA, which aims to provide a comprehensive investment regime throughout the ASEAN area, is an important component of the ambitious economic community plan (ASEAN, 2013a; Desierto, 2013). Its aims include progressive liberalisation of investment regimes in five main sectors (manufacturing, agriculture, fisheries, forestry, mining and quarrying) and incidental services, enhanced protection, improved transparency, promotion of investment and cooperation to provide favourable conditions for investment (Article 1). The ACIA reflects a phased plan for liberalisation pursuant to which member states should liberalise their investment regimes by providing MFN and national treatment to investors and investments from other member states in relation to admission, establishment, management and operation of investments (Articles 5 and 6). This applies initially in relation to investments in manufacturing, agriculture, fisheries, forestry, mining and quarrying, and related service sectors (Article 3(3)), but may be extended to other sectors if the member states so agree. Article 7 prohibits restrictive performance requirements, and Article 8 places limits on nationality requirements for directors and senior managers. In addition, the ACIA allows foreign investors who are established in an ASEAN state to benefit from the regime established by the ACIA, thus potentially extending the benefits of a more liberalised investment regime to investors beyond the region (Article 19). These commitments are, however, qualified by 'reservation lists', which may be submitted by members setting out limitations and restrictions (Article 9), and are further limited by exclusions relating to taxation, subsidies, government procurement and other measures (Article 3(4)).

In the mid-term report on progress under the Blueprint for the Economic Community (ERIA, 2012), it was noted that there had been considerable progress in relation to investment liberalisation in the target sectors, but that there was space for the addition of industries to be liberalised. The World Bank (2014) takes the view that progress in liberalisation has been mixed. In particular, liberalisation in the oil and gas and agricultural sectors is proving challenging.

In addition to the ASEAN agreements, two major cross-regional initiatives have recently been negotiated. The expanded TPP (signed on 4 February 2016) involves a number of APEC members; the RCEP involves the ASEAN nations and its six partners in free trade agreements – Australia, New Zealand, China, Japan, Korea and India. The Guiding Principles and Objectives for Negotiating the Regional Comprehensive Investment Agreement (ASEAN et al., 2012: 2) state that 'RCEP will aim at creating a liberal, facilitative, and competitive investment environment in the region. Negotiations for investment under the RCEP will cover the four pillars of promotion, protection, facilitation and liberalization.' Although several RCEP negotiation rounds of negotiations have been held (DFAT, 2014c), it is not clear what has been proposed or agreed regarding investment liberalisation and facilitation. Although investment is part of the TPP, the confidentiality surrounding the actual negotiations meant that there was limited information on the likely content of the investment chapter, although it did not include an investor–state dispute settlement provision (Nottage, 2016).

In summary, it can be said that Asian nations nowadays generally support and encourage FDI, at least in principle; and that many nations have committed – at the domestic, bilateral and regional levels –to further encourage and facilitate FDI and, as part of that process, to liberalise market access to FDI. In practice, however, the FDI regimes of a considerable number of Asian economies continue to be restrictive. This indicates that the process of liberalisation remains difficult for many countries and that progress will continue to be gradual, notwithstanding domestic and regional initiatives aimed at facilitating and liberalising both trade and investment.

International arbitration mechanisms supporting investment in Asia

The boom in foreign investment into and within Asia has also been underpinned by new treaties and national laws supporting the use of international arbitration to resolve investment disputes, rather than merely recourse to national courts. Many inter-company disputes directly or indirectly involve cross-border investments, which are increasingly resolved by parties agreeing to the incorporation of international commercial arbitration (ICA) clauses in their underlying contracts.[8] Similar clauses can also be included in investment or 'concession' contracts negotiated between private investors and host government authorities, although these have become rarer.[9] Nowadays, as outlined above, investment treaties (including FTAs) increasingly contain substantive commitments from Asian host states for the benefit of all foreign investors from the treaty partner (home) state. Furthermore, these rights can often be enforced through investor–state arbitration (ISA) or other investor–state dispute settlement procedures set out in such treaties (Hwang and Thio, 2012).

Using the ICA system to resolve disputes between investors or with states

As occurred earlier in other parts of the world, ICA has emerged in Asia as the preferred method for resolving international disputes involving international trade and investment, especially among private firms over the last decade (Ginsburg and Ali, 2013). The dramatic growth in Asia-related ICA filings, as well as the emergence of major arbitration centres in the region (notably in Singapore, Hong Kong and Beijing/Shanghai), reflects more than just the underlying expansion of trade and investment – with more transactions leading to greater scope for disputes to emerge and then proceed to a binding decision from an agreed neutral third party (Fan, 2013). Businesses and their legal advisers have also been educated to realise that it may be better to entrust such decisions to private arbitrators, rather than to judges in local courts. This is especially true in developing countries, where the judiciary may be inexperienced in cross-border dispute resolution, inefficient and even corrupt or susceptible to political influence.

Governments throughout Asia, encouraged by international organisations such as the United Nations Commission on International Trade Law (UNCITRAL), as well as regional bodies (for example APEC, 1999), have also increasingly provided legislative support for ICA. First, almost all Asian states have acceded to the 1958 New York Convention on the Recognition and Enforcement of Foreign Arbitral Awards (NYC).[10] This convention limits the grounds for contesting enforcement in that state of an award rendered by an arbitral tribunal with an overseas seat agreed by the parties to the dispute, and it also promotes ICA by requiring local courts to decline to hear the dispute and instead refer it to arbitration when faced with a valid agreement to arbitrate abroad.

Secondly, the Asian region (including Australia and New Zealand) has one of the highest rates of uptake of the UNCITRAL Model Law on ICA.[11] The Model Law provides a template for national legislation setting out an efficient process for dealing with ICA proceedings before arbitrators and local courts at the agreed seat, for example by essentially limiting the grounds to set aside arbitral awards to those provided by the NYC when it comes to later enforcing the award overseas. In particular, such grounds do not include scope for the enforcing jurisdiction to annul awards where the arbitral tribunal has simply made errors of fact or even errors of law. Some governments in Asia, including Singapore and recently Korea, also provide significant financial and other in-kind support for national ICA centres – aiming to make those states even more attractive seats for ICA services, compared to traditional venues in Europe and the United States (Fan, 2013).

This strong contemporary support for ICA among firms and most governments in Asia has confounded some earlier 'culturalist' commentators who had perceived and anticipated little uptake of such a binding, law-based dispute resolution process, in contrast to negotiated or mediated settlements. They tended to tie this expectation to an ostensible preference in Asia for more harmonious and consensus-based processes, whereas the reality appears much more complex and nuanced (Taylor and Pryles, 2006).

ICA agreements and proceedings can occur not only between private parties involved in trading or investment relationships, but also between private investors and host states. However, the latter scenario typically requires the parties to agree too on an underlying cross-border investment contract, setting out all of the rights and obligations assumed by the state (such as tax breaks or non-discrimination principles) and the investor (such as certain minimum investments). Another impediment may be national law limiting the ability of host states to enter into such ad hoc agreements, including the provision for binding ICA in the event of a dispute, or limits to the enforcement of ICA awards resulting from such agreements in the host state. In addition, the dispute resolution process may take place under agreed arbitration rules that are better suited for inter-firm disputes, by favouring expediency over accuracy or transparency in decision making.[12] Lastly, the applicable substantive law governing the arbitration may be exclusively or partly based on a national law (usually contract law), which gives one party an unfair advantage and which does not necessarily reflect public law principles usually applicable to states (such as non-discrimination or 'due process').

Using treaty-based ISA to resolve investor–state disputes

Treaty-based ISA provisions have emerged as a response to problems using the ICA system where one party is a sovereign state (Greenberg, Kee and Weeramantry, 2011: 492–493). The host state provides express advance consent to arbitration of disputes in a BIT or FTA concluded with the investor's home state and the treaty also sets out substantive protections (such as non-discrimination or national treatment, fair and equitable treatment or 'due process', and compensation for expropriation), which are governed primarily by public international law. The treaty also typically provides options for arbitration rules that are appropriate for investor–state disputes, such as the UNCITRAL Arbitration Rules (which are also popular for ad hoc arbitration of purely commercial disputes) or the Rules of the International Centre for the Settlement of Investment Disputes (ICSID), affiliated with the World Bank. The ICSID Arbitration Rules are especially attractive for investors when both the home and host states are also parties to the Framework 1965 Washington Convention (also known as the ICSID Convention),[13] because the arbitration procedure is extensively 'delocalised' from intervention by local courts. In particular, complaints about the resultant award can be heard only by an ad hoc annulment committee of (newly appointed) arbitrators, not by local courts at the seat, as with ISA (or ICA) proceedings conducted, for example, under the UNCITRAL Rules.

Another reason why ISA provisions have become popular as an additional option for investors seeking to claim against host states for violating substantive protections, instead of inter-state arbitration (also often provided in investment treaties), is because the latter process tends to become more 'politicised'. In particular, if and when a dispute arises, the disgruntled investor may not be able to persuade its home state to initiate and pursue appropriately the inter-state process.[14]

Accordingly, ISA provisions have become commonplace in investment treaties, including in those agreed to by Asian states. Most involve a capital-exporting state and a developing country, but there are also now many examples involving more developed or middle-income states (such as Malaysia). In addition, Asian states such as Korea often agreed to ISA in investment treaties at the bequest of more developed states; now that Korea is itself a capital-exporting state, it presses for inclusion of ISA protections – as in the recent Korea–Australia FTA (DFAT, 2014b). In addition, especially since the late 1990s, China has switched from a restrictive to an expansive approach to ISA protections in its treaties.[15] Japan has belatedly stepped up its treaty negotiation programme and almost always secures ISA protections (Hamamoto and Nottage, 2013). Among ASEAN member states, ISA protections were included in ASEAN's 1987 IGA and significantly elaborated in the 2009 ACIA (Maxwell and Wegner, 2009). Unsurprisingly, therefore, ISA is found in most 'ASEAN+' FTAs except for the FTA with Japan (omitting an investment chapter altogether). ISA is also on the agenda for RCEP and was also part of the longer-standing negotiations for an expanded TPP – involving five states from Asia (plus Australia, New Zealand and five others).[16]

However, ASEAN's FTAs already have multiple features that retain significant sovereignty for host states with respect to ISA proceedings. In particular, the ACIA (Article 40) and AANZFTA (Article 27) allow the partner states to issue joint interpretations on treaty provisions. These and most other ASEAN agreements also allow the states' tax authorities to consult and decide whether a host state's taxation measure amounts to 'expropriation', with such decisions to be given 'serious consideration' by the arbitral tribunal ruling on such an ISA claim (Bath and Nottage, 2015; cf. Nottage, 2014c). The treaties also establish committees of officials to monitor implementation, which might extend to advising on interpretation of disputed provisions and certainly can help to avoid disputes arising or escalating.[17]

Nonetheless, it is far from certain whether and precisely how ISA protections may be incorporated into future regional FTAs such as the RCEP and the TPP, if and when the latter comes into effect. ISA has been targeted by some civil society groups as taking away too much power from host states to act or legislate in good faith for their national interests (cf. Campbell, Nappert and Nottage, 2014). Australia's Productivity Commission shared a similar concern about ISA more generally, in a 2010 report that led the Gillard government to declare in April 2011 that it would eschew any form of ISA in future treaties. Economists in the Commission also questioned the received wisdom that offering ISA resulted in significant increases to inbound FDI and that (Australia's) outbound investors relied on ISA when engaging even with developing countries. These concerns have been queried, particularly in the current Asian context (Nottage, 2013), and the Liberal-led Australian government has, since 7 September 2013, reverted to Australia's case-by-case assessment of whether and how to include ISA provisions.[18] Nonetheless, similar concerns have attracted considerable attention worldwide and deserve ongoing scrutiny.[19]

Potential backlash against ISA could spread in parts of Asia. Some longer-standing reservations about inbound FDI in general, and (to a lesser extent) arbitration as opposed to national court processes, can be inferred from the fact that some states have still not joined the ICSID Convention.[20] Sornarajah (2011: 246–250) adds that several ASEAN countries have had 'negative experiences' with investment arbitration, although so far few cases have been filed generally under treaties – mainly because of provisions requiring that the claimant show that an investment has been preapproved for treaty protection and/or made (and maintained) in accordance with national FDI laws, as well as often broadly worded general exception clauses (for example concerning public health measures).[21] He is worried about the 'great danger . . . that the richer states of the region – Singapore, Malaysia and possibly Australia – will seek to make use of treaties as a sword, provoking negative reactions from the other states' in the region (Sornarajah, 2011: 251).

Australian investors have indeed subsequently prevailed, quite controversially, in an UNCITRAL Rules arbitration against India arising out of a mining project (Kachwaha, 2013). Australian investors are now involved in ICSID arbitrations against Pakistan and Indonesia.[22] However, Australia itself was also subject to its first ever claim, under UNCITRAL Rules with the seat in Singapore, brought by Philip Morris Asia under the 1993 BIT with Hong Kong in relation to Australia's strict new tobacco plain packaging legislation.[23] Almost all other ASEAN states have now been subject to ISA claims as well.[24] India announced in 2013 that it was reviewing its treaties with ISA and Indonesia indicated in March 2014 that it would review its BITs as they come up for renewal.[25]

Yet, so far, the numbers and proportions of Asia-related ISA proceedings remain comparatively low. Rather than this being attributable directly to Asian cultural norms generally favouring harmony, the paucity appears to be linked to organisational and other features characteristic of parties from specific Asian countries,[26] as well as to insufficient information and other 'institutional barriers' related to the ISA system (Nottage and Weeramantry, 2011). As Asian state respondents start to become more familiar with treaty-based ISA, with examples emerging of even least-developed countries prevailing in formal proceedings,[27] we may see more claims being contested rather than being settled informally – as may have occurred in the past. There is also a slow increase in ISA claims being filed by Asian investors, which may also help to generate confidence in this dispute resolution mechanism (Kim, 2013).[28] However, this tendency may also exacerbate concerns about ISA even among some developed countries in the region, such as Australia.[29]

Conclusions

In summary, the policies and approaches within Asia in relation to FDI appear to reflect a certain amount of ambivalence. On the one hand, the opening up of markets to FDI through revisions to domestic legislation, supported by bilateral and regional initiatives directed towards investment encouragement and liberalisation, has been accompanied by substantial growth in FDI across the region. Asian nations actively engage in and negotiate regional agreements directed at the facilitation and liberalisation of trade and investment, which necessarily involve commitments to remove or modify domestic restrictions on FDI and to submit to dispute resolution mechanisms, including at a state level through ISA. On the other hand, a significant number of Asian nations continue to maintain investment regimes that are regarded as highly restrictive by the OECD, APEC and the World Bank, reflecting difficulty at a domestic level in taking the necessary steps substantially to modify and remove FDI restrictions. Given the range of legal and economic systems in the region, it can be expected that this conflict between the desire to regionalise and liberalise both trade and investment, and the economic and political pressures imposed at a domestic level, will continue to have an impact on progress in developing investment policy in Asia.

In relation to investment dispute resolution, treaty-based ISA stands now at something of a crossroads in the Asian region. The more developed countries may be able to 'opt out' of ISA provisions in bilateral and even regional treaties.[30] Yet this will require concessions on other matters or otherwise complicate and delay negotiations, especially in regional treaties, as well as undermining efforts from developed countries to credibly insist on ISA protections vis-à-vis their developing country parties. A more likely scenario is therefore that ISA provisions will continue to be included in Asian treaties, but with extensive exceptions and limitations to balance public and private interests. These will probably remain along the lines of existing ASEAN investment treaties (Wongkaew, 2014), but may include further limitations or transparency measures seen or proposed recently particularly for developed countries, including the United States and European Union member states (Campbell et al., 2014). After all, ISA retains significant advantages in 'depoliticising' investment dispute resolution compared to an inter-state process, especially when compared to litigating against host states in developing countries in Asia.

Notes

We thank Lucy Cameron, 2014 student intern at the Sydney Centre for International Law, for editorial assistance and research especially into recent investment treaty arbitrations involving Asian and Australian parties.

1 For the purposes of this chapter, the Asian region includes North, Southeast and South Asia, but not the Middle Eastern countries generally referred to by UNCTAD as 'West Asia'.

2 Covering ASEAN states, China, Korea, Japan, India, Australia and New Zealand (Australian Government Department of Foreign Affairs and Trade (DFAT), 2014c).

3 Covering Australia, Brunei Darussalam, Chile, Japan, Malaysia, Mexico, New Zealand, Peru, Singapore, United States and Vietnam (Nottage, 2016).

4 State Council of the People's Republic of China (2013) *Notice on the Printing and Distributing the Overall Plan for the China (Shanghai) Pilot Free Trade Zone*.

5 The National Development and Reform Commission (NRDC) (2014) *Administrative Measures for the Verification and Approval and the Recordation of Foreign Investment Projects*.

6 The rules are complex and restrictions are imposed by nature of investor (particularly Bangladeshi and Pakistani nationals), type of target entity (and equity interests) and type of industry. Investments subject to the government route include foreign investment in up to 26 per cent of defence projects, investment of between 49–74 per cent in broadcasting carriage services, investments of more than 74 per cent in existing airports and majority ownership of telecom services, private banking or single-brand product retail trading.

7 It should be noted that Hong Kong also acts as a conduit for Chinese inbound and outbound investment. In 2012, US$30 billion was invested in Hong Kong by Chinese investors and $65 billion was invested in China by Hong Kong investors (UNCTAD, 2014b).

8 The Singapore International Arbitration Centre, for example, has experienced a burgeoning caseload over the last decade – reaching 619 cases by the end of 2013 (SIAC, 2014). Out of an indicative sample of thirty-nine cases, five involved Asian parties to joint ventures and/or shareholder agreements.

9 An example is the highly controversial 'Bangkok Second Stage Expressway' thirty-year concession contract, concluded between the Thai government and a company 65 per cent owned (originally) by Kumagai Gumi from Japan (Fisman and Werker, 2006).

10 Myanmar is the latest Asian state to accede to the NYC: see UNCITRAL (2014).

11 Agreed in 1985 and revised in 2006. See generally Greenberg et al. (2011).

12 For example, there may be strict confidentiality obligations (typically favoured by commercial parties, but potentially conflicting with citizens' expectations of their state) or more powers given to the presiding arbitrator. See Nottage and Miles (2010).

13 Convention on the Settlement of Disputes between States and Nationals of Other States, available online at https://icsid.worldbank.org/ICSID/Index.jsp [accessed 10 February 2014].

14 Comparing similar problems in international tax disputes in the Asia-Pacific region and the recent emergence of an interesting hybrid dispute resolution process, see Burch, Nottage and Williams (2012).

15 See further references, and a focus on its 2010 FTA with ASEAN, in Bath and Nottage (2015).

16 On 'ASEAN+' FTAs and the TPP, see ASEAN (2015) and Nottage (2016), respectively.

17 See Wongkaew (2014: 5.6.4); more generally, Burch et al. (2012). Wongkaew (2014: 5.6.3) also mentions the constraints on the ISA tribunal's remedial powers (restitution or monetary damages excluding punitive damages) and scope to appoint experts to report on public health and other matters, as well as limitation periods for ISA claims and preliminary rulings on jurisdiction or merits (Wongkaew, 2014: 5.6.2). Substantively, moreover, the ASEAN agreements also tend to set out general and security exceptions, enhanced discretion in economic crises, and carve-outs for government grants, services or procurement (Wongkaew, 2014: 5.4), as well as compulsory licences of intellectual property rights and some national laws regarding expropriation of law (Wongkaew, 2014: 5.3).

18 See DFAT (2014a); Trakman and Sharma (2015).

19 See Armstrong et al. (2014). On renewed problems of costs and delays associated with both ICA and ISA, see also Nottage (2015b).

20 Note especially the absence of India, Vietnam, Laos, Myanmar and Thailand (signed, but not yet deposited, instruments of ratification) (ICSID, 2016).

21 See generally Sornarajah (2011), describing investment arbitrations against the Philippines in particular, as well as Myanmar, Pakistan, Malaysia, Indonesia and Thailand – although the last two cases were based on investment agreements rather than treaties. See also Wongkaew (2014: 5.1).

22 See, respectively, *Tethyan Copper Company Pty Ltd v Islamic Republic of Pakistan*, ICSID Case No. ARB/12/1; *Churchill Mining PLC and Planet Mining Pty Ltd v Republic of Indonesia*, Consolidated ICSID Case Nos ARB/12/40 and 12/14. The Tribunal upheld jurisdiction in the latter case, but only on the basis of consent to ISA included in a mining licence granted by the Indonesian authorities, not under the consent provided to all foreign investors under the (peculiarly worded) BIT with Australia (Nottage, 2015a).

23 See Mitchell and Wurzberger (2011). Australia won its jurisdictional challenge in 2015: *Philip Morris Asia Ltd (Hong Kong) v The Commonwealth of Australia*, UNCITRAL, PCA Case no. 2012-12, 17 December 2015.

24 See, e.g., the discussion of two claims against Vietnam under its BIT with France, for investments related to health care and food assistance, in Peterson (2014).

25 See *The Economic Times* (2013); Nottage (2015a).

26 Such as risk-averseness and a long-term perspective, traditionally, on the part of large Japanese companies, cf. Tsuchiya and Wells (2011). Nonetheless, pursuant to an aluminium smelter joint venture contract with Indonesia rather than an investment treaty, a formal ICSID claim was lodged against Indonesia – then settled – by a consortium of blue-chip Japanese companies (Smith and Browning, 2014).

27 See, e.g., *Cambodia Power Company v Kingdom of Cambodia*, ICSID Case No. ARB/09/18, 22 March 2011 (rejecting a US investor's claim under a power plant investment contract).

28 In addition to the thirteen ISA claimants found to have Asian nationality as of 1 August 2011, listed in Nottage and Weeramantry (2011: 43–44), there have been at least six more filed from Asia or Australia (three from Australia – against Pakistan, Indonesia and India; one from Macau/China – against Laos; one from Singapore – against Papua New Guinea). Others claims that have been threatened against India include one from a Malaysian investor (Axiata). There are also reports of two claims lodged or forthcoming from Korean investors, against an Asian state and an African state. See Nottage and Butt (2015).

29 On domestic political difficulties facing the Australian government in ratifying its FTA with Korea signed on 8 April 2014, see Nottage (2014a). However, a Senate Committee has recommended against enactment of a Bill proposed by a Greens Party senator that would preclude Australia from entering into any treaties providing for ISA (or, indeed, investor-state mediation): see Nottage (2014b).

30 See, e.g., the omission of ISA from the 2011 Protocol to the Australia–New Zealand FTA, available online at http://www.info.dfat.gov.au/Info/Treaties/treaties.nsf/AllDocIDs/E6F1AE822746BA39CA25784200205358 [accessed 25 July 2016]. See also the same omission, only between those two countries, in the 2009 AANZFTA 'Official Documents', available online at http://www.dfat.gov.au/fta/aanzfta/ (accessed 13 March 2014). See further the Malaysia–Australia FTA (signed 22 May 2012), available online at http://www.dfat.gov.au/fta/mafta/ [accessed 13 March 2014], although its omission of ISA has limited significance because it exists anyway under AANZFTA and the Malaysia FTA was concluded under the now-superseded (Labour) Gillard Government Trade Policy Statement of 2011. Nonetheless, ISA was also omitted in the Japan–Australia Economic Partnership Agreement, concluded by Australia's new (Liberal-led) Government on 7 April 2014: see Nottage (2014c).

References

APEC (1994a) *APEC Non-binding Investment Principles*, available online at http://www.apec.org/Press/News-Releases/2010/~/media/965E37FDA6D848B4A0350D68D2A4BE1C.ashx [accessed 14 April 2014].

APEC (1994b) *Bogor Declaration: APEC Economic Leaders' Declaration of Common Resolve*, available online at http://www.apec.org/Meeting-Papers/Leaders-Declarations/1994/1994_aelm.aspx [accessed 10 April 2014].

APEC (1995) *The Osaka Action Agenda: Implementation of the Bogor Declaration*, available online at http://www.apec.org/~/media/Files/Groups/IP/02_esc_oaaupdate.pdf [accessed 26 July 2016].

APEC (1999) *International Commercial Disputes: A Guide to Arbitration and Dispute Resolution in APEC Member Economies, 1999*, available online at http://publications.apec.org/publication-detail.php?pub_id=705 [accessed 14 April 2014].

APEC (2007) 'APEC Transparency Standards', available online at http://www.apec.org/Groups/Committee-on-Trade-and-Investment/APEC-Transparency-Standards.aspx [accessed 14 April 2014].

APEC (2011) *2010 Guide to Investment Regimes of APEC Member Economies*, 7th edn, available online at http://publications.apec.org/publication-detail.php?pub_id=1120 [accessed 10 April 2014].

APEC (2012) *APEC's Bogor Goals Progress Report*, 13 August, available online at http://www.apec.org/About-Us/About-APEC/Achievements-and-Benefits/~/media/Files/AboutUs/AchievementsBenefits/20120822_APECsBogorGoalsProgressReport.ashx [accessed 10 April 2014].

APEC (2013) 'Action Plans', available online at http://www.apec.org/About-Us/How-APEC-Operates/Action-Plans.aspx [accessed 10 April 2014].

APEC (2014a) 'About APEC, Mission Statement', available online at http://www.apec.org/About-Us/About-APEC/Mission-Statement.aspx [accessed 28 February 2014].

APEC (2014b) 'Regional Economic Integration Agenda and the Evolution of Economic Integration in the Asia-Pacific Region', available online at http://www.apec.org/About-Us/About-APEC/Fact-Sheets/Regional-Economic-Integration-Agenda.aspx [accessed 14 April 2014].

APEC (2014c)' Individual Action Plan Submissions', available online at http://www.apec.org/About-Us/How-APEC-Operates/Action-Plans/IAP-Submissions.aspx [accessed 10 April 2014].

Armstrong, S., Kurtz, J., Nottage, L., and Trakman, L. (2014) 'The Fundamental Importance of Foreign Direct Investment to Australia in the 21st Century: Reforming Treaty and Dispute Resolution Practice', *Australian Centre for International Commercial Arbitration (ACICA) Review*, 2(2): 22–35.

ASEAN (1987) *ASEAN Agreement for the Promotion and Protection of Investments*, available online at http://asean.org/?static_post=the-1987-asean-agreement-for-the-promotion-and-protection-of-investments [accessed 26 July 2016].

ASEAN (1998) *Framework Agreement on the ASEAN Investment Area*, available online at http://www.asean.org/storage/images/archive/7994.pdf [accessed 26 July 2016].

ASEAN (2008) *Charter of the Association of South-East Asian Nations*, available online at http://www.asean.sec/publications/ASEAN.Charter.pdf [accessed 26 July 2016].

ASEAN (2009) *ASEAN Comprehensive Investment Agreement*, available online at http://www.asean.org/storage/images/2013/economic/aia/ACIA_Final_Text_26%20Feb%202009.pdf [accessed 26 July 2016].

ASEAN (2013a) *ASEAN Comprehensive Investment Agreement: A Guidebook for Businesses and Investors*, available online at http://investasean.asean.org/files/upload/ACIA%20guidebook%20Business.pdf [accessed 26 July 2016].

ASEAN (2013b) *ASEAN Investment Report 2012: The Changing FDI Landscape*, available online at http://www.asean.org/storage/images/2013/other_documents/AIR%202012%20Final%20(July%202013).pdf [accessed 26 July 2016].

ASEAN (2015) 'List of Instruments', available online at http://agreement.asean.org/ [accessed 26 July 2016].

ASEAN (2016) 'A Blueprint for Growth, ASEAN Economic Community 2015: Progress and Key Achievements', available online at http://www.asean.org/wp-content/uploads/images/2015/November/aec.php [accessed 22 August 2016].

ASEAN, Australia, New Zealand, China, Japan, Korea and India (2012) *Guiding Principles and Objectives for Negotiating the Regional Comprehensive Economic Partnership*, available online at http://dfat.gov.au/trade/agreements/rcep/Documents/guiding-principles-rcep.pdf [accessed 26 July 2016].

Australian Government Department of Foreign Affairs and Trade (DFAT) (2014a) 'Investor–State Dispute Settlement', available online at http://dfat.gov.au/trade/topics/pages/isds.aspx [accessed 19 July 2016].

Australian Government Department of Foreign Affairs and Trade (DFAT) (2014b) 'Korea–Australia Free Trade Agreement, Fact Sheet: Investment', available online at http://dfat.gov.au/trade/agreements/kafta/Documents/fact-sheet-investment.pdf [accessed 26 July 2016].

Australian Government Department of Foreign Affairs and Trade (DFAT) (2014c) 'Regional Comprehensive Economic Partnership Negotiations', available online at https://www.dfat.gov.au/fta/rcep/ [accessed 27 February 2013].

Bath, V. (2011) 'The Quandary for Chinese Regulators: Controlling the Flow of Investment into and out of China', in V. Bath and L. Nottage (eds) *Foreign Investment and Dispute Resolution Law and Practice in Asia*, London: Routledge, 68–89.

Bath, V., and Nottage, L. (2015) 'The ASEAN Comprehensive Investment Agreement and "ASEAN Plus": The Australia–New Zealand Free Trade Area (AANZFTA) and the PRC–ASEAN Investment Agreement', in M. Bungenberg, J. Griebel, S. Hobe and A. Reinisch (eds) *International Investment Law*, Oxford: Hart, 283–303.

Bourassa, B. (2013) 'U.S. and China Breakthrough Announcement on the Bilateral Investment Treaty Negotiations', *Treasury Notes*, 15 July, available online at http://www.treasury.gov/connect/blog/Pages/U.S.-and-China-Breakthrough-Announcement-.aspx [accessed 9 April 2014].

Burch, M., Nottage, L., and Williams, B. (2012) 'Appropriate Treaty-based Dispute Resolution for Asia-Pacific Commerce in the 21st Century', *UNSW Law Journal*, 35(3): 1013–1043.

Campbell, C., Nappert, S., and Nottage, L. (2014) 'Assessing Treaty-based Investor–State Dispute Settlement: Abandon, Retain or Reform?', *Transnational Dispute Management*, 1, available online at http://transnational-dispute-management.com/article.asp?key=2024 [accessed 11 April 2014].

Chirathivat, S., and Srisangnam, P. (2013) 'The 2030 Architecture of Association of Southeast Asian Nations Free Trade Agreements', ADBI Working Paper Series No. 419, available online at http://papers.ssrn.com/sol3/papers.cfm?abstract_id=2256824 [accessed 14 April 2014].

Desierto, D. (2013) 'Investment Treaties: ASEAN', in H. Hill and M. Socorro Gochocco-Bautista (eds) *Asia Rising: Growth and Resilience in an Uncertain Global Economy*, Cheltenham: Edward Elgar, 284–201.

Economic Research Institute for ASEAN and East Asia (ERIA) (2012) *Mid-term Review of the Implementation of AEC Blue Print: Executive Summary*, October, available online at http://www.eria.org/Mid-Term%20Review%20of%20the%20Implementation%20of%20AEC%20Blue%20Print-Executive%20Summary.pdf [accessed 9 April 2014].

The Economic Times (2013) 'Investment Pacts Can't Be Subject to Foreign Laws', 17 April, available online at http://articles.economictimes.indiatimes.com/2013-04-17/news/38616367_1_canada-india-business-council-indian-high-commissioner-protection-agreement [accessed 11 April 2014].

Fan, K. (2013) 'International Dispute Resolution Trends in Asia' *Transnational Dispute Management*, 10(4), available online at http://www.transnational-dispute-management.com/article.asp?key=1970 [accessed 11 April 2014].

Fisman, R., and Werker, E. (2006) 'The Search for Security', *Financial Times*, 23 March, available online at http://www.ft.com/intl/cms/s/2/28cc44b8-ba86-11da-980d-0000779e2340.html#axzz2ypPT4IU2 [accessed 14 April 2014].

Ginsburg, T., and Ali, S. (eds) (2013) *Arbitration in Asia*, New York: Juris.

Government of India Ministry of Commerce and Industry (2014) *Consolidated FDI Policy, Effective 7 April 2014*, available online at http://dipp.nic.in/English/Policies/FDI_Circular_2014.pdf [accessed 14 April 2014].

Greenberg, S., Kee, C., and Weeramantry, J. R. (2011) *International Commercial Arbitration: An Asia-Pacific Perspective*, Cambridge/New York: Cambridge University Press.

Hamamoto, S., and Nottage, L. (2013) 'Japan', in C. Brown (ed.) *Commentaries on Selected Model Investment Treaties*, Oxford: Oxford University Press, 347–391.

Hwang, M., and Thio, N. (2012) 'Investment Treaty Arbitration in Asia: Contemporary Issues and Challenges', *Transnational Dispute Management*, 9(3), available online at http://www.transnational-dispute-management.com/article.asp?key=1829 [accessed 11 April 2014].

ICSID (2016) 'List of Contracting States and Other Signatories to Convention', available online at https://icsid.worldbank.org/ICSID/FrontServlet?requestType=ICSIDDocRH&actionVal=ContractingStates&ReqFrom=Main [accessed 19 July 2016].

Kachwaha, S. (2013) 'The *White Industries Limited–India* BIT Award: A Critical Assessment', *Arbitration International*, 29(2): 275–293.

Kim, J. (2013) 'A Pivot to Asia in Investor–State Arbitration: The Coming Emergence of Asian Claimants', *ICSID Review*, 27(2): 399–415.

Kundi, I. A. (2013) 'Cabinet Approves Draft of Investment Policy 2013', *The Nation*, 14 March, available online at http://www.nation.com.pk/business/14-Mar-2013/cabinet-approves-draft-of-investment-policy-2013 [accessed 9 April 2014].

Liu, M., Berry S., and Tam, E. (2012) 'Hong Kong', in O. Borgers (ed.) *Foreign Investment Review: Mergers, National Interest and National Security in 26 Jurisdictions Worldwide 2012*, 47–51, available online at https://www.lw.com/thoughtLeadership/foreign-investment-review-china-and-hong-kong-2012 [accessed 14 April 2014].

Maxwell, I., and Wegner, K.-J. (2009) 'The New ASEAN Comprehensive Investment Agreement', *Asian International Arbitration Journal*, 5(2): 167–189.

Mitchell, A., and Wurzberger, S. (2011) 'Boxed in? Australia's Plain Tobacco Packaging Initiative and International Investment Law', *Arbitration International*, 27(4): 623–651.

Nicolas, F., Thomsen, S., and Bang, M. H. (2013) 'Lessons from Investment Policy Reform in Korea', available online at http://www.oecd-ilibrary.org/finance-and-investment/lessons-from-investment-policy-reform-in-korea_5k4376zqcpf1-en [accessed 27 February 2014].

Nottage, L. (2013) 'Throwing the Baby with the Bathwater: Australia's New Policy on Treaty-based Investor–State Arbitration and its Impact in Asia', *Asian Studies Review*, 37(2): 253–272.

Nottage, L. (2014a) 'Investor–State Arbitration Down Under: KAFTA Review and the Anti-ISDS Bill', 5 September, available online at http://blogs.usyd.edu.au/japaneselaw/2014/09/kafta_2.html [accessed 15 September 2014]

Nottage, L. (2014b) 'The "Anti-ISDS Bill" before the Senate: What Future for Investor–State Arbitration in Australia?', *International Trade and Business Law Review*, 18: 245–293.

Nottage, L. (2014c) 'Why No Investor–State Arbitration in the Australia–Japan FTA?', 9 April, available online at http://www.eastasiaforum.org/2014/04/09/why-no-investor-state-arbitration-in-the-australia-japan-fta/ [accessed 15 September 2014]

Nottage, L. (2015a) 'Do Many of Australia's Bilateral Treaties Really Not Provide Full Advance Consent to Investor–State Arbitration? Analysis of *Planet Mining v Indonesia* and Regional Implications', *Transnational Dispute Management*, 1, available online at https://www.transnational-dispute-management.com/article.asp?key=2177 [accessed 19 July 2016].

Nottage, L. (2015b) 'In/Formalization and Globalization of International Commercial Arbitration and Investment Treaty Arbitration in Asia', in J. Zekoll, M. Baelz and I. Amelung (eds) *Formalisation and Flexibilisation in Dispute Resolution,* The Netherlands: Martinus Nijhoff, 211–249.

Nottage, L. (2016) 'The TPP Investment Chapter and Investor-State Arbitration in Asia and Oceania: Assessing Prospects for Ratification', *Melbourne Journal of International Law,* 17(2): forthcoming, available online at http://ssrn.com/abstract=2767996 [accessed 22 August 2016].

Nottage, L., and Butt, S. (2015) 'Recent International Commercial Arbitration and Investor–State Arbitration Developments Impacting on Australia's Investments in the Resources Sector', in P. Evans and G. Moens (eds) *Arbitration and Dispute Resolution in the Resources Sector: A Comparative Perspective,* Berlin: Springer, 153–179.

Nottage, L., and Miles, K. (2010) 'Revising Investor–State Arbitration Rules in Australia and Japan to Meet Public Interests', in L. Nottage and R. Garnett (eds) *International Arbitration in Australia,* Sydney: Federation Press, 222–252.

Nottage, L., and Weeramantry, J. R. (2011) 'Investment Arbitration in Asia: Five Perspectives on Law and Practice', in V. Bath and L. Nottage (eds) *Investment Law and Dispute Resolution Law and Practice in Asia,* London: Routledge, 25–52.

Organisation for Economic Co-operation and Development (OECD) (2009) *India: Investment Policy Review – OECD,* Paris: OECD.

Organisation for Economic Co-operation and Development (OECD) (2013) 'FDI Regulatory Restrictiveness Index 2013', available online at http://www.oecd.org/investment/fdiindex.htm [accessed 27 February 2014].

Organisation for Economic Co-operation and Development (OECD) (2014) *OECD Investment Policy Reviews: Myanmar,* available online at http://www.oecd.org/daf/inv/investment-policy/Myanmar-IPR-2014.pdf [accessed 10 April 2014].

Palit, A. (2009) 'India's Foreign Investment Policy: Achievements and Inadequacies', available online at https://www.ifri.org/sites/default/files/atoms/files/av18palitfinal.pdf [accessed 26 July 2016].

Peterson, L. (2014) 'As Vietnam Explores Collection of Costs Award against Unsuccessful Investor, Another Claimant Sticks Its Head above the Parapet', *Investment Arbitration Reporter,* 14 February, available online at http://www.iareporter.com/articles/20140214 [accessed 11 April 2014].

Reserve Bank of India (2014) 'FAQs, Foreign Investments in India, Foreign Direct Investment', available online at http://www.rbi.org.in/scripts/FAQView.aspx?Id=26 [accessed 9 April 2014].

Scollay, R. (2012) 'APEC's Regional Economic Integration Agenda and the Evolution of Economic Integration in the Asia-Pacific Region', Korea Institute of International Economic Studies APEC Study Series No. 12–02, available online at http://papers.ssrn.com/sol3/papers.cfm?abstract_id=2319745 [accessed 16 September 2014].

Singapore International Arbitration Centre (SIAC) (2014) 'Facts and Figures; Profiles of Cases', available online at http://www.siac.org.sg/2014-11-03-13-33-43/facts-figures/profile-of-cases [accessed 26 July 2016].

Smith, M., and Browning, L. (2014) 'Indonesia and Nippon Asahan Aluminium Consortium Reach Settlement', Ashurst Dispute Resolution Newsflash, available online at http://www.ashurst.com/publication-item.aspx?id_Content=10053 [accessed 11 April 2014].

Sornarajah, M. (2011) 'Review of Asian Views on Foreign Investment Law', in V. Bath and L. Nottage (eds) *Investment Law and Dispute Resolution Law and Practice in Asia,* London: Routledge, 242–254.

Taylor, V., and Pryles, M. (2006) 'The Cultures of Dispute Resolution in Asia', in M. Pryles (ed.) *Dispute Resolution in Asia,* The Hague: Kluwer Law International, 1–28.

Trakman, L., and Sharma, K. (2015) 'Locating Australia on the Pacific Rim: Trade, Investment and the Asian Century', *Transnational Dispute Management,* 1, available online at https://www.transnational-dispute-management.com/article.asp?key=2178 [accessed 19 July 2016].

Tsuchiya, C., and Wells, L. (2011) 'Japanese Multinationals in Foreign Disputes: Do They Behave Differently, and Does It Matter for Host Countries?', *Transnational Dispute Management*, 5, available online at http://www.transnational-dispute-management.com/article.asp?key=1795 [accessed 11 April 2014].

UNCITRAL (2014) 'Status', available online at http://www.uncitral.org/uncitral/en/uncitral_texts/arbitration/NYConvention_status.html [accessed 14 February 2014].

UNCTAD (2008) *Identifying Core Elements in Investment Agreements in the APEC Region*, New York/Geneva: UNCTAD.

UNCTAD (2013) *World Investment Report 2013: Global Value Chains – Investment and Trade for Development*, available online at http://unctad.org/en/PublicationsLibrary/wir2013_en.pdf [accessed 9 April 2014].

UNCTAD (2014a) 'Bilateral FDI Statistics', available online at http://unctad.org/en/Pages/DIAE/FDI%20Statistics/FDI-Statistics-Bilateral.aspx [accessed 16 September 2014].

UNCTAD (2014b) *World Investment Report 2014: Investing in the SDGs – An Action Plan*, available online at http://unctad.org/en/PublicationsLibrary/wir2014_en.pdf [accessed 16 September 2014].

UNCTADStat (2014) 'Inward and Outward Foreign Direct Investment Flows, Annual, 1970–2013', available online at https://knoema.com/UNCTADFDI2014Sep/inward-and-outward-foreign-direct-investment-flows-and-stock-annual-1970-2013 [accessed 26 July 2016].

Wongkaew, T. (2014) 'A Resilient Boat in Stormy Seas: ASEAN Investment Agreements and the Current Investor–State Dispute Settlement Regime', *Transnational Dispute Management*, 11(1), available online at http://www.transnational-dispute-management.com/article.asp?key=2040 [accessed 11 April 2014].

World Bank (2014) *East Asia Pacific Economic Update*, available online at http://www.worldbank.org/content/dam/Worldbank/document/EAP/region/eap-update-april-2014-full-report.pdf [accessed 10 April 2014].

Part III

Asian traditions and their transformations

12 National control over local law making in Indonesia

Simon Butt

Indonesia's post-Soeharto decentralisation experiment was put into action from 2001. Since then, local governments have enjoyed greatly expanded power to devise policy and enact 'regional regulations' (*peraturan daerah*, commonly abbreviated to *Perda*), issuing many thousands of them.[1] Legally speaking, however, the central government has retained almost unbridled control over regional law making: the central government can override or annul almost any Perda.

This chapter examines the process by which the national government reviews Perda and the grounds upon which it can invalidate them. Its main focus is the so-called *Klarifikasi* (clarification) stage of the process, under which the Ministry of Home Affairs (MoHA) examines by-laws local governments submit to it for review. If MoHA uncovers legal flaws in a by-law, then it sends a formal letter – which is also referred to as a *Klarifikasi* – to the head of the local government from which the by-law originates, outlining the flaws it has identified. The letter calls on the head to coordinate with the regional parliament to revise the Perda, taking account of the 'suggestions' made in the Klarifikasi letter. Even though these letters are cast as 'suggestions', responding to them is clearly intended to be mandatory. If local governments fail to respond by amending, they leave their Perda susceptible to annulment on the grounds or flaws identified in the Klarifikasi.

By focusing on Klarifikasi, this chapter identifies some of the flaws in regional laws and problems in regional law making – or at least those commonly highlighted by the central government during the Klarifikasi process. It also reveals ways in which the central government exercises its control over local law making. As we shall see, the central government is certainly rather selective in the laws it chooses to subject to the Klarifikasi process and, ultimately, tends to invalidate only a narrow category of Perda.

This chapter is divided into two parts. The first provides background to the introduction of regional autonomy in Indonesia and outlines its main features, including the relative law-making jurisdictions of national and regional governments. It then draws on existing research to discuss the mechanisms by which the central government can review by-laws and describes how this control has been exercised to annul Perda.

The second part outlines the Klarifikasi process, before examining some of the 'suggestions' that MoHA has conveyed to local governments for improving their by-laws. This analysis is based on original research that involved reading the Klarifikasi sent by the Ministry to local governments that were available on the Ministry's website at time of writing.[2] The regular issuance of Klarifikasi, and their publication on this website, appear to be relatively recent phenomena, enabling a more detailed examination of central–local relations in law making in general, and of the review process in particular, than was possible in previous research.

As we shall see, the central government appears to be reluctant to *invalidate* Perda unless they seek to impose a tax or fee that is not authorised by a national law. However, this chapter demonstrates that, based on the data available, the Ministry appears to be more willing to address a much broader range of subject matter during the Klarifikasi process and has even raised deficiencies in local legal drafting practices. Based on the evidence presented in this chapter, it is now not strictly accurate to conclude, as has previous research (Butt, 2010; Butt and Parsons, 2012, 2014), that, in its control over local government law making, the central government is concerned *only* with keeping local imposts within the legal limits of national law, presumably to guard its own revenue flows.

Decentralisation and central government control

When Soeharto was forced to step down in May 1998, reformists made several key demands, all of which sought to disperse the power of the state, which had, for thirty-two years, been concentrated in the presidency. Many of these demands were met during the *Reformasi* period – the first few years after Soeharto's fall. The most significant of them were introduced through constitutional amendments, deliberated and enacted annually from 1999 until 2002. These amendments, and accompanying statutory reforms, radically reconfigured Indonesia's political and legal systems, taking Indonesia from a strong authoritarian system backed by the military, to one of Southeast Asia's most democratic (Ramage, 2007).

Most of these reforms were genuine and far-reaching. Soeharto's authoritarian system – which was often violent, repressive and exploitative – had become deeply unpopular during his presidency, particularly in its later stages. One of the first areas to which Indonesia's new president, President Bacharuddin Jusuf Habibie, turned was electoral reform, with new laws enacted to govern elections held in 1999.[3] These were the first free and fair elections since 1955, filling Indonesia's national Parliament with a large number of reformists who had previously been in opposition. Even Soeharto sympathisers who were re-elected in 1999 were said to have been swept along by the reform process, afraid that they might not survive in office if they were to resist (Crouch, 2010). Some of them feared that if these reforms were not made, or if they were made, but were not genuine, then Indonesia might descend into further violent unrest, or even 'Balkanise' (Horowitz, 2013: 34).

Some of the more important reforms were as follows.[4] The national Parliament was given far greater powers, including over national law making, justified by the fact that it was now democratically elected. In 2004, a direct presidential election system was introduced. The Supreme Court and the courts from which it could hear appeals were made institutionally independent of government. An Anti-corruption Commission and a Constitutional Court were established, and began operating in late 2003 and early 2004, respectively. Other institutions important for maintaining transparency and accountability were introduced, including an Ombudsman, which receives complaints from citizens about government services and investigates those complaints (Crouch, 2007), a Judicial Commission, which investigates allegations of judicial impropriety (Colbran, 2009), and an Information Commission, which assists citizens and legal entities to obtain 'public' information from government institutions (Butt, 2013).

Among these reforms was decentralisation, or 'regional autonomy' (*otonomi daerah*). Its significance lies not only in the improvements to governance expected by bringing government 'closer to the people', thereby increasing the accountability and transparency of government (World Bank Independent Evaluation Group (IEG), 2008; Tanzi, 1995; Litvack and Seddon, 1999); decentralisation was also designed to relieve pressure – building through Soeharto's reign and increasing in intensity immediately before, during and after his fall – brought to bear on the national government by separatist groups. Many regions of Indonesia had long complained about Soeharto's oppressive rule. The national government had dictated to local governments, who had very little, if any, say in the running of local affairs. This was problematic in some parts of Indonesia where local identity was given insufficient 'space' within national structures imposed in the regions. So, for example, the Independent Aceh Movement (*Gerakan Aceh Merdeka*) pushed for independence from Indonesia, at least in part because it sought to enforce Islamic law in the province. Another major grievance was that most of the proceeds of natural resource exploitation in the regions were directed to the central government, particularly Soeharto's inner circle, with very little channelled back to the regions, including for much-needed development programmes in poorer areas. This led to decades-long and much-publicised conflict in West Papua and Aceh, but also occurred in many other resource-rich provinces such as Sumatra, Sulawesi and Kalimantan.

The constitutional and statutory framework for decentralisation

For most of Indonesia's regions, decentralisation was initiated by way of statute in 1999, which provided for decentralisation to commence from 2001.[5] Aceh and Papua achieved 'special' regional autonomy under separate legislation (Butt and Lindsey, 2012). The powers of local governments were then constitutionally recognised in the Second Amendment to the Constitution made in 2000, with articles 18, 18A and 18B now providing the basic framework for regional autonomy.[6] Article 18(1) states that Indonesia is divided into provinces (*propinsi*); provinces are divided into counties (*kabupaten*) and cities (*kota*); and each province, county and city is to have its own regional government. Provincial, county and city governments are to regulate and administer matters of government themselves (article 18(2)). In exercising this power and their autonomy, regional governments can enact regional regulations (Perda) and other regulations (article 18(6)). Provincial, county and city governments are to have regional people's representative councils (*Dewan Perwakilan Rakyat Daerah*, or DPRD), whose members are voted in by general election (article 18(3)). Governors (*gubernur*), regents (*bupati*) and mayors (*walikota*) are the heads of the executive governments of provinces, counties and cities, respectively, and are also to be democratically elected (article 18(4)).

The Constitution also touches on jurisdictional issues. Under article 18(5), regional governments are granted power to exercise wide-ranging autonomy, except in matters that national legislation reserves for the central government. The Constitution requires that the relative authority of the central, provincial, county and city governments, and between provincial, county and city governments, be exercised having regard for regional uniqueness and diversity (article 18A(1)). Finally, the relationship between the central and regional governments in matters of finance, public services, and the utilisation of natural and other resources is to be regulated and implemented with justice and harmony (article 18A(2)). The Constitution requires that other aspects of decentralisation are to be further regulated by statute (articles 18(7) and 18A(2)).

The primary statute giving flesh to these bare-bone constitutional provisions, including local law making, is, at time of writing, Law 32 of 2004 on Regional Government.[7] The 2004 Regional Government Law has been 'implemented' through the issuance of various regulations – mainly government, presidential and even ministerial regulations – some of which are discussed below.

In summary, then, three levels of regional government – provinces, cities and counties, and villages – now have legal power to make policy and to bring it into effect by issuing Perda.[8] (Counties and cities are the same 'level', or 'tier', of government, distinguished primarily by their population density and the size of their territory.[9]) One effect of this has been to dramatically increase the number of institutions and individuals with law-making powers in today's Indonesia (Butt, 2010). By early 2014, Indonesia had 34 provinces, 412 counties and 93 cities.[10] Each tier now has both a legislature and executive, both with significant law-making powers, to which I now turn.

Local government law-making powers

As mentioned, article 18(5) of the Constitution gives regional governments the 'broadest autonomy', and article 18(6) gives regional governments the 'right' to issue Perda and other regulations to exercise this autonomy.

According to the 2004 Regional Government Law, law-making power is to be exercised to 'increase the prosperity of the community, public services and regional competitiveness' (section 2(3)). Perda can be initiated by the regional head or the local legislature and should be directed towards 'implementing regional autonomy' (section 136(2)) – that is, addressing matters over which the 2004 Regional Government Law grants local governments jurisdiction. Perda should accommodate the special characteristics of the region in which they are enacted (section 136(3)), and must not contravene the public interest or higher-level laws (section 136(4)). Once deliberated and approved by the local parliament, they are brought into law (*ditetapkan*), or assented to, by the regional head (section 136(1)). Also granted law-making powers are heads of the executive arm of regional governments, who can implement Perda by issuing regulations or decisions (section 146(1)).[11]

Even though the terms 'Perda' or 'by-law' are often used to refer to all types of law issued by local governments, whether executive or legislative, there are, in fact, several recognised categories of local laws. Strictly speaking, 'Perda' refers to laws issued by regional parliaments that apply generally to their constituents.[12] 'Perkada' (*peraturan kepala daerah*) are regulations issued by governors, regents or mayors.[13] These regulations can be issued by individual officials, or can be issued as 'joint regulations' with regional heads from other provinces, cities or counties.[14] Regional parliaments can also determine their own standing orders, usually by way of regional parliament regulation (*peraturan DPRD*).[15]

While the 2004 Regional Government Law appears to give local governments significant power, it also imposes quite onerous obligations upon them. In particular, sections 13 and 14 establish various 'obligatory matters' (*urusan wajib*) for which local governments are legally responsible. These are certainly not trifling matters. They include development planning, public order and security, public infrastructure, health, education, labour, small and medium-sized enterprises, the environment, land affairs, public administration and investment.

Law-making powers retained by the central government

As mentioned, article 18(5) of the Constitution establishes that the law-making powers of regional legislatures and executive governments are not unlimited: some matters remain within the exclusive jurisdiction of the national government. These matters are not set out in the Constitution itself; rather, they are listed in section 10(3) of the 2004 Regional Autonomy Law as foreign affairs, defence and security, national monetary and fiscal matters, justice sector matters and religion. More important still is that, under section 10(5), the central government retains power to regulate *any* issue. It is not constrained in its law making to the matters listed in section 10(3). In other words, the jurisdiction granted to local governments is not exclusive.

Critically, if national and regional laws conflict, the national law will usually prevail over the regional law, rendering it invalid, at least to the extent of any inconsistency. This is clear from applying the so-called hierarchy of laws – a list of laws commonly used in the Indonesian legal system and their relative status – set out in section 7(1) of Law 12 of 2011 on Law Making. The hierarchy is as follows.

(a) 1945 Constitution (*Undang-undang Dasar 1945*)
(b) Decrees of the People's Consultative Assembly (*Ketetapan MPR*)
(c) Statutes/interim emergency laws (*Undang-Undang/Peraturan Pemerintah Pengganti Undang-Undang*)
(d) Government regulations (*Peraturan Pemerintah*)
(e) Presidential regulations (*Peraturan Presiden*)
(f) Provincial regulations (*Peraturan Daerah Propinsi*)
(g) County/city regulations (*Peraturan Daerah Kabupaten/Kota*)

The main premise of the hierarchy is that every law, except for the Constitution, derives its legal authority from a law of a type higher than its own in the hierarchy. It follows that each law must not contradict a higher-level law. So, for example, a city Perda will be valid when enacted if it fulfils two primary requirements: first, it must specify the legal authority upon which it relies – such as the provisions of the Constitution and the 2004 Regional Government Law, which give the city government power to enact that Perda; and secondly, it must not breach the law from which it derives its authority nor any other law higher than it on the hierarchy. This means that Perda must comply with articles 18 and 18A of the Constitution and the provisions of the 2004 Regional Government Law, which, as mentioned, delineate the matters over which regional governments have, and do not have, jurisdiction. In other words, Perda cannot regulate matters over which regional governments have no formal jurisdiction. Perda must also comply with statutes that establish procedures and practices for law making, including in their drafting and enactment, which are set out in the 2011 Law-making Law itself. Finally, the substance of a Perda cannot breach the substance of a law above it in the hierarchy. For example, a Perda cannot set a particular tax at 10 per cent if a government regulation sets it at 5 per cent.

Before turning to discuss the mechanisms for central government review of Perda, it bears noting that many types of law very frequently employed in Indonesia are not specifically mentioned on the list contained in section 7(1). This is pertinent to the following discussion because the vast majority of Perda annulled by the central government have been annulled by MoHA decree – a type of law not listed in the hierarchy. Some legal commentators have questioned whether such decrees can therefore purport to override, let alone invalidate, legal instruments that are explicitly mentioned on the hierarchy, including provincial, city and county Perda. On this issue, section 8 of the 2011 Law-making Law is relevant. It states that legal instruments issued by ministers and various specified government institutions have legal force provided that they 'are required by higher-level laws or on the basis of authority'. However, neither the Law-making Law nor any other law of which this author is aware stipulates their precise status vis-à-vis laws on the hierarchy, including Perda. Formally, then, it is unclear whether these decrees can prevail over Perda. The central government's use of MoHA decrees to invalidate Perda is discussed next.

Central government review

In summary, then, under the 2004 Regional Government Law, the national government has retained exclusive authority to regulate several matters and also has jurisdiction, held concurrently with regional governments, over all other matters. Legally, because many types of national law trump regional laws, the space in which Perda can operate is limited to matters of regional import that the national government has not yet regulated.

When regional autonomy was being designed in 1999, its architects adopted mechanisms for central government review of Perda. Maintaining this control was undoubtedly necessary while local bureaucrats and politicians built the necessary skills and experience to run the affairs of their regions. After all, the central control of the Soeharto era had left most local officials and parliaments unprepared for making policy or drafting laws. This 'bureaucratic review' (Butt, 2010) mechanism was, however, retained when, as mentioned, the regional autonomy laws were replaced in 2004. The central government was therefore keen to reserve this power to review Perda, even though local administrators had, by this stage, gained several years' experience.

The 2004 Regional Governance Law provides two grounds for review of all types of regional law: non-compliance with the public interest or higher-level laws. This chapter limits itself to consideration of the ground based on higher-level law.[16]

The review process is extremely complex and outlined in several laws,[17] but can be briefly described as follows. Specific categories of Perda – namely, those seeking to impose regional taxes and user charges, those setting regional budgets and those containing spatial plans – must be conveyed for review within three days of passage through local parliament, but before their formal enactment.[18] All by-laws – including those concerning other matters – are reviewed post enactment.[19] Section 145 of the 2004 Regional Government Law requires that they be submitted to the central government within seven days of passage. The central government then has sixty days in which to review the Perda and to invalidate it by presidential regulation if, in its view, the Perda breaches either a higher-level law or the public interest. Once the sixty days pass, the submitted Perda continues into force by default.[20] If any of the regional governments 'cannot accept' the invalidation, they can appeal to the Indonesian Supreme Court (section 145(6)).[21] The process of the central government reviewing Perda and then notifying local governments that the Perda under review contradicts higher-level laws or the public interest is called Klarifikasi, and is the main focus of the second part of this chapter.

Shortcomings of the review process

Although reported statistics vary, MoHA appears to have invalidated almost 3,000 Perda between 2002 and 2012, with the Home Affairs Minister predicting that his Ministry would review another 2,500 in 2013 (Parlina and Aritonang, 2013).[22] Nevertheless, the review process does not appear to function in line with the 2004 Regional Government Law and regulations. In particular, some local governments appear not to have submitted their by-laws for review as required (DITJENPP, 2008; *Hukumonline*, 2012). While some local governments undoubtedly employ this as a deliberate strategy to avoid revocation, it seems reasonable to speculate that others might be genuinely confused by the review process. As mentioned, this process varies depending on the subject matter of the law, and the arm and tier of local government issuing it, and is described differently in each of the plethora of laws that regulate it. Further, local governments appear to have very little to lose by failing to submit their Perda because no formal sanctions apply for non-compliance, at least for Perda that do not impose a tax or user charge.[23] One result is that many by-laws that might contradict national statutes and regulations remain on the books simply because they are not reviewed.

The central government is also commonly criticised for choosing to invalidate some types of Perda, while ignoring many others that appear to be both illegal and deleterious. The central government has, based on the available data, invalidated only Perda that raise revenue for local governments by imposing taxes, user charges or licence fees that are not permitted by national law (Butt, 2010).[24] This theme appears to be confirmed in statements made by a MoHA spokesman reported in the *Jakarta Post* in 2013 (Parlina and Aritonang, 2013). He said that, of the 1,878 by-laws invalidated by the Home Affairs Ministry between 2002 and 2009, almost 1,800 imposed regional taxes and levies. Twenty-nine also sought to raise revenue, such as by regulating third-party political donations and the sale and distribution of alcoholic beverages.

Perhaps one explanation for the emphasis on revenue raising Perda is that MoHA is hamstrung by limited resources, with the result that reviews are periodic and carried out by relatively small teams (Butt and Parsons, 2011; Ray, 2003: 18; MoHA Regulation 1 of 2014, article 77). This is clearly insufficient to handle the many thousands of laws produced by local law makers each year. In this context, the focus on revenue-raising laws appears to reflect a priority to guard central government revenue flows (Butt, 2010), and, as former Vice President Boediono has stated, to prevent the creation of a 'high cost economy' that harms investment and therefore development (*Tempo*, 2013) or hampers internal trade (Hidayat, 2006).[25]

Discriminatory by-laws

Perda regulating subject matter other than revenue tend not to be invalidated, even if they appear to contradict a higher-level law or are otherwise undesirable. One such category is the so-called *Perda Syariah* – by-laws said to be inspired by Islamic law, of which there are, by some estimates, several thousand across almost 300 of Indonesia's cities and counties (Media Indonesia, 2010; Parlina and Aritonang, 2013).[26] Many of these by-laws are said to be targeted towards Muslim women and discriminatory, such as by requiring those women to wear Islamic headdress and separating them from men in public places (Salim, 2007). Others have sought to marginalise or even ban religious minorities, such as Shi'ite Muslims and the Ahmadiyyah sect (Crouch, 2012). These Perda are thought to have political appeal, helping politicians and candidates to establish moral legitimacy (Bush, 2008; Cochrane, 2013), even though these Perda draw the ire of many civil society groups and citizens.

The main legal objection to these by-laws appears to be that Indonesia's Constitution, and several national statutes, provide citizens with the right to freedom from discrimination, including on the basis of gender and religion (Parsons and Mietzner, 2010; Crouch, 2009).[27] This right is also provided by international conventions that Indonesia has ratified.[28] It formally binds central and regional governments alike. Another legal objection is that local governments have no power to issue Perda regulating religion; as mentioned, this matter falls within the exclusive jurisdiction of the central government.

Many of these Perda do not simply 'slip through' the review process, as described above; rather, they draw significant controversy and are widely reported in the media. Consider, for example, the proposed by-law being deliberated by the parliament of Bengkulu, a province in Southwest Sumatra, apparently to increase religiosity in the region under the so-called *Bengkuluku Religius* (literally, 'my Bengkulu is religious') programme. The by-law, if enacted, would require residents to attend Friday prayer meetings and to pray five times per day. In January 2014, Indonesia's Home Affairs Minister Gamawan Fauzi publicly criticised the by-law. He said that the by-law would not have been problematic if it were 'only a call advising people to go to the mosque to pray, or to go to the church for the Christians' (Pasandaran, 2014). Minister Fauzi observed, however, that the Bengkulu local government lacked power to impose sanctions for non-compliance with this by-law. He said: 'They don't have the authority, as religious affairs are under the authority of the central government.' The Minister added that if the Bengkulu government were to enact the by-law, MoHA would review it and decide whether to annul it or allow it to remain in force.

Despite being well aware of these Perda *Syariah*, there is little evidence to suggest that the national government has reviewed more than a handful of them, let alone invalidated them for being discriminatory. This appears to be indicative of a general reluctance of the Indonesian central government to intervene in religious matters. Many commentators have argued, for example, that the state has failed to protect the constitutional rights to religious freedom of minority religious groups (Colbran, 2010; Crouch, 2012; Pearson, 2014).

While these by-laws raise issues of discrimination and religious freedom, they also raise broader issues about the extent to which the national government can and should intervene in the affairs of regional governments. No doubt some government officials, including those in MoHA itself, argue that because regional governments are democratically elected, they should therefore be given significant latitude in their law making. For them, the central government should not, as a general rule, interfere in local political and legal matters, including by invalidating even the most oppressive by-laws, provided that they do not intrude on central government interests. If their constituents disapprove, they can be removed from office at the next election (Butt and Parsons, 2014).

Klarifikasi

As mentioned, all Perda submitted to the central government for review – and potential invalidation – undergo Klarifikasi. Under this process, a MoHA team, which should also contain members from ministries whose portfolios are relevant to the subject matter of the Perda under review,[29] assesses that Perda for compliance with higher-level laws and/or the public interest.[30] If the team decides that the relevant Perda breaches either ground, then it 'issues a letter about the results of the *klarifikasi* to the regional head . . . containing a recommendation that the regional government perfect (*melakukan penyempurnaan*) the Perda and/or revoke the Perda'.[31] If the regional government does not heed the recommendation, MoHA can recommend to the President that the Perda be revoked.[32]

As mentioned, the central government has, almost exclusively, only invalidated Perda for seeking to raise revenue in breach of national laws. Many Klarifikasi, too, have found fault with Perda on similar grounds. For example, some by-laws sought to:

- impose a tax or user charge that falls outside categories permitted by national law;[33]
- set tax rates higher than permitted by national laws;[34]
- establish renewal fees for particular permits, even though national laws do not require renewal;[35]
- shorten the duration of particular fishing licences, presumably with the aim of extracting additional fees when licences were renewed;[36]
- impose a fee for issuing birth certificates, even though national laws require that these be provided at no cost to citizens;[37]
- impose a service charge for commercial vehicles using roads that lead from one city to another (according to MoHA, this created a 'high-cost economy' and impeded the 'mobility of people, the passage of goods and services between regions, and import–export activities');[38] and
- categorise fines as regional income (*penerimaan daerah*) rather than state income (*penerimaan negara*), as specified under the 2009 Tax Law.[39]

However, a reading of the available Klarifikasi clearly reveals that MoHA is concerned with a much broader range of issues than illegal imposts. In fact, more Klarifikasi were directed towards Perda that did not seek to raise revenue than those that did.

Drafting errors

Perhaps the most commonly breached statutes were the 2011 Law-making Law, which establishes drafting principles for national and regional law makers, and the 2004 Regional Government Law, which imposes many of the same drafting standards and delineates the jurisdictions of local governments. As for maintaining drafting standards, one Perda, for example, was criticised for containing a flawed cross-reference.[40] Article 15 of the Perda had referred to supervisors (*pengawas*) of regional state-owned enterprises (SOEs). Article 16 referred to the 'appointment of *managers* and supervisors as referred to in article 15' (emphasis added). Although the Klarifikasi did not clearly specify the objection to article 16, it appears that the perceived shortcoming was that article 15 did not mention managers, but only supervisors. According to MoHA, the reference to both managers and supervisors caused uncertainty. This conclusion is not persuasive, however, if the purpose of the reference to article 15 was intended to be directed towards supervisors only. In other words, article 16 could simply be referring to the appointment of managers, on the one hand, and the appointment of supervisors as referred to in article 15, on the other.[41]

Several other Klarifikasi appear to have picked up typographical errors. For example, one Perda sought to establish prerequisites for appointment as a civil servant investigator (PPNS).[42] One prerequisite, contained in article 8(g) of the Perda, was the need to 'complete education and training in the area of education (*pendidikan*)', which did not accord with a national law and human rights ministerial regulation concerning PPNS.[43] It seems clear that law makers intended it to be that candidates 'complete education and training in the area of investigation' (*penyidikan*).

Unlimited or excessive delegation of power

The most common fault with Perda identified by MoHA during the Klarifikasi process was *delegasi blangko* ('unlimited delegation'). This is a delegation of power deemed to be excessively wide, primarily because it fails to confine the delegate to specified subject matter. More than 50 per cent of the Klarifikasi studied mentioned this ground.[44] *Delegasi blangko* is prohibited by point 210 of Appendix II of the 2011 Law-making Law, which does not define the term, but rather provides two examples to illustrate the concept for drafters. The first example is a mock provision expressed as follows: 'Matters that are not sufficiently regulated in this statute are to be further regulated by government regulation.' A clear example of such a provision, identified in one Klarifikasi,[45] is article 27 of Balangan County Regulation 25 of 2012 on Public Service, which states that 'issues not regulated in this Perda will be further regulated by Bupati regulation'. This provision appears to fall afoul of the prohibition because it does not specify the issues about which the *bupati* can regulate.

The second example of a *delegasi blangko* provided in point 210 of Appendix II is article 24 of Aceh Perda 4 of 2010 on the Creation of the Organisational Structure and Procedures for the Regional Disaster Management Agency. It reads: 'Matters that are not yet regulated in this [Perda] are to be regulated by Bupati Regulation, provided that they are implementing regulations.' Many Klarifikasi also pick up this second type of delegation. For example, article 35(2) of Buton County Regulation 1 of 2014 on Parking Taxes states: 'Matters not regulated in this Perda, provided that they are about its implementation, are to be further regulated by Bupati Regulation.'[46]

This second type of *delegasi blangko* is problematic, however, because the delegation is *not* unconstrained. The regent is, in fact, limited to implementing the Perda; he or she cannot seek to regulate new issues or even to expand the scope of the Perda, which, presumably, is what the *delegasi blangko* prohibition seeks to prevent. This prohibition also appears to contradict section 146(1) of the 2004 Regional Government Law, which specifically authorises regional heads to issue laws to implement Perda. Section 146(1) states: 'To implement Perda . . . the regional head is to issue regional head regulations and or regional head decisions.'

Also identified in Klarifikasi are Perda that delegate regulatory power to officials that have not been granted that power by national law. For example, two regulations issued by the mayor of Surabaya in 2013 purported to grant regulatory powers to the head of the local government education office and the head of the local office for social affairs. In the Klarifikasi, MoHA asked the Surabaya mayor to revise these Perda on the ground that heads of local government offices had not been granted law-making powers under either the 2004 Regional Government Law or the 2011 Law-making Law.[47]

Several Klarifikasi 'picked up' Perda for flaws in their 'Preambles'. This section, set out at the beginning of most Perda – indeed, most types of Indonesian law – contains a list of the higher-level laws upon which the Perda rests for its formal legal authority. For example, Lampung Provincial Regulation 10 of 2012 on the Management of Cooperatives was deemed problematic because it did not refer to the national Law 17 of 2012 on Cooperatives.[48] Similarly, several Perda relating to non-smoking areas did not list MoHA Decree 7 of 2011 on Guidelines for Implementing Non-smoking Areas in their respective *mengingat* sections.[49] The need for such a list appears to flow from the hierarchy of laws, which, as mentioned, requires that every law be 'based on' a higher-level law. Another Perda referred to a higher-level law as a legal basis, which was, in fact, no longer valid.[50]

Finally, several Klarifikasi chided local parliaments (DPRD) for issuing Perda that purported to give themselves authority to perform functions outside those listed in section 42 of the 2004 Regional Government Law. Section 42(1) sets out the official 'tasks' (*tugas*) and 'authority' (*wewenang*) of local parliaments.[51] For example, one Klarifikasi suggested amendment to a Perda that sought to entrust the local parliament with approving the merging or takeover of a particular company.[52] Another criticised a Perda for requiring a local parliament to choose the head of a local public radio institution council.[53] Neither of these functions is listed in section 42(1).

There is, however, little to commend these Klarifikasi that seek to confine DPRD functions. The list of DPRD functions contained in section 42(1) is clearly not intended to be exhaustive. Section 42(2) states that, in addition to the tasks and authority referred to in section 42(1), the DPRD is to 'perform other tasks and has other powers as regulated by law (*peraturan perundang-undangan*)'. Perda clearly fall within the types of 'law' anticipated by section 42(2), because Perda are listed in the hierarchy of laws. It is therefore quite appropriate for a local parliament to give itself additional tasks, provided that it does so by way of Perda and does not otherwise breach a higher-level law or the public interest. In any event, there seem to be no reasons of public policy that make it undesirable for the DPRD to approve specified mergers and acquisitions, or to select heads of important regional institutions.

Offences and sanctions

The second most commonly identified fault of Perda in the Klarifikasi are provisions that impose criminal sanctions without specifying the norms that, if breached, attract those sanctions. A Perda provision imposing a sanction for breaching a norm must specify the provisions of the Perda in which those norms are contained.[54] According to these Klarifikasi, this degree of specificity is required by point 118 of Appendix II of the 2011 Law-making Law, and failure to comply will breach section 5(f) of the 2011 Law-making Law and section 137(f) of the 2004 Regional Government Law, both of which require 'clarity of formulation' (*kejelasan rumusan*) in law-making.

For breach of this prohibition, MoHA recommended amendment to Wajo County Regulation 4 of 2012 on Fishery Resource Management.[55] Article 43(1) of this Perda stated: 'Any person who breaches the rules (*ketentuan*) of this regulation faces a maximum of six months imprisonment or a maximum of 50 million rupiah in fines.' For MoHA, the reference to 'the rules of this regulation' lacked clarity in formulation, because it did not specify the offences to which the sanctions attached and the provisions of the Perda in which they were contained.

Provisions that *do* clearly refer to the relevant norms and the articles in which they are contained, but fail to specify the *sanction*, have also been singled out in Klarifikasi for breach of point 118 of Appendix II of the 2011 Law-making Law. For example, article 35 of Lampung Provincial Regulation 11 of 2012 on the Management of Air Quality and Pollution Control states that anyone who breaches environmental standards – including pollution emission limits – is subject, for those breaches, to the criminal sanctions imposed in the 2009 Environmental Management Law.[56] Article 57 of West Nusa Tenggara Provincial Regulation 1 of 2013 on Protection of Sustainable Agricultural Land was even vaguer, specifying various crimes and the provisions in which they were defined, but not specifying sanctions for breach;[57] instead, the sanctions applied would be 'in accordance with the law'. In MoHA's view, both Perda breached provisions in the 2011 Law-making Law that required laws to have 'legal order and certainty'.[58]

In these Klarifikasi, MoHA appears to be solely concerned to ensure conformity with the 2011 Law-making Law, which reflects long-standing Indonesian legal drafting practices, the main purpose of which is to avoid ambiguities or confusion. Statutes, for example, contain near their end a chapter on 'Criminal Provisions'. In addition to establishing new norms, this chapter often creates criminal offences for breach of provisions in other chapters of the statute. This makes it readily apparent from a glance whether a statute establishes criminal offences, and if so, what they are. It also clarifies which of the various norms established by the statute are intended to carry criminal penalties for breach. After all, many types of norm are clearly not amenable to criminal penalties. So, for example, article 42 of the Wajo Perda itself sets out many of the tasks of PPNS. These are cast as rules, but it would be surprising if law makers had intended to make the same criminal penalties applicable to illegal fishers and civil servants who were merely negligent in the performance of their duties.

Nevertheless, it is easy to see why local legislatures might be frustrated with suggestions such as these. For example, why should the Wajo parliament be required to specify each provision in which an offence is defined, provided that it evidences this intent unambiguously and that the Perda clearly defines these 'norms' as offences or breaches? Indeed, many of its provisions contain numbered lists of norms under the heading of 'rules' (*ketentuan-ketentuan*). And why does the Lampung Perda need to be entirely self-contained? The sanctions it imposes are readily ascertainable, even if they are not listed in the Perda itself. The offences and the sanctions applicable under it are those described in the 2009 Environmental Management Law[59] – a national statute that can be easily obtained. Only if the definitions or sanctions in that statute were unclear would the reference to them in the Perda cause any real confusion or lack of clarity.

Usurping jurisdiction and contradicting 'higher level' laws

Many Klarifikasi identified Perda that contradicted 'higher-level national laws'. Examples from these Perda include:

- permitting junior public servants to work as PPNS, in breach of the national Code of Criminal Procedure, which requires that these investigators have a particular minimum rank;[60]
- authorising regional governments to guarantee third-party debts, in breach of a government regulation on regional borrowing;[61]
- requiring investors to prioritise employing locals, which was held to be discriminatory, thereby breaching section 5 of Law 13 of 2003 on the Workforce;[62]
- establishing third-party contributions as mandatory when national law required them to be voluntary;[63] and
- regulating international-standard education programmes in Indonesian schools, which contravened an Indonesian Constitutional Court decision[64] that effectively dissolved those school programmes.[65]

Relatively few Klarifikasi accused local governments of usurping the jurisdiction of another tier of government. A handful of city and county Perda regulated matters falling within the jurisdiction of provincial governments, such as cross-regional welfare[66] and surface water (*air permukiman*).[67] As for usurping the jurisdiction of the national government, several Perda were identified for purporting to bind or otherwise apply to the central government or to regulate the national budget.[68] MoHA categorised this as a breach of the 2011 Law-making Law requirement that the substance of a law reflect its type and position on the hierarchy.[69] In other words, a local government cannot, by way of Perda, seek either to dictate to the central government or to draw from the national budget.

An appropriate legal instrument to achieve this would be a national statute, government regulation or presidential regulation.[70]

Perhaps the most significant in Klarifikasi in this regard was the review of Tasikmalaya County Regulation 10 of 2012 on Islamic Education in the County of Tasikmalaya.[71] According to MoHA, this entire Perda concerned religion and was therefore inconsistent with sections 10(1) and (3) of the 2004 Regional Government Law, which, as mentioned, gives the central government exclusive jurisdiction over religion. Religious issues could not therefore be regulated by Perda. Further, the Klarifikasi pointed out that even though the Perda applied to all citizens, it related only to the education of those following one religion – yet all people had a right to education, regardless of their religion. In short, by applying only to education for Muslims, the Perda discriminated against non-Muslims, thereby contradicting higher-level laws, including article 28I(2) of the Constitution and section 1(3) of the 1999 Human Rights Law, which establish freedom from discrimination as a human right that local governments must respect, as must the central government. Finally, MoHA declared that the Perda breached the principle of *Bhineka Tunggal Ika* – Indonesia's national motto, usually translated as 'Unity in Diversity' – with which local government must comply by virtue of section 6(f) of the 2011 Law-making Law. This principle requires observance of the diversity of the Indonesian population, including its religious diversity, and equality before the law and government. This also prohibited discrimination, including on the basis of religion.

Also found to be discriminatory was Papua Provincial Regulation 1 of 2011 on Restoration of the Rights of Papuan Female Victims of Violence and Human Rights Violations.[72] The Perda aimed to rehabilitate victims by giving them financial and institutional support 'as a form of state accountability' for providing 'protection, empowerment and enforcement of the human rights of Papuan women'. According to MoHA, various provisions of the Perda were discriminatory because they were specifically directed towards the indigenous women of Papua. This thereby breached sections 6(b), (f) and (h) of the 2011 Law-making Law, which requires that laws be humanitarian, and reflect *Bhineka Tunggal Ika* and equality before the law and in government. Unfortunately, the Klarifikasi did not consider whether the Perda was issued by the local government to give effect to an important constitutional right – 'to special treatment to obtain the same opportunities and benefits to achieve equality and justice' (article 28H(3)). This provision would presumably justify a discriminatory Perda if it were directed towards a disadvantaged group – a group into which Papuan women may well fall.

Critiques of Klarifikasi: Lack of clear guidance

The legal infrastructure for local law making gives the central government predominance over regional governments. However, this chapter has demonstrated, through an analysis of Klarifikasi, that the central government sometimes exercises its control in a questionable manner. Some Klarifikasi are, in fact, flawed in at least two additional ways that appears to undermine their very purpose. First, most Klarifikasi are vague, insufficiently identifying the defects in the Perda that need to be remedied, providing little or no guidance to law makers about how the identified defects might be remedied. For example, several require simply that the Perda 'be brought into line with drafting techniques in accordance with Appendix II of the 2011 Law-making Law';[73] without more detailed information, this advice has no utility. Appendix II contains almost 300 separate clauses that provide advice to drafters. If MoHA does not specify the clauses to which the Perda drafters should have regard when revising their Perda, local governments must, in essence, guess what deficiencies to address.

This leads to the second shortcoming of the Klarifikasi: none of them provide guidelines that local governments might follow when revising their Perda to remedy the defect identified, even though the Klarifikasi are clearly cast as suggestions that must be followed if local governments want to avoid invalidation. It is possible, then, that local governments will revise their Perda, genuinely intending to respond to the Klarifikasi, but fail to do so in the way anticipated by MoHA, thereby making their Perda susceptible to further scrutiny – perhaps even invalidation.[74]

Concluding remarks

The research presented in this chapter is, unfortunately, necessarily preliminary owing to the limited availability of data. Pages on the MoHA website that host the decrees by which the Ministry purports to invalidate Perda do not appear to have been regularly updated in recent years. Yet if various media statements of MoHA officials are to be believed, annulments have been taking place and the trend of invalidating only revenue-raising Perda appears to have continued. Similarly, the collection of Klarifikasi included on the MoHA website at time of writing does not appear to be complete: posted there are only Klarifikasi issued in early-to-mid 2013. Presumably, Klarifikasi were issued before and have been issued since that period, but they have simply not been made available. Nevertheless, if these available Klarifikasi are indicative of MoHA's general approach to Perda review, illegal revenue raising is but one among many national government concerns about local law making.

Official data on local government compliance with Klarifikasi is unavailable. A handful of local governments have reportedly announced amendments to, or annulments of, their own Perda in response to Klarifikasi (*Kompas*, 2007). Among them was the Tasikmalaya Perda on Islamic Education, mentioned above (*Kabar Priangan*, 2013). However, it is quite possible that many, if not most, Klarifikasi are simply ignored by local governments and that the central government moves to invalidate only those Perda that appear to most directly affect its interests – namely, its revenue flows. If this is true, then Klarifikasi directed at other 'flaws' such as excessive delegation and usurpation of jurisdiction, or even discrimination, can be safely ignored by local governments. Once sixty days pass, the Perda comes into force in any event.

Local governments have few incentives to respond to Klarifikasi anyway. As mentioned, Klarifikasi generally do not specifically advise local law makers about how they might amend their Perda to improve them. A local government that cannot be confident that any amendments it makes will be acceptable to MoHA will be unlikely to bother allocating resources to drafting, and then submitting, any amendments. Reluctance is all the more likely if local governments perceive, rightly or wrongly, that the reasons outlined in the Klarifikasi are unnecessary, pedantic, debatable, or perhaps even contrary to law themselves. After all, MoHA itself makes mistakes in its Klarifikasi and is not free from credible claims that it has breached, and continues to breach, the hierarchy when reviewing Perda, by breaching a higher-level law. The 2004 Regional Government Law and the 2009 Regional Tax and User Charges Law require that Perda invalidation be effected by presidential regulation, yet all Perda invalidations, except one,[75] have been by MoHA decree.

Nevertheless, it seems that local citizens still need protection from local governments, who, while democratically elected, might be incompetent, predatory or opportunist. Indeed, there is emerging evidence that decentralisation has been a 'mixed bag' for many citizens and that, in some important areas such as health and education, public services have deteriorated since decentralisation (Lewis, 2014). Worse, as mentioned, some local governments appear willing to breach national legal protections, including the human rights provided under national laws and international conventions that Indonesia has ratified. The failure of the central government to invalidate Perda that are discriminatory or otherwise illegal serves to underline the need for an effective objective arbiter to resolve real disputes that arise between the central and regional governments, and to protect the human rights of citizens. MoHA, however, is probably not the best institution to perform this function.

Notes

1 In Indonesian, *peraturan daerah* is often translated as 'by-law' or 'by-laws'. I likewise use the word Perda as both a singular or plural noun in this chapter.
2 Of which there were ninety-three. See the Ministry of Home Affairs Legal Documents and Information Network website (http://www.jdih.setjen.kemendagri.go.id/).
3 See Law 3 of 1999 on General Elections.
4 See generally Butt and Lindsey (2012); Hosen (2010).
5 Law 22 of 1999 on Regional Government; Law 25 of 1999 on Fiscal Balance between the Central and Regional Governments.
6 The following translations draw from Butt and Lindsey (2012).
7 This statute replaced Law 22 of 1999 on Regional Government.
8 Only limited powers were granted to village administrations. This chapter does not discuss them.
9 See s. 1(4)(5) of Law 32 of 2004 on Regional Government; Government Regulation 38 of 2007 on the Division of Government Affairs between Central Government, Province, Regency and District.
10 See the Ministry of Home Affairs Regional Autonomy website (http://otda.kemendagri.go.id/index.php/data-otda-158/seputar-otda). By contrast, in 1998 Indonesia had fewer than 300 cities and counties. This number has almost doubled, because various provinces, cities and counties have since split (Booth, 2011).
11 A civil police unit (*pamong praja*) can be established to help the regional head to enforce these laws (art. 148(1)).
12 MoHA Regulation 1 of 2014, art. 4.
13 MoHA Regulation 1 of 2014, art. 5.
14 MoHA Regulation 1 of 2014, art. 6.
15 MoHA Regulation 1 of 2014, art. 7.
16 The Elucidation to s. 136(4) of the 2004 Regional Government Law defines 'inconsistent with the public interest' as 'policies that disturb harmonious relations between members of society, public services, and public order and [which are] discriminatory'. However, to this author's knowledge, this ground has rarely, if ever, been employed as a ground to review, let alone invalidate, a Perda (Butt, 2010).
17 While the starting point is the 2004 Regional Governance Law, guidelines are contained in a plethora of lower level national regulations. These include Government Regulation 79 of 2005 on the Guide to the Supervision of Regional Governance, and MoHA Regulation 1 of 2014 on Local Law making. Law 28 of 2009 on Regional Taxes and User Charges deals specifically with review of laws imposing taxes and user charges. For more detailed discussion about the review process, see Butt (2010); Butt and Parsons (2012, 2014).
18 MoHA Regulation 1 of 2014, arts 76, 81.

19 MoHA Regulation 1 of 2014 appears to delegate to provincial governments the responsibility to review city and county Perda. This responsibility has, in fact, been imposed for several years, but, to the author's knowledge, provincial governments have not yet commenced performing these reviews. They simply forward any Perda they receive on to the central government (Butt and Parsons, 2011).

20 2004 Regional Government Law, s. 147(3) and (7).

21 This chapter does not consider judicial review by the Indonesian Supreme Court of the validity of Perda or their revocation by the central government. For a detailed discussion of this issue, see Butt and Parsons (2014).

22 Unfortunately, more up-to-date statistics were not available at time of writing. In particular, it was not possible to verify whether 2,500 Perda were, in fact, reviewed in 2013, as predicted by the spokesperson.

23 The central government can impose financial penalties upon regional governments that fail to submit their tax and user charge by-laws for review: Law 28 of 2009 on Regional Taxes and User Charges, s. 159(1).

24 Several hundred of the legal instruments through which these invalidations were effected are available online on the MoHA website (http://www.depdagri.go.id). However, this database is almost certainly incomplete.

25 Another possible factor is that, at least prior to the enactment of Law 28 of 2009 on Regional Taxes and User Charges, Perda that imposed taxes or user charges could be annulled by MoHA rather than the President, who was thought to be too busy, and even somewhat reluctant, to invalidate Perda (Butt and Parsons, 2011).

26 According to Human Rights Watch (2014: 343–344), sixty new discriminatory regulations were enacted in 2013, joining the 282 already issued.

27 In particular, Ch. XA of the 1945 Constitution; Law 39 of 1999 on Human Rights.

28 For example, Indonesia has ratified the International Covenant on Civil and Political Rights (ICCPR) by enacting Law 12 of 2005 on the Ratification of ICCPR and the Convention on the Elimination Discrimination against Women (CEDAW) was ratified by Law 7 of 1984.

29 MoHA Decree 1 of 2014, art. 89(1).

30 MoHA Decree 1 of 2014, art. 90(2).

31 MoHA Decree 1 of 2014, art. 91(1).

32 MoHA Decree 1 of 2014, art. 91(4).

33 Klarifikasi 188.34/2698/SJ, 188.34/2854/SJ and 188.34/2269/SJ.

34 Klarifikasi 188.34/3219/SJ.

35 Klarifikasi 188.34/3213/SJ, 188.34/1060/SJ, 188.34/1654/SJ, 188.34/529/SJ, 188.34/2936/SJ, 188.34/3274/SJ and 188.34/2269/SJ.

36 Klarifikasi 188.34/1057/SJ.

37 Klarifikasi 188.34/2945/SJ.

38 Klarifikasi 188.34/2270/SJ.

39 Klarifikasi 188.34/3218/SJ, 188.34/1055/SJ and 188.34/2855/SJ.

40 For examples of Klarifikasi referring to similar grounds, see 188.34/3399/SJ, 188.34/3217/SJ and 188.34/3768/SJ.

41 Klarifikasi 188.34/3767/SJ.

42 Klarifikasi 188.34/3268/SJ. *Penyidik Pegawai Negeri Sipil* (PPNS) are civil servants who, by law, are granted powers to assist police. Their functions and powers differ, depending on the rules issues by the department in which they work. Generally speaking, however, PPNS are granted power to receive complaints about crimes, to conduct initial investigations, seize items and documents, and to call in suspects and witnesses for questioning. PPNS must coordinate with police during their investigations (s. 7(2) of the Code of Criminal Procedure): they must inform the police that they are investigating and must hand over their findings to police for further action. The police are generally entitled to ignore any or all PPNS findings. Indeed, police may proceed without seeking the assistance of the PPNS at all.

43 Law and Human Rights Minister Regulation M.HH.01.AH.09.01.TAHUN 2011 on Appointment, Dismissal, Transfer, and Taking the Oath of Office for Civil Servant Investigators, and the Form, Shape, Court and Format of the Civil Servant Investigators Identity Cards, art. 2(2)(g).

44 Fifty-one out of ninety-three Klarifikasi studied.

45 Klarifikasi 188.34/2272/SJ.

46 Identical provisions are found in many Perda that were subjected to the Klarifikasi process, including art. 7 of Banggai County Regulation 10 of 2008 on Contributions for Use of Syukuran Aminudin Amir Bubung Luwuk Airport (Klarifikasi 188.34/3273/SJ) and art. 96 of Bangka County Regulation 4 of 2011 on Public Service User Charges (Klarifikasi 188.34/2945/SJ).

47 Klarifikasi 188.34/2268/SJ.

48 Klarifikasi 188.34/3262/SJ.

49 Klarifikasi 188.34/1899/SJ.

50 Klarifikasi 188.34/2100/SJ.

51 The list is also contained in art. 3 of Government Regulation 16 of 2010 on Guidelines for Drafting Standing Orders of Regional Parliaments.

52 Klarifikasi 188.34/6525/SJ.

53 Klarifikasi 188.34/3279/SJ.

54 Around 20 per cent (nineteen of ninety-three) of the Klarifikasi studied contained this ground.

55 Klarifikasi 188.34/3278/SJ.

56 Klarifikasi 188.34/2938/SJ.

57 Klarifikasi 188.34/3399/SJ.

58 See s. 6(1)(i) of the 2011 Law-making Law.

59 Law 32 of 2009 on Environmental Management.

60 Klarifikasi 188.34/3277/5J.

61 Klarifikasi 188.34/1052/SJ.

62 Klarifikasi 188.34/2950/SJ.

63 Klarifikasi 188.34/3273/SJ.

64 Constitutional Court Decision 5/PUU-X/2012 reviewing Law 20 of 2003 on National Education.

65 Klarifikasi 188.34/2946/SJ and 188.34/2944/SJ.

66 Klarifikasi 188.34/6274/SJ. Law 11 of 2009 on Social Welfare stipulated that this was a provincial matter.

67 Klarifikasi 188.34/1465/SJ. Government Regulation 38 of 2007 on the Division of Tasks between the Central, Provincial and City/County Governments determined that this was a provincial matter.

68 Klarifikasi 188.34/3762/SJ, 188.34/2858/SJ, 188.34/2947/SJ, 188.34/2946/SJ and 188.34/1662/SJ.

69 See ss. 137(c) and 5(c) of the Law-making Law.

70 Another Perda had sought to regulate the maintenance of graveyards, which Law 11 of 2009 on Social Welfare had determined to be a central government matter: Klarifikasi 188.34/6274/SJ.

71 Klarifikasi 188.34/1051/SJ.

72 Klarifikasi 188.34/2694/SJ.

73 See, e.g., Klarifikasi 188.34/2271/SJ, 188.34/5329/SJ and 188.34/1899/SJ.

74 Klarifikasi 188.34/3262/SJ required that provisions of the Perda under review be brought into line with a specified national statute. While MoHA referred to the Perda provisions that needed to be brought into line with the statute, it did not state with which articles of the statute they needed to be brought into line.

75 Presidential Regulation 87 of 2006 on the Invalidation of arts. 33(2)(n) and 34(8) of Aceh Regulation 7 of 2006 (the Second Amendment to Aceh Regulation 2 of 2004 on the election of governors/deputy governors, *bupati*/deputy *bupati* and mayors/deputy mayors in the Province of Aceh).

References

Booth, A. (2011) 'Splitting, Splitting and Splitting Again: A Brief History of the Development of Regional Government in Indonesia since Independence', *Bijdragen Tot de Taal-, Land- En Volkenkunde*, 167(1): 31–59.

Bush, R. (2008) 'Regional "Sharia" Regulations in Indonesia: Anomaly or Symptom?', in G. Fealy and S. White (eds) *Indonesia: Islamic Life and Politics*, Singapore: Institute of Southeast Asian Studies, 174–191.

Butt, S. (2010) 'Regional Autonomy and the Proliferation of Perda in Indonesia: An Assessment of Bureaucratic and Judicial Review Mechanisms', *Sydney Law Review*, 32(2): 177–191.

Butt, S. (2013) 'Freedom of Information Law and Its Application in Indonesia: A Preliminary Assessment', *Asian Journal of Comparative Law*, 8(1): 1–42.

Butt, S., and Lindsey, T. (2012) *The Indonesian Constitution: A Contextual Analysis*, Oxford: Hart.

Butt, S., and Parsons, N. (2011) 'Analytical Paper: Perda Review Mechanisms', Report prepared for AusAID (on file with author).

Butt, S., and Parsons, N. (2012) 'Reining in Regional Governments? Local Taxes and Investment in Decentralised Indonesia', *Sydney Law Review*, 34(1): 91–106.

Butt, S., and Parsons, N. (2014) 'Judicial Review and the Supreme Court in Indonesia: A New Space for Law?', *Indonesia*, 97(1): 55–86.

Cochrane, J. (2013) 'Touting Islam to Draw Votes in Indonesia', *New York Times*, 17 June.

Colbran, N. (2009) 'Courage under Fire: The First Five Years of the Indonesian Judicial Commission', *Australian Journal of Asian Law*, 11(2): 373–301.

Colbran, N. (2010) 'Realities and Challenges in Realising Freedom of Religion or Belief in Indonesia', *The International Journal of Human Rights*, 14(5): 678–704.

Crouch, H. (2010) *Political Reform in Indonesia after Soeharto*, Singapore: ISEAS.

Crouch, M. (2007) 'The Yogyakarta Local Ombudsman: Promoting Good Governance through Local Support', *Asian Journal of Comparative Law*, 2(1): Article 11.

Crouch, M. (2009) 'Regional Regulations in Indonesia: Failing Vulnerable Groups', *Review of Indonesian and Malaysian Affairs*, 43(2): 53–103.

Crouch, M. (2012) 'Judicial Review and Religious Freedom: The Case of Indonesian Ahmadis', *Sydney Law Review*, 34(3): 545–572.

Direktorat Jenderal Peraturan Perundang-undangan (DITJENPP) (2008) *Panduan Praktis Memahami Perancangan Peraturan Daerah*, Jakarta: Direktorat Jenderal Peraturan Perundang-undangan Departemen Hukum dan HAM bekerjasama dengan United National Development Programme; CAPPLER Project.

Hidayat, N. (2006) 'Sisi Lain Perda-Perda Bermasalah: Perspektif Remodel Lebih Dominan', *Jawa Pos*, 14 November.

Horowitz, D. L. (2013) *Constitutional Change and Democracy in Indonesia*, New York: Cambridge University Press.

Hosen, N. (2010) *Human Rights, Politics and Corruption in Indonesia: A Critical Reflection on the Post-Soeharto Era*, Dordrecht: Republic of Letters.

Hukumonline (2012) 'Banyak Perda Abaikan Kaidah Yang Berlaku', 16 March, available online at http://www.hukumonline.com/berita/baca/lt4f62f0e755b55/banyak-perda-abaikan-kaidah-yang-berlaku [accessed 20 July 2016].

Human Rights Watch (2014) 'World Report 2014: Events of 2013', New York: Human Rights Watch.

Kabar Priangan (2013) 'Revisi Perda Pendidikan Keagamaan Islam, Dua Bulan Selesai', 14 May.

Kompas (2007) 'Perda Bermasalah Di Seluruh Sulawesi Dihapus', 4 August.

Lewis, B. D. (2014) 'Decentralised Government: Greater Demand Needed to Raise Service Quality in Indonesia', *East Asia Forum*, 22 March, available online at http://www.eastasiaforum.org/2014/03/22/decentralised-government-greater-demand-needed-to-raise-service-quality-in-indonesia/ [accessed 20 July 2016].

Litvack, J., and Seddon, J. (eds) (1999) 'Decentralisation Briefing Notes', World Bank Institute Working Papers, available online at http://siteresources.worldbank.org/WBI/Resources/wbi37142.pdf [accessed 20 July 2016].

Media Indonesia (2010) '3200 Perda Bertentangan Dengan HAM', 7 July.

Parlina, I., and Aritonang, M. (2013) 'After Straddling Proposal, Ministry to Review Bylaws', *Jakarta Post*, 18 January.

Parsons, N., and Mietzner, M. (2010) 'Sharia By-laws in Indonesia: A Legal and Political Analysis', *Australian Journal of Asian Law*, 11(2): 190–217.

Pasandaran, C. (2014) 'Home Affairs Minister Speaks out against Mandatory Prayer Bylaw', *Jakarta Post*, 17 January.

Pearson, E. (2014) 'Indonesia's Growing Religious Intolerance Has to Be Addressed', *Guardian Australia*, 6 February.

Ramage, D. (2007) 'Indonesia: Democracy First, Good Governance Later', *Southeast Asian Affairs*, 7: 135–160.

Ray, D. (2003) 'Decentralization, Regulatory Reform, and the Business Climate', in *Decentralisation, Regulatory Reform, and the Business Climate*, Jakarta: Partnership for Economic Growth, 1–40.

Salim, A. (2007) 'Muslim Politics in Indonesia's Democratisation: The Religious Majority and the Rights of Minorities in the Post-New Order Era', in R. H. McLeod and A. J. MacIntyre (eds) *Indonesia: Democracy and the Promise of Good Governance*, Singapore: Institute of Southeast Asian Studies, 35–75.

Tanzi, V. (1995) 'Fiscal Federalism and Decentralization: A Review of Some Efficiency and Macroeconomic Aspects', in World Bank (ed.) *Annual World Bank Conference on Development Economics*, Washington, DC: World Bank, 295–316.

Tempo (2013) 'Boediono Minta Perda Bermasalah Dicabut', 12 February, available online at https://m.tempo.co/read/news/2013/02/12/078460851/boediono-minta-perda-bermasalah-dicabut [accessed 20 July 2016].

World Bank Independent Evaluation Group (IEG) (2008) *Decentralisation in Client Countries: An Evaluation of the World Bank Support, 1990–2007*, Washington, DC: World Bank.

Klarifikasi

Klarifikasi 188.34/529/SJ, 5 February 2013, reviewing Bandung City Regulation 19 of 2012 on Nuisance Permits and Nuisance Permit User Charges.

Klarifikasi 188.34/1051/SJ, 27 February 2013, reviewing Tasikmalaya County Regulation 10 of 2012 on Islamic Education in the County of Tasikmalaya.

Klarifikasi 188.34/1052/SJ, 27 February 2013, reviewing Southeast Sulawesi Provincial Regulation 4 of 2011 on Regional Borrowings.

Klarifikasi 188.34/1055/SJ, 23 September 2013, reviewing West Ogan Komering Ulu Regulation 3 of 2012 on Regulation of the Use of County Roads and Village Roads for Rock Mining Transportation.

Klarifikasi 188.34/1057/SJ, 27 February 2013, reviewing Riau Provincial Regulation 6 of 2006 on the Fishing Industry in Riau Province.

Klarifikasi 188.34/1060/SJ, 27 February 2013, reviewing Karanganyar County Regulation 6 of 2012 on User Charges for Specific Approvals.

Klarifikasi 188.34/1465/SJ, 18 April 2012, reviewing Karimun County Regulation 9 of 2007 on Amendments to Regional Regulation 5 of 2004 on Management of Underground and Surface Water and Regional User Charges.

Klarifikasi 188.34/1654/SJ, 1 April 2013, reviewing Tanah Laut County Regulation 3 of 2011 on Nuisance Permit User Charges.

Klarifikasi 188.34/1662/SJ, 1 April 2013, reviewing Surabaya City Regulation 16 of 2012 on Education.

Klarifikasi 188.34/1899/SJ, 27 December 2012, reviewing Pontianak City Regulation 10 of 2010 on Non-smoking Areas.

Klarifikasi 188.34/2100/SJ, 25 April 2013, reviewing Jambi Provincial Regulation 5 of 1987 on Receipt by Regional Governments of Third-party Contributions.

Klarifikasi 188.34/2268/SJ, 3 May 2013, reviewing Surabaya Mayor Regulation 19 of 2013 on Technical Guidelines for the Provision of Education Grants to Private Schools in 2013.

Klarifikasi 188.34/2269/SJ, 3 May 2013, reviewing Tasikmalaya City Regulation 8 of 2003 on Nuisance Permits.

Klarifikasi 188. 34/2270/SJ, 3 May 2013, reviewing Binjai City Regulation 5 of 2011 on Business Service User Charges.

Klarifikasi 188.34/2271/SJ, 3 May 2013, reviewing Cilegon City Regulation 13 of 2009 on Procedures to Resolves Regional Damages Claims.

Klarifikasi 188.34/2272/SJ, 3 May 2013, reviewing Balangan County Regulation 25 of 2012 on Public Service.

Klarifikasi 188.34/2694/SJ, 12 July 2012, reviewing Papua Provincial Regulation 1 of 2011 on Restoration of the Rights of Papuan Female Victims of Violence and Human Rights Violations.

Klarifikasi 188.34/2698/SJ, 12 July 2012 reviewing Kerinci County Regulation 2 of 2010 on Industry and Trade Approval Services.

Klarifikasi 188.34/2854/SJ, 4 June 2013 reviewing Pelalawan County Regulation 2 of 2012 on Public Service User Charges.

Klarifikasi 188.34/2855/SJ, 4 June 2013, reviewing Pelalawan County Regulation 4 of 2012 on User Charges for Specific Approvals.

Klarifikasi 188.34/2858/SJ, 4 June 2013, reviewing Gunung Mas County Regulation 2 of 2012 on the Management of Natural Disasters.

Klarifikasi 188.34/2936/SJ, 10 June 2013, reviewing Padangsidimpuan City Regulation 6 of 2010 on User Charges for Specific Approvals.

Klarifikasi 188.34/2938/SJ, 10 June 2013, reviewing Lampung Provincial Regulation 11 of 2012 on the Management of Air Quality and Pollution Control.

Klarifikasi 188.34/2944/SJ, 10 June 2013, reviewing West Tanjung Jabung County Regulation 10 of 2012 on the Education System.

Klarifikasi 188.34/2945/SJ, 10 June 2013, reviewing Bangka County Regulation 4 of 2011 on Public Service User Charges.

Klarifikasi 188.34/2946/SJ, 10 June 2013, reviewing Banten Provincial Regulation 7 of 2012 on Education.

Klarifikasi 188.34/2947/SJ, 10 June 2013, reviewing Bogor City Regulation 9 of 2012 on Garbage Management

Klarifikasi 188.34/2950/SJ, 10 June 2013, reviewing North Maluku Provincial Regulation 7 of 2012 on Investment of Regional Capital in North Maluku Province.

Klarifikasi 188.34/3213/SJ, 20 June 2013, reviewing Gayo Lues County Regulation 5 of 2011 on User Charges for Specific Approvals.

Klarifikasi 188.34/3217/SJ, 18 July 2013, reviewing Melawi County Regulation 6 of 2012 on Hotel Taxes.

Klarifikasi 188.34/3218/SJ, 20 June 2013, reviewing East Aceh County Regulation 1 of 2011 on Land and Building Tax.

Klarifikasi 188.34/3219/SJ, 20 June 2013, reviewing Gayo Lues County Regulation 4 of 2011 on Regional Taxes.

Klarifikasi 188.34/3262/SJ, 21 June 2013, reviewing Lampung Provincial Regulation 10 of 2012 on the Management of Cooperatives.

Klarifikasi 188.34/3268/SJ, 21 June 2013, reviewing West Kalimantan Provincial Regulation 2 of 2013 on Civil Servant Investigators in West Kalimantan.

Klarifikasi 188.34/3273/SJ, 21 June 2013, reviewing Banggai County Regulation 10 of 2008 on Contributions for Use of Syukuran Aminudin Amir Bubung Luwuk Airport.

Klarifikasi 188.34/3274/SJ, 21 June 2013, reviewing Palembang City Regulation 18 of 2011 on Administration and Nuisance Permit User Charges.

Klarifikasi 188.34/3277/5J, 21 June 2013, reviewing South Halmahera Country Regulation 14 of 2011 on Civil Servant Investigators in Halmahera Country.

Klarifikasi 188.34/3278/SJ, 21 June 2013, reviewing Wajo County Regulation 4 of 2012 on Fishery Resource Management.

Klarifikasi 188.34/3279/SJ, 21 June 2013, reviewing Wajo County Regulation 8 of 2012 on the Establishment of the Wajo Local Public Radio Broadcast Institute.

Klarifikasi 188.34/3399/SJ, 27 June 2013, reviewing West Nusa Tenggara Provincial Regulation 1 of 2013 on Protection of Sustainable Agricultural Land.

Klarifikasi 188.34/3762/SJ, 18 July 2013, reviewing Banjarnegara County Regulation 2 of 2013 the Management of Regional Natural Disasters.

Klarifikasi 188.34/3767/SJ, 18 July 2013, reviewing Bangli County Regulation 5 of 2012 on Guidelines for Establishment and Managing Village Owned Enterprises.

Klarifikasi 188.34/3768/SJ, 20 June, reviewing Melawi County Regulation 4 of 2012 on Entertainment Taxes.

Klarifikasi 188.34/5329/SJ, 27 December 2012, reviewing Pontianak City Perda 9 of 2001 on Amendments to Perda 13 of 2006 on Monitoring, Control and Management of Bird Nest Cultivation in Pontianak.

Klarifikasi 188.34/6274/SJ, 12 September 2013, reviewing Bandung City Regulation 23 of 2012 on Social Welfare.

Klarifikasi 188.34/6525/SJ, 25 September 2013, reviewing Bandung County Regulation 29 of 2012 on Changing the Name and Legal Form of the People's Credit Bank of Bandung to a Limited Liability Company named the Kerta Raharja People's Credit Bank.

13 Forestry law, *masyarakat adat* and struggles for inclusive citizenship in Indonesia

Noer Fauzi Rachman and Mia Siscawati

Introduction

On 16 May 2013, the Constitutional Court of the Republic of Indonesia ruled that customary forests (*hutan adat*) were no longer to be regarded as part of state forests (*hutan negara*). The Court ruled to delete the word 'state' from article 1.6 of Forestry Law No. 41 of 1999. The article now reads '*Adat* forests are ~~state~~ forests located in the territory of customary law communities (*masyarakat hukum adat*)'. The ruling determines the category of forest to which a 'customary forest' (*hutan adat*) belongs. 'Customary forest' has been removed from the category of 'state forest' (*hutan negara*), and moved into 'forest subject to rights' (*hutan hak*). The Constitutional Court ruling in Case 35/PUU-X/2012 is a landmark achievement for the forest reform process in Indonesia.

This chapter presents a critical analysis of the Constitutional Court ruling – particularly the implications of the ruling in favour of *masyarakat hukum adat*[1] and their *adat* forests, as well as the implications it has for state institutions in terms of implementation. The chapter identifies the ways in which the ruling was influenced by civil society, which advocated for the recognition of the rights of *masyarakat adat* over lands, natural resources and territory. We discuss the struggle over lands, natural resources and territory in the context of the territorialisation of forest control in Indonesia.

We argue that the Constitutional Court ruling is a remarkable and historic landmark in Indonesian agrarian politics, especially in relation to the status of *masyarakat hukum adat* (hereinafter *masyarakat adat*) as rights-bearing subjects, by which they have a 'right to have rights', including rights over lands and territories. Treating 'customary forests' in the category 'forests subject to rights' means that *masyarakat adat* are recognised as rights-bearing subjects that have the legal authority to exercise rights, duties and capacities as they pertain to those forests. However, the Constitutional Court ruling views *masyarakat adat* as homogeneous entities, and has paid limited attention to the gender dimension of the control of customary lands and territories by *masyarakat adat*. This is linked to a limited gender perspective in the efforts to reclaim control over indigenous-owned forests as initiated by the Indigenous Peoples Alliance of the Archipelago (*Aliansi Masyarakat Adat Nusantara*, or AMAN).

In analysing the Indonesian Constitutional Court ruling, this chapter discusses the concept of 'the right to have rights', which we adopt from Hannah Arendt through the work of Margaret Somers (2008). Based on Arendt's idea that citizenship is the necessary condition for all types of right-bearing, we argue that AMAN advocates inclusive citizenship, calling on the Ministry of Forestry and other Indonesian statutory institutions to recognise the status of *masyarakat adat* as rights-bearing subjects.

As we illustrate in this chapter, we adhere to the point of view found in critical legal studies such as the following:

> [R]ights take shape and are constituted by and through struggle. Thus, they have the capacity to be elements of emancipation, but they are neither a perfect nor exclusive vehicle for emancipation. Rights can only be operative as constituents of a strategy of social transformation as they become part of an emergent 'common sense' and are articulated within social practices . . . They articulate a vision of entitlements, of how things might be, which in turn has the capacity to advance political aspiration and action.
>
> (Hunt, 1991: 247)

Moreover, in line with the above approach, we follow the methodological observation that:

> [T]he social forces at work in any particular conjuncture are not random. They are formed out of history. They're quite particular and specific, and you have to understand what they are, how they work, what their limits and possibilities are, what they can and cannot accomplish. . . . But what is the outcome of the struggle between those different contending relations or forces is not 'given', known, predictable. It has everything to do with social practice, with how a particular contest or struggle is conducted.
>
> (Hall, 2007: 280)

This chapter also illustrates how the Constitutional Court ruling challenges the state's territorialisation of forests in Indonesia, while at the same time providing an opportunity for changing the trajectory of systemic agrarian conflicts. In analysing the state's territorialisation of forests and inhabitants in Indonesia, we adopt the concept of state territorialisation of forests and inhabitants, as defined by Peter Vandergeest and Nancy Peluso (1995) in their historical analysis of territorial control over the forests of Thailand since the late nineteenth century. Their article addresses the way in which state power is territorialised within the borders of a politically defined space, and the relationship of this process to the allocation and realisation of resource access rights, in addition to control over the people who use such resources (Vandergeest and Peluso, 1995: 387). They employ Sack's (1986: 19) concept of territoriality as 'the attempt by an individual or group to affect, influence, or control people, phenomena, and relationships by delimiting and asserting control over a geographic area'. This involves the inclusion and exclusion of people and activities within a circumscribed, delimited area and the space of the state is further defined as abstract space. In a separate article, Vandergeest (1996: 159) defines territorialisation as 'the process by which states attempt to control people and their actions by drawing boundaries around a geographical space, excluding some categories of individuals from this space, and proscribing or prescribing specific activities within the boundaries of that space'.

Vandergeest and Peluso (1995: 391) examine the territorialisation of resources and people in rural areas, particularly in the following three processes: the territorialisation of civil administration in rural areas of Siam/Thailand; state attempts to control the use of major portions of national territory by demarcating it; and finally defining it as forest. Elsewhere, Vandergeest (1996) further identifies three stages of territorialisation of the state's control of forests. First, the state claims all lands considered to be 'nobody's land' (*terra nullius*) as state property. At this stage, the state intends to earn income from the extraction of natural resources. The next stage is the establishment of the boundaries of the land declared to be state property in order to assert the state's territorial control over the natural resources; after the territorial boundaries of a certain area are established, the state forbids anyone access the area and its natural resources unless the state issues a permit or a concession to the land. The final stage of territorialisation of the state's control of forests is when the state launches a programme that can be called 'functional territorialisation'. In the case of Thailand, this approach was established in 1960; it was also adopted in the United States in land use management models whereby the states divided forests into types of suitability for various functions or exploitation based on scientific criteria, such as slope, rainfall and soil type. The main output of this programme was the zoning of areas, aimed at regulating the types of activity that would be allowed in each zone (Vandergeest, 1996).

This process in the state's territorialisation of forests and their inhabitants has also occurred in Indonesia. Indonesia's territorialisation practices took root during its colonial period and continue into the contemporary era. The process has not been linear, but rather dynamic, and has been operationalised through negotiation and interaction between state institutions and actors and non-state ones over certain periods. The establishment of state territorialisation during the colonial era was preceded by the extensive use of tropical timbers from the Indonesia's archipelago as raw material for the Dutch shipbuilding industry.

This chapter starts with a historical overview of the state's territorial claim to – and control over – forests. It also describes the contemporary process of the government's claim to, and control over, forests in Indonesia, including the establishment of *kawasan hutan* ('forest zones'), and how this approach was influenced by the approach taken by Indonesia's former colonial government. In the second part of this chapter, we closely analyse the struggles of *masyarakat adat* and the role that AMAN has played in agrarian conflicts in the Indonesian archipelago. AMAN's agenda has largely been influenced by the *masyarakat adat* experience of being excluded from their own lands and territories, and of being criminalised by the Ministry of Forestry, other statutory institutions and concession holders. We focus on the ways in which AMAN's significant contribution has been to give the *masyarakat adat* visibility and to garner respect for their rights. Their action includes the 2013 petitioning for a judicial review of Forestry Law No. 41 of 1999 by the Constitutional Court. We also discuss the limited participation of *adat* women, as well as the limited attention to gender issues in the whole process of the judicial review. The third part of this chapter contextualises the Constitutional Court ruling as a landmark in the trajectory of Indonesian agrarian politics.

Territorialisation of forest control in Indonesia

Control over land and natural resources that are within *adat* territories (*wilayah adat*), both by state institutions and corporations who receive concessions from the state, cannot be separated from the multilayered history of the territorialisation of state control over forests that was laid down in the colonial period and has been extended into the contemporary era. A particular product of territorialisation of forest control is the classification of areas that have no private entitlement as state forests, which Peluso and Vandergeest (2001) call 'political forests'. The institutionalisation of 'political forests' during Indonesia's colonial era contributed to the formulation of forest tenure and forest governance in post-colonial Indonesia. The legacy of the political forest concept is still strongly reflected in access to, control of and exclusions from forests and forest resources. We see this in the continued authority exerted over heterogenic groups of men and women, as well as over space, in contemporary Indonesia (Elmhirst, 2010). This continuous authority, which is exerted through a variety of power-wielding techniques, establishes and shapes resource access by reinforcing the identification of certain geographical areas, including uplands and remote islands, as empty, alienated, backward or uncivilised, providing justification for the territorial ownership and managerial control over these areas to be in the hands of the state (Ribot and Peluso, 2003; Li, 2000, 2001).

The extraction of timbers from Indonesia's forests began in the early 1600s. At this time, the Dutch East India Company (known as *Vereenigde Oost-Indische Compagnie*, or VOC, in Dutch), which operated in the Indonesian Archipelago from 1602 to 1800, began ruling the port cities, gradually building several shipyards and becoming a major consumer of Indonesia's timber, which was then largely teak (Boomgaard, 1992: 4). The VOC not only extracted timber and other resources, but also began to exert territorial control over the areas in which it operated. Over the next two centuries, the Company acquired additional ports as trading bases and safeguarded its interests by taking over surrounding territories. It remained an important trading concern and paid an 18 per cent annual dividend for almost 200 years (Ricklefs, 2008: 143)., However, because of the problems of corruption it faced in the late eighteenth century, the Company went bankrupt and was formally dissolved in 1800. Its possessions and debt were taken over by the Dutch government, and with the area already in Dutch hands, the VOC's territories became the territories of the Dutch East Indies (Ricklefs, 2008: 144), formally declared a colony in 1806. The Dutch East Indies continued to expand until it occupied what is now recognised as the Indonesian archipelago.

Forestry was, from the earliest colonial times, a concern. Governor-General Willem Herman Daendels, who served as governor-general of the Dutch East Indies during 1808–11, enacted the first regulations on centralised forest management in colonial Java in 1803 and established the colonial Forest Service (*Boschwezen*) (Boomgaard, 1992). In 1865, the colonial government enacted the colonial Forestry Law for Java and Madura, which was implemented by the Forest Service. This law officially adopted the approach of state control over forest lands and resources. In 1870, a further regulation known as the *Domeinverklaring* was adopted. It claimed that all forest lands were state lands, except the lands under private entitlement (Peluso, 1992; Peluso and Vandergeest, 2001; Simon, 2001). This was the first step in state territorialisation (Vandergeest, 1996). The second stage of the state's territorialisation of the forests and their inhabitants in colonial Indonesia occurred when the colonial Forest Service (*Dienst van het Boschwezen*) delineated boundaries between agricultural and forest lands, and organised the establishment of state-controlled territories of forested areas. This stage completed the adoption of the notion of 'political forests' within the colonial state (Peluso and Vandergeest, 2001). The final stage of territorialisation of the state control of forests, 'functional territorialisation' (Vandergeest, 1996), occurred when the Dutch colonial Forest Service zoned forest areas according to different functions, such as production and protection.

The process of the state's territorialisation of forests and its inhabitants in post-colonial Indonesia reached its peak during the New Order era when President Soeharto was in power. The foundation stones of this regime were political control and economic development, based on the utilisation of natural resources. To secure this process, Soeharto's administration enacted the Basic Forestry Law No. 5 of 1967 (*Undang Undang No. 5/1967 tentang Ketentuan-Ketentuan Pokok Kehutanan*). This law adopted the colonial Forestry Law and claimed that all forest areas – outside the small enclaves of private-owned lands – were state-controlled property and therefore should be managed under the state-controlled system.

The Basic Forestry Law of 1967 also established the allocation of forest zones based on different functions. According to article 3 of the Law, forest zones in Indonesia were divided into the following four functions:

1 protected forest, owing to its natural characteristics, designated for water catchment, and prevention of floods and erosion, as well as maintaining soil fertility;
2 production forest, designated for the purpose of managing forest products to meet the needs of society in general and the needs of development, industry and export in particular;
3 natural preserved forest, owing to its special characteristics, designated for the protection of biological resources – which function divided into natural preservation (*cagar alam*) and wildlife sanctuaries (*suaka margasatwa*); and
4 recreation forest.

Following the enactment of the Basic Forestry Law of 1967, a forest land use planning policy using the allocation of forest zones based on the different functions was established under Government Regulation No. 33 of 1970 and formalised in a set of decrees enacted by the Minister of Agriculture in 1980 and 1981. These policies then continued with the development of *Tata Guna Hutan Kesepakatan* (TGHK) or 'Forest Land Use by Consensus'. Based on TGHK, which was completed in 1994, the permanent forest was categorised into:

1 permanent production forest (*Hutan Produksi*, or HP) (33.4 million hectares);
2 limited production forest (*Hutan Produksi Terbatas*, or HPT) (27.57 million hectares);
3 convertible production forest (30 million hectares), which category includes areas able to be converted to other uses, including the development of infrastructure, industrial agriculture (including palm oil plantations) and mining;
4 protected forest (*Hutan Lindung*, or HL) (29.65 million hectares); and
5 natural conservation areas (*Kawasan Perlindungan Alam*, or KPA) or conservation forest (*Hutan Konservas, or* HK), which includes national parks, nature preserves (*Cagar Alam*, or CA) and recreation forests (19.15 million hectares).

These policies clearly reinforced the practice that Vandergeest (1996: 160–161) refers to as 'functional territorialisation' – that is, the remapping of forest and other areas according to scientific criteria such as slope, soil type and watershed classification, which then became the basis for laws prohibiting and prescribing specific activities in these areas.

The TGHK served as a legal reference for timber extraction on the Outer Islands. Using this policy – in particular, the section on the allocation for production forests – the Indonesian Ministry of Forestry licensed forest lands to both private and state-owned logging companies, as well as to industrial plantation companies. By applying timber-based extractive forestry, and by licensing forest lands to both private and state-owned logging companies during the 1970s and the early 1980s, the New Order regime facilitated a massive process of forest exploitation. Timbers harvested under this process were mainly exported as round logs. Most of the companies that received logging concessions were closely associated with military institutions (such as military cooperatives) or high-ranking military officers. The strong connection with the military, along with the extremely high revenue from the timber, drove the excessive logging that occurred (Dauvergne, 1997: 71–72).

The framework of political forests and industrial forestry adopted by the New Order regime ignored the existence of communities and systems of forest resource management that had been developed by indigenous and other local communities across Indonesia. The arrival of logging companies and the massive extraction of forest resources in areas that were the homelands of indigenous communities impacted on women and men differently. Indigenous women suffered more and, in certain areas, women managed to organise themselves against the extractive companies (Siscawati, 2014b).

The State's territorialisation of forests and inhabitants in post-New Order Indonesia through Forestry Law No. 41 of 1999

After the end of the Soeharto period, there was change of emphasis in the forestry regime. The new Forestry Law No. 41 (unlike the Basic Forestry Law No. 5 of 1967) subscribed to a narrower definition, defining forests as the area covered by trees, and this law also adopted an ecosystem approach. Article 1 of Forestry Law No. 41 of 1999 states that a 'forest is an ecosystem unit as a plot of land containing bio-natural resources dominated by vegetation in an integrated unity of the environment thereof'. Nevertheless, this Law adopted a relatively conventional approach in seeing an ecosystem as an entity of which people are not considered a part.

In defining 'forest zones' (*kawasan hutan*), article 1 of Forestry Law No. 41 of 1999 refers to 'any particular area determined or designated by the government to be permanent forest'. Based on the status of the forest, article 5 of Forestry Law No. 41 of 1999 maintains two categories of forest: state forest (*hutan negara*) and forest subject to rights (*hutan hak*). 'State forest' refers to any forest on land over which there is no land title held. The category known as *hutan hak* refers to any forest situated on land in which land title exists. This category is commonly regarded as (and translated as) 'private forest'. Article 1 of the Forestry Law No. 41 of 1999, however, does not explicitly state that this category comprises private forest.

This Law recognises the existence of customary forest (*hutan adat*); however, it categorises customary forest as state forest. Article 1 states that '*adat* forest is a state forest that is located in the territory of *masyarakat hukum adat*'. Article 5(2) states that 'State forest as referred to in point 1 can be customary forest'. Article 5(3) states that '[t]he Government shall stipulate the status of a forest as referred to in points (1) and (2) of Article 5', and customary forest shall be stipulated if there is any and its existence is acknowledged. Point 4 of article 5 concludes that, '[i]n the case [of] development, the *masyarakat hukum adat* in question no longer exists, [and] the management right of customary forest shall be returned to the Government'. All of the above demonstrates that Forestry Law No. 41 of 1999 does not address the claim made by *masyarakat hukum adat* that their customary forests existed long before the modern state of Indonesia was established. Moreover, Forestry Law No. 41 of 1999 has not recognised the rights of *masyarakat adat* over forest lands and resources.

This new forestry law serves as the legal basis for Government Regulation (*Peraturan Pemerintah*, or PP) No. 6/2007 on Forest Allocation, Forest Management Planning and Land Utilisation, later revised and replaced by PP No. 3/2008 on the Amendment to Government Regulation No. 6/2007 Forest Allocation, Forest Management Planning and Land Utilisation. This Regulation provides a legal basis for managing conservation forests, protected forests and production forests through the integrated forest management system known as *Kesatuan Pengelolaan Hutan* (KPH), or 'Forest Management Unit'. At the same time, this Regulation provides a legal basis for state-sponsored community forestry, such as village forestry (*hutan desa*, or HD), community-based forestry (*hutan kemasyarakatan*, or HKm), community-based timber plantations (*hutan tanaman rakyat*, or HTR), and partnerships (*kemitraan*).

The recognition of state-sponsored community forestry has been relatively slow. Official data released by the Ministry of Forestry in August 2009 showed that the state forest areas officially allocated totalled 11,990.06 hectares for HKm. These areas are located in eleven districts and seven provinces. Other areas were still pending, with 175,556 hectares in the process of being officially allocated for HKm. These areas are located in twenty-six districts and twelve provinces. The government had plans to expand 400,000 hectares of HKm areas for 2009 and 2.1 million hectares of HKm areas for 2015. It had also set a target of 5 million hectares of village forest to be released in 2015 (Ministry of Forestry, 2009; Kementerian Kehutanan Republik Indonesia, 2009). The total number of areas to be officially allocated for HKm and HD (village forests) is relatively small compared to forest areas managed by companies that have forest concession licences from the Ministry of Forestry. The slow progress in communities being able to realise their user rights to manage state forests is clearly linked to the main substance of Forestry Law No. 41 of 1999 and all other forestry policies that do not view local communities as subjects that 'have the right to have rights'. Moreover, the 1999 Forestry Law and other forestry policies enacted to further regulate the state forest zone show that the state's territorialisation of forests, including 'functional territorialisation', has strengthened, rather than weakened.

Contemporary state territorialisation of forests and systemic agrarian conflicts

Systemic agrarian conflicts are protracted conflicts arising from opposing claims made on rights and access to particular pieces of land, or over natural resources and territories, between local rural communities and concessionaries (mostly huge corporations) in the business of infrastructure, production, resource extraction and conservation, and where each side is taking direct or indirect action to negate the claim of the other (Rachman, 2012c). This type of agrarian conflict arises from the granting of agrarian concessions and licences to corporations by public officials, including the Minister of Forestry, which exclude communities' previous rights and their access to the land, the natural resources or the territories.

The agrarian conflicts in 'forest zones' also have gender dimensions. The lack of access to land has economic and social dimensions that have particularly impacted on women of many different *adat* communities and local communities – especially women of landless families and other minority social groups – who have been facing various forms of gender injustice (Siscawati and Mahaningtyas, 2012; Siscawati and Rachman, 2014), such as loss of lands they inherited from their parents, internal discrimination in education resulting from poverty created by the loss of access to lands and resources, and more burdens as male members of their families leave their villages to obtain cash incomes. Girls from poor families are also vulnerable to inducements offered to the families and to the girls themselves to leave the villages to become child labourers. They are also at risk of falling victim to trafficking in women and children, a problem that has been particularly widespread in agrarian conflict areas (Siscawati, 2014b). This situation has led a number of indigenous women in different areas to lead grassroots actions against extractive industries since the late 1980s (Siscawati, 2014a). However, the majority of agrarian protests and grassroots resistance movements are still dominated by male leaders.

New forms of agrarian protests have begun to emerge during the last two years. One of these new protests was the long march of 1,000 kilometres over forty-two days undertaken by thirty-two male peasants and one female peasant from contested areas in an ecosystem restoration concession in Jambi (Sumatra). During the march, which took place between December 2012 and January 2013, fellow victims of land exclusions, including farmers from Mesuji, Lampung (Sumatra), joined them. Prior to the long march, another group of more than 100 villagers from the same areas set up protest tents in front of the headquarters of the Ministry of Forestry in Jakarta. A small number of peasant women participated in these activities. The women who participated in the long march stated that the women of their villages played significant roles in the preparation of the march. Many of them wanted to participate, but they were unable to do so because of various domestic responsibilities.[2] The three groups then decided to jointly organise a march from the Ministry of Forestry's building to the Presidential Palace on 23 January 2013. These collective activities served as part of their attempt to voice their demands, which they strategically connected with rights, as contained in the Constitution of 1945, requesting the recognition and the protection of their rights as citizens of the Republic of Indonesia.

These agrarian conflicts in Jambi and Lampung are not isolated instances. The way in which the Forestry Law and other policies are dealt with is reflected in these cases. This includes the use of force and the criminalisation of local community members, as well as the use of manipulation, fraud and coercion, all of which are seen to be used widely and systematically. Such tactics are often used to deny local peoples' land claims or to transfer control over land, natural resources and territories into the hands of giant corporations for their business projects. They also exclude local people from, or limit their access to, their lands, natural resources and territories.

Aside from having to confront systemic agrarian conflicts, the Ministry of Forestry has also been facing a significant challenge because of the Constitutional Court ruling in the Case 45/PUU-IX/2011 regarding Article 1(3) of Forestry Law No. 41 of 1999. The case was officially submitted by the heads of five districts in Central Kalimantan Province. Article 1(3) defines the process by which Indonesia's Forest Zone (*Kawasan Hutan*) is established by the national government (represented by the Ministry of Forestry). A large proportion of administrative districts have been designated as forest zone, causing the local governments to depend upon the Ministry of Forestry for permission to undertake development activities. The five district heads who submitted an application for judicial review of Forestry Law No. 41 of 1999 to the Constitutional Court argued that article 1(3) of that Law, stating that a '[f]orest zone is a certain area designated and or established by the government intended to be maintained as permanent forest area' – especially the phrase 'designated and or established by the government' – results in an injury to the applicants' constitutional rights, causing, among other things:

- a lack of legal certainty in their exercise of their authority, particularly regarding the issuance of new permits and extension of permits that had previously existed in regard to plantations, mining, housing and residences, and other structures and infrastructure;
- an inability to implement/execute autonomy in the widest sense; and
- an inability to implement the local regulations of Central Kalimantan Province regarding the Plan for Spatial Management of both Regency and Provincial Areas (Arizona, Mary and Nagara, 2012).

The Constitutional Court declared the phrase 'designated and or established by the government' in article 1(3) to be unconstitutional and unenforceable. Article 1(3) now reads: 'A Forest Zone [*Kawasan Hutan*] is a particular area gazetted [*ditetapkan*] by the Government to be maintained as permanent forest [*Hutan Tetap*].' This ruling raises questions concerning the rights of local communities to refuse the designation of their land and territories as land to be included in the forest zone.

AMAN and the struggles to make *masyarakat adat* visible and their rights protected

As mentioned previously, the state's territorialisation of forests and their inhabitants, as a policy adopted by the New Order through the establishment of state forest zones (*kawasan hutan negara*), ignored the existence of *masyarakat adat* and other local communities. In other words, *masyarakat adat* and local communities were not recognised by the state, particularly by the Ministry of Forestry. Forestry laws, both the Basic Forestry Law No. 5 of 1967 and its successor Forestry Law No. 41 of 1999, supported the expansion of forest extraction by forest-related industries and other industries operating on the basis of the commodification of forests in various regions in Indonesia. Many of the areas in which companies operate with licences for logging concessions, timber plantations and newly established ecological restoration concessions are customary territories of *masyarakat adat*. In the case of forest areas allocated for conservation purposes (such as national parks and nature reserves), the management is in the hands of agencies under the Ministry of Forestry. This has caused agrarian conflicts between *masyarakat adat* and companies, as well as government agencies. In handling agrarian conflicts, government agencies and companies often use various forms of coercion, including military and paramilitary methods. In response to such situations, *masyarakat adat* in various places in Indonesia have utilised a variety of resistance tactics. Although most of the resistance operations of *masyarakat adat* have been led by male leaders, female leaders have emerged in several places.

In May 1993 some leaders of *masyarakat adat* who had led the struggles of *masyarakat adat* met with environmental movement activists at a meeting organised by the Forum for the Environment (*Wahana Lingkungan Hidup Indonesia*, or WALHI) held at Tana Toraja (South Sulawesi). The Toraja meeting resulted in agreement on the term '*masyarakat adat*' and its definition as 'a group of people with origins (hereditary) in certain geographical areas, who have an ideological, political, economic, socio-cultural value system, and their own territory' (Sangaji, 2007). Although several female leaders of *masyarakat adat* attended the meeting, the issue of indigenous women was not specifically discussed.

Together with other activists and a variety of non-governmental organisations (NGOs) that joined Indonesian social movements, the *Jaringan Pembalaan Hak-hak Masyarakat Adat* (JAPHAMA), or Indigenous Peoples Rights Advocacy Network, encouraged community initiatives in different places in Indonesia's archipelago. *Masyarakat adat* who intensively developed resistance against state and company control of their territories welcomed the activists' efforts. This collaboration resulted in the development of a plan for the first national conference of *masyarakat adat*. The conference was finally held in Jakarta in March 1999. The Congress was organised by networks of Indonesian NGOs. Congress participants, who were representatives of *masyarakat adat* from all over Indonesia, agreed to establish AMAN as a formal organisation to represent *masyarakat adat* from across the Indonesian archipelago. The establishment of AMAN also aimed at finding ways in which to render the existence of *masyarakat adat* visible, their rights respected and their citizen status confirmed.

By engaging in the politics of indigeneity, AMAN frames the Indonesian *masyarakat adat* as 'indigenous peoples' as defined by international human rights instruments.[3] They have succeeded in developing effective networks within indigenous peoples' organisations at the regional and international levels. The presence of AMAN as a national organisation of 'indigenous peoples' in Indonesia has been important and influential in global forums for promoting indigenous peoples' rights, including in the context of developing international human rights standards, international environmental treaties and climate change negotiations.

Aside from the politics of indigeneity, AMAN's perspectives and its organisational agenda have been shaped too by the everyday experiences of *masyarakat adat* dealing with systemic agrarian conflicts.[4] The harsh realities experienced by many *masyarakat adat* under the New Order regime (1967–98) and its successors were created when their territories were treated as a resource-rich frontier.[5] The central statutory institutions are frequently present, and their presence significantly transforms the lives of *masyarakat adat* in remote and rural areas, both inland and coastal, through coercive social engineering, including the granting of licences to private or state-owned corporations or government agencies to establish land, mining, plantation and forestry concessions, as well as conservation areas. Such concessions are generally accompanied by the dispossession and displacement of *masyarakat adat* from their lands, with or without resettlement projects.

Masyarakat adat have special characteristics as the owners of their lands and territories because of their original rights (*hak-hak asal-usul*). As an archipelagic country, Indonesia is well known for the varied socio-ecological characteristics of its indigenous territories: dense-forested river and lake landscapes, agro-forestry in lowland and upland areas, coastal and marine customary territories, savannah grasslands, and so on. The diversity of the regions also affects indigenous livelihoods, which range from hunting and gathering forest species, fishing and collecting marine resources, rotational cultivation, sedentary farming, and so on, to various combinations of the foregoing. *Masyarakat adat* are among the population groups who were directly victimised by, and subsequently suffered under, the regulations, policies and practices of the New Order regime in granting land, mining, forestry and plantation concessions from 1967 onward.

Granting concessions is, of course, within the ambit of the government's legal authority. The problem stems from decisions made by government officials to grant licences/permits/use rights for *adat* lands and territories to corporations, and the creation of *adat* land territories as national parks. This might not have been a problem if the *masyarakat adat* whose lands and resources were affected had been able to exercise their right to free, prior and informed consent, as guaranteed in the UN Declaration on the Rights of Indigenous Peoples. In most cases, corporations and government agencies that have licences to manage natural resources decide to displace the communities by force. The competing claims collide when the licences/permits/use rights holders attempt to delegitimise the existence of the communities, their territorial rights, and rights to access land and resources, and then the communities resist. Thus it can be said that the main source of agrarian conflicts lies in the decisions of public officials who have the authority to allocate land/natural resources to state-owned or privately owned companies/institutions involved in producing global commodities and/or ecological services.

AMAN's strategies

In its *Pandangan Dasar* ('fundamental view'), AMAN (1999: 1) expresses the juxtaposed relations between the Indonesian state and the existence of *masyarakat adat*:

> [L]ong before the Republic of Indonesia was established, a variety of *masyarakat adat* lived scattered around the Indonesian archipelago. We, *masyarakat adat*, are living based on ancestry for generations in an indigenous territory, which extends to land and natural resources, and is governed by traditional institutions that manage the sustainability of community life.[6]

The establishment of AMAN has enabled the scattered *masyarakat adat* around the archipelago to develop a unified collective action framework that is represented in AMAN's motto, 'If the state does not recognise us, we do not recognise the state'.[7] The motto concisely and precisely represents the position that AMAN has decided to maintain – that is, its problematic and contingent relation to the state:

> It is clear [that the State] has recognised the diversity of '*masyarakat adat*' cultures across the Indonesian archipelago, as has been formulated in the phrase *Bhineka Tunggal Ika* (Unity in Diversity). But, in fact, we did not obtain recognition of sovereignty. *Masyarakat adat* in the Republic of Indonesia have experienced serious hardships. Our sufferings are essentially derived from the non-recognition of the sovereignty of *masyarakat adat* by the sovereignty of the Indonesia State as exemplified in their government practices.[8]
>
> (AMAN, 1999: 1)

AMAN started with a confrontational strategy by clearly articulating its criticism of government policies and practices, mobilising protests against forest/mining/plantation concessions, and demanding that statutory institutions recognise the existence of *masyarakat adat* and their rights over lands and territory. AMAN demonstrated that the violations of their rights over lands and territory would be fatal to the future of *masyarakat adat*.

AMAN's working strategies have changed over time because of the changes in the political spaces within which it works. When the Indonesian government moved to introduce democratic-decentralised governance in 2001, AMAN's leaders and its NGO supporters began launching strategic collaborative initiatives with selected district level political elites to leverage their political agendas. An NGO network, the *Jaringan Kerja Pemetaan Partisipatif* (JKPP), or Indonesian Network for Participatory Mapping, has, since its establishment in 1996, been helping *masyarakat adat* to create a map of customary territories, and has encouraged local governments to develop workable mechanisms to identify and recognise the existence of *masyarakat adat* and their territories.

AMAN congresses and national workshops, which always take place in district or provincial cities, have been well attended by its national, and also international, supporters.

It has received credible coverage in local and national newspapers. At its Fourth Congress in Tobelo (Halmahera Island in North Maluku), more than 2,000 people came to participate and celebrate the Congress, which was also officially and financially supported by the district government of Tobelo.[9]

AMAN's strategies have also included actions directly dealing with particular legislation and regulations. These are outlined next.

AMAN and the Judicial Review of Forestry Law No. 41 of 1999

As mentioned at the beginning of this chapter, AMAN is fully aware that many of Indonesia's key sectoral laws, especially Forestry Law No. 41 of 1999, do not recognise the Indonesian indigenous peoples' rights. These laws have been used to legalise the claim over customary lands as state forest lands. This situation led AMAN to challenge the Forestry Law in Indonesia's Constitutional Court on 19 March 2012, when an official request for a judicial review of the Law was submitted by AMAN and two indigenous communities, the Kasepuhan Cisitu people from Banten (Java), and the Kenegerian Kuntu people from Riau (Sumatra).

In its 2012 petition for the judicial review of Forestry Law No. 41 of 1999, AMAN refers to the articles in the 2002 Amendment to the Indonesian Constitution that recognise the rights of *masyarakat adat*. Article 18B(2) of the 2002 Amendment to the Indonesian Constitution (which appears in Chapter VI on 'Regional Authorities') asserts that:

> [T]he state recognises and respects the individual communities of traditional law and their traditional rights [*masyarakat hukum adat*] as long as they survive, and in accordance with the development of the community and the principle of the Unitary State of the Republic of Indonesia, as regulated by law.

Article 28I(3) of the Constitution asserts that the 'cultural identity and the rights of *masyarakat adat* [traditional communities] are respected in accordance with the continuing development of civilisation over time'. It is clear that the rights referred to in article 28I are to be regarded as a 'human rights', because this article appears in Chapter XA of the Constitution, entitled 'Human Rights'; thus they are to be respected, upheld and protected as such. Traditional rights, argued AMAN, include the right to govern and regulate one's own resources. AMAN also argued that cultural identity and traditional rights are human rights, to be recognised as such.

AMAN's request for a judicial review of the Forestry Law is in line with the idea of agrarian constitutionalism. Constitutionalism here, generically, can be understood as a specific point of view based on the constitution of a country, which in principle 'arranges two connected relations: first, the relationship between government and citizens and, second, the relationship between one government agency with another' (Asshiddiqie, 2009: 27). Agrarian constitutionalism is a framework for bringing the 1945 Constitution of the Republic of Indonesia to bear as the foundation for the agrarian reform processes, which include the reform of forest tenure. The government of Indonesia must observe the 1945 Constitution not only as the main legal reference, but also as a source of knowledge and its socio-political mandate. In its Preamble, the 1945 Constitution clearly instructs the government of Indonesia 'to protect all the people of Indonesia and the entire country of Indonesia and to promote the welfare of the public for the purposes of realising social justice for all Indonesian people' (Rachman, 2012b).[10] Agrarian constitutionalism is not a new approach. It was applied during the preparation of the establishment of the Basic Agrarian Law in 1960 (Notonagoro, 1972; Rachman, 2012c). At the time of writing, this approach is being adopted by AMAN as the foundation of its demands and struggles for the state to recognise and protect the existence of indigenous peoples and their basic rights, with particular focus on article 1.6, stating that customary forests are categorised as state forests. AMAN's demands and its legal action must be seen as a call for state agencies and government officials, as well as members of the parliament, to fulfil their constitutional obligations.

In the Constitutional Court, AMAN's lawyers demonstrated the way in which the existence of *masyarakat adat* is denied and how their rights have been violated, as illustrated in the testimonies of six community leaders who served as witnesses. These witnesses represented the cases of:

- the Bentian in Kutai Barat District, East Kalimantan Province;
- the Manggarai, East Manggarai District, East Nusa Tenggara Province;
- the Talang Mamak, Indragiri Hulu District, Riau Province;
- the Semunying, Bengkayang District, West Kalimantan;
- the Sekatak, Bulungan district, East Kalimantan Province; and
- the Pagaruyung of Bukit Dua Belas National Part, Jambi Province.

All of the witnesses from the communities were men. The male witnesses who represented their communities did not address the gender dimension of the marginalisation of *masyarakat adat* nor the various injustices faced by indigenous women and other marginalised groups in their community. No stories of the struggles of *adat* women and those of marginalised members of communities appeared in the entire series of this Constitutional Court hearing process. As a result of the absence of exploration and discussion of the gender dimension of marginalisation during the hearing process, gender issues were not covered in the text of the Constitutional Court ruling either.

Through the stories narrated by the witnesses, who represented *masyarakat adat* who have been losing their territory and the main sources of their livelihood, as well as resources that are linked to their identities and socio-cultural and spiritual needs, AMAN's lawyers presented a number of common examples whereby *masyarakat adat* suffered after their *adat* territories were categorised as part of the state forests.

In the expert testimony delivered at the Constitutional Court by Noer Fauzi Rachman, two mechanisms by which *masyarakat adat* are dispossessed were explored. The first is categorisation, by which customary lands and indigenous territories are defined to be included in the rubric of state land (*Tanah Negara*) or the state forest zone (*Kawasan Hutan Negara*). Rachman calls this categorisation 'state-ising' *adat* territory (*negara-isasi wilayah adat*).

The second mechanism involves the exercise of bureaucratic power in producing permits/licences/use rights to particular corporations/government agencies after they have met all eligibility requirements. After the corporations/government agencies obtain the permits/licences/use rights (completely or partially), they begin to mobilise their resources to work in the field. It is at this point that their field officers are confronted with actual expressions of local claims over lands, resources and territory within the concession in which they work (Rachman, 2012c; Mahkamah Konstitusi Republik Indonesia, 2013: 66–68).

For leaders of *masyarakat adat* in the Bentian, Manggarai, Talang Mamak, Semuying, Sekatak and Pagaruyung cases who testified before the Constitutional Court, AMAN has not only served as a good ally in articulating their position and concerns, but it has also provided, and continues to provide, a framework, a stage, resources, networks and political leverage by which they can make strategic use of the status of *masyarakat adat* and their identity as customary leaders in their everyday struggle over land, resources and territory.[11] Because *masyarakat adat* in Indonesia is not a self-evident category, we argue that, in order to assert themselves as *masyarakat adat*, communities have to enter into a relationship with civil society organisations, such as AMAN and its NGO supporters, and adopt a particular type of indigeneity politics. This process resonates well with the experiences and aspirations of many dispossessed rural communities in Indonesia, and indeed 'indigenous peoples' around the world (Djuweng and Moniaga, 1984; Afiff and Lowe, 2007; Fauzi, 2003).

AMAN's initiative in advocating a Law on the Recognition and Protection of Indigenous People's Rights

In addition to submitting a petition for a judicial review of Forestry Law No. 41/1999 (particularly in relation to a number of articles) to the Constitutional Court, AMAN prepared a draft Law on the Recognition and Protection of the Rights of Indigenous Peoples (*Rancangan Undang-Undang Pengakuan dan Perlindungan – Hak – Hak Masyarakat Adat*, or RUU PPHMA), and formally handed it to the head of the Indonesian Parliament during the National Congress of AMAN in May 2012 (Down to Earth, 2013). AMAN continues to intensively monitor the ongoing parliamentary processes for this Draft Law, as well as to lobby potential political actors to support it. AMAN also encouraged the legislative body in the national Parliament (*Dewan Perwakilan Rakyat Republik Indonesia*, or DPRRI) to take the initiative in drafting a new Law on the Recognition and Protection of Indigenous Peoples Rights. In April 2013, after a year-long drafting process, the General Assembly of the DPRRI approved the draft as the official draft and submitted it to the Indonesian president.[12]

If the Indonesian Parliament passes this draft Law, Indonesian indigenous peoples will experience a major breakthrough, because the Law will provide legal recognition for indigenous peoples and their rights to land, natural resources and traditional knowledge.[13] The Law will also provide them with the firm basis under national law to exercise their right to give or withhold their free prior and informed consent (FPIC) to plantations, mining, logging and other projects affecting their lands.

More recently, growing environmental concerns have fuelled further recognition, with twelve government agencies and state institutions declaring support for the recognition and protection of indigenous peoples' rights in efforts to reduce deforestation. This effort is known as the Forest Management and Governance Reform Pact (*Nota Kesepahaman Bersama*, or NKB). The Pact is a memorandum of understanding of joint actions between twelve government agencies and state institutions, established on 11 March 2013 (two months before the Constitutional Court ruling on customary forests in 2013). The president of Indonesia attended the official signing of the NKB. The key objectives of the NKB are the harmonisation of forest-related regulations, the resolution of forest related conflicts and the alignment of the technical procedures for forest gazetting. The NKB is facilitated by the National Corruption Eradication Commission (*Komisi Pemberantasan Korupsi*, or KPK). The KPK is a statutory institution that had strong public support until recently.[14] The twelve government institutions and state institutions that have signed the NKB are: the Ministry of Internal Affairs; the Ministry of Justice and Human Rights; the Ministry of Finance; the Ministry of Energy and Mineral Resources; the Ministry of Agriculture;

the Ministry of Forestry; the Ministry of Public Works; the Ministry of the Environment; the Ministry of National Development and Planning/National Development Planning Agency; the National Land Agency; the National Geospatial Information Agency; and the National Human Rights Commission. However, although the Law has been approved as a draft, it has yet to be enacted or implemented, while a national inquiry has been launched into continued violation of the laws by extractive companies and others. To say that this state of affairs is disappointing, after the recent progress in regard to the forestry legislation, is a major understatement. In mid-2014, public hearings of the National Human Rights Commission of the National Inquiry on Indigenous Peoples were under way, whereby a number of conflicts were being brought to the attention of parliamentarians and others. A number of court cases and constitutional rulings are also worth noting as contributing to the goal of greater indigenous rights, and a more sensitive and just forestry policy.

The Constitutional Court ruling in Case 35/PUU-X/2012: Addressing the territorialisation of the state's control of forests and determining the citizenship status of *masyarakat adat*

The Constitutional Court ruling in Case 35/PUU-X/2012 is a landmark decision in agrarian politics. The Constitutional Court has used the Indonesian Constitution to show that locating customary forests under state-owned forests is unconstitutional, because *masyarakat adat* are rights-bearing subjects and the owners of their customary territories. Thus the ruling has put legal and political pressure on the Ministry of Forestry and other statutory institutions to advance forest tenure reform agendas, which include removing *adat* territories from the state forests zone (*Kawasan Hutan Negara*).

Responding to the judicial review submitted by AMAN in November 2012 (known as Case 35/PUU-X/2012), the Constitutional Court then had to address the problems faced by *masyarakat adat* in relation to forestry regulations and related policies. Forestry Law No. 41/1999, which replaced the Basic Forestry Law No. 5/1967, provided the legal foundation for the Ministry of Forestry of the Republic of Indonesia to treat *adat* territories (*wilayah adat*) as resource-rich frontiers, or biodiversity hotspots, or for other reasons, and for categorising such *adat* territories (*wilayah adat*) as part of state(-owned) forests. By doing so, the Ministry of Forestry used its legal authority to include *adat* territories within areas allocated for logging, industrial tree plantations, conservation, ecological restoration or other purposes and issued forestry licences for corporations or government agencies to operate in those areas without the consent of the appropriate *masyarakat adat*. These communities, whose territories are scattered across the Indonesian archipelago, have been struggling against what they basically perceive as land and resource grabs by concessionaries and the Ministry of Forestry. The cases mentioned earlier clearly reflect the characteristics of systemic agrarian conflict (and are echoed in more recent conflicts). These have become chronic and pervasive because of (a) the affected parties' persistent and disruptive challenges against concessionaries and the Ministry of Forestry, and (b) the demonstrated inadequacy of the existing institutional mechanisms to manage the conflict.

By submitting a petition calling for the judicial review of Forestry Law No. 41 of 1999 to the Constitutional Court, AMAN promoted the need for the government to recognise customary territory and to provide inclusive citizenship – that is, to make sure that Indonesian statutory institutions recognise *masyarakat adat* as rights-bearing subjects. This struggle could also be understood as a struggle for *tanah-air*. *Tanah* literally means 'land' and *air* means

Table 13.1 Constitutional Court Ruling in Case Number 35/PUU-X/2012, 16 May 2013 (Judicial Review of Articles in Forestry Law 41/1999)

What was changed	*Original Indonesian wording in Law 41/1999*	*English translation (unofficial translation)*	*Indonesian revision by Constitutional Court*	*English revision (unofficial translation)*
Article 1.6	*Hutan adat adalah hutan negara yang berada dalam wilayah masyarakat hukum adat.*	*Adat* forest means state forests located in *masyarakat adat*'s territories.	*Hutan adat adalah hutan yang berada dalam wilayah masyarakat hukum adat.*	*Adat* forest means forests located in *masyarakat hukum adat*'s territories.
Article 4.3	*Penguasaan hutan oleh Negara tetap memperhatikan hak masyarakat hukum adat, sepanjang kenyataannya masih ada dan diakui keberadaannya, serta tidak bertentangan dengan kepentingan nasional.*	Forests controlled by the State shall respect the rights of *masyarakat hukum adat*, as long as they exist and their existence is recognised, and they do not contradict national interests.	*Penguasaan hutan oleh Negara tetap memperhatikan hak masyarakat hukum adat, sepanjang masih hidup dan sesuai dengan perkembangan masyarakat dan prinsip Negara Kesatuan Republik Indonesia yang diatur dalam undang-undang.*	Forests controlled by the State shall respect the rights of *masyarakat hukum adat*, as long as they remain in existence and are compatible with societal development, and with the principle of the Unitary State of the Republic of Indonesia as regulated by law.
Article 5.1	*Hutan berdasarkan statusnya terdiri dari:* *a. hutan negara, dan* *b. hutan hak.*	Forest status consists of two types: a. state forests, and b. forests subject to rights.	*Hutan negara sebagaimana dimaksud pada ayat (1) huruf a, tidak termasuk hutan adat.*	State forests as referred to in paragraph (1) point a, does not include *adat* forests.
Article 5.2	*Hutan negara sebagaimana dimaksud pada ayat (1) huruf a, dapat berupa hutan adat.*	State forests as referred to in paragraph (1) point a, can be in the form of *adat* forests.	—	—
Article 5.3	*Pemerintah menetapkan status hutan sebagaimana dimaksud pada ayat (1) dan ayat (2); dan hutan adat ditetapkan sepanjang menurut kenyataannya masyarakat hukum adat yang bersangkutan masih ada dan diak ui keberadaannya.*	The Government shall determine the status of forests as referred to in paragraph (1) and paragraph (2); and *adat* forests shall be determined as long as the indigenous peoples concerned remain in existence and their existence is recognised.	*Pemerintah menetapkan status hutan sebagaimana dimaksud pada ayat (1); dan hutan adat ditetapkan sepanjang menurut kenyataannya masyarakat hukum adat yang bersangkutan masih ada dan diakui keberadaannya.*	The Government shall determine the status of forests as referred to in paragraph (1); and *adat* forests shall be determined as long as the *masyarakat hukum adat* concerned remain in existence and their existence is recognised.

Source: Mahkamah Konstitusi Republik Indonesia (2013); adapted from Down to Earth (2013).

Note: One of the authors of this chapter (Noer Fauzi Rachman) was involved in the development of this table.

'water'. When the two words are paired as *tanah-air,* the meaning goes beyond expressing the vital resources for human life; the expression symbolically and materially means the territorial struggle for the motherland or native land, as well as the struggle against political oppression, economic colonisation and cultural domination (hence *tanah-air* may be translated as 'motherland' or 'native land').[15] At the Tobelo Congress (North Maluku) in April 2012, AMAN declared a new motto, 'If the state is not with us, we are still sovereign over our *tanah-air*',[16] in addition to the previous motto launched at the First Congress of AMAN in 1999, 'If the state does not recognise us, we do not recognise the state'.[17]

The Constitutional Court ruling of Case 35/PUU-X/2012 should be considered a landmark policy in the context of forest tenure reform, because it treats *masyarakat adat* as rights-bearing subjects (*penyandang hak*). By legally recognising the status of *masyarakat adat* as rights-bearing subjects, the Indonesian Constitutional Court has created the highest norm for Indonesian statutory institutions to advance forest tenure reforms, which need to address discriminatory categorisation over lands of indigenous people's communities. Attention also needs to be paid to defining indigenous communities accurately and justly. Margaret R. Somers (2008), who developed Hannah Arendt's core argument on citizenship, states that citizenship is the necessary condition for all kinds of right-bearing. After observing the trajectory of AMAN's working strategies in the discursive and practical arenas, we argue that AMAN promotes the struggle for inclusive citizenship, by which the Ministry of Forestry and other Indonesian statutory institutions are exposed to the status of *masyarakat adat* as rights-bearing subjects. The Constitutional Court Ruling has validated the AMAN claim.

We approach the issue of citizenship not simply as a legal concept or as a question of formal rights inscribed in the state laws, but rather as an everyday practical term. We follow Somers' (2008: 25) effort to rework Arendt's conception of citizenship as 'the right to have rights', which is 'not any single civil, juridical, or even social right, but the primary right of recognition, inclusion, and membership both in political and civil society'. Moreover, we use the framework that she offers on the relationships between the state, the market and civil society. Her main argument is that market fundamentalism is deeply corrosive of the foundations of citizenship by making social inclusion dependent upon successful participation in market transactions – that is, that the market transforms 'inalienable citizen rights' into 'conditional privileges' contingent upon successful labour market performance.

Students of Indonesian agrarian politics learn how the global market has come to life since the rise of the New Order regime, established after the bloody political transition in the mid-1960s. The regime established an authoritarian-military repressive government structure to ensure that any tendency to organise rural/urban protests was eradicated once and for all. Those who resisted such treatment were punished by the repressive state apparatus, with the use of violence being not infrequent (Southwood and Flanagan, 1983). Because of the macroeconomic policy orientation of the ruling regime, property relations between local rural peoples and their land-territory, and land use patterns, drastically changed through state territorialisation projects, including extractive mining and logging concessions, transmigration projects, national parks and, last, but not least, plantations.

During the New Order regime period from 1966 to 1997 (before Indonesia was hit by the Asian financial crisis), Indonesia's macroeconomic policy was shaped mainly by four major paradigms, which were competing with one another – namely, nationalism, populism, predatory bureaucracy and liberalism (Robison, 1986, 1997; Rosser, 2002). Soeharto fell after the intense political dynamics of the first quarter of 1998, largely because of the Asian financial crisis, and in response to overwhelming mass protests and the existence of factionalised political elites that could not deal successfully with the crisis. The configuration of oligarchic powers in Indonesia has changed considerably since Soeharto's fall after thirty-two years in power. Political liberalisation and the adoption of a democratic decentralisation policy have altered the political landscape (Hadiz, 2001, 2006, 2010). Soon after the New Order regime collapsed, a group consisting of activists and progressive academicians that had formulated an alternative academic draft of the Forestry Law during 1997–98 intensively lobbied the government and Parliament to adopt it. In this alternative academic draft, Indonesian civil society organisations suggested that the state should recognise the rights of indigenous peoples in managing forest resources within their territories by excluding customary forests (*hutan adat*) from the state forests. However, the main concepts this group intensively advocated were not fully accepted. The new Forestry Law No. 41 of 1999 was signed on 30 September 1999 by President B. J. Habibie without significant changes in terms of state control over forest resources. This new Forestry Law continued to support centralised control over forest lands not legally claimed as private lands. It also continued to ignore the rights of indigenous peoples over lands and forest resources. The era of President Abdurrahman Wahid (1999–2001) was marked by the political reform that allowed social movements to further develop. President Wahid attended the First Congress of Indigenous Peoples held in Jakarta in March 1999, at which the declaration of the establishment of AMAN was made. In addition, Wahid's presidency was marked by the establishment of decentralisation policies that aimed at providing autonomy to regional governments. However, these policies had unintended consequences relating to the more aggressive resource extraction triggered by economic and political interests at regional levels (provincial and district levels). During the era of President Megawati Soekarnoputri (2001–04), there was no significant effort at addressing aggressive resource extraction and its complex impacts. In addition, although there was a series of significant efforts to develop transparency within state institutions and corruption eradication, transparency and corruption within technical sectors related to natural resources continued.

After President Susilo Bambang Yudhoyono came to power in 2004, central and local governments decided to expand existing projects, and to accelerate the growth in the number of sites for extraction and production of natural-resource-based commodities (both mineral and agricultural) by expanding and extending large- and middle-scale concessions, including for extraction of oil and gas, nickel and bauxite, copper, manganese, silver and gold, coal, palm oil, and timber for plywood, pulp-and-paper manufacture, and woodchip and pallet production, etc. The Indonesian government's Master Plan for Accelerating and Expanding Economic Development (MP3EI) 2011–25 was created as the official frame of reference by which massive infrastructure development projects were designed, through public and public–private investment schemes, in so-called economic corridors. It is very clear that market fundamentalism dominated the MP3EI and, in examining it, we see the efficacy of Ellen M. Wood's (1994, 2002) notion of 'market-as-imperative' in understanding how state institutions allocate licences to companies, thereby denying *masyarakat adat* access to their land, resources and territory. In an Indonesian setting, systemic agrarian conflicts occur on an unprecedented scale because of communities' persistent, disruptive and collective challenges to statutory institutions and concession holders that rely on force (including violence in various forms), regulation and the use of money to achieve their goals (Lucas and Warren, 2013).

In examining the struggle for *adat* territory in relation to the existing systemic agrarian conflicts,[18] we conceive of the systemic agrarian conflicts as prolonged competing claims on who has the rights over lands, natural resources and territories, between rural communities and land, plantation, forestry, mining and infrastructure concession holders.

The conflicting claims are protracted because of the persistent resistance of community leaders in mobilising their communities and the significant role of social movement organisations, such as AMAN, in delegitimising concession holders' domination. Theoretically speaking, this effort is different from what Polanyi (1957) calls counter-movements against the market (Block, 2008). This is more a counter-movement against the state, which is creating the conditions – including the mechanisms with which to transfer existing property rights in land to concessionaires as a commodity – that it deems necessary for building a market-based society. Social movement organisations are not autonomous of state institutions; social institutions are, of necessity, part of the society in which they operate. They may be ostensibly independent of the state, but they nevertheless operate within it, and in some cases their operations may be encouraged or hampered by government policy. They can be invited to be part of the decision-making apparatus or rejected. They need a particular character of state institution – what Somers (2008) calls 'a social State'. She argues that:

> A healthy civil society is not autonomous of markets and states. Indeed the contrary is true; civil society's very capacity for resistance against external market incursions requires support from the state in the form of market regulations, social insurance policies, public services, redistributive tax schemes and mechanisms to institutionalize and enforce the rights to livelihood.
>
> (Somers, 2008: 31)

The Constitutional Court of Indonesia has performed and promoted such a role for social movement organisations. AMAN leaders and their NGO supporters are very aware of their power to influence state institutions. They have observed, and actively and continuously shaped, the ways in which state institutions work differently; however, their agendas and positions have often been in conflict with one another. On the other hand, they are also aware that the state institutions are not monolithic and homogeneous units. There are those state institutions, such as the Constitutional Court, which clearly stand for the constitutional rights of Indonesian citizens. The Constitutional Court has performed its function, which is to revise defective existing laws by which government practices endanger the constitutional rights of Indonesian citizens.

The Constitutional Court judges have approached their role as constitutional guardians through the lenses of 'responsive law' (Nonet and Selznick, 2001), and 'progressive law' (Rahardjo, 2006), by which they have criticised the practices of the predatory state and of market fundamentalism that endanger the constitutional rights of Indonesian citizens. In the context of systemic agrarian conflicts, it is important to understand their concerns about social injustices because of the growing economic disparity that state institutions create by handing licences to control land and natural resources over to both private and state-owned corporations, on the one hand, and by annexing customary rights over land and resources, on the other.

One of the judges of the Constitutional Court, Ahmad Sodiki, presented a clear view on this issue:

> From the perspective of the constitution, this creates increasing social injustices that are rooted in misallocation of the existing natural resources. When we apprehend this issue through the lens of Article 33(3), of the Constitution, it is the state's obligation to ensure that natural resource allocation, that is, land, waters and natural

> resources are [to be] utilized for the sake of [the] people['s] prosperity ([and in a] fair and equitable [manner] [as per Article 18A(2)]). This aim could not be achieved by enforcing the existing land and natural resource related laws *because the laws are defective. When such defective laws are enforced, it will create social injustices. Enforcing such defective natural resource laws will endanger the existence of* masyarakat adat *who are vulnerable to [exclusion] by those who have power in the name of the State or by permission of state institutions.*[19]
>
> (Sodiki, 2012, emphasis added)

It is worth noting that, in his paper presented at a workshop in June 2012, Sodiki inserts in the reference to article 33(3) a reference to the wording of article 18A(3), where it is stated that 'the use of natural and other resources shall be regulated and administered *with justice and equity* according to law' (emphasis added). Thus it seems that he believes that 'fair and equitable', which here appears, is also clearly implied or intrinsically related to in the wording of article 33(3) (in Chapter XIV on 'National Economy and Social Welfare') – namely, that, where natural resource utilisation is to occur, it could be argued that it should occur both in a manner and with outcomes that are 'to the greatest benefit of the people'. It should also perhaps be noted that this phrase may be taken to further imply more than economic prosperity, but rather to mean social welfare and other benefits (given the title of Chapter XIV) and to include, but not necessarily be limited to, economic benefits.

Based on the Constitution of the Republic of Indonesia, especially article 18B, the Constitutional Court has established the constitutional norm that the state has to recognise and respect the status of *masyarakat adat* as rights-bearing subjects who hold the right to have rights. By removing customary forests from the 'state-owned forests' (*hutan negara*) category and moving them into the 'forests subject to rights' (*hutan hak*) category, the Court has begun to announce that *masyarakat adat* are rights-bearing subjects. Some might say that, with this recognition, the gong was struck to mark the beginning of a play. The question then remains as to what characters we will see, what role they will play and for what reason.

Undoing categorial inequality

As stated above, the Constitutional Court ruling in Case 35/PUU-X/2012 raises a critical question about the kind of case that this ruling is actually addressing. We argue that this is an instance of undoing categorial inequality. We refer to the concept of 'categorial inequality' as suggested by Tilly (1998: 8), who (referring to 'categorical distinctions') asserts that:

> [D]urable inequality among categories arises because people who control access to value producing resources solve organizational problems by means of categorical (*sic*) distinctions. Inadvertently or otherwise, those people set up systems of social closure, exclusion and control. Multiple parties – not all of them powerful, some of them even victims of exploitation – then acquire stakes in these solutions.

Tilly (1998: 10) identifies four basic mechanisms that make inequality durable – namely, exploitation, opportunity hoarding, emulation and adaptation. He argues that '[e]xploitation and opportunity hoarding favor the installation of categorical [*sic*] inequality, while emulation and adaptation generalize its influence' (Tilly, 1998: 10). 'Exploitation' takes place when people in one social group expropriate resources produced by members of another social group and prevent them from realising the full value of their effort in producing it. 'Opportunity hoarding' takes place when one social group restricts access to a scarce resource through outright denial and/or exercising monopoly control that prevents access by outgroup members. Either way, opportunity hoarding is enabled through a socially defined process of exclusion.

Moreover, Tilly (1998) explains that, within any social structure setting, exploitation and opportunity hoarding are reinforced by emulation and adaptation. 'Emulation' occurs when one group of people copies a set of social distinctions and interrelationships from another group. or transfers the distinctions and interrelationships from one social setting to another. Lastly, 'adaptation' occurs in everyday behaviours that follow ranked categories in ways that assume the existence and importance of asymmetric social categories. Emulation and adaptation work, over time, to institutionalise categorial distinctions and to embed them in social relations.

Undoing categorial inequality is a necessary step in advancing policies toward recognition.[20] From the struggles of *masyarakat adat*, it is clear that undoing categorial inequality requires particular forms of adequate visibility, representation and participation by discriminated groups/populations in formal policy processes in both statutory and non-statutory institutions in multiple arenas and at multiple levels. Adequate forms of visibility, representation and participation are three key determinants by which *masyarakat adat* may transform their position into a potentially significant social force that may work not only in strengthening their position in systemic agrarian conflicts, but also for legalising their citizenship status. We have shown how AMAN performs its role in advancing the struggles for *adat* territory across the Indonesian archipelago and has scaled those efforts in the national arena, including through a recent effort to petition for a judicial review of the constitutionality of categorising customary forests as state-owned (*negaraisasi*).

Concluding remarks

It is clear that, on 16 May 2013, the Constitutional Court of the Republic of Indonesia, through its ruling in Case 35/PUU-X/2012, declared the status of *masyarakat hukum adat* as rights-bearing subjects. We have elucidated the ways in which this ruling is a landmark in Indonesian agrarian politics, especially by challenging state control over forests and territorialisation projects. The Court legitimises the main position of AMAN that the state has to recognise the status of *masyarakat adat* as the owners of their *adat* territories.

What we have shown in this chapter are the difficulties in legally recognising the status of *masyarakat adat* as rights-bearing subjects in the context of systemic agrarian conflicts. We conclude that the formal recognition of the status of *masyarakat adat* as rights-bearing subjects, especially related to their rights over *adat* territory, is very difficult to assert, because the political commitment of high-level parliamentary and government elites to lead the realisation processes is weak, and state institutions are fragmented.

We observe that none of the elites have committed to assuming a leadership position for administering the process. Consequently, efforts by AMAN and other civil society organisations encounter difficulties when working with members of the Parliament, the Senate and various government institutions. Thus the efforts to coordinate activities are severely limited, which limits speed and efficacy in moving the formal recognition of these rights forward.

Although then Indonesian President Susilo Bambang Yudhoyono expressed his personal commitment to initiate 'a process that registers and recognises the collective ownership of *adat* territories in Indonesia' (Yudhoyono, 2013), these words have not been translated into concrete action. It will also be very interesting to observe what impacts this ruling has on the ways in which statutory institutions interrelate and the role that social movement organisations will play in creating such inter-institutional dynamics.

The election of President Joko Widodo (2014) – former mayor, then governor, of Jakarta – adds another dimension. A forestry graduate who was, at one juncture, a timber furniture manufacturer, he has been described as the first president not to have emerged from existing political elites, nor to be closely associated with the military. Because of the nature of this research, which observes highly dynamic subjects, involving both the actors and the issues, it is important to follow and engage with policy processes at multiple sites of the power struggle, contestation and negotiation.

Notes

1 The term *masyarakat adat* was officially adopted at the first congress of the Indigenous Peoples Alliance of the Archipelago (*Aliansi Masyarakat Adat Nusantara*, or AMAN) in 1999. AMAN defines *masyarakat adat* as 'a group of people who have lived in their ancestral domain for generations, have sovereignty over the land and natural resources, and govern their community by customary law and institutions which sustain the continuity of the livelihoods'. In the context of social movements, we follow AMAN's translation of *masyarakat adat* as indigenous peoples, or indigenous communities. Indonesian legal scholars have inherited the concept of *masyarakat hukum adat* (*adatrecht gemenschap*) as a particular legal personality in Indonesia (previously the Netherlands East Indies) from the literature of *adat* studies developed by colonial *adat* scholars. See Van Vollenhoven (1981); Ter Haar (1962); also Hooker (1981). In this chapter, we use the terms *masyarakat hukum adat, masyarakat adat* and indigenous peoples or indigenous communities interchangeably.

2 Personal communication between Mia Siscawati and three women from Jambi and Lampung who joined the long march to the Presidential Palace in Jakarta. The conversation took place in Jakartaon on 23 January 2013.

3 See AMAN, ICRAF and FPP (2003); Colchester, Sirait and Wijardjo (2003). AMAN supporters started by considering ILO Convention No. 169 concerning indigenous and tribal peoples in independent countries (Djuweng and Moniaga, 1984). Later, AMAN and its supporters referred to the United Nations Declaration on the Rights of Indigenous Peoples (UNDRIP), which was declared in 2007.

4 There has been rich scholarship in analysing the politics of indigeneity in contemporary Indonesia and the role of AMAN. For some of the reports, see Persoon (1998); Li (2000, 2001, 2010); Afiff and Lowe (2007); Moniaga (2007); Sangaji (2007); Henley and Davidson (2007); Baker (2009).

5 For the concept of the frontier in relation to state formation in Kalimantan (Indonesia), see Tsing (2005) and Eilenberg (2012).

6 The English translation of the Indonesian original is provided by the authors.

7 '*Kalau Negara tidak mengakui kami, kami pun tidak mengakui Negara*'.

8 The English translation of the Indonesian original is provided by the authors.

9 See Down to Earth (2012).

10 See also Arizona (2011) and Arizona et al. (2012) for analysis of Indonesian Constitutional Court decisions regarding agrarian and natural-resource-related laws.

11 By reworking Michel-Rolph Trouillot's (1991) 'savage slot', Li (2000) critically explicates how the notion of 'tribal slot' has been used by AMAN in Indonesia.

12 See Dewan Perwakilan Rakyat Republik Indonesia (2013).

13 See AMAN's website (http://www.aman.or.id/).

14 There have been recent efforts to weaken KPK, including the plan of the House of Representatives to revise the 2002 Corruption Eradication Law, which serves as the legal foundation of KPK.

15 In order to address and popularise their struggles against political oppression, economic colonisation and cultural domination, AMAN leaders reuse the *trisakti* (three principles) mantra, which was invented by the first president of Indonesia, Soekarno, i.e. 'politically sovereign, economically autonomous, and culturally dignified' (*berdaulat secara politik, mandiri secara ekonomi, dan berkepribadian secara budaya*).
16 '*Kalau Negara tidak bersama kami, kami tetap berdaulat atas tanah air kami*'.
17 '*Kalau Negara tidak mengakui kami, kami pun tidak mengakui Negara*'.
18 See Fauzi (1999, 2002); Rachman (2011).
19 The English translation of the Indonesian original is provided by the authors.
20 Nancy Fraser (2003) opposes the argument that the representation and the political struggle between the politics of recognition and the politics of redistribution are mutually exclusive alternatives. Her famous motto is 'justice today requires both redistribution and recognition' (Fraser, 2003: 9).

References

Afiff, S., and Lowe, C. (2007) 'Claiming Indigenous Community: Political Discourse and Natural Resource Rights in Indonesia', *Alternatives: Global, Local, Political*, 32(1): 73–97.

AMAN (1999) *Pandangan Dasar Kongres Masyarakat Adat Nusantara 1999 tentang Posisi Masyarakat Adat terhadap Negara*, Jakarta: AMAN.

AMAN, ICRAF and FPP (2003) *In Search of Recognition*, Bogor: AMAN/ICRAF (World Agroforestry Centre)/FPP (Forest Peoples Program).

Arizona, Y. (2011) 'Perkembangan Konstitusionalitas Penguasaan Negara atas Sumber Daya Alam dalam Putusan Mahkamah Konstitusi', *Jurnal Konatitusi*, 8(3): 257–314.

Arizona, Y, Mary, S. R., and Nagara, G. (2012) *An Annotation of the Constitutional Court Decision No. 45/PUU-IX/2011 Regarding Constitutionality of Forest Areas in Article 1 Paragraph 3 Law No. 41 Year 1999 Regarding Forestry*, Jakarta, Epistema Institute.

Asshiddiqie, J. (2009) *Menuju Negara Hukum yang Demokratis*, Jakarta: BIP-Gramedia.

Baker, L. (2009) 'Who Owns the Land? Looking for Law and Power in Reformasi East Kalimantan', Unpublished thesis, Nijmegen University.

Block, F. (2008) 'Polanyi's Double Movement and the Reconstruction of Critical Theory', *Revue Interventions économiques*, 1 December, available online at http://.interventionseconomiques.revues.org/274 [accessed 26 May 2013].

Boomgaard, P. (1992) 'Forest Management and Exploitation in Colonial Java, 1677–1897', *Forest and Conservation History*, 36(1): 4–14.

Colchester, M., Sirait, M., and Wijardjo, B. (2003) *The Application of FSC Principles 2 & 3 in Indonesia: Obstacles and Possibilities*, Jakarta: Wahana Lingkungan Hidup (WALHI), Aliansi Masyarakat Adat Nusantara (AMAN)/Rainforest Foundation.

Dauvergne, P. (1997) *Shadows in the Forest: Japan and the Politics of Timber in Southeast Asia*, Cambridge, MA: MIT Press.

Dewan Perwakilan Rakyat Republik Indonesia (2013) 'Pimpinan: RUU Hak Masyarakat Hukum Adat Ditetapkan Menjadi RUU DPR RI', 11 April, available online at http://www.dpr.go.id/id/berita/pimpinan/2013/apr/11/5640/ruu-hak-masyarakat-hukum-adat-ditetapkan-menjadi-ruu-dpr-ri [accessed 26 May 2013].

Djuweng, S., and Moniaga S. (eds) (1984) *Konvensi ILO 169 mengenai Bangsa Pribumi dan Masyarakat Adat di Negara-negara Merdeka*, Jakarta: Elsam dan LBBT.

Down to Earth (2012) 'Indonesia's Indigenous Peoples Continue to Struggle for Recognition', available online at http://www.downtoearth-indonesia.org/story/indonesia-s-indigenous-peoples-continue-struggle-recognition [accessed 26 May 2013].

Down to Earth (2013) 'A Turning Point for Indonesia's Indigenous Peoples', 7 June, available online at http://www.downtoearth-indonesia.org/story/turning-point-indonesia-s-indigenous-peoples [accessed 8 June 2013].

Eilenberg, M. (2012) *At the Edges of States: Dynamics of State Formation in the Indonesian Borderlands*, Leiden: KITLV.

Elmhirst, R. (2010) 'Migrant Pathways to Resource Access in Lampung's Political Forest: Gender, Citizenship and Creative Conjugality', *Geoforum*, 42(2): 173–183.

Fauzi, N. (1999) *Petani dan Penguasa, Dinamika Perjalanan Politik Agraria Indonesia*, Yogyakarta: Insist Press/KPA bekerja sama dengan/Pustaka Pelajar.

Fauzi, N. (2002) 'Konflik Tenurial: yang Diciptakan Tapi Tak Hendak Diselesaikan', in A. Lounela and R. Y. Zakaria (eds) *Berebut Tanah: Beberapa Kajian Berspektif Kampus dan Kampung*, Yogyakarta: Karsa, 322–352.

Fauzi, N. (2003) *Bersaksi untuk Pembaruan Agraria, Dari Tuntutan Lokal hingga Kecenderungan Global*, Yogyakarta: Karsa/KPA bekerja sama dengan/Insist Press.

Fraser, N. (2003) 'Social Justice in the Age of Identity Politics: Redistribution, Recognition and Participation', in N. Fraser and A. Honnet (eds) *Redistribution or Recognition? A Political–Philosophical Exchange*, London: Verso, 7–107.

Hadiz, V. (2001) 'Capitalism, Oligarchic Power and the State in Indonesia', *Historical Materialism*, 8(1): 119–151.

Hadiz, V. (2006) 'Corruption and Neoliberal Reform: Market and Predatory Power in Indonesia and Southeast Asia', in R. Robison (ed.) *The Neo-liberal Revolution, Forging the Market State*, New York: Palgrave Macmillan, 79–97.

Hadiz, V. (2010) *Localising Power in Post-authoritarian Indonesia: A Southeast Asia Perspective*, Stanford, CA: Stanford University Press.

Hall, S. (2007) 'Epilogue: Through the Prism of an Intellectual Life', in B. Meeks (ed.) *Culture, Politics, Race, and Diaspora: The Thought of Stuart Hall*, Kingston: Randle, 269–291.

Henley, D., and Davidson, J. S. (2007) 'Introduction: Radical Conservatism – The Protean Politics of Adat', in J. S. Davidson and D. Henley (eds) *The Revival of Tradition in Indonesian Politics: The Deployment of Adat from Colonialism to Indigenism*, London/New York: Routledge, 1–49.

Hooker, M. B. (1981) *Adat Law in Modern Indonesia*, Oxford: Oxford University Press.

Hunt, A. (1991) *Explorations in Law and Society: Towards a Constitutive Theory of Law*, New York/London: Routledge.

Kementerian Kehutanan Republik Indonesia (2009) 'Menhut Serahkan SK Areal Kerja Hutan Kemasyarakatan di NTB', Pusat Informasi Kehutanan nomor S.389/PIK-1/2009, available online at http://www.dephut.go.id/index.php/news/details/5857 [accessed 8 January 2014].

Li, T. (2000) 'Articulating Indigenous Identity in Indonesia: Resource Politics and the Tribal Slot', *Comparative Studies in Society and History*, 42(1): 149–179.

Li, T. (2001) '*Masyarakat Adat*, Difference, and the Limits of Recognition in Indonesia's Forest Zone', *Modern Asian Studies*, 35(3): 645–676.

Li, T. (2010) 'Indigeneity, Capitalism, and the Management Of Dispossession', *Current Anthropology*, 51(3): 385–414.

Lucas, A. and Warren C. (eds) (2013). *Land for the People: The State and Agrarian Conflict in Indonesia.* Athens, OH: Ohio University Press.

Mahkamah Konstitusi Republik Indonesia (2013) *Putusan Nomor 35/PUU-X/2012*, Jakarta: Mahkamah Konstitusi Republik Indonesia.

Ministry of Forestry (2009) 'Menhut Serahkan SK Areal Kerja Hutan Kemasyarakatan di NTB', Press release, 4 August, available online at http://www.dephut.go.id/index.php/news/details/5857 [accessed 8 January 2014].

Moniaga, S. (2007) 'From *Bumiputera* to *Masyarakat Adat*: A Long and Confusing Journey', in J. S. Davidson and D. Henley (eds) *The Revival of Tradition in Indonesian Politics: The Deployment of Adat from Colonialism to Indigenism*, London/New York: Routledge, 275–294.

Nonet, P., and Selznick, P. (2001) *Law and Society in Transition: Toward Responsive Law*, New Brunswick, NJ: Transaction.

Notonagoro (1972) *Politik Hukum dan Pembangunan Agraria di Indonesia*, Jakarta: Pantjuran Tudjuh.

Peluso, N. L. (1992) *Rich Forests, Poor People: Resource Control and Resistance in Java*, Berkeley, CA: University of California Press.

Peluso, N. L., and Vandergeest, P. (2001) 'Genealogies of the Political Forest and Customary Rights in Indonesia, Malaysia, and Thailand', *Journal of Asian Studies*, 60(3): 761–812.

Persoon, G. A. (1998) 'Isolated Groups or Indigenous Peoples: Indonesia and the International Discourse', *Bijdragen tot de Taal-, Land- en Volkenkunde*, 154(2): 281–304.

Polanyi, K. (1957) *The Great Transformation: The Political and Economic Origins of Our Time*, Boston, MA: Beacon Press.

Rachman, N. F. (2011) 'The Resurgence of Land Reform Policy and Agrarian Movements in Indonesia', Unpublished dissertation, University of California, Berkeley, CA.

Rachman, N. F. (2012a) 'Masyarakat Adat dan Perjuangan Tanah Airnya', Pidato pada acara Pembukaan Kongres Masyarakat Adat Nusantara Ke-4, 19 April, Tobelo, Halmahera Utara, available online at http://www.kongres4.aman.or.id/2012/05/masyarakat-adat-dan-perjuangan-tanah-airnya.asp [accessed 27 May 2013].

Rachman, N. F. (2012b) 'Masyarakat Adat dan Perjuangan Tanah Airnya', *Kompas*, 11 June, available online at http://regional.kompas.com/read/2012/06/11/03572833/Masyarakat.Adat.dan.Perjuangan.Tanah-Airnya [accessed 27 May 2013].

Rachman, N. F. (2012c) 'Meralat Negaraisasi Tanah Adat. Memperbaiki Rute Transformasi Kewarganegaraan Masyarakat Adat dan Mengukuhkan Kembali Eksistensi Negara Bangsa', Expert statement delivered to the Constitutional Court during judicial review of Forestry Law No. 41, available online at http://huma.or.id/pembaruan-hukum-dan-resolusi-konflik/info-terkait-pembaruan-hukum-dan-resolusi-konflik/meralat-negaraisasi-tanah-adat.html [accessed 27 May 2013].

Rahardjo, S. (2006) *Membedah Hukum Progresif*, Jakarta: Kompas.

Ribot, J. C., and Peluso, N. (2003) 'A Theory of Access', *Rural Sociology*, 68(2): 153–181.

Ricklefs, M. C. (2008) *A History of Modern Indonesia since c. 1200*, Stanford, CA: Stanford University Press.

Robison, R. (1986) *Indonesia: The Rise of Capital*, Sydney: Unwin & Hyman.

Robison, R. (1997) 'Politics and Markets in Indonesia's Post-oil Era', in G. Rodan, K. Hewison and R. Robison (eds) *The Political Economy of Southeast Asia: An Introduction*, Melbourne: Oxford University Press, 26–63.

Rosser, A. (2002) *The Politics of Economic Liberalisation in Indonesia: State, Market, and. Power*, Richmond: Curzon Press.

Sack, R. D. (1986) *Human Territoriality: Its Theory and History*, Cambridge: Cambridge University Press.

Sangaji, A. (2007) 'The Masyarakat Adat Movement in Indonesia: A Critical Insider's View', in J. S. Davidson and D. Henley (eds) *The Revival of Tradition in Indonesian Politics: The Deployment of Adat from Colonialism to Indigenism*, London/New York: Routledge, 319–336.

Simon, H. (2001) *Pengelolaan Hutan Bersama Rakyat, Teori dan Aplikasi pada Hutan Jati di Jawa*, Yogyakarta: Bigraf.

Siscawati, M. (2014a) 'Pertarungan Penguasaan Hutan dan Posisi Perempuan Adat [Struggles of Forest Control and the Position of Indigenous Women]', *Jurnal Wacana*, 33(16): 157–197.

Siscawati, M. (2014b) 'The Neglectful State', *Down to Earth Newsletter*, Oct: 99–100.

Siscawati, M., and Mahaningtyas, A. (2012) 'Gender Justice: Forest Tenure and Forest Governance in Indonesia', Washington, DC: Right and Resource Initiative.

Siscawati, M., and Rachman, N. F. (2014) 'Gender dan Politik Konsesi Agraria: Dimensi Gender dalam Mekanisme-Mekanisme Penguasaan Tanah, Perubahan Tata Guna Tanah, dan Krisis Sosial-Ekologis dalam Perkebunan Kelapa Sawit, Pertambangan Batu Bara, Hutan Tanaman Industri, dan Restorasi Ekosistem', Working Paper No. 12, Bogor: Sajogyo Institute.

Sodiki, A. (2012) 'Konstitusionalitas Masyarakat Adat dalam Konstitusi', Paper presented at Simposium Masyarakat Adat: Mempersoalkan Keberadaan Masyarakat Adat sebagai Subjek

Hukum, Perkumpulan Pembaruan Hukum berbasis Masyarakat dan Ekologis (HuMa), Jakarta, 27–28 June.

Somers, M. R. (2008) *Genealogies of Citizenship: Market, Statelessness, and the Right to have Rights*, Cambridge: Cambridge University Press.

Southwood, J., and Flanagan, P. (1983) *Indonesia: Law, Propaganda and Terror*, London: Zed Press.

Ter Haar, B. (1962) *Adat Law in Indonesia*, Jakarta: Bhrarata.

Tilly, C. (1998) *Durable Inequality*, Berkeley, CA: University of California Press.

Trouillot, M.-R. (1991) 'Anthropology and the Savage Slot: The Poetics and Politics of Otherness', in R. Fox (ed.) *Recapturing Anthropology*, Santa Fe, NM: School of American Research, 17–44.

Tsing, A. L. (2005) *Friction: An Ethnography of Global Connection*, Princeton, NJ: Princeton University Press.

Van Vollenhoven, C. (1981) *Van Vollenhoven on Indonesian Adat Law: Selections from Het Adatrecht van Nederlandsch-Indië (Volume I, 1918; Volume II, 1931)*, The Hague: Martinus Nijhoff.

Vandergeest, P. (1996) 'Mapping Nature: Territorialization of Forest Rights in Thailand', *Society and Natural Resources*, 9(2): 159–175.

Vandergeest, P., and Peluso, N. L. (1995) 'Territorialization and State Power in Thailand', *Theory and Society*, 24(3): 385–426.

Wood, E. M. (1994) 'From Opportunity to Imperative: The History of the Market', *Monthly Review*, 46(3): 14–40.

Wood, E. M. (2002) *The Origin of Capitalism: A Longer View*, London: Verso.

Yudhoyono, S. B. (2013) 'Presidential Opening Speech', Presidential speech at the International Workshop on Tropical Forest in Jakarta, 27 June, available online at http://www.forestpeoples.org/sites/fpp/files/news/2013/06/27%20Juni%202013%20-%20Opening%20Speech%20President%20RI%20-%20TFA%202020%20Workshop%20(Rev%202%20SBY)%20check%20against%20delivery.pdf [accessed 20 December 2013].

14 Legal and cultural landscapes

Cultural and intellectual property concepts, and the 'safeguarding' of intangible cultural heritage in Southeast Asia[1]

Christoph Antons

Introduction: The emergence of intangible cultural heritage

Intangible cultural heritage is a relatively recent add-on to a long-standing debate about the safeguarding of cultural heritage that was previously focused on tangible heritage, such as the Elgin marbles,[2] and displayed a tendency to what heritage scholar Laurajane Smith (2006: 109) has called a 'discourse of monumentality'. The inclusion of intangible cultural heritage in the safeguarding programmes of the United Nations Educational, Scientific and Cultural Organization (UNESCO) was meant to restore the balance between developed and developing countries in this field, because developing countries were regarded as particularly rich in intangible cultural heritage (Forrest, 2012: 365). Heritage in general, and intangible cultural heritage in particular, has recently become an area of great interest for a diverse group of 'stakeholders', ranging from tourism operators, and regional and national development planners, to the representatives of indigenous peoples and other ethnic minorities. One of the chief reasons for this increasing interest is the embrace of culture in more recent development strategies,[3] which include the emergence of cultural and heritage tourism, as well as high hopes in various countries for the creative industries (Suharmoko, 2008; Theparat, 2012; *Borneo Post Online*, 2010). UNESCO heritage listings become important symbols and quality seals for tourist attractions, whether they are natural parks or entire parts of cities.[4] In the case of intangible cultural heritage, the skills, knowledge, crafts and performances of local people are often an attraction that is marketed in addition to the special appeal of the site itself.

In a rather unexpected development for UNESCO as the sponsor of the extension of heritage programmes to the intangible, the use of intangible cultural heritage in tourism promotion campaigns and in other areas of commercialisation of traditional culture has led to considerable diplomatic tensions between neighbouring countries with the same, or similar, cultural heritage. It is perhaps less surprising that many of these disputes about heritage are to be found in Southeast Asia, an area that historically has always been at the crossroads of, and receptive to, different cultural influences (Antons, 2013a). In addition, as elsewhere during the centuries of colonial expansion, the borders in this region were drawn by European colonial powers with little knowledge of, or regard for, local ethnic and cultural affiliations. They often permanently divided local communities that henceforth belonged to different colonies and, following decolonisation in the twentieth century, to different nation states (Antons, 2012a, 2013b).

Competition between countries laying claim to the same or similar cultural heritage for tourism, or the commercialisation of, for example, traditional medicine or music, has led to attempts to monopolise the relevant aspects of a culture, relying on a mixture of cultural property claims derived from UNESCO conventions and intellectual property rights, such as copyrights and patents. To facilitate such claims, national governments often collect and represent a variety of local cultures at the national level and in negotiations with neighbouring and other foreign countries. Local communities more often than not find themselves on the margins of subsequent commercialisation discussions. Rather than strong rights to their cultural expressions, they often have to be content with compensation mechanisms for the contributions that their cultural expressions, traditions and ideas have made to the development of new products or services.

This chapter will present the origin of the concepts of cultural property and intellectual property as they relate to intangible cultural heritage, and demonstrate how these concepts have influenced relevant national laws in Southeast Asia. It will illustrate the cross-border conflicts that have emerged as a result of the mixing of the different laws and of nationalist rhetoric meant predominantly for a domestic audience. It will further analyse the different concepts of geographical space that were used in nation-building processes in Southeast Asia, on the one hand, and in the legal construction of 'cultural space' for heritage conservation and intellectual property rights, on the other.

Cultural and intellectual property and claims to intangible cultural heritage in Southeast Asia: The disputes between Indonesia and Malaysia

In 2007, a diplomatic row erupted between Indonesia and Malaysia, after a rap version of the folk song 'Rasa sayang' in the various languages of the largest ethnic communities in Malaysia was used in the tourism promotion campaign 'Malaysia truly Asia'. Indonesians believed that the song originated in the Moluccan islands, whereas Malaysia saw it as widely used in island Southeast Asia and as *kebudayaan Nusantara*, common heritage of the archipelago (*Star Online*, 2007; Antons, 2009). Subsequently, Indonesian politicians and government ministers urged an investigation into the question of whether the material was copyright protected under Indonesian law, and whether it was possible to sue Malaysia for its appropriation of what was regarded as Indonesian heritage (*Jakarta Post*, 2007; Antons, 2009). A similar case developed two years later following the use of *pendet*, a Balinese temple dance, for another tourism promotion series, 'Enigmatic Malaysia', on the Discovery Channel (*Asia Sentinel*, 2009; Fitzpatrick, 2009; Antons, 2009; Chong, 2012). Further disputes developed regarding batik, the shadow puppet theatre of *wayang kulit*, the ceremonial dagger *kris*, the Malaysian national anthem 'Negaraku', the music instruments *gamelan* and *angklung* (Chong, 2012, with further references) and the patenting by the Massachusetts Institute of Technology (MIT), together with the Malaysian government, of the bioactive fraction of *pasak bumi*, a plant used in traditional medicine in both countries and known in Malaysia as *tongkat Ali* (Antons, 2015; Antons and Antons-Sutanto, 2009, with further references). In the field of agriculture, both countries have used geographical indications to market organic red rice varieties from the borderlands of Sarawak and North Kalimantan. These rice varieties are grown by related forest-dwelling communities on both sides of the border. However, since the Indonesian community is landlocked and has no road access to the provincial capital, growers are forced to sell their rice on the Malaysian side of the border (Chew, 2004). This has triggered claims that the organic rice sold in Malaysia is, in fact, grown in Indonesia (Susilo, 2012).

In view of shared history and cultural expressions, and the common origin of the respective national languages, it is hardly surprising that many disputes develop between neighbouring countries such as Indonesia and Malaysia. However, the Indonesian media has long reported similar cases concerning companies from elsewhere, such as the patenting of a process for creating traditional medicines and the patenting of traditional cosmetics in Japan, the patenting of processes for using cane (*kerajinan rotan*) and making *tahu* and *tempe*, and the copyright registration of Indonesian designs in the United States, as well as the patenting of local strains of corn by a majority Thai-owned company (*Kompas*, 2006; Budiningsih, 2007; Wisnu, 2008). While some of these cases were not correctly reported in the media (Antons, 2015), especially copyright claims as in the 'Rasa sayang' dispute hardly came as a surprise for long-standing observers of Indonesian copyright law developments. Indonesian politicians referring to copyright were probably thinking of article 10 of the then Copyright Act of 1982. It provided in article 10(2) that the state should hold the copyright in folklore and so-called products of popular culture that become common property, and listed a whole range of examples that also included songs and dances. Article 10(3) provided further that foreigners needed permission from the relevant authorities to use such material. Further, article 10(1) effectively attempted to create a copyright in heritage by providing that the state would also hold the copyright in pre-historical and historical works and 'other national cultural objects' (Antons, 2009).

Article 10 was introduced into the Copyright Act as early as 1982 (Antons, 2000), but in practice never implemented, because a government decree to regulate the details required in article 10(4) was never issued. In 2014, the Indonesian Copyright Law was revised and a new provision on 'traditional cultural expressions', a term now widely used in intellectual property discussions instead of 'folklore', replaced article 10. The new Copyright Act (Law No. 28 of 2014 on Copyright) deleted the subsection related to pre-historical and historical works and 'other national cultural objects', but retained in article 38 the copyright of the state to traditional cultural expressions.

Because the whole approach again requires implementation via a government regulation, the 'traditional cultural expression' provision of the new 2014 Act may well share the fate of the previous 'folklore' provision and remain unimplemented. Still, it constitutes a symbolically powerful claim of the government to administer and control traditional cultural expressions at the central level. If one examines the development of the legislation over time, it clearly sends the important message that the representation of culture at the national level and internationally is a matter for the national government. This understanding is in accordance with the Indonesian Constitution, which provides in article 32(1) that 'the state shall advance the national culture of Indonesia among the civilisations of the world by assuring the freedom of society to preserve and develop cultural values'. But when precisely does culture become 'national' and how does this process relate to cultural expressions that are essentially 'regional' or 'local'?

International models, and the drafting of intellectual property and heritage laws in post-colonial Southeast Asia

Such questions are not new in Indonesia. Although the relationship between the central government and the regions was a sensitive topic during the years of the authoritarian Suharto government centred on Jakarta, they were already being asked during the drafting process of Indonesia's first national Copyright Act of 1982.[5] According to the writer Ajip Rosidi (1984: 79), who followed the debate at the time, the idea to place the copyright to expressions of folklore into the hands of the state encountered 'sharp protests' in the early 1980s. Factions in the Indonesian Parliament expressed their concern, and urged for an amendment and for a clarification that the state did not own the copyright in such cases (Simorangkir, 1982: 224). As a compromise, the government inserted the qualification that it would exercise the copyright only 'with regard to foreign countries'.[6] Observers and copyright experts therefore concluded from this at the time that Indonesian citizens were generally free to use the folkloristic material described in section 10 (Rosidi, 1984: 79–80; Simorangkir, 1982: 136).

A great deal of confusion has been generated by the inclusion of 'works of pre-historic, historic and paleo-anthropologic remains' and 'other national cultural objects' in article 10(1). Although the paleo-anthropologic remains were dropped from the wording as early as 1987 (Hutagalung, 2012: 184), article 10(1) remained concerned with heritage protection, and with material that had nothing to do with copyright and no place in a copyright law. In fact, the protection of 'national cultural objects' turned up in early drafts of Indonesian copyright laws for the first time in 1966 and then again in 1972 (Simorangkir, 1979: 19, 151). Its further development was probably influenced by discussions in the World Intellectual Property Organization (WIPO) and UNESCO about folklore protection and the protection of national cultural property, which culminated in the WIPO/UNESCO-sponsored Tunis Model Law on Copyright of 1976 (Weiner, 1987) and in the 1970 UNESCO Convention on the Means of Prohibiting and Preventing the Illicit Import, Export and Transfer of Ownership of Cultural Property (Hoffman, 2006).

The 1970 UNESCO Convention was the product of an immediate post-colonial period during which developing countries were demanding the return of cultural objects looted from their territories by colonial powers. The same arguments would soon also be mounted by indigenous peoples both vis-à-vis former colonial powers and the governments of post-colonial settler societies (Hoffman, 2006; Vrdoljak, 2008: 206–211). As for copyright, the Tunis Model Law was drafted by a Committee of Governmental Experts convened by the Tunisian government, with assistance from WIPO and UNESCO (International Bureau of WIPO, 1998). It too was clearly drafted in the spirit of a time when economic development was regarded as a state-led and state-planned process in which communities played only subsidiary roles. Its main provision speaks of 'works of national folklore' (Antons, 2012b: 147–48) and the Model Law attempts a national regulation of folklore with the use of copyright principles. All of these various international debates became influential at a time when developing countries, often under considerable pressure from developed-country trading partners, were drafting their first national copyright laws. Thus the Indonesian Copyright Law mixes intellectual property models for folklore protection with nationalistic cultural property claims based on the principles of UNESCO conventions at the time, although the latter were drafted for tangible objects and not for the intangible heritage typically expressed in folklore.

Indonesia is not alone in Southeast Asia in this particular approach. Laos protects 'artistic works' and folklore under the copyright part of its Intellectual Property Law of 2008, designating as potential owners of folklore the local community, but explaining further that the ownership can be exercised by individuals and organisations, as well as the state. Further, the Law on National Heritage of 2005 provides that the state asserts copyright ownership of Lao national and cultural historical heritage if it is outside Laos in the illegitimate possession of other countries, or if other countries have asserted copyright ownership in an illegitimate manner. In a rather cryptic provision, it is further explained that the state will also consider copyright ownership in national heritage items that have high value or are rare and of unique national character, and propose them for 'registration of ownership and copyright in the name of the nation with international organisations' (article 28) (Antons, 2012a: 89–90). Since no international copyright registration for this kind of material is available, what is meant is presumably inscription of this material on one of the UNESCO lists for the safeguarding of intangible cultural heritage.

In the Philippines, the Indigenous Peoples' Rights Act of 1997 provides for the most far-reaching recognition and protection of indigenous rights in Asia. Chapter VI of the Act is particularly important and establishes, among other provisions, community intellectual rights, including the right to the restitution of cultural, intellectual, religious and spiritual property taken without free and prior informed consent or in violation of customary laws and traditions (section 32), and the right to special measures to control of, develop and protect indigenous knowledge systems and practices, sciences and technologies, and cultural manifestations (section 34). These theoretically far-reaching rights could potentially come into conflict with the National Cultural Heritage Act of 2009, which uses the terms 'cultural heritage' and 'cultural property' side by side. It creates restrictive conditions for the sale and export of cultural property, and for 'important cultural property' and 'national cultural treasures'. For 'indigenous properties', therefore, the national cultural agency in charge (such as a museum or an archive) shall consult with the National Commission on Indigenous Peoples to establish relevant regulations (section 21).

From community traditions to national cultural and intellectual property

What is, further, remarkable in this field is the increasing role of the state and the appropriation of heritage material by national agencies. In view of the abovementioned importance of heritage for tourism, nation building, and national and regional development projects, it is hardly surprising that the state wants to control it. In this section, three examples will be discussed: expressions of folklore; traditional agricultural knowledge; and traditional medicine.

Traditional cultural expressions/expressions of folklore and copyright

In the development of the Indonesian copyright legislation related to folkloristic expressions discussed above, the initial compromise between national and community interests was that the state was to exercise the copyright to so-called products of popular culture only towards foreign countries (article 10(2)b. of the Copyright Act of 1982) (Simorangkir, 1982: 96). While this position remained unchanged in two revisions in 1987 and 1997, the qualification disappeared in a new Copyright Act in 2002. Instead, the new Act provided that foreign citizens needed a licence from the relevant government agency to publish or reproduce what was called 'folklore and products of popular culture'. The point that the provision was mainly aimed at foreigners, which had appeased opponents when it was introduced, was now to be found only in the government's explanatory note to the provision. Here, it was stated that the provision was intended to 'prevent actions by foreign parties which could damage the relevant cultural values' (Antons, 2009: 111).

The latest Copyright Act of 2014 continues this trend towards affirmation of the increasingly strong role of the state. It now no longer mentions the licensing requirements for foreigners or the fact that the copyright should be exerted only in this context; instead, it speaks of the duty of the state to make an inventory of, and protect and conserve, traditional cultural expressions (article 38(2)), and provides that any use of the material has to be conscious of the values that exist within the society that developed it (article 38(3)). According to the government's explanatory memorandum accompanying the provision, this refers to a community's *adat* and other social norms. *Adat*, as has often been pointed out, is a complex term referring to both the supernatural and secular social reality (von Benda-Beckmann, 1979: 113–114; Lowenhaupt Tsing, 2009). Originally from the Arabic language and translated as 'custom' or 'tradition' (Lowenhaupt Tsing, 2009: 41), as *adat* law, it became part of the colonial legal system of the Dutch, who regarded it as helpful in their efforts to contain Islam (Lowenhaupt Tsing, 2009: 48–49). To a considerable extent, this system survived the transition to independence (Lev, 1965: 305–306; Holleman, 1981: lix).

During most of the post-colonial period, as a legal concept *adat* led a somewhat embattled life between state law and Islamic law as the other pillars of Indonesia's pluralist legal system. It has seen a renewed importance, however, since the downfall of Suharto and the subsequent decentralisation policies that were designed to satisfy long-standing demands for greater autonomy of the regions and provinces (Hadiz, 2010: ch. 1). In particular, it has become an important argument for forest-dwelling communities to claim recognition of their rights as minorities, and of their status as not dissimilar to that of indigenous peoples in settler colonies in North and South America, Australia and New Zealand (Lowenhaupt Tsing, 2009). The basis for such claims is article 18B(2) of the revised Indonesian Constitution of 1945, which recognises and respects the integrity of 'customary law communities' (*masyarakat adat*, henceforth '*adat* communities'), as well as their traditional rights, 'as long as these remain in existence and are in accordance with the development of society and the unitary state of the Republic of Indonesia'. A similar qualified recognition is seen in article 28I(3) in a newly introduced Part on 'Human Rights'. Accordingly, the cultural identity and rights of traditional communities are respected 'in accordance with the development of the times and civilization'.

Although this leaves much room for discretion and further argument, the representatives of customary law communities have meanwhile fought successfully for basic recognition of their rights in the Indonesian Constitutional Court.[7] For our discussion of rights related to heritage and culture, it means that the protection of local cultural expressions is now becoming enmeshed in the complicated regulation of regional decentralisation. The complication stems from the fact that Indonesia's administrative and legislative decentralisation takes place in a country that continues to stress its character as a unitary state (article 1 of the Constitution).[8] A chapter in the Constitution on regional government, therefore, regulates only the basic framework. The details of legislative and administrative powers are regulated in Law No. 23 of 2014 on Regional Government Administration, and especially in a list of responsibilities for central, provincial and district/city authorities in the Annex to that Law. The manner of putting different levels of government in charge according to what is regarded as most effective for the respective subject matter may well lead to overlaps and disputes about responsibilities in the case of subject matter that concerns different categories.[9] An example is the recognition of *adat* communities and their traditional knowledge, which plays such an important role for cultural heritage, but also in the context of natural resource management. Here, the section on responsibility for the field of culture puts the central government in charge of community intellectual property rights in the field of culture (Annex to Law No. 23 of 2014 under V). The section on the environment, however, prescribes that the recognition of locally living *adat* communities, including their environment-related traditional knowledge, is a matter for the district or provincial level, unless the respective *adat* community lives across the borders of two or more provinces, in which case the central government is again responsible (Annex to Law No. 23 of 2014 under K). In this way, the Law assumes that environment-related knowledge and other forms of culture can be easily separated – but as the long-standing debate about traditional knowledge at WIPO shows (Antons, 2012b), this is not the case.

Hence rights derived from local culture and tradition become subject to a complicated bargaining process between the central government and government branches at provincial and district levels, on the one hand, and between all of them and *adat* communities, whose rights are now recognised by the Constitution and by the Constitutional Court, on the other. Given this strengthened legal position of communities in the constitutional discourse, it is perhaps not completely surprising that the central government is countering the trend in fields such as intellectual property law, in which rights related to commonly held knowledge and cultural practices are placed firmly into the hands of the state. In the new Copyright Act of 2014, the communities producing the traditional cultural expressions and holding communal rights to them are reduced to a role in 'safeguarding, developing and preserving' them (Explanatory Memorandum to section 38(3)).

Even more concerning is the list of examples of traditional cultural expressions in the explanatory memorandum to article 38(2) of the 2014 Copyright Act. Besides classical material, which had been mentioned previously in this context, such as dances and shadow theatre (*wayang*) performances, the list now also includes *adat* rituals. To make the national government the copyright holder to such ceremonies, which are essential for the traditions and religious beliefs of communities, is a very controversial proposition. It could generate controversies with regards to mainstream *adat* communities on Java and those following recognised minority religions, such as the Hindus on Bali. It is particularly controversial, however, in the case of forest-dwelling *adat* communities, previously referred to as 'isolated communities' (*masyarakat terasing*), with traditions based on animism. Animist belief systems are not recognised as religion in Indonesia; the government officially recognises only the world religions of Islam, Catholicism, Protestantism, Hinduism and Buddhism (Persoon, 2009: 201). This, and the threat of being regarded as communist during the days of the anti-Communist Suharto government, prompted conversion among many tribal communities. Such communities would see any central government attempt to become involved in *adat* rituals, or to deny their religious character, as a further violation of their rights and their private sphere. Perhaps what the government wants to regulate in the context of copyright law is the artistic character of performances (such as dances) connected with *adat* rituals. However, because of the religious connotation of the rituals, such a limiting view cannot be maintained and would be regarded as inappropriate. In any case, the inclusion of such rituals could also be regarded as a further sign that Indonesian legislators are influenced by intellectual property models, as well as by concepts derived from UNESCO conventions concerned with heritage. After all, the 2003 UNESCO Convention for the Safeguarding of Intangible Cultural Heritage includes 'rituals and festive events' among the list of examples of intangible cultural heritage (see article 2(2)).

Traditional agricultural knowledge and plant variety laws

Elements of Indonesian heritage are also protected in the form of local plant varieties developed by farmers, often over many generations, in section 7 of Law No. 29 of 2000 on Plant Variety Protection. Regarding the rights in such varieties, the provision states that they are owned by the community, but controlled by the state. As is often the case in Indonesia, what precisely this means follows from implementing decrees. Depending on the geographical spread, Government Regulation No. 13 of 2004 concerning the naming, registration and use of the initial variety for the making of essentially derived varieties puts the governor of a province (*Gubernur*) or district (*Bupati*), the mayor of a city (*Walikota*) or, if the variety is spread over several provinces, the Plant Variety Registration Office within the Ministry of Agriculture in charge of representing the community in registering the variety (articles 5 and 7). Article 9 stipulates that any individual or legal entity using a local variety to produce an essentially derived variety needs to conclude an agreement with those registering authorities. The text makes no exception from this requirement for members of the variety-owning community themselves. Compensation to the variety-owning community for such use 'may' be included in the agreement, but this is not a compulsory component of such agreements (articles 9(4) and 10). If compensation is included in the agreement, the registering authorities are required to use it for several broadly worded purposes: raising the prosperity of the community, the conservation of the local variety and conservation efforts related to genetic resources in the locality of the variety (article 10). These regulations leave the 'owning communities' without any real rights with regards to their traditional varieties; on the contrary, the authorities have substantial discretion as to whether to negotiate compensation for them and how to use it in a manner they regard as conducive to those local interests. Unlike the earlier folklore protection provisions in the Copyright Act, the text of the 2004 Regulation does not even exclude local community members from the requirement to conclude an agreement to use the variety.

The regulation of traditional medicine

The tendency for intangible cultural heritage and traditional knowledge to come under national control is also visible in the field of traditional medicine, where public benefit considerations and the need for standardisation are argued. In Thailand, for example, Thai traditional medicine has seen a revival over the last few decades. The Institute of Thai Traditional Medicine was set up in 1993 and the Department for Development of Thai Traditional and Alternative Medicine established in 2002. The latter proclaimed as its aims, among others, the revival of the body of knowledge of Thai traditional medicine, its promotion and integration into the healthcare system and research into, and development of, Thai traditional medicine, complementary and alternative medicine, folk medicine, and traditional and herbal products (Chokevivat, Chuthaputti and Khumtrakul, 2005: 1–2). The value of traditional herbal medicines, both locally produced and imported, rose almost tenfold from 1990 onwards, and accounted in 2010 for 3,500 million baht (US$109.4 million at 2010 rates) (Thongruang, 2014: 87). The use of such traditional knowledge for drug administration and the production of herbal medicines raises intellectual property issues, which the Thai government has attempted to solve by issuing the Act on the Protection and Promotion of Traditional Thai Medicinal Intelligence of 1999. The Act distinguishes between national, general and personal formulas of traditional Thai drugs. 'General formulas' are widely used formulas in the public domain, which will be notified by the Minister of Public Health. 'Personal formulas' allows individuals or groups of individuals to apply for intellectual property rights, provided that they are Thai nationals and have invented, improved or developed or inherited the formula. Any of these, however, can be declared by the Minister as a 'national formula' if it has special medical or public health value, or is simply 'of benefit' (section 17). The 1999 Act has also detailed provisions on the protection of herbs. Writing in 2009, Robinson and Kuanpoth (2009: 393–395) questioned quite correctly the extent to which such conservation provisions would affect the access of local communities to the herbs and thought that constitutional safeguards for local knowledge under the 2007 Constitution would prevent such a development. However, following the military coup in Thailand in 2014, the 2007 Constitution was replaced by an interim Constitution, which no longer includes such safeguards for local knowledge. In any case, even such limited constitutional safeguards for local knowledge as those available under the 2007 Constitution would be ineffective against competing intellectual property rights, making it likely that some local communities will try to maintain informal modes of protection and secrecy (Robinson and Kuanpoth, 2009: 393). Equally likely is that the strong use and listing of medicinal plants for purposes of the national health policy (Chokevivat et al., 2005: 2) will trigger the transformation of public domain 'general formulas' into 'national formulas' under the discretionary powers of the Ministry of Public Health.

Continuing controversies about the relationship between intangible cultural heritage, cultural property and intellectual property

The various laws in Southeast Asia show how different international discourses promoting cultural and intellectual property have been influential. When these international models were first promoted in the 1950s and 1960s, cultural property did not yet extend to the intangible and intellectual property, and did not yet consider the wide-ranging concepts of traditional cultural expressions and traditional knowledge that are now under discussion at WIPO. Since then, there has been a subtle move away from the terminology of cultural property (Prott and O'Keefe, 1992: 307), most notably in the 2003 UNESCO Convention for the Safeguarding of Intangible Cultural Heritage, which no longer uses the term. At the same time, WIPO took up work on traditional cultural expressions, traditional knowledge and associated genetic resources in the late 1990s, and has overseen negotiations for international instruments in these fields since 2001. Because the 2003 UNESCO Convention also covers 'knowledge and skills', there is overlap with the work of WIPO. The UNESCO Convention addresses this overlap and states that nothing in the Convention shall affect intellectual property rights. Some international law experts have further argued that intangible cultural heritage can be distinguished from those aspects negotiated at WIPO, because intellectual property rights focus on the end product of a creative process, whereas intangible cultural heritage focuses on the entire process (Francioni, 2001, as quoted in Aikawa-Faure, 2008: 29; Lixinski, 2013: 8). Others have recognised that '[f]orms of intangible cultural heritage fall within the scope of an overlapping and multifaceted international regime', and that the overlap between intellectual property rights and intangible cultural property in particular requires 'close collaboration between the two regimes in order to ensure consistency' and to address the overlaps 'in a way that does not undermine either one' (Forrest, 2012: 363–364). WIPO itself seems to regard the areas as overlapping, having pictured them in a 2001 report as overlapping circles, with heritage as the widest, including the smaller circles of traditional knowledge, indigenous knowledge and expressions of folklore (WIPO, 2001).

The governments of developing countries have often used these various concepts in ways that empower young nation-states (Antons, 2005, 2009, 2012a, 2013a, 2013b,

2015; Aragon, 2012; Aragon and Leach, 2008). In spite of their very different origins in international law, on the one hand, and as predominantly individual rights drawn from an area of commercial law, on the other, both cultural and intellectual property are understood as helping to strengthen national culture and as benefiting the nation. In the process, the cultural property concept developed for tangible material is extended to the intangible and intellectual property becomes national property. As shall be explained further below, these national level claims are then bound to clash with claims in neighbouring countries that practise the same or similar cultures, as will often be the case.

Apart from with national governments, the cultural property concept has also been popular with indigenous peoples that seek restoration of their cultural material from former colonial powers, as well as from governments in newly independent countries that succeeded former colonial governments. Because cultural property was developed as part of international law, there is much unfinished business in this field, in particular in the developing world. Academic commentators have noted the rise over the last few decades of an international indigenous movement that started in settler colonies in North and South America, Australia and New Zealand, as well as in Scandinavian countries.[10] For many years, as the historian Coates (2004: 8) points out, '[m]uch of the political agitation has focused on the activities of European colonial powers and on the small, indigenous societies displaced by intrusions associated with the transplanting of European settlements'. He notes that this emphasis 'ignores equally disruptive and authoritarian invasions of indigenous territories by Asian, African and other societies and skips over the experience of indigenous societies separate from their contact with and conquest by outsiders' (Coates, 2004: 8). In recent years, however, the international indigenous movement has come to include minorities from Asia and Africa (Sissons, 2005: 22–23), although this extension has been controversial and has prompted some to question the extent to which it might weaken the specific concerns of indigenous movements in settler societies (Niezen, 2003: 74). For the same reason, Benjamin (Chapter 20 in this volume) proposes to distinguish between true place-linked 'indigeny' and 'indigenism' as self-conscious political stances.

In spite of such concerns about terminology, an indigenous movement is making its presence felt in Asia, where it has long been resisted by governments concerned about national unity (Kingsbury, 1999: 336–377). The exception has been the Philippines, which, prior to independence, was a colony of the United States and thus inherited a system of administering ethnic minorities that drew comparisons with the position of native Americans there (Eder and McKenna, 2004: 60–61). 'The rights of indigenous cultural communities to their ancestral lands' were recognised in the Constitution in 1987, followed in 1997 by the Indigenous Peoples Rights' Act covering, among other things, claims for certificates of ancestral domain titles (Eder and McKenna, 2004: 64–67). In Malaysia, the Constitution recognises the 'natives of Sabah and Sarawak', but refuses to do the same for aboriginal groups on the Malayan peninsula, lumped together since the days of the British colonial administration under the term *orang asli*. Demonstrating the ambiguity of the term 'indigenous' in Malaysia, the former share with the Malay 'indigenous' majority[11] the special position and access to preferential treatment under article 153 of the Constitution, while the *orang asli* paradoxically are not included in the definition of Malay or *Bumiputra*, and have to be content under article 8(5)(c) with the administrative 'provision for the protection, well-being or advancement of the aboriginal peoples of the Malay peninsula (including the reservation of land) or the reservation to aborigines of a reasonable proportion of suitable positions in the public service' (Harding, 2012: 186). According to Harding (2012: 188–191), case law from Canada and Australia was influential in a string of cases in Malaysia since 1997 recognising aboriginal rights, and culminating in decisions in 2002 and 2005 recognising 'customary community title' at common law to their lands.[12] In Indonesia, as discussed by Rachman and Siscawati in Chapter 13 in this volume, the Constitutional Court recently revised the Forestry Law, which now no longer categorically includes 'customary forests' in 'state forests', and has thereby opened up the space for the recognition of customary rights for the 'customary law communities' (*masyarakat adat*) living in and dependent on forests.

Although the main concerns of such communities in Asia are largely identical with those of the international indigenous movement, when it comes to cultural and intellectual property, use of the term 'indigenous' will not work for the benefit of such communities if the terminology is also employed and monopolised at the official level by state authorities. Commentators sympathetic to the indigenous movement have advocated the use of the concept of 'cultural property' in the relationship of indigenous peoples to the state (Carpenter, Katyal and Riley, 2009; Tsosie, 2012). Geismar (2013: 213) goes further and speaks approvingly, for Pacific island countries, of the way in which 'key actors are fusing international discourses of indigenous rights, cultural heritage, cultural property, and traditional knowledge to create their own brands of [intellectual property] IP', thinking that this 're-articulation of IP provides a powerful re-envisioning of the market for culture'. While this fusion may lead to interesting discussions in her case studies of majority 'indigenous' *ni-Vanuatu* (Geismar, 2013: 30), and in a liberal and wealthy settler society such as New Zealand, the examples from Southeast Asia in this chapter show that the fusion in fact works against indigenous and other discriminated minorities in the context of Asian nation-building processes, in which the concept of 'indigenous' is monopolised and exclusively interpreted by state institutions. In such settings, the fusion of 'hard' intellectual property rights and 'soft' cultural property claims in the interest of national development is used as a justification for the appropriation of heritage material originating from communities within the country and for heritage claims against neighbouring countries.

The exercise of rights within territorial boundaries defined by culture

The turn to culture in development policies discussed by Coombe (2009) has not only triggered rights discourses drawing on intellectual and cultural property as well as human rights, but also generated debate about the boundaries of the territories in which such rights are exercised. Because cultures move with people across state boundaries, the realms in which cultures are predominantly practised are rarely in accordance with the boundaries of nation-states that adopt rules related to such cultures (Antons, 2013b; 2015). Von Benda-Beckmann, von Benda-Beckmann and Griffiths, (2009) have drawn attention to the relatively recent literature on law and space (for example Blomley, Delaney and Ford, 2001), and how it becomes more complex under conditions of legal pluralism whereby '[d]ifferent notions of space and spatially grounded rights and obligations become pitted against one another in strategic interactions over contested forms of political authority in the (sometimes violent) fight for control over resources' (von Benda-Beckmann et al., 2009: 7). They also point to the political discourse of cartography and the fact that 'law defines space in its own terms' (von Benda-Beckmann et al., 2009: 19). But they also point out that this is an interactive, rather than one-way, process, quoting Manderson's (2005: 1) statement that 'the law both structures our understanding of certain spaces, while at the same time those spaces themselves radically transform the experience, application and effect of the law' (von Benda-Beckmann et al., 2009: 3).

Thongchai Winichakul (1994) and other historians writing on mainland Southeast Asia (for example Ivarsson, 2008) have shown the historical development of such political discourses of cartography. Winichakul (1994) presents the arrival of modern geography in Thailand and how it came to influence negotiations with Thailand's new neighbours, the colonial powers of Britain and France. Prior to the arrival of modern cartography, political power in Southeast Asia was exercised via tributary relationships that were more important than the exact drawing of borders. Wolters (1999: 27–28) has described the *Mandala* concept of political rule as a 'vaguely definable geographical area without fixed boundaries', 'wherein smaller centres tended to look in all directions for security'.[13] In between such 'vaguely definable geographical areas' were often buffer zones that were difficult to access. Scott (2009: xiv) explained how these buffer zones became 'regions of refuge' for those seeking to escape military conscription or taxation by feudal rulers. Frequently, the refugees included cultural minorities pushed into the interior by expanding hegemonic nation-states, thus forming the basis for the forest-dwelling, tribal communities that now often collectively negotiate their rights as 'indigenous peoples'.

Different understandings of space and boundaries are now also playing a role in the disputes between Southeast Asian neighbours such as Indonesia and Malaysia, or Thailand and Cambodia. In both cases, there is a narrower reading, defining culture within current national borders, as opposed to a wider reading that looks at cultures within the borders of former empires. This is visible in the interpretation of Khmer culture in Thailand and Cambodia, with Thailand laying claim to this heritage as part of its territory prior to European colonial intervention, and with its view of the Thai monarchy and the ethnic Khmer population living in the North Eastern provinces of Thailand as the heirs of the Angkor civilisation (Keyes, 2002; Denes, 2015). The symbolic value of this heritage is high. In 2008, a serious military conflict erupted between Thailand and Cambodia over the temple complex of Preah Vihear (*Asia Sentinel*, 2008). Although the conflict was primarily about the exact line of the border, it erupted after Cambodia's application for world heritage status of the site was approved by UNESCO.

Similar differences in the perception of ancient territorial boundaries as the basis for claims to culture are also seen in the disputes between Indonesia and Malaysia. Malaysians like to speak of being of 'Malay stock' (*rumpun Melayu*) and of a 'Malay world' (*dunia Melayu*) that stretches across several current Southeast Asian nation-states (Liow, 2008). In Malaysia, this space is imagined as following in the footsteps of the ancient Malay kingdom of *Srivijaya*, with its centre in Sumatra, which was later succeeded by the Sultanate of Melaka (Andaya, 2004). Indonesia's reading of history, on the other hand, shows the dominant influence of Java. For those seeking for the space of a 'greater Indonesia' in history, such space is often found in the Javanese kingdom of *Majapahit*, a rival of *Srivijaya* (Liow, 2008: 50). Thus, while the concept of the 'Malay world' extends the borders of present-day Malaysia on the basis of 'Malay' as an ethnic category, for Indonesians it is just one ethnic community among many in their multi-ethnic country, and the space of 'Indonesian culture' is confined by the borders of the nation-state (Reid, 2004: 20).

It is clear, therefore, that one reason for the recent conflicts about heritage is different delineations of the space in which cultures are practised, and that this depends on different readings of history and the role of ancient kingdoms in the identity formation of current nation-states. Yet another reason is the recent embrace of cultural diversity in various fields of law.[14] They have introduced conceptions of space that are different from the classical territory of law in modern nation-states, defined as that of the nation itself and of states, provinces, towns or other administrative units of the nation-state. Different conceptions of space can apply, for example, in those countries that recognise customary laws of different communities and the spaces associated with them (von Benda-Beckmann et al., 2009). However, there are also examples of national laws that introduce different conceptions of space. A prime example are laws for the protection of geographical indications as a relatively recent addition to the range of intellectual property instruments. Originally promoted and introduced into the World Trade Organization (WTO) discussions leading to the Agreement on Trade-related Intellectual Property Rights (TRIPS) by European countries to protect their wines, spirits and agricultural products (UNCTAD and ICTSD, 2005: 279–281), geographical indication protection has meanwhile been embraced by a significant number of developing countries, many of them situated in Asia (Blakeney, 2009: 104).

Geographical indications are quality indicators for tradition and craftsmanship involved in production processes in certain regions, and they are administered by associations authorised to monitor this quality. The potential of geographical indications to contribute to the safeguarding of heritage is debated (Gangjee, 2012). Madhavi Sunder (2007: 115) fears that, within a recognised association for the protection of geographical indications, 'traditional leaders may impose their will on members, reifying traditional hierarchies'. It is important, however, not to confuse such legally constructed associations with traditional communities or traditional craft associations. An examination of the composition of associations for the protection of geographical indications in Indonesia, for example, shows that they are often a mixture of government personnel, local manufacturers and producers, and various supporting associations, such as institutions responsible for the training of craftspeople. Although referred to as 'communities' for the protection of a geographical indication (*masyarakat perlindungan indikasi geografis*), potential applicants for registration of such rights can be producer communities, consumer groups or authorised organisations, which is a reference to the local government (article 56(2) of the Trade Marks Act No. 15 of 2001; article 5(3) of Government Regulation No. 51 of 2007 on Geographical Indications). Furthermore, although such communities or associations are formed at the local level, draft a 'book of regulations' for the use of the geographical indication and recommend new members, the ultimate decision about such matters is made by an expert committee in Jakarta, which is staffed from various ministries and research institutes (articles 8, 14, 16 and 19 of Government Regulation No. 51 of 2007). Under such circumstances, most of the geographical indications currently protected in Indonesia have more to do with regional and rural development under the leadership of the central government than with the safeguarding of community heritage. This raises questions, particularly in countries such as Indonesia with a history of transmigration. If ostensible community rights are used to delineate a 'cultural space' that can be marketed and from which profits can be derived, then who is allowed to operate within that space? Community associations may well want to restrict such economic opportunities to locals who have grown up with a culture, but often this may be difficult to argue in a nation-state that imposes no restrictions on people as to where to settle and which occupation or trade to choose.[15]

Conclusion

During the globalisation debate of the 1990s and early 2000s, it was often discussed that the new international environment, with its transnational networks and new forms of communication, puts great pressure on nation-states (Held and McGrew, 2002). While countries in Europe and North America were moving towards larger regional forms of governance, the young nation-states in the developing world, often still ruled in a very centralised fashion, became increasingly concerned about their still relatively recent and fragile national unity. Decentralisation and the partial diversion of power to regions and provinces have been embraced as one way in which to reduce the pressure without losing control of the process. Not surprisingly, this has led to a revival of local traditions, but at the same time also to debates about national identity and attempts to strengthen discourses about culture and tradition at the central level. In legal terms, it has triggered a revival of customary and religious laws, while national governments try to ensure that these alternative legal orders remain embedded in a framework of national laws. As this chapter has shown, the different legal orders relate to different spaces for which they can claim validity. While most national laws still bind all citizens, alternative legal orders may go beyond the boundaries of the nation-state, or create exclusive spaces with preferential rights for some within the nation-states. In many cases, tradition, custom and religion not only are important as symbols of identity, but also relate to resources and the question of who should be allowed to control them.

The discussion around intangible cultural heritage is a good example of these contradicting tendencies. Although the UNESCO Convention for the Safeguarding of Intangible Cultural Heritage of 2003, with its focus on the role of 'communities, in particular indigenous communities, groups and, in some cases, individuals', seems progressive and in tune with recent decentralisation policies, the examples from Southeast Asia in this chapter show that national governments remain in control of heritage discourses. They are selectively using elements from various UNESCO conventions and national intellectual property laws to construct powerful claims to cultural and intellectual property vis-à-vis neighbouring countries. Heritage is big business in Asia, particularly in relation to tourism, agriculture and medicinal products. An excellent example is the 2015 International Day of Yoga, heavily promoted by the Indian government for health benefits, but (according to observers) also to attract tourists to India and to prevent attempts by yoga teachers in the West to claim intellectual property rights in yoga poses (Suri, 2015; Burke, 2010). As the examples in this chapter show, some governments have gone further, and have appropriated local and regional heritage at the national level to defend it against foreign interests. While relevant laws are often not immediately implemented against locals, or are declared as not being relevant for them, locals may soon become more critical towards such centralisation of heritage, depending on the benefits to be obtained, in which case the legal regulation of heritage could become part of wider and ongoing debates about the recognition of customary rights and rights to natural resources.

Notes

1 Research for this chapter was supported under the Australian Research Council's Discovery Projects funding scheme (Project Number DP130100213).

2 For examples of disputes about tangible heritage, including the Elgin marbles, see Gillman (2010: 9–40).

3 Rosemary Coombe (2009: 402) has referred to that extent to the 'cultural turn in development policies'.
4 See the contributions in Picard and Wood (1997).
5 The 1982 Copyright Act replaced an outdated Dutch colonial law that had survived the declaration of independence, but not been relevant in practice (Antons, 2000: 53–54).
6 See the official government response in Simorangkir (1982: 196).
7 See Rachman and Siscawati, Chapter 13 in this volume.
8 Hadiz (2010) has pointed towards the historical reasons for the deep distrust of federalism among Indonesian politicians. After the struggle for independence ended with the formal recognition of the new republic by the Netherlands, Indonesia was formed in 1949 as the federated 'United States of Indonesia', but Dutch influence and interference in the affairs of some of the states led to the return to a unitary republic under a new, provisional Constitution barely nine months later (Abdullah, 2009: 191–199; Ricklefs, 2001: 284–285).
9 See also Butt, Chapter 12 in this volume.
10 Minde (2003: 79–87) reports an article appearing in Sweden in 1963 with the title 'The Sami are the Indians of Sweden' and visits from native American leaders to Sami towns in the early 1970s.
11 The term *bumiputra* literally means 'sons of the soil'.
12 *Government of Selangor v Sagong Tasi* [2002] 2 MLJ 591, aff'd [2005] 5 MLJ 289, as quoted in Harding (2012: 189).
13 An excellent example are the Northern Khmer, discussed by Denes (2015: 4), who are descendants from the ancient Khmer empire, but were, from the eighteenth century onwards, offering tribute to the Siamese court.
14 See, e.g., the contributions in Nafziger, Kirkwood Paterson and Dundes Renteln (2010); Calboli and Ragavan (2015).
15 See also Butt, Chapter 12 in this volume, who mentions a 'clarification letter' (*Klarifikasi*) of the central government criticising a local law, which prioritised employing locals, as discriminatory and in breach of national Law No. 13 of 2003 on the Workforce.

References

Abdullah, T. (2009) *Indonesia: Towards Democracy*, Singapore: Institute of Southeast Asian Studies.

Aikawa-Faure, N. (2008) 'From the Proclamation of Masterpieces to the Convention for the Safeguarding of Intangible Cultural Heritage', in L. Smith and N. Akagawa (eds) *Intangible Heritage*, London: Routledge, 13–44.

Andaya, L. (2004) 'The Search for the "Origins" of Melayu', in T. P. Bernard (ed.) *Contesting Malayness: Malay Identity Across Boundaries*, Singapore: Singapore University Press, 56–75.

Antons, C. (2000) *Intellectual Property Law in Indonesia*, London/The Hague: Kluwer Law International.

Antons, C. (2005) 'Traditional Knowledge and Intellectual Property Rights in Australia and Southeast Asia', in C. Heath and A. Kamperman Sanders (eds) *New Frontiers of Intellectual Property Law: IP and Cultural Heritage, Geographical Indications, Enforcement and Overprotection*, Oxford/Portland, OR: Hart, 37–51.

Antons, C. (2009) 'What is "Traditional Cultural Expression"? International Definitions and Their Application in Developing Asia', *WIPO Journal*, 1(1): 103–116.

Antons, C. (2012a) 'Geographies of Knowledge: Cultural Diffusion and the Regulation of Traditional Knowledge/Cultural Expressions in Southeast Asia', *WIPO Journal*, 4(1): 83–91.

Antons, C. (2012b) 'Intellectual Property Rights in Indigenous Cultural Heritage: Basic Concepts and Continuing Controversies', in C. B. Graber, K. Kuprecht and J. C. Lai (eds) *International Trade in Indigenous Cultural Heritage: Legal and Policy Issues*, Cheltenham/Northampton, MA: Edward Elgar, 144–174.

Antons, C. (2013a) 'At the Crossroads: The Relationship between Heritage and Intellectual Property in Traditional Knowledge Protection in Southeast Asia', *Law in Context*, 29(1): 74–94.

Antons, C. (2013b) 'Asian Borderlands and the Legal Protection of Traditional Knowledge and Traditional Cultural Expressions', *Modern Asian Studies*, 47(4): 1403–1433.

Antons, C. (2015) 'Epistemic Communities and the "People without History": The Contribution of Intellectual Property Law to the "Safeguarding" of Intangible Cultural Heritage', in I. Calboli and S. Ragavan (eds) *Diversity in Intellectual Property: Identities, Interests and Intersections*, Cambridge: Cambridge University Press, 453–471.

Antons, C., and Antons-Sutanto, R. (2009) 'Traditional Medicine and Intellectual Property Rights: A Case Study of the Indonesian *Jamu* Industry', in C. Antons (ed.) *Traditional Knowledge, Traditional Cultural Expressions and Intellectual Property Law in the Asia-Pacific Region*, Alphen aan den Rijn: Kluwer Law International, 363–384.

Aragon, L. V. (2012) 'Copyright Culture for the Nation? Intangible Property Nationalism and the Regional Arts of Indonesia', *International Journal of Cultural Property*, 19(3): 269–312.

Aragon, L. V., and Leach, J. (2008) 'Arts and Owners: Intellectual Property Law and the Politics of Scale in Indonesian Arts', *American Ethnologist*, 35(4): 607–631.

Asia Sentinel (2008) 'Thailand and Cambodia Agree to Cool Things Off', 17 October, available online at http://www.asiasentinel.com/new/politics/thailand-and-cambodia-agree-to-cool-things-off/ [accessed 20 July 2016].

Asia Sentinel (2009) 'Indonesian Outrage over a Dance' 25 August, available online at http://www.asiasentinel.com/new/society/indonesian-outrage-over-a-dance/ [accessed 20 July 2016].

Blakeney, M. (2009) 'Protection of Traditional Knowledge by Geographical Indications', in C. Antons (ed.) *Traditional Knowledge, Traditional Cultural Expressions and Intellectual Property Law in the Asia-Pacific Region*, Alphen aan den Rijn: Wolters Kluwer, 87–108.

Blomley, N., Delaney, D., and Ford, R. T. (eds) (2001) *The Legal Geographies Reader*, Oxford/Malden, MA: Blackwell.

Borneo Post Online (2010) 'Creative Industries a Major Driver of Economic Growth', 1 January, available online at http://www.theborneopost.com/2010/01/01/creative-industries-a-major-driver-of-economic-growth/ [accessed 28 May 2015].

Budiningsih, C. B. (2007) 'Menyoal Paten Pengetahuan Tradisional', *Pikiran Rakyat*, 30 July.

Burke, J. (2010) 'Yoga Heritage: Don't Even Think about Stealing It, Says Indian Government', *The Guardian*, 8 June, available online at https://www.theguardian.com/world/2010/jun/08/yoga-heritage-india-filming-asanas [accessed 20 July 2016].

Calboli, I., and Ragavan, S. (eds) (2015) *Diversity in Intellectual Property: Identities, Interests and Intersections*, Cambridge: Cambridge University Press.

Carpenter, K. A., Katyal, S. K., and Riley, A. R. (2009) 'In Defense of Property', *Yale Law Journal*, 118(6): 1022–1255.

Chew, D. (2004) 'Borders of Kinship and Ethnicity: Cross-border Relations between the Kelalan Valley, Sarawak, and the Bawan Valley, East Kalimantan', *Borneo Research Bulletin*, 1 January, available online at http://www.thefreelibrary.com/_/print/PrintArticle.aspx?id=134382059 [accessed 20 July 2016].

Chokevivat, V., Chuthaputti, A., and Khumtrakul, P. (2005) *The Use of Traditional Medicine in the Thai Health Care System*, 27 May, available online at http://www.thai-institute.net/thai-massage-herbs-articles/Thai%20Healthcare.pdf [accessed 20 July 2016].

Chong, J. W. (2012) '"Mine, Yours or Ours?" The Indonesia–Malaysia Disputes over Shared Cultural Heritage', *SOJOURN: Journal of Social Issues in Southeast Asia*, 27(1): 1–53.

Coates, K. S. (2004) *A Global History of Indigenous Peoples*, Basingstoke/New York: Palgrave Macmillan.

Coombe, R. (2009) 'The Expanding Purview of Cultural Properties and Their Politics', *Annual Review of Law and Social Science*, 5: 393–412.

Denes, A. (2015) 'Foklorising Northern Khmer Identity in Thailand: Intangible Cultural Heritage and the Production of "Good Culture"', *SOJOURN: Journal of Social Issues in Southeast Asia*, 30(1): 1–34.

Eder, J. F., and McKenna, T. M. (2004) 'Minorities in the Philippines: Ancestral Lands and Autonomy in Theory and Practice', in C. R. Duncan (ed.) *Civilising the Margins: Southeast Asian Government Policies for the Development of Minorities*, Ithaca, NY/London: Cornell University Press, 56–85.

Fitzpatrick, S. (2009) 'Malaysia "Steals" Bali Dance', *The Australian*, 26 August, available online at http://www.theaustralian.com.au/news/world/malaysia-steals-bali-dance/story-e6frg6so-1225766191831 [accessed 20 July 2016].

Forrest, C. (2012) *International Law and the Protection of Cultural Heritage*, London: Routledge.

Gangjee, D. (2012) 'Geographical Indications and Cultural Heritage', *WIPO Journal*, 4(1): 92–102.

Geismar, H. (2013) *Treasured Possessions: Indigenous Interventions into Cultural and Intellectual Property*, Durham, NC/London: Duke University Press.

Gillman, D. (2010) *The Idea of Cultural Heritage*, rev'd edn, Cambridge: Cambridge University Press.

Hadiz, V. R. (2010) *Localising Power in Post-authoritarian Indonesia: A Southeast Asia Perspective*, Stanford, CA: Stanford University Press.

Harding, A. (2012) *The Constitution of Malaysia: A Contextual Analysis*, Oxford/Portland, OR: Hart.

Held, D., and McGrew, A. (2002) *Globalisation/Anti-globalisation*, Cambridge: Polity Press.

Hoffman, B. T. (2006) 'Exploring and Establishing Links for a Balanced Art and Cultural Heritage Policy', in B. T. Hoffman (ed.) *Art and Cultural Heritage: Law, Policy and Practice*, Cambridge: Cambridge University Press, 1–18.

Holleman, J. F. (ed.) (1981) *Van Vollenhoven on Indonesian* Adat *Law*, The Hague: Martinus Nijhoff.

Hutagalung, S. M. (2012) *Hak Cipta: Kedudukan & Peranannya dalam Pembangunan*, Jakarta: Sinar Grafika.

International Bureau of WIPO (1998) 'The Protection of Expressions of Folklore: The Attempts at International Level', available online at http://itt.nissat.tripod.com/itt9903/folklore.htm [accessed 28 May 2015].

Ivarsson, S. (2008) *Creating Laos: The Making of a Lao Space between Indochina and Siam, 1860–1945*, Copenhagen: NIAS Press.

Jakarta Post (2007) 'Malaysia Urges Indonesia to Drop Plans to Sue over Folk Song', 8 October.

Keyes, C. F. (2002) 'The Case of the Purloined Lintel: The Politics of a Khmer Shrine as a Thai National Treasure', in C. J. Reynolds (ed.) *National Identity and its Defenders: Thailand Today*, Chiang Mai: Silkworm Books, 212–237.

Kingsbury, B. (1999) 'The Applicability of the International Legal Concept of "Indigenous Peoples" in Asia', in J. R. Bauer and D. A. Bell (eds) *The East Asian Challenge for Human Rights*, New York: Cambridge University Press, 336–377.

Kompas (2006) 'Lemah, Perlindungan Negara pada Pengetahuan Tradisional', 17 March.

Lev, D. S. (1965) 'The Lady and the Banyan Tree: Civil-law Change in Indonesia', *American Journal of Comparative Law*, 14: 282–307.

Liow, J. C. (2008) *The Politics of Indonesia–Malaysia Relations: One Kin, Two Nations*, London/New York: Routledge.

Lixinski, L. (2013) *Intangible Cultural Heritage in International Law*, Oxford: Oxford University Press.

Lowenhaupt Tsing, A. (2009) '*Adat*/Indigenous: Indigeneity in Motion', in C. Gluck and A. Lowenhaupt Tsing (eds) *Words in Motion: Toward a Global Lexicon*, Durham, NC/London: Duke University Press, 40–64.

Manderson, D. (2005) 'Interstices: New Work on Legal Spaces', *Law Text Culture*, 9(1): 1–10.

Minde, H. (2003) 'The Challenge of Indigenism: The Struggle for Sami Land Rights and Self-Government in Norway 1960–1990', in S. Jentoft, H. Minde and R. Nilsen (eds) *Indigenous Peoples: Resource Management and Global Rights*, Delft: Eburon Academic, 75–104.

Nafziger, J. A. R., Kirkwood Paterson, R., and Dundes Renteln, A. (2010) *Cultural Law: International, Comparative and Indigenous*, New York: Cambridge University Press.

Niezen, R. (2003) *The Origins of Indigenism: Human Rights and the Politics of Identity*, Berkeley, CA: University of California Press.

Persoon, G. A. (2009) ' "Being Indigenous" in Indonesia and the Philippines', in C. Antons (ed.) *Traditional Knowledge, Traditional Cultural Expressions and Intellectual Property Law in the Asia-Pacific Region*, Alphen aan den Rijn: Kluwer Law International, 195–216.

Picard, M., and Wood, R. E. (eds) (1997) *Tourism, Ethnicity and the State in Asian and Pacific Societies*, Honolulu: University of Hawai'i Press.

Prott, L. V., and O'Keefe, P. J. (1992) '"Cultural Heritage" or "Cultural Property"?', 1 *International Journal of Cultural Property*, 1(2): 307–320.

Reid, A. (2004) 'Understanding *Melayu* (Malay) as a Source of Diverse Modern Identities', in T. P. Bernard (ed.) *Contesting Malayness: Malay Identity across Boundaries*, Singapore: Singapore University Press, 1–24.

Ricklefs, M. C. (2001) *A History of Modern Indonesia Since c. 1200*, 3rd edn, Stanford, CA: Stanford University Press.

Robinson, D., and Kuanpoth, J. (2009) 'The Traditional Medicine Predicament: A Case Study of Thailand', *The Journal of World Intellectual Property*, 11(5/6): 375–403.

Rosidi, A. (1984) *Undang-Undang Hak Cipta 1982 – Pandangan Seorang Awam*, Jakarta: Penerbit Djambatan.

Scott, J. C. (2009) *The Art of Not Being Governed: An Anarchist History of Upland Southeast Asia*, New Haven, CT/London: Yale University Press.

Simorangkir, J. C. T. (1979) *Hak Cipta Lanjutan*, Jakarta: Penerbit Djambatan.

Simorangkir, J. C. T. (1982) *Undang-Undang Hak Cipta 1982 (UHC 1982)*, Jakarta: Penerbit Djambatan.

Sissons, J. (2005) *First Peoples: Indigenous Cultures and Their Futures*, London: Reaktion Books.

Smith, L. (2006) *The Uses of Heritage*, London/New York: Routledge.

Star Online (2007) 'Rasa Sayang Belongs to All', 3 October, available online at http://www.thestar.com.my/news/nation/2007/10/03/rasa-sayang-belongs-to-all/ [accessed 20 July 2016].

Suharmoko, A. (2008) 'Govt Plans Blueprint for Creative Industries', *Jakarta Post*, 10 March.

Sunder, M. (2007) 'The Invention of Traditional Knowledge', *Law & Contemporary Problems*, 70(2): 97–124.

Suri, M. (2015) 'India and the Politics of Yoga', *International New York Times*, 19 June, available online at http://www.nytimes.com/2015/06/20/opinion/india-and-the-politics-of-yoga.html?_r=0 [accessed 20 July 2016].

Susilo. H. (2012) 'Beras Adan Resmi Dipatenkan', *Kompas*, 15 January, available online at http://regional.kompas.com/read/2012/01/15/18453496/Beras.Adan.Resmi.Dipatenkan [accessed 17 March 2015].

Theparat, C. (2012) 'New Agency to Give Creative Industries an Infusion of Funds', *Bangkok Post*, 27 August, available online at http://www.bangkokpost.com/print/309507 [accessed 28 May 2015].

Thongruang, C. (2014) *The Barriers to the Adoption of Thai Traditional Medicine Services in Thai Community Hospitals: A Case Study of Community Hospitals in Phitsanulok Province*, PhD thesis, Sydney Business School, University of Wollongong, available online at http://ro.uow.edu.au/theses/4064 [accessed 20 July 2016].

Tsosie, R. (2012) 'International Trade in Indigenous Cultural Heritage: An Argument for Indigenous Governance of Cultural Property', in C. B. Graber, K. Kuprecht and J. C. Lai (eds) *International Trade in Indigenous Cultural Heritage: Legal and Policy Issues*, Cheltenham/Northampton, MA: Edward Elgar, 221–245.

UNCTAD and ICTSD (2005) *Resource Book on TRIPS and Development*, Cambridge: Cambridge University Press.

von Benda-Beckmann, F. (1979) *Property in Social Continuity: Continuity and Change in the Maintenance of Property Relationships through Time in Minangkabau, West Sumatra*, The Hague: Martinus Nijhoff.

von Benda-Beckmann, F., von Benda-Beckmann, K., and Griffiths, A. (2009) 'Space and Legal Pluralism: An Introduction', in F. von Benda Beckmann, K. von Benda-Beckmann and

A. M. Griffiths (eds) *Spatialising Law: An Anthropological Geography of Law in Society*, Aldershot: Ashgate, 1–29.

Vrdoljak, A. (2008) *International Law, Museums and the Return of Cultural Objects*, Cambridge: Cambridge University Press.

Weiner, J. (1987) 'Protection of Folklore: A Political and Legal Challenge', *International Review of Industrial Property and Copyright Law*, 18(1): 56–92.

Winichakul, T. (1994) *Siam Mapped: A History of the Geo-body of a Nation*, Honolulu: University of Hawai'i Press.

Wisnu, A. (2008) 'Copyright Law Fails to Protect Artisans: Experts', *Jakarta Post*, 24 September.

Wolters, O. W. (1999) *History, Culture and Region in Southeast Asian Perspective*, rev'd edn, Ithaca, NY/Singapore: Cornell Southeast Asia Program/Institute of Southeast Asian Studies.

World Intellectual Property Organization (WIPO) (2001) *Intellectual Property Needs and Expectations of Traditional Knowledge Holders: WIPO Report on Fact-finding Missions on Intellectual Property and Traditional Knowledge*, Geneva: WIPO.

Part IV

Law, the environment, and access to land and natural resources

15 Transnational sustainability certification as a new extraterritoriality?

Peter Vandergeest

Introduction

In recent years, a variety of non-state agencies operating transnationally have emerged with the express purpose of claiming rule-making authority with respect to ecological and social practices. Specifically, they seek to identify operators who can demonstrate compliance with standards as verified by 'third-party' certification.[1] In this chapter, this world of rule-making and assessment will be referred to as 'transnational sustainability certification' (TSC). The term 'sustainability' will be defined broadly, in reference to both ecological and social standards. In the area of resource management and food production, such agencies include organisations set up to certify forest management (such as the Forestry Stewardship Council, or FSC), fisheries (the Marine Stewardship Council, or MSC) and aquaculture (the Aquaculture Stewardship Council, or ASC). In addition, industry groups and non-government organisations (NGOs) have collaborated to establish organisations that certify many controversial crops and activities, most of which are oriented towards export to Europe and North America (such as palm oil, sugar, fish oil and fish meal, jewellery and tourism).[2] In some sectors, distinct certification organisations compete with each other in providing certification services – the multiple certifying organisations involved in producing sustainable, fair trade or organic coffee being among the more visible to affluent consumers. Finally, the turn towards certification has spawned a rapidly growing sector of companies and non-profit organisations that audit producers against standards (certifying bodies), or which help producers to comply with often extremely complex certification requirements, much of which involves supplying detailed documentation of the producers' daily activities.

In this chapter, we take up the question of how TSC interacts with state authority in Southeast Asia. Specifically, we consider specific ways in which TSC rule-making and rule-enforcement activities overlap with the mandates of distinct state agencies. The chapter begins by comparing legal extraterritoriality of the colonial period to contemporary TSC authority claims. It then explains in detail the operation of schemes for shrimp farming, to show how it parallels the legal extraterritoriality claimed by imperialist powers during the colonial era, albeit with some important differences. It finishes by briefly comparing the distinct ways in which state agencies have responded to these regimes in Thailand and Vietnam.

Extraterritoriality and sustainability certification

The term 'extraterritoriality' generally refers to a legal regime whereby 'a state claims exclusive jurisdiction over its citizens in another state' and is situated within an assumption that Westphalian territorial sovereignty holds outside of these exceptions (Kayaoglu, 2010: 2). In the latter case, 'a state claims exclusive jurisdiction over all people within its territorial boundaries regardless of their nationality', hence excludes external authority structures from domestic authority (Kayaoglu, 2010: 2). Extraterritoriality evolved in Europe to protect embassies or embassy staff – essentially islands in the midst of an assumed absolute territorial sovereignty of the modern state (for example Sassen, 1996: 4–5).

When extraterritoriality was extended to Asian and African states that were not directly colonised, however, it took a very different form. In these areas, the extraterritorial provisions protecting subjects of imperial states were not reciprocated with provisions protecting subjects of countries such as Siam who were living in territories claimed by imperial states. This relationship was widespread throughout Asia and Africa. Kayaoglu (2010: 5) lists countries subject to this one-sided extraterritoriality as including China, Japan, Egypt, Tunisia, Algeria, Morocco, Tripoli, Iran, Korea, the Ottoman Empire/ Turkey, Zanzibar, Tonga, Madagascar, Samoa, Congo and Siam. Extraterritorial empires transformed extraterritoriality as an equal relationship of mutual exceptions to an unequal relationship of one-sided exclusions that embodied the semi-colonial status of these states (Kayaoglu, 2010: 2).

A comparison to TSC suggests, first, that territorial sovereignty is best understood not as exclusive in a Westphalian sense, but as disaggregated (Slaughter, 2004) variegated, or graduated (Ong, 2006). Sovereignty can be broken down into components that can be shifted or shared between state and non-state actors (Sassen, 1996: xii). Similarly, TSC can thus be understood as referring to situations in which specific components of state territorial control are supplemented or pre-empted (Neilson and Prichard, 2009: 184–185) by non-state entities who claim rule-making authority in specified territories. Linking TSC not only to extraterritoriality in general (Gulbrandsen, 2005), but also specifically to the unequal extraterritorialities imposed on Siam and other Asian and African states during the colonial period, draws our attention to the ways in which TSC can be considered imperialist or neo-colonial when it is implemented in sites that were previously colonised or which were subjected to imperial extraterritoriality (Neilson and Prichard, 2009: 184–185).

Transnational certification is largely legitimised by a standard narrative portraying the state as ineffective with respect to protecting vulnerable ecologies, workers and communities, as will be detailed below. This narrative is applied to all states; it is not unique to the global South or to Asia. However, when it concerns Asian states, it takes specific forms that often invoke Orientalist stereotypes about Asia. These narratives, along with the way in which most organisations that promote TSC are based in the global North, are helping to produce a regulatory regime that parallels colonial extraterritoriality, which pre-empts state territorial sovereignty in order to apply rules created primarily by organisations from the North that are designed to protect ecologies, workers and communities. We can call these the 'new subjects' of extraterritorial authority.

The next section will examine these intersecting authority claims in the context of aquaculture, focusing on shrimp farming in Thailand (previously Siam), as well as southern Vietnam.

Aquaculture certification

Seafood produced through aquaculture now makes up half of global seafood consumption (Bush et al., 2013), with wild-caught fisheries in decline and rapid advances in aquaculture technologies. Most aquaculture production by volume comprises relatively low-value carps, seaweed and shellfish, produced primarily in Asia, for primarily domestic and inter-regional markets (Belton and Bush, 2014: 8). But what has drawn most attention from academics, activists and certification proponents is the high-value, intensive and export-oriented aquaculture industry – especially shrimp, although pangasius, tilapia and a few other species are also important. Of the aquaculture species cultivated for export in Asia, shrimp has the longest history, spanning about three decades. Shrimp farming generates considerable revenue, especially for processors, exporters and suppliers of inputs, of which the most costly is shrimp feed. Thailand and Vietnam have been among the world's leading producers: both were producing around 500,000 tonnes annually before volume dropped during 2012–13 as a result of an epidemic of early mortality syndrome (EMS). Shrimp in Thailand are grown by about 20,000, mostly small, highly intensive farms ranging in size from less than 1 hectare to large corporate farms; in Vietnam, the sector also includes more extensive farms, many of which are set up as mixed shrimp farm–mangrove ecologies. The processing industry is dominated by large agrofood corporations, which are sometimes transnational in their scope – particularly those based in Thailand. Two of the most important are brand-conscious Thai Union and Charoen Pokphand, both of which also operate processing plants in Vietnam, and both of which are important suppliers to Europe and North America, and, as such, the targets of criticisms when scandals emerge involving the shrimp supply chain.

Shrimp farming has been intensely controversial for its impacts on coastal ecologies, including the destruction of mangrove forests to make way for shrimp farms in some areas (although in Thailand most shrimp farms are in former rice fields), the degradation of livelihood resources through pollution and blocked access for people who live in the coastal zones, and the conditions of hired workers (Bene, 2005; Vandergeest, Flaherty and Miller, 1999). With respect to workers, it is the 'slave'-like situation of many of the migrant workers in seafood-processing facilities and on the fishing boats that supply inputs for shrimp feed that has generated critical international attention (for example EJF, 2013; Hodal, Kelly and Lawrence, 2014). In Europe and North America, the response to this and other scandals involving seafood produced in Asia has been to hold corporate buyers partly accountable for working conditions among their suppliers – much like the highly publicised scandal involving the unsafe and poorly paid work in textile factors in Bangladesh following the collapse of the Rana Plaza factory in April 2013. Buyers in turn respond by claiming that they are working to clean up their supply chains – which they often do by requiring their suppliers to obtain third-party sustainability or labour certifications.

Three transnational certification systems are currently important in shrimp farming in Asia. First, the ASC was founded by the World Wide Fund for Nature (WWF) and the Dutch Sustainable Trade Initiative in 2009 to certify aquaculture operations. Like the MSC and the FSC, after which the ASC was patterned, the ASC is transnational, operating across states and not welcoming of the participation of states in its governance structure. ASC standards have been created for twelve major aquaculture species through eight Aquaculture Dialogues run by the WWF. The Global Steering Committee that ran the Shrimp Aquaculture Dialogue (ShAD), which included eight members identified with NGOs and six identified with various parts of the industry – but nobody identified with governments or relevant intergovernmental organisations, such the United Nations Food and Agriculture Organization (FAO). ShAD completed its work in early 2014, sending its shrimp standards to the ASC in March 2014. Although it only began to administer certification in 2014, by time of writing the ASC had already received commitments from many major buyers, especially in Europe.

The second important TSC for farmed shrimp is the Global Aquaculture Alliance's (GAA) Best Aquaculture Practices (BAP) programme, also known as the Aquaculture Certification Council (ACC), which administers the BAP standards. The GAA is an industry organisation based in the United States and was established in 1997 to counter intense criticism of shrimp farming, which had, at the time, resulted in increasing state regulation and the tightening of conditions for financial support for shrimp-farming projects among development banks (Bene, 2005: 590). The GAA subsequently developed standards for aquaculture, the BAP, and set up the 'independent' ACC to administer these standards (Lee and Connelly, 2006: 61). When Walmart announced in 2006 that it planned to buy only seafood that was certified for sustainability, it identified the ACC as the certification that it would require for its aquaculture suppliers. The ACC has a significant presence in Thailand because of the need to respond to Walmart and other buyer requirements for sustainability certification. Because it is the processor who sells to Walmart and other North American buyers, it is the processor who is thus required to find and supply certified shrimp. Processors have therefore been active in helping farms to become certified under group certification provisions in the ACC standards. Thus the ACC's list of certified shrimp farms in Thailand shows that many are certified as groups, sponsored by processing companies.

In the case of shrimp farming, more than other aquaculture species, the impact on marginalised coastal communities has received considerable attention, and many of the groups who oppose shrimp farming and certification are partly oriented towards working with coastal communities to defend their right to use and manage coastal ecologies. They oppose TSC with the argument that the standards do not fully address all of the environmental and social problems caused by shrimp farming, and that certification will merely encourage more consumption of unsustainable shrimp in wealthy countries.[3] This chapter, however, does not focus on coastal communities,[4] but the relationship with state agencies whose mandate it is to regulate shrimp farming and coastal ecologies. Our interviews and observations at industry events suggest that many state and inter-state organisations that are either mandated to regulate shrimp farming or are involved in projects to improve sustainability also regard TSC with considerable suspicion, although for reasons very different from those of the community-oriented environmental groups. In contrast to these groups, they often see transnational certification as a neo-colonial imposition by North-based groups or as a hidden trade barrier targeting Asian countries. The next section focuses on the question of how transnational certification could indeed be considered neo-colonial, by comparing it to colonial-era extraterritoriality.

Certification territories and extraterritoriality

In a very useful analysis of extraterritoriality in Siam, Tomas Larsson (2007) has shown how extraterritoriality not only mapped protections onto persons, but also created territories for protecting these persons. Extraterritoriality was introduced into Siam by the Bowring Treaty of 1855, under which the Siamese government ceded jurisdiction over British subjects to British consular authority and British law (Larsson, 2007: 778). Extraterritoriality is often understood as territorial in relation to how British subjects were protected while in Siamese national territory. But Larsson (2007) shows that the treaties also produced kind of variegated sovereignty (Ong, 2006) within the national territory. Larsson (2007: 778) quotes the following provision from the Treaty with the British,

'British subjects, their persons, houses, premises, lands, ships or property of any kind shall not be seized, injured, or in any way interfered with by the Siamese', which curtailed not only Siamese state jurisdiction over British subjects living in Siam, but also the ability of Siamese government agencies to rule and regulate activities in the territories defined as the 'houses, premises, lands' controlled by British subjects. A subsequent sentence illustrates how extraterritoriality not only limited territorial sovereignty, but also helped to produce it: 'On the other hand, Siamese subjects, their persons, houses, premises, or property of any kind, shall not be seized, injured, or in any way interfered with by the English . . .' (quoted in Larsson, 2007: 778).

In effect, the exception also produced the rule (Ong, 2006: 101, citing Carl Schmitt). The treaty simultaneously situated the Siamese state in a subordinate position and recognised it as sovereign in relation to the English state, as long as English property and persons were excluded from this sovereignty.

The treaties with the British became models for a series of other unequal treaties with foreign powers, including many European countries, the United States and, eventually, Japan. These treaties and extraterritoriality remained in force until new treaties were negotiated during the 1920s and 1930s that ended extraterritoriality, after the Siamese government had created a European-style legal system. The population and territories covered by extraterritorial provisions were very large because people residing in Siam, but born in adjacent British and French colonies – known as 'alien Asiatics' (Larsson, 2007: 780) – were considered British or French subjects. The effect was a perception that the state's authority and prestige was severely compromised, and that it was not considered a fully modern state with a status equal to that of the imperial powers. At a more practical level, the Siamese worked to limit the extent of these extraterritorial spaces by setting limits on the rights and abilities of foreign subjects to purchase land (Larsson, 2007). The struggle against what was perceived as the encroachments of colonial powers on the territorial integrity of Thailand (both through the direct annexation of territory claimed by the Siamese state and through extraterritoriality) helped to produce a nationalism linked to the territorial Thai geo-body that persists even today (Winichakul, 1997).

Turning to the ASC and ACC standards, we see that they have important similarities and differences compared to colonial-era extraterritoriality. A key *difference* lies in provisions that seem designed to counter the perception that certification could compromise domestic sovereignty. The first principles of both the ASC and ACC standards echo the guidelines of the FAO in stating that farms must comply with all applicable national laws and local regulations, and must provide documentation that the farms are following these laws. The ACC standard specifically mentions that farmers need to show documents (including land title documents and permits) that they have appropriate land rights, as well as the right to use water, and to construct, operate and dispose of waste. Neither set of standards indicates that the auditor should report any legal violations to relevant state authorities. Principle 1 of the ASC Shrimp Standard,[5] however, states that government-issued permits and licences should be made publicly available upon request within one month, with the rationale that the affected communities should have access to this information.

The rationale accompanying Principle 1 of the ASC standard also states that 'where necessary in subsequent principles, the ASC Shrimp Standard goes beyond the minimum legal requirements to produce more rigorous standard'. It is the 'going beyond' that produces the extraterritorial space, through provisions that supplement the rule-making authority of states with that of transnational, non-governmental agents.

The more cautious ACC standards make no mention of a need to 'go beyond' national law, leaving that implicit.

The ACC and ASC combine to create at least two distinct kinds of certification territories. The first is the space of the farm itself, much like the treaties that turned the premises and property of foreign subjects into an extraterritorial space. That space is defined in Principle 1, which requires farmers to have appropriate land documents. This would normally involve some kind of cadastral mapping of the property. Within this territory, the standards then go on to claim the authority to regulate a series of practices, as well as the authority to regulate how the farm interacts with ecologies and people across the spatial boundaries of the farm. To illustrate this, we can examine the principles on labour.

The ACC lists thirty-three requirements in its principle on 'Worker Safety and Employee Relations', many of which direct farmers to follow (with documentation) national and local labour laws. Examples include paying minimum wages, employing foreign workers who are documented, using employment agencies that are licensed and meeting government standards for employee housing. But many requirements do not specifically refer to local or national regulations, for example those involving transparency in contracts, safe or healthy working conditions, the right to collective bargaining or representation and 'equal opportunity' with respect to recruitment, compensation, etc. The ASC goes much further than the ACC in bypassing local and national labour regulation. Principle 4 of the ASC Shrimp Standard begins by stating that national labour laws are 'often not consistent in a global context and sometimes fall below internationally agreed-upon levels', and that the ASC standards are based on core principles of the International Labour Organization (ILO) and other fundamental rights of human beings according to the United Nations. The template document for the WWF's eight Aquaculture Dialogues (which produced ASC standards for twelve species) indicates that the WWF worked closely with the NGO Social Accountability International (SAI) to align standards with best labour practices. The labour standards thus transform the farm into a space where labour regulation can be accomplished through certification. The document includes ten criteria for labour, which are listed and explained over twenty pages of text; for each criterion, the document lists (as with the other standards) one or more *indicators*, *requirements* for each indicator, a *rationale* and a *guidance for implementation*. The document in fact resembles the charters of human rights that are often attached to state constitutions. Among the requirements we find, among other things: a minimum age of 18 for permanent hired employees; a ban on forced, bonded or compulsory labour; adoption of an anti-discrimination policy addressing gender, age, race, caste, national origin, religion, sexual orientation, union membership, political affiliation, maternity or any other condition that might give rise to discrimination; provisions for worker health and safety; a requirement that wages not only meet legal minimum wages, but also are fair in the sense that they are sufficient to allow workers to support the average-sized family above the poverty line; access to freedom of association and collective bargaining; maximum weekly working hours; overtime pay; minimum wages; a minimum fourteen-week maternity leave; fair and transparent contracts; and decent and safe living conditions for on farm accommodation.

These standards go very far in their support for worker rights in an industry that often relies on migrant workers, discriminatory labour practices (for example Islam, 2008; Resurreccion and Sajor, 2010) and unfree working conditions. Discriminatory or unfree labour practices are hardly unique to shrimp farming or processing – industrial agriculture in the global North, as well as the global South, often relies on migrant workers, who frequently have precarious legal status or whose labour relations are less than free. The millions of workers from Burma, Cambodia and Laos who are working in Thailand often experience exploitation and abuse, including, but not limited to, those employed in shrimp farming and processing. But the key question for this chapter is not whether these or any other labour standards are adequate for protecting workers on certified shrimp farms; the point is that the ASC standards aim to produce the farm as a delimited territory within which labour practices can be regulated through the ASC and its associated network of accredited certifying bodies, consultants and so on, by means of auditing documents and soliciting worker testimonies. This regulation is effectively outside of government regulatory processes and, more specifically in Thailand, regulation by the Department of Labour Protection and Welfare, as well as the Department of Fisheries. The question that follows this observation is not whether these standards will or will not be effective, but whether they will address labour conditions in the fisheries and aquaculture sector more broadly, where production is primarily for local or inter-regional markets, or indeed the broader worker relations that produce these situations, especially the widespread use of non-documented or low-paid migrant labour. It is indicative of the state-avoiding character of TSC that the draft standards are unclear about what would happen if these, or other provisions, were to contradict national laws – as they would in Ontario, Canada, where farm workers are banned from forming unions and where many farm workers are seasonal workers brought from other countries to work in conditions considerably less than 'free'.[6]

So far, this chapter has discussed labour standards to illustrate how transnational certification agents claim rule-making authority in certification spaces. In the case of shrimp farming, the ACC and ASC claim rule-making authority in the farm's territory for a series of other management practices as well, including the siting of the farm (not in mangroves), pollution control and disease management. They also have standards with respect to what kinds of feed are permissible, given the controversies around the fishmeal and fish oils that go into shrimp feed. The ACC requires that farmers obtain their feed from suppliers providing reliable information on the protein, fishmeal and fish oil content in the feed, but does not make shrimp farmers responsible for sustainability and working conditions in the fisheries that supply feed mills. In contrast, the ASC requires that fishery products in shrimp feed be traceable and certified by certification bodies that meet specific criteria with respect to accreditation or membership of international associations.

The second kind of certification territory produced by these standards extends the target zone for regulation to areas outside of the farm itself. ACC standards are limited in the extent to which they expect farmers to manage land outside the space of the farm, requiring only that farmers restore or contribute to restoring three times the area of any wetlands (mangroves) lost in the area of the farm since 1999, that the restored area be properly maintained and that the hydrological conditions around the farm not be disturbed. The ASC goes much further, setting out a series of provisions concerning the ecological relationship between the farm and the surrounding biophysical environment, including the protection of endangered species as defined by the International Union for Conservation of Nature and Natural Resources (IUCN), and the maintenance of 'undisturbed vegetation' on 'buffer zones' that are supposed to separate shrimp farms from aquatic or marine environments and waterways.

Justifications

During the colonial period, Europe, the United States and Japan justified extraterritorial protection for their subjects through their depiction of Siamese (and Chinese, etc.) laws as not modern – that is, as personal, arbitrary, irrational or barbaric. For example, Loos (2006: 101–102) argues that Siam's sovereignty was very much a gender and legal issue, in that extraterritorial provisions were eliminated only after adopting modern family law, including a requirement that marriage should be monogamous. In a broader context, Kayaoglu (2010: 7–8, 43) emphasises that imperialist extraterritoriality has to be understood broadly as based not only in material power, but also in ideas about civilisation, Christianity and morality. He notes how extraterritoriality was not imposed on weaker European or Latin American states, while even small European states acquired extraterritorial rights in major Asian states. With the exception of Japan, no Asian or African state obtained extraterritorial powers in other states.

Today, proponents similarly justify certification as a means for advancing more humane and enlightened eco-governance. Non-governmental action is depicted as necessary because government laws and regulations for protecting ecologies and vulnerable people are inadequate, poorly enforced, corrupt, and so on. There are differences: colonial-era extraterritoriality positioned arbitrary state authority as the threat to the subjects of imperialist states, whereas sustainability certification poses the externalities associated with self-interested entrepreneurship as the threat. Inadequate state regulation is repositioned as neglect, or a failed solution to these problems. The argument regarding the ineffective state is included in the various rationales in the ASC standards, which state that government regulations are often inadequate, as noted above. Although this argument applies to all states in principle, southern and Asian states are depicted as particularly inadequate.

During the colonial era, extraterritoriality was intended to protect vulnerable national subjects of imperial states, as well as their properties, from the authority of less-civilised Asian or African states. Kayaoglu (2010: 31) shows how Orientalist images of Asia as despotic, stagnant and so on helped to provide the rationale for legal extraterritoriality in Asia. More specifically, he labels as 'legal Orientalism' the claims of Western jurists and politicians that Western legal systems were ethically and intellectually superior to Asian systems – claims that helped to justify the removal or replacement of non-Western judicial systems.

Today, TSC similarly aims to protect vulnerable subjects located in the territorial jurisdiction of Asian states. The new subjects in need of protection are coastal ecologies, workers, children, affected communities, or IUCN-identified endangered species – subjects that proponents consider to be of concern to a 'global' community. Central to the justification for TSC is idea that it is the obligation of North-based agents, such as the ASC, the ACC, NGOs (especially the WWF), supermarket chains, restaurants and consumers, to protect these subjects. Media depictions of the problems associated with industrial production of shrimp and other aquaculture species in Asia continue to invoke Orientalist narratives about unethical or 'shocking' practices in developing countries that, for example, have 'less stringent or poorly enforced labour laws' (Food and Water Europe, 2011: 7).[7] The American catfish industry, for example, has portrayed pangasius produced in Vietnam as 'smooth talking', 'slippery' 'Asian imposters' of real American catfish (Mansfield, 2003: 332).[8] In parallel to past justification for legal extraterritoriality in Asia, these depictions invoke strong images associating these practices with a deficit of morality and civilisation. They are intended to produce a certain kind of ethical consumerism:

consumers are being urged to buy only those commodities that can be reliably certified as untainted by these practices or, more importantly, urged to buy from branded retailers who have committed to buying only sustainably produced and ethical seafood.

We are not trying to suggest that there are not serious environmental and social problems associated with aquaculture (or fishing) in Asia; rather, the point is how these problems are linked in popular depictions in Europe and North America to Orientalist images of Asia, and how transnational certification is portrayed as a way of assuring consumers in Europe and North America that they can consume Asian-produced seafood without guilt and fear. Vulnerable subjects located in Asia are in fact not the only actors that are protected through sustainability certification; certification also protects North-based supermarkets and restaurant chains from brand devaluation through scandals associated with their suppliers, and consumers from both the possible guilt of supporting unsustainable shrimp farming and the potential health consequences of the chemicals used in industrial shrimp farming.

A final useful comparison concerns the way in which rule-making authority is ultimately enforced. Extraterritoriality was famously imposed on many Asian states through gunboat diplomacy. As Cashore (2002) points out, in the long run a successful TSC system must rely on broad-based acceptance by participating actors, not on coercion. But in the short run, what replaces violence as the key coercive mechanism is market access. In both Vietnam and Thailand, shrimp sold into domestic markets obtain a significantly lower prices than shrimp sold to processors for export. The proponents of TSC aim to make access to these markets conditional on certification – that is, following rules put in place by transnational standards for shrimp farming, in addition to compliance with state regulations. States are responding to this apparent encroachment on their jurisdictions in diverse ways, as illustrated next in the context of Thailand and Vietnam.

State response in Thailand and Vietnam

Different state agencies in Asia have responded to TSC initiatives in distinct ways. In some cases, these differences can be explained by the organisational interests of the specific agency concerned, but other differences – especially national-level differences – can be attributed to national political cultures and distinct approaches to national economic development.

In Thailand, interviews conducted by the author and collaborators[9] over several decades have consistently shown that the Department of Fisheries regards TSC for aquaculture with great suspicion, if not outright hostility. Above all, fisheries officials thought that it was properly the role of the Thai government to deal with environmental and social problems in Thailand, not what they labelled 'foreign' organisations promoting certification. They articulated their arguments primarily in terms of nationalism and sovereignty. Typical comments included 'Thailand is our home', and 'We cannot let anyone do things in our home without our knowledge and permission'. Officials also talked about ACC and other transnational standards as a way in which rich countries could control and take advantage of developing countries, and stated that their role was to 'protect Thailand' (personal interview, 21 January 2009). Finally, along with many shrimp farmers, state officials were of the opinion that 'foreign' certification constituted a hidden trade barrier and could be an indirect way for importers to favour certain countries over Thailand. Overall, there was a lot of suspicion around the possible motives driving transnational certification.

The Department of Fisheries was not opposed to internationalisation of standards for shrimp farming, but it argued that internationalisation needs to work through inter-state cooperation, rather than through North-based private institutions. Thus its key criticism of the certification system run by the ACC, and of the WWF's standard-setting process for creating the ASC's Shrimp Standards, is that they were not the result of this kind of international cooperation. It specifically argued that the FAO is the appropriate agency for creating international standards, because member governments can participate in the standards-setting process.

The Thai Department of Fisheries has done much more than simply criticise and reassert its own mandate to regulate shrimp farming; it has also completely reoriented how it regulates shrimp farming, replacing top-down regulations regarding pollution and other practices with a state-run certification scheme. It has further revamped state-run certification so that it can argue that certification is consistent with international standards not only for shrimp farming, but also in terms of how to organise a third-party certification system. The Thai Department has done this by participating in, and then adhering to, FAO standards for both aquaculture and aquaculture certification. The Thai Department of Fisheries has been active in both of these FAO processes, including acting as the host for a session on developing standards for credible aquaculture certification held in Phuket during 2010. The FAO's Code of Conduct for Responsible Fisheries, which encompasses aquaculture, identifies 'states' as responsible for regulating aquaculture, in contrast to both the ACC and the ASC. The FAO guidelines for aquaculture certification additionally begin with the requirement that aquaculture certification schemes must recognise the sovereign rights of states, and must comply with all relevant local, national and international laws and regulations.

The Department of Fisheries has created several government-run sustainability certification systems. The most important has been the Good Aquaculture Practices (GAP) certification, launched in 2002. In its initial form, the GAP certified mainly for chemical residues and traceability, with inspections performed by fisheries officials. By around 2005, the Department had succeeded in making this certification mandatory and universal for all farmers seeking to sell their shrimp to processors for export. In 2009, it launched a new GAP that added environmental and social criteria similar to the ACC standards. Implementation was also restructured so that that the Department could claim it adhered to International Organization for Standardization (ISO) and FAO guidelines for 'third-party' certification, including a turn towards inspections being undertaken not by government officials, but by accredited third-party 'certifying' bodies. The new GAP standards were developed by a separate government body, the Bureau of Agricultural Commodity and Food Standards (ACFS), in accordance with international guidelines requiring that standard development be done by a body separate from the standards-holding body. The ACFS has been aggressive more broadly in creating standards for agricultural certification schemes run by other government departments, in part to compete with transnational certification. It has also issued standards for organic agriculture and Good Agriculture Practices. Along with the Department of Fisheries, the goal is to have importers recognise these various standards and certification processes as equivalent to transnational certification. The work of the ACFS is indicative of a broader response in Thailand to TSC, which is to see it as an encroachment to sovereignty and to respond with competing state-run certification. Thus the most important impact of transnational certification in Thailand may be not the creation of sustainability in delimited certification territories, but the reorientation of state regulation into certification systems.

In contrast to Thailand, some Asian governments are collaborating with TSC. An example is the organic shrimp farming project in Ca Mau province in Vietnam, which has drawn considerable attention from both activists and academics (for example Ha et al., 2012; Omoto, 2012). The project initially used Naturland[10] organic standards, while recently the Netherlands Development Organisation (SNV) and IUCN have taken over this project with a goal of creating an 'organic coast' (*Vietnam News*, 2014). In a separate project in the area, the transnational consultancy company Blueyou has created a branded shrimp product (Selva Shrimp) in which shrimp farmer groups are assessed against the new ASC standards.[11]

The initial impetus for the certification came from the way in which the shrimp farms were located in a mangrove area under the jurisdiction of a state-owned forestry company (Omoto, 2012: 63). After the war ended in the mid-1970s, the government settled people into this area and the settlers later took up extensive shrimp aquaculture (Omoto, 2012: 65) that involved maintaining about 50 per cent mangrove cover amidst the farms. For the state forestry company, organic certification provided an indirect means for monitoring farmer's land use and halting further reduction of the mangrove area, as the key standard was a requirement that mangrove cover be maintained or restored to 50 per cent of each farm's total area. The organic certification involved close collaboration with state agencies, as well as European-based NGOs and private companies, for which it was means for reinforcing state territorial control and strengthening the jurisdiction of the state forestry company.

The Vietnamese government has supported TSC in various sectors, including aquaculture and fisheries. For example, it is the site of the first MSC-certified fishery in Asia, the Ben Tre clam fishery, and Vietnam was touted by proponents of sustainability certification as the first nation-state to use MSC certification to regulate fishing.[12] The government supports transnational organic and other sustainability certification schemes as a way of facilitating agrofood exports (Ha and Bush, 2010; Anh et al., 2011), and to enhance its ability to regulate farmers, albeit indirectly through private agencies. But even in Vietnam interviews and observations at seafood industry events suggest that cooperation with TSC as way of facilitating access to export markets does not necessarily indicate that officials always view TSC positively. The Vietnamese government, like the Thai government, has also created national state-run certification and best management practices (BMP) programmes based on the FAO standards (Anh et al., 2011). Ha and Bush (2010: 1109) report that some government staff even opposed the Naturland organic shrimp certification programme because they saw this private standard as diminishing the government's sovereign control over the industry.

Conclusions

This chapter has focused on aquaculture certification in general and the certification of shrimp farming in particular. There are significant differences in how various transnational sustainability schemes (the ASC, FSC, MSC, organic, the Roundtable on Sustainable Palm Oil, etc.) regimes are organised (Gale and Howard, 2004; Eden and Bear, 2010) and in how they remake state sovereignty. For example, unlike the ASC, the MSC accepts government units as clients, and its emphasis on certifying management systems means that it can have the effect of endorsing and reinforcing state management while at the same time inducing a reorganisation of these management practices to conform to MSC requirements. There are also important differences in how governments have engaged these distinct regimes, both in Asia and more broadly. For example, some governments are more or less turning over the determination of what constitutes sustainable fisheries management to the MSC,[13] while other governments (such as Iceland and Sweden) are developing national sustainability certification schemes as a counter to the MSC (Foley, 2013), much like the Thai government.

During discussions with proponents of certification for aquaculture, I have often raised the question of working more with local and national government agencies to implement sustainability certification or to regulate the aquaculture sector more broadly – more like the MSC, or even the FSC, for example. A common response is that the turn towards transnational eco-certification was motivated by the inability or unwillingness of governments to regulate shrimp farming properly in the first place and that there is little to be gained from working directly with governments. We might note that while this account might be reasonably accurate for forestry and the FSC (Cashore et al., 2006a, 2006b), it is contradicted in the case of shrimp farming by the history outlined in this chapter, whereby sustainability certification initially emerged out of industry attempts to stave off increased state regulation.

Many academic authors also describe TSC as emerging as a response to insufficient state regulation. For example, the political science literature cites neoliberalism or globalisation (Auld et al., 2009: 189) as reducing the state's ability to regulate effectively. This literature is primarily on the global North (Cashore et al., 2006b: 18–19), with some exceptions, especially in relation to the FSC (Cashore et al., 2006b). Popular, NGO and academic portrayals of state agencies located in Asia or the global South however, additionally invoke corruption, lack of state capacity, the prioritising of economic growth and Orientalist images implying that Asians are not sufficiently civilised with respect to protecting workers, animals and ecologies. With respect to international FAO standards, TSC proponents point out that government resource agencies (fisheries, forestry, mining, etc.) and related intergovernmental agencies such as the FAO are oriented towards promoting and defending the industries that they are supposed to regulate.

It is indicative that TSC in the South is largely for products exported to Europe and North America. The geographical locations of the main proponents of TSC and the orientation towards global North markets has led many government agencies and Asian participants in the industry to understand TSC as an attempt by powerful Northern actors to push aside Southern governments, to create trade barriers and use market access to force compliance with Northern moralities. These views are held not only for aquaculture certification, but also for the certification of other crops in other parts of Asia where TSC is increasingly a condition of access to high-value markets in the North.[14]

In contrast to both the proponents and opponents of TSC for shrimp aquaculture, the aim in this chapter was not to assess whether either TSC or government regulation is adequate or not; rather, it has shown how TSC is, in effect, a claim to have the authority to make rules that overlap with, supplement or even contradict state authority in ways that invoke and parallel legal extraterritoriality. The narratives that position Asian states as lacking effectiveness or basic morality reinforces a common view in Asian countries that TSC is an attempt by rich countries to tell poorer countries what to do with respect to the environmental and social aspects of farming and resource extraction.

This chapter has been an attempt to explain these critical perspectives by highlighting how TSC and its narratives have much in common with the colonial-era extraterritorial empires described by Kayaoglu (2010). Much like the extraterritorial empire, the sustainability certification empire does not aim to displace state rule through direct colonisation; instead, it acknowledges the existing legal system, and then goes on to create certification territories where certification agencies claim rule-making and rule-enforcement authority in ways that pre-empt government authority. It has also shown how there are parallels in how sustainability certification seeks to protect valued subjects and in how TSC is justified through a narrative of deficient states. What has changed is that it is no longer the subjects of Western countries that are protected, but endangered non-human species, local communities, workers, women and children. The source of the threat has also shifted: in sustainability certification, it is unregulated industrial shrimp farmers who are presumed to act in their individual economic interests at the expense of ecologies, communities and workers. Finally, the new extraterritoriality is partial: it does not challenge the legality of state regulation of shrimp farming, while at the same time claiming the right to assess whether farms follow state regulations and to add more regulations.

In Thailand, the government response to this perceived encroachment on state sovereignty has been to create certification schemes run by government agencies and to seek recognition for these schemes from intergovernmental agencies, while arguing that transnational certification is a trade barrier. A strongly nationalist political culture tied up with the Thai geo-body (Winichakul, 1997) helps to explain why the Thai government has taken the lead among Asian states in the fight to counter TSC in aquaculture. Vietnam's government has responded in ways that are distinct: the government is less concerned with protecting agency mandates and state sovereignty, and more willing to cooperate so as to facilitate exports in the service of rapid economic growth, as well as, in some cases, enhancing state capacity to control farmer practices.

The final argument that can be offered is that the creation of certification territories will, by themselves, not have a major impact on the problems associated with industrial aquaculture or fisheries. At most, this approach will create 'sustainability enclaves' (Whitington, 2012), monitored by primarily private agencies, producing primarily for export to North America and Europe. These enclaves might be successful in building brand value among buying corporations and in assuring Northern consumers that they can safely consume Asian-produced seafood that is not implicated in unsustainable and unjust production practices. Transnational certification might also protect North-based supermarkets and restaurant chains from brand devaluation through scandals associated with their suppliers, and protect consumers from both the possible guilt of supporting unsustainable shrimp farming and the potential health consequences of the chemicals used in industrial shrimp farming. But the direct impact on ecologies and social justice will be limited, at least in the near future, in that the demand for certification has so far been confined to Northern markets, which excludes the larger and more rapidly growing Asian markets, and by the narrow take on sustainability, in that the use of the farm as the unit of certification excludes many cumulative or broader-scale impacts (Bush et al., 2013). If these schemes have any broader impact, it will be through the way in which they can leverage governments to regulate the entire sector more effectively. Overall, actions to address unsustainability and injustice might be more effective if they were to directly engage both relevant state agencies and the social movements in Asia who are challenging injustice and unsustainability in these sectors.

Notes

1 Certification by independent accredited certifying bodies. According to international standards for certification, the standards-holding body should also be independent from the entities (certifying bodies) doing the inspections and assessments.
2 The members of the International Social and Environmental Accreditation and Labeling (ISEAL) Alliance, an association of standards organisations, give an indication of the sorts of products and activities that are currently covered. See online at http://www.isealalliance.org/our-members/full-members [accessed 21 July 2016].
3 See Asia Solidarity against Industrial Aquaculture (2012).
4 For more on which, see Anh et al. (2011); Vandergeest (2007).
5 Available online at http://www.asc-aqua.org/upload/ASC%20Shrimp%20Standard_v1.0.pdf [accessed 21 July 2016].
6 Under the Canadian Agricultural Employees Protection Act, 2002 (AEPA). See Ontario Ministry of Agriculture, Food and Rural Affairs (2003).
7 For example, the WWF film *Pangasius Lie*, shown on German television in March 2011 (generating considerable criticism for its portrayal of the Vietnamese industry), and the Solidarity Center's (2008) film about Burmese workers in the shrimp industry in Thailand.
8 See also Little et al. (2012) for similar portrayals in Europe.
9 Primarily Anusorn Unno, who conducted interviews with Department of Fisheries officials, as well as shrimp farmers, nearby residents, processors and staff at certifying bodies. These interviews were conducted during 2008 and 2009. In addition, the author of this paper has discussed shrimp farm regulation with government officials over the past twenty years, including, most recently, during a workshop on aquaculture certification in 2012. See also NACA (2001–16).
10 Naturland is the main German organic standards body.
11 See Blueyou (undated).
12 According to WWF (2009).
13 See, e.g., Foley (2013) on Canada.
14 See e.g., Neilson and Prichard (2009) on tea in India.

References

Anh: T., Bush, S. R., Mol, A. P. J., and Kroozo, C. (2011) 'The Multi-level Environmental Governance of Vietnamese Aquaculture: Global Certification, National Standards, Local Cooperatives', *Journal of Environmental Policy & Planning*, 13(4): 373–397.

Asia Solidarity against Industrial Aquaculture (2012) 'Open Letter to the GSC of the WWF Shrimp Aquaculture Dialogue, 4 May 2011', 21 February, available online at http://asiasolidarity.org/2012/02/worldwide-opposition-to-wwfs-shrimp-standards/ [accessed 27 July 2016].

Auld, G., Balboa, C., Bernstein, S., and Cashore, B. (2009) 'The Emergence of Non-state Market-driven (NSMD) Global Environmental Governance: A Cross-sectoral Assessment', in M. A. Delmas and O. R. Young (eds) *Governance for the Environment*, Cambridge: Cambridge University Press, 183–215.

Belton, B. and Bush, S. R. (2014) 'Beyond Net Deficits: New Priorities for an Aquacultural Geography', *The Geographical Journal*, 180(1): 3–14.

Bene, C. (2005) 'The Good, the Bad, and the Ugly: Discourse, Policy Controversies and the Role of Science in the Politics of Shrimp Farming Development', *Development Policy Review*, 23(5): 585–614.

Blueyou (undated) 'Selva Shrimp', available online at http://www.blueyou.com/page/Programmes/Selva_Shrimp [accessed 21 July 2016].

Bush, S., Belton, B., Hall, D., Vandergeest, P., Murray, F. J., Ponte F. J., Oosterveer, P., Islam, M. S., Mol, A. P., and Hatanaka, M. (2013) 'Certify Sustainable Aquaculture?', *Science*, 341(6150): 1067–1068.

Cashore, B. (2002) 'Legitimacy and the Privatization of Environmental Governance: How Non-state Market-driven (NSMD) Governance Systems Gain Rule-making Authority', *Goverance*, 15(4): 503–529.

Cashore, B., Gale, F., Meidinger, E., and Newsom, D. (2006a) *Confronting Sustainability: Forest Certification in Developing and Transitioning Countries*, New Haven, CT: Yale School of Forestry and Environmental Studies.

Cashore, B., Gale, F., Meidinger, E., and Newsom, D. (2006b) 'Introduction: Forest Certification in Analytical and Historical Perspective', in *Confronting Sustainability: Forest Certification in Developing and Transitioning Countries*, New Haven, CT: Yale School of Forestry and Environmental Studies, 7–24.

Eden. S., and Bear, C. (2010) 'Third-sector Global Environmental Governance, Space, and Science: Comparing Fishery and Forestry Certification', *Journal of Environmental Policy & Planning*, 12(1): 83–106.

Environmental Justice Foundation (EJF) (2013) *The Hidden Cost: Human Rights Abuses in Thailand's Shrimp Industry*, London: EJF.

Foley, P. (2013) 'National Government Responses to Marine Stewardship Council (MSC) Fisheries Certification: Insights from Atlantic Canada', *New Political Economy*, 18(2): 284–307.

Food and Water Europe (2011) *De-coding Seafood Eco-labels: How the European Commission Can Help Consumers Access Sustainable Seafood*, available online at http://documents.foodandwater europe.org/doc/EUecoLabels-web.pdf [accessed 6 May 2011].

Gale, F., and Howard, M. (2004) 'Public Accountability in Private Regulation: Contrasting Models of the Forest Stewardship Council (FSC) and Marine Stewardship Council (MSC)', Paper presented at the Australasian Political Studies Association Conference, University of Adelaide, 29 September–1 October.

Gulbrandsen, L. H. (2005) 'Explaining Different Approaches to Voluntary Standards: A Study of Forest Certification Choices in Norway and Sweden', *Journal of Environmental Policy and Planning*, 7(1): 43–59.

Ha, T. T. T., and Bush, S. R. (2010) 'Transformations of Vietnamese Shrimp Aquaculture Policy: Empirical Evidence from the Mekong Delta', *Environment and Planning C: Government and Policy*, 28(6): 1102–1119.

Ha, T. T. T., Bush, S. R., Mol, A. P. J., and van Dijk, H. (2012) 'Organic Coasts? Regulatory Challenges of Certifying Integrated Shrimp–Mangrove Production Systems in Vietnam', *Journal of Rural Studies*, 28(4): 631–639.

Hodal, K., Kelly, C., and Lawrence, F. (2014) 'Revealed: Asian Slave Labour Producing Prawns for Supermarkets in US, UK', *The Guardian*, 10 June, available online at https://www.theguardian.com/global-development/2014/jun/10/supermarket-prawns-thailand-produced-slave-labour [accessed 21 July 2016].

Islam, M. S. (2008). 'From Sea to Shrimp Processing Factories in Bangladesh: Gender and Employment at the Bottom of a Global Commodity Chain', *Journal of South Asian Development*, 3(2): 211–236.

Kayaoglu, T. (2010) *Legal Imperialism: Sovereignty and Extraterritoriality in Japan, the Ottoman Empire, and China*, Cambridge: Cambridge University Press.

Larsson, T. (2007) 'Intertextual Relations: The Geopolitics of Land Rights in Thailand', *Political Geography*, 26(7): 775–803.

Lee, D., and Connelly, J. (2006) 'Global Aquaculture Alliance on Best Aquaculture Practices: An Industry Prepares for Sustainable Growth', *Sustainable Development Law & Policy*, 7(1): 60–62.

Little, D., Bush, S. R., Bolton, B., Phuong, N. T., Young, J. A., and Murray, F. (2012) 'Whitefish Wars: Pangasius, Politics and Consumer Confusion in Europe', *Marine Policy*, 36(3):738–745.

Loos, T. (2006) *Subject Siam: Family, Law, and Colonial Modernity in Thailand*, Ithaca, NY: Cornell University Press.

Mansfield, B. (2003) 'From Catfish to Organic Fish: Making Distinctions about Nature as Cultural Economic Practice', *Geoforum*, 34(3): 329–342.

Neilson, J., and Prichard, B. (2009) *Value Chain Struggles: Institutions and Governance in the Plantations Districts of South India*, Chichester: Wiley-Blackwell.

Network of Aquaculture Centres in Asia-Pacific (NACA) (2001–16) 'Aquaculture Certification, available online at http://www.enaca.org/modules/certification [accessed 15 July 2014].

Omoto, R. (2012) 'Small-scale Producers and the Governance of Certified Organic Seafood Production in Vietnam's Mekong Delta', Unpublished PhD dissertation, Department of Geography, University of Waterloo, Waterloo, ON.

Ong, A. (2006) *Neoliberalism as Exception: Mutations in Citizenship and Sovereignty*, Durham NC: Duke University Press.

Ontario Ministry of Agriculture, Food and Rural Affairs (2003) *Factsheet: Agricultural Employees Protection Act, 2002*, available online at http://www.omafra.gov.on.ca/english/busdev/facts/03-045.htm [accessed 21 July 2016].

Resurreccion, B. P., and Sajor, E. E. (2010) '"Not a Real Worker": Gendering Migrants in Thailand's Shrimp Farms', *International Migration*, 48(6): 102–131.

Sassen, S. (1996) *Losing Control? Sovereignty in an Age of Globalisation*, New York: Columbia University Press.

Slaughter, A. M. (2004) 'Disaggregated Sovereignty: Towards the Public Accountability of Global Government Networks', *Government and Opposition*, 39(2): 159–190.

Solidarity Center (2008) *The True Cost of Shrimp: How Shrimp Industry Workers in Bangladesh and Thailand Pay the Price for Affordable Shrimp*, available online at http://www.solidaritycenter.org/wp-content/uploads/2014/12/pubs_True_Cost_of_Shrimp.pdf [accessed 9 May 2011].

Vandergeest, P. (2007) 'Certification and communities: Alternatives for regulating the environmental and social impacts of shrimp farming'. *World Development*, 35(7): 1152–1171.

Vietnam News (2014) 'Shrimp Project Helps to Create "Organic Coast"', 12 January, available online at http://vietnamnews.vn/sunday/features/250091/shrimp-project-helps-create-organic-coast.html#1hCEekRxdzIw0drp.97 [accessed 27 July 2016].

Whitington, J. (2012) 'The Institutional Condition of Contested Hydropower: The Theun Hinboun–International Rivers Collaboration', *Forum for Development Studies*, 39(2): 231–256.

Winichakul, T. (1997) *Siam Mapped: A History of Geobody of a Nation*, Honolulu: University of Hawai'i Press.

World Wide Fund for Nature (WWF) (2009) 'Famed Clam Fishery First to Receive MSC Certification in Southeast Asia', 10 November, available online at http://wwf.panda.org/wwf_news/?180081/Famed-clam-fishery-first-to-receive-MSC-certification-in-Southeast-Asia [accessed 21 July 2016].

16 The regulation of innovation in agriculture and sustainable development in India and Southeast Asia

Rajeswari Kanniah and Christoph Antons

Legislative developments in agriculture follow innovations and technological advances. The Green Revolution, for example, introduced high-yielding hybrid technology, heralding an era of intensive monoculture farming, mechanisation, and increased use of pesticides and oil-based fertilisers. Seed quality and certification laws followed this advancement. When technology developed even further to enable genetic modification of plants, concerns over safety aspects led to the enactment of biosafety laws. In addition, the gene revolution brought about a massive shift in the paradigm of ownership over plant genetic resources. In step with these technological innovations, new forms of intellectual property rights (IPR) over plants were established, and thus was born the new concept of 'plant breeders' rights' (PBR), or 'plant variety rights' (PVR), in addition to amendments in patent laws being made to allow for property rights over plants, microorganisms and biotechnological processes. Yet another new law on geographical indications was introduced to guarantee consumers authenticity of the geographical origin and territorial attributes of agricultural products, and to protect the original producers from misappropriation and unfair competition from imitators and counterfeiters.

This chapter will review the development of these laws and their impact on farmers, breeders, consumers, biotechnology companies and seed producers, as well as researchers, in five Asian developing countries with substantial agricultural sectors consisting of both small holdings and commercial agriculture: India, Indonesia, Malaysia, the Philippines and Thailand. The impact on developing countries of recent rounds of free trade agreements (FTAs), many of which have included demands for stronger protection of IPR including in the agricultural sector, will also be covered (Antons and Thampapillai, 2015: 48–49).

The enclosure of a commons: The emergence of intellectual property and other property rights in agriculture

Technological innovations in agriculture in Europe and the United States in the nineteenth and twentieth centuries contributed to the creation of a new regime of control over seeds. The work of Gregor Mendel, who 'discovered' the laws of heredity,[1] published in an obscure journal in 1866, was 'rediscovered' in 1900 by K. E. Correns in Germany, E. Von Tschermak in Austria and Hugo de Vries in the Netherlands, all at the same time (Heitz, 1987: 62; Aoki, 2008: 16). The agricultural boom was beginning in Europe, with mechanical equipment and chemical fertilisers being introduced in agriculture. There began a reliance on specialised farmers for seed supplies, which led to seed-breeding programmes and the evolution of the seed trade, and an associated plant breeding industry with a strictly commercial bent. Breeders associations were set up,[2] national research institutes established,[3] seed testing systems introduced and seed registration laws[4] enacted.

Similar specialisation was taking place in the United States. The American Seed Trade Association (ASTA) was first convened in 1883 with a membership of thirty-five companies (Aoki, 2008: 15). The seed industry began as an informal, 'over the fence' local business created by farmers. It eventually grew into a specialised business – growing, collecting and bagging seed became yet another service provided for farmers, just as was selling grain and feed. By the 1930s, hybrid corn[5] had been developed in the United States and the commercial seed industry took off. Doyle (1985: 33–35) regards hybrid corn as the single most important development in the creation of the American seed industry. While there were some forty or fifty seed companies operating in the United States prior to the arrival of hybrid corn, there were nearly 300 new seed companies forty years later, most of them in the business of selling hybrid corn (Doyle, 1985: 33–35). At the same time, seed certification programmes were beginning to be established in the various states.

Plant breeders began to build their own private collections of exotic species in seed banks and botanic gardens. Until the early 1900s, breeders' practices were still relatively friendly vis-à-vis competitors. Sample-sized bags of seeds were sent, usually free of charge, to many competitors on request, without restriction on use (Smolders, 2005: 5). The creation of the hybrids[6] brought about a significant change. Open pollinated plants[7] and asexually reproducing plants[8] are capable of being easily multiplied. Breeders therefore could not engage in repeat sales: farmers could use the seeds of their produce and competing breeders could use the seeds for development of other varieties. This is not the case with hybrids, which come with built-in security for their breeders and rights owners: their progeny do not produce the same yield as the parent; the farmer therefore has to purchase seeds for every new planting season. Kloppenburg (2014: 1227) describes this as the technical way of achieving commodification of seeds, as opposed to the legal path, which focuses on intellectual property, contract law and seed regulation.

Parental lines of the newly created hybrids became trade secrets, closely guarded by their breeders. Plant breeders pushed for IPR protection of their seeds, but still kept the door open for free exchange of breeding material amongst themselves, because they knew that their livelihoods depended upon continuous innovation in existing species of plant varieties. Hence the PBR system was created as the model to protect the interests of classical breeders, since it allowed breeding material from protected seeds to be freely available for further breeding, without prior approval having to be obtained from the rights owner/breeder (Kloppenburg, 2014: 1228).

Unlike the large-scale, mechanised farming practices in the United States and Europe, farming in Asian developing countries is dominated by a large number of small, fragmented subsistence farm holdings. The formal seed sector is still dominated by government agencies, publicly funded universities and research institutions, while the private seed industry focuses on a small number of commercially viable crops and animal feed sectors. Farmers in the informal seed sector remain the largest producers of seeds. The United Nations Food and Agriculture Organization (FAO) estimated in 2004 that, for the Asia Pacific region, community-based seed systems account for 80–90 per cent of total seed consumed (FAO, 2004). In most developing countries in Asia, the informal seed system (farm-saved seeds, seed exchanges between farming communities, village markets) remains the predominant source of seed supply.

In developing countries, the Green Revolution arose in the 1960s amidst growing concerns about food security and declining farm productivity (Aoki, 2008: 23).

High-yielding hybrid varieties of corn from the United States, and rice developed by national and international breeding centres, were freely distributed to farmers to raise their productivity. Seed quality and certification laws came much later in the developing countries of Asia.[9] These laws were introduced to protect farmers as the consumers of seeds and to enable them to claim compensation from losses sustained from spurious seeds or seeds that did not produce the yields claimed on their labels. In most countries of Asia, seed quality and certification laws were initially applied only to seeds in the formal sector, while farm-saved seeds were exempted.

The advance of biotechnology – the gene revolution – brought another wave of change. With rDNA technology enabling the movement of genes across species barriers, new concerns about the biosafety of the laboratory-created plants and organisms surfaced. Thus began a highly polarised debate about the safety of genetically modified (GM) plants for human and animal consumption. To address these concerns, new international laws controlling the transboundary movement of GM organisms (GMOs) were adopted, and national laws relating to biosafety issues for growing and consuming GM foods were passed.

With the widespread usage of GM technology in plants, gaining proprietary rights over parts of plants became the norm. Seeds, genes, gene fragments, tissues, cells, cell lines – in fact, every microscopic piece of the seed and the biotechnological processes to enable these gene transfers – became capable of protection, and therefore the private property of the persons who first succeeded in isolating and identifying their uses. The biotech companies that invested billions in research and development to produce new varieties of GM seeds became the new seed barons. Competition and the race to bring to the market the latest new varieties of seeds set in. Investment had to be protected and hence breeding material was no longer to be shared. The biotech companies sought an increased and more stringent form of IPR protection – that is, patents – for their GM seeds, stretching the argument that their seeds fulfilled the same patent criteria as industrial inventions (Kloppenburg, 2014: 1228–1229).

Before long, IPR for plants became available. Depending on the law of the country and the type of plant material that was to be protected, the IPR protection ranged from the most stringent (in terms of criteria for protection, as well as the rights accorded to the owners) – that is, the patent system – to the less stringent – that is, the PVP system (Leskien and Flitner, 1997; Helfer, 2002). In the United States, the Plant Variety Protection Act of 1970 has offered patent protection to asexually reproduced plants since 1930 and utility patent protection for living organisms altered by human intervention became available after the Supreme Court's landmark decision in 1980, in the case *Diamond v. Chakrabarty*[10] (Aoki, 2008: 4; van Overwalle, 1999). Patents are used to protect not only plants and plant varieties, but also parts of plants, such as tissues, cells, genes, microbiological processes and microorganisms (Correa, 2012: 5–6). They accord the owners monopoly rights over their inventions for a fixed duration, usually between twenty and twenty-five years. Misappropriation of another's seed or any part of the seed is subject to litigation and a claim for damages. Researchers and other breeders have to pay licence fees to access breeding material from the patent owners. Exemptions from such requirements have been used in many countries, but, as will be explained further below, their reach under the World Trade Organization (WTO) Agreement on Trade-related Aspects of Intellectual Property Rights (TRIPS Agreement) is disputed (Correa, 2005: 31, 34–66). The biotech companies have preferred the patent route, because it accords them greater protection and a better guarantee of recouping returns on their huge investments in research and development. Plant patents are used to protect asexually propagated plants, and sui generis[11] PVP certificates have been used to protect both asexually and sexually reproducing plant varieties. The PVP system has been favoured by classical breeders, because it provides for exceptions to breeders' rights, granting breeders access to the protected varieties for further breeding without having to obtain consent and pay royalties. Depending on the law of the country, more than one, or even all, of the different forms of IPR may be available with regard to the same plants (Kanniah, 2011).

The concepts of IPR on plants in international laws have their origins in, and evolved from, the laws of the United States[12] and the European Union.[13] These countries/federal union of states and their multinational seed industries then heavily influenced the introduction and development of IPR on plants in international laws – the International Convention for the Protection of New Varieties of Plants 1961 (the UPOV[14] Convention), revised in 1972, 1978 and 1991, and the WTO's 1995 TRIPS Agreement. These international conventions provided for the expansion of the rights of the commercial plant breeders and biotechnologists, and placed limitations on the rights of farmers and researchers. Such protections were subsequently subsumed in the national laws of developing countries that became members of the WTO. Prior to TRIPS, developing countries in Asia did not have any IPR laws relating to plants (Kanniah, 2011).

The concept of private property rights over plants underpins the UPOV Convention and TRIPS. Two other international conventions relating to plants are the Convention on Biological Diversity (CBD), adopted in 1992, and the FAO International Undertaking on Plant Genetic Resources, later reconstituted as the International Treaty on Plant Genetic Resources for Food and Agriculture (ITPGRFA), adopted in 2001 (OECD, 2012). By contrast, instead of private ownership, the CBD calls for the recognition of national sovereignty over plant genetic resources (PGRs), while the ITPGRFA facilitates multilateral access and benefit sharing of PGRs between countries.

Seed quality laws

With the exception of India, organised seed systems in developing countries were a post-Green Revolution phenomenon. With development assistance from the World Bank, FAO and US Agency for International Development (USAID), India and countries in Southeast Asia began to establish formal seed systems that linked research and breeding activities to seed production, and multiplication, marketing and distribution to farmers. In all five countries, the public sector continues to play a centralised role in producing breeder and foundation seeds for distribution to farmers for low-value, high-volume crops such as rice, wheat, vegetables and fruits, while the private sector deals in high-value, low-volume crops, and especially technology-embedded crops such as hybrid maize and GM cotton.

Once seed systems became more established, laws were introduced to ensure that only 'registered' seeds were legally available for sale in the market. These laws were not only intended to protect farmers, but also to provide incentives for the development of the private seed breeding and marketing industry (Kloppenburg, 2014: 1232). The preamble of Indonesia's Law No. 12 of 1992 on the Plant Cultivation System, for example, speaks of 'developed, efficient and strong agriculture' and its role in achieving the aim of national development. Among the five countries surveyed here, India had an early start in enacting the Seed Act 1966. Then came Thailand, with its Plant Act of 1992, and the Philippines Republic Act No. 7308, Seed Industry Development Act, 1992,[15] followed by Indonesia's Law No. 12 of 1992 on the Plant Cultivation System and Government

Regulation on Plant Seed Management 1995, while Malaysia is still in the process of drafting a law. Unlike in the other four countries, seed certification in Malaysia is still not legally mandatory and has been undertaken by government agencies for different crop types since the 1970s (Ginibun and Ugap, 2012).

The seed laws have focused on specified species of crops that are considered important to the food security of the country and regulate only the quality of the 'registered' plant species (in India, based on 'value for cultivation and use', or VCU, criteria, originating in the European countries). Seed certification to ensure conformity with specified standards is not always compulsory. Farmers' seeds are mostly exempted, although this is a recent development in Indonesia that required a constitutional challenge of the law and a rephrasing of key provisions of Law No. 12 of 1992 by the Constitutional Court. Such laws enable both the formal and informal seed systems to coexist, at least for the time being, and ensure the availability of commercially viable high-yielding plant varieties, as well as farmers' plant varieties.

These basic premises have recently come under pressure, however. India attempted to bring farmers' seeds within the ambit of the Seed Act 1966, ostensibly to protect farmers from poor-quality seeds (GRAIN and Sharma, 2005; Bala Ravi, 2009; Shiva, 2005). The proposed amendments contained in the Seed Bill 2004 were vehemently opposed by farmers' groups and civil society organisations, because they required all seeds for sale to conform to VCU criteria (Madhavan and Sanyal, 2006). In fact, while the Bill was concerned with compensation for farmers if commercial seeds did not perform to expected levels, it referred claimants to the Consumer Protection Act 1986 and was therefore less straightforward than similar compensation mechanisms under the Protection of Plant Varieties and Farmers' Rights Act 2001. It was further charged that such a ruling would serve the interests of the private seed industry by wiping out competition from farm-saved seeds, which are unlikely to meet VCU criteria. There were also concerns that genetic variability of plant species would be affected if VCU were required for all plant varieties and that farmers' costs of production would increase if they were forced to purchase new seeds for every planting season. Control over agriculture would shift from the farmer to the private seed industry. With so much opposition, the government referred the Seed Bill 2004 to a Parliamentary Standing Committee on Agriculture, which prepared a report in 2006. An amended Seed Bill introduced in 2008 has not been enacted at time of writing (Ranjan, 2009: 234–238).

In Indonesia, there was a string of court cases in East Java from 2005 onwards involving farmers reusing protected seeds. The case that became most widely publicised and discussed was that of a farmer named Tukirin, who was growing corn in the Regency of Nganjuk. He apparently managed to develop seeds of a lower quality in a cross-breeding process using protected seeds of the Indonesian subsidiary of a Thai multinational company, which had been given to him as part of a collaborative programme with the local government. He sold the seeds obtained from the cross-breeding process to his neighbours at a low price and without labelling them (Jhamtani and Patria, 2006). The company filed a case against Tukirin and a fellow farmer in the local district court. The court found that Tukirin had violated section 14(1) of Law No. 12/1992 on the Plant Cultivation System, which makes any seed certification required for propagating seeds under section 13(2) the prerogative of the government or of authorised individuals or legal entities. Applying the criminal provisions of the Law, the court gave Tukirin a suspended one-year jail sentence and prohibited him from planting his own corn seeds for one year. Similar cases were reported from other regencies in East Java (*Tempo*, 2005; Indonesian Human Rights Committee for Social Justice, 2013).

This string of prosecutions prompted an alliance of individual farmers with human rights and farmers' organisations from various parts of Java to challenge the constitutionality of key provisions of Law No. 12/1992 on the Plant Cultivation System in Indonesia's Constitutional Court. In 2013, the Court agreed with regards to two of the criticised provisions. Article 9 of the Law declared a monopoly right in favour of the government to search for and collect genetic resources for plant breeding; individuals or legal entities required a licence from the government for such activities (article 9(3)). The Constitutional Court decided that this provision had to be rephrased to make it plain that individual small farmers were exempted from this requirement. Similarly, article 12(1) made the circulation of varieties resulting from plant breeding or introduction from abroad dependent on prior release by the government. Again, the Court found that this provision had to be rephrased to exempt the results of plant breeding achieved at the domestic level by individual small farmers.[16] While the Constitutional Court rephrased Law No. 12 of 1992, it did not comment on the implementing of Government Regulation No. 44 of 1995 on the Plant Nursery Sector. As with such decrees in Indonesia in general, this government regulation is important for detailed implementation and it repeats much of the wording of the law to which the Constitutional Court has objected. It must therefore be assumed that this wording has to change in accordance with the main provisions of the law.

With globalisation came trade liberalisation and the opening up of domestic seed markets to foreign seed companies. Governments began to scale back public research and breeding expenditure to allow the private seed industry to enter, and they now encourage complementary, rather than competitive, work by public institutions, often out of concern not to infringe IPR (Kloppenburg, 2014: 1226, 1230–1231). A case study with hybrid maize shows that the entry of the private sector in the hybrid maize seed market has resulted in the public sector cutting back in Asia (excluding China), increased prices (in India) and increased concentration (in India, the Philippines and Thailand) (Morris, 2002; 201–207). Clearly, the seed quality laws have played a role in providing the entry point for the private sector to dominate the market in technology-embedded crops.

Biosafety laws

The legislative treatment accorded to GM seeds presents a completely different picture. In developing countries, consumers and farmers have been cautious about accepting GM foods and crops for a variety of reasons, including health concerns, cross-contamination of local plant varieties, monopoly of the technology by a few corporations that may render access to GM seeds unaffordable in the future, and sensitivity of export markets such as the European Union, Australia and Japan, which require mandatory labelling of GM foods (Gupta, Karihaloo and Khetarpal, 2008). Hence GM materials for food, feed or processing are highly regulated and addressed not only in biosafety laws, but also in other related laws, such as seed quality laws, plant quarantine laws, food safety laws, biodiversity laws, environmental laws and PVP laws. All five countries have developed national policies, established national agencies, enacted laws and issued administrative guidelines relating to biosafety in compliance with their obligations under the Cartagena Biosafety Protocol. The main GM laws are:

- *India* – Rules for the Manufacture, Use/Import/Export and Storage of Hazardous Micro Organisms/Genetically Engineered Organisms or Cells 1989 (under the provisions of the Environment (Protection) Act 1986);

- *Indonesia* – Regulation of the Government of Republic Indonesia No. 21 of 2005 on Biosafety of Genetically Engineered Products;
- *Malaysia* – Biosafety Act 2007 (Act No. 678);
- *Philippines* – Administrative Order No. 8, Series of 2002, Rules and Regulations for the Importation and Release into the Environment of Plants and Plant Products Derived from the Use of Modern Biotechnology; and
- *Thailand* – Plant Quarantine Act B.E. 2507, amended by Plant Quarantine Act (No. 2) B.E. 2542 and Plant Quarantine Act (No.3) B.E. 2551.[17]

These laws are aimed at protecting humans, animals, plants and the environment from GM materials.[18] While it has been feared that stringent regulatory frameworks may pose a disincentive to life science corporations entering the markets for biotech products in these five countries owing to the increased cost of getting approval for marketing their GM products, in some countries, such as India and the Philippines, there have been accusations that the regulatory framework has been rather lax and that GM field trials have been indiscriminately allowed without proper procedures being followed (James, 2012: 33–35).

India and the Philippines have been the early contenders in planting GM crops in the Asia-Pacific region since 2000, with India planting Bt[19] cotton and the Philippines growing Bt maize. Both countries are among the top mega-biotech crop-growing countries in the world, with India (positioned fifth among twenty-eight countries) planting 10.8 million hectares with Bt cotton and the Philippines (positioned twelfth) growing 0.8 million hectares of Bt maize in 2012 (James, 2012: 4). By 2013–14, Bt cotton had taken up 95 per cent of the total cotton-growing area in India and Bt maize covered 62 per cent of the total area planted with maize in the Philippines (Gupta, Karihaloo and Khetarpal, 2014).

While there are many case studies demonstrating the ability of GM crops to resist disease and pests, there are as many case studies pointing towards crop failures. In India, farmers' suicides have been attributed by some groups to crop failures resulting from the planting of Monsanto's Bt cotton (Shiva, 2013; Sewell, 2012), as well as to the rise of the costs of input such as seeds, fertilisers and pesticides (Lai, 2013). An Indian parliamentary select committee released a damning report criticising abuses in the regulatory system for approval of GM crops, calling for an end to all field trials of GM crops and recommending an in-depth probe into the release of Bt cotton (Parliamentary Committee on Agriculture, 2012). In the meantime, a technical expert committee set up by the Indian Supreme Court has called for an indefinite moratorium on field trials of GM crops until gaps in regulatory systems have been addressed (Chauhan, 2013; Rodrigues, 2013). In the Philippines, the Court of Appeal granted a stop order for field trials of GM aubergine (eggplant) in a case filed by Greenpeace, Filipino non-government organisation (NGO) MASIPAG and other interested individuals (Panada, 2013). According to Indonesian media reports, the biotechnology industry there is waiting for a presidential decree allowing the more widespread use of GMOs in agriculture (Wiyanto, 2014).

With the legislative instruments and administrative institutions in place, governments in all five countries began permitting the imports of GM food and animal feed, and approving GM crop field trials and the growing of a limited number of GM crops. In the Philippines, forty-four GMOs have been approved, of which forty are for direct use as food, animal feed and food processing, while four are planted as crops. Most of these are GM corn, canola, soybean, cotton, potato, sugar beet and alfalfa (Panada, 2013). Malaysia has granted approval for the import/use of GM corn, soybean, carnations and papaya,[20] while Indonesia has granted approval for field trials of herbicide-tolerant transgenic corn, cotton and soybean, as well as insect-resistant corn and cotton (Gupta et al., 2014). While Thailand has still not allowed the growing of GM crops, field trials of cotton, rice, tomato and pepper have begun (Gupta et al., 2008).

The plant variety protection laws

Plant variety protection (PVP) in much of the developing world came about as a result of the WTO TRIPS Agreement. Article 27(3)(b) of TRIPS, dubbed the 'biotechnology clause', imposes a mandatory requirement for the protection of plants, but gives options for such protection – a sui generis PVP system or patent, or a combination of both. In complying with Article 27(3)(b), all five countries chose to enact sui generis PVP laws for plant varieties and rejected the option of patenting plant varieties. Although developing countries have had considerable freedom under TRIPS on how to design a sui generis PVP system (Gervais, 2008; Aoki, 2008), in general they have not made much use of that freedom (Correa, 2012: 3). The five countries examined here all looked to the UPOV Convention, then the only sui generis system in operation, when drafting their PVP laws. The UPOV-style PVP system therefore became the preferred model, even though not many developing countries, especially from Asia, had ratified the UPOV Convention 1978 or the UPOV Convention 1991. The main attraction of the UPOV PBR model (especially the UPOV Convention 1978) is that it permits exemptions to the breeders' rights and thus, to an extent, mitigates the exclusive ownership model of the patent system. This addresses a major concern of developing countries over granting private rights over plants, since they are vital for food security.

Because the philosophical basis of the CBD and ITPGRFA fundamentally diverges from that of TRIPs, reconciling the differing and often opposing obligations was a difficult task for the five countries studied. An option would have been to ignore the CBD and ITPGRFA, since these treaties, unlike TRIPS, do not contain sanctions for non-compliance.[21] There was general acceptance in these countries that the CBD and ITPGRFA were, unlike TRIPS, more development-friendly and in the interests of developing countries. This was certainly the view of civil society groups in these five countries; in several of these, the civil society groups mounted a sustained campaign to ensure that the obligations under the CBD and the ITPGRFA were kept to the fore (Kanniah, 2011).

Although TRIPS imposes a mandatory requirement to enact IPR laws for plant varieties, as noted, it offers three choices – the patent, a sui generis system, or a combination of both – as long as the introduced system is 'effective'. With each of these choices there are also flexibilities that members can exercise. The five countries are attempting to utilise these to reconcile their national interests, the demands of their civil societies, and their differing obligations under TRIPS and the CBD and ITPGRFA. However, bilateral FTAs have begun to restrict the freedom of design offered under the WTO TRIPS Agreement by taking a narrower view on what is 'effective' and making adherence to the stricter 1991 version of UPOV mandatory (Kanniah and Antons, 2012: 3, 12–13). Critics have also questioned the complementarity of intellectual property and farmers' rights, with some dismissing farmers' rights as a rhetorical construct (Peschard, 2014: 1089–1099).

Since the adoption of TRIPS, the International Union for the Protection of New Varieties of Plants (UPOV) has been actively promoting its PBR Model Law throughout Asia.[22] Yet relatively few countries from Asia are among the seventy-two members of UPOV.[23] There are currently fourteen countries in East, Southeast and South Asia with PVP laws in force: five are members of UPOV and nine are not. The five members (with earliest enacted PVP legislation footnoted) are Japan,[24] China,[25] South Korea,[26] Singapore[27] and Vietnam.[28] The nine non-members (with relevant PVP legislation footnoted) are Hong Kong (1997),[29] Thailand (1999), Indonesia (2000), India (2001), Philippines (2002), Taiwan (2004),[30] Malaysia (2004), Cambodia (2008)[31] and Laos (2008).[32]

UPOV has had a constant presence in the five countries in this study, ostensibly to provide technical expertise in the drafting of the PVP law, but in effect to promote its own PBR model. Despite UPOV's efforts, the PVP laws of each of these countries are not carbon copies of the UPOV model; indeed, some depart quite radically from the UPOV model, and integrate elements of the CBD and ITPGRFA. They could hope to achieve a degree of reconciliation of the disparate objectives of the three treaties only by way of a sui generis PVP law.

Apart from TRIPS and UPOV, there have been many other domestic and external pressures and influences that have shaped the final outcome of the PVP laws in the five surveyed countries, including national aspirations for biotechnological advancement and commercialisation of agriculture, threatened action for IPR violations under the US section 301 procedure, domestic and foreign seed industry demands, agitation from civil society and farmers' organisations, obligations in bilateral trade agreements (BTAs), expert advice from the FAO, and development assistance from UPOV member countries such as the United States and Japan (Kanniah and Antons, 2012; Kanniah, 2005: 283).

The respective PVP acts of the selected countries, in chronological order, are:

- *Thailand* – Plant Varieties Protection Act B.E. 2542 (1999);
- *Indonesia* – Plant Variety Protection Act (No. 29 of 2000);
- *India* – Protection of Plant Varieties and Farmers' Rights Act (Act No. 53 of 2001);
- *Philippines* – Plant Variety Protection Act of 2002 (Republic Act No. 9168); and
- *Malaysia* – Protection of New Plant Varieties Act 2004 (Act No. 634).

A comparative review of the PVP laws shows that all five countries have attempted to temper their PVP laws by introducing unique features that mitigate the power of the rights holders (Kanniah, 2011). They have sought to balance the rights of the PVP owners with the interests of other stakeholders and the public interest in a number of ways: introducing exemptions to breeders' rights; explicit provisions for farmers' right to save, use, sow and sell protected seeds; disclosure of origin/source; prior informed consent and benefit sharing; and compulsory licensing. Compulsory licensing opens up the possibility for government intervention in the public interest, since plant varieties have enormous implications for food security. Further, the laws recognise new rights that hitherto did not exist in international IPR laws, such as farmers' rights to local varieties and to their traditional knowledge.

The sui generis PVP laws that they designed are a conflation of the objectives of the international laws and are not typical IPR laws. The PVP laws of these five countries contain elements of private property rights that coexist with the sovereign rights of the country to protect its biological diversity and biosafety. The PVP laws provide an interface with the relevant national laws relating to biodiversity and biosafety – and, in the case of India, even seed quality. Indeed, each of them is truly a sui generis PVP law.

India's PVP Act is regarded as the standard bearer of PVP laws for a developing country. India is the only country among the five to provide for a positive farmers' right that reiterates farmers' traditional rights to deal with seeds even if they are protected under the Act, as long as the seeds are not sold under a brand name. Indeed, there is a separate Chapter on farmers' rights in the Indian PVP Act (Chapter VI). India has therefore opted to introduce farmers' rights within the PVP legislation, and to give farmers and plant breeders rights. In doing so, India has gone further than any other country in recognising farmers' rights in its PVP legislation. In addition, the Indian PVP Act provides for a guarantee of seed performance,[33] usually found in seed quality laws, and bans the use of terminator technology in any genes or gene sequence,[34] an element also present in its biosafety laws. Again, critics have pointed out that the treatment of farmers and breeders under the Act is not really equal, and that much of the farmers' rights protection is impressive mainly on paper (Peschard, 2014). More recently, however, and as explained in detail below, there has been a dramatic and impressive upsurge in applications for, and registrations of, farmers' varieties that should help to correct such negative perceptions about the Indian legislation to some extent.

Implementation of PVP

Although these countries began the process for the development of their PVP laws soon after the TRIPS Agreement came into force in 1995, they were slow to implement them. PVP offices had not been set up, staff had not been appointed and trained, administrative and technical guidelines and regulations had not been issued, and even budgets for the implementation of the PVP Acts had not been approved until well after the TRIPS deadline of 2000 had passed. However, once they were ready, the PVP applications came flooding in and PVP certificates were granted. The following commentary provides a general overview of PVP implementation in the five countries.

India

In India, the PVP Act was passed in 2001, the implementing rules issued in 2003 and the PVP Office established in 2005. At time of writing (July 2015), registration of varieties is available for ninety-two crops.[35] Applications for registration may be received for new plant varieties, extant varieties (notified under the Seed Act 1966), essentially derived varieties (EDVs), extant varieties (variety of common knowledge) and farmers' varieties. From 2007 to 13 July 2015, the Protection of Plant Varieties and Farmers' Rights Authority received 9,565 applications for the registration of plant varieties, including open pollinated varieties, hybrids, parental lines and transgenic varieties, from farmers and the public and private sector, including multinationals.[36] The majority of the applications were for farmers' varieties (59 per cent), followed by extant varieties and new varieties. Of the applications received, 1,831 were granted certificates of registration (CoRs). Cereals (such as maize, bread wheat, rice, pearl millet and sorghum), cotton and pulses made up 70 per cent of the CoRs granted, with rice alone receiving a total of 785. This is to be expected, because rice varieties are endemic in India. The highest number of CoRs (54 per cent) was issued for extant varieties, followed by farmers' varieties (31 per cent) and new varieties (13 per cent). In 2009, three farmers' varieties of rice became the first farmers' plant varieties in India to receive CoRs. The conversion ratio (that is, the ratio of applications to successful registrations) shows an interesting development for farmers' varieties: while it was less than 1 per cent for farmers' varieties, 3.5 per cent for new varieties and 25.5 per cent for extant varieties in 2013 (Manjunatha et al., 2013), two years later the figures had shown a marked improvement for farmers' varieties at 10.5 per cent, almost closing the gap with new varieties at 13 per cent, while extant varieties remain dominant at 45 per cent. The upsurge in applications and successful registration of farmers' varieties appears to be a direct result of the efforts of the Protection of Plant Varieties and Farmers' Rights Authority and organisations supporting farmers. The Authority initiated a number of awareness-raising activities to educate and assist farmers, such as conducting regional workshops and opening up regional offices. The criteria for registration and the registration process were also simplified for farmers (Peschard, 2014).

Indonesia

The Centre for PVP was established under the Ministry of Agriculture in August 2002 and began accepting applications only in 2004. The first PVP certificate for a new variety was granted in 2007 to an Indonesian company and the first local variety to be granted a certificate was in 2005 to the governor of a district. As at 2014, a total of 829 PVP certificates had been granted – 501 for local varieties[37] and 328 for new varieties.[38] In addition, there are 1,047 varieties registered for use as propagating material.[39] Local varieties are protected under section 7 of Law No. 29 of 2000 on Plant Variety Protection. Rather cryptically, the provision states that they are owned by the community, but controlled by the state. Further details can be obtained from Government Regulation No. 13 of 2004 concerning the naming, registration and use of an initial variety for the making of essentially derived varieties. The Regulation authorises the governor of a province (*Gubernur*) or district (*Bupati*), the mayor of a city (*Walikota*) or, if the variety is spread over several provinces, the Plant Variety Registration Office within the Ministry of Agriculture to register the local variety. As Antons points out in Chapter 14 in this volume, individuals or legal entities using a local variety to produce an essentially derived variety need to conclude an agreement with these registering authorities. Unlike with other IPR held or administered by the state, the Regulation does not exempt community members from this requirement. The Regulation provides that there 'may' be compensation of the community, which the authorities should use for a range of broadly worded purposes. In the end, the Regulation grants a substantial amount of discretion to the authorities, but no real rights to the communities.

Malaysia

Malaysia followed a similar pattern of a long lag between the enactment of the PVP Act in 2004 and its implementation. The Malaysian PVP Act came into force on 1 January 2007 and implementation began only when regulations were issued in 2008.[40] Although application is open to all plants excluding micro-organisms, the Department has issued a crop priority list of twenty plant genera for which applications will be accepted. While applications for other crops will be received, the time taken for review may be longer owing to a lack of technical expertise. The twenty crops on the priority list comprise ornamentals (five genera), forest plantation crops (six), industrial crops (four), fruits (four) and cereals (one).[41]

PVP applications were accepted from 2008 and at time of writing (July 2015), from a total of 207 PVP applications that had been filed with the Department of Agriculture, thirty-nine had been granted.[42] Of the applications received, ornamentals formed the largest number, at 119 applications, followed by cereals and forest plants (twenty each), fruits (nineteen), vegetables (twelve), and herbs and mushrooms (three each). Of the thirty-nine PVPs granted, the majority (nineteen) have been for forest plants (owned jointly by the Sabah Forestry Development Authority and a private company), followed by eleven ornamentals (eight for chrysanthemum flowers, owned by a Dutch private company, and three for orchid flowers, owned by MARDI, a Malaysian public sector agricultural breeding institution), six for cereals (all for rice, owned by Universiti Kebangsaan Malaysia), one for fruit (for durian, owned by a private Malaysian company), one for an industrial crop (for roselle, owned by Universiti Kebangsaan Malaysia, or UKM) and one for a vegetable (for a chilli, owned by MARDI). No farmers' varieties have so far been registered for PVP. Even though foreign applicants (Dutch, American, Australian and Japanese) dominated with 53 per cent of all PVP applications, the Malaysian public sector was more successful in gaining PVP registrations, at 77 per cent. In fact, all twenty applications for cereals came from the public sector – all for rice submitted by MARDI and UKM. Foreign applicants were active in only three categories – ornamentals, fruits and vegetables. In addition to the plants granted PVP certificates, the Department of Agriculture has also examined extant plant varieties to be listed on the national crop list. At time of writing, a total of 523 varieties has been listed – fruits (480), vegetables (8) and cereals (35).

Philippines

The Philippines acted faster than the other four countries in developing implementing regulations in 2003, a year after its PVP Act was passed. However, while applications were received from 2003, the granting of PVP certificates has been slowed down by testing for distinctness, uniformity and stability, and the first certificates were finally granted in 2007. Some 237 applications were submitted between 2003 and 2015.[43] By May 2015, 187 PVP certificates had been granted. The majority of the applications and PVP certificates granted were for corn and rice, followed by vegetables and fruits. Private domestic and multinational seed companies (Pioneer HiBred, Monsanto, Bayer Crop Science, Dole, Del Monte and Syngenta) dominated applications and successful grants of PVP certificates. In fact, Pioneer, Monsanto, Bayer and Syngenta together account for close to 50 per cent of the PVP certificates granted, and these were in respect of just two crops – rice and corn.

Thailand

In Thailand, although the PVP Act was passed in 1999, the process of developing implementing regulations went on for several years. Thailand has specified sixty-two genera and species for protection (Holthius, 2015). PVP applications were accepted only from 2003 (Ratanasatien, 2008). Between 2003 and 2013, 1,074 applications had been submitted and PVP certificates had been granted to 138 plant varieties (East Asia Plant Variety Protection Forum Office, 2013). However, the Thai PVP Act is, at time of writing, being amended. The Plant Variety Protection Bill 2013 seeks to introduce revisions in four areas: criteria for protection, specifying novelty in addition to uniformity, stability and distinctness in line with UPOV criteria; duration of protection, increased from between twelve and seventeen years to between twenty and twenty-five years; scope of PBR, expanded to include rights to EDVs; and registration of local communities, providing for details of what constitutes a local community and a system of registration (Lerdhamtewe, 2014a).

Patent protection

TRIPS made patents mandatory for plants and animals derived from non-biological and microbiological processes and micro-organisms. All five countries have provided for this under their patent laws:

- *India* – Patents (Amendment) Act 2002;
- *Indonesia* – Patent Law No. 14/2001;
- *Malaysia* – Patents Act 1983, amended by Patents (Amendment) Act 1993 (Act No. A863);
- *Philippines* – Intellectual Property Code (Republic Act No. 8293); and
- *Thailand* – Patents Act B.E. 2522 (1979), as amended by Patents Act (No. 3) B.E. 2542 (1999).

The 1991 UPOV Convention reversed a previous prohibition of simultaneous protection under both patent and plant variety laws (Correa, 2012: 4). Whether and to what extent a country grants patent protection besides PVP depends on what precisely is excluded from the scope of patent law and how the courts will interpret this. Although they are all modelled on the TRIPS requirements, exclusion provisions differ widely, with India excluding 'plants and animals in whole or any part thereof other than micro-organisms, but including seeds, varieties and species and essentially biological processes for production or propagation of plants and animals' (section 3(j) of the Patents Act). This, however, has been interpreted as meaning, conversely, that micro-organisms and biotechnological process inventions that require substantial human intervention are, in fact, patentable (Kumar and Wilson, 2006; Shiva, 2005). Blakeney (2011: 5) has also pointed out that there is no definition of 'micro-organisms' in TRIPS and that this may allow countries to permit patents for all kinds of microscopic biological material, including for cells and genes. For Indonesia, which excludes in section 7(d) 'all living creatures, except micro-organisms' and 'any biological process which is essential in producing plants or animals, except non-biological or micro-biological processes', commentators have similarly concluded that, conversely, biotechnological and micro-biological processes are patentable (Barisah, 2012).

Additional pressure to allow for patent protection of plant material comes from BTAs. In BTAs, the United States has restricted the choice granted under the TRIPS Agreement and obliged developing-country partners in Asia, Africa and Latin America to make patents available in this field, or at least to 'endeavour' to do so (Kanniah and Antons, 2012: 3; Correa, 2012: 6; Antons, 2016). Patent protection for plant material is therefore increasingly on the agenda in the developing world in spite of the flexibilities granted by TRIPS. Depending on their willingness to accept such stringent conditions in FTAs and BTAs, and in the wording and interpretation of exclusion clauses, developing countries may then face similar discussions about exclusions and exceptions as are currently conducted in countries with much more commercialised agricultural and much further advanced biotechnology sectors. These options are exclusions from patentability to protect '*ordre public* or morality, including to protect human, animal or plant life or health or to avoid serious prejudice to the environment' (Article 27.2 TRIPS), exclusions under Article 30 TRIPS for research and experimental purposes or specifically for breeders, and compulsory licensing in favour of plant breeders (Article 31 TRIPS). In view of WTO Panel decisions interpreting these provisions narrowly (Dreyfuss, 2009: 258–259), views range from continuing optimism about the remaining flexibilities in TRIPS (Correa, 2005, 2012; Dinwoodie and Dreyfuss, 2007; Haugen, 2007, 2009; Haugen, Muller and Narashiman, 2011) to those who see the space constrained by such decisions (Strandburg, 2009; Dent, 2011). Under the circumstances, analysts have considered broadly worded experimental use exemptions that include farmers and breeders (Antons, 2016), or an 'open source' licence in analogy to the free software movement (Kloppenburg, 2014; Hope, 2008). As for the majority of developing countries, and in particular for those with large-scale smallholder agriculture, they are probably well advised to explore the scope of Article 27.3.b. TRIPS for sui generis protection and to interpret the conditions of the Agreement for patenting in this field as narrowly as possible.

Geographical indications law

As with PVPs, the protection of geographical indications (GIs) is also a TRIPS-mandated form of IPR. Article 22.1 TRIPS defines GIs as 'indications which identify a good as originating in the territory of a Member, or a region or locality in that territory, where a given quality, reputation or other characteristic of the good is essentially attributable to its geographical origin'. Article 22.2 instructs members to provide for legal means to prevent the use of GIs to mislead the public and to prevent unfair competition.

TRIPS provides for three levels of protection of GIs: a base level protection for all products; additional protection for wines and spirits; and an extra protection only for wines (Banerji, 2012). Because TRIPS does not define 'goods', there is flexibility in enlarging the definition beyond natural and agricultural goods, and indeed the five countries in this study have taken advantage of this.

Geographical indications are distinguishable from other IPR in two ways: first, they are collective rights shared by producers from a specific locality, while other IPR are available only to individuals; and secondly, they can exist in perpetuity if producers uphold the quality that justifies the protection, while other IPRs are for a fixed duration. Further, it has been argued that embedded in GIs are the traditional culture and knowledge of the producers, and in that sense they are not only economic rights, but also protect cultural rights and heritage (Banerji, 2012; Gangjee, 2012). This is apparent in the registered GIs in the five countries studied, where handicrafts, textiles, local foodstuff and manufactured goods have been given GI status, along with natural and agricultural products.

India

In India, the Geographical Indications of Goods (Registration and Protection) Act of 1999 (No. 48 of 1999) came into force on 15 September 2003, after the Geographical Indications of Goods (Registration and Protection) Rules 2002 were promulgated. Section 1(3)(f) of India's GI Act specifies that '"goods" means any agricultural, natural or manufactured goods or any goods of handicraft or of industry and includes food stuff'. Section 1(3)(e) provides that the category of eligible GIs includes manufactured goods, where any one of the activities of production, processing or preparation of the goods takes place in a given place, territory or locality. Between September 2003 and July 2015, there were 236 GIs registered in India.[44] The registered GIs have been categorised as handicrafts, agricultural, manufactured goods, foodstuffs and textiles. Foreign GIs registered in India include Pisco from Peru, Champagne from France, Napa Valley wine from the United States, Scotch Whisky from the United Kingdom, Prosciutto di Parma from Italy, Cognac from France, Porto and Duoro from Portugal, and Tequila from Mexico.

Indonesia

In Indonesia, GI protection is regulated under Law No. 15 of 2001 on Trade Marks, in Chapter IV on 'Protection of GI and Source of Origin'. The details of the GI system are, however, to be found in Government Regulation No. 51 of 2007 about Geographical

Indications. A GI is defined as a 'sign, which indicates the geographical origin of a good which gives a certain characteristic and quality to a good because of the factor of the geographical environment, including the factor of nature, the human factor or a combination of the two' (article 56(1) of the 2001 Act; article 1(1) of the 2007 Regulation). Potential applicants for GI protection are organisations representing local producer communities, authorised organisations (usually at government level) and groups of consumers of the relevant goods (article 56(2) of the 2001 Act; article 5(3) of the 2007 Regulation). Of thirty-one GIs registered before the end of March 2015,[45] none were registered by consumer organisations, while two were registered by government organisations – in this case, the government of the District of Sumedang. Three GIs were registered by foreigners for Champagne (France), Peruvian Pisco (Peru) and Parmigiano Reggiano (Italy). All of the remaining ones were registered by organisations representing local producer communities.

The law defines these 'producer communities' as consisting of parties cultivating commodities resulting from nature or natural wealth, producers of agricultural commodities and of craft or industrial goods, and traders selling such goods. Many of the organisations representing the 'producers' call themselves 'Community for the Protection of . . . ' a specified GI; in one case (from Kalimantan), the *Adat* Community Association for the Protection of Adan Krayan Rice. The leadership of many of these associations consists of a mixture of local government personnel, local manufacturers, producers and training providers. They are authorised to draft 'books of regulations' with the details of the protected goods and the local conditions, and to recommend new authorised users and members. The ultimate decision about such matters, however, is made by an expert team for GIs in Jakarta, consisting of staff from various ministries, research institutes and the Indonesian intellectual property office (articles 8, 14, 16, 19 of the 2007 Regulation). As Antons points out in Chapter 14 in this volume, because of their heavy reliance on local culture and heritage, there is a danger that GIs could be drawn into the difficult politics of Indonesia's decentralisation process,[46] because communities could well take a more restrictive view about membership and authorised use of certain traditions than the national government does. In any case, the government has high hopes – expressed in the government explanation accompanying the 2007 Regulation – that GIs will contribute to environmental conservation, and to the strengthening of natural and human resources in Indonesia's regions, as well as helping to prevent the migration of the workforce from regions to the cities. It is further interesting that, in a country rich in cultural traditions, GIs have been used so far intensively and almost exclusively for agricultural products such as coffee, pepper, tobacco, fruits, vegetables and rice, and for fish farming, but only for a single craft product – the famous furniture from Jepara on the North Coast of Central Java.

Malaysia

In Malaysia, the Geographical Indications Act 2000 (Act No. 602) and the Geographical Indications Regulations 2001 govern the GI system. The types of good covered include natural and agricultural products and products of handicraft or industry. Between 2003 and 2015, a total of ninety-five products were the subject of GI application, of which eighty-eight were Malaysian and seven were foreign. At time of writing, forty-seven GIs had been successfully registered – forty-two were Malaysian and five were foreign (Pisco, Scotch Whisky, Cognac, Champagne, Parmegiano Reggiano). The range of Malaysian GIs registered include agricultural crops, horticultural products, handicrafts, foodstuffs and textiles.

Philippines

Section 4 of the Intellectual Property Code of the Philippines (Republic Act No. 8293) provides for GIs as an IPR. A system of GI registration is not yet in place in the Philippines. At time of writing, the Intellectual Property Office of the Philippines (IPOPHIL) has drafted the Rules and Regulations on Geographical Indications, and is inviting comments and conducting public consultations on the draft. The latest such consultation was scheduled for 25–26 June 2015.[47] The draft Rules define goods as agricultural products, foodstuff, any handicraft product, or wines and spirits (rule 2(b)). The draft Rules follow closely the TRIPS prohibitions on the use of GIs to mislead the public or cause unfair competition (rule 4). GI applications may be made by natural or juridical persons directly involved in the extraction or production of the product, by individuals or organisations producing the goods or involved in the trade of products bearing the GI, by government agencies or local government units having areas of responsibility covering the geographical origin of the goods, by foreign governments and by associations specifically entrusted with responsibility for protection or regulating GIs (rule 7).

Thailand

In Thailand, the Protection of Geographical Indications Act B.E.2546 (AD2003) entered into force on 28 April 2004. Other rules and regulations governing GIs are the Ministerial Regulation 2004, the Ministerial Notification 2004 and the Department of Intellectual Property Notification 2004. The GI Act of Thailand provides for three types of protection: general protection; protection for specific goods; and protection for foreign goods. Those eligible to apply for GIs are the local governments, local communities, consumers and foreign holders. As at 2014, sixty-one GIs were registered in Thailand (Lerdhamtewe, 2014b). The registered GIs were classified as rice, silk, wines and spirits, agricultural products, cultural products and foodstuffs. There were nine foreign products registered, all except one under the wines and spirits category – Pisco, Brunello Di Montalcino, Champagne, Prosciutto Di Parma, Scotch Whisky, Napa Valley wine, Tequila, Barbaresco and Barolo.

Conclusion

New laws have followed technological innovations in agriculture in the fields of seed quality, biosafety, IPR laws (PVPs, patent laws and GIs) in India, Indonesia, Malaysia, the Philippines and Thailand. The laws have more or less mirrored the commitments made in the international treaties to which these countries have adhered and demonstrate policy shifts from purely national concerns to trading in the liberalised globalised markets (Seshia and Scones, 2003). At the same time, they have heralded a regime change in the domestic agriculture sector, with the public sector gradually withdrawing from research and breeding, and the private sector gaining greater market access and market share, and more concentration and consolidation of power in the markets, for technology-embedded new plant varieties and commercially cultivated crops (Kloppenburg, 2014).

For the time being, the nature of agricultural holdings and farming practices in these five countries provides some limited security for farming communities that farm-saved seeds and the informal seed sector will continue to play a role. Studies from international agencies such as the United Nations Economic and Social Commission for Asia and the Pacific (UNESCAP, 2009) and United Nations Conference on Trade and Development

(UNCTAD, 2013), and the recent report drafted by Olivier De Schutter for the UN Human Rights Council (De Schutter, 2014), have also restated the need for a focus on farmers in developing countries and a paradigm shift away from monocultures and industry-driven agriculture towards agriculture that is ecologically sustainable and promotes rural development.

The seed industry is continuing to agitate for greater access to markets for seeds, but governments in these countries are also facing vociferous protests from farmers' organisations and civil society groups when any attempts are made to curtail the freedom of farmers to practise their traditional farming rights. The struggle for and against IPR is particularly fierce, although seed laws and other forms of regulation are also important. Of particular concern is the relatively limited use that the governments of developing countries have made of the freedom granted in Article 27.3.b. TRIPS to design their own PVP systems. Instead, with one eye on the market, they have often imported solutions tested elsewhere, but not in the local context. Even the more inventive approaches, such as the Indian Protection of Plant Varieties and Farmers' Rights Act of 2001, often seem to suffer from the attempt to do too much and to please too many 'stakeholders' at the same time. In the end, such mixed laws leave the traditional farming sector in a second-tier position.

Even more concerning is the recent move towards the patenting of plant material in BTAs to which a number of developing countries have agreed, presumably in exchange for trade benefits in other sectors. If this trend continues, it will force developing countries to consider the rather limited exclusion or exemption provisions from patent rights under TRIPS in the interests of their researchers and farmers, or to impose compulsory licences. At the same time, there is discussion about a contractual approach by developing 'open source' licensing in the seed sector. Somewhat less controversial and strongly promoted by many developing countries are GIs, which help to market particular agricultural products with a strong reputation. However, because GIs are connected to the communities and the regions in which the traditions are practised, decisions will have to be made on how exclusively membership of such communities is to be defined, and there could be different views about this at different levels of the governance structure. The fierce contest about all these different types of rights, therefore, will continue to be played out at the local and global levels, between different sections of the farming community, between farmers and industry and the modernising governments that often support them to a considerable extent, and between developing-country and developed-country governments.

Notes

1 Mendel worked with pea plants. He was the first to prove, by keen observation and painstaking record-keeping, that plants carried hereditary 'elements' from one generation to the next and that they inherited these traits from their parents. His theory was that it took two 'elements', one from each parent (although only one would be expressed), to determine the final outcome of any trait.

2 The Swedish Seed Association was founded in 1886. Germany set up a seed control system under the Farmers' Union in 1895, and drafted a Seed and Seedlings Law in 1930, which was never passed. Another attempt in 1953 – the Law on the Protection ofVarieties and Seeds of Cultivated Plants – eventually played a substantial part in the drafting of the International Convention for the Protection of New Varieties of Plants 1961 (UPOV Convention). Czechoslovakia passed a law on seeds in 1921; France introduced a seed control and registration system in 1922; The Netherlands introduced a Breeders Ordinance in 1941 (Heitz, 1987: 68–76).

3 The Austrian Federal Institute of Agriculture and Seed Testing was established in 1881 (Heitz, 1987: 63).

4 Regulations setting standards for selling seeds and regulating competition began to appear in European countries in the 1920s. Official registration rules for superior new varieties began to be introduced around the same time – 1925 in France, 1933 in Germany, 1938 in Austria and 1941 in the Netherlands. They applied first to major crops, such as wheat, maize, potato and sugar beet, and were later extended to other crops. Vegetables, especially those in which the private breeding sector was not active, came much later (Vellve, 1992: 58).

5 Hybrid corn is developed by inbreeding and cross-breeding. An inbred line is a variety of corn that has been cross-bred with its own kind for several generations to the point at which certain valued characteristics in that line are fixed and retained in subsequent generations. Such inbred lines are used for cross-breeding with other inbred lines to produce first-generation or single-cross hybrids. There are also double-cross hybrids, which are produced by crossing two different single-cross hybrids (Doyle, 1985: 37–38).

6 A hybrid is a cross between two different plant races, varieties, species or genera, produced through human intervention to exhibit specific characteristics.

7 Open pollinated plants are plants that reproduce themselves in one of two ways: cross-pollination between two plants by wind, insects, birds, water or other natural means; or self-pollination between the male and female flower parts within the same flower or between flowers in the same plant.

8 Asexually reproducing plants are propagated by using parts of the plant, e.g. stems, bulbs, roots, leaves, etc.

9 For a discussion on the stages for the development of seed systems in developing countries, see Pray and Bharat (1991); Morris (2002).

10 *Diamond v. Chakrabarty*, 447 U.S. 303 (1980).

11 *Sui generis* is Latin meaning 'of its own kind'. It is used for IPR systems that are designed for a particular type of product, such as plants in the PVP system, rather than general in scope, such as copyright or patents.

12 US Patent Act (35 USC 101); US Plant Patent Act of 1930 (35 USC 161); US Plant Variety Protection Act of 1970.

13 International Convention for the Protection of New Varieties of Plants 1961 (revised 1972, 1978 and 1991); Convention on the Unification of Certain Points of Substantive Law on Patents for Invention 1963 (Strasbourg Convention); European Patent Convention (EPC) 1973; Regulation on Community Plant Variety Rights 1994; Directive on the Legal Protection of Biotechnological Inventions 1998.

14 'UPOV' deriving from the French *Union Internationale pour la Protection des Obtentions Vegetales* – that is, the International Union for the Protection of New Varieties of Plants.

15 Section 4(24) of the Philippines Republic Act No. 7607, Magna Carta of the Small Farmer, defines 'good seeds' as 'seeds that are the progeny of certified seeds so handled as to maintain a minimum acceptable level of genetic purity and identity and which is selected at the farm level'. Under Republic Act No. 7900, the High-Value Crops Development Act of 1995, recommended varieties must be registered and certified.

16 Constitutional Court Decision in Case 99/PUU-X/2012, 9 July 2013, 128–129.

17 For a detailed listing of other rules and regulations, see the Biosafety Clearing House for the Convention on Biological Diversity, online at http://bch.cbd.int/database/laws/ [accessed 13 July 2015].

18 The laws and guidelines are too numerous to list. For a detailed listing of the laws and comprehensive information on biosafety in India, Indonesia, Malaysia, Philippines and Thailand, see Biosafety Clearing House (2011).

19 That is, genetically modified by the insertion of genes from the soil bacterium Bacillus thuringiencsis (Bt).

20 See the Biosafety Clearing House on the Convention on Biological Diversity, online at http://bch.cbd.int/database/results?searchid=591355 [accessed 13 July 2015].

21 Non-compliance with TRIPS attracts sanctions under its Dispute Settlement Undertaking.

22 UPOV organised regional seminars on the Nature and Rationale for the Protection of Plant Varieties under the UPOV Convention in 1990 (Tokyo), 1991 (Tsukuba), 1992 (Suweon), 1993 (Beijing), 1995 (Medan) and 1996 (Bishkek). UPOV also conducted eleven national seminars in Asia, in Beijing, Harbin, Xian, Nanjing, Jakarta, Kuala Lumpur, Manila, New Delhi, Dhaka and Hanoi. In addition, UPOV conducted: technical guidance workshops in 1997 (Brisbane), 1998 (Cambridge), 1999 (Kunming and Cambridge); Asian regional technical meetings in 2000 (Tsukuba), 2001 (Beijing), 2002 (Seoul), 2003 (Manila) and 2004 (Hanoi); national technical seminars in Manila, Singapore, Serdang, New Delhi (two such seminars), Peradeniya, Jakarta, Bangkok, Vientiane, Hanoi, Cuttack, Hyderabad, Pune, Phnom Penh (two), Ho Chi Minh City and Yangon. UPOV has continued to organise such national stakeholder seminars, as well as regional technical training workshops, not only in Asia, but also all over the world.

23 For current list of UPOV members, see online at http://www.upov.int/export/sites/upov/members/en/pdf/pub423.pdf [accessed 13 July 2015].

24 Plant Variety Protection and Seed Act 1998 (Japan).

25 Regulations of the People's Republic of China (PRC) on the Protection of New Varieties of Plants 1999 (entered into force 1997) PVP Gazette 85, October 1999; Implementing Rules for the Regulations of the People's Republic of China (PRC) on Protection of New Varieties of Plants (Forestry Part) 1999; Implementing Rules for the Regulations of People's Republic of China (PRC) on Protection of New Varieties of Plants (Agriculture Part) Decree of the Ministry of Agriculture, Decree No. 13, 27 April 1999.

26 Industry Seed Law 1997 (Republic of Korea), sometimes referred to as the Plant Varieties Protection Law of Korea 1997.

27 Plant Varieties Protection Act, Act 22 of 2004 (Singapore).

28 Ordinance on Plant Varieties, Order No. 03/2004/L-CTN of 5 April 2004 (Vietnam); Intellectual Property Law, Law No. 50/2005/QH11 [Rights for the Plant Variety] 2005 (Vietnam).

29 Plant Varieties Protection Ordinance 1997 (Hong Kong). Following the transfer of Hong Kong sovereignty from the United Kingdom to the PRC in 1997, this has been superseded by Chapter 490 of the Plant Varieties Protection Ordinance (PRC).

30 Plant Variety and Plant Seed Act 2004 (Republic of China [Taiwan]).

31 Law on Seed Management and Breeders' Rights of 2008 (Cambodia).

32 Law on Intellectual Property of 2008 (Laos).

33 Indian PVP Act 2001, s. 39(2).

34 Indian PVP Act 2001, s. 18(1)(c). Terminator technology renders seeds sterile after first germination and therefore seeds cannot be saved for future planting.

35 See online at http://www.plantauthority.gov.in/CropSpeciesnotified1.htm [accessed 13 July 2015].

36 See online at http://www.plantauthority.gov.in/pdf/application&20status.pdf [accessed 13 July 2015].

37 See online at http://ppvt.setjen.pertanian.go.id/ppvtpp/statis-52.html [accessed 28 July 2015].

38 See online at http://ppvt.setjen.pertanian.go.id/ppvtpp/statis-75.html [accessed 28 July 2015].

39 See online at http://ppvt.setjen.pertanian.go.id/ppvtpp/statis-53.html [accessed 28 July 2015].

40 Protection of New Plant Varieties Regulations 2008 (Malaysia); Protection of New Plant Varieties (Size of Holdings) Regulations 2008 (Malaysia); Administrative Guidelines on Application and Registration of New Varieties of Plants 2008 (Malaysia).

41 See online at http://pvpbkkt.doa.gov.my/Legislation/Guidelines/Species.html [accessed 13 July 2015].

42 See online at http://pvpbkkt.doa.gov.my/ [accessed 13 July 2015].

43 Plant Variety Protection Office, Department of Agriculture, Republic of the Philippines, online at http://www.pvpo.bpinsicpvpo.com.ph/ [accessed 14 July 2015].
44 See online at http://ipindia.nic.in/girindia/ [accessed 13 July 2015].
45 See online at http://www.dgip.go.id/images/adelch-images/pdf-files/publikasi/publikasi_ig/ig_terdaftar_maret_2015.pdf [accessed 28 July 2015].
46 See, in this volume, Butt, Chapter 12, and Rachman and Siscawati, Chapter 13.
47 See online at http://www.ipophil.gov.ph/releases/archive-2015/316-notice-to-submit-comments-and-invitation-to-the-3rd-public-consultation-on-the-revised-draft-rules-and-regulations-on-geographical-indication [accessed 23 July 2016].

References

Antons, C. (2016) 'Article 27.3.b TRIPS and Plant Variety Protection in Developing Countries', in R. M. Hilty and H. Ullrich (eds) *TRIPS + 20: Beyond Trade Rules*, Berlin/Heidelberg: Springer, 389–414.

Antons, C., and Thampapillai, D. (2015) 'An Overview of Free Trade Agreements in the Asia-Pacific Region with a Particular Focus on Intellectual Property', in C. Antons and R. M. Hilty (eds) *Intellectual Property and Free Trade Agreements in the Asia-Pacific Region*, Berlin/Heidelberg: Springer, 27–53.

Aoki, K. (2008) *Seeds Wars: Controversies and Cases on Plant Genetic Resources and Intellectual Property*, Durham, NC: Carolina Academic Press.

Bala Ravi, S. (2009) 'The Conflict between Seed Bill and PPVFR Act of India', SAWTEE Policy Brief No. 19, available online at http://www.sawtee.org/publications/Policy-Brief-18.pdf [accessed 23 July 2016].

Banerji, M. (2012) 'Geographical Indications: Which Way Should ASEAN Go?', *Boston College Intellectual Property & Technology Forum*, 1–11, available online at http://bciptf.org/wp-content/uploads/2012/06/Geographical_Indications.pdf [accessed 17 July 2015].

Barisah, N. (2012) 'Undang-undang Paten dan Hak Petani', 16 April, available online at http://twnindonesia.info//content/blogcategory/0/42/ [accessed 6 July 2015].

Biosafety Clearing House (2011) *Second National Regular Report on the Implementation of the Cartagena Protocol on Biosafety*, available online at http://bch.cbd.int/protocol/cpb_natreports.shtml#natrep2 [accessed 10 November 2013].

Blakeney, M. (2011) *Trends in Intellectual Property Rights Relating to Genetic Resources for Food and Agriculture*, Background Study Paper No. 58, Rome: FAO.

Chauhan, C. (2013) 'SC Committee Says No to GM Crops for Time Being', *Hindustan Times*, 22 July, available online at http://www.hindustantimes.com/delhi/sc-committee-says-no-to-gm-crops-for-time-being/story-cJdrETdlD3RjhWtxHrDIaP.html [accessed 6 November 2013].

Correa, C. M. (2005) *The International Dimension of the Research Exception*, Washington, DC: American Association for the Advancement of Science SIPPI Project (on file with the authors).

Correa, C. M. (2012) *TRIPS-related Patent Flexibilities and Food Security: Options for Developing Countries*, Geneva: Quaker United Nations Office (QUNO)/ICTSD.

De Schutter, O. (2014) *The Transformative Potential of the Right to Food: Final Report of the Special Rapporteur on the Right to Food*, UN Doc. A/HRC/25/57, 24 January, available online at http://www.ohchr.org/EN/HRBodies/HRC/RegularSessions/Session25/Documents/A_HRC_25_57_ENG.DOC [accessed 21 July 2016].

Dent, C. (2011) 'The TRIPS Agreement and an Experimental Use Exception for "Research Tools"', *Australian Economic Review*, 44(1): 73–78.

Dinwoodie, G. B., and Dreyfuss, R. C. (2007) 'Diversifying without Discriminating: Complying with the Mandates of the TRIPS Agreement', *Michigan Telecommunications Technology Law Review*, 13(2): 445–456.

Doyle, J. (1985) *Altered Harvest: Agriculture, Genetics and the Fate of the World's Food Supply*, New York: Viking Penguin.

Dreyfuss, R. (2009) 'Fostering Dynamic Innovation, Development and Trade: Intellectual Property as a Case Study in Global Administrative Law', *Acta Juridica*, 237–282.

East Asia Plant Variety Protection Forum Office (2013) 'Report on the Overall Achievements of the First Five Years of the Forum', Presentation at the Sixth East Asia Plant Variety Protection Forum Meeting, Kuching, Sarawak, Malaysia, 3 July.

Gangjee, D. (2012) 'Geographical Indications and Cultural Heritage', *WIPO Journal*, 4(1): 92–102.

Gervais, D. (2008) *The TRIPS Agreement: Drafting History and Analysis*, 3rd edn, London: Thomson Reuters.

Ginibun, F. C., and Ugap, A. W. (2012) 'Current Status of the Integrated Seed Sector in Malaysia', available online at http://q.datakultur.se/~svalofco/wp-content/uploads/2012/12/Malaysia-Seed-Sector-Status-Paper.pdf [accessed 13 July 2015].

GRAIN and Sharma, D. (2005) 'India's New Seed Bill', *Seedling*, July: 22–27, available online at https://www.grain.org/es/article/entries/457-india-s-new-seed-bill [accessed 21 July 2016].

Gupta, K., Karihaloo, J. L., and Khetarpal, R. K. (2008) *Biosafety Regulations of Asia Pacific Countries*, Rome: FAO.

Gupta, K., Karihaloo, J. L., and Khetarpal, R. K. (2014) *Biosafety Regulations of Asia Pacific Countries*, Rome: FAO.

Haugen, H. M. (2007) *The Right to Food and the TRIPS Agreement, With a Particular Emphasis on Developing Countries' Measures for Food Production and Distribution*, Leiden: Martinus Nijhoff.

Haugen, H. M. (2009) 'Human Rights and TRIPS Exclusion and Exception Provisions', *Journal of World Intellectual Property*, 11(5/6): 345–374.

Haugen, H. M., Muller, M. R., and Narashiman, S. M. (2011) 'Food Security and Intellectual Property Rights: Finding the Linkages', in T. Wong,and G. Dutfield (eds) *Intellectual Property and Human Development: Current Trends and Future Scenarios*, Cambridge: Cambridge University Press, 103–138.

Heitz, A. (1987) 'The History of Plant Variety Protection', in *The First Twenty-five Years of the International Convention for the Protection of New Varieties of Plants December 2, 1961–December 2, 1986*, Geneva: UPOV, 62–86.

Helfer, L. R. (2002) 'Intellectual Property Rights in Plant Varieties: An Overview with Options for National Governments', FAO Legal Papers Online #31, available online at http://www.fao.org/fileadmin/user_upload/legal/docs/lpo31-2.pdf [accessed 13 July 2015].

Holthius, J. V. M. (ed.) (2015) *Global Agriculture Law: A Global Guide from Practical Law*, London: Thomson Reuters.

Hope, J. (2008) *Biobazaar: The Open Source Revolution and Biotechnology*, Cambridge, MA: Harvard University Press.

Indonesian Human Rights Committee for Social Justice (2013) 'Our Seed, Our Sovereignty: Seed Law Victory in Indonesia', available at https://www.grain.org/bulletin_board/entries/4774-our-seeds-our-soveriegnty-seed-law-victory-in-Indonesia [accessed 3 July 2015].

James, C. (2012) *The Global Status of Commercialised Biotech/GM Crops*, International Service for the Acquisition of Agri-biotech Applications Executive Summary Brief 44, available online at https://www.isaaa.org/resources/publications/briefs/44/executivesummary/pdf/Brief%2044%20-%20Executive%20Summary%20-%20English.pdf [accessed 6 November 2013].

Jhamtani, H., and Patria, D. (2006) 'Case Documentation: Indonesian Farmers Prosecuted for Breeding Their Own Seeds', 20 October, available online at http://www.asianfarmers.org/?p=208 [accessed 6 July 2015].

Kanniah, R. (2005) 'Plant Variety Protection in Indonesia, Malaysia, the Philippines and Thailand', *Journal of World Intellectual Property*, 8(3): 283–310.

Kanniah, R. (2011) *Breeders vs Farmers: The Contest for Rights over Plant Varieties in Selected Asian Countries*, Saarbucken: VDM Verlag Dr. Muller.

Kanniah, R., and Antons, C. (2012) 'Plant Variety Protection and Traditional Agricultural Knowledge in Southeast Asia', *Australian Journal of Asian Law*, 13(1): 1–23.

Kloppenburg, J. (2014) 'Repurposing the Master's Tools: The Open Source Seed Initiative and the Struggle for Seed Sovereignty', *Journal of Peasant Studies*, 41(6): 1225–1246.

Kumar, S., and Wilson, N. (2006) 'Biotechnology in the Limelight', *Managing Intellectual Property*, available online at http://www.managingip.com/Article/1321387/Biotechnology-in-the-limelight.html [accessed 21 July 2016].

Lai, N. (2013) 'Farmer Suicides in India', *Asia Sentinel*, 4 February, available online at http://www.asiasentinel.com/society/farmer-suicides-in-india/ [accessed 21 July 2016].

Lerdhamtewe, P. (2014a) 'Recent Developments in Thailand's Plant Variety Protection Law', *Journal of Intellectual Property Law and Practice*, 8(1):1–2.

Lerdhamtewe, P. (2014b) 'The Protection of Geographical Indications in Thailand', *Journal of World Intellectual Property*, 17(3–4): 114–128.

Leskien, D., and Flitner, M. (1997) *Intellectual Property Rights and Plant Genetic Resources: Options for a Sui Generis System*, Issues in Genetic Resources No. 6, Rome: International Plant Genetic Resources Institute.

Madhavan, M. R., and Sanyal, K. (2006) *Legislative Brief: The Seeds Bill, 2004*, available online at http://www.prsindia.org/uploads/media/1167468389/legis1167477737_legislative_brief_seeds_bill.pdf [accessed 21 July 2016].

Manjunatha, B. L., Rao, D. U. M., Dastagiri, M. B., Sharma, J. P., and Burman, R. R. (2013) 'The Legal Protection of Public and Private Plant Varieties in India: A Comparative Analysis', *Journal of Bioremediation Biodegradation*, 4(7): 1–5.

Morris, M. L. (2002) 'The Development of the Seed Industry under Globalization', in D. Bigman (ed.) *Globalisation and the Developing Countries: Emerging Strategies for Rural Development and Poverty Alleviation*, Oxford: CABI, 201–207.

Organisation for Economic Co-operation and Development (OECD) (2012) *OCED Seed Schemes: A Synthesis of International Regulatory Aspects that Affect the Seed Trade*, available online at http://www.oecd.org/tad/code/internationalregulatoryaspectsseedtrade.pdf [accessed 6 November 2013].

Panada, R. (2013) 'PH Most "GMO Friendly" Country in Southeast Asia?', *The Rappler*, 14 September, available online at http:www.rappler.com/business/industries/247-agriculture/38878-gmo-philippines-golden rice [accessed 13 July 2015].

Parliamentary Committee on Agriculture (*Lok Sabha*) (2012) *Cultivation of Genetically Modified Food Crops: Prospects and Effects*, New Delhi: Lok Sabha Secretariat.

Peschard, K. (2014) 'Farmers' Rights and Food Sovereignty: Critical Insights from India', *Journal of Peasant Studies*, 41(6): 1085–1108.

Pray, C. E., and Bharat, R. (1991) *A Framework for Seed Policy Analysis in Developing Countries*, Washington, DC: International Food Policy Research Institute.

Ranjan, P. (2009) 'Recent Developments in India's Plant Variety Protection, Seed Regulation and Linkages with UPOV's Proposed Membership', *Journal of World Intellectual Property*, 12[3]: 219–243.

Ratanasatien, C. (2008) 'Current Situation of PVP Legislation in Thailand', Presentation to the Asian Seed Congress, Hyderabad, India, 9–12 November.

Rodrigues, A. (2013) 'Nip this in the Bud', *The Hindu*, 12 August, available online at http://www.thehindu.com/opinion/lead/nip-this-in-the-bud/article5012989.ece [accessed 21 July 2016].

Seshia, S., and Scones, I. (2003) 'Tracing Policy Connections: The Politics of Knowledge in the Green Revolution and Biotechnology Eras in India', Institute of Development Studies Working Paper No. 188, available online at http://www.ids.ac.uk/publication/tracing-policy-connections-the-politics-of-knowledge-in-the-green-revolution-and-biotechnology-eras-in-india [accessed 21 July 2016].

Sewell, A. (2012) 'Ministry Blames GMO Cotton for Farmer Suicides', *Digital Journal*, 25 April, available online at http://www.digitaljournal.com/article/323656 [accessed 6 November 2013].

Shiva, V. (2005) 'The Indian Seed Act and Patent Act: Sowing the Seeds of Dictatorship', *GRAIN*, 14 February, available online at https://www.grain.org/article/entries/2166-india-seed-act-patent-act-sowing-the-seeds-of-dictatorship [accessed 6 November 2013].

Shiva, V. (2013) 'The Seeds of Suicide: How Monsanto Destroys Farming', *Asian Age and Global Research*, 5 April, available online at http://www.globalresearch.ca/the-seeds-of-suicide-how-monsanto-destroys-farming/5329947 [accessed 6 November 2013].

Smolders, W. (2005) *Disclosure of Origin and Access and Benefit Sharing: The Special Case of Seeds for Food and Agriculture*, Geneva: QUNO.

Strandburg, K. J. (2009) 'Evolving Innovation Paradigms and the Global Intellectual Property Regime', *Connecticut Law Review*, 41(3): 861–920.

Tempo (2005) 'Penjara Bagi Petani Kreatif', 28 August, available online at https://m.tempo.co/read/news/2005/08/28/05865842/penjara-bagi-petani-kreatif [accessed 21 July 2016].

United Nations Conference on Trade and Development (UNCTAD) (2013) *Trade and Environment Review 2013: Wake up before It Is Too Late – Make Agriculture Truly Sustainable Now for Food Security in a Changing Climate*, Geneva: UNCTAD.

United Nations Economic and Social Commission for Asia and the Pacific (UNESCAP) (2009) *Sustainable Agriculture and Food Security in the Asia Pacific*, available online at http://www.refworld.org/pdfid/49f589db2.pdf [accessed 21 July 2016].

United Nations Food and Agriculture Organization (FAO) (2004) *Seed Policy and Regulations in the Light of the International Treaty on PGRFA and the Cartagena Protocol on Biosafety*, Twenty-seventh FAO Regional Conference for Asia and the Pacific, Beijing, 17–21 May, available online at ftp://ftp.fao.org/unfao/bodies/aprc/aprc27/J1701e.doc [accessed 29 June 2006].

van Overwalle, G. (1999) 'Patent Protection for Plants: A Comparison of American and European Approaches', *IDEA Journal of Law and Technology*, 39(2): 143–194.

Vellve, R. (1992) *Saving the Seed: Genetic Diversity and European Agriculture*, London: Earthscan.

Wiyanto (2014) 'Pemanfaatan Biotek Tanaman Pangan Tunggu Perpres', *Inilahcom*, 28 February, available online at http://ekonomi.inilah.com/read/detail/2078449/pemanfaatan-biotek-tan-man-pangan-tunggu-perpres [accessed 7 July 2015].

17 Institutionalising property

New land law in a new nation-state

Daniel Fitzpatrick

How does property emerge as an institution in a new nation-state? At time of writing, the National Parliament of Timor-Leste is shortly expected to consider (and pass) a new law to establish property rights in land. In common with a number of other countries in the Asian region, Timor-Leste has long-standing customary authority systems, and a history of armed conflict and population displacement. As in all societies, but particularly in these types of circumstance, it is clear that the shape and content of property in land will not be a product of law alone. While the design of law is important, because it sets the parameters for state–citizen interaction, the interaction of law with non-state mechanisms of property coordination will determine the way in which property emerges as an institution in the new state context.

The notion that institutions matter is a core principle of current approaches to development. Broadly, the economic literature defines institutions as the rules of the game – the constraints that humans devise to shape social interaction (Calvert, 1995; Searle, 2005: 1–22; Shepsle, 1986). Much of the literature on institutions as rules of the game suggests that institutions emerge through processes of conflict and interest-group bargaining (Calvert, 1995: 80). For example, Itai Sened (1997: 67) argues that property is the product of political interactions that establish rules for lower-order games of resource competition. This is a public choice conception of institutions that draws attention to processes of legislative design. But there remains a question of institutionalisation: why would resource users necessarily comply with rules established through political interaction, especially when there are existing conventions of property coordination generated by resource users themselves? How do legal rules of property establish compliance with individual claims to property, given that coercive enforcement alone is too costly to provide a viable basis for a property system?

This chapter analyses the potential pathways for the emergence of property in land in Timor-Leste. Timor-Leste provides a useful case study of the formation of property. The new state is emergent and still distant from many of its citizens, both in terms of enforcement of *de jure* rights and supply of information on law. The draft law on land establishes a layered set of interacting rules: a default presumption of state title to land; a principle of adverse possession as the basis for private ownership of land; and notions of community property and community protection in areas of customary domain. At the same time, there are historical mechanisms for property coordination based on localised principles of respect for ancestral authority and highly contextualised notions of rights based on possession. Not only are there plural sources of authority, but also there is little or no epistemic consensus on core terms such as 'possession', 'community' and 'property'. The chapter argues based on the case study that the emergence of property – not simply as a set of legal rules, but as an effective constraint on human interaction – involves more than processes of legislative design or interest-group interaction, and requires attention to the process by which law traverses social mechanisms of communication and authority.

Custom and possession in traditional Timorese land systems

Timor-Leste is a new nation-state that lies northwest of Australia in the Lesser Sunda Islands at the eastern end of the Indonesian archipelago. It has a land area of approximately 14,600 km^2, and a population of over 1.1 million. While national income is relatively high as a result of offshore oil and gas reserves, almost all East Timorese pursue livelihoods outside the oil and gas sector. Around a third rely exclusively on subsistence agriculture. After independence in 2002, over 39 per cent lived below the poverty line (estimated at less than US$0.55 a day) (International Finance Corporation and Asian Development Bank, 2007: 2). After the political crisis in 2006, which displaced around 100,000 East Timorese, real per capita income in the non-petroleum sector decreased by as much as 20 per cent and youth unemployment spiked from 40 per cent to 58 per cent. There are relatively low levels of private sector activity or employment, and emerging allegations of official rent-seeking involving access to land, including for agribusiness developments (International Finance Corporation and Asian Development Bank, 2007: 7).

The rural population is relatively dispersed. Some 600,000 hectares, or 42 per cent of the land mass, is viable agricultural land. The soil is generally shallow, and susceptible to landslides and flooding. Most agricultural activity is subsistence farming (corn, rice, root crops, vegetables and fruit), although there is some cash crop production of coffee, tobacco, cloves, cocoa, vanilla and areca nuts. Large areas of Timor-Leste are not cultivated because 44 per cent of the land mass lies at an incline of greater than 40 per cent (International Finance Corporation, 1997: 2). Since 1999, there has been a migration of people from rural to urban areas, and from eastern to western districts. In Dili District, which includes the capital city of Dili, there have been rapid population increases from around 7,000 in the 1960s to 175,000 in 2004 (Government of Timor-Leste, 2004: 8). While there is increasing competition for land in urban areas and around rural towns such as Ainaro, there is sufficient land for cultivation in most rural districts of Timor-Leste. Current pressures on local land systems arise more from contested authority over land, particularly as a result of relocations during Indonesian times, than from the availability of land itself.

There are approximately twenty-six ethno-linguistic groups in East Timor. Each has a distinct mythology of origin, whereby authority over land is claimed by lineages that trace descent to a founding ancestor or a common source of identity (Bellwood, Fox and Tryson, 1995; Fox, 1996; McWilliam, 2002). Typically, the senior lineage (or 'source house') of origin group is designated as the 'lord of the land' (Fox, 1980). Elders of the senior lineage claim privileged information on the rituals required to mediate access to land through relations with local guardian spirits. Across rural East Timor, there are sacred sites marking symbolic acts by mythical founding ancestors that involved intermediation with local guardian spirits (Forbes, 1989; McWilliam, 2007). These sites include coastal altar posts marking the first landing of ancestor-sectors, abandoned hilltop villages that were sites of first settlement and sacred houses that contain objects of origin group legitimacy (Fitzpatrick, McWilliam and Barnes, 2013). Periodic rituals at sacred sites reproduce the privileged status and authority of origin group elders (Fitzpatrick and Barnes, 2010: 213–214).

In customary areas, Timorese narratives of origin are focal points for property coordination, because they provide a basis for shared expectations of priority in relation to land (Fitzpatrick and Barnes, 2010). In-migrants, in particular, know they can avoid costly forms of conflict, and obtain access to land, through cooperative incorporation into customary order. Historically, elders of the senior lineage allocated new land for settlement and farming to new arrivals through mechanisms of marriage, or a traditional contract known as *juramento* (Fitzpatrick and Barnes, 2010; McWilliam, 2007). The incorporation of in-migrants into customary order through marriage creates reciprocal 'wife-giver/wife-taker' relations between the origin lineage and the in-migrant group (Clamagirand, 1982; Traube, 1986). Long-term exchange relations between lineages, or 'houses', provide the basis for future generations of in-migrants to access land. In a context of abundant land, the option to access land through exchange relations provides a low-cost alternative to conflict over land. Pervasive beliefs in spiritual relations with land, including sickness as a retribution for transgression of origin norms, also contributes to localised mechanisms for the coordination of property in land (Fitzpatrick et al., 2013: 2–36).

Susana Barnes (2011: 34–35) provides the following example from the northeastern district of Viqueque. Shortly before World War II, a group of Afalocai people left their traditional lands in the district of Viqueque and settled on land claimed as sacred by the neighbouring Darlari origin group, without seeking permission from Darlari elders. The land cleared for settlement and cultivation by the Afalocai was not under active use by the Darlari. According to the customary narratives of the Darlari, the Afalocai in-migrants soon fell ill because they had not respected the guardian spirits of the land. Their leader, Gregorio, then sought help from the Darlari elders. The result was a marriage alliance between the two groups, with Gregorio marrying a woman from the senior Darlari lineage. Darlari elders allocated land to Gregorio's followers at a number of sites within the customary domain of the Darlari. This first group of Afalocai migrants into the area claimed by the Darlari holds heritable rights to land, based both on acts of residence and cultivation and their status as a 'wife-taker' group, subject to the acknowledgement of Darlari customary authority in the agreement with Darlari elders.

Inter-group warfare was common on the island of Timor prior to the arrival of the Portuguese colonialists. Most early settlements were fortified hilltop forts rather than villages close to fields and sources of water (Fitzpatrick et al., 2013: 159–169). For groups with access to means of violence, warfare offered an alternative means to access land to cooperative processes of in-marriage and incorporation into customary order. Successful warfare also provided a supply of slave labour. The tapestry of customary group interaction in Timor contains multiple examples of alliance, agreement, conquest and subjugation. These historical examples illustrate the point that while origin narratives may serve as a potential focal point for property coordination, strategic calculations also allowed the possibility of conflict as an alternative to cooperative respect for claims of ancestral precedence (Fitzpatrick and Barnes, 2010).

Even within customary groups, there were (and are) strategic acts that test property coordination mechanisms based on respect for ancestral origin. At times, in-migrant households have sought to strengthen their entitlements by purporting to transfer land to areas, claim land left fallow and, in more recent times, construct concrete housing. Some in-migrant lineages have claimed authority to represent the group in relations with outsiders, as an articulation of political power that is distinguished from the ritual authority of the senior lineage. Other lineages claim authority over land allocation, or certain types of ritual, while professing overall acknowledgement of the privileged relations between senior lineage elders and the guardian spirits of the land. Over time, demographic growth and changes in external circumstances have increased the potential for property conflict within a customary group, as interactions among households and lineages of the group created the potential for changes in strategy that disrupt the equilibrium mechanisms for property coordination (Fitzpatrick et al., 2013).

The emergence of land claims based on possession

The intrusion of colonial authority in Timor-Leste increased the potential for property claims based on actual possession rather than grant or permission from holders of customary authority. Early in the twentieth century, the Portuguese sought to clear forested areas, particularly in the fertile lowlands of the southern coast, for rice fields and other forms of intensive cultivation (Gunn, 1999: 25–49). Much of this land had not been the subject of swidden (shifting) cultivation by customary groups and, as a result, access to cleared land was not necessarily determined through customary mechanisms, but by village heads acting under authority from the Portuguese administration (Gunn, 1999: 25–49). The Portuguese did not issue formal documents of title to those who had cleared land, but did often provide a hoe or other type of agricultural implement (Gunn, 1999: 25–49). As a consequence of colonial Portuguese land-clearing policies, many individual claims to land in fertile lowland areas are now based not on customary allocation pursuant to origin narratives, but on histories of actual possessory acts, including clearing and digging irrigation channels (Gunter, 2007).

Initial participation in clearing land and constructing irrigation channels, through work groups organised by hamlet and village heads, led to allocation of individual plots for housing and cultivation. According to Fitzpatrick and colleagues (2013: 239–264), these plots are subject to heritable rights of control and exclusion, and could even be leased or sold to residents of other hamlets of villages. In many areas, these transactions are documented, with the local village head acting as a witness to the agreement. However, a number of land-holders also acknowledged the traditional claims of a local origin group to ritualised stewardship of land, and participated in ceremonies organised by the group to celebrate harvests and the like. Some even sought customary elder permission for transactions involving their land. Even in areas first cleared or settled under colonial supervision, therefore, there are still property legitimation strategies involving reference to custom, as well as historical acts of possession.

A brief history of land law and administration in East Timor

Portugal held Timor as a colony from 1701 to 1974, interrupted by Japanese military occupation between 1942 and 1945. In 1975, the Indonesian military invaded East Timor, shortly after Portugal withdrew from all of its colonies. From 1974 to 1999, at least 102,800 and as many as 183,000 East Timorese died from conflict-related causes (Government of Timor-Leste, 2005: 44). According to the Truth and Reconciliation Commission established by the new state of East Timor (Government of Timor-Leste, 2005: 73):

> The people of Timor Leste experienced repeated periods of displacement, often in massive numbers, between 1975 and 1999. Most individual East Timorese alive today have experienced at least one period of displacement. Many have experienced several . . .

In 1999 the Indonesian government agreed, over the objections of its military command, to hold a popular consultation on independence for East Timor. Almost 80 per cent of East Timorese voted for independence, notwithstanding a campaign of intimidation planned by Indonesian military forces and executed by pro-Indonesian militia groups (Fitzpatrick, 2002: 1–2). Following the vote, the Indonesian military and its militia proxies carried out a 'scorched earth' campaign of property destruction and forced population displacement. Most land title offices and records were destroyed. More than half the housing stock was seriously damaged or destroyed. More than 400,000 people were internally displaced within East Timor itself and a further 300,000 fled, or were forcibly transported, across the border to West Timor. This widespread displacement – more than 75 per cent of the population – created a humanitarian crisis, while also reawakening cycles of land conflict as some took advantage of displacement or abandonment to repossess lands allegedly lost as a result of dispossession in either the Portuguese, Japanese and Indonesian periods of control of East Timor (Fitzpatrick, 2002: 5–7). Not surprisingly, in the capital city of Dili, there was a rush to occupy habitable houses when displaced people returned to seek shelter. Much of the housing subject to ad hoc occupation had been held by Indonesian citizens, who fled once order was established by the International Force for East Timor (INTERFET), a UN-led military force (Fitzpatrick, 2002: 6).

As a result of the war-torn history of East Timor, there are multiple bases for land claims and a legacy of contestation over past events of possession and dispossession. The potential bases for private claims to land in contemporary East Timor include custom, possession, Portuguese title documents, Indonesian title documents and eminent domain (Fitzpatrick, 2002: 136). According to Indonesian government records, the colonial Portuguese Timor administration issued and registered 2,843 land titles between 1900 and 1974 (Da Cruz, 1999: 44). Between 1976 and 1996, the Indonesian administration issued and registered a total of 34,965 Indonesian property titles, covering approximately 10 per cent of East Timor's total land mass. Most titles issued by the Portuguese and Indonesians took the form of limited-term leasehold interests rather than indefinite ownership interests (Fitzpatrick, 2002: 88–89, 158–160). By 1998, according to Pedro de Sousa Xavier (2000: 2), the total number of Indonesian titles had increased to 44,091. In theory, these Indonesian titles included converted Portuguese titles pursuant to conversion regulations issued by the Indonesian government for East Timor. However the number of converted Portuguese titles was relatively small, as Indonesian government files record that only 142, out of a possible 1,503 in the capital city, Dili, were converted and that, moreover, there was never any application for conversion by non-Indonesian citizens – that is, East Timorese exiles in Portugal or Australia (Da Cruz, 1999: 11, 49).

On 25 October 1999, the United Nations Security Council passed Resolution No. 1272 establishing the United Nations Transitional Authority in East Timor (UNTAET). Article 1 vested all legislative and executive authority with respect to East Timor, including the administration of justice, in the hands of UNTAET. After democratic elections, East Timor attained independence in March 2002. The Fretilin Party, which had been closely associated with the armed (Falantil) resistance to Indonesian occupation, formed the new government, with a majority of ministers drawn from a group of Portuguese-speaking Timorese that had been exiles in Mozambique or Portugal during the Indonesian occupation.

Law No. 1 of 2003: The default rule of state title to land

East Timor became the independent state of Timor-Leste in March 2002. In 2003, the National Parliament of Timor-Leste approved Law No. 1 of 2003 on the regulation of state land and abandoned land. The Law is most significant for its definition of state land. It defines land held under the 'private domain' of the state to include unclaimed private land without an identifiable owner. This provision provides a bright-line default: the burden of proving private title lies with the claimant. It seems that the interests of key regulatory agents – the political elite and international legal advisers – converged on the need to strengthen the state. The then-governing party Fretilin, in particular, had a long-standing ideological preference for state control over land, as a result of its socialist revolutionary history as the party of resistance to Indonesian occupation and to the concentration of landed property ownership under Portuguese rule (Braithwaite et al., 2010: 17). International advisers were also comfortable with default presumptions of state title, both because of their legal training and because of international aid donor concerns for state viability.

Default presumptions of state ownership lie within orthodox common and civil law conceptual frameworks (McAuslan, 1998). A default rule of state title to land supports the territorialisation of state power because it includes certain projections and assumptions of state sovereign authority. Yet, in post-conflict circumstances of competitive racing for control over resources, there are considerable incentives and opportunities for government officials to claim large areas as unowned land to facilitate rent extraction from the grant of state land leases. There will likely be widespread uncertainties of private ownership because of population displacement, destruction of records and undocumented forms of land-holding. There will be economic pressures to generate employment and investment. In all of these circumstances, a bright-line rule on state land may provide a low-cost interpretive pathway for government actors to obtain rents and grant land concessions to investors who would otherwise face uncertain negotiations with purported groups of private landowners (Alden Wily, 2009: 36 –8). Law No. 1 of 2003 allows this result, because officials from the Land and Property Directorate may determine that an area of land lacks an identifiable owner and is therefore subject to proof of ownership by a private claimant, available for grant to an outside investor.

The effects of the housing conflicts of 2006–07

In 2006, political conflict between the Fretilin prime minister and the president, a former Falantil military leader, degenerated into circumstances of temporary state failure, as elements of the police and army engaged in armed combat, and latent tensions over post-1999 land occupations escalated into large-scale house burnings and evictions in Dili (Harrington, 2007). In the lead-up to the violent events of 2006, supporters of the prime minister and president had armed and funded competing private militia, which were associated with martial arts gangs and elements of the police and military (Scambary, 2006). The conflict soon took on so-called Easterner–Westerner distinctions, which contributed to violent housing conflicts in Dili as 'Westerners' – long-term residents of Dili – took advantage of widespread lawlessness to engage in tit-for-tat forced evictions of 'Easterners', who had occupied houses largely owned by Indonesians before their departure in late 1999. The return of UN-led military and police forces led to restoration of order in 2007, the resignation of the prime minister and the election of the president as prime minister under a coalition of parties known as the Association with a Parliamentary Majority (AMP). Fretilin becamse the major opposition party.

The tragic events of 2006–07 highlighted the fragility of the East Timorese state and the risks of conflict over post-1999 occupation of land and housing. The conflict over housing, in particular, increased appreciation among legal advisers and the political elite of the risks of disorder if the state were to attempt mass evictions as part of a programme of restitution of pre-independence titles to land. Whereas, until 2006, most international legal advisers had advocated a simple rule of restitution of possession as at 5 October 1999, to facilitate the return of displaced persons, a draft 2009 Land Law replaced restitution of titles with recognition of rights based on possession. East Timorese citizens could claim ownership on the basis of possession since 31 December 1998, even where there was a competing claim based on titles issued by the Portuguese or Indonesian administrations. The recognition of possession represented an acknowledgement of the likelihood of violent resistance to eviction by possessors and the effects of further housing violence on state stability.

The proposed rule of 'special adverse possession' first appeared in a draft Land Law issued for discussion in June 2009. The draft Law did not allow for restitution of Portuguese or Indonesian titles at all; instead, a claimant would receive an ownership right if she peacefully took possession of a vacant property before 26 April 2006, without the authority of the previous possessor, and maintained possession in good faith for at least five consecutive years (section 13). While the draft Law privileged possessory claims over ones of restitution, it did provide that, where there was no special adverse possession, a claim based on Portuguese or Indonesian titles – including long-term use rights – would be entitled to conversion to a registered ownership right. The privileging of possession over restitution in the draft 2009 Law had an orthodox policy rationale: to reduce the costs of proving title. As in stable socio-political environments, the rule of adverse possession reduced the costs of proving rights in circumstances in which other mechanisms of proof were lost or costly to establish (Merrill, 1984: 1122). Yet there were context-specific issues of social ordering affecting the design of the possessory rule, including a desire to minimise the likelihood of forced evictions, which would strain the enforcement capacity of a state still subject to the possibility of violent instability.

In early 2010, the Minister of Justice commissioned Portuguese lawyers to review the 2009 draft Law. The advisers recommended restitution of pre-independence ownership titles while retaining ownership rights based on long-term possession. This would favour members of the Portuguese-speaking elite who had received ownership, rather than limited-term, titles under the Portuguese administration. The draft Law, as approved by the National Parliament of East Timor in February 2012, combined restitutionary and possessory principles. Claims of ownership may be based on Portuguese or Indonesian ownership titles and, where there is no such title, on continuous, peaceful and notorious possession that commenced on or before 31 December 1998.[1] Under this formulation, the great majority of ownership claims would be based on possession rather than restitution, because Portuguese and Indonesian ownership titles were relatively few in number and limited in terms of areas covered, with most pre-independence titles limited-term leasehold interests. In Dili, for example, 88 per cent of all titles issued under the Indonesian administration were limited-term in nature (*hak guna bangunan*) (Fitzpatrick, 2002: 88).

On 20 March 2012, however, the president refused to assent to the law and referred it back to Parliament with a list of proposed revisions. The veto reasons included concerns over the definition of state land and a lack of consultation with civil society groups.[2] After presidential elections in April 2012 and parliamentary elections in June 2012, the

AMP formed a new government and a new president was appointed. At time of writing, the Council of Ministers has approved a new draft of the Land Law, which retains the essential features of the 2012 draft. Once there is a quorum, the National Parliament is expected to consider (and pass) the draft Land Law.

The draft Land Law provides that mere occupants cannot acquire ownership rights to land by means of special adverse possession. 'Mere occupants' are defined to include people using land with no intention of acting as owners, people 'who took advantage of the tolerance of legitimate possessors', and representatives and agents of the legal possessor (section 10(1)). These categories establish distinctions between actual and legal possession that are common to civil and common law systems. They allow possessory doctrines to accommodate transactions such as bailment, leases and licences. Yet the law does not extend the distinction between mere occupants and legal possessors to customary districts. Section 10(3) defines possessors to include those who reside in, have erected buildings on or have cultivated land claimed by another party based on the belief of ancestral customary domain, even when rent is being paid to that party. Fitzpatrick and colleagues (2013: 106–111) argue that this definition potentially allows large numbers of persons displaced during the Indonesian occupation to claim alienable ownership of land within ancestral customary domains, even though they might otherwise fall within the definition of 'mere occupant'. Entitlement to ownership on the basis of individual possession alone, with unrestricted powers to sell land to other Timorese citizens, will be inconsistent with localised understandings of the rights of displaced persons and, in some cases, will lead to violent conflict should those who were displaced, or their descendants, claim alienable rights of ownership.

Chapter V of the draft Land Law: Community protection zones and community property

The application of a rule of adverse possession to areas of customary domain is further complicated by new legal categories of community property and community protection zones in Chapter V of the draft Land Law. Section 21 defines community protection zones as areas protected by the state for the purpose of safeguarding common interests of local communities. A community protection zone does not take the form of a right to property. Individuals, communities and the state may own land in a community protection zone, with the ordinary rights and incidents of ownership, subject only to the protective safeguards set out in sections 22 and 25. The nature of state protective obligations in community protection zones includes responsibilities to ensure that all customary practices: conform to the Constitution and are participatory, non-discriminatory and respect gender equality; promote environmental and socio-cultural sustainability in the uses of natural resources and the way of life of each local community; and protect immovable property in the community from real estate speculation (section 22). Section 25 further provides that economic activity by a third party in a community protection zone is subject to a number of conditions, including requirements that the activity: be preceded by consultation with the local community; benefit the local community as a whole in an inclusive and non-discriminatory fashion; be performed in a sustainable way, from environmental and socio-cultural points of view; and respect community ways of life and access to natural resources.

At this stage, all domestic land actors in East Timor are unfamiliar with the notion of a 'community protection zone'. The notion was taken from Mozambican law, primarily as a result of conversations among international legal advisers. There was a belief among international actors that key political and bureaucratic figures in East Timor would not support explicit recognition of customary rights or authority relating to land, that a reference to Mozambique would provide legitimacy and a cognitive shortcut for East Timorese political figures who were exiles in Mozambique during the Indonesian occupation, and that the experience in Mozambique would provide a useful template for the implementation of Chapter V in East Timor. The development of land law in Mozambique involved similar circumstances to East Timor of a former Portuguese colony emerging from war and a political elite antagonistic to recognition of customary authority (Tanner, 2002). As is also allowed under the law on community protection zones in East Timor, the state in Mozambique may grant state land leases to investors in rural areas subject to requirements of community consultation and partnership.

The importation of Mozambican legal concepts by foreign advisers had little to do with public choice models of legislative design and interaction among political representatives. Their incorporation into the law reflected a conscious effort by foreign legal advisers to work within political constraints on recognising customary rights to land. However their implementation will be influenced by the rent-seeking incentives of key actors in the state. In particular, at present there are no incentives for Land and Property Directorate officials to identify or demarcate community protection zones in a timely or expansive manner, because that will trigger costly consultation and protection measures and reduce the opportunity for rent-seeking gain from rapid grant of leases over state land.[3] A lower-cost interpretive pathway will involve declaration by the Land and Property Directorate that an area sought by an investor is state land outside a community protection zone. This will allow the direct grant of rights to an investor without incurring community protection zone obligations, including, in particular, the requirements of consultation prior to third-party economic activity.

The new category of community property

The first version of the 2010 draft Law did not provide for customary ownership of land, whether individual or collective. After some debate, a second version included the possibility of collective ownership of land through incorporation as a cooperative. After further advice that customary groups were unlikely to form cooperatives, in circumstances of limited access to legal information, the draft Law was amended to establish communities as juridical entities for the purposes of community property. A community may thus hold and register ownership of community property without the need for legal incorporation. 'Community property' is defined as land acknowledged by the community as being of common and shared use, by a group of individuals or families, organised in accordance with local practices and customs (section 25(1)). The reference to local practices and customs is significant, because the notion of community property is intended to apply in customary districts.

Section 26 provides that the Land and Property Directorate shall assist each local community in the process of community property demarcation and consult with local and community authorities, as well as the elders residing locally, as sources of essential information. However, even more so than is the case with community protection zones, Land and Property Directorate staff have few incentives to identify and demarcate areas of community property in a timely or expansive manner. In conversations with the author, senior Land and Property Directorate officials interpreted the notion of community property by reference to restrictive Indonesian conceptions of customary land – that is, as limited to areas of actual residence and cultivation (Fitzpatrick, 1997: 171–212). There is little funding, capacity and political will to undertake any process for demarcating areas of community property. Wherever possible, the state is likely to grant rights directly to investors through claims of state land or compulsory acquisition of private land, rather than to facilitate agreements between a community and an outside investor. In these circumstances, the category of community property will likely not be a bright-line right of exclusion vested in a customary community and enforced by agencies of the state, but a symbolic legal artefact – a product of compromises in the drafting of the law – that, at best, acts as an element in the localised negotiation of entitlements to customary land and, at worst, contributes to widespread uncertainty and confusion surrounding the effects of private property rules in the draft Law.

The potential implementation of the draft Land Law in rural districts

How might the draft Land Law affect the institutionalisation of property in independent Timor-Leste? To analyse the potential pathways of property in Timor-Leste, this section considers the relationship between the law and customary land arrangements in rural districts. The analysis distinguishes two broad areas of land relations in rural districts. The first involves districts of acknowledged customary domain. Resource users predominately obtain rights through membership of, agreement or intermarriage with lineages descended from a mythologised source of origin. The second area involves districts first cleared for settlement by work groups organised under colonial agricultural programmes. Resource users predominately derive rights from historical acts of cultivation and construction, accompanied at times by the grant of agricultural implements from sources of colonial authority. While land users in areas cleared or cultivated under colonial supervision may acknowledge the underlying land stewardship of nearby origin groups, or even attempt to mythologise their forebears' acts of first possession as productive of customary legitimacy, the key land allocation and conflict-management actors tend to be hamlet and village heads rather than origin group elders. Hamlet and village heads may consult with origin elders, particularly where they are family or marriage relations, but nevertheless retain a primary role in local questions of land management.

In areas of acknowledged customary domain, it is likely that any attempt to apply a legal rule of adverse possession will be productive of conflict or uncertainty, as a result of both competing epistemic understandings of possession as a basis for entitlement and the potential for possessory claims to undermine long-standing systems of customary authority. In customary systems, the relevant acts of possession enumerated by the Land Law – construction, settlement, cultivation – have significance for property entitlements only in a context of social status and affiliation. There is no customary rule or norm that length of time in possession alone gives rise to property entitlements, because the possessory significance of acts of clearing, cultivation and residence is negotiated with reference to customary order. Whether or not possessory acts lead to property entitlements depends on issues such as affiliation with an origin group, participation in rituals, respect for customary prohibitions and acknowledgement of the land stewardship of customary authority holders. Moreover, not only do local understandings of possession and property differ substantially from legal definitions, at least among members of origin groups, but there is also an inherent potential for legal rules of possession to challenge customary systems of land authority, particularly by supporting the claims of displaced groups that have not been incorporated into customary systems of order. The potential application of the possessory rule to areas of customary domain thus involves a combination of epistemic distance and authority plurality as between customary systems and the state.

In areas first cleared and settled under colonial supervision, where rights to land were not allocated through customary mechanisms, a legal rule of long-term possession is preferable to its primary legal alternatives, which include restitution of pre-independence rights to land, or nationalisation followed by state processes of land grant or option. In areas first cleared under colonial supervision, it seems more likely that a legal rule of possession will apply according to its legislative intent, with less indeterminacy or interpretive contestation than in areas of customary domain, because there is greater epistemic consensus on the meaning of possessory acts and less competition among customary and state-based systems of property enforcement. However, it is also suggested that a possessory rule in areas first cleared or settled under colonial supervision should be based on fuzzy, rather than bright-line, formulations of possessory entitlements, in order to allow space for situational processes of adjustment that minimise the possibility of violent conflict. Fuzzy formulations of possessory entitlements include the discretion not to apply a rule of possession where the state has limited property enforcement capacity and dispossessed claimants retain access to means of group violence.

Conclusion: Property rules in a post-conflict state

An emerging body of literature considers institutions and their path-dependent effects on economic growth (North, 1979: 1319–1332; Robinson, Acemoglu and Johnson, 2005: 386–472). The literature focuses on the incentive effects of institutions: as is often stated, secure property rights provide incentives for investment, whereas insecure property rights provide an explanation for chronic underdevelopment. While the incentive effects of institutions are much explored, the definition of institutions, and the process by which they form, is less understood. These questions are important, because the notion that institutions are the rules of the game fails to explain the way in which rules become constraints on human behaviour. Without a theory of institutionalisation of legal rules, there are assumptions of the effectiveness of formal institutions, for example that there is a well-functioning legal system with a state monopoly on the use of force. This is patently not the case in an emergent state such as Timor-Leste.

The early stages of state formation provide circumstances in which the idea of constitutional order is not a focal basis for property coordination. As is the case in most rural districts of Timor-Leste, the citizens of an emergent state tend to identify themselves as members of subgroups, distinguished by language, geography or ethnicity, rather than members of a constitutional order. There are diverse authority systems relating to land and divergent epistemic understandings of core notions such as possession and property. Moreover, there is limited capacity to enforce *de jure* rights to land. How, then, does an emergent state establish the institution of property in land? The Timor-Leste example suggests that the emergence of a simple, uniform institution of property in a new state requires a foundation of epistemic consensus as to the meaning of property, as well as a process of accrual of legitimacy on the part of the state, such that notions of law and constitutional order become a focal basis for property coordination. Yet the paradox of land policy in an emergent state is that these preconditions for the institutionalisation of property rules are unlikely to be present, because the incentives of legislative design result in layered sets of rules that provide rent-seeking opportunities for powerful state-connected actors.

Notes

1 See s. 22, 2009 draft Land Law. It seems that the decision to push the commencement date of possession back to 31 December 1998 was motivated by a desire not to reward ad hoc occupiers of land after 1999, in part because of fears of renewed possessory conflicts in Dili. It may also be that the coalition government was concerned not to recognise post-1999 claims to valuable coastal land by Fretilin-connected actors.

2 The reasons for the decision of the President are set out in La'o Hamatuk (2012). The other two laws subject to presidential veto were the Expropriation Law and the Real Estate Financing Law.

3 The draft Land Law does not define the process of identifying community protection zones or the line agency responsible for demarcating their boundaries. These lacunae will be filled by separate regulation or legislation. Based on conversations with a legal adviser in the Ministry of Justice, it is likely that the Land and Property Directorate will take responsibility for identifying and delineating community protection zones. This responsibility would be consistent with Land and Property Directorate authority over the demarcation of state land.

References

Alden Wily, L. A. (2009) 'Tackling Land Tenure in the Emergency to Development Transition in Post-conflict States: From Restitution to Reform', in S. Pantuliano (ed.) *Uncharted Territory: Land, Conflict and Humanitarian Action*, Rugby: Practical Action, 27–50.

Barnes, S. (2011) 'Origins, Precedence and Social Order in the Domain of Ina Ama Beli Darlari', in A. McWilliam and E. Traube, E. (eds) *Land and Life in Timor-Leste*, Canberra: ANU Press, 23–46.

Bellwood, P., Fox, J. J., and Tryson, D. (1995) *The Austronesians: Historical and Comparative Perspectives*, Canberra: Research School of Pacific and Asian Studies, Australian National University.

Braithwaite, J., Dinnen, S., Allen, M., Braithwaite, V., and Charlesworth, H. (2010) *Pillars and Shadows: Statebuilding as Peacebuilding in Solomon Islands*, Canberra: ANU E-Press.

Calvert, R. L. (1995) 'Rational Actors, Equilibrium and Social Institutions', in J. Knight and I. Sened (eds) *Explaining Social Institutions*, Ann Arbor, MI: University of Michigan Press, 132–145.

Clamagirand, B. R. (1982) *Marobo: Une société ema de Timor*, Langues et Civilisation de L'Asie du Sud-Est et du Monde Insulindien 12. Paris: SELAF.

Da Cruz, P. (1999) 'Studi Tentang Penguasaan dan Penggunaan Tanah Bekas Hak Portugis yang Ditunda Konversinya Dengan PP No. 34 Tahun 1992 di Kabupaten Dili Propinsi Timur-Timur [Study Concerning the Control and Use of Former Portuguese Title Land that was Converted under Presidential Decision No. 34 of 1992 in the Dili Region of East Timor Province]', Unpublished thesis, Sekolah Tinggi Pertanahan Nasional [National Land College], Yogyakarta.

de Sousa Xavier, P. (2000) 'Aspek-Aspek Terbaru Pertanahan Timor Lorosae [Current Aspects Concerning the Land in Timor Lorosae]', unpublished, on file with author.

Fitzpatrick, D. (1997) 'Disputes and Pluralism in Modern Indonesian Land Law', *Yale Journal of International Law*, 22(1): 171–212.

Fitzpatrick, D. (2002) *Land Claims in East Timor*, Canberra: Asia Pacific Press.

Fitzpatrick, D., and Barnes, S. (2010) 'The Relative Resilience of Property: First Possession and Order without Law in East Timor', *Law and Society Review*, 44(2): 205–238.

Fitzpatrick, D., McWilliam, A., and Barnes, S. (2013) *Property and Social Resilience in Times of Conflict: Land, Custom and Law in East Timor*, Farnham: Ashgate.

Forbes, H. O. (1989) *A Naturalist's Wanderings in the Eastern Archipelago*, Oxford/New York: Oxford University Press.

Fox, J. J. (1980) *The Flow of Life: Essays on Eastern Indonesia*, Cambridge, MA: Harvard University Press.

Fox, J. J. (1996) 'The Transformation of Progenitor Lines of Origin: Patterns of Precedence in Eastern Indonesia', in J. J. Fox and C. Sather (eds) *Origins, Ancestry and Alliance: Explorations in Austronesian Ethnography*, Canberra: Research School of Pacific and Asian Studies, Australian National University, 21–35.

Government of Timor Leste (2004) The 2004 Population and Housing Census of Timor-Leste, available online at http://www.dne.mof.gov.tl/census/2004_census/2004_population_housing/index.htm [accessed 21 July 2016].

Government of Timor Leste (2005) *Chega! The Report of the Commission for Reception, Truth and Reconciliation in East Timor (CAVR)*, available online at http://www.cavr-timorleste.org/en/chegaReport.htm [accessed 21 July 2016].

Gunn, G. (1999) *Timor Loro Sae: 500 Years*, Macao: Livros do Oriente.

Gunter, J. (2007) 'Communal Conflict in Viqueque and the "Charged" History of 59', *Asia Pacific Journal of Anthropology*, 8(1): 27–42.

Harrington, A. (2007) 'Ethnicity, Violence, and Land and Property Disputes in Timor-Leste', *East Timor Law Journal*, 2(1): 35–37.

International Finance Corporation and Asian Development Bank (2007) *Timor Leste: Economic and Social Development Brief*, available online at http://www.adb.org/Documents/Books/ESDB-Timor-Leste/ESDB-Timor-Leste.pdf [accessed 15 October 2009].

La'o Hamatuk (2012) 'President Vetoes Three Land Laws', 26 March, available online at http://www.laohamutuk.org/Agri/land/2012/12PNpassPRveto.htm [accessed 21 July 2016].

McAuslan, P. (1998) 'Making Law Work: Restructuring Land Relations in Africa', *Development and Change*, 29(3): 525–527.

McWilliam, A. R. (2002) *Paths of Origin, Gates of Life: A Study of Place and Precedence in Southwest Timor*, Leiden: KITLV Press.

McWilliam, A. R. (2007) 'Austronesians in Linguistic Disguise: Fataluku Cultural Fusion in East Timor', *Journal of Southeast Asian Studies*, 38(2): 355–375.

Merrill, T. (1984) 'Property Rules, Liability Rules, and Adverse Possession', *Northwestern University Law Review*, 79: 1122–1154.

North, D. (1979) 'Institutions and Economic Growth: An Historical Introduction', *World Development*, 17(9): 1319–1332.

Robinson J., Acemoglu, D., and Johnson, S. (2005) 'Institutions as a Fundamental Cause of Long-run Growth', *Handbook of Economic Growth*, 1A: 386–472.

Scambary, J. (2006) A Survey of Gangs and Youth Groups in Dili, Timor-Leste: A Report Commissioned by Australia's Agency for International Development, AusAID, available online at http://www.etan.org/etanpdf/2006/Report_Youth_Gangs_in_Dili.pdf [accessed 1 October 2012].

Searle, J. R. (2005) 'What Is an Institution?', *Journal of Institutional Economics*, 1(1): 1–22.

Sened, I. (1997) *The Political Institution of Private Property*, Cambridge: Cambridge University Press.

Shepsle, K. A. (1986) 'Institutional Equilibrium and Equilibrium Institutions', in H. F. Weisberg (ed.) *Political Science: The Science of Politics*, New York: Algora, 51–81.

Tanner, C. (2002) *Law Making in an African Context: The 1997 Mozambican Land Law*, FAO Legal Papers Online No. 26, Rome: FAO.

Traube, E. (1986) *Cosmology and Social Life: Ritual Exchange Among the Mambai of East Timor*, Chicago, IL: University of Chicago Press.

18 Water law in India

Philippe Cullet

Introduction

Water law in India is a relatively old and complex area of law. The long-standing focus on regulating access to, and control over, water reflects its importance for human survival, livelihoods and economic growth. At the same time, these different dimensions have often been addressed separately, resulting in a composite structure that is difficult to comprehend as a single comprehensive framework.

A large part of water law developed around the use of water as an input for productive activities. For decades, water law was thus essentially concerned with land rights and with irrigation. It is only progressively that there has been movement towards giving priority to the two biggest gaps that existed, the lack of a particular focus on drinking water and on water conservation and protection.

The existence of substantive gaps in Indian water law remains one of its defining characteristics in most states. In certain cases, it has proved difficult to fill identified gaps in part because the links between access to water and access to land have led to the development of resistance by beneficiaries of the present system against proposals to overhaul it. Water law has thus remained to some extent more conservative than other areas of law. For instance, while water is a central part of environmental law that has developed rapidly since the 1970s, water legislation, including recent Acts, is still largely devoid of an environmental perspective. One of the most visible signs of this dichotomy is the fact that the most important piece of legislation in India concerning water pollution is seen as being part of environmental law rather than water law.[1] Similarly, groundwater law has remained based on a set of principles developed in the nineteenth century in England. This has proved increasingly untenable, but landowners' claims over groundwater constitute a political challenge that few state governments want to tackle (Cullet, 2014: 73).

On the whole, regulating water is of immense importance in India because it is central to every aspect of life. This includes, first, the provision of sufficient and safe basic water to every person – something that is not yet fully achieved. Water is also central to livelihoods, particularly agriculture, which remains by far the primary sector in terms of individual livelihoods. Simultaneously, it needs to be regulated in a manner that privileges its protection and preservation in the short and longer terms to ensure the sustainability of human uses. This represents an immense challenge in a context in which water regulation has been largely conceived around either the predominance of the state as the actor controlling all water for 'public purposes',[2] or of individual landowners having unrestrained control over groundwater found under their land, including at the cost of similar use by other landowners. The challenge is compounded by the fact that the priority position of basic/drinking water has not been effectively implemented in India in terms of substantive regulation, as highlighted by the fact that existing drinking water quality standards are not backed by statutory recognition.

This chapter provides an overview of the regulatory framework for water in India, with a focus on rights to water and water rights. The first section offers a broad overview of the framework for water regulation and some of the specificities of the water sector, such as the increasing use of non-justiciable instruments. The next section then moves on to analyse the basic rights framework governing water, including the fundamental right to water and the different forms of appropriation that have developed over time, largely linked to control over land. In the context of the sectoral regulation of water, the third section then highlights the complexity of groundwater regulation, which is both one of the oldest areas of water law and the most important, since India today relies primarily on groundwater to meet its water needs (Planning Commission, 2012: 145). The final section then moves on to introduce the reforms that have been initiated in various areas of water law in India over the past couple of decades, as well as the links between domestic law and policy reforms and the changing international framework.

Regulation of water use and protection

The regulation of water in India is a complex affair. This results in part from the fact that water law developed progressively over many decades, with the legislature's codification effort focusing each time on specific water bodies or water uses. This is also because of the fact that the need for some form of decentralisation was understood long ago in a continent-sized country, with the consequent development of different regulatory frameworks in different parts of the country. The result is a multifaceted area of law that largely eluded lawyers' attention for a long time.

Constitutional scheme

The Constitution of India delineates the respective competences of the Union Government, states and local bodies (panchayats and municipalities). The broad division of powers between the Union and states follows the scheme of Government of India Act, 1935, which gave power to provinces (now 'states') over water supply, irrigation, canals, drainage and embankments, water storage and hydropower.[3] Under the Constitution, the primary competence for regulating water is thus given to states[4] – a scheme that appropriately reflects the variety of conditions and needs prevailing in different parts of the country.

The Union nevertheless plays an important role in water regulation. First, the Constitution gave Parliament the power to legislate concerning the adjudication of inter-state water disputes.[5] It is in this context that the Inter-State River Water Disputes Act, 1956, under which several disputes have been adjudicated, was adopted. Secondly, certain powers were reserved for the Union in the Seventh Schedule. This includes the regulation of inter-state rivers concerning which Parliament enacted the River Boards Act, 1956, a law that has been noticeable mostly for being largely dormant and the replacement of which has now been proposed. Thirdly, the Union has made use of article 252 of the Constitution, which allows Parliament to adopt an Act in a field in which states are competent provided that the states have given their assent. This was, for instance, the basis for the adoption of the Water (Prevention and Control of Pollution) Act, 1974, which is to date the most important Union legislation related to water. Article 252 is also the proposed basis for the adoption of a Framework Water Act at the Union level, three drafts of which have been prepared since the beginning of this decade.[6]

The relatively limited framework for interventions by the central government in water regulation has led it to use other avenues to influence water sector law and policy. This has included developing national water policies on several occasions (1987, 2002, 2012), as well as prodding states to take action in areas that fall under their competence. This has been the case with regards to drinking water supply, an area of high political importance in which the Union has adopted various administrative directions over time that it implements in cooperation with states through the provision of tied funding (Government of India Ministry of Drinking Water and Sanitation, 2013). The Union has also used financial levers at its disposal, as reflected in the Thirteenth Finance Commission's report that made the setting up of a water regulatory authority a precondition for the release of water sector grants (Government of India, 2009: para. 12.58).

The division of competences between the Union and states provides only one part of the relevant framework. Indeed, the Seventy-third and Seventy-fourth Amendments to the Constitution adopted in 1992 gave local bodies of governance in rural and urban areas significant powers in the water context. In rural areas, this includes powers and responsibilities over drinking water supply, minor irrigation, water management and watershed development, as well as fisheries.[7] In urban areas, this includes powers over water supply for domestic, industrial and commercial purposes.[8] These important changes in the Constitution are well entrenched in principle, but are yet to be fully implemented in certain parts of the country.

Multi-sectoral framework

The development of water law in India over many decades makes it a complex, although not necessarily comprehensive, area of law. This relatively strange combination is in part a reflection of the importance of water in each of its forms and uses, and the perceived need to adopt regulation progressively concerning relatively narrowly defined topics. Thus, during the colonial era, the focus was on the regulation of irrigation, as a result of which we still have separate laws for irrigation today. On the whole, water law has grown over time in a sectoral manner, with different rules and statutes being developed for different water bodies and different water uses.

The sectoral nature of water is positive from the point of view of the recognition of the importance of water in many sectors. However, even within a narrowly defined water sector, this sectoral framework has proved increasingly difficult to sustain, because it is built on a series of fictions that hamper equitable access to water and sustainable water protection. This is nowhere best illustrated than in the case of the existence of completely different rules governing surface and groundwater. The 'fiction' that sustained the development of different legal rules was the lack of perceived connection between the two at the time that the rules for groundwater were developed in the mid-nineteenth century.[9] Two elements stand out here: first, this missing connection was disproved decades ago, but the basic rules in place are still those developed by the case law in the nineteenth century;[10] and secondly, while groundwater was a minor source of water – although crucial for drinking water – when the rules were developed, it is today overwhelmingly the first source of water for all main water uses (Vijay Shankar, Kulkarni and Krishnan, 2011). The legal framework that is currently heavily biased towards complex statutes focusing on surface water is thus not aligned with the reality on the ground.

The complex nature of what is usually identified as belonging to water law, such as irrigation and groundwater laws, constitutes only one part of the overall regulatory framework concerning water. Indeed, over the past few decades, significant developments have taken place in other areas of law. This is the case with regard to environmental law, which includes water as one of the key elements covered.[11] In fact, it is ironic that while water law, including statutes adopted since the 1970s, remains largely or completely silent on water conservation and protection, one of the early and central pieces of legislation of 'environmental law' is the Water (Prevention and Control of Pollution) Act, 1974. This adds to the fragmentation of water law and to its complexity. Theoretically, neither fragmentation nor complexity are necessarily negative, since the regulation of water in India will never be simple. At the same time, the reality has been that the sectoral development of water law has led to the building of institutional competence in different ministries and departments, none of which has an effective mandate to look after water in a broad sense, so as to coordinate the implementation of relevant laws and policy developments. Indeed, even at the Union level, at which there is a Ministry of Water Resources,[12] the name is misleading in the sense that its umbrella function is limited and it has functioned in effect as a ministry focusing largely on the development of water-related infrastructure, such as dams.

The problems arising from the sectoral and fragmented nature of water law have been noticed, but there is little by way of concrete response to date. A generic response has been the development of water policies at the Union and state levels, starting with the National Water Policy, 1987.[13] This gives a generic context to the water sector, but fails to fill in the gaps left by a sectoral legal framework. Over the past decade, the recognition of the need to adopt framework water legislation has progressed. Jammu and Kashmir was one of the first states to take concrete steps towards consolidating its water law, and its Water Resources (Regulation and Management) Act, 2010 consolidates several sectors of water law in one statute. Some states have moved towards adopting comprehensive framework legislation. In the case of Rajasthan, two draft Bills have been prepared in recent years, but legislation has not yet been adopted. This does not amount to much in practice, but the fact that the draft Nagaland Water Policy, 2016, specifically calls for the enactment of comprehensive water legislation confirms that change can be expected in years to come.

At the national level, several drafts of framework water legislation have been prepared in recognition of the need for some form of coordination mechanism and for water law to be based, for instance, on principles that apply to all water bodies. The difficulty is that, at the national level, Parliament needs to rely on states' willingness to delegate their power to the Union under article 252 of the Constitution. States have remained wary of such initiatives because they fear that this may open the door to bringing water on the concurrent list,[14] something that has been proposed on various occasions. Indeed, the Parliamentary Standing Committee on Water Resources recently stated that:

> In view of the need to adopt a holistic approach for tackling the problem in a comprehensive and equitable manner, the Committee, therefore, reiterate their earlier recommendation . . . and urge the Government to initiate earnest efforts to build national consensus to bring the subject of 'Water' in the Concurrent List of the Constitution.
>
> (Standing Committee on Water Resources, 2015: 105)

With a view to steering clear of such controversial positions, the Ministry of Water Resources, River Development and Ganga Rejuvenation's Draft National Water Framework Bill, 2016, limits itself to providing a set of common principles and addressing issues that require the concurrence of more than one state.

Policies and administrative directions

As noted above, water law in India is sectoral, fragmented and often not comprehensive. Further, certain areas suffer from limited coverage in water legislation. This is, for instance, the case with regard to drinking water, universally recognised as the first priority by all actors in the sector. This is not to say that there is no regulation of drinking water supply at all, but there is no legislation that provides a general framework for drinking water supply. What this means in practice is that there are local laws that provide a framework for water supply, for example through water utilities, but there is no law that lays down water quality standards.[15] Even more surprisingly, there is no legal framework that specifically reflects the fundamental right to water that has been judicially recognised for more than two decades.[16]

In a context in which drinking water cannot but be the main water priority for any democratically elected government, it is not surprising to find that the lack of a statutory framework has been counterbalanced by other measures. For decades, the executive has increasingly invested the space left by the absence of legislation and devised a series of policy frameworks that act in effect as the regulatory framework concerning drinking water. The importance of these interventions is most marked in rural areas, where local people often understand these governmental policy interventions as the applicable law.

On the whole, the role of the executive in the water sector is more important than might be expected and warrants consideration while mapping 'water law'. As mentioned above, the executive's intervention starts at the broadest level, with the adoption of water policies – both generic, such as the National Water Policy 2012, and specific policies, such as the Rajasthan Rural Sanitation and Hygiene Policy, 2011. At a more specific level, there are various administrative directions that shape specific sectors, such as the National Rural Drinking Water Programme Guidelines in the case of rural drinking water supply (Government of India Ministry of Drinking Water and Sanitation, 2013).

Right to water and water rights

The development of water law in India over time has focused in large part on rights of access to, and control over, water by different actors. Given the link between land and water, water rights developed until recently in relation to land rights. This has started to change over the last few decades. First, there have been attempts to define water rights that are delinked from land rights in an attempt to foster the development of tradable water entitlements; secondly, there has been an increasingly vigorous formalisation of the fundamental right to water. This section starts by highlighting the fundamental right to water, since it is hierarchically superior, even though the body of water law concerned with water rights is much more substantial, having informed modern water law since the nineteenth century.

Fundamental right to water

The existence of a fundamental right to water in any legal system that includes a catalogue of fundamental human rights is beyond doubt. As argued by Gleick (1999: 493), given the intrinsic link between life and water, this implies that water is included as a right in any human right instrument or bill of rights, whether it is formally included in the list of recognised rights or not. The Constitution of India recognises a right to life, but does not specifically recognise a right to water. This is not particularly surprising, since it is only constitutions adopted recently that specify water as fundamental right.[17] At the same time, the higher judiciary read the right to water within the right to life already in the early 1990s – long before the right to water became a subject of interest at the international level.[18]

The case law of the early 1990s has been reiterated and further developed over time. The right is thus enshrined in the Indian legal framework. More specifically, courts have achieved the following with regard to the recognition of the fundamental right to water.

1 The Supreme Court has repeatedly derived a human right to water from the right to life recognised at article 21 of the Constitution.[19]
2 Courts have also derived the human right to water from article 47 (the duty of the state to raise the level of nutrition and the standard of living and to improve public health). This was, for instance, the case in *Hamid Khan*, in which the High Court found that, under article 47, the state has a duty 'towards every citizen of India to provide pure drinking water'.[20]
3 Courts have found on repeated occasions that the human right to water includes a duty on the part of the state to provide water. This was, for instance, the position in *Vishala Kochi Kudivella Samarkshana Samithi*, in which the High Court of Kerala found that:

   We have no hesitation to hold that failure of the State to provide safe drinking water to the citizens in adequate quantities would amount to a violation of the fundamental right to life enshrined in Article 21 of the Constitution of India and would be a violation of human rights. Therefore, every Government, which has it priorities right, should give foremost importance to providing safe drinking water even at the cost of other development programs.[21]

On the whole, the fundamental right to water is well structured and partly delineated in the case law. Yet the actual entitlements that ensue from the recognition of this right are not well determined in water law. Thus, as mentioned above, there is no broad-based drinking water legislation that would take forward the fundamental rights mandate at the legislative level. This can prove problematic, as illustrated by a 2014 interim order of the Bombay High Court that reconfirmed the right to water, but introduced the idea of a right the realisation of which can be different for different categories of people – in this case, depending on the legal status of their dwelling.[22]

State control and public trust

Water law developed in the nineteenth century in part as a consequence of the government's desire to be able to control water resources to apply them for productive use – at that point, mostly for irrigation. In legal terms, an attempt was thus made by the government to justify its control over water as an extension of its sovereign control over all resources under its jurisdiction. This was formalised, for instance, in the Canal and Drainage Act, 1873, which asserted the right of the government to 'use and control for public purposes the water of all rivers and streams flowing in natural channels, and of all lakes'.[23] This later culminated in the assertion of full control, for instance, in the Madhya Pradesh Irrigation Act, 1931, asserting that '[a]ll rights in the water of any river, natural stream or natural drainage channel, natural lake or other natural collection of water shall vest in the Government'.[24] While this could be dismissed as an outdated position, the much more recent Bihar Irrigation Act, 1997, restates word for word the provision of the earlier Act. Similarly, a recent Jammu and Kashmir legislation includes a section entitled 'Property of the government' that asserts that '[e]very water source in the State is, and shall remain, the property of the Government'.[25]

The case law also provides a continued reassertion of the controlling interest of the state over water. A relatively early decision of 1936 specifically indicated that the state had the sovereign right to regulate the supply of water in public streams.[26] Much more recently, the Supreme Court has restated that 'undoubtedly the state is the sovereign dominant owner' of water.[27]

In the past couple of decades, challenges to the state's assertion of complete power over water have been raised. The most significant development in legal terms has been the assertion by the Supreme Court that all surface waters fall under the doctrine of public trust. The underlying idea of the concept of public trust is that the state holds certain resources in trust for the public because they are intrinsically valuable to the public and cannot be owned by any person (Takacs, 2008). It also implies that the trustee has a fiduciary duty of care and responsibility to the general public. In the words of the Supreme Court:

> The State is the trustee of all natural resources, which are by nature meant for public use and enjoyment. Public at large is the beneficiary of the sea-shore, running waters, airs, forests and ecologically fragile lands. The State as a trustee is under a legal duty to protect the natural resources. These resources meant for public use cannot be converted into private ownership.[28]

The introduction of the doctrine of public trust to water is a significant step forward in curtailing the power of the state over water. Yet this has had little impact in practice beyond the specific decisions in which courts have used this principle. Indeed, neither have states amended legislation that recognises state ownership of water nor have any of the enactments concerning water adopted since 1997 taken notice of this principle, as witnessed in section 3 of the Jammu and Kashmir legislation, cited above.

Individual rights

Individual entitlements over water include a variety of rights of access to water, rights to use water or rights to use water-based resources such as fish. Most of these rights are linked to control over land and, as a result, access to land has, until recently, been the main precondition for asserting water rights.

In certain cases, landowners have been granted entitlements to appropriate water flowing past their land. This amounts to a usufructuary right to use a portion of the flow of a watercourse (Hodgson, 2004). Another type of individual entitlement concerns rights to use a specific quantity of water. This can take the form of a water licence for different uses, such as irrigation (Meinzen-Dick and Nkonya, 2007). These entitlements are usually linked to property rights in land and transferred with the same.[29] There is no right to the water itself, but a right to a certain allocation of water, which may be conditioned, for instance, by actual availability in a given year.

Different rights obtain in other cases. For example, as mentioned above, groundwater rights are also linked to land ownership, but based on a different set of principles.[30] In addition, two other evolving kinds of entitlements need mentioning. The first is the case of tradable entitlements whereby the right to the water is delinked from the right to the land. This is something that has been proposed in legislation, but not implemented on a large-scale yet.[31] The second is the granting of an individual entitlement to a stretch of a river flow, its use and resources. This should, in principle, not happen under the extant legal framework, but such a form of privatisation was in fact attempted in the case of a stretch of the river Sheonath in the state of Chhattisgarh (Das and Pangare, 2006).

Sectoral regulation of groundwater: Exemplifying the limits of the current framework

As indicated above, water law in India is in fact an aggregate of the regulation of the use of various water bodies and the regulation of separate water uses. Since it is difficult to be specific without analysing a specific sector, this section looks in more detail at groundwater. This choice is driven in part by the facts that groundwater is now the main source of water for most water uses and that the basic legal framework has not changed over the course of more than 150 years. This is so despite dramatic changes in scientific understanding of the links between surface and groundwater (Sophocleus, 2002), despite the introduction of mechanised pumping decades ago and despite the fact that groundwater is now the main source of water from which people access drinking water for survival.

Groundwater regulation is based around a set of water rights linked to land ownership. These rights were framed in nineteenth-century case law that gave landowners virtually unimpeded control over groundwater. The control given to landowners was so extensive that it was not restricted by other landowners' use of groundwater found under their plot.[32] Surprisingly, this is still the basic position that applies today in India. This framework has various problematic impacts in today's scenario.

First, the legal framework assumes that no landowner can suck out significant quantities of water from under neighbouring plots. This is no longer the case, given the technological options available. Nevertheless, in a dispute between the Coca Cola Company and a local community in Kerala, a two-judge bench of the High Court of Kerala upheld the principle and ruled that there is a need to 'assume that a person has the right to extract water from his property unless it is prohibited by a statute. Extraction thereof cannot be illegal.'[33]

Second, the current framework provides in effect for atomised regulation, since it is concerned only with landowners' access to groundwater. This prevents any attempt to regulate the use of, or to protect, groundwater on an aquifer basis, which would include not only all pieces of land owned by someone within the aquifer, but also all other areas that may not be under private ownership. This makes the existing regulation essentially outdated from an environmental point of view, since it does not provide any entry point for aquifer-wide protection measures.

Third, the current framework is essentially incapable of reflecting the central role of groundwater in the realisation of the fundamental right to water for the overwhelming majority of the population. Indeed, by giving control to landowners over groundwater, it de facto excludes everyone else from this control and puts access by the landless in a hierarchically inferior position. This is socially inequitable in a context in which some 40 per cent of the population does not have access to land, and provides an inappropriate basis on which to plan the realisation of equal access to sufficient and safe drinking water for all.

In the context of water law in general, the existing groundwater rights framework illustrates the limits of the sectoral development of water law without reference to a common set of principles. Indeed, while there are many issues that need to be addressed specifically with regard to groundwater, such measures cannot be based on principles that differ from those applied to surface water. This is primarily so because we now know that there exists a direct connection between the two. Yet even when the Supreme Court introduced the idea that water is a public trust in the mid-1990s, it did so in a context that did not make it specifically clear that it was supposed to apply to all water.[34] There is at least one subsequent case in which the Supreme Court appeared to extend the scope of the application of the public trust to groundwater, but this calls for a more specific confirmation that has not yet taken place.[35]

The inadequacy of the basic legal framework has had various consequences over time. First, the problem of depleting groundwater tables and the inadequacy of the groundwater rights framework in arresting it in the context of the multiplication of mechanised pumps led the Union government to propose a groundwater model Bill to states for adoption as early as 1970.[36] Law reform was, however, not taken up by states before the late 1990s and legislation adopted on the basis of this 1970 model (proposed again in substantially the same form in 2005) does not modify the inappropriate framework for controlling groundwater introduced in the nineteenth century.

Second, the system put in place in the nineteenth century progressively led to the creation of vested interests whereby landowners came to understand control over groundwater as an integral part of their right of ownership. This explains in part why governments have been unwilling to reform the system, since there is a strong link between land ownership and capacity to lobby politicians. Nevertheless, reforms may have happened earlier if groundwater had not been the 'ideal' buffer that could be simply extracted for some time beyond replenishment levels. This short-term solution happens to fit political agendas, which are often not geared towards long-term solutions. In addition, over-extracting groundwater is less 'visible' than in the case of surface water and is therefore less politically sensitive, at least for a while.

Third, in a context in which governments have been unwilling to legislate, other groundwater regulation mechanisms have been developed. There is thus a particularly important link between access to energy and groundwater extraction. Indeed, it has not been enough for the government to refrain from prohibiting over-extraction of groundwater, since the cost of extraction increases with falling water tables. This implies laying ever-deeper tubewells and increasing energy consumption. Various states thus gave in to the temptation to subsidise groundwater use through cheap or free electricity rather than having to regulate (and thus restrict) its use. This worked for quite some years in some parts of the country, but, as anyone analysing the situation could have predicted long ago, there is a point at which even this ends up being unsustainable. Indeed, Gujarat was the first state that ended up having to separate electricity supply to pumps and to households in a bid to control groundwater extraction (Shah and Verma, 2008).

Fourthly, the stalemate that has developed over time whereby governments have refrained from reforming the rights framework while subsidising groundwater use has been used to argue that law is neither relevant nor needed for groundwater regulation. The idea is that, in the context of the existence of millions of users, 'laws are unlikely to check the chaotic race to extract groundwater because of the logistical problems of regulating a large number of small, dispersed users' (Shah et al., 2003: 138). This is an important point that needs to be integrated in thinking around groundwater regulation, but it misses the fact that it is the present legal framework that is at the root of the problems now being faced. This was recognised by the Planning Commission, which drafted a new groundwater model Bill in 2011.[37] This new instrument is based on the premise that groundwater regulation is needed and is a central part of any reforms that will bring more equity and sustainability to groundwater use. The premise is thus that groundwater must be seen as a public trust and that it needs to be regulated on the basis of principles that recognise the primacy of the fundamental right to water, as well as the need for protection and conservation of groundwater. This text was subsequently revisited by a committee set up by the Ministry of Water Resources, River Development and Ganga Rejuvenation, and is now known as the Model Groundwater (Sustainable Management) Act, 2016.

Water sector reforms and water law reforms

Water law has developed over decades and, in this sense, can be said to have been evolving. However, this has not been a linear process. On the one hand, as indicated above, we find the very same basic principles underlying the Bihar Irrigation Act, 1997 that we already find in legislation adopted more than six decades earlier. On the other hand, the past two decades have seen the introduction of various new Acts that reflect a fast-changing water policy framework.

The analysis of these recent water law changes needs to be made in a context that looks beyond law itself to analyse the broader policy and governance reforms known as 'water sector reforms' (Cullet, 2009). Water sector reforms are a set of proposals for reforming the water sector that has evolved in parallel at the national and international levels. One of its most central principles was enunciated in the Dublin Statement of 1992 that '[w]ater has an economic value in all its competing uses and should be recognised as an economic good'.[38] This has been the basis for introducing the principle that water services must be based on (full) cost recovery (World Bank, 1998). This is true in the context of irrigation, in which farmers are made to pay for operation and maintenance costs. This is also true in the context of drinking water, in which users are made to pay for operation and maintenance charges linked to the provision of water.[39] There were attempts to go beyond this and to impose partial capital cost recovery for drinking water schemes in rural areas, but this has largely been abandoned in the meantime.[40] Interestingly, cost recovery is seen not only as an economic instrument, but also as linked to the environment. The Asian Development Bank went as far as to present cost recovery as the first instrument for conserving water.[41]

Another principle found in the Dublin Statement was that '[w]ater development and management should be based on a participatory approach, involving users, planners and policy-makers at all levels'.[42] The rationale for decentralisation is the perceived inability of the state to deliver appropriate benefits. The state is thus called upon to change its role from that of a service provider to that of a regulator (Asian Development Bank, 2003: para. 37). In the case of irrigation, for instance, this implies transferring part or full control of irrigation systems to users by both allowing them, even forcing them, to take responsibility for the upkeep of irrigation systems, as well as for the financial costs involved and for sharing the water allocated among themselves.[43]

This has been the basis for Acts focusing on the setting up of water user associations (WUAs).[44] These Acts are noteworthy because they provide for decentralisation of the management of irrigation systems, but they fail in providing any answer to the more central questions raised by existing irrigation acts that vest all powers over water in the state. First, these acts do not change the basic principles of existing irrigation legislation; secondly, in a case such as the Maharashtra Management of Irrigation Systems by Farmers Act, 2005, the 'appropriate authority' has the power to determine the command area of an irrigation project for which a WUA must be constituted. Further, the same authority can also amalgamate or divide existing WUAs on a hydraulic basis and 'having regard to the administrative convenience'.[45] In other words, the power granted at the local level is limited by the fact that authorities have the largely discretionary power to make and break WUAs.

Water sector reforms are, in effect, a new policy framework for water law. This is unexpected. The instruments that shape water sector reforms at the international level are all soft law instruments that do not bind any country. Similarly, at the national level, the principles of water sector reforms found in instruments such as water policies are not legal principles underlying water law reforms. In fact, what should have been guiding law reforms since the early 1990s are elements such as the fundamental right to water first confirmed by the Supreme Court in 1991 and the constitutional amendments of 1993 devolving various water-related functions to local bodies of governance.[46] This dichotomy leads to surprising results. Thus while panchayats[47] have been given control over minor irrigation,[48] WUAs are set up besides panchayats and yet fail to integrate some of their basic principles. Differences include the fact that WUAs include only landowners and do not make reservation either for women or scheduled castes/scheduled tribes.[49] The universal framework linked to reservation is seen as one of the big advances brought by the Seventy-third Amendment to the Constitution, something that WUAs laws simply ignore.

Water law reforms introduced since the mid-1990s are thus surprising from a legal perspective, even if they can easily be explained by looking at the broader policy context within which they have taken place. This is illustrated by the case of so-called independent water regulatory authorities. A landmark Act adopted in Maharashtra, and since then followed by several other states, promised to set up a new institutional structure that would provide results that the government had failed to deliver for decades.[50] While the need for governance reform in the water sector is widely accepted, in part because its complexity does not provide the basis for concerned government departments to deliver expected benefits, the specific form of the reform was linked to the call for less government intervention in the water sector, rather than for improving or reforming the existing system. In fact, water regulatory authorities were not devised with the water sector in mind, but were copied from an earlier avatar that had already been used in the electricity sector (Dubash, 2008). The limitations of a framework that fails, for instance, to recognise the political nature of water were quickly highlighted in the case of Maharashtra, where an amendment had already been passed in 2011 with the aim of repatriating some powers to the government, including a clear statement that it is for the government to determine sectoral allocation.[51]

Conclusion: The challenge of regulating water in a context of increasing water use and global environmental change

Water law in India is both mired in the past and changing rapidly. Its slow development over decades makes it difficult to reform. At the same time, the enormous importance of water for survival, livelihoods, the environment and economic activities makes it a topic at the centre of political, policy and legal attention. Further, while the basic principles of water law linking access to water to land rights have failed to evolve, changes affecting its nature have been effected by the Supreme Court and through constitutional amendments. In addition, new areas of law, such as environmental law, have covered issues that water law should have developed if it had responded to changing circumstances quickly enough.

The various laws that have been introduced over the past two decades confirm that water is taken seriously. Yet they also confirm that there is strong resistance to reform that would ensure more equitable access to water, and better conservation and protection of water. The problem is the result, in part, of the focus of water law reforms on policy and economic principles that are not enshrined in law, such as the proposal to conceive water as an economic good and the focus on bringing in participation of the private sector. This is problematic from two different perspectives: first, there is no reason why law reforms that are needed, according to Supreme Court directives and constitutional amendments, should be guided by economic principles; and second, even if, say, physical scarcity is a relevant basis on which to work in many parts of India, it cannot become the overwhelming organising notion, since some states happen to be concerned more by floods than by water scarcity.

The underlying problem is that, despite a framework that recognises the need for decentralisation and responses specific to the situations of individual states, the reality is quite different. This partly because of pressure from the Union, which makes states conform to a given model, as in the case of water regulatory authorities, whereby all states have been invited to follow the model introduced in Maharashtra,[52] and partly because of the fact that states fail to sufficiently adapt frameworks to their situation, as is the case with existing groundwater Acts that all closely shadow the model Bill.[53]

There is no denying that the country in general, and many states specifically, face a bleak future with regard to overall water availability. This requires adequate responses to ensure that there will be no widespread physical water scarcity in the next few decades. At the same time, focusing on this is not the only challenge that states should address nor, possibly, is it the main one at their level. First, physical water scarcity is not yet a big issue at an aggregate level in most parts of the country, but inequalities in access to water, fast-diminishing water quality and lack of sewerage are some of the problems that need immediate attention. Secondly, physical water scarcity is something that can be addressed from the local to the national levels, starting, for instance, with rainwater harvesting – something that people in desert areas of the country, such as western Rajasthan, have been doing for centuries. Yet, in today's context of fast global environmental change, it would be inappropriate to attempt to sort out problems only at the local, state or national level. Ongoing climate change is affecting rainfall patterns. This happens to be of primary importance, since most of the country relies overwhelmingly on the monsoons to replenish water sources. Water law must thus be considered today in a context that includes the global.

At this juncture, the most important need seems to be to ensure that further law making be informed by the priorities of the majority of people within a state or within the country in general. The policy reforms that developed in parallel at the international and national levels starting in the 1990s do not provide the kind of starting point that is needed. First, the Constitution and legal principles introduced by the Supreme Court should be the basis for further law reforms, rather than policy and economic principles; second, law making needs to be based on processes that go beyond 'public participation', currently envisaged as the necessary standard; third, new laws need to be based on principles, such as the subsidiarity principle, which requires that decisions be taken as closely as possible to citizens. Such measures will ensure the effective realisation of decentralisation and participation in a democratic framework.

The future of water law is not necessarily more challenging than that of other areas of law. However, the very central role that water plays in everyone's life and as an essential element sustaining the environment makes it more crucial than many other areas of law. This is also the reason why it is an area of law that cannot be left to 'experts', but must be the subject of effective democratic legislative processes. In 2016, there are reasons to be cautiously positive, since a number of states and the Union have started taking the drafting of water laws that reflect a much broader set of concerns more seriously. This will need to go beyond the drafting stage and will also need to be built not only on drafting by committees, but also on sufficient debates in bodies of democratic governance, such as Parliament and legislative assemblies.

Notes

1 Water (Prevention and Control of Pollution) Act, 1974.
2 For example, Canal and Drainage Act, 1873, Preamble.
3 Government of India Act, 1935, ss 130–134.
4 Constitution of India, Sch. 7, List II.
5 Constitution of India, art. 262.
6 Planning Commission of India, National Water Framework Bill, 2011; Ministry of Water Resources, Draft National Water Framework Bill, 2013; Ministry of Water Resources, River Development and Ganga Rejuvenation, Draft National Water Framework Bill, 2016.
7 Constitution of India, art. 243G and Sch. 11.
8 Constitution of India, art. 243W and Sch. 12.
9 *Acton v Blundell* [1843] 152 ER 1223. For further developments, see later in this chapter.
10 India is not the only country that has failed to move ahead of this scientifically wrong premise among Commonwealth countries. Yet change is needed and can be brought about, as witnessed in s. 3 of South Africa's National Water Act, 1998.
11 Environment (Protection) Act, 1986.
12 Renamed Ministry of Water Resources, River Development and Ganga Rejuvenation in 2014.
13 National Water Policy, 1987.
14 Article 246 of the Constitution of India divides the power to make laws between the Union and states by allocating some powers exclusively to the Union and some to the states, and includes an additional category whereby the power is shared (the 'concurrent list').

15 Non-statutory-backed standards exist, such as the Indian Standard Specifications for Drinking Water, IS 10500 (Bureau of Indian Standards, 2012).
16 Several Bills drafted in the past few years mention or reflect the fundamental right to water, but none has been passed at time of writing.
17 For example, South African Constitution, 1996, art. 27.
18 For example, UN Committee on Economic, Social and Cultural Rights (2002).
19 For example, *Subhash Kumar v State of Bihar* AIR 1991 SC 420.
20 *Hamid Khan v State of Madhya Pradesh* AIR 1997 MP 191, [6].
21 *Vishala Kochi Kudivella Samarkshana Samithi v State of Kerala* 2006 (1) KLT 919, [3].
22 *Pani Haq Samiti v Brihan Mumbai Municipal Corporation*, Public Interest Litigation No. 10 of 2012, Interim Order of 15 December 2014.
23 Preamble, Canal and Drainage Act, 1873 (Act VIII of 1873).
24 Madhya Pradesh Irrigation Act, 1931, s. 26.
25 Jammu and Kashmir Water Resources (Regulation and Management) Act, 2010, s. 3.
26 *Secretary of State v PS Nageswara Iyer* AIR 1936 Mad 923.
27 *Tekaba AO v Sakumeren AO* (2004) 5 SCC 672, [24].
28 *MC Mehta v Kamal Nath* (1997) 1 SCC 388, [34].
29 For example, Orissa Irrigation Act, 1959, s 24.
30 *Chasemore v Richards* [1859] 7 HLC 349, 374.
31 See Maharashtra Water Resources Regulatory Authority Act, 2005, s. 11(i)(i).
32 *Acton v Blundell* [1843] 152 ER 1223.
33 *Hindustan Coca-Cola Beverages v Perumatty Grama Panchayat* 2005(2) KLT 554, [35]. The only concession made was to set an upper limit of 500,000 litres per day (at [53]). At time of writing, the case is being appealed to the Supreme Court.
34 *MC Mehta v Kamal Nath* (1997) 1 SCC 388.
35 *State of West Bengal v. Kesoram Industries* (2004) 10 SCC 201.
36 Model Bill to Regulate and Control the Development and Management of Ground Water, 1970/2005.
37 Model Bill for the Conservation, Protection and Regulation of Groundwater, 2011.
38 Dublin Statement on Water and Sustainable Development, adopted at the International Conference on Water and the Environment, Dublin, 31 January 1992, Principle 4.
39 For example, National Water Policy, 2002, s. 11. Note that the National Water Policy, 2012, is less specific on this point and states only that '[p]ricing of water should ensure its efficient use and reward conservation' (s. 7.1).
40 See Government of India Ministry of Rural Development, Department of Drinking Water Supply (2002: para. 3.1); Government of India Ministry of Drinking Water and Sanitation (2013).
41 See Asian Development Bank (2003), para. 43 of which (within section E, 'Conserving Water') is entitled 'Cost recovery'.
42 Dublin Statement, Principle 2.
43 For example, Uttar Pradesh Water Policy, 1999, s. 17(1).
44 Andhra Pradesh Farmers Management of Irrigation Systems Act, 1997; Madhya Pradesh Sinchai Prabandhan Me Krishakon Ki Bhagidari Adhiniyam, 1999; Odisha Pani Panchayat Act, 2002; Rajasthan Farmers' Participation in Management of Irrigation Systems Act, 2000.
45 Maharashtra Management of Irrigation Systems by Farmers Act, 2005, s. 5.
46 *Subhash Kumar v State of Bihar* AIR 1991 SC 420; Constitution (Seventy-third Amendment) Act, 1992; Constitution (Seventy-fourth Amendment) Act, 1992.
47 Panchayats are defined at art. 243(d) of the Constitution of India as institutions of self-government for the rural areas.
48 Constitution of India, Sch. 11, (art. 243G), s. 3.
49 An exception is Chhattisgarh sinchai prabandhan me krishkon ki bhagidari adhiniyam 2006, s. 5.
50 Maharashtra Water Resources Regulatory Authority Act, 2005.

51 Maharashtra Water Resources Regulatory Authority (Amendment and Continuance) Act, 2011, s. 5, inserting s. 16A into the 2005 Act.
52 For example, Government of India Ministry of Finance (2011).
53 Model Bill to Regulate and Control the Development and Management of Ground Water, 1970/2005.

References

Asian Development Bank (2003) *Water for All: The Water Policy of the Asian Development Bank*, available online at http://www.adb.org/sites/default/files/institutional-document/32042/water-policy.pdf [accessed 21 July 2016].

Bureau of Indian Standards (2012) *Drinking Water: Specification*, IS 10500, 2nd revision, New Delhi: Bureau of Indian Standards.

Cullet, P. (2009) *Water Law, Poverty and Development: Water Law Reforms in India*, Oxford: Oxford University Press.

Cullet, P. (2014) 'Groundwater Law in India: Towards a Framework Ensuring Equitable Access and Aquifer Protection', *Journal of Environmental Law*, 26(1): 55–81.

Das, B., and Pangare, G. (2006) 'Privatisation: In Chhattisgarh, a River Becomes Private Property', *Economic & Political Weekly*, 41(7): 611–612.

Dubash, N. K. (2008) 'Independent Regulatory Agencies: A Theoretical Review with Reference to Electricity and Water in India', *Economic & Political Weekly*, 43(40): 46–54.

Gleick, P. H. (1999) 'The Human Right to Water', *Water Policy*, 1(5): 487–503.

Government of India (2009) *Report of the Thirteenth Finance Commission (2010–20 15, Vol. I*, available online at http://fincomindia.nic.in/ShowContentOne.aspx?id=28&Section=1 [accessed 21 July 2016].

Government of India Ministry of Drinking Water and Sanitation (2013) *National Rural Drinking Water Programme: Movement towards Ensuring People's Drinking Water Security in Rural India – Framework for Implementation*, available online at http://mdws.gov.in/sites/default/files/NRDWP_Guidelines_2013.pdf [accessed 21 July 2016].

Government of India Ministry of Finance (2011) *Implementation of Recommendation of Thirteenth Finance Commission*, Doc. No. F.No.25 (1) FCD/2010, 25 April, available online at http://finmin.nic.in/TFC/Guidelines_Water_Sector_Management.pdf [accessed 21 July 2016].

Government of India Ministry of Rural Development, Department of Drinking Water Supply (2002) *Guidelines on Swajaldhara, 2002*, available online at http://www.ielrc.org/content/e0212.pdf [accessed 21 July 2016].

Hodgson, S. (2004) *Land and Water: The Rights Interface*, FAO Legislative Study 84, Rome: FAO.

Meinzen-Dick, R., and Nkonya, L. (2007) 'Understanding Legal Pluralism in Water and Land Rights: Lessons from Africa and Asia', in B. van Koppen, M. Giordano and J. Butterworth (eds) *Community-based Water Law and Water Resource Management Reform in Developing Countries*, Wallingford: CABI, 12–27.

Planning Commission (2012) *Twelfth Five-Year Plan (2012–2017): Faster, More Inclusive and Sustainable Growth, Vol. 1*, New Delhi: Government of India.

Shah, T., and Verma, S. (2008) 'Co-management of Electricity and Groundwater: An Assessment of Gujarat's Jyotirgram Scheme', *Economic & Political Weekly*, 43(7): 59–66.

Shah, T., Roy, A. D., Qureshi, A. S., and Wang, J. (2003) 'Sustaining Asia's Groundwater Boom: An Overview of Issues and Evidence', *Natural Resources Forum*, 27(2): 130–141.

Sophocleus, M. (2002) 'Interactions between Groundwater and Surface Water: The State of the Science', *Hydrogeology Journal*, 10(1): 52–67.

Standing Committee on Water Resources (2015) *Review of Ground Water Scenario, Need for a Comprehensive Policy and Measures to Address Problems in the Country with Particular Reference to (I) Dark Blocks; and (II) Contamination of Underground Water by Certain Industries – Fifth Report*, available online at http://164.100.47.134/lsscommittee/Water%20Resources/16_Water_Resources_5.pdf [accessed 21 July 2016].

Takacs, D. (2008) 'The Public Trust Doctrine, Environmental Human Rights, and the Future of Private Property', *New York University Environmental Law Journal*, 16(3): 711–765.

UN Committee on Economic, Social and Cultural Rights (2002) *General Comment No. 15: The Right to Water (Arts. 11 and 12 of the Covenant)*, UN Doc. E/C.12/2002/11, available online at http://www.ielrc.org/content/e0221.pdf [accessed 21 July 2016].

Vijay Shankar, P. S., Kulkarni, H., and Krishnan, S. (2011) 'India's Groundwater Challenge and the Way Forward', *Economic & Political Weekly*, 46(2): 37–45.

World Bank (1998) *India: Water Resources Management Sector Review – Report on the Irrigation Sector*, Report No. 18416 IN, Washington, DC: World Bank.

Part V

People in Asia and their rights

19 Islamic courts or courts for Muslims?

Shari'a and the state in Indonesia, Malaysia and Singapore[1]

Tim Lindsey

After achieving independence in the decades following World War II, the nationalist leaders of Southeast Asian countries with Muslim populations naturally treated their Muslim populations very differently than had their former colonial overlords. In Indonesia and Malaysia, Muslims were a majority and now became the rulers, as well as the ruled. In Singapore, they were still largely excluded from power, but remained a significant minority. Despite this, the new ruling elites in each of these countries rejected calls for an Islamic state; instead, they chose forms of modern nation-state in which Islam was given limited voice in formal governance. Only heavily institutionalised and regulated (and thus restricted) roles in public life were allowed for the selected Islamic legal traditions[2] that they were willing to apply to their Muslim citizens. To achieve this, each of these three new states preserved much of the formal colonial system for managing religious and ethnic diversity that they had inherited upon independence. This meant that the new states continued to apply colonial models of legal pluralism, albeit in altered forms and to different extents.

'Legal pluralism' is, as Hooker (1975: 6) puts it, 'the situation in which two or more laws interact' within the jurisdiction of a single state. He was describing the accretional layering of different legal traditions in a single jurisdiction as result of historic processes. Hooker (1975) saw laws that obtain legitimacy by virtue of their issuance by legislatures or bureaucracies – usually colonial in origin – as a type different from those older kinds that derive legitimacy from local 'native' traditional beliefs, for example religious or customary laws. He demonstrated how European powers in archipelagic Southeast Asia systematically privileged the former over the latter. He showed that, in the plural legal systems left behind by European colonialism, these different systems still overlap and interact with one another, such that the administration of law requires (often complex) negotiation and coordination between them. The result is that different types of law typically apply in different circumstances, with their application usually determined by the ethnicity or beliefs of the citizens involved. This is a system that reflects the racial divisions fundamental to European colonialism in Southeast Asia, which were the key to their administration of Muslim populations in the archipelago. Race and religion therefore still operate, albeit to different extents, as legal classifiers in Indonesia, Malaysia and Singapore, and are frequently conflated, particularly in the latter two countries.

'The relationship of two or more systems [of law]' (Hooker, 1975: 6), modern and traditional, within a given state, how the state regulates them, and the nature of the resulting legal nexus between state, religion and race is the usual subject of studies of legal pluralism in Southeast Asia. This chapter is no exception and focuses on how state administration of post-colonial legal pluralism through *shari'a*[3] courts has affected Islamic legal traditions in the three countries selected. It begins with a brief theoretical discussion of the effect of state intervention on *shari'a* before examining the relationship between state policy on Islam and the operation of *shari'a* courts in Indonesia, Malaysia and Singapore, using Islamic *talak* divorce as a case study.

State and *shari'a*

Governments with Muslim citizens are often motivated to select and reinvent Islamic legal traditions by a perceived need to respond to the challenges they see as implicit in Islam as a rival pole of political authority. In developing legal policies for their Muslim communities, such governments are frequently preoccupied by the question of the extent to which Islam should formally be recognised as a source of formal, state-sanctioned law, enforceable by state institutions.

This is highly problematic for most contemporary governments, because, as Abdullahi An-Na'im (2008: 322–324) argues, the modern state is 'necessarily secular' and is always so, 'regardless of claims to the contrary'. For all of their rhetoric to the contrary, this is certainly true of governments that have ruled since independence in Indonesia and Malaysia, while Singapore's government has been express in its claim to be secular (Lindsey and Steiner, 2012a: 1–10, 258–261). Each has been concerned to influence the trajectory, content and style of the legal traditions of its Muslim citizens to match wider policy objectives and to 'manage' Muslim communities, and they have usually been effective in doing so.

They have, in fact, little choice but to intervene. In modern states with Muslim populations, Muslim leaders typically demand state recognition of legal traditions associated with their religion. Like most others, the governments of Indonesia, Malaysia and Singapore have responded by selecting from Islamic legal traditions to enforce some as formal state law. But when the state becomes involved in the application of Islamic religious norms, the transmission of those norms through the legal mechanisms of modern state politics and administration inevitably alters them, whether or not this is intended (and typically, it is). Islamic legal traditions are reinterpreted – and often reinvented – by institutions that are 'necessarily a product of mundane, human politics, and not divine command, as such' (An-Na'im, 2008: 322):

> [A]ny Shari'a principle that is enforced through the coercive authority of the state ceases to be part of the normative system of Islam and becomes an expression of the political will of the state . . . This does not mean that Shari'a principles cannot be a source of state law, but the outcome of the enactment and enforcement of its principles by state institutions is always a matter of secular law and not of Shari'a as the religious normative system of Islam.

The result is that *shari'a* (Islamic law, understood as norms and rules derived from the *Qur'ān* and *ḥadītih*[4]) becomes 'less than law', because its enforcement as law requires the intervention of 'legislative, judicial and administrative organs of state' (An-Na'im, 2008: 323) that inevitably distort and subordinate *shari'a*. The result is a 'tension between perceptions of the "divinity" of Shari'a and [the] realities of the secular experiences of Islamic societies' (An-Na'im, 2008: 324). The 'status of Shari'a is ambiguous, even when it is claimed to be the actual legal system' of a community (An-Na'im, 2008: 324). In other words, revelation filtered through the bureaucratic agencies of the state cannot remain intact.

Just as mediation by the state and its legal mechanisms inevitably alters Islamic legal traditions, so too engagement with Islamic legal traditions inevitably alters the state. As An-Na'im (2008) also argues, when a modern state seeks to regulate a religion by passing laws and creating legal and bureaucratic institutions to control that religion's expression and application, it usually finds itself called upon to determine its substance too. In other words, once the state uses law to regulate and administer Islam, it cannot avoid a normative role as well. The state 'standing in the middle' thus finds itself the context in which disputes about the substance and legal status of *shari'a* are fought out, for example through elections, in the legislature, in the production of regulation, and so on. In many cases, it also finds itself the judge of those contests, for example through the courts, the bureaucracy, law-enforcement agencies and the policies it develops in response to such contests. It is thus forced to grapple with the question of the extent to which the nation-state itself is normatively 'Islamic', and its response is usually ambiguous and often conflicted – largely as a result of the inevitable tension between its need for Islamic identity and the reality of its essentially secular nature.

This has meant that the three Southeast Asian governments selected have often (but not always) used recognition and enforcement of legal traditions as – ironically – means of marginalising, containing or controlling the influence of Muslim authority. In doing so, these governments have chosen modes of intervention that differ both between states and within each state over time, but which all share common strategies of institutional control, most often through co-option. This is true even when it seems that the application of Islamic legal traditions is expanding, not contracting, as in Malaysia.

As mentioned, this chapter seeks to locate, map and describe these patterns in the complex relationship between state and *shari'a* in Southeast Asia by using *shari'a* courts in Indonesia, Malaysia and Singapore as a comparative case study. In doing so, it will also seek to show that the form and substance of state regulations and legal institutions applicable to Muslims are fundamental to understanding the wider role Islam plays in these three societies. This is because it is very often at this level that key decisions are made that determine the minutiae of Muslims private religious lives – even if that is sometimes forgotten by observers, both foreign and local.

Indonesia's religious courts

The Indonesian courts that have authority to apply Islamic legal traditions comprise three tiers: the *Pengadilan Agama* (religious courts), the *Pengadilan Tinggi Agama* (Religious High Courts) and the *Mahkamah Agung* (Supreme Court).[5] The religious courts are the exclusive courts of first instance[6] for cases in which the parties are Muslim[7] and which concern, among other things,[8] marriage.[9] Marriage-related cases are understood as those regulated by the Marriage Law No. 1 of 1974[10] and the courts' business is overwhelmingly dominated by divorce. It also, however, includes a much smaller number of cases involving a range of other related matters, including, among other things, applications for polygamy, division of property, child custody and guardianship, child maintenance, spousal maintenance, the legal status of children, marriage legalisation, and decisions relating to 'mixed marriages' between Indonesian and non-Indonesian citizens.

Despite their restricted jurisdiction, the religious courts are among the busiest courts in Indonesia. In 2009, for example, litigants brought 257,798 cases to the religious courts, compared with 202,754 cases brought to the general courts (*Pengadilan Umum*).[11] The religious courts thus heard 27 per cent more cases than the general courts in that year, despite both the broad civil and criminal jurisdiction of the general courts and the tightly restricted jurisdiction of the religious courts, which, as mentioned, are dominated by divorce trials. These figures will, of course, fluctuate from year to year, but the religious courts are likely to have a trial caseload similar to that of the general courts for the foreseeable future.

The size of the religious courts' caseload also reflects the fact that divorce cases now form the single largest group of cases in the Indonesian judicial system, comprising 50 per cent of all cases, with criminal cases following at only 33 per cent (Direktorat Jenderal Badan Peradilan Agama, 2006: 3, 269).[12] The domination of the Indonesian judicial system by divorce cases is even more striking in the context of civil litigation. In 2009, for example, there were approximately 310,000 civil cases or matters heard in the religious and general courts combined, of which approximately 230,000 were divorce cases. Divorce cases that year thus represented 74 per cent of all civil cases heard in Indonesian courts.

As mentioned, the religious courts hear divorces for Muslims. Non-Muslim divorces are heard by the general courts. Of the total of divorces decided in Indonesia, the religious courts decide 98 per cent and the general courts, only 2 per cent.[13] Accordingly, despite suffering decades of neglect by the Indonesian state, the religious courts are today arguably the most active branch of the Indonesian judiciary, and thus that which has the broadest engagement with the Indonesian public and, in particular, with Indonesian Muslim families.

Sources of decision making

The legislation applicable to the religious courts does not expressly state the sources of law on which religious courts judges may rely in coming to their decisions. In practice, however, the panels of three judges who hear cases generally apply the version of Islamic law embodied in national regulation – chiefly Law No. 1 of 1974 on Marriage and its implementing Government Regulation No. 9 of 1975, as well as a range of ministerial regulations and circular letters (*surat edaran*). The chief source, however, is the state-sanctioned *Kompilasi Hukum Islam* (Compilation of Islamic Law, Presidential Instruction No. 1 of 1991), issued by former President Soeharto as a 'guide' for religious court judges. The *Kompilasi* is narrow in scope, covering only marriage, inheritance and *wakaf*, and its provisions allow only a very restricted application of Islamic legal traditions. For nearly two decades, the religious court judges have, in fact, relied heavily on the *Kompilasi*, the 1974 Marriage Law and its 1975 Implementing Regulation to deal with divorce and related cases.

In fact, traditional Islamic legal sources are seldom cited in religious court judgments – and then usually only to support propositions of law in national regulation. In only 30 per cent of the eighty-five cases analysed for this chapter was any sort of Islamic legal source referred to at all. None of the Supreme Court decisions studied cited any Islamic sources at all. Across all three levels of the Islamic judicial system, the *Qur'ān* and *ḥadīth* – the basic scriptural sources of Islam – were relied upon less frequently then *fiqh*.[14] *Fiqh* textbooks[15] were cited in 72.7 per cent of the small number of cases in which Islamic sources were used. Next, came the *Qur'ān*, cited in 54.5 per cent of cases that relied on Islamic sources, while only 27 per cent cited *ḥadīth*. In none of the cases studied were *fatāwā*[16] cited at all, despite being the basic tool by which *fiqh* is applied in traditional Islamic jurisprudence.

Nurlaelawati (2010) has suggested that the religious courts are more ambivalent toward the *Kompilasi* and more ready to rely on *fiqh* sources than the selection in this chapter suggests, although her selection of cases is much smaller. Wahid (2010: 13–14), however, refers to research conducted by the Directorate of Religious Justice in 2001, which concluded that 100 per cent of 1,008 decisions of the religious courts surveyed were based on the *Kompilasi*, with 71 per cent explicitly stating this in the judgment itself. This is understandable: from a formalist point of view, it is perhaps surprising that the courts cite sources of Islamic law at all. There is no express authority to do so in the legislation that establishes and regulates them, unlike in Singapore, for example, where, as will be seen, the judges are expressly required to apply 'Muslim law' by the governing statute.[17] Accordingly, even when the religious courts do consider Islamic law, they can never use religious sources of law to contradict or set aside national (non-Islamic) law and, indeed, they virtually never do so.

Indonesian religious court judgments, like the procedures these courts follow, thus differ little from decisions of Indonesia's secular courts and both are influenced heavily by European 'civil law' traditions of judicial decision making. This is unsurprising given that the religious courts are supervised by the secular Supreme Court, both through administrative oversight and the appeal process, and it is a strongly civil law institution.[18] The Supreme Court almost never gives detailed attention to Islamic sources of law in its judgments, instead restricting itself to state regulation.

Talak *divorce*

This can be clearly seen from the principles applied by the religious courts in the overwhelming majority of cases it decides – divorce cases. Even in this core area of the jurisdiction of Indonesia's courts for Muslims, the applicable law has diverged significantly from classical Islamic legal traditions by reason of the national regulations that now set the jurisprudential boundaries of the religious courts. One clear example of this is the absence of extrajudicial unilateral *talak* divorces effected by the husband.

According to traditional Islamic jurisprudence, a husband has the right to divorce a wife at will by declaring '*talak*' to her three times. The Indonesian legislation provides, however, that a husband must first make an application to the religious courts for permission to pronounce *talak* for it be effective. Permission will be granted only if the court is satisfied of at least one of the six conditions set out in Government Regulation No. 9 of 1975 (discussed below). If the court grants the permission, this will then allow the husband to pronounce *talak* to his wife in court once the decision has binding legal status. This essentially abolishes the husband's unilateral right to *talak* divorce as it stood at traditional *fiqh*. In an effort to appear to be adhering to Islamic legal tradition – nominally, at least – the religious courts are usually meticulous in only ever granting permission for the husband to pronounce *talak* to his wife. They never actually declare the parties to be divorced per se. In other words, in *talak* cases, the parties are legally divorced not when the court upholds the husband's application for permission to divorce, but – in theory – only after the husband, with the court's permission, pronounces (or is deemed to have pronounced) *talak* to his wife.

At traditional *fiqh*, a Muslim wife in Indonesia generally has three grounds of divorce, albeit on much more limited grounds: a *taklik*[19] divorce, if she can show that her husband breached the marriage contract; a *khuluk*[20] divorce, whereby she pays a sum of money to obtain her husband's consent to divorce; and a *fasakh*[21] divorce, which covers several limited circumstances, including where her husband has committed adultery or is impotent. In Indonesia, however, a wife may bring an action for divorce, known as *cerai gugat* (complaint divorce), on the same grounds as a husband – namely those listed in regulation 19 of Government Regulation No. 9 of 1975:

(a) One party commits adultery, becomes an alcoholic, addict, gambler, or other such thing that is hard to cure;
(b) One party leaves the other party for 2 (two) years consecutively without the leave of that other party and without a valid reason or any other circumstance outside their control;
(c) One party receives a prison sentence of 5 (five) years or greater punishment subsequent to the marriage;
(d) One party commits an act of severe abuse or brutality that endangers the other party;
(e) One party incurs a physical disability or sickness that results in them being unable to fulfill their obligations as a husband/wife;
(f) Between husband and wife there is an on-going conflict and disagreement and there is no more hope of living together harmoniously in the one household.

The most common ground of divorce relied upon is (f), because the other grounds are much narrower. While, under classic Islamic law, a husband could divorce his wife on such grounds, they would certainly not be sufficient for a wife to obtain a divorce if she did not have her husband's consent to do so.

One result of this legislative displacement of *fiqh* in the field of divorce is that Indonesia's religious justice system has come to favour female litigants over men. Women now bring twice as many applications for divorce in the religious courts as men and are usually successful (Sumner and Lindsey, 2010). This pattern was clear from the cases studied for this chapter, in which all divorces initiated by women were successful, while only 60 per cent of men ultimately received judicial permission to pronounce the *talak* to which they would have had an automatic right at traditional *fiqh*. Equally significantly, the cases in which the husband was ultimately unsuccessful in obtaining permission to divorce his wife were usually those in which the wife had expressly contested the divorce. In cases in which the husbands had ultimately received judicial permission for divorce, wives typically did not contest the divorce, but only disputed an ancillary matter, such as division of property or maintenance. The result of this approach is, as Lev (1996: 193) argued decades ago, that:

> The Indonesian Islamic family law regime has long been one of the most liberal in the Muslim universe. Contracts of marriage are elaborate and flexible, partly because of pressure and advice by women's organisations in recent decades. In addition, the religious offices and courts have been quietly sympathetic to women in bad marriages. In my own research on the Islamic judiciary, to which initially I brought a few common misconceptions, it gradually dawned on me that in reality the courts were by and large oriented to women, their primary clientele. Seldom did they reject appeals for divorce by women . . .

In summary, viewed from the perspective of the sources of law that they cite, Indonesian religious courts decisions differ little from their secular counterparts and are heavily influenced by European traditions of judicial decision making. They almost never consider Islamic sources of law, instead being narrowly restricted to the positive laws of Indonesia's secular, largely Dutch-derived, legal system. Further, the religious courts derive their existence solely from statute and have no express jurisdiction or reserve power to decide matters according to Islamic law. They therefore may consider Islamic sources of law only where given the opportunity to do so by national regulation – and even that is usually done obliquely, by reference to the distillation of state-sanctioned *fiqh* contained in the *Kompilasi*. Even when the courts do consider traditional religious sources of law, they cannot use them to contradict or set aside national law.

In other words, the religious courts are courts for Muslims, for whom their jurisdiction is compulsory, but they are not Islamic courts, in the sense that they usually do not seek to apply Islamic legal tradition and instead refer almost exclusively to state regulation.

Malaysia's Syariah courts

As in Indonesia, the administration of law for Muslims in contemporary Malaysia is, to a great extent, a product of colonial rule. Many of the policies, regulations and institutions relied on by the state today are continuations or modifications of those developed under the British – particularly from the late nineteenth century onward. Some are better understood as deliberate repudiations of those policies, regulations and institutions, but in all cases the colonial influence still looms large as a reference point.

As part of their overall colonial strategy of co-opting Islam as an agent of colonial rule, the British in Malaya relied on the judiciary to develop Islamic legal doctrine and the courts were dominated by British-trained common lawyers. Islamic legal traditions were therefore interpreted through regulatory and judicial institutions of common law origin to create a body of 'Islamic law' that, as in contemporary Indonesia, had only very limited connection with traditional *shari'a*. Hooker has labelled the resulting hybrid body of law the 'Anglo-Malay *madhhab*'.[22] While this model was initially followed by the Malaysian administration post-independence, recent decades have seen a significant re-emergence of traditional *fiqh* in judicial decision making in the Syariah courts and a corresponding decline in the prominence of British common law influence.

The 1957 Constitution of Malaysia allocates powers between the federal and state governments, with the latter receiving the largest share. Under the British, Islamic matters had become closely linked to the individual states and their respective hereditary rulers (rajas or sultans). These retained only limited authority in the colonial period, but were allowed to act as guardians of the Islamic religion and Malay traditions in their own kingdoms, a role they jealously guarded. It was therefore not surprising that this principle came to be enshrined in the Constitution upon independence.

Legislative and executive powers over most aspects of Islamic legal tradition other than Islamic banking and finance were given to the states by item 1 of the State List (List II) of the Ninth Schedule of the Constitution. The individual states also retained power over their own Syariah courts, while the federal government obtained executive and legislative power over criminal and civil law, and the courts that dealt with these matters, pursuant to item 4 of the Federal List (List I) of the Ninth Schedule of the Federal Constitution, as well as the Syariah courts in the federal territories, which it administers directly. As discussed below, this constitutional arrangement has since led to much controversy regarding the relationship between the secular federal courts and the state-run Syariah courts.

Unlike the religious courts in Indonesia, the Syariah courts of Malaysia have a criminal jurisdiction, but their civil jurisdiction is far busier and, as in Indonesia, divorce cases are the greatest part of their work. This is a product of history: under colonial rule, family matters of Muslims overwhelmingly dominated the work of the *Kadi* (*qāḍī*, meaning judge) courts, as they were then known. Upon independence, this was also confirmed in the Constitution. Item 1 of State List (List II) of the Ninth Schedule granted all states (except the Federal Territories of Kuala Lumpur and Labuan) the power to enact legislation regarding, among other things, Islamic law and the personal and family law of persons professing the religion of Islam, including Islamic law relating to betrothal, marriage, divorce, dower, maintenance, adoption, legitimacy and guardianship.[23]

In 1981, a committee was established to undertake a study of the Syariah courts and to propose a model for their restructure (Muhammad, 2009: 199). As a result of its recommendations, the three-tier structure developed in the Federal Territories was ultimately followed by most of the states (Ibrahim, 1986: cxl). The modern Syariah court systems in the majority of individual states now have three levels: Syariah subordinate courts, a Syariah High Court and a Syariah Appeal Court.

In 1988, the Malaysian Constitution was amended to provide that the High Courts were to 'have no jurisdiction in respect of any matter within the jurisdiction of the Shariah Courts' (Horowitz, 1994: 269). This highly significant change created a 'zone of autonomous legal development for Islamic courts' by stopping appeals from the Islamic courts to the secular courts (Horowitz, 1994: 237). By contrast to the situation in Indonesia, the Syariah courts of Malaysia were promoted to a parallel, instead of subordinate, place in the legal system.

There have, however, since been significant jurisdictional conflicts between the civil and Syariah courts, most of which relate to article 11(1) of the Federal Constitution, the provision dealing with religious freedom (Karean, 2006: 51). While article 11(1) guarantees the right of every person to profess and practise his religion, state legislation empowers the rulers, state religious authorities (including religious councils and their *fatwā*-issuing agencies) and Syariah courts to determine the personal law of Muslims. This includes the personal rights and duties of Muslims who seek to convert *from* Islam (Karean, 2006: 51). This has serious implications, with some Malaysian states allowing for the detention of apostates, among other forms of punishment.[24] As a result of a complex series of recent and very controversial cases,[25] the civil courts have now largely deprived themselves of jurisdiction over issues concerning the rights of individuals who no longer want to be Muslim, leaving the issue for determination by the Syariah courts (Karean, 2006: 52).

The power relationship between the courts has, in fact, changed dramatically since independence. The once-subjugated Syariah courts have greatly expanded both their jurisdiction and their influence. This is not only a result of extensive legislative reform or the newly assertive character of the Syariah court judges themselves, but also, in part, a creation of the restraint – even timidity – that the secular judges show in exercising their civil jurisdiction when it touches on Islam. They seem to have generally (although not entirely) accepted that the jurisdiction of the Syariah courts can be arrived at by implication, thus allowing the latter a virtual monopoly on cases in areas considered 'sensitive' by secular courts because they involve Islamic legal traditions.[26]

This has ramifications for understanding the relationship between Islam, law and the state in Malaysia that go well beyond the issues of apostasy and religious freedom, important though these are. It also represents a departure from the various models for the judicial administration of laws for Muslims inherited from the colonial period, which gave the final say to the secular courts, as is still the case in Indonesia. It is therefore not surprising that – again, in stark contrast to the situation in Indonesia – the formation of an independent and expanded jurisdiction for Malaysia's newly empowered courts for Muslims has also been accompanied by judicial efforts to prefer the *fiqh* over statutes and even case law.

Sources of decision making

In fact, the feature that most distinguishes Malaysian Syariah courts from both Indonesia's civil law tradition religious courts, Singapore's common law Syariah courts (discussed below) and Malaysia's other, secular, courts, which are located firmly in the British common law tradition, is, as mentioned, the sources of law on which they principally rely: the *Qur'ān*, *ḥadīth* and *fiqh*. They also consider the words and deeds of the Prophet's companions, the opinions and rulings of various caliphs, scholarly consensus (*'ijmā'*) and judicial analogy (*qiyās*), as well as the legal opinions or *fatāwā* of scholars. The courts generally refer to qur'ānic passages before considering any other sources of law, but then use the other sources to elucidate and apply them. Notwithstanding the priority given to the *Qur'ān* and *ḥadīth*, the majority of the material to which the court refers is *fiqh* or, more precisely, scholarly books on *shari'a*. It is also the influence of these scholarly works that differentiates the lower-level courts from the higher-level courts and appeal boards. The latter typically analyse the primary materials through a much deeper examination of *fiqh* texts, often engaging in research to do so. Most significantly, case law is, as mentioned, rarely referred to and almost never treated as binding.

Talak *divorce*

Because traditional sources of Islamic law make up the bulk of the courts' reference material, state and federal legislation is mentioned only sparingly. Even on issues of jurisdiction – the area in which the courts are arguably most dependent on legislation – a court will often consider legislation only after first establishing that it has jurisdiction at Islamic law to hear the matter in the first place.[27]

This approach has sometimes been criticised. In several decisions in the early 1990s in which he delivered the decision of the Syariah Appeal Board of Kuala Lumpur, Professor Ahmad Ibrahim, a senior member of that Board, spoke out against the tendency of the Syariah courts to ignore express legislative provisions in favour of adhering to traditional *fiqh*.[28] He was specifically concerned with the courts' practice of ratifying *talak* divorces pronounced by men outside court. Ibrahim pointed out that the Islamic Family Law Act (No. 303) of 1984 (Federal Territories) at that time made no provision for extrajudicial *talak* and that section 124 of that Act, in fact, made it an offence for anyone to pronounce *talak* to his wife without court permission (although Ibrahim noted that this provision was never enforced by the courts). The widespread flouting of section 124 eventually led to the introduction of amendments in 1994 that now allow the courts to ratify extrajudicial *talak*, thus defeating the original prohibition.[29]

In any event, in his decisions in the early 1990s, Ibrahim referred to Islamic sources of law that supported the divorce mechanism then established under the legislation. He referred to two recorded *ḥadīth*, cited in Abu Dawud's *Kitab al-Talaq*, to the effect that both Muharib and Ibn Umar had reported the Prophet as saying that, of all permissible acts, that most hated by God was divorce. Moreover, he cited the principal qur'ānic passages that set out the procedure for divorce (Al-Baqara, 4: 229, 230, 231; Al-Talaq, 65: 1, 2) and interpreted these as meaning that:

> [D]ivorce should not be pronounced at the whim and fancy of the husband, but should be effected only for good reason and where it is clear that the parties can no longer live within the limits ordained by God and that the marriage has irretrievably broken down.[30]

According to section 54 of the Islamic Family Law Act (No. 303) of 1984 (Federal Territories):

> A husband or wife who desires divorce shall present an application for divorce to the Shariah court. The Shariah Court will then ensure that every effort is made to effect reconciliation between the parties and only if the court is satisfied that the marriage has irretrievably broken down, will the court advise the husband to pronounce one talaq [*talak*] before the court.

Ibrahim concluded that many injustices would be avoided if the provisions of the Islamic Family Law Act were followed. He called on all parties (judges, lawyers and officers) involved to ensure that God's commands were obeyed by strict adherence to the provisions of the Islamic Family Law Act. What is significant here is that Ibrahim was seeking to compel the courts to give priority to legislation not by arguing that legislation had supremacy per se, but by arguing that the legislation in question gave effect to *shari'a*. Judging from their subsequent decisions, the Syariah courts paid little heed to Ibrahim's plea and, indeed, the Federal government also seems to have given up on efforts to prohibit extrajudicial *talak* – another factor that clearly distinguishes the practices of these courts from Indonesia's religious courts.

In summary, the once-subjugated Syariah courts have greatly expanded both their jurisdiction and their influence, and have gradually given a much greater place to Islamic legal tradition in their judgments, usually at the expense of common law tradition. This fits with the agenda of Islamisation that has been pursued since at least the 1980s by the United Malays National Organisation (UMNO), the Malay party that leads the *Barisan Nasional* (National Front) coalition that has ruled Malaysia since independence. Its vote now under threat from the Islamist *Parti-Islam Se-Malaysia* (PAS, or Pan-Malaysia Islamic Party), UMNO has sought to consolidate support from Malay voters – who, as will be seen, constitutionally must be Muslim – by overtly presenting itself as strengthening Islamic institutions and thus the Malay community. To speak of Islam in Malaysia is now necessarily to speak of Malay identity and, indeed, the state itself.

Not all Malaysians welcome these changes. The non-Muslim (and thus non-Malay) population is highly sceptical of recent developments that threaten to leave them without judicial recourse in disputes with Muslims. Many fear the increased – and increasingly conservative – power of the Syariah courts over everyday life, particularly on matters of public morality. Malay Muslims themselves are not unified on the benefits of increasingly conservative interpretation of Islamic legal traditions applied in the Syariah courts.[31] Many are concerned that judgments are delivered that seem unpredictable or lack a clearly reasoned basis, even if they generally follow the party line of Malay-Muslim chauvinism, particularly where non-Malays are before the court. As a result, the question of the expanding jurisdiction of Malaysia's Syariah courts and the nature of the understanding of Islam that they promote has become part of a continuing, much wider and increasingly heated national debate about the relationship between *shari'a* and the state.

In Malaysia, the divisions and controversies over Islam and its legal traditions are a product of – and sometimes a proxy for – the divisions and controversies created by the political dominance of the Malays and their control of the Malaysian polity. Tunku Abdul Rahman, the first prime minister (1957–69), famously said, in the early years of independence, '[u]nless we are prepared to drown every non-Malay, we can never think of an Islamic Administration'.[32] He was speaking against Islamisation of the state, but an uncomfortable truth about Malaysian politics is implicit in his remark: when Malays *do* 'think of an Islamic administration' (and it is a common theme of public discourse in rapidly Islamising Malaysia), then that implicitly suggests that they are also contemplating 'drowning' non-Malays – politically and legally, at least. In the last few decades, this possibility has seemed much less unlikely than Abdul Rahman could have expected. As Malays have watched the slow erosion of the their numerical majority (which traditionally reliably delivered them government), so their willingness to demand an Islamic – and thus necessarily Malay – administration has increased and this is, to a degree, reflected in the recent 'Islamisation' of the Syariah courts.

Malaysia's Syariah courts are certainly 'courts for Muslims' and, like the Indonesian religious courts, their jurisdiction is compulsory. Increasingly, they are also courts for non-Muslims who happen to be married to, or kin of, Muslims, usually to the former's disadvantage. They are now becoming 'Islamic courts' too, in the sense of applying Islamic traditions that originate outside the state regulatory framework – which makes them unique among the three countries examined in the chapter. It is also highly controversial because of the embedded nature of race and religion in Malaysia, and the sense that these courts are taking part in a wider process of Islamising the state at the cost of non-Malay Malaysians.

Singapore's Syariah Court

As mentioned, the British colonial administration established Kadi courts in the Malay states, but for a long time Singapore, which became the seat of British colonial power in the region, lacked such an institution. Islamic law was instead left to English-trained judges working in the secular legal system. The absence of a court for Muslims became a grievance of many Singaporean Muslims, and not without reason, given that Muslims across the straits in British Malaya enjoyed them.

The Syariah Court was finally established in in 1958 by the Muslims Ordinance (No. 25) of 1957, which granted it jurisdiction over matters related to Islamic family law in disputes between Muslims or persons married under *shari'a*. After Singapore's independence, the Administration of Muslim Law Act (AMLA), cap 3, (No. 27) of 1966 came into force. The AMLA created a comprehensive scheme for the administration of laws for Muslims through a range of agencies – including the Syariah Court – and it delivered major change to the system established in 1958.

It seems, however, that the Syariah Court of Singapore is not, in fact, a judicial body. Article 93 of the 1965 Constitution of the Republic of Singapore provides that the 'judicial power of Singapore is vested in the Supreme Court and in such subordinate courts as may be provided by any written law for the time being in force'. The Supreme Court Judicature Act, cap. 322, (No. 24) of 1969, revised in 1999, and the Subordinate Courts Act, cap. 321 (No. 19) of 1990, revised in 1999, implement article 93 of the Constitution by establishing the power of the courts. Because it does not appear at all in any of these statutes, the Syariah Court is not considered a 'subordinate court' in the sense of section 2 of the Supreme Court of Judicature Act of 1969, which defines a subordinate court as 'a court from which an appeal to the Supreme Court is possible'. Instead, the Syariah Court draw its authority solely from the AMLA and appeals from the Syariah Court run to an Appeal Board, set up under AMLA section 55, the decisions of which are final. There is thus a parallel system of courts that deals with the administration of Muslim personal laws in Singapore and the Syariah Court appears to sit outside the secular judicial system, in a formal constitutional sense at least.

Recent amendments to the AMLA have furthered weakened the authority of the Syariah Court, in effect, creating a partially overlapping jurisdiction between the Islamic jurisdiction and that of the secular courts – particularly in respect of certain private law matters. Unlike Malaysia or Indonesia, where jurisdiction is compulsory, Muslims have choice of jurisdiction in Singapore. They may now opt at first instance for either the Syariah Court or the secular courts. They may choose only the Syariah Court, however, only if both parties are Muslim (unlike Malaysia, where only one needs be Muslim to found jurisdiction). Again unlike either Indonesian or Malaysia, if the parties choose the Syariah Court, they may still seek leave to bring parallel civil proceedings in the secular courts for certain property or child custody matters.

The reforms also introduced into the AMLA elements of substantive secular family law taken from the Women's Charter, cap. 353 (No. 18) of 1961. This is significant because different legal regimes apply to marriages, depending on whether the marriage was registered under the AMLA or the secular 1961 Women's Charter. The Women's Charter regulates family law in Singapore in general, but provides that certain provisions do not apply to Muslims.[33] The state's rationale for these exemptions was based on divergences between secular laws and Islamic legal traditions, as understood in Singapore, in both matters of substance and procedure.

Under this bifurcated system, the Singapore Family Court hears petitions for divorce of non-Muslim marriages under the Women's Charter, while the Syariah Court exercises a similar jurisdiction in relation to Muslim divorces. One of the main differences between the two jurisdictions is that until a divorce application has been filed with the Syariah Court, it cannot hear ancillary issues such as payment of *nafkah iddah*,[34] payment of *mut'ah*,[35] custody and access to children, or the division of matrimonial assets. The Family Court, however, is not restricted in the same manner and can hear such matters before a divorce application is filed. Since the 1999 amendments, Muslim litigants in the Syariah Court may now seek leave from that court to bring civil proceedings in the secular court on disposition or division of property or custody of children. In addition, elements of the Women's Charter of 1961 dealing with property in divorce now also appear in section 52 of the AMLA. These reforms have thus blurred what were previously much clearer distinctions between the two systems, to the cost of the Syariah Court.

Government statistics on divorces in 2002–08 show that a large majority of divorces filed in Singapore are now filed under the Women's Charter and that the number of women seeking a divorce under the Women's Charter is consistently at least double that of those seeking one under the AMLA.[36] The number of men filing under the Women's Charter is also about twice as high as the number of men filing under the AMLA, with the gap continuing to increase. There are also significant differences between the gender of the initiator in divorces initiated under the two statutes. Muslim women still find it difficult to get a divorce under the AMLA and consider their entitlements at more risk in the Syariah Court than in the Family Court. Consequently, the percentage of women compared with men filing for divorce under the Women's Charter is now proportionally higher than under the AMLA.

Talak *divorce*

As mentioned, the laws applied in both the Syariah Court and Family Court in Singapore are now very similar when it comes to the custody of children and the division of matrimonial assets. The difference between both courts lies, however, in the grounds for divorce, which are much broader under the Women's Charter, because it allows for no-fault divorce initiated by either the wife or the husband. By contrast, the Syariah Court has consistently upheld the position that only the husband is permitted to dissolve the marriage without cause.

According to section 35(2)(b) of the AMLA, the Syariah Court has jurisdiction over disputes relating to 'divorces known in the Muslim law as . . . talak'.[37] As mentioned, *talak* is a man's right under traditional Islamic law to unilaterally divorce his wife whenever he wishes, for any reason. A man may pronounce *talak* to his wife one, two or three times. Each *talak* is cumulative and, after one or two utterances, the man may *rujuk* (reconcile) with his wife, in which case they resume lawful status as man and wife. After three utterances, however, the ex-husband and ex-wife may not remarry unless the wife has married another man, consummated that marriage, divorced and completed her three months of *iddah*.

The Singapore Syariah Court's position (which is far from being a universal one) seems to be that the triple *talak* divorce can be effected by making three utterances either at once or in close succession,[38] and that this can be done via telephone or in writing, thus making it very easy for men to obtain a quick divorce at will. The case of *Mohd Rashid bin Mohd Hussein*[39] is an example of this. It concerned a man who had pronounced triple *talak* to his wife over the phone by saying 'I divorce you with triple *talak*'.[40] He subsequently applied for divorce, signing a declaration that he intended to used the term 'triple' so as not to reconcile with his wife again. As is required by section 102(4) and (5) of the AMLA, the application was referred to the Syariah Court, where the husband again confirmed his intention to divorce his wife by triple *talak*, and the Court ordered that the divorce be registered.[41]

Decisions like this, which many see as motivated by a traditionalist concern to support male authority within marriage, doubtless contribute to the decline in appeal of the Syariah Court for Muslim women in Singapore.

Sources of decision making

Another reason for the fall in divorce cases in Singapore's Syariah Court may relate to the fact that its judgments, while usually very socially conservative and showing little concern for the gender issues that motivate the Indonesian religious courts, also do not offer a particularly Islamic alternative. The Singapore Syariah Court tends, like the Indonesian courts, simply to apply legislation and, unlike the Malaysian Syariah courts, gives relatively little weight to Islamic tradition except where directed to do so in the legislation (as in the case of *talak*). They also generally give little space to explaining their reasoning, particularly in their Malay-language decisions (judges may use either Malay or English in their judgments).

According to section 35(3) of the AMLA, the law to be applied in all matters within the jurisdiction of the Syariah Court is the colonial trope, 'Muslim law, as varied where applicable by Malay custom'. The only limitation on this is that it is stated to be subject to the provisions of the Act. The Act is, however, largely silent on this issue, beyond the standard cursory reference in section 11 to archaic colonial texts prescribed under British colonial rule in the earlier ordinances for Muslims.[42] It does not, for example, specify a *madhhab* (school of Islamic law) to which the Court should adhere.[43] Moreover, it is not stated whether decisions of the Syariah Court or its Appeal Board are binding or whether the Court can look at the decisions of other Syariah courts for precedents, although this is often done in in practice. Decisions from Malaysian courts have particular significance given that the law to be applied is Muslim law 'as varied where applicable by Malay custom', an issue to which the courts of Singapore's majority-Malay neighbours have given considerable attention. In practice, the sources of law for the Syariah Court are thus legislation (in particular, AMLA), case law from Singapore and Malaysia, and 'Muslim law' – usually in that order.

The fifty decisions surveyed for this chapter were generally united by the fact that they give primacy to legislation and in none of them did the Court ever refuse to follow a precedent on the grounds that it deviated from traditional notions of Islamic law (although Malaysian courts certainly do this). In other words, in addition to legislation, case law is also given greater weight than traditional sources of Islamic law.

The result is that the Court operates in much the same way as common law courts, with the addition that it applies 'Muslim law' as well as the typical common law sources of law. As well as applying legislation and case law, the Court also relies (albeit to a much lesser extent) on the *Qur'ān*, but only to fill gaps left by statutes and cases over secondary sources, such as *fiqh* textbooks or *fatāwā*, which are rarely decisive. As a result, although the (now outdated) texts in section 11 of AMLA are rarely cited by Syariah Court judges, precedent alone is enough to ensure that they retain lingering influence on the development of Islamic law in Singapore today. In other words, the so-called Anglo-Muslim law of colonial times that is being fast jettisoned in Malaysia survives in post-colonial Singapore.

In summary, Singapore's Syariah Court is an institution that was provided reluctantly to Muslims to satisfy their demand for formal, institutional recognition of their legal traditions. It was, however, established outside the formal judicial system of Singapore, and lacks the full panoply of authority and powers enjoyed by the secular courts, particularly as regards enforcement. Its jurisdiction too has always been limited, being largely confined to family law – and even that has, over time, been further constricted and diminished. The Syariah Court must now compete with the secular courts for litigants at first instance. Even where it has jurisdiction over an action, it may face competition from related proceedings in the secular courts under the Women's Charter of 1961. While not offering the comforts of faith, the Women's Charter of 1961 proceedings offer greater convenience and more benefits for women, and this is now reflected in litigants' growing preference for the Family Court over the Syariah Court.

All courts are, of course, jealous of their jurisdictions, but the Syariah Court of Singapore now seems to have little capacity to defend its authority. Its core business – divorce – is therefore being eroded. This may also be linked to the often poor quality of decision making in this Court, a product of its inability to act convincingly as either a traditional Islamic judicial institution or a modern common law court. A more conservative, traditionalist approach to Islamic law is typically linked to a judicial assertion of Malay identity, as Abdul Rahman (2004) has persuasively argued. The bilingual nature of the Syariah Court helps to demonstrate this, with the most conservative judgments in the sample selected for this chapter being written in the Malay language, while the more liberal decisions are often written in English.

This is, in itself, significant, because it suggests that, despite the reach of the secular state in Singapore and its long-standing and consistent success in marginalising and debilitating Islamic legal tradition as a way of managing the Malay Muslim population, resistance continues – albeit in a limited and contained fashion. It is precisely the judges of the Syariah Court who prefer to adjudicate in Malay who most often assert understandings of

Islamic legal tradition that diverge from the 'sanitising' and secularising ambitions of the avowedly secular Singapore state.[44] Unfortunately, the resulting inconsistency in judicial decision making in the Syariah Court often works to the disadvantage of Malay Muslims in Singapore and, it seems, women in particular.

Conclusion

It is the premise of this chapter that the most important among a range of factors determining the nature of the *shari'a* courts of Indonesia, Malaysia and Singapore is state policy on Islam.

In Indonesia, over 80 per cent of the population are Muslim (CIA, 2014), but the Constitution does not give that religion a privileged place; instead, the national ideology, the *Pancasila* (five principles) embodied in the Preamble to the Constitution simply requires that citizens hold a 'belief in an almighty God'.[45] Upon independence in 1945, this was adopted in place of *Piagam Jakarta* (Jakarta Charter) proposals that Muslims be obliged to observe Islamic law.[46] This claim was again solidly rejected in 2002 in the course of post-Soeharto amendment of Constitution to create new, democratic polity (Butt and Lindsey, 2012: 232–234).

Today, notwithstanding a number of local regulations, or *Peraturan Daerah* (PerDa), seeking to enact norms seen as Islamic, *shari'a* has formal status only as a separate source of law in a single province, Aceh, where it was recognised as part of a peace deal to end separatist conflict. Elsewhere, the Dutch 'reception theory' policy that *shari'a* applies only insofar as received into local laws continues to hold, such that Islamic legal traditions are subject not to only local custom but, more importantly, to state secular law.[47] The *Mahkamah Konstitusi*, or Constitutional Court, recognised this in 2008 when it rejected a challenge to the constitutional validity of Law No. 7 of 1989 on the Religious Courts.[48] The applicant had argued that, by excluding Islamic criminal law from the jurisdiction of the religious courts, this statute infringed rights to religious freedom guaranteed to Muslims by articles 28 and 29 of the Constitution. The Constitutional Court, however, relied on articles 24(2) and 24A(5) of the Constitution, which provide that the jurisdiction of these courts is to be determined by legislation and thus is a matter left to the discretion of the *Dewan Perwakilan Raykat* (DPR, or People's Representative Assembly), the national legislature, because 'the highest law is the 1945 Constitution, not the Quran'.[49]

Reluctance by the state to enforce Islamic legal traditions is long-standing in Indonesia and reflects Dutch policy that saw Islamic authority as a direct threat to the colonial state (Feener, 2007: 89–72). *Shari'a* courts – the so-called Priest Courts (*Priesterraad*) – were allowed, but were absorbed into the colonial bureaucracy and their jurisdiction confined to personal law – chiefly, family law (Lindsey, 2012: 12, 268–270; Nurlaelawati, 2010: 46–47). The Indonesian system of courts for Muslims today reflects its origins, and remains highly bureaucratic and largely symbolic in its religiosity. The sources of law relied upon are predominantly national legislation, with Islamic sources such as the *Qur'ān* and *ḥadīth* being referred to only sparingly and, importantly, in such a way as not to contravene the rules in the legislation. Their jurisdiction is limited by statute to only a few aspects of Islamic legal tradition and even within these restricted areas the substantive law applied by the courts sometimes deviates so significantly from the orthodox schools of *fiqh* as to make it questionable whether it is particularly Islamic at all. The decisions of these courts are, however, usually more consistent with the sort of decisions that Indonesia's general courts make in non-Muslim 'secular' divorces and both courts are under the close supervision of the apex court, the Supreme Court, a secular, civil law European tradition court. This is a state of affairs that has rendered the religious courts effectively bureaucratic divorce-on-demand courts for women.

In Malaysia, although the British also saw Islamic authorities as a potential threat, their strategy was generally one of co-option, closely linking Islam to the status of the Malay rulers through whom they governed, conflating Malay identity with statehood and Muslim religious identity. This system was preserved upon independence and enshrined in the Constitution, with article 160(2) defining all Malays as Muslim. The High Court recently held that this means that a Malay 'remains in the Islamic faith until his or her dying days'.[50]

Since independence, Malay leaders have asserted rights to hegemony or *ketuanan Melayu* (Malay supremacy) as a separate, privileged class among other Malaysians. This notion is premised on their identity as Muslims and the 'Islamicity' of the state that they claim the right to govern. Malay leaders have argued – particularly since the 1980s – that these special rights of Malay-Muslims were part of a grand political bargain or 'social contract' struck at independence by which non-Malays were recognised as citizens of the new, 'Malay' state, although the existence of such a bargain is disputed (Kessler, 2010).

Religious issues relating to Islam are thus also political issues in Malaysia and, very often, legal ones as well, and the relationship between law, the state, its institutions and Islamic legal traditions is at the very heart of the modern Malay polity. Debate over these issues has now become a discourse 'conducted in an increasingly intolerant, authoritarian and chauvinist manner' in Malaysia (Whiting, 2002: 7). In part, this is because political competition for Malay support and increasing conservatism among Muslims in recent decades has led to a 'competitive denigration of secularism' (Whiting, 2002: 4). This has increased rhetorical support for the notion of an 'Islamic state', although the question of what that state should be like remains hotly contested among all leading parties, including those that compete for Malay support, such as UMNO and PAS.

The increasing reliance by the Malaysian Syariah courts on Islamic tradition reflects these factors. The structure of written reasons for Syariah court decisions derives from the common law tradition, but the substance of their decisions are increasingly influenced by Islamic legal doctrines taken from traditional *fiqh*. The two primary sources of Islamic law, the *Qur'ān* and the *Sunna (ḥadīth)*, are now given the greatest priority of any of the sources of law considered by the Syariah courts. In fact, in these courts they often displace the regulatory and judicial sources paramount in common law. The *Qur'ān* and the *Sunna* are, however, broad and inherently imprecise as jurisprudential texts. Being essentially spiritual in nature, they are often expressed as norms and parables rather than as specific rules, hence they are open to interpretation to a great extent. This means that it is usually the writing of legal scholars that is, in practice, the most influential source of Islamic legal tradition in Malaysia's Syariah courts. The *fiqh* is often determinative of the outcome of a judicial decision on any particular scriptural point, because it offers interpretations of the *Sunna* and *Qur'ān* expressed in legal forms that are more immediately useful to judges in formulating decisions. By comparison, the legislation dealing with law for Muslims in Malaysia is procedural, rather than substantive, in nature, and so is cited only sparingly and usually only on questions of jurisdiction – and even then often in conjunction with traditional Islamic sources. These changes have, however, been seen as weakening the position of women and religious minorities who come before these courts, particularly in divorce cases.

In Singapore, unlike Indonesia and Malaysia, Muslims are minority and they were marginalised when the island was directly ruled by the British, who shared neither race, language nor religion with them. This remains the case today, with Singapore ruled since independence by single party, the People's Action Party, which is dominated by non-Muslim ethnic Chinese.

In Singapore, as in Malaysia, religion and race are conflated, and in both countries the Syariah courts are also principally courts for Malays. In Malaysia, however, the government is Malay-dominated; in Singapore, Malays are largely excluded from government. The result is that while the courts for Malays in Malaysia have support from the state, those in Singapore remain marginalised and the state has consistently adopted policies that make the secular courts a more attractive venue for Muslims, particularly women seeking divorce. Consequently, Singapore's Syariah Court is not formally a 'court' and, while it may be conservative in its interpretation of the AMLA, it is not really 'Islamic' either, because it rarely goes beyond the terms of that statute and never uses Islamic tradition to contradict it. Even its role as a 'court for Muslims' is diminishing as Muslims increasingly take their disputes elsewhere for resolution, just as the state intends.

In conclusion, then, this brief comparative study suggests that the question of what Muslims in archipelagic Southeast Asia want from their *shari'a* courts is rarely the key to understanding the form that these courts take. It has long been true that what the state wants is more often decisive.

Notes

1 This chapter draws extensively on material published in Lindsey (2012); Lindsey and Steiner (2012a, 2012b); and Sumner and Lindsey (2010). The author is grateful to his two co-authors for permission to do so and for the opportunity to work with them. The research on which these publications and this chapter are based was funded by an ARC Federation Fellowship (2006–11).

2 The term 'Islamic legal traditions' is a broader category than *shari'a* and better reflects the diversity of interpretation and debate regarding 'law' for Muslims in Southeast Asian Islam. It may, for example, embrace descriptors such as *shari'a*, *fiqh* (Islamic jurisprudence), 'Muslim law', 'Islamic law' or even *adat* (traditional customary law), among others. In this chapter, 'Islamic legal traditions' is used as an umbrella term, in the broader sense suggested by Muhaimin (1995), who argues that it is possible to posit the tradition of Islam as something that involves '"tradition" wherein the owner or performer intends to do or claims that his actions come from, is [*sic*] associated with . . . Islam; and that his intended or claimed behaviour is verifiable through, and finds its roots and justification in Scriptures' (Muhaimin, 1995: 10).

3 For convenience, *shari'a* is used here for the Arabic *sharī'a*. Original spelling is retained for quotations and the names of institutions, for example '*Syariah* court'. In fact, there is no consistency in spelling across Southeast Asia, or even within individual countries or institutions, with local forms including *syariah*, *shariah*, *shari'a*, *syari'e*, *syariat*, *syara'*, *syariaa* and *syaria*, among others. There is sometimes even variation within individual documents.

4 *Ḥadīth* (traditions), i.e. the recorded words and deeds of the Prophet Muhammad, one of the main sources of Islamic law.

5 Law No. 7 of 1989, s. 4(1).

6 Law No. 7 of 1989, s. 6(1).

7 Law No. 7 of 1989, ss. 1(1), 49(1).

8 The other areas that fall within the jurisdiction of the religious courts are: inheritance (Law No. 7 of 1989 on Religious Justice, s. 49(b)); Muslim wills and testaments (s. 49(c)); *hibah* (charitable bequests) (s. 49(d)); *wakaf* (s. 49(e). *Waqf* is the permanent dedication by a Muslim of property, usually land, for purposes recognised by Islamic law as pious, religious or charitable; Islamic

philanthropy (s. 49(f)–(h)), comprising *zakat* (obligatory charitable payments), *infaq* and *sadaqah* (voluntary charity), and *ekonomi syari'ah* (*shari'a* economy) issues (s. 49(i)). The Elucidation (or explanatory memorandum) to s. 37 of Law No. 3 of 2006 provides that '*shari'a* economy' includes Islamic banking, Islamic microfinance, Islamic insurance, Islamic contracts, Islamic securities, Islamic pawnbroking (*penggadaian*) and 'Islamic business'. For more descriptions of these areas of jurisdiction, see also the Elucidation to s. 49(2) of Law No. 7 of 1989 on Religious Justice, and the Elucidation to s. 49(a), as inserted by Law No. 3 of 2006, s. 37.

9 Law No. 7 of 1989 on the Religious Courts, s. 49(1), as amended by Law No. 3 of 2006, s. 37.

10 Elucidation to s. 49(2) of Law No. 7 of 1989 on Religious Justice; and Elucidation to s. 49(a), as inserted by Law No. 3 of 2006, s. 37.

11 These data are taken from the Supreme Court Annual Report 2009, and from subsequent data provided by the statistical units of the directorates-general for the general courts (*Badilum*) and religious courts (*Badilag*). Case numbers for the general courts exclude summary or short cases (such as traffic fines), which are heard in an expedited way by the general courts. Heard by only one judge, these are essentially bureaucratic proceedings rather than trials. They thus require a much lower commitment of time and resources. However, uncontested cases are included in the calculation of cases to enable a more direct comparison of the caseload between the general and religious courts, because both jurisdictions deal with this kind of case. Until the 2007 Annual Report of the Supreme Court, the number of general court cases was obscured by several million summary traffic offences, which are processed in an expedited way. Traffic and other summary cases are now presented separately in the Supreme Court annual reports, resulting in a clearer picture of the judicial workloads of the general and religious courts (Sumner and Lindsey, 2010).

12 See also e-profile documents for the religious courts for 2004, 2006 and 2007, available online at http://www.badilag.net [accessed 9 June 2012].

13 This is despite the fact that Indonesia's non-Muslim population (mainly comprising Christians, Hindus, Buddhists and Confucians) is approximately 15 per cent of the total population of 270 million.

14 *Fiqh* (Islamic jurisprudence, i.e. the contested body of scholarly interpretation).

15 Namely, Asbah Wanadhair, Ghayatul Murom Lis Syaehil Majdi, Muhadz-zab, Tanbih, Bidayatul Mujtahid, Risalatus Syiqaq, Mada Hariyatur Zaijain, Mughnil Muhtaj, Tuhfah, Nash, Bughyatul Mustarsyidin, Tarsyihul Mustafidien and Subulus Salam.

16 *Fatāwā* (plural of *fatwā*, meaning legal opinion of a religious scholar).

17 Singaporean Administration of Muslim Law Act (AMLA), cap. 3, (No. 27) of 1966.

18 As indicated above, appeals from the religious courts are first made to the Religious High Court (located at the provincial level). Appeals can be made on wide-ranging grounds, pursuant to Law No. 7 of 1989 on Religious Justice, ss. 6(1) and (2), 51(1). Law No. 7 of 1989, s. 4(2), allows the Religious High Court to send the case back to the first-instance religious court for further examination if it thinks it necessary, to uphold the original decision in full or in part or quash it, rehear the case itself and alter orders, as it sees fit. The Supreme Court, located in Jakarta, is the final appellate court on matters within the jurisdiction of the religious courts, as it is for most branches of the Indonesian judicial system, other than the Constitutional Court (*Mahkamah Konstitusi*). Appeal lies from the Religious High Courts to the Supreme Court solely on grounds of error of law and Supreme Court decisions can then be reviewed through a further *Peninjauan Kembali* (PK), or reconsideration, process, which is the final level of appeal in the Indonesian system.

19 *Taklik* (*talīq*, meaning divorce initiated by the wife, provided that a breach of a lawful condition agreed to at the time of marriage has occurred).

20 *Khuluk* (*khul*', meaning divorce initiated by the wife by redemption, whereby she agrees to pay compensation to the former husband, often by repaying the dowry that was initially given to her).

21 *Fasakh* (*faskh*, meaning divorce initiated by the wife if the husband has not fulfilled certain obligations).

22 *Madhhab*, *madhab*, *madzhab*, *mazhab*, etc. (*madhhab*, meaning school of Islamic legal thought). The comment was made in a personal communication between the author and M. B. Hooker. See also Lindsey and Steiner (2012b: 5).

23 The full text of this provision is as follows:
Islamic law and personal and family law of persons professing the religion of Islam, including the Islamic law relating to succession, testate and intestate, betrothal, marriage, divorce, dower, maintenance, adoption, legitimacy guardianship, gifts, partitions and non-charitable trusts; Wakafs and the definition and regulation of charitable and religious endowments, institutions, trusts, charities and charitable institutions operating wholly within the State; Malay customs. Zakat, Fitrah and Baitulmal or similar Islamic religious revenue, mosques or any Islamic public places of worship, creation and punishment of offences by persons professing the religion of Islam against precepts of that religion, except in regard to matters included in the Federal List; the constitution, organisation and procedure of Syariah courts, which shall have jurisdiction only over persons professing the religion of Islam and in respect only of any of the matters included in this paragraph, but shall not have jurisdiction in respect of offences except in so far as conferred by federal law, the control of propagating doctrines and beliefs among persons professing the religion of Islam; the determination of matters of Islamic law and doctrine Malay custom.

24 See, e.g., Syariah Criminal Offences Enactment (No. 3) of 1995 (Sabah), s. 63.

25 See, e.g., *Soon Singh a/l Bikar Singh v Pertubuhan Kebajikan Islam Malaysia (PERKIM) Kedah* [1999] 1 MLJ 489; *Tongiah Jumali v Kerajaan Negeri Johor & ors* [2004] 1 MLJ 40; *Lina Joy v Majlis Agama Islam Wilayah Persekutuan* [2004] 6 CLJ 242, 271.

26 For a detailed discussion of recent decisions on the controversial and still opaque division of jurisdiction between the two court systems, see Steiner (2014).

27 See, e.g., *ex parte Siti Aisyah Janthip Aisam* (1427H) 21 (2) JH 262; *Hajah Ramlah bt Syarif v Nor Husin bin Othman* (1420H) 13 (1) JH 103.

28 See *Re: Mohd Hussin bin Abdul Ghani & Anor* [1990] 2 MLJ 75, (1412H) 7 (1) JH 189; *Rojmah bte Abdul Kadir v Mohsin Bin Ahmad* [1991] 3 MLJ 30; *Mejar Mohammad Sultan Bin Ismail Dan Saodah bt Haji Abdul Kadir* (1414H) JH 266 (Civil Appeal No. 6 of 1990); *Jasni bin Abdul Rahim v Rahmah bte Mohd Jono* [1992] 1 MLJ 143.

29 See Islamic Family Law Act (No. 303) of 1984 (Federal Territories), s. 55A, as amended.

30 *Rojmah bte Abdul Kadir v Mohsin Bin Ahmad* [1991] 3 MLJ 30, 31, (1990) JH 265.

31 For Malay Muslim criticisms of Syariah court decisions, see Steiner (2014).

32 *Straits Times*, 1 May 1959, as quoted in von der Mehden (1963: 611).

33 These include, significantly, Parts II–VI (Monogamous Marriages; Solemnization of Marriages; Registration; Penalties and Miscellaneous Provisions relating to Solemnization and Registration of Marriages; Rights and Duties of Husbands and Wives); Part X (Divorce), Part XII (Miscellaneous), s. 181 (marriages solemnised before 15 September 1961 deemed to be registered under this Act); and s. 182 (voluntary registration of marriages solemnised under religion or custom).

34 *Nafkah iddah* (*nafaqa ʻidda*). *Iddah* is the period that must elapse before a widow or divorcee can remarry – roughly three months – and *nafkah iddah* is the payment made by the husband for this period.

35 *Mut'ah* (*muṭʻa*), meaning a consolatory gift, i.e. a gift to a wife on divorce if no dowry has been settled.

36 Singapore Department of Statistics, formerly available online at http://www.singstat.gov.sg/stats/themes/people/marriages.pdf [accessed 14 July 2008].

37 Section 35(2)(c) also gives the Court jurisdiction to hear disputes relating to 'nullity of marriage or judicial separation'. These terms presumably refer to secular law concepts and the Court has not (in the sample decisions examined) relied on these heads of jurisdiction. It is therefore unclear whether subsection (c) could be a basis for a woman to receive a divorce where she did not have grounds for *taklik* or *fasakh* divorce and the husband refused to give a *talak* or *khuluk*.

38 With the possible exception for adherents of the Hanafi *madhhab*, when the wife is pregnant: *Mohd Rashid bin Mohd Hussein* (Appeal Case No. 01/1988).

39 *Mohd Rashid bin Mohd Hussein* (Appeal Case No. 01/1988).
40 *Saya ceraikan Awak dengan talak tiga.*
41 The husband later regretted the divorce and appealed against the Syariah Court's decision, claiming to have been enraged at the time of pronouncing the *talak* and unaware of the consequences. This was rejected by the Appeal Board because of the number of times he had confirmed the divorce in the Syariah Court. For more detail of this case, see Lindsey and Steiner (2012a: 211, 219–222).
42 These are the same as those in AMLA, s. 44(1), which provides that, in deciding the questions of inheritance and succession, the Court may accept as proof of Islamic law the contents of all or any of: (a) the English translation of the *Qur'ān*, by Yusuf Ali or Marmaduke Pickthall; (b) *Mohammedan Law*, by Syed Ameer Ali; (c) *Minhaj et Talibin*, by Nawawi, translated by E. C. Howard from the French translation of Van den Berg; d) *Digest of Moohummudan Law*, by Neil B. E. Baililie;(e) *Anglo-Muhammadan Law*, by Sir Roland Knyvet Wilson, 6th edn, revised by A. Yusuf Ali; (f) *Outlines of Muhammadan Law*, by A. A. Fyzee; and (g) *Muhammadan Law*, by F. B. Tyabji.
43 AMLA, s. 33(1), directs that the *Majlis Ugama Islam Singapura* (MUIS, or Islamic Religious Council of Singapore), and its Legal Committee 'ordinarily follow the tenets of the *Shafi'i* school of law', but the same is not stipulated for the Syariah Court. There is an exception if the MUIS or the Legal Committee considers that following the *Shafi'i* school of law would be 'opposed to the public interest', in which case they may follow any of the other 'accepted schools of Muslim law' (s. 33(2)) or, if the requested ruling is in relation to a particular school of law, the ruling may be made in accordance with that particular school of law (s. 33(3)). Again, there is no guidance given to the Court.
44 On the avowedly secular ideology of the Singapore government and its willingness to use what it calls 'social engineering' to 'sanitise' religion, see Lindsey and Steiner (2012a: 1–10, 258–263).
45 For an account of the formation of the *Pancasila*, see Lindsey (2012: 35–44).
46 On the Jakarta Charter and efforts to implement Islamic law as binding for Muslims in Indonesia, see Butt and Lindsey (2012: 226–232).
47 On reception theory, see Lindsey (2012: 11–15); Feener (2007: 89–72).
48 Constitutional Court Decision 16/PUU-VI/2008.
49 The words are Justice Muhammad Alim's, spoken during hearings prior to judgment.
50 *Lina Joy v Majils Agama Wilayah Persekutuan & anor* [2004] 6 CLJ 242, 271.

References

An-Na'im, A. A. (2008) 'Shari'a in the Secular State: A Paradox of Separation and Conflation', in P. Bearman, W. Heinrichs and B. G. Weiss (eds) *The Law Applied: Contextualising the Islamic Shari'a – A Volume in Honour of Frank E. Vogel*, London/New York: I. B. Tauris, 44–56.

Butt, S., and Lindsey, T. (2012) *The Constitution of Indonesia: A Contextual Analysis*, Oxford/Portland, OR: Hart.

Direktorat Jenderal Badan Peradilan Agama (2006) *Himpunan Data Statistik Perkara di Lingkungan Peradilan Agama Seluruh Indonesia Tahun 2005*, Jakarta: Mahkamah Agung, Direktorat Jenderal Badan Agama.

Feener, M. (2007) *Muslim Legal Thought in Modern Indonesia*, Cambridge: Cambridge University Press.

Hooker, M. B. (1975) *Legal Pluralism: An Introduction to Colonial and Neo-colonial Laws*, Oxford: Clarendon.

Horowitz, D. (1994) 'The Qur'an and the Common Law: Islamic Law Reform and the Theory of Legal Change', *American Journal of Comparative Law*, 42(2/3): 233–293.

Ibrahim, A. (1986) 'The Shariah Court in Malaysia', *Malayan Law Journal*, 2: cxxx–cxlvi.

Karean, V. S. (2006) 'The Malaysian Constitution and Its Identity Crisis: Secular or Theocratic?' *LAWASIA Journal*, 1: 47–61.

Kessler, C. (2010) 'What Social Contract?', *The Malaysian Insider*, 6 September.

Lev, D. (1996) 'On the Other Hand', in L. J. Sears (ed.) *Indonesia in Transition: Social Aspects of* Reformasi *and Crisis*, Durham, NC/London: Duke University Press, 191–205.

Lindsey, T. (2012) *Islam, Law and the State in Southeast Asia, Vol. I: Indonesia*, London: I. B. Tauris.

Lindsey, T., and Steiner, K. (2012a) *Islam, Law and the State in Southeast Asia, Vol. II: Singapore*, London: I. B. Tauris.

Lindsey, T., and Steiner, K. (2012b) *Islam, Law and the State in Southeast Asia, Vol. III: Malaysia and Brunei*, London: I. B. Tauris.

Muhaimin, A. G. (1995) *The Islamic Traditions of Cirebon:* Ibadat *and* Adat *among Javanese Muslims*, Canberra: ANU E-press.

Muhammad, R. W. (2009) *The Administration of Islamic Judicial System in ASEAN Countries with Particular Reference to Malaysia*, Kuala Lumpur: Lambert Academic.

Nurlaelawati, E. (2010) *Modernisation, Tradition and Identity: The Kompilasi Hukum Islam and Legal Practice in the Indonesian Religious Courts*, Amsterdam: Amsterdam University Press.

Rahman, N. A. B. A. (2004) 'Traditionalism and Its Impact on the Administration of Justice: The Case of the Syariah Court in Singapore', *Inter-Asia Cultural Studies*, 5(3): 415–432.

Steiner, K. (2014) 'The Case Continues? The High Courts in Malaysia and Unilateral Conversion of a Child to Islam by One Parent', *Australian Journal of Asian Law*, 14(1): Article 10.

Sumner, C., and Lindsey, T. (2010) Courting Reform: Indonesia's Islamic Courts and Justice for the Poor, Lowy Institute Paper 31, Double bay, New South Wales: Lowy Institute.

US Central Intelligence Agency (CIA) (2014) *World Factbook: East and Southeast Asia*, available online at https://www.cia.gov/library/publications/the-world-factbook/wfbExt/region_eas.html [accessed 22 July 2016].

von der Mehden, F. R. (1963) 'Religion and Politics in Malaya', *Asian Survey*, 3(12): 609–615.

Wahid, M. (2010) 'Reformation of Islamic Family Law in post-New-Order Indonesia: A Legal and Political Study of the Counter Legal Draft of the Islamic Land Compilations', in O. Atsushi, O. Masaaki and A. Suaedy (eds) *Islam in Contention: Rethinking Islam and the State in Indonesia*, Kyoto/Jakarta/Taiwan: Kyoto University Press, The Wahid Institute and the Centre for Asia-Pacific Area Studies, 75–118.

Whiting, A. (2002) 'Secularism, the Islamic State and the Malaysian Legal Profession', *Asian Journal of Comparative Law*, 5(1): 1–34.

20 Indigenous peoples

Indigeneity, indigeny or indigenism?

Geoffrey Benjamin

Introduction

The terms 'indigenous people', 'indigenousness' and 'indigeneity' are most commonly understood to refer to tribal or endangered minorities suffering political, cultural, legal or economic disadvantages that are not borne by the majority sectors of their countries' populations. Typically, the question of who is 'indigenous' and who is not arises with regard to land-rights claims, but the label is also employed on occasion by members of dominant 'majority' populations, as well as by dominated minorities, when asserting ethnic hegemony, cultural authenticity and other such concerns.[1] However, the 'tribal' sense is the generally accepted default meaning of 'indigenous', even though the concepts 'tribal' and 'indigenous' actually refer to different, albeit overlapping, social realities.

In the Americas, Australasia and much of Russia, 'indigenous' usually refers unambiguously to those members of the population whose ancestors did not arrive from Europe, or from Africa during the trans-Atlantic slave trade. The 'indigenous' peoples of those regions are therefore usually distinguishable from the exogenous European- and African-descended members by their genetic, cultural and linguistic characteristics. Regardless of the demographic facts, the indigenes normally constitute a political 'minority', with many of them following tribal or peasant patterns of social organisation. This sometimes leads the exogenous mainstream to regard them as living in a 'traditional', or even 'primitive', manner, needing enlightenment or protection.

In Asia, however, and despite the colonisation formerly undergone by most of the region, there was no large-scale or persistent European settlement. Without further qualification, therefore, 'indigenous' could be applied in some of its various senses to almost *all* of Asia's inhabitants, regardless of their specific social circumstances.[2] (The main exceptions are people of Chinese or South Asian ancestry in those Southeast Asian countries in which they form a significant part of the population.) Consequently, the distinction between presumed indigenes and the dominant population is less clear in Asian countries than in other parts of the world. The two sectors have shared so many millennia of interlinked history that the differences between them cannot easily be captured simply by the term 'indigenous'. Thus being 'indigenous' in Asia often has less to do with purportedly distinct origins than with processes of deliberate dissimilation between different patterns of social and cultural organisation within the same overall framework – although this is not to deny that distinct origins may also play a part. Moreover, Asian polities differ in the uses they make of the 'indigenous' concept and in the extent to which they accord official recognition to 'indigenous' status. Sometimes, the term 'indigenous' is applied officially to sections of the population other than the relatively disadvantaged people who would normally be so labelled elsewhere in the world.

Clearly, 'indigenous' and its relatives are multiply ambiguous terms, which suggests that a more careful vocabulary is required, especially in relation to Asia. This chapter aims to clarify the issues by proposing a more appropriate way of discussing the various social circumstances that are currently described as 'indigenous' and the different senses in which a population may therefore be referred to as an 'indigenous people'.

Who gets to be called 'indigenous'?

In Asia and elsewhere, there are at least six different senses in which individuals or populations might come to regard themselves or be regarded by others as 'indigenous':

1. those whose familial ancestors have always, as far as is known, inhabited the specific places that their present-day descendants still live in, the distinctive cultural consequences of which circumstance are discussed shortly in terms of 'indigeny';
2. those who have resisted incorporation into centralised states by organising themselves into autonomous segmentary social formations, which is discussed below in terms of 'tribal' or 'tribality';
3. those claiming protection of traditional land rights that have been denied to them in the modern political sphere – currently the most widespread self-ascribed use of the label 'indigenous';
4. those regarded as having arrived earlier into a territory (however defined) that later also came to be inhabited by populations regarded as originating elsewhere – although this is not a homogeneous phenomenon and such populations cannot be described *simply* as 'indigenous', largely because of the varying time-depths that would have to be taken into account;[3]
5. those who are regarded as members of the self-declared 'definitive' founding population of a national political tradition, which sometimes overlaps with circumstance 4, and is discussed later in the chapter as an example of 'indigenism'; and
6. those who are regarded as the ancient originators of a distinctively named archaeological 'tradition'. (To avoid confusion with present-day usages of 'indigenous' or with present-day populations – always difficult to determine – such 'traditions' are better referred to as 'endogenous'.)

Since each of these circumstances generates its own set of political and legal consequences, they are clearly not all 'indigenous' in the same sense or to the same extent. Despite a degree of overlap, they should therefore not be placed under a single undifferentiated label, especially if the concept 'indigenous people' is to be the object of judicial deliberations. Unfortunately, current social-science practice regularly disguises these distinctions by applying the newly coined term 'indigeneity' to all or most of the meanings listed above,[4] thereby dissolving away the distinction between true place-linked *indigeny* (an unself-conscious condition of life) and territory-based *indigenism* (a self-conscious political stance), perhaps on the post-modernist grounds that both are supposedly just rhetorical constructs.[5] Indigeny, however, is not a rhetorical construct of any kind, being constituted of the historically maintained connections of particular individuals and families to particular places. It should therefore not be treated in the same way as the rhetorically asserted indigenist connections of whole populations to whole territories – especially when those populations are defined 'ethnically'.

Paradoxically, indigenism actually constitutes a manifestation of the covert *exogeny* experienced by people who have moved away from the places inhabited by their presumed familial ancestors. This now characterises a high proportion of the world's population, both rural and urban. More generally, exogeny is a precondition for the generation and maintenance of societal modernity and the formal rationality on which it depends, and without which the mounting of explicitly indigenist claims would not be possible.[6] Sociologically, true place-linked indigeny should therefore not automatically be regarded as synonymous with 'indigeneity', which in many cases turns out to be a form of modern political identity characteristic of culturally exogenous contexts. The overlap between indigeny and indigeneity is, at best, only partial.

'Tribal' versus 'indigenous'

The widespread use of the word 'indigenous' to label social formations that are more properly characterised as 'tribal' also generates conceptual and legal problems. Tribespeople are indeed typically indigenous (in the 'indigeny' sense discussed shortly) to the places they inhabit,[7] but most of the populations who can justifiably claim to be indigenous to their places of habitation are state-dominated peasants rather than segmentary and historically autonomous tribespeople.

The two intergovernmental bodies most closely involved in this issue, the United Nations and the International Labour Organization (ILO), have differed slightly in terms of how they handle it. The United Nations declared 1993 the 'International Year of Indigenous Peoples'. In September 2007, the General Assembly followed through by adopting the UN Declaration on the Rights of Indigenous Peoples. A further World Conference on Indigenous Peoples was held in September 2014. No mention of 'tribal peoples' is made in these proceedings nor is any unambiguous definition offered of the term 'indigenous peoples'. Nevertheless, the text of the 2007 Declaration clearly implies that tribespeople were its intended focus, by expressing a 'concern' that:

> [I]ndigenous peoples have suffered from historic injustices as a result of, inter alia, their colonization and dispossession of their lands, territories and resources, thus preventing them from exercising, in particular, their right to development in accordance with their own needs and interests . . .
>
> (UN Declaration on the Rights of Indigenous Peoples, Preamble)

The failure to define 'indigenous' or to employ the term 'tribal' has allowed some Asian signatory governments to interpret the Declaration in a manner considerably at deviance from its intended purpose. The 1989 ILO Convention No. 169 on Indigenous and Tribal Peoples attempted to ameliorate the deficit by differentiating explicitly between 'tribal' and 'indigenous' peoples. The status of 'tribal' peoples, it suggested, is regulated 'wholly or partially by their own customs or traditions or by special laws or regulations' (Article 1(a)), whereas that of 'indigenous' peoples results from their having been conquered or colonised and who, 'irrespective of their legal status, retain some or all of their own social, economic, cultural and political institutions' (Article 1(b)). The stated differences are so slight that the remainder of the Declaration 'for practical reasons' applies 'indigenous' to *both* categories, but adds 'self-identification' as a criterion for determining to which populations the provisions of the Convention should apply.

The latter requirement, however, is not clear-cut. In Asia especially, 'self-identification' leaves the question of just who is 'indigenous' open to political manipulation. Moreover, the ability to self-identify as 'indigenous' or 'tribal' depends crucially on the specific language in which the discourse is mounted. Almost always, this will be a standardised official language rather than the language or dialect that the people themselves employ in their daily lives. Consequently, such indigenist discourse will necessarily have to be carried on in the exogenist standard-language context, as too would any pro-indigene campaigns organised by non-governmental bodies. (The latter, though, are usually run by persons who are well aware of the specific local issues, including the question of language.) In this chapter, both 'tribal' and 'indigenous' are employed as far as possible with objective, sociologically verifiable meanings that do not depend on the linguistic usages of the people or peoples referred to.

Most anthropologists now recognise that 'tribes' as discrete, bounded social units hardly ever occur in reality,[8] but social formations organised on a segmentary *tribal* (the adjective) basis certainly have existed in many parts of Asia and continue to do so. In Southeast Asia especially, 'tribal' refers to uncentralised, segmentary societies that have organised themselves to resist the inroads of the state, which they have wished to keep off their backs.[9] Segmentary tribal formations *of the kind described in the ethnographic and historical literature* (a crucial proviso) first came into being in abreaction to the creation of centralised states. This millennia-old dissimilatory process led to the emergence of three distinct, but mutually defining, pre-modern forms of sociality: rulers, peasants and tribespeople. *Rulers* and their accomplices placed themselves in control. *Peasants*' lives were controlled by agencies of the state, which they provisioned in exchange for a little reflected cultural and religious glory, but no counter-control, while continuing to support themselves through their own subsistence activities. *Tribespeople* resisted the state and its rulers by organising themselves in a segmentary ('tribal') manner, and by retaining distinctive languages, cultural practices, religions and subsistence modes, rather than assimilating to the more widespread 'majority' ways of life. Nevertheless, the character of tribal society – in Asia especially – has been shaped by the proximity of the state.

The tribal/peasant/ruler framework is therefore not a ranked evolutionary series constituted of supposedly different types of people, but the consequence of somewhat similar people reacting in different ways to ever-shifting political circumstances. Segmentary tribal formations are thus neither primordial nor 'primitive', nor are they necessarily long-lived, for constant ethnogenetic process ensures that named 'tribal' identities last for just two or three generations before they eventually merge with some other identity. (Centralised administrations act to terminate this fluidity by instituting fixed ethnic classifications that are resistant to both ethnogenetic change and the insertion of new ethnological discoveries.[10]) There has also been movement in and out of tribality by individuals and families, mostly in the majority direction through peasantisation, but also in the opposite direction through secondary tribalisation.[11]

Such was the immediate pre-modern situation in most of Asia until the end of the Second World War. Subsequent decolonisation and modernisation led to the absorption of the pre-modern polities into a much smaller number of modern nation-states, with a consequent progressive dissolution of the ruler/peasant/tribespeople distinctions in favour of a more uniform 'citizen' status, at least in *de jure* terms. Citizenries are inimical to the maintenance of true indigeny: they are required to work within the transcendental 'there and then' worldview of 'nation building' rather than the 'here and now' orientation that has characterised most tribespeople and some peasants. Centralised political domination is maintained by imposing the hegemony of the administrative and financial capitals over other places within the state's territory. Modern states therefore seek to destroy indigeny-based forms of consociation, often by breaking the linkage to specific places through enforced population movements euphemistically described as 'resettlement' or 'relocation'.[12]

By entering the cash economy, therefore, tribespeople increasingly become rural proletarians, or even middle-class urbanites. In the process, they lose control over the land and maritime resources on which their families' subsistence was previously, and often still is, based. When this happens, they and their supporters typically adopt an explicitly 'indigenous' identity, to reinforce their land-rights claims and reject unwelcome cultural influences. The latter include restrictions against their language and pressure to undergo religious conversion, changes that their peasant neighbours succumbed to centuries ago as tokens of the reflected civilisational glory (through conversion to Buddhism, Islam or Catholicism) of which they mostly came to feel proud.

Thus, although Asian tribespeople and peasants might both be thought of as 'indigenous peoples' in various respects, they inhabit different social worlds. The widespread fusing of the terms 'indigenous' and 'tribal' fails to capture this distinction. Consequently, whenever the primary reason for asserting 'indigenous' rights is to protect the circumstances of current or recent tribespeople, the label 'indigenous' may prove self-defeating. Indeed, the problems experienced by peasants are sometimes *opposed* to those of tribespeople and may lead to conflict between them. This is further aggravated whenever the majority population employs the label 'indigenous' to assert its political dominance over other sectors of the population: peasants usually fall religiously, linguistically and ethnically *within* the majority sector. Consequently, the label 'indigenous' sometimes draws attention away from the problems experienced by Asia's tribal populations.

Indigeny versus exogeny

Tribespeople and some peasants in Asia regularly suffer varying degrees of disadvantage, ranging from racial or class prejudice to expropriation of their land without consultation, compensation or considerations of legality. The latter occurs frequently, whether carried out by state agencies or by private actors with the state's compliance. However, the difficulties confronted by the removed people in attempting to remedy the situation do not result primarily from their tribality or peasant status; rather, it is their *place-linked indigeny* that puts them at a peculiar disadvantage when confronted by this kind of enforced social change. (In this section, 'indigenes' refers solely to those living under true indigeny and not to the other social circumstances that are sometimes also referred to as 'indigenous'.)

'Indigeny' labels the distinctive sociocultural circumstances that characterise people who continue to inhabit the places that their immediate familial ancestors lived in for as long as social memory can recall. In the strictest sense, 'indigeny' should therefore cease to characterise those who have moved away from their ancestral places. But this criterion is not absolute, because the interaction of place, time and descent ensures that the degree of indigeny is variable, relational and graded. A person can be variously *more* or *less* indigenous with respect to any or all of several features. First, place can be more narrowly or more broadly defined.

Second, because indigeny attaches primarily to individuals and families rather than to whole populations considered as undifferentiated 'peoples' or 'ethnic groups', an individual's own ancestors may have lived there longer than someone else's, which leads to a further potential distinction of 'priority' or 'precedence', as analysed in Fox and Sather (1996), between the more and the less 'aboriginal' indigenes (Gray, 1995: 39).

Third, some ancestors may be considered more salient than others, especially in the unilineal or unilaterally biased systems found in several parts of Asia. Moreover, individuals may frequently be of mixed descent with respect to indigeny.

The contrast between indigeny (embodiment *by* place) and exogeny (estrangement *from* place) is fundamental (Benjamin, 2016: 513). True indigenes carry out most of their activities in the same place, with the same people, over long periods of time. Their understanding of their own circumstances is typically tacit, non-articulated and constantly sustained by the embedded practices of their daily lives, in which home and workplace are the same, and there is no distinction between family and co-workers. Under indigeny, 'place' is informal and subjective. Being transmitted primarily in families rather than through the politico-jural institutions of wider society, indigeny is therefore embedded in a web of many-stranded, multiplex social relations. In turn, this has an elective affinity with the various non-formal modes of thought that Max Weber (1978: 979–980) characterised as 'substantive rationality', exemplified especially in the informal, 'ethical' and restitutive legal procedures to which he referred as '*kadhi* justice'. (Weber had practised as a lawyer and earned a doctorate in legal history.)

For those living under indigeny, tribespeople especially, the land itself is a mainstay of the sociocultural framework – a 'subject', so to speak, rather than commoditisable object.[13] Indigenes may therefore find it difficult to get their views across appropriately when acting within the formally rational framework required by modern exogenous institutions, including the law courts. Exogenes, in contrast, being less attached to land in this way, typically find the indigenous framework difficult to comprehend. Under exogeny, land and territory are formally and objectively defined, with home and workplace spatially separated, and family different from co-workers. Exogenes are therefore emotionally and cognitively free to take an exploitative approach to their and others' surroundings. They may even come to think of 'culture' – religion, language, music, dance, etc. – as an object ripe for exploitation. Exogeny is therefore frequently associated with religious conversion – the move from an unnamed local religion towards a named 'world' religion' – in an instrumental process that ultimately sustains a more detached view of the people's relation to land.

Exogeny is thus associated with the kinds of separated, less-embedded lives typical of the relatively single-stranded, social relations that characterise socially differentiated social formations in general, and modern society especially. These have a close affinity with the framework that Weber (1978) characterised as 'formal rationality' – summarisable as the belief that one can do just one thing at a time in a calculable manner, which Weber showed to favour those who already held power or who might wish to gain power. A major factor in this is adherence to an externally imposed, bureaucratically codified judicial system based on formal equality before the law, rather than to the interpersonal specificities that typify the multi-strandedness of indigeny. Exogenes can thus easily think of their own and others' land as an objectified commodity open to exploitation by alteration and sale, once it is 'registered' under a modern legal system and hence viewable *solely* in that light.

Indigenes' unregistered land, on the other hand, regardless of the immensely long periods over which it may have served as their subsistence and cultural base, is treated under the law as not belonging to them, but to the state. In the absence of 'registered' documentary evidence, such customary prior residence is hard to prove in court, regardless of the real circumstances. Since the phrase 'indigenous people' is most frequently invoked in relation to land rights and since land-rights cases are increasingly coming before the courts, conflict thus arises between the true indigeny-based principles underpinning 'native' land title and formal exogeny-based principles by which the courts are usually constrained to abide. Lawyers acting on behalf of indigenes whose rights are threatened thus face the problem of translating between distinct and barely bridgeable systems of land tenure. The judges before whom such cases are argued must therefore sometimes consider judicial precedents emanating from other parts of the world, such as Canada, Australia and the United States, where issues of tribal land rights have been brought before the courts.

Thus it is necessary to incorporate a concern for the sociology of indigeny when dealing not only with tribal societies, but also, under modernisation, with state-based societies and macro-economic issues. Exogenes' political and economic dominance, even when they adopt a purportedly indigenist stance, may lead them to misconstrue the real indigenes' difficult socioeconomic position as being the result of laziness, or even primitivity, rather than as resulting from usurpation of their subsistence base.

Indigenism

Unlike indigeny and exogeny, indigen*ism* identifies a set of overt political ideologies. Indigenist discourse relates explicitly to politically defined territories, rather than to concrete individuated places, and is therefore necessarily espoused within an exogenous, rather than indigenous, frame of action. As Hirtz (2003), with reference to the Philippines, and Dove (2006), more generally, have argued, mounting an indigenist campaign requires a degree of exogenous and modern life experience on the part of its proponents (which assertion is not intended to denigrate or minimise the importance of such efforts).

There are several kinds of indigenism, of which two are particularly significant with respect to legal issues. First, there is the local-level 'indigeneity' or 'indigenousness' asserted by tribespeople, former tribespeople and peasants when trying to protect and guarantee their land rights. Internationally, this is the type of indigenism most commonly regarded as deserving of attention and support, as in the stances taken by the United Nations, the ILO and several non-governmental organisations (NGOs), such as the World Council of Indigenous Peoples, the International Work Group for Indigenous Affairs and Survival International.

Second, and in contrast, there is the overtly national-level indigenism of which the *Bumiputera* and *Pribumi* ideologies of Malaysia and Indonesia are examples.[14] *Bumiputera* and *Pribumi* are primarily *political* terms, relating to nation-state concerns; they are not proper tools of sociological analysis and do little to aid understanding of the specific life circumstances of the people they label.

Moreover, unlike true indigeny, political indigenism – especially where it affects inter-group relations – is open to the state's manipulation of the notions of 'place' and 'territory'. These are sometimes recategorised as 'indigenous' land reserves in the ethnic-nationalistic sense, while the people who formerly lived there under true indigeny lose their ownership rights. This is the case, for example, of several declared 'Malay reserves' in Peninsular Malaysia that were formerly occupied solely by aboriginal Orang Asli. In Asia, then, these two varieties of indigenism often lead to conflict. Advances made on behalf of the nationalist approach tend to override the wished-for advances asserted at the local level. The latter typically involves the desire for a degree of nativist autonomy *from* the state; the former, however, refers to a stance adopted *by* the state for its own purposes.[15]

A related phenomenon in Asia is what might be called the *submerged indigenousness* of several relatively large-scale, mostly non-tribal populations. Vail (2007) describes one such example, the Khmers of northeast Thailand, as an 'invisible minority'. These constitute points of potential indigenist agitation for autonomy or independence and their presence tends to further heighten the 'exogenous' cultural character of the more dominant sector of the population. Examples include:

- the Mons and other non-Burmans in Burma;
- China's complex history of creeping Sinicisation of originally non-Chinese populations, some of whom are still not (Han) 'Chinese';
- India's complicated fusion of the caste hierarchy and occupational specialisation with graded degrees of indigeny;
- Indonesia's appropriation of Malay as the Indonesian national language, and the relations between 'transmigrated' and local populations;
- Japan's Burakumins and Ainus (the latter not officially recognised as an 'indigenous people' until 2008);
- Singapore's part-indigenous Malay presence;
- Sri Lanka, with respect to the Veddas and Tamils;
- Taiwan's Austronesian-speaking Aboriginal populations;
- Thailand's very complex ethnic makeup, some (such as the Mons, Khmers, 'Sakais' and Karens) pre-dating the advent of Thai civilisation and others (Meos, Hmongs) post-dating it; and
- Vietnam, with respect to the Chams in the south and the tribal 'Montagnards' in the highlands.

'Indigenous peoples' in Asia: Some examples

The following selected country sketches illustrate the kinds of problem that have arisen in Asian states that have employed the idea of 'indigenous people'. The various interpretations of the phrase demonstrate that there is no generally recognised synonymy between 'tribal' and 'indigenous' throughout the region, nor is there a clear distinction between 'indigenous people' defined ethno-nationally and 'indigenous people' defined by their place-linked indigeny. Accordingly, when steps are taken to protect the rights of tribal, or recently tribal, people, employment of the term 'indigenous' without further qualification will prove insufficient. The specific details must be spelled out in each case, down to the individual, family or community level. This requires research into the people's documented local history, which is more likely to be found in administrative archives and ethnographers' notebooks than in published works. Unfortunately, the coverage of such materials is usually partial. The courts must therefore also consider the evidence of oral history and be willing to accommodate the special circumstances of people whose land-attachments are expressed in a radically different manner from that of the established law codes.

Malaysia

In Malaysia, 'indigenous' has become the preferred English translation of the politically loaded term *Bumiputera* ('son of the soil'), which has been deployed for decades as a label justifying the provisioning of special privileges to just some of the country's citizens.

In Peninsular Malaysia, *bumiputera* is normally taken to refer to the Malays – a population that has long continued to assimilate individuals of non-Peninsular origin.

In his opening speech at the government-sponsored International Seminar on Indigenous People in Kuala Lumpur on 29 November 1993, Anwar Ibrahim (later to become Malaysia's deputy prime minister) inserted the name *Melayu* ('Malay') into the middle of a long list of 'indigenous' Malaysian groups. In terms of senses 4 and 5 listed earlier in this chapter, he could be regarded as correct in doing so. But the Conference had been convened to address the problems of minority *tribal* societies worldwide – 'indigenous' in senses 1–3 – whereas the Malays of Malaysia constitute a non-tribal political dominant majority. Further confusion has emerged since then. In his 2009 address to the General Assembly of the United Nations, Malaysia's delegate referred explicitly to the aboriginal tribal Orang Asli as 'indigenous people'. In so doing, he showed that his government – or at least, its foreign ministry – understood the United Nations' use of 'indigenous' to mean 'tribal'. Malaysia, as a signatory to the 2007 Declaration on the Rights of Indigenous Peoples, is therefore morally bound to apply all of its terms to the Orang Asli.

Within Malaysia, however, official sources, including at least two of the country's former prime ministers, have on several occasions asserted publicly that the Orang Asli are *not* 'indigenous'. For them, 'indigenous' identifies not the people whose ancestors have inhabited the Peninsula for the longest time, but solely the descendants of those – the Malays – who supposedly first brought 'civilisation' to the country. The deputy director of the Department of Orang Asli Development (himself an Orang Asli) reasserted this view publicly in 2012. In other words, the rhetoric of indigenism in Malaysia relates solely to the nation-state construct and has nothing to do with temporal priority. Officially, therefore, only the Malays qualify as 'indigenous' to Malaysia (in sense 5 above) – a practice that continues to relegate the Orang Asli to a historical and legal limbo, especially with regard to land rights.[16]

Singapore

Since the late 1980s, there have been no tribal populations in Singapore. The last such were the non-Muslim Orang Seletar living on the island's north coast, who, like most other Singaporeans, have since been resettled into high-rise apartment blocks, thereby ceasing to be tribal. Other formerly tribal populations were also living under place-linked indigeny until the 1950s or later. They too have now been resettled and merged into the so-called Malay sector of the population, *all* of whom, according to article 152 of the Singapore Constitution, are the 'indigenous people' of the Republic, regardless of their specific familial origins. Nevertheless, according to studies in the 1980s, there were significant cultural and socio-economic differences within the Singapore 'Malay' community between the locally indigenous ones and those who were descended exogenously from migrants. The latter displayed significantly higher degrees of educational attainment and of religious (Islamic) orthodoxy (Ali, 2002). Conversely, Malays of more indigenously Singaporean descent exhibited relatively less educational success and lower degrees of Islamic orthodoxy.[17]

Indonesia

Pribumi, similar to the Malaysian term *Bumiputra* and regularly translated as 'indigenous', normally refers to those whose ancestors originated from anywhere within the vast territory of the current Republic of Indonesia in contrast with those whose ancestors came from outside Indonesia, especially China. Thus people who have 'transmigrated' from Java to Sumatra, for example, are officially still *Pribumi*, even though they are no longer indigenous in the place-linked 'indigeny' sense. However, local usage sometimes differs: in southern Sumatra, for example, *pribumi* is also used to distinguish the local, more truly indigenous, people from those who have migrated from elsewhere in Indonesia. In West Borneo (Kalimantan Barat) province, local 'indigenous' feelings led to an unexpected alliance between Malays, ethnic Chinese and tribal Dayaks in sometimes violent opposition to non-'indigenous' migrants from the island of Madura.

A more traditional approach is followed in Riau Islands (Kepulauan Riau) province, where the local Malays sometimes distinguish between those who are *Melayu asli* ('indigenous Malays') and those who are *Melayu murni* ('pure Malays') (Wee, 1988: 212–214). The *Melayu asli* are members of locally derived populations, often tribal in social organisation, but the *Melayu murni* are mostly higher-ranking people of non-Melayu (usually Bugis) origin, whose members have often tried to decide for the other Malays just what constitutes cultural Malayness, in yet another example of the appropriation of indigeny by exogeny for political purposes.

Indonesia's many tribal populations, along with some other rural communities, were formerly categorised in official publications as *masyarakat terasing* ('unintentionally separated societies') rather than indigenes (Persoon, 1998), but are now referred to officially and in the Constitution as *masyarakat adat* ('customary-law societies'). *Masyarakat* ('society') is sometimes replaced by *suku* ('societal segment'), as in the distinction between *Orang Suku Laut* ('tribal sea people') and *orang laut* ('[any] sea people'). But *suku* is also employed more generally in relation to so-called ethnic groups, as in Malalatoa's official and comprehensive 1995 *Ensiklopedi Suku Bangsa di Indonesia* [Encyclopaedia of Indonesian Ethnic Groups], which treats such large-scale populations as the Javanese no differently from the many small-scale and under-described tribal populations that it also describes. As Persoon (1998: 281) reports, the associated view that the population of Indonesia is predominantly indigenous justified the government's decision to ignore the UN Year of Indigenous People in 1993. Tribality, as such, therefore mostly goes unremarked in Indonesian usage.

Neither indigeny nor temporal priority feature in these terminologies; rather, the implication is that the various *terasing/adat* communities are 'separated' from the national mainstream through no fault of their own and that their problems would be solved simply by integration into that mainstream. But Li (2000: 21) reports that, in parts of Indonesia, outsiders have an interest in maintaining the tribality of certain populations because their supposed 'failure to improve (to turn nature's bounty to a profit)' can then be used to justify assigning their land and resources 'to people who will make better use of them'. This deliberate misrecognition of the special life circumstances of true indigenes has led to expropriation and damaging of their land and forest resources in favour of commercial crop estates or paper pulp enterprises. Nevertheless, the indigenes' long-established swidden farming is often blamed for generating the toxic 'haze' that envelopes the region annually, but which is actually the product of the industrial-scale enterprises that destroyed their subsistence base in the first place. Legal solutions to remedy this situation have proved extremely difficult to establish.

Philippines

Unlike Indonesia, the Philippines explicitly recognises that its population contains many tribal/indigenous peoples. This was recognised legally by the passing of a national Indigenous Peoples Rights Act (IPRA) in 1997 and is also apparent in the open presence of many NGOs concerned with their welfare. Persoon (2009: 206–214) presents a comprehensive account of the highly variable situation of the country's tribal and post-tribal populations.

In some respects, however, ideas about indigenousness in the Philippines are similar to the Malaysian case. William Scott (1974: 7) wrote that the tribal hill populations are regarded by the lowlanders as 'non-Filipinos' – hence not 'indigenous' – because the former were the only true *resisters* to Spanish colonialism. Similarly, Aguilar (2005: 612–620) has shown that a popular Philippine version of the obsolete ethnic migratory wave theory accords indigenous status not to the various tribal populations, but to the supposedly 'third-wave' lowland-dwelling *Indios*, because they were the reputed bringers of civilisation. As in the Riau-Malay and Malaysian cases, Philippine rhetoric thus fuses an ideology of 'indigeny' with the notion of civilisational purity. This, as in Malaysia and the Riau Islands, allows exogeny to appropriate indigeny to itself, thereby legitimising a proclaimed exogeny as the basis of the right to rule.

Thailand

Although it displays differences from the Malaysian and Philippine examples, the Thai state's ideological underpinnings also exhibit an interplay between exogeny and indigenism. Despite the historically exogenous and suppletive character of Thai cultural traditions (although not necessarily of the people), official ideology insists that the state's rule is based on an overarching homogeneity compounded of language (Central Thai), religion (Theravada Buddhism) and indigenousness (Hamilton, 1991). The Thai political domain finds it difficult to accommodate anything, such as its many tribal populations (including several clearly aboriginal ones), that might hint at an alternative, exogenous, origin for Thai culture. Consequently, even the highly aboriginal Maniq 'negritos' of the south are commonly characterised as originating from outside Thailand. Confusion also results from the dual denotation of the word 'Thai', which refers both to Thai citizenship regardless of ethnicity and to Thai ethnicity. As Dorairajoo (2009) shows, the 1.8 million Malays of the south are therefore sometimes 'Thais' and sometimes 'non-Thais', a 'problem' further complicated by their 'ethnic' adherence to Islam rather than ethnic-Thai Theravada Buddhism. (In Malaysia, the equivalent distinction is solved by talking of 'Malaysians' and 'Malays', respectively.)

India

Despite a persistent belief that India was populated anciently by waves of migrants coming from elsewhere and that some Indians are therefore more 'indigenous' than others, the vast majority of the population must be considered broadly indigenous to the country. Nevertheless, in Indian (as well as Nepalese, Bangladeshi and Sri Lankan) usage, the most usual word for 'indigenous', *adivāsi*, implying a distinctively aboriginal status, applies to only around 8 per cent of the population, but with great regional variation, from 38 per cent in Chhattisgarh to just 0.9 per cent in Bihar. The term *adivāsi* (from *adi*, meaning 'earliest times', and *vāsi*, meaning 'inhabitant') was invented in the 1930s, but it has met with opposition on the grounds that it is supposedly employed primarily by landless people as a means of asserting aboriginal priority in access to land.

Also well established in official usage are the terms 'scheduled castes' and 'scheduled tribes', established by the pre-independence colonial administration and now specifically listed in Schedules annexed to the Indian Constitution. A subcategory of the latter consists of so-called Particularly Vulnerable Tribal Groups, who are regarded as isolated and as maintaining a distinctive cultural identity. These are presumably more likely to be living in circumstances of true place-linked indigeny than the members of other 'scheduled' castes and tribes. However, these categorisations are not normally understood as indicating that they are 'indigenous peoples'.

Fluidity, not fixity, marks these categorisations. Just as fully Hindu subcastes are known to change their positions in the ritual purity–pollution hierarchy over the generations by altering their customary behaviours, so also do people move *into* the caste hierarchy from 'scheduled caste' or 'scheduled tribe' status by becoming more formally Hindu. Since such changes tend to alter the basis of their former endogamous practices, this also leads to the generation of new 'tribes', who break away to reinforce their local endogamy. An alternative pathway for lower-ranking people is to employ conversion to supposedly caste-rejecting Christianity or Islam as a means of getting outside the caste system altogether. While this succeeds to some extent at the individual level, especially when it is associated with improved access to formal education, it has not prevented the local groups from being considered essentially as new sub-castes in the wider all-Indian framework, at least in those areas in which the ties of locality remain strong.

Conclusion

The terms 'indigenous people(s)' and 'indigeneity' are multiply ambiguous. Their use without further qualification obscures key differences between the various real-world circumstances to which they are typically applied. This leads to confusion when the label 'indigenous' is employed in formal deliberations over political, cultural and land rights. To achieve clarity, some further distinctions need to be observed, most importantly between 'indigeny' and 'indigenism', between 'tribal' and 'indigenous', and between 'indigeny' and 'exogeny'.

Indigeny (the continued habitation of the same specific places that one's familial ancestors always lived in) differs qualitatively in its cultural, economic and psychological consequences from all other circumstances that are labelled 'indigenous'. The latter usages typically make reference not to specific families and places, but to politically defined populations ('ethnic', 'national' or otherwise) and territories (states, regions or claimed 'homelands'). Moreover, most such cases arise within the tacitly exogenous context that underpins modernity, made possible by *not* living continuously where one's ancestors lived. The latter usages of 'indigenous' are examples of 'indigenism' in its several varieties, rather than indigeny. The exogenous framework emphasises formal rationality and codified legal systems, which makes it difficult for the 'native title' concerns of truly indigenous people to be argued for and judged fairly in court. Without due care, therefore, indigenist arguments may sometimes act against the interests of true place-linked indigenes.

The conventional use of 'indigenous' as a synonym of 'tribal' brings together two distinct, and sometimes antithetical, social circumstances under a single label. In Asia, tribespeople are those who have resisted incorporation into centralised states by organising themselves into culturally autonomous, segmentary social formations. Such tribespeople are indeed mostly indigenous (in the 'indigeny' sense) to the places they inhabit. However, this is also true of many peasants in the region, even though they have historically adopted the dominant cultural framework of the states in which they live. The shared indigeny of tribespeople and many peasants generates the 'traditional' character of their lives and the consequent disadvantages that they experience in the face of modernisation. However, the persisting cultural differences between tribespeople and peasants relate not to their indigeny, but to their distinct patterns of linkage to the state. Treating both of these rural populations in an undifferentiated manner as simply 'indigenous' peoples therefore misrepresents their life circumstances, with regard especially to matters of religion, language and mode of attachment to land.

Examples drawn from several different Asian countries demonstrate the varying and sometimes antithetical ways in which the idea of 'indigenous peoples' has been applied – or ignored – and hence the necessity to employ it with more care than has usually been the case.

Notes

1 More restricted uses of 'indigenous' also appear in scholarly social-scientific and biological writing, but these are not discussed in this chapter.
2 Bowen (2000: 13) also draws attention to the key distinction between the Old World and the New World in the differing significance of the phrase 'indigenous people'. The English word 'indigenous' is easily translatable into other European languages, but the question of its translatability into Asian languages is not so straightforward. A few examples are given later, but the issue is not otherwise discussed in this chapter.
3 The term 'aboriginal' is employed in this sense in Australia and Canada, and was formerly employed in Peninsular Malaysia in relation to the populations now known as *Orang Asli* ('original people'). In all three cases, 'indigenous' is also sometimes employed in reference to these populations.
4 The adjective 'indigenous' is well established, but the nouns 'indigeneity' and 'indigenism' have only recently entered the lexicon, with their usage limited to recent social-science discussions. 'Indigeneity' does not even appear in the 2005 edition of the *Oxford English Dictionary* or in the more historically orientated *Shorter Oxford English Dictionary*. 'Indigenousness', however, occurs in both dictionaries, although it is rarely employed in the kinds of context referred to in this chapter. 'Indigeny' is an older word that was formerly employed with the same undifferentiated range of meanings currently covered by the term 'indigeneity'. However, as suggested in this chapter, it has proved appropriate not to treat this family of words as synonyms, but to deploy them separately as labels of distinct sets of social circumstances.
5 For a critical review of some of the uses to which the term 'indigeneity' has been used, see Trigger and Dalley (2010). The term may retain some residual utility, however, as hinted at by Hirtz (2003) and Dove (2006), with reference to the image of the 'indigenous' produced by non-indigenous (exogenous) individuals concerned with environmental or traditional-knowledge issues. For a detailed discussion of the situation of 'traditional'/'indigenous' knowledge in the modern world, see Antons (2008).
6 The contrast between indigeny and exogeny is also a major factor underlying many of the closely related contrasts proposed in the classical social-science literature. In chronological order, these include: Karl Marx on 'species-being' (*Gattungswesen*) versus 'alienation'; Ferdinand Tönnies

on *Gemeinschaft* ('community') versus *Gesellschaft* ('association, society'); Émile Durkheim on 'mechanical' versus 'organic' solidarity; Max Weber (throughout his writings) on 'substantive rationalities' versus 'formal rationality'; Georg Simmel on 'subjective culture'/'heart' versus 'objective culture'/'intellect'; Edward Sapir on 'genuine' versus 'spurious' culture; Lucien Lévy-Bruhl on 'participatory' versus 'discursive' mentalities, a clarification of his earlier discussion in terms of 'primitive' mentality; Louis Wirth on 'primary' versus 'secondary' social contacts; Marcel Mauss on the evolution of the various notions of the self and the person; and Robert Bellah on 'compact' versus 'differentiated' symbolic systems.

7 A few present-day tribal populations are not strictly indigenous to the places they currently occupy, as they are known to have migrated there from elsewhere within the past few generations.

8 The very few possibly authentic cases in Asia include the Sentinelese and (less clearly so) the Jarawas, who both inhabit remoter parts of India's Andaman Islands. For anthropological critiques of the concept of 'tribe', see Fried (1966); Godelier (1977).

9 This approach to tribality has been examined for the Malay World by Benjamin (2002: 7–17) and Wawrinec (2010), and for mainland Southeast Asia more extensively by James Scott (2009).

10 In this regard, Jonsson (2011: 109) warns that 'any scientific account of human diversity in Southeast Asia that takes for granted contemporary ethnolinguistic classification serves, deliberately or not, to reinforce particular state regimes (colonial, national, etc.) of truth'.

11 Some instances of secondary tribalisation in Southeast Asia are listed and discussed by Fortier (2014), who clearly regards such cases as not especially rare. Dove (2006: 192) draws attention to the parallel process by which peasants relabel themselves as 'indigenous people' (virtual tribespeople, so to speak) to claim protection for their 'traditional' rights in the modern sphere.

12 Such resettlement does not take into account a community's resource zone: the people are treated as if they were simply moving house. As pointed out by Colwell-Chanthaphonh and Ferguson (2006), sites that outsiders see as physically abandoned may still remain connected directly with a living population through such spiritual tokens as the perennial fruit trees, spirit-charged sites and cemeteries that they leave behind to keep their indigeny intact. Urbanites' concern for the preservation of 'heritage' hardly ever extends to such non-monumental remains. The traditional owners are therefore usually powerless to prevent the bulldozing that precedes urbanisation or the setting up of commercial plantations or garbage-dumping sites.

13 Laird (1979) discusses an unusually complicated Orang Asli example from Malaysia. Delang (2003: 160–178) explicitly applies the contrast between indigeny and exogeny, and the contrast between many-stranded and single-stranded relations to his extensive study of land-linked social and economic change among the Karens, a peasantising tribal population of northern Thailand.

14 For informed discussions of the terms *Bumiputera* and *Pribumi*, see Siddique and Suryadinata (1982), Aguilar (2001) and Nah (2006). The *Pribumi* category is supposed to have been abandoned in 2006, following the passing of a national citizenship law (Wawrinec, 2010: 102), but there has been no such relaxing of the *Bumiputera* concept in Malaysia.

15 A recent development has attempted to obviate some of these problems by replacing the idea of 'indigenous peoples' with that of 'fourth-world nations', regarded as culturally distinct populations numbering in the thousands that constitute 'nations without states'. One such list (Hirch, 2007) brings together 'the Roma in Europe, pre-WWII Ashkenazi in the region of the Pale of Settlement, Kurds and Palestinians in the Middle East, and Native American Nations / First Nations, Alaskan Natives, Hawaiians and Indian peoples throughout the Americas'. Although these populations have undoubtedly suffered social disabilities of various kinds, their circumstances differ greatly. Moreover, by referring to them as 'nations', it is implied that they should eventually come to form ethnically based states of their own. However, that too would probably lead to the further cultural and political disadvantaging of any people within their domain who were still living under true place-linked indigeny, tribal or otherwise.

16 For reviews of the land-rights situation of the Orang Asli and other such Malaysian populations, see Bulan (2007); Idrus (2010); Subramaniam (2013). These studies include reports on the court cases that have passed judgments, frequently in their favour, on land-rights claims made on behalf

of various Malaysian tribal populations. Perhaps because of the disagreements in Malaysia about the meaning of 'indigenous', government agencies have usually chosen to mount appeals against these judgments, greatly delaying the eventual carrying out of the courts' decisions. Unfortunately, the Malaysian Department of Orang Asli Development (JAKOA) has hitherto lent its support not to the Orang Asli claimants, but to the parties against whom the claims were being made.

17 Like most other Singaporeans, these populations have now been resettled into standard public housing, thereby becoming more 'exogenous', with a probable loss of their former distinctively 'indigenous' characteristics. The majority population of Singapore is highly exogenous, which has predisposed it to accept one of the highest degrees of formal rationality in the world.

References

Aguilar, F. V., Jr (2001) 'Citizenship, Inheritance, and the Indigenizing of "Orang Chinese" [*sic*] in Indonesia', *Positions: East Asia Cultures Critique*, 9(3): 501–533.

Aguilar, F. V., Jr (2005) 'Tracing Origins: Ilustrado Nationalism and the Racial Science of Migration Waves', *Journal of Asian Studies*, 64(3): 605–637.

Ali, M. (2002) 'Singapore's Orang Seletar, Orang Kallang, and Orang Selat: The Last Settlements', in G. Benjamin and C. Chou (eds) *Tribal Communities in the Malay World: Historical, Social and Cultural Perspectives*, Leiden/Singapore: International Institute for Asian Studies (IIAS)/Institute of Southeast Asian Studies (ISEAS), 273–292.

Antons, C. (2008) 'Traditional Cultural Expressions and Their Significance for Development in a Digital Environment: Examples from Australia and Southeast Asia', in C. B. Graber and M. Burri (eds) *Intellectual Property and Traditional Cultural Expressions in a Digital Environment*, Cheltenham: Edward Elgar, 287–301.

Benjamin, G. (2002) 'On Being Tribal in the Malay World', in G. Benjamin and C. Chou (eds) *Tribal Communities in the Malay World: Historical, Social and Cultural Perspectives*, Leiden/Singapore: International Institute for Asian Studies (IIAS)/Institute of Southeast Asian Studies (ISEAS), 7–76.

Benjamin, G. (2016) 'Indigeny–Exogeny: The Fundamental Social Dimension?', *Anthropos: International Review of Anthropology and Linguistics*, 111: 513–531.

Bowen, J. (2000) 'Should We Have a Universal Concept of "Indigenous Peoples' Rights"?' Ethnicity and Essentialism in the Twenty-first Century', *Anthropology Today*, 16(4): 12–16.

Bulan, R. (2007) 'Native Title in Malaysia: A Complementary *Sui Generis* Proprietary Right under the Federal Constitution', *Australian Indigenous Law Review*, 11(1): 54–78.

Colwell-Chanthaphonh, C., and Ferguson, T. J. (2006) 'Rethinking Abandonment in Archaeological Contexts', *SAA Archaeological Record: Magazine of the Society for American Archaeology*, 6(1): 37–41.

Delang, C. O. (2003) 'Social and Economic Adaptations to a Changing Landscape', in C. O. Delang (ed.) *Living at the Edge of Thai Society: The Karen in the Highlands of Northern Thailand*, London: Routledge Curzon, 155–182.

Dorairajoo, S. (2009) 'Peaceful Thai, Violent Malay (Muslim): A Case Study of the "Problematic" Muslim Citizens of Southern Thailand', *Copenhagen Journal of Asian Studies*, 27(2): 61–83.

Dove, M. R. (2006) 'Indigenous People and Environmental Politics', *Annual Reviews in Anthropology*, 35: 191–208.

Fortier, J. (2014) 'Regional Hunter-gatherer Traditions in Southeast Asia', in V. Cummings, P. Jordan and M. Zvelebil (eds) *The Oxford Handbook of the Archaeology and Anthropology of Hunter-gatherers*, Oxford: Oxford University Press, 1010–1030.

Fox, J. J., and Sather, C. (eds) (1996) *Origins, Ancestry and Alliance: Explorations in Austronesian Ethnography*, Canberra: Australian National University Department of Anthropology, available online at http://epress.anu.edu.au/austronesians/origins/pdf/origins-whole.pdf [accessed 21 July 2016].

Fried, M. H. (1966) 'On the Concepts of "Tribe" and "Tribal Society"', *Transactions of the New York Academy of Sciences, Series II*, 28(4): 527–540.

Godelier, M. (1977) 'The Concept of the "Tribe"', in *Perspectives in Marxist Anthropology*, London: Cambridge University Press, 70–96.

Gray, A. (1995) 'The Indigenous Movement in Asia', in R. H. Barnes, A. Gray and B. Kingsbury (eds) *Indigenous Peoples of Asia*, Ann Arbor, MI: Association for Asian Studies, 35–58.

Hamilton, A. (1991) 'Rumours, Foul Calumnies and the Safety of the State: Mass Media and National Identity in Thailand', in C. J. Reynolds (ed.) *National Identity and Its Defenders: Thailand 1939–1989*, Clayton: Center of Southeast Asian Studies, Monash University, 341–375.

Hirch, M. (2007) 'Indignant Peoples Want to Be Free', 9 August, available online at http://cwis.org/FWE/2007/08/09/indignant-peoples-want-to-be-free-2/ [accessed 27 September 2014].

Hirtz, F. (2003) 'It Takes Modern Means to Be Traditional: On Recognizing Indigenous Cultural Communities in the Philippines', *Development and Change*, 34(5): 887–914.

Idrus, R. (2010) 'From Wards to Citizens: Indigenous Rights and Citizenship in Malaysia', *PoLAR: Political and Legal Anthropology Review*, 33(1): 89–108.

Jonsson, H. (2011) 'Ethnology and the Issue of Human Diversity in Mainland Southeast Asia', in N. J. Enfield (ed.) *Dynamics of Human Diversity: The Case of Mainland Southeast Asia*, Canberra: Pacific Linguistics, 109–122.

Laird, P. (1979) 'Ritual, Territory and Region: The Temoq of Pahang, West Malaysia', *Social Analysis*, 1: 54–80.

Li, T. (2000) 'Articulating Indigenous Identity in Indonesia: Resource Politics and the Tribal Slot', *Comparative Studies in Society and History*, 42(1): 149–179.

Malalatoa, M. J. (1995) *Ensiklopedi Suku Bangsa di Indonesia* [*Encyclopaedia of Indonesian Ethnic Groups*], two vols, Jakarta: Departemen Pendidikan dan Kebudayaan RI.

Nah, A. M. (2006) '(Re)Mapping Indigenous "Race"/Place in Postcolonial Peninsular Malaysia', *Geografiska Annaler*, 88B: 285–297.

Persoon, G. (1998) 'Isolated Groups or Indigenous Peoples: Indonesia and the International Discourse', *Bijdragen tot de Taal-, Land- en Volkenkunde*, 154(2): 281–304.

Persoon, G. (2009) '"Being Indigenous" in Indonesia and the Philippines', in C. Antons (ed.) *Traditional Knowledge, Traditional Cultural Expressions and Intellectual Property Law in the Asia-Pacific Region*, Alphen aan den Rijn: Kluwer Law International, 195–216.

Scott, J. C. (2009) *The Art of Not Being Governed: An Anarchist History of Upland Southeast Asia*, New Haven, CT: Yale University Press.

Scott, W. H. (1974) *The Discovery of the Igorots: Spanish Contacts with the Pagans of Northern Luzon*, Quezon City: New Day.

Siddique, S., and Suryadinata, L. (1982) '*Bumiputra* and *Pribumi*: Economic Nationalism (Indiginism) [*sic*] in Malaysia and Indonesia', *Pacific Affairs*, 54(4): 662–687.

Subramaniam, Y. (2013) 'Affirmative Action and the Legal Recognition of Customary Land Rights in Peninsular Malaysia: The Orang Asli Experience', *Australian Indigenous Law Review*, 17(1): 103–122.

Trigger, D. S., and Dalley, C. (2010) 'Negotiating Indigeneity: Culture, Identity, and Politics', *Reviews in Anthropology*, 39(1): 46–65.

Vail, P. (2007) 'Thailand's Khmer as "Invisible Minority": Language, Ethnicity and Cultural Politics in North-eastern Thailand', *Asian Ethnicity*, 8(2): 111–130.

Wawrinec, C. (2010) 'Tribality and Indigeneity in Malaysia and Indonesia', *Stanford Journal of East Asian Affairs*, 10(1): 96–107.

Weber, M. (1978) *Economy and Society: An Outline of Interpretive Sociology*, two vols, ed. G. Roth and C. Wittich, Berkeley, CA: University of California Press.

Wee, V. (1988) 'Material Dependence and Symbolic Independence: The Construction of Melayu Ethnicity in Island Riau, Indonesia', in A. T. Rambo, A. Terry, K. Gillogly and K. L. Hutterer (eds) *Ethnic Diversity and the Control of Natural Resources in Southeast Asia*, Ann Arbor, MI: University of Michigan, Center for South and Southeast Asian Studies, 197–226.

21 *Lèse-majesté*, Asian style

Crisis of monarchy in pre-war Japan and present-day Thailand*

David Streckfuss

As long as there have been monarchies during the past two millennia, there have been *lèse-majesté* laws at the core of their legal systems, protecting royal privilege, sacred status and eminent persons from physical or verbal assaults. Revolutions in Europe championing free speech forced most monarchies to moderate their *lèse-majesté* laws. Elsewhere, European colonialism often tossed out indigenous monarchs along with their indigenous *lèse-majesté* laws.

Lèse-majesté has rarely been the subject of academic study, perhaps because the law played a leading role only in certain periods, such as in the Roman Empire (Lear, 1965) or Absolutist France (Le Bret, 1632). Outside of the Middle East, Asia's only sovereign kingdoms/empires in 1930 were Afghanistan, Nepal, Japan and Siam. There is nothing to suggest that *lèse-majesté* became an issue in Afghanistan, whereas in Nepal, insult of the monarchy was part of a treason law mentioned by human rights observers for a period (Amnesty International, 1987: 253–254). In the Empire of Japan and the Kingdom of Thailand, though, *lèse-majesté* played such an important role that we might even say that the law largely came to define the institution of monarchy itself. They are truly the two great Asian exemplars of *lèse-majesté* regimes. Especially in the period 1928–45 in Japan and since 1976 to the present day in Thailand, use of the *lèse-majesté* law was, and is, a sign of an immense socio-political imbalance – of a crisis auguring a decisive shift in the institution of the monarchy itself.

This chapter begins with a descriptive analysis of the ideological and legal framework in each national context that provided the foundation for the crisis that followed. It follows this with an examination of how *lèse-majesté* cases were adjudicated, and how such adjudication articulated with the ideological and legal framework. Finally, we draw comparisons between the *lèse-majesté* experiences of each country. In both cases, perhaps unsurprisingly, we discover that fledgling democratic institutions and movements were overwhelmed by right-wing movements that sought to make the monarchy the centre of a state ideology that vigorously opposed basic values such as equality and popular sovereignty.

A few conditions need to be stated at the outset. First, we are looking at *lèse-majesté* as a crime of words or symbolic actions, not actual bodily attacks on the royalty. Further, we are privileging the Japanese side of the comparison. We delve into some depth on the ideological foundations and the details of specific cases, because the story of *lèse-majesté* in Japan has yet to be told in Japanese or English, especially in the Taishō (1912–26) and early Shōwa (1926–45) periods. We describe the Thai case in rather broad historical strokes, because there is already a fairly substantial literature on the topic (Streckfuss, 1995, 2011; Leyland, 2010), but we do zero in on how *lèse-majesté* and the role of the monarchy have defined the contours of Thailand's latest political crisis of 2013–14.

Japanese political context and the *lèse-majesté* law

As Japan moved from a somewhat more fragmented polity to become a politically centralised and industrial state, there were four components relating to *lèse-majesté* in constructing the new state's ideology: emperor, religion, national polity (*kokutai*) and law.

In the seventeenth century, the shogunate effectively became rulers of Japan and kept the emperor so well out of view that a Japanese scholar in 1914 had to admit that 'loyalty to the Emperor . . . was confined largely to the warriors of the imperial guard, and to those who enjoyed close relations to the court' (Tasuku, 1914: 119–121). The main thrust of the Meiji elite was to make the emperor 'the sole object of popular devotion' (Tasuku, 1914: 119–121; Gluck, 1985: 79–80). From 1868 to 1890, Emperor Meiji made 102 trips throughout Japan (Gluck, 1985: 74). Government authorities then replaced his imperial appearances with imperial rescripts, pronouncements and photographic portraits distributed to every government office, foreign consulate, university and high school, making the emperor 'more fully public property than he had ever been before' (Gluck, 1985: 82–84). It was really only at the end of the Meiji period that 'virtually all Japanese were conscious of the emperor's existence for the first time in Japanese history' (Gluck, 1985: 95–101).

The Meiji elite also incorporated Shintō, the nativist, polytheistic 'religion' of imperial Japan, into the imperial state ideology. Shintōism would revive 'the unity of religion and government' by tying the emperor to the origin of the Japanese people:

> The Heavenly Deities and the Great Ancestress [*Amaterasu Omikami*] established the throne and made the succession secure. The line of Emperors in unbroken succession entered into possession thereof and handed it on. Religious ceremonies and government were one and the same.
>
> (Quoted in Holtom, 1942: 5–6)

Shintōists organised themselves into a national association that established 1,000 new shrines per year. The number of Shintō shrines empire-wide peaked at 196,357 in 1901. Smaller shrines were merged with larger ones and placed within a twelve-grade hierarchy of shrines, which 'culminates in the imperial throne' (Holtom, 1942: 38–43).

The Imperial Constitution of the Empire of Japan of 1889 established the legal status of the emperor and 'consecrated the sovereignty of the emperor according to divine principle' (Yoichi, 1990: 52):

> **Article 1.** The Empire of Japan shall be reigned over and governed by a line of Emperors unbroken for ages eternal.
>
> [. . .]
>
> **Article 3.** The Emperor is sacred and inviolable.
>
> **Article 4.** The Emperor is the head of the Empire, combining in Himself the rights of sovereignty, and exercises them, according to the provisions of the present Constitution.

Emperor, religion and Constitution were bound together by the concept of *kokutai*. In the 1880s, the term originally meant something like 'national characteristic/essence/polity'. It was assumed that every country had its own *kokutai* that changed over the time.

But, by 1915, *kokutai* had become more fixed and, at the same time, so uniquely and exclusively Japanese that no foreigner could possibly fathom its meaning (Gluck, 1985: 36–37; Byas, 1943: 279). Gluck (1985: 102) writes that, under the auspices of *kokutai*, '[e]thical, national, and historical values were gradually intertwined in various renderings', resulting in an 'ideological amalgam' that served as 'a catechism of citizenship that joined code and country in a newly generalised civil morality'. Advocates of Shintōism interpreted the constitutional provision that declared the emperor as 'sacred and inviolable' to mean that the emperor was a 'manifest deity', 'the living representative of a divine imperial line' (Gluck, 1985: 142). Shintō became the de facto state religion as it successfully embedded itself within the definition of *kokutai* and became a way of 'disseminating the code of imperial loyalism' (Mitchell, 1983: 106; Gluck, 1985: 102, 138, 142). Elder statesman and compiler of the 1915 history of the Meiji Era, Kaneko Kenarō, described *kokutai* as:

> . . . the Emperor of a line unbroken through the ages, holding the three sacred treasures and ruling over the people, is the basis on which our country is founded, the Imperial throne for this reason being eternal and the Kokutai august.
>
> (Quoted in Byas, 1943: 279)

What later became known as the emperor system developed in the late nineteenth century and early twentieth centuries. Takagi (2011: 51) argues that 'the core of the emperor system, as it was invented in modern times, lay in the discourse of an "unbroken line of emperors"' and that, in turn, the core of the *kokutai* ideology was the emperor system. Along with state Shintō, compulsory education served as a key vehicle for dissemination. In a school textbook on ethics, for instance, students were exhorted to 'always revere the Imperial Ancestress and, [be] regardful of the exalted foundations of our national structure', and to 'support the Imperial Destiny, which is as imperishable as heaven and earth' (quoted in Holtom, 1942: 61).

Committee members drafting Japan's first 'modern' Criminal Code of 1882 were at first reluctant to include a *lèse-majesté* provision, for even acknowledging that a Japanese person might commit the crime seemed to be *lèse-majesté* itself (Heng-Chao, 1987: 29; Ishii, 1958: 343). Despite such reluctance, authorities obviously warmed up to it when the Code came into effect: nearly half of the total 101 *lèse-majesté* cases before promulgation of the revised Code of 1907 occurred within the first four years of the Code's initial implementation, while from 1886 to 1906 there was an average of a mere two cases. Under categories laid out by Omata (2010), author of the only monograph on *lèse-majesté* of the period, the law was used to knock the wind out of the fledgling democracy movement.

After 1890, the *lèse-majesté* law was linked to the constitutional status of the emperor. In commentaries, one of the key framers of the Prussian-inspired 1889 Charter, Itō Hitobumi (1889: 6), points out that, constitutionally, '[n]ot only shall there be no irreverence for the Emperor's person, but also shall He neither be made a topic of derogatory comment nor one of discussion'.

Compared to the 1882 Code, the 1907 revised Criminal Code added protection to a wider range of persons. A new provision reads:

> **Article 74.** Acts of an insulting and disrespectful nature committed against the Emperor, the Emperor's Grandmother, the Empress Dowager, the Empress, the Crown Prince, or the heir presumptive shall be punished with penal servitude for a period of not less than three months and not exceeding five years.

But it is also important to note that symbols of the emperor – such as the 'Imperial shrines or Imperial Mauselea' – are protected to the same degree as are lesser members of the imperial family:

> **Article 76.** Acts of an insulting and disrespectful nature committed against members of the Imperial family shall be punished with penal servitude for a period of not less than two months and not exceeding four years.

By 1910, the legal foundation of the Japanese *lèse-majesté* regime was established in the Constitution and Criminal Code. The Constitution confirmed the emperor's sacredness. Sovereignty over the empire was constitutionally bequeathed to the emperor. One might even say that these foundations were absolutely fixed. Decades later, Matsunami (1940: 63, 65) contended that amending the Constitution was 'unthinkable': if changed, 'there would no longer exist in Japan any constitution at all'; 'We, Japanese subjects,' he wrote, 'tremble at the mere thought of such a change.'

Siamese/Thai political context and the *lèse-majesté* law

Like Japan, Siam was not colonised by the West, providing a compelling continuity with pre-modern values. As in Germany and Russia, the Bangkok elite carried out centralisation under an ideology that posited the rights of 'moral' leaders to govern. This ideology was protected in Siam's first modern Criminal Code of 1908, as expressed in the *lèse-majesté* laws (Streckfuss, 2011: 420):

> **Section 98.** – Whosoever displays malice toward or defames the King, the Queen Consort, the Heir-apparent, or Regent when he is carrying out his duties to the King, shall be liable to imprisonment not exceeding seven years or a fine of not more than five thousand baht, or both.

> **Section 100.** – Whosoever displays malice toward or defames the princes or princesses from whichever reign, the punishment shall not exceed three years or a fine of not more than two thousand baht, or both.

Section 104, an anti-sedition measure, also protected the monarchy, punishing those who sought to 'create disloyalty or to insult the king, the government, or the country' with up to three years' imprisonment and a hefty fine of 1,000 baht (Streckfuss, 2011: 418–419).

While the monarchies in Japan and Siam in 1910 were in comparable positions in terms of legal protection, in other respects the Siamese elite set the country on a very different trajectory. Japan had a more unified state ideology expressed by *kokutai* by the early twentieth century. The Siamese elite had only a vague notion of *chat* (nation); the 'nationalism' of the time was expropriated by the king and always expressed in terms of absolute monarchy. Rather clumsily, King Rama VI (r. 1910–25) defined 'Thainess' as 'Thai history, Thai art, Thai language, Thai literature, Thai Buddhism, Thai love of the royal leader, and an essential Thai spirit, a fierce devotion to *thai* in the sense of "free," warrior spirit . . .' (Vella, 1978: 178). In a more concise form, he borrowed the Russian czar's formulation and made it into, 'Nation, Religion, Kingship'. By the end of the absolute monarchy, the components of what later would be called 'Thainess' 'justified and sustained the political structure of centralized power, and the social structure that divided people into hierarchical classes in accordance with their birthright' (Saichol, undated: 8). As a final legal act to protect absolute monarchy, the penalty for section 104 was substantially increased in 1927: imprisonment of between three and ten years and a maximum fine of 1,000–5,000 baht awaited any who would, through writing, 'bring into hatred or contempt the Sovereign, the Government or the administration of the State' (Streckfuss, 2011: 418–419).

The first Constitution, enacted immediately following the overthrow of the absolute monarchy in 1932, did not accord the king a sacred or inviolable status. All subsequent constitutions, though, have placed the king 'in a position of revered worship' (for example article 8 of the 2007 Constitution of the Kingdom of Thailand). However, the 1933 Protection of the Constitution Act supported new democratic institutions, outlawing any action that was 'in any way in opposition to or in order to have the people lose their faith in or to be afraid of governance under the constitution system of Siam' (section 3). With a maximum penalty of twenty years, the law in a sense valued constitution over monarchy by nearly three to one. Relatedly, a revised section 104 forbade bringing the monarchy 'into hatred or contempt', but it also included a saving clause if such communication 'merely be an expression of good faith or amount to a critical and unbiased comment on governmental or administrative acts within the spirit of the Constitution or for the public interest'. Significantly, the 1933 Act and section 104's saving clause were soon repealed (Streckfuss, 2011: 98, 418–419).

The monarchy began its revitalisation in the late 1940s, both ideologically and financially, with much of its assets and property 'returned'. The phrase 'the democratic regime with the king as head of state' was used for the first time in the military-inspired 1949 Constitution and has appeared in every constitution since. The phrase has come to indicate not a democracy with the monarchy under the Constitution, but rather 'Thai-style' democracy: a limited democracy dominated wholly or partially by appointees. The royalist ideology was largely consolidated in the early 1960s (Hewison, 2009; Thak, 2007). The revised Criminal Code of 1957 did not register that the country had become a constitutional monarchy, specifying the very same punishment as under absolute monarchy but adding 'insults' into the mix (Streckfuss, 2011: 420):

> **Section 112.** – Whosoever defames, insults or threatens the King, the Queen, the Heir-apparent, or the Regent shall be punished with imprisonment not exceeding seven years.

In the political realm, the core of 'Thainess' became known as 'Thai-style democracy'. Developed in the early 1960s under military dictatorship, 'Thai-style democracy' envisioned a 'society without politics' under a strong paternalistic ruler, negatively juxtaposed against greedy politicians. A key proponent of this system, Kukrit Pramoj, argued that Thai people are best 'under the military regime', where they 'should be confident that the country is ruled by a "good man" and that this is very different from being governed by politicians who seek only their own interest' (Saichol, 2007: 69, as quoted in Hewison, 2009; Thak, 2007).

As in the first fifty years of modern Japan, there were relatively few cases of *lèse-majesté* in Thailand (as Siam was renamed in 1939) between 1908 and 1960. In the 1950s, there was an average of only one case per year, mostly for what was deemed to be personally insulting. Even through to 1975, there was an average of about five cases per year, usually in relation to new security measures to counter communism.

Types of *lèse-majesté* in Japan

Lèse-majesté *for the elite (catastrophic* **lèse-majesté***)*

As the Japanese state began to turn to *lèse-majesté* or related measures, four types can be identified, the final one developing last and being covered in the next section. The first type was *lèse-majesté* for the elite – in a sense, the least common. In most cases, accusation did not lead to actual *lèse-majesté* prosecutions; rather, they commonly led to recantations, dismissals, resignations, ruined careers, fallen governments or assassinations. Foreign journalist Hugh Byas (1943: 233–234) reported that '[t]here is nothing a Japanese dreads more than a charge that he has failed in respect to the Emperor'. Occasionally, though, suspicions of disloyalty could have fatal consequences. A government minister, Mori Arinori, was assassinated by a zealous Shintō priest in 1889 'for irreverence to the throne' – and his crime? It was reported that the priest's motive was to punish Mori for an incident two years prior when Mori visited the Shrine of Ise and failed to take off his shoes where he should have and pulled back a sacred veil with his walking stick (*The Times* (London), 18 February 1889, quoted in Gluck, 1985: 85; Smith, 1997: 87–88).

Lèse-majesté *for the people (common* **lèse-majesté***)*

Common *lèse-majesté* (articles 74 and 76) was reserved for common folk who had some (quite often off-hand) gripe with the monarchy or who had been caught up by socialist ideology, but were not typically socialists as such. We examine the period 1921–27 in some detail, given excellent data on *lèse-majesté* cases compiled in 1978 (*Shakaimondai shiryō kenkyūkai*, 1979). The analysis of these cases comes from an unpublished manuscript (Streckfuss, 2013a). Of the 130 cases, a little less than two-thirds were dismissed. About 38 per cent of those charged had some secondary school training and another 50 per cent had gone to primary school. No one arrested during this period had any university experience. In all but three cases, defendants tried were found guilty – a conviction rate of 93.3 per cent. In short, if arrested for *lèse-majesté* during this period, there was a 32.3 per cent chance of being convicted for the crime.

Professional, educated suspects were almost three times less likely to be tried. Cases dropped included those of four teachers, one junior high school student, five secondary school students, eight farmers, a civil contractor, a salesperson, a newspaper editor and six journalists. Conversely, 79 per cent of those convicted were 'the poor': carrot peddlers, apprentice cooks, blacksmiths, day labourers, print shop workers and rickshaw drivers. Among those tried, there were no 'elite' present at all – no politicians, no business owners and no civil servants. The one student tried was one of the three found not guilty.

The justice system was efficient. For those whose cases were dismissed, the average time from arrest to the date on which the case was dropped was 100 days, with a median period of 49 days. The shortest time was a mere eight days. Prosecutors took more than twenty months to dismiss the case of an unemployed youth from Osaka, who wrote in his diary: 'When the prince visits local towns, all the people, even students, stop their own work and have to give him a welcome. This is a great nuisance for us!'

For the forty-nine persons found guilty, the average sentence was 2.7 years – 15 per cent lower than the length of sentence for which prosecutors had called. Appeals generally also worked down the sentence by the same percentage, although no case was ever overturned. In the one case appealed to the Supreme Court, the Court of Appeal's sentence was upheld.

Strangely, perhaps, in this period, espousal of socialist sentiment did not automatically condemn a defendant and many cases pursued against socialists were dropped. But, when tried, socialists often suffered longer sentences. One unemployed man from Kofu had written on the wall of a business office, 'To people: Kill the Emperor and radically destroy the government. We must ally militarily and economically with the Soviet Union and then defeat capitalistic states.' He was sentenced to four years in prison. In Kobe in 1923, two prisoners wrote a letter in their own blood, pledging 'to assassinate the Imperial Family, nobility, and plutocrats' as part of 'the first step of the Japanese revolution'. One was sentenced to ten years; the other, to five.

Non-socialist political commentators or activists were twice as likely as declared socialists to be prosecuted. A young Yasu-Nouzu carrot peddler was sentenced to one year for tearing up a portrait of the emperor and empress in a country inn. An apprentice cook from Matsuhama was given three years for saying, 'Both we and the Emperor have equal rights. He is a man who commits the crime of murder!' A 21-year-old yarn-maker from Maehashi sent a complaint to the police station, stating, 'I saw the procession of the prince as he returned from foreign countries. Why were there so many police guards there! I didn't like that! He's still wet behind the ears!' A 54-year-old man from Oita in 1924 wrote in a letter to a friend, 'Japanese society must guarantee equality. So the Imperial family must be totally abolished. We people always live in abject misery, but on the other hand the Imperial family seems to enjoy luxury. It's stupid!' For that, and for cutting down trees planted by the crown prince and imperial family in the park, he was sentenced to two-and-a-half years.

Three persons were found not guilty. A 23-year-old labourer in Tokyo wrote in his notebook, 'To people: I worry about everyone believing in the Imperial family, although they are only foolish icons. People should stop celebrating over the marriage of the Crown prince.' When a 23-year-old student from Kyoto finally appeared in court more than four-and-a-half years after his being charged, prosecutors had asked for a sentence of four years. In his diary had been discovered the following entry:

> Patriotic education is delusional. I saw people waving flags at the Imperial procession and I thought Japan will have a rocky road ahead. . . . At the national holiday of the Emperor's birthday, all of the people participated in the celebration, bowing their heads to his portrait, and reading out loud the imperial rescript. I felt like crying because it's absurd. I had so such a strong anger and sadness that I wanted to be a rebel.

He was found not guilty, because the court had determined that it was not a serious infraction and had noted that he came from a good family. The other two found not guilty – both young farmers hailing from Nagano – were found such because the court noted that they had shown regret.

A core attribute of modern *lèse-majesté* laws is their vagueness and lack of clear standards. What could be said or done in Japan and what could not were not clearly defined. In these cases, no obvious pattern emerges. At face value, it is difficult to discern guilt or innocence, or why similar comments or actions received such varying sentences – why a socialist ballad singer from Nagoya who destroyed a royal portrait at a friend's house in anger was given a four-year sentence, while the case of a man from Osaka who defaced a portrait at a factory was dismissed.

For more serious infractions, it is hard to see why the comment in a letter to a friend that announced an assassination attempt on the crown prince merited a seven-year jail sentence – 'We must defeat the Emperor to achieve the purpose of democracy. The unbroken imperial line under the provision of the Constitution is vicious' – when the following comments were given significantly lighter sentences:

> Death penalty!→Emperor and Crown Prince!
>
> (1924 in Kobe, written in twenty-six public places, such as on the walls of shrines and toilets; two-year prison sentence)
>
> In society people can't eat well however they work very hard. On the other hand, the emperor can eat the bread of idleness without working. There is a great inconsistency! So we must kill him! Both we and the emperor equally eat, defecate and mate like humans!
>
> (1927 in Asahikawa, said in a bar to friends; two-year prison sentence)

Or then there were the following cases, all of which were dismissed:

> Our emperor is a tyrant. He pilfers the people's property and his hands are heavily tainted by corruption. Also you are one of his satellites. You and the police must accept bribes! You should resign as soon as possible and clean up politics. Otherwise we will kill the Emperor with 100,000 rioters and planes by cooperating with China and Korea.
>
> (1922 in Nagano, written in a letter to the governor of Nagano prefecture)
>
> The Emperor system should be abolished! Kill the Emperor and Crown Prince! They are all stupid!
>
> (1922 in Kyushu, in letters sent twelve times to the police chief, the ward mayor and the postmaster)
>
> The Emperor is an enemy of civilization and freedom. His ancestors deprived us of our primary lands. We have a right to kill them. Our purpose is to kill the Emperor, the Crown Prince, and the Imperial Family and give a chance to the anarchists.
>
> (1925 in Tokyo, written in a diary)

The reach of *lèse-majesté* in Japan was alarming: a quarter of infractions arose from sentiments expressed in strictly private or semi-private venues. Many convictions came from personal diaries, notebooks and private correspondence either intercepted by censors or turned over to the police. A quarter occurred in semi-private circumstances – words said in a private home, in small bars or among just a few listeners. Only about a third of cases involved actions intended for 'the public'. There did not seem to be a correlation between the public-ness of what was said or done and the length of sentence. One 27-year-old unemployed man of Kobe wrote in his diary, 'The government forces us to venerate the Emperor as a god to protect the national polity' and 'to be slavishly devoted. Such mindless deference to an icon is just a big joke.' Because the crime was essentially a thought crime, police could not even specify a date of the 'incident', saying only that it happened between 1 September and late November 1924. For this irreverent thought, however, the man was sentenced to three years in prison.

Lèse-majesté *for liberals (lesser* lèse-majesté*)*

Rather than *lèse-majesté*, it was much more likely for 'liberal' intellectuals – such as journalists, university academics, schoolteachers – to come under the purview of a wide array of laws designed to limit free speech in imperial Japanese society. This set of laws included newspaper laws, publication laws and, pre-emptively, censorship laws, and could result in prison terms of (generally) not more than two years, fines, or the banning of publications, plays, movies or broadcasts. For instance, section 32 of the *Shinbushi Hō*, Law No. 9 of 1897, forbade any publication that could 'debase the dignity of the imperial house'. Along with *lèse-majesté*, this law 'added another sharp weapon to the censorship bureaucrats' arsenal' and was 'part of the ongoing effort of the authorities to build a wall of reverence around the throne' (Mitchell, 1983: 129–131). The average sentence was between one and three months with no hard labour, unlike those convicted of *lèse-majesté* who were subject to hard labour and whose sentences averaged almost three years.

Under Taishō democracy, censorship rules provided protection to the nation, the Constitution and the imperial family. According to Kasza (1988: 64–65), 'ever the foremost dictates of state censorship' were for items that would 'desecrate the sanctity of the imperial family'. Censors sought out items that might denigrate 'the imperial regalia (sword, jewels, and mirror), Shintō shrines and the Imperial Mausoleum, and all members of the imperial household past and present. This last provision encompassed every Emperor in history, including not a few mythical personages' (Kasza, 1988: 64–65).

A notable case of 'lesser *lèse-majesté*' was that of Aoki Tetsuji, who was prosecuted for violation of the press law in 1920. In the offending article, Aoki called for abolition of the *lèse-majesté* law, rejected the concept of *kokutai* and argued that seeking legitimacy for the imperial institution based on the 'unbroken imperial line' put the monarchy on shaky ground. Aoki's lawyer actually tried to argue in court that the idea of the unbroken line was wrong; the prosecution's only argument was the people's faith in the unbroken imperial line could not be challenged. The court gave Aoki the opportunity to recant. When he refused and after an appeal to the Supreme Court failed, Aoki was imprisoned for four months in 1922 (Mitchell, 1983: 187–189).

There was only an average of five *lèse-majesté* cases per year up to 1927. However, if we take into account the fact that about 15 per cent of press law cases involved 'slandering the imperial house', then the number of *lèse-majesté*-related cases jumps to an annual average of twenty-two – a significant increase, but also a signifier that the domain of *lèse-majesté* was increasing.

***Lèse-majesté* goes to war (1928–1945)**

As Japan geared up for war in Asia and the Pacific, the number of *lèse-majesté* cases shot up sharply as the vestiges of liberal democracy collapsed. The focus of right-wing groups and dominant factions in the military was the emperor system, which consolidated within the idea of *kokutai*. Any perceived slight to the throne was zealously pursued and suppressed.

Emblematic of this shift is the fate of a socialist member of the National Diet. When the Emperor opened the Diet in 1929, newly elected Yamamoto Senji appeared in 'ordinary clothes'. A stevedore named Kuroda took affront at this grave slight, visited Yamamoto at his home and killed him. Upon his arrest, Kuroda simply said: 'I told Yamamoto I held to the Emperor-centric principle, His sneer at this infuriated me. We fought, and he died' (*New York Times*, 7 March 1929, quoted in Byas, 1943: 320).

The most famous case of this period was that of Minobe Tatsukichi. A constitutional law professor at Tokyo Imperial University and a member of the House of Peers, Minobe had developed the 'organ theory' of the state, which argued that the emperor was part of, rather than above or beyond, the state. The idea, drawn from German state theory, became generally accepted and was not controversial when first published decades prior. But in the political milieu of the 1930s, Minobe's organ theory had become an intolerable insult. His books were burnt in front of Meiji Shrine in Tokyo. Clamouring for his prosecution, right-wing groups denounced Minobe for his 'non-Japanese, blasphemous, Europe-worshipping ideology which ignores our . . . tradition' (Mitchell, 1976: 153). He was initially accused of *lèse-majesté*, but prosecutors reasoned that Minobe had not intended to commit it; instead of a sentence, his books, well known in academic circles and used as textbooks in universities, were banned or ordered to be revised. Minobe resigned from the House of Peers and made a 'written admission of error'. The Cabinet issued a declaration late that year on *kokutai* that 'affirmed that the emperor was sovereign and that any theory which held differently would be suppressed' (Mitchell, 1983: 275–277). But Minobe's woes did not end there. After evading Minobe's bodyguards, an ultra-nationalist confronted him. When Minobe asked if his assailant had even read his books, the man in response shot Minobe through both knees (Behr, 1989: 121).

The most important legal change – the enactment of the 1925 Peace Preservation Law and the legal recognition of *kokutai* – created a fourth type of *lèse-majesté*. To counter the perceived rise of socialistic ideas, the 1925 Law forbade forming any 'society with the objective of altering the national polity or the form of government' (section 1), with a maximum prison sentence of ten years. In 1928, an amendment allowed those found harming the *kokutai* to be executed.

There are three important consequences of the Peace Preservation Law. First, it brought the concept of *kokutai* – a term the definition of which was still evolving just decades before – into the legal discourse, which gave the justice system a potent new tool. In fact, in a 1929 decision, the Supreme Court hazarded a definition of the term (Streckfuss, 2013a).

Secondly, it carved out within the justice system a space for the concept of 'thought crimes', which officials defined as 'anyone who appears as if they might want to change the absolutism of the emperor' or 'the kokutai' (Mitchell, 1983: 201–203).

Thirdly, because the core feature of *kokutai* was the emperor system, these efforts of the Japanese imperial state created an alternative route to *lèse-majesté*, but one that was more encompassing and damning.

The new Law was used with utter abandon. Between 1928 and 1935, almost 60,000 Japanese were arrested under this 'super-*lèse-majesté*' Law, of which 4,175, or 7 per cent, were prosecuted. If the case came to trial, the conviction rate was an impressive 99 per cent. Compared to common *lèse-majesté*, sentences were severe. Between 1925 and 1930, the average sentence was three-and-a-half years. Almost half were given sentences of hard labour for more than three years; 17 per cent were given sentences of more than five years. In comparison, the average sentence for common *lèse-majesté* was twenty-one months and only 13 per cent received sentences of more than three years.

Between 1928 and 1935, the average annual number of persons prosecuted for *lèse-majesté* jumped thirteen-fold to sixty-five. As Japan went to war, that number more than tripled, peaking in 1937 with 399 persons tried. If we were to include those convicted of monarchy-related violations of the press law and the much more numerous convictions under the Peace Preservation Law, as many as 1,000 Japanese were removed from society every year for views deemed anti-monarchical from 1936 to the early 1940s.

A reason for the increase is that the expanding domain of *lèse-majesté* was no longer to protect the monarch from mere insults, but to protect an entire thought complex. Charges of *lèse-majesté* often made no reference at all to the emperor or imperial family. The head of what eventually became the Sōka Gakkai Buddhist movement and a number of his followers were arrested and jailed for *lèse-majesté* in the early 1940s. They were convicted of 'refusing to enshrine a deity tablet . . . from the Grand Shrine of Ise', on grounds that such an action amounted to slandering the Dharma, which had somehow become an aspect of the monarchy (Baffelli, 2011: 221–222).

The emperor system had become essentially an orthodoxy reigning over a sacred, Japanese universe and protected by multiple forms of *lèse-majesté*.

The rise of *lèse-majesté* in Thailand (1976–present)

Following the massacre of students at Thammasat University and a coup in October 1976, a military government attempted to set up a 'dhammocracy', or rule by virtuous men with no need for the messy and corrupt features of democracy. A whole national security apparatus and a host of government agencies such as the National Identity Board placed the monarchy at the centre of 'Thainess'. Most emblematic of this change was the remarkable amendment to the Act Promulgating the Criminal Code, B.E. 2499 (1956), (the *lèse-majesté* law), article 112, increasing the maximum sentence from seven to fifteen years in prison for each count (Streckfuss, 2011: 420).

The increase can generally be attributed to the shift in the law from protecting the reputation of the king to protecting an institution. With the new emphasis on the centrality of the monarchy after 1976, the average annual number of cases doubled (Streckfuss, 2011: 107–108, 190–194). In the aftermath of Black May 1992, which expelled those behind the 1991 coup, there was an upsurge of enthusiasm for democracy. A very deliberative process of public consultations created Thailand's most democratic Constitution in 1997. The number of *lèse-majesté* cases dropped and many predicted that the vicious coup cycle had finally come to an end. Thai-style democracy, and indeed Thainess itself, seemed to be giving way to a new identity for Thailand within the community of democratic nations. The *lèse-majesté* law seemed set to become a historical relic as in so many other democratic constitutional monarchies around the world.

However, another military coup in 2006 seemed to turn the clock back. Despite the king's own calls for the law not to be invoked in late 2005, the number of *lèse-majesté* cases skyrocketed, increasing by an incredible 1,500 per cent between 2005 and 2010.

An overview of *lèse-majesté* over the last few years provides some sense of the nature of the law and its current use. There is a 43 per cent chance that an arrest for *lèse-majesté* will lead to prosecution. As much as 75 per cent of those charged are denied bail during pre-trial and when the case has been appealed. Because of the severity of the punishment, most defendants admit guilt, thereby cutting their sentence in half and allowing them to ask for a royal pardon. But between 2006 and 2012, about 45 per cent appealed their convictions. The conviction rate for *lèse-majesté* is 94 per cent and the average initial sentence is about ten years – seven years if admitting guilt (Streckfuss, 2013b). A sample of *lèse-majesté* convictions from 2008 to May 2013 follows, with the length of number of years sentenced/sentence if admitting guilt, in parenthesis:

- distributing material offensive to the monarchy (20 years sentenced/reduced to 15 years);
- posting comments insulting to the monarchy on the Internet (20 years/10 years);
- saying that the king had killed his brother and backed the 2006 coup (no admission, 18 years);
- posting anti-monarchy content on a website (13 years);
- saying that the king had ordered the killing of students on 6 October 1976 (10 years);
- distributing videos showing royals in compromising sexual situations, saying that the king was seriously ill (9 years/4.5 years);
- defaming the queen (6 years/3 years);
- stating that the king sided with pro-royalist protesters (6 years/4 years);
- selling VCDs offensive to the monarchy (6 years/3 years);
- making reference in a novel to a prince that implied criminal activity (6 years/3 years);
- selling videos saying that the crown prince was unpopular (4 years/3 years);
- attacking the head of the Privy Council by using royal title (3 years/3 years); and
- saying that the king interfered with politics (3 years/2 years).

There are three causes for the explosion in the number of cases in recent years. First, the monarchy or those associated with it have acted incautiously: backing coups, undemocratic constitutions, pro-royalist agitation, annulment of elections and manipulation of public bodies.

Second, the pro-democracy United Front for Democracy against Dictatorship (UDD), or 'red shirts', have a nationwide following and represent the majority of the population. Members of the UDD have been increasingly critical of the role of extra-constitutional powers. The Internet has provided new windows to both Thailand and the world that are not provided by state-run media or the Thai education system. Through it, Thai society has gained access to new and previously restricted information, including a new perspective on the monarchy. In turn, UDD members have almost all been exclusively the victims of *lèse-majesté* charges.

Finally, the state and social network groups have expanded surveillance of Thai society and Thai Internet users. Increasingly, the state has used powers under the Computer Crime Act of 2007 to block websites and apprehend those deemed to have committed *lèse-majesté*.

Two recent court cases show how deeply and widely the domain of *lèse-majesté* has expanded. The first case concerned a radio announcer on a community radio, who stated (in a rather rambling way) that 'we [Thais] now live with dignity and liberty and we mustn't live like we [did] under the Fourth Reign' (King Mongkut, or Rama IV, r. 1851–68). From this, prosecutors construed the meaning of the words to be 'that His Age [of his royal person, Rama IV] was one in which one had to be a slave, there was no freedom, there was poor governing'. Hearing this would apparently be earth-shattering for listeners, because it would cause 'the people to lose their faith completely, in a manner that is likely to bring disrepute and dishonor to, and cause contempt and hatred, of the fourth reign' (Streckfuss, 2013c).

The case is particularly bizarre because past kings are not designated for protection in the law; even if they were, the defendant was talking about a reign and not about King Rama IV. And if it were about a reign, was it true? Were there slaves and serfs? Was the system despotic? The Supreme Court pointed out that article 112 of the 1956 Revised Criminal Code (the *lèse-majesté* law) does not actually specify which king, queen, or heir apparent is to be protected by the law; therefore, all of the kings of the

Chakri Dynasty could be covered, because 'defamation of a past king will inevitably affect the present king who still reigns'. If past kings were not protected by the law, words of the defendant could 'still have a negative effect on the feelings of the people that would lead to dissatisfaction and might affect the security of the kingdom' (Streckfuss, 2013c).

A second case involved a man who was found guilty of posting a message deemed to be *lèse-majesté* twice on a website and who was sentenced to five years' imprisonment for each post. A third charge was for attempted *lèse-majesté*, because 'the defendant's computer showed that he had prepared to post another *lèse majesté* message on the web forum' – an attempt that was foiled when twenty police arrested him in his home and seized his computer. The court used the logic that anyone who 'commences' to commit a crime can be found guilty. The man was consequently sentenced to an additional forty months (Thaweeporn, 2013).

The category of 'attempted crime' may apply to other, more physical crimes, such as robbery or murder. But can it really apply to defamation, a discursive and complicated crime? The decision opens the door to a whole new and troubling area for *lèse-majesté*, truly placing it in the realm of thought crimes.

These cases show that the scope of the *lèse-majesté* law has spread as never before, stretching legal logic to a breaking point.

Sacredness, history and sovereignty in Japan and Thailand

There are many similarities and differences that we could explore between the *lèse-majesté* experiences of Japan and Thailand, but let us explore only one – the sacred or divine status of the monarch. From this, we can go on to discuss orthodoxy, history, the impulse toward totalitarianism, and the tension between royal and popular sovereignty.

Western classical historians such as Lear (1965: 13) point vaguely to the 'East' (of Rome) in explaining the origins of 'divine' kingship. Divine kingship made its way to Europe via Christianity, as did, eventually, its companion, *lèse-majesté*. But how far 'East' did divine kingship go? Certainly, there was (and is?) a belief throughout South and East Asia in a separation of the physical and spiritual worlds. Japan based many of its political models on Chinese ones; Siam, on Hindu ones. Through Buddhism, pre-modern Japan and Siam both developed suspicions of heterodoxy and an impulse towards understanding difference as a form of heresy (Josephson, 2012: 43–70). Indigenous monarchies were discredited when they fell to Western colonial powers. Of the larger states of East Asia, only the Japanese and Siamese monarchies survived, providing a rather uninterrupted continuity of beliefs surrounding their monarchies. The Japanese and Siamese monarchs stepped out from behind the veils of their palaces, and they became symbols of drives for centralisation (or 'modernisation').

In Japan, Meiji elite very consciously mobilised Shintōism to help to establish 'imperial authority'. Local deities were placed within a hierarchy under the ancestral god of the imperial family, in an effort to:

> replace the simple faith of the people by the political worship of all the deities of heaven and earth, the Emperor, Imperial Family as well as the royal subjects, who had supported the Imperial Regime. They were also designed to instill the idea to the people that the Emperor was the descendant of Amaterasu, the supreme goddess

above all the other deities and that the Emperor was the one in this world to give ranks to these deities and offer grades to shrines to glorify them, thus proving his sanctity beyond these deities.

(Yokoyama, 1976: 99)

The Meiji elite also sought to impose orthodoxy by turning a blind eye to anti-Buddhist movements and effecting a 'continuous suppression' of Christianity and other belief systems that might interfere with emperor worship. In an effort to counter ideas of the Freedom and Popular Rights Movement, the Meiji elite engineered grand processions of the Emperor Meiji throughout Japan. There were surprisingly few formal *lèse-majesté* cases throughout the Meiji period, but Yokoyama (1976: 99–101) argues that *lèse-majesté* at the time was 'flexible' and that its main suppression was in the form of a 'relentless crackdown by the police'. Even by 1893, it seems that the imperial ideology was in place. An official history prepared by the Ministry of Education for the 1893 World's Columbian Exposition in Chicago, IL, boldly stated that, '[i]n the long period of more than twenty-five centuries . . . never has there been found a single subject of the realm who sought to impair the Imperial prestige' (Japan et al., 1893: 18).

But it was really only in the early Shōwa period (1926–45) that Japan came together as a *lèse-majesté* regime. Right-wing movements flourished to counter what were seen as corrupt politicians and greedy capitalists, calling on the emperor to take direct power. The military was involved in imperialist adventures abroad and domestic political intrigues at home. Assassinations of prime ministers had become commonplace. Thousands of those suspected of disloyalty to the throne were imprisoned. Historians who questioned the authenticity of 'a line of Emperors unbroken for ages eternal' were charged and silenced (Brownlee, 1997).

The middle classes, and much of the intelligentsia, came to eschew democratic reform and joined the masses enthralled by the throne under the immutable Constitution. Western-educated, former diplomat Matsunami Niichirō (1940) pointed out to Western audiences that the emperor in Japan was not like kings in Europe, who were merely 'God's minister on earth', meaning that they were 'only under God'; in Japan, emperors were:

the ministers on earth of the Imperial Ancestors in Heaven, everybody is under the Emperor and the Emperor is under nobody . . . We look upon our Emperor as almighty just as Western Christians look upon their God . . . we worship Him respectively as . . . our holy entity [whose person] is sacred and His decisions are looked upon as actually coming from Heaven . . . as those of God.

(Matsunami, 1940: 126, 158, 160–162)

With such a god-ruler, the Japanese state itself is made divine. Matsunami (1940: 108, 151, 173, 178) proclaimed that 'the Emperor is the State itself', and that, because 'Our people consider that they all form one vast family with the Imperial House as its head', they too become part of the divine state: 'The Japanese sense of the Divine State is peculiar to our people and there is nothing of this sort in foreign countries, East and West.'

Unlike under dictatorships in Italy, Germany and the Soviet Union wherein consent of the governed is achieved by coercion, in Japan, divine right is accepted by the ruled and 'the consent of the governed is all voluntary and with pleasure' (Matsunami,

1940: 175). European fascism was 'state worship', but the state was invisible; unlike fascist state worship, said Matsunami (1940: 166); in Japan the emperor is 'in a sense, visible' – 'the state is a human institution, but our Emperor is superhuman existing before human history began'. Rejecting the fascist 'will to power', Matsunami (1940: 168) asserted that Japan's mission is peaceful and that 'the will to power and morality are compatible and may be reconciled' – that world peace is possible through universal worship of the Japanese emperor, who 'is worthy of respect as God and as the embodiment of benevolence and justice' and may be entrusted 'the prerogative of administration forever' over humankind.

Japan had become essentially a totalitarian state under the emperor. And what circumscribed the boundaries of acceptable thought, speech and actions was the *lèse-majesté* law, the scope of which had:

> logically [come] to encompass not only the criticisms, the display of suspicions or insults against the ideologies of the Imperial Regime as a mythos (the sum of history, tradition, and mythology that would help to explain the origin of the royal authority), but also the criticisms and the display of suspicions against the regime as a political system (the ruling system), under which all the political powers were concentrated in the hands of the Emperor (while the civil officials and military attaché under the direct control of the Emperor wielded the power) and its material foundation (the land ownership as a landlord or as a capitalist).
>
> (Yokoyama, 1976: 102)

In Siam, the monarchy adopted two models, of the Hindu *devaraja* (god-king) and *dhammaraja* (king possessing Buddhist virtues). There was an effort among royalists in the 1950s to emphasise the *dhammaraja* model. Under military dictatorship in the early 1960s, certain *devaraja* features were reintroduced. An even clearer *devaraja* feature was the increased penalty for *lèse-majesté* in 1976. For thirty years, there was an uneasy tension between these two models – one claiming that all Thais loved the king, the other threatening draconian punishment – and between royal versus popular sovereignty. The scale seemed to be tipping in favour of popular sovereignty with the 1997 Constitution, but the 2006 military coup – and all of the attendant anti-democratic forces, including the *lèse-majesté* law – rather violently tipped the scale back the other way.

The Japanese Constitution of 1889 could never be altered, because it came from the hand of the emperor; under similar logic, the eighteen Thai constitutions were the work of corrupt politicians and so could be torn up at any time. Two things that have not changed are the king's being 'in a position of revered worship' and, since 1949, the affirmation that Thailand is governed by 'the democratic regime with the king as head of state'. Article 68 of the 2007 Constitution reads:

> No person shall exercise the rights and liberties prescribed in the Constitution to overthrow the democratic regime of government with the King as Head of the State under this Constitution or to acquire the power to rule the country by any means which is not in accordance with the modes provided in this Constitution.

In late 2013, the Constitutional Court not only ruled that a Bill to amend the Constitution passed by Parliament to allow for a fully elected senate was an attempt to 'overthrow the democratic regime of government with the King as Head of State', but also that legislators who voted for the Bill could lose their seats. Moreover, the Court ruled as peaceful and lawful the People's Democratic Reform Committee (PDRC), which has openly declared its intention to overthrow the government since late 2013, physically blocked elections in February 2014 and been involved in various acts of violence.

The PDRC has claimed exclusive loyalty to the throne and has outlined policies to provide greater protection of the monarchy and to counter any efforts to amend the *lèse-majesté* law. In April 2014, parents filed a complaint against their own daughter for *lèse-majesté*; soon after, the 'Rubbish Collection Organisation' was set up by a PDRC supporter with 100,000 Facebook followers, aiming to 'clean up the rubbish' – that is, to track down and 'exterminate' perpetrators of *lèse-majesté* acts (Samabuddhi, 2014; Dawson, 2014). Shortly after, a poet who had spoken out against the *lèse-majesté* law was gunned down in broad daylight. At the end of April, the Senate set up an Ad Hoc Committee on Studying and Monitoring Problems Concerning Law Enforcement and Measures for the Protection of the Royal Institution that was 'to create measures to counter those offending the royal institution', and which found that 'information and communication technology was being used improperly to insult the royal institution, and attempts were being made to link the monarchy to current political movements' (Wangkiat, 2014). In Thailand, it has become brother against brother, parents against child and royalists on a witch hunt against traitors. Columnist Kong Rithdee (2014) notes that the recent surge in *lèse-majesté* cases 'demonstrates the complex knot of paranoia, intolerance and legal decapitation that Section 112 has exerted in the minds of the people'.

As effusive as Japanese monarchists were in their praise of the emperor in the 1930s, it is doubtful that a Japanese court ever went to the lengths of the Thai Constitutional Court in October 2012. In a response to a petition challenging the constitutionality of the *lèse-majesté* law, the Court rejected the claim and, in its ruling, harkened back to Sukhothai, the 'first' Thai kingdom of the thirteenth century, in which the king was 'head of state:

> Up until the current constitution of the kingdom, the form of regime remains one with the king as head of the state. This demonstrates the great respect, esteem, and admiration held by the people for the institution of the monarchy. The place of the Thai king as the respected and beloved center of the Thai people has been continuous, as shown in age-old royal traditions and legal conventions. The king has administered with virtue and taken action with the intention of the well-being of the people. In particular, King Bhumipol Adulyadej, the current monarch, greatly contributes to the nation and gives royal grace to the Thai people. He visits the people and bestows royally-conceived projects in different areas in order to alleviate the suffering and solve the problems and troubles of the people. . . . Ordinary people are aware of the king's conduct and his generosity. They therefore have deep-seated respect, trust, and loyalty for the king and the institution of the monarchy. The long-standing patronage of the Thai king has made the Thai people to continually respect, love, and admire the king. This is a unique characteristic of Thailand held by no other country.
>
> (Quoted in Haberkorn, 2013)

Well-known Thai scholar Nidhi Eoseewong has pondered on the drift in Thai politics toward totalitarianism (Haberkorn, 2014). Totalitarian dictatorship becomes possible when people are alienated from all traditional ties. Primarily from the middle classes, they are 'atomised' and have become the centre of their own worlds, which they find empty. They are bored of politics and corruption and democracy. Totalitarian dictatorship, according to Nidhi, 'destroys the principle of the democratic majority entirely', because '[a] majority that holds that every person is politically equal is the very problem'; totalitarianism instead views that '[e]veryone should not be politically equal – not when they have different levels of education, hold different shares in the country, and view the collective differently' (quoted in Haberkorn, 2014). Joining the 'Great Mass of the People' (as the leader calls the PDRC movement), these profoundly anti-democratic protesters find a meaning: expressing loyalty to the monarchy (quoted in Haberkorn, 2014).

Although their respective constitutions were based on Western models, the cultural and political contexts in Japan and Thailand were quite different. Heresy had risen in common with absolute monarchies in Europe and both fell victim to the Enlightenment. Nineteenth-century constitutions in Europe may have still claimed their monarchs as sacred and that they were answerable to none but God, but the tendency was toward de-sacralisation and mass politics: humans were left to themselves to work out politics. Intransigent regimes attempting to re-sacralise their kings merely hastened the end of monarchy. By 1890, the components of Japan's emperor system ideology were in place; forty years later, the forces creating totalitarianism also essentially made the Japanese emperor a god. In Thailand, the components of 'Thainess' were in place by the mid-1960s; forty years later, the re-sacralisation of the monarchy was engaged. In many ways, monarchism became the official religion of the two regimes, which acted more like theocracies demanding orthodoxy, ferreting out heresy and protected by a powerful blasphemy law (Streckfuss, forthcoming).

Yet it is strange to note that, despite the popular impression that all Japanese were enthralled by the emperor system, the cases described in this chapter show a certain pluckiness in the criticisms made of the emperor. It was the common people who made these bold attacks, while the elite and educated shuddered at any suggestion of disloyalty. In comparison, Thai attacks on the monarchy have been much milder, while fetching longer sentences.

The tension between oligarchic or royal sovereignty versus popular sovereignty in Japan was 'solved' in a sense by the imposition of the American occupation, during which full suffrage was extended to all Japanese, the emperor denied his own divinity and the *lèse-majesté* law was abolished. In doing so, though, the occupation in some ways deprived Japanese society of the formative democratic struggle that it might otherwise have had. This chapter has shown that anti-monarchy sentiments were both strongly expressed and seemingly widespread. Although Japan turned into a police state, we can only speculate what might have happened had Japanese society had its own democratic revolution.

Conclusion

Both Japan and Thailand considered themselves to have a unique monarchy that shared a unique relationship with its people. It is curious to note that Thai kings or their defenders, at least publicly, have never made the grandiose claims to historical continuity that their Japanese counterparts had nor, seemingly, have they ever placed the king at such exalted heights – or have they? Future historians will have difficulty explaining why the punishment for insulting a *dhammaraja* was three times more severe than Japan's protection of a veritable god. Japan's veneration for its emperor was an impetus for its entrance into war. The position of the Thai monarchy has denied its society a truly democratic revolution championing the cause of equality for eighty-two years. Structural inequality has always been clothed in Thainess, Thai-style democracy or Thai culture. In that span of time, have the people ever really been sovereign, or has popular sovereignty merely been thwarted time and again when it infringed on oligarchic or royal privilege?

Thai society is now facing its own moment of truth. The rise of *lèse-majesté* cases and their successful suppression is not a triumph for monarchy, but rather a warning of an escalation of crisis. A similar rise in cases in Japan in the 1930s might have been taken as a warning of impending destruction wreaked by its pursuing war in Asia and in the Pacific. Imperial Germany had also seen one of the richest concentrations of *lèse-majesté* cases in modern history from the 1880s through into the early 1900s. Within a decade, Germany was devastated and its monarchy abolished.

After the overthrow of the absolute Thai monarchy in 1932, 'the people' supposedly became sovereign. But, eight decades later, an oligarchy that never grew up and the monarchy it claims as its own have refused to allow this dream to be realised. As Michael K. Connors (2003: 147) has written:

> The people were the sources of sovereignty, but they were not yet able to divest it to legitimate representatives. The people were sovereign and yet this was an imagined state, needing state development and cajolement. The people were sovereign and yet rule should be according to enlightened elites. The people were Thai, but expressions of Thainess [were] to be cultivated, policed and socialized.

The orthodoxy and underlying violence of Thainess, of 'the democratic regime with the king as head of state', of a culture of impunity and of a blind loyalty to the throne, are either coming to an end or will all be realised in totalitarian dictatorship (Saichol, undated: 2).

The lesson of *lèse-majesté* is that a massive increase is a sign of crisis. When one faction within modern societies is too zealous in imposing orthodoxy, such societies are liable to break. Japan did not learn this lesson. Thailand has not either and it is fast approaching ruin.

Note

* I should thank first the Center for Southeast Asian Studies (CSEAS) at Kyoto University for the opportunity as a Visiting Guest Fellow to have the time and funding to do research on *lèse-majesté* in Japan. I would also like to thank the many staff at CSEAS who assisted me in various ways, including Shin Egishi and Hinata Shinsuke for assistance in translation, and David Malitz and Simon Creak for the comments and criticisms. A special thanks to Richard Mitchell for his kind correspondence.

References

Amnesty International (1987) *Amnesty International Report*, London: Amnesty International Publications.

Baffelli, E. (2011) 'The Gakkai is Faith; the Kōmeitō is Action: Sōka Gakkai and "Buddhist Politics"', in R. Starrs (ed.) *Politics and Religion in Modern Japan: Red Sun, White Lotus*, New York: Palgrave Macmillan, 216–239.

Behr, E. (1989) *Hirohito: Behind the Myth*, New York: Villard Books.

Brownlee, J. S. (1997) *Japanese Historians and the National Myths, 1600–1945: The Age of the Gods and Emperor Jinmu*, Vancouver, BC/Tokyo: University of British Columbia Press/University of Tokyo Press.

Byas, H. (1943) *Government by Assassination*, London: George Allen & Unwin.
Connors, M. K. (2003) *Democracy and National Identity in Thailand*, London/New York: Routledge Curzon.
Dawson, A. (2014) 'The Big Issue: Redefining Defamation', *Bangkok Post*, 27 April.
Gluck, C. (1985) *Japan's Modern Myths: Ideology in the Late Meiji Period*, Princeton, NJ: Princeton University Press.
Haberkorn, T. (2013) 'On the Uses of History', *Prachatai*, 2 April, available online at http://www.prachatai.com/english/node/3558 [accessed 24 March 2014].
Haberkorn, T. (2014) 'Hannah Arendt, Nidhi Eoseewong, and the Spectre of Totalitarianism in Thailand', *Asia-Pacific Journal*, 12(14): Article 4, available online at http://japanfocus.org/-Jeff-Kingston/4105 [accessed 8 April 2014].
Heng-Chao Ch'en, P. (1987) *The Formation of the Early Meiji Legal Order*, Oxford: Oxford University Press.
Hewison, K. (2009) '"Thai-style Democracy": A Conservative Struggle for Thailand's Politics', *Prachatai*, 7 July, available online at http://www.prachatai.com/english/node/1292 [accessed 25 March 2014].
Holtom, D. C. (1942) *Modern Japan and Shinto Nationalism: A Study of Present-day Trends in Japanese Religions*, Chicago, IL: University of Chicago Press.
Ishii Ryosuke (1958) *Japanese Legislation in the Meiji Era*, trans. and adapted W. J. Chambliss, Tokyo: Centenary Culture Series, Kasai/Pan-Pacific Press.
Itō, H. (1889) *Commentaries of the Constitution of the Empire of Japan*, Tokyo: Igirisu-Hōritosu Gakko.
Japan, Brinkley, F., & Japan. Imperial Japanese Commission to the World's Columbian Exposition. (1893) *History of the Empire of Japan*. Tokyo: Published by the Dai Nippon Tosho Kabushiki Kwaisha, by order of the Dept. of Education, Printed at the Japan Mail Office, Yokohama.
Japanese Department of Education (1893) *History of the Empire of Japan*, Tokyo: Dai Nippon Tosho Kabushiki Kwaisha.
Josephson, J. A. (2012) *The Invention of Religion in Japan*, Chicago, IL/London: University of Chicago Press.
Kasza, G. J. (1988) *The State and the Mass Media in Japan, 1918–1945*, Berkeley, CA/London: University of California Press.
Kong, R. (2014) 'Free Speech Tied in *Lèse-majesté* Knot', *Bangkok Post*, 19 April.
Le Bret, C. (1632) *De Sourerainere du Roy*, Paris.
Lear, F. S. (1965) 'The Crime of Majesty in Roman Public Law', in *Treason in Roman and Germanic Law: Collected Papers*, Austin, TX: University of Texas Press, 3–48.
Leyland, P. (2010) 'The Struggle for Freedom of Expression in Thailand: Media Moguls, the King, Citizen Politics and the Law', *Journal of Media Law*, 2(3): 115–137.
Matsunami Niichirō (1940) *The Constitution of Japan and Politics*, Tokyo: Maruzen.
Mitchell, R. H. (1976) *Thought Control in Prewar Japan*, Ithaca, NY/London: Cornell University Press.
Mitchell, R. H. (1983) *Censorship in Imperial Japan*, Princeton, NJ: Princeton University Press.
Omata, N. (2010) *Meijiki ni okeru fukei jiken no kenkyū* [*Lèse-majesté* in the Meiji Period], Kyōto-shi: Shibunkaku Shuppan.
Saichol, S. (undated) 'The Construction of Mainstream Thought on "Thainess" and the "Truth" Constructed by "Thainess"', available online at http://www.fringer.org/wp-content/writings/thainess-eng.pdf [accessed 23 March 2014].
Saichol, S. (2007) *Kukrit lae kan sang kuam pen thai 2: yuk jom phon sarit tung tossawat 2530* [Kukrit and the Construction of Thainess, Vol. 2: From Sarit's Era to 1997], Bangkok: Matichon.
Samabuddhi, K. (2014) 'Call to Stop *Lèse-majesté* Witch Hunts', *Bangkok Post*, 20 April.
Shakaimondai shiryō kenkyūkai [Social Concern Research Group] (ed.) (1979) *Fukei jiken Ji Taishō 10-nen itari Shōwa 2-nen* [*Lèse-majesté* Cases, 1921–27], Kyoto: Tōyōbunkasha.
Smith, P. (1997) *Japan: A Reinterpretation*, New York: Pantheon.

Streckfuss, D. (forthcoming) 'European Constitutional Monarchies as Democracies vs. the Kingdom of Thailand as a Theocracy', in E. Kuhonta and V. Nethipo (eds) *Democracy and Crisis in Thailand* (provisional title).

Streckfuss, D. (1995) 'Kings in the Age of Nations: The Paradox of *Lèse-majesté* as Political Crime in Thailand', *Comparative Studies in Society and History*, 37(3): 445–475.

Streckfuss, D. (2011) *Truth on Trial in Thailand: Defamation, Treason, and Lèse-majesté*, London and New York: Routledge.

Streckfuss, D. (2013a) '*Lèse-majesté* in Imperial Japan, 1882–1947', Unpublished manuscript, on file with the author.

Streckfuss, D. (2013b) '*Lèse-majesté* as Crisis of Monarchy: A Comparison of Present-day Thailand and Prewar Japan', Paper presented at the Center for Southeast Asian Studies, Kyoto University, 31 May.

Streckfuss, D. (2013c) *Lèse-majesté* and the Thai Judiciary's Assault on History', *Prachatai*, 15 November, available online at http://www.prachatai.com/english/node/3744 [accessed 24 March 2014].

Takagi, H. (2011) 'Fabricating Antiquity in Modern Nara', *Zinbun,* 43: 51–60.

Tasuku, H. (1914) *The Faith of Japan*, New York: Macmillan.

Thak, C. (2007) *Thailand: The Politics of Despotic Paternalism*, Chiangmai: Silkworm.

Thaweeporn, K. (2013) 'Thai Man Found Guilty of Attempted *Lèse-majesté*', *Prachatai*, 12 December, available online at http://www.prachatai.com/english/node/3790 [accessed 24 March 2014].

Vella, W. F. (1978) *Chaiyo! King Vajiravudh and the Development of Thai Nationalism*, Honolulu: University of Hawai'i.

Wangkiat, P. (2014) 'Senators Start Pro-monarchy Crusade', *Bangkok Post*, 30 April.

Yoichi, H. (1990). 'The Constitution and the Emperor System: Is Revisionism Alive?', *Law and Contemporary Problems*, 53(1): 51–60.

Yokoyama, K. (1976) 'Tennosei to fukeisai: josetsu' [Emperor System and *Lèse-majesté*: preface], *Horitsu Jiho*, 48(4): 96–103.

22 The construction of ethnicity in colonial law and its legacy

The example of the *Peranakan* Chinese in Indonesia

Rosy Antons-Sutanto and Christoph Antons

Introduction

Sixteen years after the notorious anti-Chinese riots in the Indonesian capital, Jakarta, and in other cities (Purdey, 2006: 106–141), the newly elected President Joko Widodo of Indonesia inaugurated Basuki Tjahaja Purnama, his former deputy governor of Jakarta, as the new governor of the capital city (Reuters, 2014). Basuki, known popularly under his Hakka nickname 'Ahok', is Christian and the first ethnic Chinese politician appointed as governor of the capital city. His inauguration is regarded as a step forward towards ethnic and religious tolerance in Indonesia.

Nonetheless, race, ethnicity and religion continue to play an important role in Indonesian politics, with the notion of *pribumi* ('indigenous') as 'dominant ethnicity'.[1] During the presidential elections of 2014, concerns were raised as to whether Indonesia can be led by a politician of migrant descent, such as an ethnic Chinese (Kwok, 2014). A 'black campaign' of libel was run against Joko Widodo, who was alleged to be secretly of ethnic Chinese descent and a Christian himself. A fake obituary using Joko Widodo's alleged Chinese name, Hubertus Oey Hong Liong, was circulated online (*Jakarta Post*, 2014). This would have been a rather serious allegation prior to the amendment of the Constitution of 1945, article 6 of which had, up to that point, prescribed that the president must be an *orang Indonesia asli* ('autochthonous Indonesian'). Until recently, this was generally interpreted as meaning that the president must belong to the population group named *Bumiputera*. This population group was initially formed as part of an elaborate ethnic classification system that the Dutch colonial powers introduced in 1855 in the *Indische Staatsregeling*, the quasi-constitution of the colony.

Strong objections were subsequently also raised against the nomination of Basuki Purnama as governor of Jakarta. The Islamic Defenders Front (*Front Pembela Islam*, or FPI) strongly objected to Basuki's inauguration, stating that Muslims should be led only by Muslims. However, many Muslims did not share the FPI's concerns. Saiq Aqil Siradj, leader of the biggest Islamic party, *Nahdatul Ulama* (NU), supported Basuki's inauguration, arguing that leaders should be judged based on their honesty and dedication, and not their religion (Kwok, 2014).

The question of whether Indonesians of migrant descent can participate in Indonesian politics on equal terms remains a contested one, because it touches upon the political power of ethnic groups and their ranking in Indonesian ethnic stratification. This chapter explores the ambiguous position of ethnic Chinese in the context of the debates about their legal status and identity from a historical and legal perspective. We show in the following section how concepts of 'race' and 'population groups' have been constructed in many colonial and post-colonial societies to maintain the interests of dominant ethnic groups. We go on to show that the formation of the *Peranakan* Chinese as a permanent foreign minority group in what is now Indonesia is an example of this, then examine the role of the colonial institutions in such 'racial' classification and the construction of the population group of the 'foreign Orientals'. Before concluding, we discuss the 'institutional memory', the legacy of these institutions and the perceptions that they have helped to create in independent Indonesia – and we conclude that a complete eradication of the system is needed in the interests of nation building.

Ethnic identity, category and culture

One of the most important legacies of Dutch colonialism in Indonesia is the legal classification of population groups based on a concept of primordial identity, in which 'race' and ethnic groups are perceived as 'natural'. In his book *Old Societies and New States*, Clifford Geertz (1963a) argued that ethnic identities often hold back the process of nation building, because they are rooted in primordial attachments. He defined a primordial attachment as 'one that stems from the "givens" – or, more precisely, as culture is inevitably involved in such matters, the assumed "givens" – of social existence' (Geertz, 1963b, reprinted in Hutchinson and Smith, 1996: 41). Since his focus is on cultural explanations, Geertz dedicates relatively little attention to the role of institutions and authorities in shaping ethnic relationships. For Indonesia, however, the role of law and legal institutions in this process is very clear, and we examine this role later in this chapter. There is little conceptual distinction being made in the country between ethnic categories and identity, leading to a static view of the latter.

Building on Geertz' view, Harold Isaacs (1975) argued that ethnic identity is unchangeable, because it is a person's 'basic group identity'. By 'basic group identity', he meant:

> the identity derived from belonging to what is generally and loosely called an 'ethnic group'. It is composed of what have been called 'primordial affinities and attachments'. It is the identity made up of what a person is born with or acquires at birth. It is distinct from all other multiple and secondary identities people acquire because unlike all the others, its elements are what makes a group, in Clifford Geertz' phrase, a 'candidate for nationhood'.
>
> (Isaacs, 1975: 30)

Cornell and Hartmann (2007: 51) have summarised Isaacs' eight elements that directly make up a person's identity as:

> the physical body (including size, shape, skin color and so on), a person's name (both individual and family), the history and origins of the group one is born into, one's nationality or other group affiliation, the language one first learns to speak, the religion one is born into, the culture one is born into and the geography and topography of the place of birth.

According to Isaacs, racial and ethnic identities are fixed, because they are rooted in the unchangeable elements of birth.

Because Geertz defined ethnic identity as *a priori* to all experiences or interactions, he implied that all social interactions are carried out within such a primordial reality

(Eller and Coughlan, 1993: 187). This suggests the concept of culture as *Geist*, a kind of idea or spirit that provides a basis for the characterisation of a society and which seems to have a life of its own (Geertz, 1963b, reprinted in Hutchinson and Smith, 1996: 42). In that regard, institutions, as well as cultural elements such as religion, knowledge, art, law and custom, are somehow perceived as the work of transcendental forces. Hence, in this view, culture appears as a coherent set of values and ideas transmitted in an undifferentiated manner from one generation to another. In this context, members of ethnic groups are supposed to share common cultural characteristics in an identical way and hence the concept of an ethnic group is that of a homogeneous cultural group.

Such primordialism is rejected here. It is clear to us that racial and ethnic identities are categories constructed through social interactions. Just as Cornell and Hartmann (2007: 25) assert, these categories become 'socially significant [only] to the extent that we use them to organise and interpret experience, to form social relations, and to organise individual and collective action'. We believe that it is important to make a clear conceptual distinction between identity and category, as does Jenkins (2008: 56), who refers to ethnic identity as being constructed within a group on the basis of a concept formulated by its members, whereas an ethnic category is externally constructed (Jenkins, 1994: 200). It is important to note that a concept of identity is often not entirely freely constructed by individuals or groups, because such perceptions run the risk of underestimating the power of others to impose ethnic categories. Because ethnic communities do not live in isolation, the perception of others influences the options of self-identification. In fact, ethnic identity is constructed within a dialogue between insiders and outsiders. It is in the meeting of internal and external definitions that the identity of persons or groups is made. The construction of ethnic identity means that 'the content of an ethnic group – in terms of both "culture" and membership – has no a priori existence or stability' (Banks, 1996: 12). Therefore ethnic identity needs to be reasserted in every generation, because its content needs each time to be negotiated within the existing structural context. This makes ethnic identity conceptually fluid, varied and inconsistent. It is a mistake to perceive an ethnic group as a homogeneous cultural group, ignoring differentiation and diversification within the group.

Following Max Weber, we believe that an ethnic group is not held together by a strong sense of identity nor by strong ethnic ties. Weber pointed out that collective interests play a very important role in the formation of ethnic groups in modern society. He defined an ethnic group as a political group (Weber, 1997: 19). Glazer and Moynihan (1975: 7–8) also argued that an ethnic group should not be defined as a cultural group, but as an interest-defined group, driven by pursuit of collective interests. In our view also, ethnic membership arises and changes according to changing circumstances and interests, which makes a person's identity far from fixed. Ethnicity can therefore be highly political, especially when it is used as a medium by which groups compete, or are made to compete, in pursue of their collective goals. As social groups can define themselves in ethnic terms, new ethnic groups may appear and disappear with changing circumstances (Cornell and Hartmann, 2007: 59). In the case of the Chinese minority groups in the colonial state of the Netherlands East Indies, and subsequently in Indonesia, the process of their formation shows that the concept of Chinese identity has been multifaceted and fluid. The ethnic Chinese community had been differentiated and diversified into various groupings, such as the *Peranakan* ('locally born') and *Totok* ('foreign born') Chinese as a result of their struggle to improve their position in a changing legal and economic structure during the late colonial period.

However, unlike in the modern European society of the early twentieth century described by Weber, the formation of an ethnic group in a colonial setting is not entirely an internal decision of a group. In a colonial setting, colonial subjects had few or no political rights. Colonial governments usually classified ethnic groups using existing ethnic labels, such as 'Chinese', but changed the way in which the labelled people defined their own identity. In the case of the Netherlands East Indies, for example, the colonial government constructed the new ethnic categories of 'natives' and 'foreign Orientals', which had not existed prior to the arrival of the colonial powers. Once such ethnic categories were introduced or changed, the relevant ethnic groups and identities were fixed along the lines of the utilitarian policy considerations of the colonial governments. Ethnic labels have been used both in informal and colloquial ways and in formal legal categorisations. Both formal and informal labelling have run parallel to each other and in different sequences, as is discussed in the following two sections of this chapter.

Peranakan Chinese: The formation of a permanent foreign minority group

Ethnic identity is not simply a personal choice; the formation of an ethnic group is also about a process of establishing boundaries, which involves the government, and is not entirely an internal decision of a group. As Joane Nagel (1994: 154) put it: 'Ethnic identity is closely associated with the issue of boundaries. Ethnic boundaries determine who is a member and who is not and designate which ethnic categories are available for individual identification at a particular time and place.' Although the process of ethnic categorisation could be consensual in the sense that external definitions confirm the group's internal perceptions of themselves, ethnic categories in such cases are nevertheless mandatory. In case of ethnic minority groups such as the *Peranakan* Chinese, they often do not have the leverage to choose their identity or to change its content, as is demonstrated by the process of the formation of foreign minority groups in Indonesia.

Although distinctions between indigenous (*pribumi*) Indonesians and ethnic Chinese are commonly viewed as biological in Indonesia, and used to explain the unease between Chinese and Javanese in particular, historical research has in fact shown that ethnicity is constructed, and that the Chinese community has been transformed into a permanent foreign minority group and represented as unchangeable (Tan, 1995; Ong, 2005: 175–178). Ethnic Chinese in Indonesia are generally referred to as *Peranakan* to indicate that they are locally born. However *Peranakan* Chinese do not form a homogeneous group, because the term *Peranakan* has over the centuries developed different meanings depending on the context in which it is being used (Ong, 1995).

Ethnic Chinese generally differentiate themselves into *Peranakan* and *Totok*. *Peranakan* see themselves as descendants of early waves of Chinese migration to Java. Before a change in Chinese migration law in 1859, Chinese could not legally emigrate and migrants could not return home without facing the possibility of severe punishment (Gautama, 1997: 51). Because women were traditionally prohibited from leaving China (Yen, 1986: 9), early Chinese migration to Java was predominantly of men (Ong, 1943: 50). The vast majority of these settled permanently on Java (Ong, 1943: 254), where they married local women; their children were called *Peranakan*. The Indonesian term *Peranakan* is derived from the Javanese word *pranakan* ('womb') and was therefore originally used for children of Javanese women married to foreigners. However, it is now being used in Indonesia mainly for ethnic Chinese, with a particular reference to the older Chinese community on Java. The dichotomy of *Peranakan* and *Totok* is hardly used for Chinese living on islands other than Java and Madura, where the majority of the Chinese population arrived only after 1859 as labourers ('coolies') in mining and on plantations (Ong, 1943: 61–73). The descendants of these coolies are called *Cina Sabrang*, in which phrase *sabrang* refers to all islands outside of Java (Ong, 1995: 144).

After the change in Chinese migration law in 1859, Chinese could emigrate out of China and many came as family units to Java (Ong, 1943: 255). This change coincided with the decline of the economic position of *Peranakan* Chinese. It also changed the way in which Chinese newcomers were incorporated into the society. Unlike in the previous time, when newly arrived migrants were incorporated into local *Peranakan* trading networks, the newcomers now formed their own networks to compete for diminishing economic opportunities for the Chinese. To enhance their chances for economic success, Chinese newcomers had to distinguish themselves from the *Peranakan* by organising their groups along the lines of dialect, family and place of origin. Hence the *Peranakan* called them *Totok*, with the double meaning of 'full-blooded' and 'newcomer'. They emerged towards the end of the colonial period as a new sub-ethnic category. The *Totok* 'newcomers' referred to the *Peranakan* as *Baba(h)* Chinese – an old reference for male *Peranakan* Chinese only, but then used for the entire group. Although distinctions between *Peranakan* and *Totok* are often regarded as different degrees of Chinese ancestry, they are merely notions of group identification. In reality, many of the newcomers also married Javanese women, because there were few Chinese migrant women. The *Totok* Chinese groups emerged during a time when the *Peranakan* Chinese middle classes felt challenged, as they began to lose their well-established position as middlemen in trade, while Chinese newcomers started to make inroads into the retail business in rural Java. Following independence, these *Totok* became the main target of a prohibition of rural trade for foreigners that the government introduced in 1959, and as a result of which many were forced to leave their villages (Sochmawardiah, 2013: 130) and opted to return to China (Coppel, 1983: 34). Coppel (1983: 37) puts the figure at more than 100,000 Chinese leaving the country, causing serious disruptions to the Indonesian economy at the time.

During the late colonial period, besides economic interests, *Peranakan* and *Totok* were shaped by their individual political needs: they formed different associations, and had different political goals and trajectories. The independence of Indonesia in 1945 set in motion a process of social change, disrupting the existing colonial stratification, and changing existing ties and relationships. The attitude of the Indonesian government towards Chinese from the very beginning was to promote assimilation, combined with restrictions, because of a belief that the colonial administration had strengthened the economic position of the Chinese at the expense of the autochthone (*asli*) Indonesian population (Coppel, 1983: 37). The relationship between the two became framed as one between a weak and a strong economic group (*golongan ekonomi lemah/kuat*) and the maintenance of the classification was justified with the need to reverse the colonial economic stratification by strengthening the 'weak economic group' (Utrecht and Djindang, 1983: 187). The Chinese thus became a target of Indonesian economic nationalism (Sochmawardiah, 2013: 129). However, it has been noted that the restrictions in fact prevented the very assimilation that was the goal of these measures (Wahid, 1991: 224–228). The common experience of discrimination during the Suharto period (1967–98) changed the relationship between *Peranakan* and *Totok*, and their perceptions of the 'self–other' distinctions. They realised that identity is a reflexive project of the self (Giddens, 1991: 33); hence *Peranakan* and *Totok* distinctions are largely personal definitions.

Because the ethnic Chinese were legally formed as a permanent foreign minority, the issue of Chinese identity in Indonesia has its historical basis in the colonial period. As is described below, it involves inter-group relationships in which ethnic categories were created and used by the colonial government to establish ethnic boundaries. Ethnic Chinese were administered as a population group based on 'race', and hence their racial identity and characterisation were externally defined by administrators. There were, and still are, huge discrepancies between the government's definitions of Chinese identity and those of the Chinese themselves. Before the establishment of China as a modern nation-state at the beginning of the twentieth century, Chinese migrants did not see themselves as belonging to a 'nation' or a 'race'. The perception of Chinese as a 'race' came with the new concept of 'nation-race' (*Minzuzhuyi*) in China, which derived from the Japanese concept *minzokushugi*. This concept was adopted by nationalist extremists among students studying in Japan during the time of the Chinese nationalist movement to promote a nationalism strongly characterised by a vivid 'racial consciousness' (Dikötter, 1990: 426). This concept of nationalism in turn was introduced to the ethnic Chinese community in the Netherlands East Indies by Chinese teachers teaching in Chinese-language schools there (Suryadinata, 1981: 5–7; Kwee, 1969: 17–21; Ong, 1943: 201–204). They encouraged Chinese living overseas, including those who were born overseas, to support the Chinese nationalist movement because they belonged to the Chinese nation. They suggested that inclusion in the new China as Chinese citizens was perhaps the only way in which they might improve their oppressive conditions and marginalised position in the colony. Such ideas encountered mixed reception among the *Peranakan*, who largely did not speak Chinese. Without ideas of 'race' or 'nation', local Chinese previously had ideas of 'being Chinese' and 'becoming un-Chinese' based only on maintaining a Chinese way of life or not (Wang, 1988: 1). In general, they considered everyone Chinese who saw themselves as such.

Unlike the nationalists, the imperial Chinese government considered emigrants to have abandoned 'Chinese values' and they were no longer considered to be members of the Chinese community (Dikötter, 1990: 421). These people could not expect any diplomatic protection from China (Phoa, 1992: 8). In contrast to the imperial Chinese government, the Dutch authority considered ethnic Chinese living in their territory to be Chinese because they were of Chinese origin. They were of the view that emigration did not change a person's 'racial' and ethnic identity; this was acquired at birth (van Mastenbroek, 1934).

The idea of 'racial groups' in Asia arrived with colonialism. While the Indonesian government after independence combined assimilation with restrictions, the colonial government had used a combination of segregation and restriction to administer the population, who were classified according to their respective places of origin. The terms 'Europeans' and 'natives' were legally constructed to divide the population into colonising and colonised groups, and the definitions changed over time. While the group of 'Europeans' during the time of the Dutch East India Company was not much differentiated, the colonised 'natives' always consisted of a plurality of ethnic groups. 'Natives' were administratively distinguished into ethnic categories and, until the end of the nineteenth century, identified by physical characteristics, religion, language and customs (Gautama, 1997: 20–22). These characteristics were regarded as the 'essence' of each ethnic group, leading to an association between people and culture. This made the social and legal position of certain groups, such as the Christian *Mardijkers*[2] and the *Peranakan* Chinese Muslims, ambiguous.

Since Chinese who left their homeland were, at that time, considered as having severed their formal link to China, the majority of them never returned home. Many who settled permanently on Java converted to Islam and assimilated into a local community. They gave up their Chinese identity by shaving their Qing-style hair and changing their names to Javanese names (The, 1993: 60). The Dutch referred to them as *geschoren* ('shaven') Chinese, again also using the term *Paranakan*[3] for them (van Mastenbroek, 1934: 26). The Dutch usage of the term *Paranakan* for Chinese Muslims indicates that most locally born Chinese were probably Muslims. As Anthony Reid (1996) has pointed out, only a small group retained their Chinese religion. It is unclear whether these *Peranakan* Muslims continued to regard themselves as Chinese, because other Chinese apparently did not regard them as such (Salmon, 1993: 283). In this regard, Reid (1996: 36–37) also points towards reports from the first Dutch traders, who mentioned meeting Javanese who said that 'they have their origin from the Chinese', a group of whom had fled China because of its oppressive demands for labour.

The Dutch authorities held the view that religious conversion did not change a person's origin. Chinese Muslims were first of all Chinese, but were also regarded as a particular group of Muslims. Hence they were placed under the supervision of the 'native' leaders (*Inlandsche hoofden*), but at the same time continued to be subjugated to all regulations applied to the Chinese. As the number of Chinese converting to Islam continued to grow, a separate administration of Chinese Muslims was established and Chinese Muslim captains, known as *Commandant der Paranakan-Chineezen*, were appointed (van Mastenbroek, 1934: 26). As such ethnic categories were constructed to administer intergroup relationships, the *Peranakan* Chinese population group was initially formed to separate Chinese Muslims both from other Chinese and from Javanese. They were prohibited from marrying non-Muslim Chinese and both Chinese population groups were prohibited by law from marrying outside of their own groups.[4] In 1901, the prohibition of interreligious marriage was abolished (Gautama, 1996: 6). By this time, however, the Chinese were classified as part of a newly formed group of 'foreign Orientals', which became formalised in 1920 when the Chinese were completely separated from the 'natives', so that the issue of inter-ethnic marriage was to return in a different form.

The marginalised position of Chinese Muslims became a disincentive for further Chinese conversion to Islam. In 1827, the office of *Commandant der Paranakan-Chineezen* was abolished and the term *Peranakan* Chinese lost its associations with Chinese Muslims. As the Chinese population group on Java consolidated, the term *Peranakan* was then used to refer to Chinese born on Java (Ong, 1991: 84–85). The Chinese population group was further consolidated by a government resolution requiring people:

> to notify the local authorities when there is some tendency by foreign Asians in Java as Malays, Buginese and Chinese to amalgamate with the native population. The government considers such tendencies inappropriate and has decided on the contrary to implement the old custom of forcing such foreigners to live in specific quarters or neighbourhoods under a chief of their own nationality so that they will be treated attentively and without any difference.
>
> (Staatsblad 1835 No. 37, as quoted in Phoa, 1992: 12)

This obligation was later confirmed in article 73 of the Constitution of 1854 and implemented in 1866 (Phoa, 1992: 12). Thus, until 1919, Chinese were obliged to live in their designated districts, which led to their concentration in the cities (Ong, 1943: 40).

Movement between districts was limited until 1914 by the so-called pass system (*passenstelsel*), requiring permits to travel for 'natives' and 'foreign Orientals' alike (Phoa, 1992: 12). The legacy of the district system (*wijkstelsel*), with designated quarters, can still be observed in the layout of the old cities of Jakarta, Semarang and Surabaya (Lohanda, 2002: 4, 19).

The term *Peranakan* Chinese further acquired 'racial' connotations during the later course of the nineteenth century. The rise of the scientific concepts of 'race' in Europe at that time introduced a new understanding of 'race' as a biological type of human being. All persons were seen as belonging to a certain 'race' or as a product of several 'races' (Miles and Brown, 1989: 39). These ideas were then brought to Java by the interim British administration (1811–16), and used to differentiate Chinese into migrants and descendants. Locally born Chinese were categorised as descendants of Chinese migrants. Because they were born of 'native' mothers, they were formally referred to by the British as *Peranakan* Chinese who were 'half-caste' (van Mastenbroek, 1934: 51). Some 80 per cent of Chinese on Java were born locally (Ong, 1943: 30), the majority of them being *Peranakan* in this racialised understanding of the term. Upon the restoration of the Dutch government, the Dutch authorities officially did not use the term *Peranakan*, which had been used for the Chinese Muslim population group, but referred to these 'half-castes' as *Indo* or *Babah* Chinese. As mentioned previously, the latter term was originally used for *Peranakan* Chinese males. After independence, the term acquired a derogative connotation in the context of so-called Ali Baba companies – that is, joint ventures in which Chinese collaborated with an Indonesian holder of import licences, who was initially defined during the 1950s as a member of *bangsa Indonesia asli* (the autochthonous Indonesian nation) (Mackie and Coppel, 1976: 13–14).

The ideas of 'race' and 'racial' characterisation of a group were also used to justify the distribution of economic roles. From the very beginning of the colonial period, the Chinese were given a role as middlemen between the Dutch authorities and the local population. They were perceived by early Dutch traders as the most suitable people to serve the Dutch trading interests, and described in contemporary Dutch sources as diligent, frugal and skilful in advancing their interests (Hoetink, 1917: 346–347). In addition, they were, in the view of the Dutch, ideal for the role assigned to them because they were a defenceless foreign community cut off from their protective networks at home (Ong, 1943: 240). Many tasks were contracted out to Chinese traders. This gradually changed the role of the *Peranakan* Chinese in the local economy. Prior to the arrival of the Dutch, they had been active in all spheres of the economy and in the administration of local rulers (Meilink-Roelofsz, 1962: 247) and, because their economic role was not limited to the role of middlemen, *Peranakan* Chinese traders also played an important role in Chinese international trade (Go, 1966: 36). When Dutch domination of the sea lanes eliminated international Chinese trade from the region, *Peranakan* Chinese traders became Dutch middlemen and played an important role in linking Dutch exporters and domestic producers, as well as Dutch industry and domestic consumers. In addition, Chinese were also leaseholders of the so-called *particuliere landerijen* ('private landholdings'), involving buying, selling and leasing of farmland, in which role they were ascribed the position of landlord (Phoa, 1992: 7–8, 10). When the government of the Netherlands East Indies, after the dissolution of the Dutch East India Company, introduced a system of forced cultivation (*cultuur-stelsel*), it initially employed *Peranakan* Chinese and Indo-European middlemen as contractors (Bosma and Raben, 2008: 105). Under this system, Javanese farmers had to reserve a part of their fields for the growth of export crops.

The system filled the state treasury of the Netherlands, but led to considerable hardship on Java (Ricklefs, 2001: 156–160). When the system was gradually abolished in the second half of the nineteenth century, the poverty on Java was blamed on the Chinese, and in the subsequent so-called ethical policy, measures were taken to protect the Javanese farmers from them, leading to further restrictions for the Chinese and changing the perception that the Javanese held of them.

With the establishment of the colonial state of the Netherlands East Indies in 1800, colonial regulation in the nineteenth century also laid the foundation of the ethnic stratification that still applies in today's Indonesia. The position of the Chinese during this century became particularly difficult and ambiguous when they were legally classified as 'natives', but subjugated to different foreign laws, such as the Dutch commercial laws and the *Ta Ching Lu Li*, the Code of China's Qing dynasty. Although the *Peranakan* after living on Java for centuries had developed their own customs (*adat istiadat*), the Dutch did not recognise those and emigration, in their view, did not change the essence of people; rather, they found it appropriate to order the Chinese community to regulate its family affairs according to the Qing Code. In fact, the customs of the *Peranakan* Chinese were considerably different from those that formed the basis for imperial legislation in China (Ong, 2005: 112). These differences were not acknowledged, however, and were attributed to a lack of knowledge of the *Peranakan* about their own customs. Appointed Chinese officers subsequently attempted to reconstruct these customs, leading to further alienation of the community. Towards the end of the colonial period, there were many diverse cultural and political orientations among the *Peranakan* (Suryadinata, 1981).

The legal construction of the population group of 'foreign Orientals'

As explained earlier in this this chapter, ethnic categorisation can also mean the imposition of external characterisations in which the categorised are formally defined by the categorisers from within their framework of meanings. It implies an unequal power relationship between categorised and categorisers, the latter being in the position of power and authority to impose their concepts on the former. This process is seen in many different administrative contexts, and often becomes an exploitative and control mechanism in the context of unequal power relationships, as in the case of the legal categorisation of ethnic groups in Indonesia. The Indonesian population was, and still is, classified into different legal categories of 'population groups' (*golongan rakyat*), constructed primarily on the basis of 'racial' and ethnic origin (Gautama and Hornick, 1983: 1). The 'population groups' (*bevolkingsgroepen* in Dutch) were originally constructed by the colonial Dutch government within the framework of colonial legal pluralism. The usage of ethnic categories for formal classification of the population was, however, common in colonial societies, because they were closely linked to the organisation of the workforce. Miles and Brown (1989: 96) refer to a process of ethnicisation that is both economic and cultural in character. The concept of 'ethnicisation' was originally introduced by Wallerstein (1983: 121–122), who argued that the division of population into various ethnic groupings in any given locality had been developed because of migration, leading to an ethnicisation of the world's workforce. Hence the markers of ethnic boundaries in countries such as Indonesia, whether skin colour, language or religion, are actually cultural constructs (Miles and Brown, 1989: 96) that are symbolising a hierarchy of ethnic groups and their power relationships. This process of ethnicisation has entailed a process of legal categorisation in which 'racial' and cultural characterisation has been used in the formation and reproduction of ethnically categorised groups as 'population groups'.

The process of formal ethnic categorisation is, in general, carried out by ethnic groups who are in a dominant position. Ashley Doane (1997: 376) has explained how dominant ethnic groups have used their position and identity strategically to shape the nature of inter-ethnic group relationships, because they have had a 'disproportionate ability to shape the sociocultural understanding of society, especially those involving group identities and intergroup interactions'. In Indonesia, the position of dominant ethnic group was held during the colonial period by the Dutch, an 'elite minority', as colonising power and law, and the politics of 'racial' and ethnic categorisation, were used to establish the boundaries between dominant and subjugated population groups.

In his book *De Historische Ontwikkeling van de Staatsrechtelijke Indeeling der Bevolking van Nederlandsch-Indië*, van Mastenbroek (1934) described how law was used to establish the mechanisms of dominant ethnicity, with segmentation of the population and the Dutch on top of a stratified colonial society. Within the 'native' population group, Indonesians were distinguished into different ethnic categories, indirectly administered via appointed ethnic leaders. This indirect administration had transformed the local society into a 'plural society', described by Furnivall (1948: 304, as quoted in Premdas, 2004: 222), speaking of Burma and Java, as follows:

> In Burma, as in Java, probably the first thing that strikes the visitors is the medley of peoples – European, Chinese, Indians, and native. It is, in the strictest sense, a medley, for they mix but do not combine. Each group holds to its own religion, its own culture and language, its own ideas and ways. As individuals they meet only at the market place, in buying and selling. There is a plural society, with different sections of community living side by side, but separately within the same unit. Even in the economic sphere there is separate division of labour along racial lines.

Once this legal and socio-economic structure had been established, it became difficult to overcome. In 1921, Tjoe Bou San commented in the *Sin Po* newspaper with regard to the Chinese community that:

> The lines of colonial politics that divide the peoples here in the Indies have already been made so thick that they are stronger than even the thickest walls of a fortress . . . This wall that divides the peoples here, evidently can no longer be destroyed by the mixing of living together for centuries.
>
> (Quoted in Gautama, 1996: 12, n. 25; translated by the authors)

Pluralism was commonly used by colonial authorities. What made the processes unusual in the case of Indonesia is the extent to which law was used by the Netherlands East Indies authorities for economic exploitation (Lev, 2000: 14). A precise legal configuration of pluralism had been developed for regulating intergroup relationships that granted privileges strategically to the Dutch as the dominant ethnic group (Ong, 1943: 238). Ashley Doane (1997: 376) defined 'dominant ethnic groups' as those ethnic groups in the society exercising 'power to create and maintain a pattern of economic, political, and institutional advantage, which in turn results in the unequal (disproportionately beneficial to the dominant group) distribution of resources'. This is also reflected in a saying from colonial times: 'The Javanese plows and sows.

The Chinese gathers it in. And the European walks away with it' (Rush, 1990: 20, quoting Fromberg in Chung Hwa Hui, 1926: 487).

Central to the colonial legal pluralism were the mechanisms of establishing the Dutch domination. The population groups of 'Europeans' (*Europeanen*), 'natives' (*Inlanders*) and 'foreign Orientals' (*Vreemde Oosterlingen*) were legally formed to establish a new ethnic stratification based on the hierarchy of 'race' and culture formulated by the colonial administrators, which was, in the words of Fasseur (1995: 140), 'the cornerstone of the colonial administration'. Because legal pluralism was designed to maintain 'Europeans' in the position of colonisers to whom disproportionate advantages were ascribed (van Doorn, 2013), it required a rather exclusive definition of who was included as 'European'. During the time of the administration by the Dutch East India Company, which ruled the colony for almost 200 years before the Dutch colonial state was established, the 'Europeans' included all people coming from Europe and their descendants born overseas. The status of such descendants, however, depended on recognition by their fathers, as well as skin colour and how much 'European blood' they were regarded as having (van Mastenbroek, 1934: 37).

On the dissolution of the bankrupt Dutch East India Company, the Dutch government took over the Company possessions in 1800. From 1847 onwards, a large number of laws, promulgated in the Netherlands in 1838, were transferred to the Netherlands East Indies, including a civil code, a commercial code and various procedural codes. Because most of the new laws initially applied to 'Europeans' only, it became necessary to formally establish who belonged to this group and who did not. Accordingly, the General Regulations for Legislation for the Netherlands East Indies (*Algemeene Bepalingen van Wetgeving voor Nederlandsch-Indië*) divided the population into 'Europeans and persons equalised with Europeans', on the one hand, and 'Natives and persons equalised with Natives', on the other.[5] Those equal with 'natives' were, according to article 8, 'Arabs, Moors, Chinese and all others, who are Muslims or heathen'.[6] Equated with the 'Europeans' were, according to article 7, all Christians, including those from the 'native population' and all other people not belonging to the groups described in article 8. Article 9 clarified that civil and commercial law applied only to Europeans and people equalised with them.

Article 10 of the General Regulations for the Legislation allowed the governor-general, however, to introduce at his discretion exceptional rules for Christian 'natives' in general, or for particular communities. This happened, in fact, when the new laws came into force in 1848 and the governor-general used his authority under article 10 to immediately reverse the position of article 7 to stipulate that 'native Christians' remained under their own laws after all, and therefore remained 'natives' in the emerging legal stratification of the colony.[7]

The year 1848 was also that of the bourgeois revolutions in several European countries. In the Netherlands, the increased revenues from the colonies had created a new middle class that was seeking economic liberalisation of the colony (Robison, 1986: 6; Ricklefs, 2001: 161). Under the revised Dutch Constitution, Parliament in the Netherlands gained influence in colonial affairs and a separate constitution had to be drafted for the Netherlands East Indies (Hall, 1981: 613). The *Regerings Reglement* enacted in 1854 came into force in 1855.[8] Article 109 of the Regerings Reglement confirmed the position reached earlier under the General Regulations for the Legislation, with the previous exception keeping native Christians under 'native' law now becoming the rule. Again, however, the governor-general could make exceptions from these categorisations by decree, now with approval from the Council of the Netherlands East Indies.

This time, however, the governor-general used this authority to declare European commercial law and much of the civil law (with exceptions mainly in family and inheritance law) applicable to that part of the 'foreign Asian' population which was equated with the 'native' population, with applicability initially on Java and Madura, but later extended to other parts of the colony (van Mastenbroek, 1934: 92). In this decree of 1855,[9] the term 'foreign Orientals' (*vreemde Oosterlingen*) is used to refer to such people.[10] The record of colonial regulation shows that the understanding of the term 'foreign Orientals' changed considerably over the period of Dutch rule. Much of this changed understanding has to do with the expansion of the territory under Dutch control and, later, with concepts of citizenship. In the early days of rule under the Dutch East India Company, 'foreign nations' included everyone outside the small colonial possession of the city of Batavia and its immediate surroundings, even Javanese and Sundanese from other places on Java. As late as 1766, the New Statutes of Batavia used the term 'foreign Orientals' to refer to 'Makassarese, Balinese . . . and others' and distinguished these people from 'Chinese and other Natives' (van Mastenbroek, 1934: 22–23). While Chinese were seen as 'native', because they were already there when the Dutch arrived in the early seventeenth century, the concept of other 'native' populations expanded with Dutch control over the archipelago. In the Decree of 1855, the 'foreign Orientals' still included all 'natives' of the Dutch East Indies archipelago who were outside their original territory and under the administration of local leaders of the native population, and who 'had not mixed with them' (Tjiook-Liem, 2009: 26). At the time, this would have included, for example, Balinese and Acehnese, because these parts of the archipelago were not yet under Dutch control.

Van Mastenbroek (1934: 62) has pointed out that an important difference between the General Regulations for Legislation and the Regerings Reglement was not only that the former was focused on private law, but that the classification system was also relevant for public law. The understanding of the 'foreign Orientals' changed once again in the twentieth century, after almost the entire archipelago was finally united under Dutch rule circa 1910 (Ricklefs, 2001: 189). While the 'native' population group now included the population of such newly acquired territories, people with origins elsewhere, such as the Chinese, Indians and Arabs, were now made to form the core of the 'foreign Oriental' group, which thus no longer included 'native' populations from elsewhere in the archipelago. These people were legally formed by the Dutch as an intermediate group (*bangsa tengah*), linking European producers and native consumers in the colonial economy (Lohanda, 2002: 26: Wertheim, 1955: 41). However, even this 'foreign Oriental' group became further differentiated in 1917, when the Chinese on Java and Madura, Sulawesi, and parts of Sumatra and Eastern Indonesia were made subject to almost the entire European civil and commercial law, with very few exceptions (van Mastenbroek, 1934: 93; Gautama and Hornick, 1983: 13). Non-Chinese 'foreign Orientals' and Chinese in other areas of the archipelago remained initially subject to European laws in the more limited way defined in the Regerings Reglement. Further decrees in 1924 extended the 1917 Decree to all of the Chinese population in the Netherlands East Indies and the application of the entire Dutch civil law to non-Chinese 'foreign Orientals', with the exceptions, however, of family and inheritance law (van Mastenbroek, 1934: 93; Gautama and Hornick, 1983: 13–14). This system was then formalised in the Indische Staatsregeling of 1925, which replaced the Regerings Reglement. The definition of 'foreign Oriental' that emerged from regulation 163 of the Indische Staatsregeling, was now negative, in the sense that it included all people *not* belonging to either of the other two categories of 'Europeans' and 'natives'.[11]

Thus, within a time frame of about 160 years, the concept of 'foreign Orientals' had changed from a reference to populations elsewhere in the archipelago, but outside Dutch possessions, to an international one focused on descent from populations elsewhere in Asia and outside the colonial state of the Netherlands East Indies. However, such population groups were not homogeneous. Each population group consisted of different ethnic groups that were again separated and stratified by the colonial government. For example, the 'foreign Oriental' group included Chinese, Indians and Arabs with different legal positions. The 'native' population group included all autochthonous ethnic groups originating from the Netherlands East Indies. The group of 'Europeans' in the late colonial period now included not only people of European descent, but also people from other countries that had 'modernised' their legal systems, such as the Japanese, who were specifically mentioned in regulation 163 of the Indische Staatsregeling as being under Dutch law. The ethnic division triggered within the 'foreign Oriental' and 'native' population groups, respectively, ethnic nationalist movements to improve their disadvantaged positions early in the twentieth century (van Doorn, 2013: 63–67).

The legal classification system was vertically differentiated between legal population groups, as well as horizontally between ethnically categorised groups within legal population groups. The foundation for boundaries between horizontally differentiated groups was laid during Dutch East India Company times. From the very beginning, the Dutch adopted a policy of segregation: they aimed to keep different 'racial' and 'ethnic' groups physically segregated. The 'native' population was subject to various legal restrictions, such as the policy requiring residence in ethnically segregated quarters (*wijkendwang*) and the system of travel permits (*passenstelsel*) to travel between different European-controlled territories. There was interference in particular in the relationship between Chinese and Javanese. While the Javanese were not allowed to mix with other Asian groups, a prohibition of marrying non-Christians initially applied to Europeans was extended to Chinese (independently of their religion) and to Christian 'natives' (van Mastenbroek, 1934: 27). Subsequently, the Chinese were prohibited from marrying outside their population group and, in a further decree, from marrying Muslims (Gautama, 1996: 27; van Mastenbroek, 1934: 31). The boundaries were further enforced by requiring from the various ethnic groups to use their own ethnic clothing and by punishing violations of this requirement (van Mastenbroek, 1934: 25; Gautama, 1996: 14–15). These restrictions created during the early colonial period continued into the twentieth century, with the system of travel permits abolished only in 1914 (van Mastenbroek, 1934: 104) and the requirements to wear ethnic clothing confirmed for the Chinese as late as 1905 (Gautama, 1997: 42).

These horizontal boundaries between ethnic groups were based on myriad decrees and were even more difficult to overcome than the vertical boundaries between legal population groups, for which the so-called *intergentiel recht* was used. This term, derived from the Latin *ius intergentes* and introduced by *adat* law scholar van Vollenhoven, ultimately prevailed over a number of other terms such as 'interlocal law' or 'intercolonial law'. Essentially referring to internal conflict-of-laws provisions, other commentators regarded it at the time as 'quasi-international private law', but the differences to international private law were emphasised by a younger generation of writers during the late colonial period and after independence (Gautama, 1993: 11–21). It was subsequently translated into Bahasa Indonesian as 'intergroup law' (*hukum antargolongan*).

The most important tools of the *intergentiel recht* were so-called equalisation, assimilation, voluntary submission and involuntary submission. 'Equalisation' could be effected in the form of a decree (*formeel-wettelijke gelijkstelling*) or by court decision. Equalisation by decree created so-called *Staatsblad* Europeans, *Staatsblad* being the word for the Netherlands East Indies Government Gazette. Gautama and Hornick (1983: 15) point out that equalisation required conversion to Christianity until 1894, whereas, in the late colonial period, the emphasis shifted to the legal needs of an applicant (Gautama, 1993: 104). Courts took into account such indicators as name, religion, lifestyle, marriage ceremonies and partners, as well as racial characteristics, such as shape of the face (Gautama, 1993: 105).

For the 'assimilation' of 'Europeans' or 'foreign Orientals', conversion to Islam was an important indicator (Gautama and Hornick, 1983: 16). Gautama's (1993: 107–109) survey of colonial jurisprudence, however, shows that conversion to Islam, while important, was not the only factor and was occasionally disregarded; with increasing application of Dutch law in the late nineteenth and twentieth centuries, 'native' Indonesians and 'foreign Orientals' could also voluntarily submit to European law or become subject to European law on the basis of legislation or case law. Submission could be complete or partial, in which latter case persons remained under their previous family and inheritance law. It could also be ad hoc for a single, exactly defined legal act, or presumptive, for example when a 'native' Indonesian participated in a legal transaction unknown in his or her *adat*, but covered by European law (Gautama and Hornick, 1983: 16–21).

The legal pluralism of the colonial administration and the dualism in the court system – in which a *Raad van Justitie* ('Council of Justice') applied European procedural rules for those under European law and a *Landraad* presided over cases of the non-Europeans, applying the simplified rules of a procedural code for the 'native' population (Mertokusumo, 2002: 7; Setiawan, 1992: 360; Lev, 2000: 6) – had important implications for the legal and economic position of those classified under the system. The classification determined the quality of justice to which one was subject, and access to positions and economic opportunities and to a commercial law that was a precondition for modern trade and business life. Hence the legal system provided crucial mechanisms of dominant ethnicity in which the European population group received disproportionate advantages. Gautama (1997: 42), quoting Wertheim, points to better criminal law jurisprudence, better rules related to investigations, greater guarantees of personal freedom, better labour law, and a better position in and vis-à-vis the defence force. While Dutch commercial law applied to 'foreign Orientals', it did not automatically apply to 'native' Indonesians, who were therefore subject to their customary law and mostly excluded from the crucial tools of modern commerce. In 1870, the colonial government introduced the prohibition for 'native' Indonesians to sell their land (*vervreemdingsverbood*), which was, in particular, meant to exclude the Chinese from acquiring land, in order to discourage further migration (van Doorn, 2013: 26; Ong, 1943: 64). Further, salaries for teachers, civil servants, army personnel and hospital personnel, as well as their pensions, depended on the question of whether they were European or not (Gautama, 1997: 72). Van Doorn (2013: 48–49) reports that, in the 1930s, 92 per cent of higher positions in government were held by Europeans, who represented only 1 per cent at the lower end of the spectrum; 'native' Indonesians occupied only 6.4 per cent of the higher-ranking positions, but 98.9 per cent of the lower. Thus Dutch policies had established a social stratification, with the Europeans at the top of the social ladder, and the 'foreign Orientals' and 'Natives' as subjugated people with different economic roles.

The classification of the population further created first- and second-class forms of citizenship for people born in the colony and had implications in public law. The legal status of 'European', for civil law purposes, had never been synonymous with being 'Dutch'

(Fasseur, 1995). As discussed earlier, the European population group included all people of European descent. Towards the end of the colonial period, it also included Asians from countries that had 'modernised' their legal systems, so that they were largely in accordance with Dutch law. However, from the middle of the nineteenth century, a distinction was made between 'Netherlanders' and 'foreigners'. The Dutch Citizenship Law of 1850 led to a distinction between 'public law Netherlander' status (*staatsrechtelijk Nederlanderschap*) and 'private law Netherlander' status. While Dutch born in the Netherlands were awarded *staatsrechtelijk* status, with all of the political rights that this entailed, people born in the Netherlands East Indies were only 'Dutch' in the sense of the civil law and with regard to diplomatic representation outside the country, but without political rights (Gautama, 1997: 22–25; Tjiook-Liem, 2009: 433–434). In 1892, a new Dutch Citizenship Law adopted the principle of *ius sanguinis* ('right of blood'), focusing on descent, for Dutch born in the Netherlands. After further regulation in 1910 in the Law on the Regulation of Dutch Subject Status for non-Netherlanders, adopting *ius soli* ('right of the soil') and focusing on the place of birth,[12] 'foreign Orientals' and 'natives' born in the colony were Dutch 'subjects' (*onderdanen*), but could no longer refer to themselves as 'Netherlander' (Supomo, 1997: 13–17).

Peranakan Chinese, on the one hand, fell within this second-class citizenship, while at the same time, for civil law purposes, they were treated as 'foreign Orientals' and therefore as Chinese migrants (Gautama, 1997: 28). They were made foreigners at home and subject to the forms of discrimination summarised by Ong Eng Die (1943: 240) as follows:

- they came under the infamous *passen en wijkstelsel*, restricting movement and living quarters until 1914 and 1919, respectively;
- until 1914, they were affected by the *politierol*, which gave administrators quasi-judicial and large discretionary powers over them;
- they paid taxes in excess of those that Europeans were paying;
- there was no government commitment to educating Chinese children; and
- access to government positions was totally denied to them.

This last was a further factor in consolidating the *Peranakan* Chinese community as a 'trading minority'. The lack of legal protection spurred the *Peranakan* Chinese to organise themselves to improve their situation in what became known as the 'Chinese emancipation movement' (Ong, 1943: 246). This movement seeking legal protection later made the Chinese appear to be seeking equalisation with Europeans for their entire population group in the eyes of the nationalist Indonesian independence movement. Ong Eng Die (1943: 243) has pointed out, however, that the members of the Chinese emancipation movement were opposed to the discrimination that they experienced vis-à-vis the Europeans, but from the very beginning never sought to avoid assimilation with Indonesians.

The legal position of *Peranakan* Chinese became even more ambiguous after a new citizenship law in China in 1909 was extended to all Chinese living overseas, including the descendants of earlier Chinese migrants who had left China generations ago (Tjiook-Liem, 2009: 425). The Dutch Law on the Status of Subjects of 1910 had the effect of now also legally splitting the Chinese community into *Peranakan* long-term residents and *Totok* newcomers, with the former being Dutch subjects and the latter newly arrived migrants being Chinese citizens, even though their Indies-born children became Dutch subjects. A diplomatic agreement in 1911 declared that the Dutch Law would determine whether

Chinese in the Indies were subjects of one or the other nation (Ong, 1943: 245). Both the Dutch colonial authorities, as well as the Chinese consulates, now started to register 'their' respective Chinese (Lohanda, 2002). A new law, introduced in 1917 for Java (Staatsblad No. 130), made civil registration, previously reserved for Europeans, compulsory for *Peranakan* Chinese (Ong, 1943: 44). Chinese claims on the basis of *ius sanguinis* were reasserted in another Citizenship Law of China in 1929 (Gautama, 1997: 11).

While Dutch claims to *Peranakan* 'subjects' had thereby prevailed, the segregation within the colony was further institutionalised in regulation 163 of the Indische Staatsregeling of 1926, the revised quasi-constitution of the Netherlands East Indies. The regulation now clearly separated the 'foreign Orientals' from the 'natives' and institutionalised this separate group, which, in practical terms and in civil law, had already been treated differently for many decades since the mid-eighteenth century. Here, in their economic roles and in contrast to the 'natives', although the *Peranakan* and *Totok* were distinguished as far as their subject status was concerned, they were nevertheless all 'foreign Orientals' and the locally born *Peranakan* had therefore become permanently migrants. Community representatives realised the discrepancy between the lack of protection granted to them as opposed to that available to other Dutch subjects, such as Indies-born Europeans, or migrants from other Asian nations, such as Japan or Thailand.

The legacy of the colonial construction of ethnicity

Perhaps surprisingly, in view of the strongly discriminative character of the colonial ethnic classification system, it not only survived the transition to independence, but also proved to leave a continuing legacy that still influences the interaction between ethnic groups and their economic and social status in Indonesia today (Lindsey, 2005: 44–45). When Indonesia's first president, Sukarno, declared independence in 1945, discriminative provisions were to be found in many different laws and decrees. For many years, introductory textbooks on Indonesian law would explain the different legal positions for 'Europeans', 'foreign Orientals' and 'Indonesians' in separate sections (for example Utrecht and Djindang, 1983). Indonesia's turbulent years of struggle for independence against the returning Dutch from 1945–49, and subsequently local rebellions in parts of Java and on the outer islands, left no time for a systematic revision of the Dutch-derived legal system. Article II of the transitional provisions of the Constitution of 1945 left all colonial law in force as long as it was not in conflict with the Constitution. Some provisions of the Civil Code were declared invalid on this basis in the early 1960s (Gautama and Hornick, 1983: 184–187). For the majority of the colonial laws, however, invalidation required a court decision in a specific case questioning the constitutionality of a discriminatory law (Gautama and Hornick, 1983: 187–189). In a politicised legal system from the late Sukarno period and throughout the long reign of Indonesia's second president, Suharto, for more than three decades, the courts generally did not have a good reputation (Pompe, 2005), and few people held out much hope for legal change via the judiciary. Suharto's military-backed government collaborated with a number of Chinese tycoons, but held the majority of the Chinese community at ransom by directing public frustration at the Chinese, who every now and then became the target of riots and outbreaks of violence (Coppel, 1983; Purdey, 2006).

More serious efforts at reforming the Indonesian legal system started only after the downfall of Suharto in 1998. Democratically elected governments initiated reviews of problematic parts of the system. The Constitution was revised three times and the amended version introduced new elements, such as a more decentralised structure with greater power for regional governments and a new chapter on human rights. Indonesia ratified the 1969 UN International Convention of the Elimination of All Forms of Racial Discrimination (ICERD) in 1999. A year earlier, Suharto's successor Habibie had issued a decree on the revocation of the terms *pribumi* and *non-pribumi* in an administrative context.[13] The terms had been used for many years to distinguish between 'indigenous' Indonesians (*pribumi*, meaning 'sons of the soil') and those of foreign descent. He also issued a presidential instruction[14] to implement another presidential decree from the Suharto period, abolishing the requirement for ethnic Chinese to hold certificates of Indonesian citizenship.[15] Ethnic and racial discrimination now also came to be regarded as a violation of human rights under a new Law No. 39 of 1999 on Human Rights.

Habibie's successor Abdurrahman Wahid followed with a further presidential decree revoking a presidential instruction from 1967 that prohibited all expressions of Chinese culture and identity in public. Such strongly discriminatory measures had been introduced in the aftermath of the events of 1965 when the army, after an alleged coup attempt by left-leaning officers, had purged members of the Indonesian Communist Party (*Partai Komunis Indonesia*, or PKI) and what they regarded as their sympathisers. Because of allegations of backing for the coup attempt from Communist China, many ethnic Chinese became victims of the ensuing violence. The colonial understanding of the Dutch saying '*Eens een Chinees, blijft een Chinees*' ('Once a Chinese, remains a Chinese') (Ong, 2005: 176; Coppel, 1983: 8–9) is clearly visible in the presidential instruction of 1967.[16] Its preamble stated that:

> [T]he Chinese religion, belief and customs in Indonesia which concentrate on the land of their ancestors and in their manifestation can cause psychological, mental and moral influence, which is not proper for Indonesian citizens and becomes a hindrance for the assimilation process and needs to be regulated as well as its function placed into proper proportion.[17]

Among other things, the presidential instruction authorised the Minister of Religion to categorise Chinese religion, beliefs and customs after consulting with the Attorney-General. The involvement of the Attorney-General's office shows that these elements of Chinese culture were regarded as potentially dangerous, disruptive and subversive.

Following Abdurrahman Wahid's decree, expressions of Chinese identity were further recognised in 2002, when President Megawati Sukarnoputri declared Chinese New Year to be a national holiday.[18] Yet the perception of the unchangeable Chinese is deeply rooted (Sochmawardiah, 2013: 121–124): as late as 2008, the Mayor of Pontianak in Kalimantan issued a decree prohibiting the performance of the Chinese dragon dance in public (*Antara News*, 2008). It has also proven difficult for Chinese in some areas to register Confucianism as a religion and to include this information on their identity cards (Effendy, 2004).

In 2006, the administration of President Yudhoyono introduced a new Citizenship Law[19] that finally gives a non-discriminative definition of *Warga Negara Indonesia* ('Indonesian citizen'), a term that had previously often been used to distinguish ethnic Chinese from *orang Indonesia asli* ('indigenous Indonesians'). While the new Citizenship Law continues to use the term *bangsa Indonesia asli* ('indigenous Indonesian people'),[20] it is now used in contrast to 'naturalised citizen' and described in an explanatory memorandum of the government as referring to people who have been citizens of Indonesia since birth and who never acquired a different citizenship of their own free will. Also in 2006, a new Law on the Administration of the Population was introduced to regulate such issues as the registration of citizens and foreigners.[21] Section 106 of the Law abolished several colonial decrees on civil registration for Europeans, Indonesians and Indonesian Christians, as well as sections of the first book of the Civil Code and a law from 1961 on family name changes. Oddly, however, in the case of the Chinese, what was abolished was a regulation related to the application of commercial law, rather than the one related to civil registry.[22] A Cabinet instruction in 1966 had instructed the Civil Registry to disregard the colonial classification of the population based on regulations 131 and 163 of the Indische Staatsregeling, and instead to distinguish simply between Indonesian citizens and foreigners. As mentioned above, the Chinese had subsequently been required to prove their citizenship via a certificate of Indonesian citizenship, which was actually meant for foreign-born Chinese migrants holding Indonesian citizenship, but came to be applied to the locally born *Peranakan* as well, although they actually held Indonesian citizenship by birth. As Winarta (2008: 65, 69, 71) and Lindsey (2005: 52–53) point out, President Habibie's instruction of 1999 to abolish the certificate of Indonesian citizenship was, in some cases, ignored.

Yudhoyono also revoked by presidential decree[23] a Cabinet circular from 1967[24] that had prescribed the term *Cina* for ethnic Chinese, instead of the term *Tionghoa* that Chinese used to refer to themselves. Not only did the circular purport to address what was called the 'Chinese problem' (*Masalah Cina*), but it also spoke of the negative 'psychopolitical associations' (*assosiasi-psikopolitis*) for the Indonesian population of the older term. The circular had further stressed that the term *Cina* was better suited, because it reflected 'the dynasty from which the Chinese race had come'.[25] Pointing to the changes in the Indonesian legal landscape, including the revised Indonesian Constitution with its chapter on human rights, as well as to the importance of the bilateral relationship with China, Yudhoyono's decree acknowledged the discriminative impact on Indonesian citizens of Chinese descent of the Suharto-era Cabinet circular, which in fact upheld a colonial legacy of racially based restrictions (Sochmawardiah, 2013: 122–124).

Importantly, in 2008, the Yudhoyono government promulgated Law No. 40 on the Elimination of Racial and Ethnic Discrimination.[26] Although this Law is an important step forward, concerns remain. Rather than questioning the racial and ethnic distinctions introduced by colonialism, the ideas of 'race' and ethnic classification remain deeply rooted in Indonesian society. This is visible in the way in which the Law defines 'race' as 'a group of the population on the basis of physical traits and principles of descent' and 'ethnic' as the 'classifying of human beings on the basis of belief, values, practices, customs and traditions, norms, language, history, geography and family relationships' (section 1(2) and (3)). This raises the concern that social issues are seen as related to ethnicity, and therefore continue to be understood as problems of different descent (*keturunan*), 'race' and 'nation' (Gautama, 1997: 33).

Rather than requiring the systematic elimination of all discriminatory provisions in all currently valid laws[27] and making it abundantly clear that the colonial classification system derived from the Indische Staatsregeling is no longer applicable, section 22 of Law No. 40 of 2008 instead declares all laws and regulations with regard to race and ethnicity to be valid as long as they are not in conflict with the 2008 Law. This ultimately makes the invalidation of discriminating laws a matter for the courts – an approach that faces the same problems as the invalidation of provisions in conflict with the Constitution that was discussed earlier (Lindsey, 2005: 63–65).

Conclusion

The history of the formation of the Chinese population group in Indonesia confirms that 'race' is a construct and that racial differentiation has been strategically used by colonial governments for the distribution of economic opportunities, as pointed out by Immanuel Wallerstein (1983) and Eric Wolf (1982), among others. Under the 'divide and rule' policies of colonial powers, trading middlemen were strategically chosen from among the population, built up and segregated from the rest (Wertheim, 1959). The Chinese in the Netherlands East Indies were denied access to political office and stripped of the ability to own land or to work in the agricultural sector of the economy (Go, 1966; Ong, 1943). These policies continued after independence, complicated further by citizenship questions and the primordial idea of an ethnic group. Because of this concept of primordial identity, social problems are often perceived as related to ethnicity, while problems related to inter-ethnic group relationships are seen as problems of descent (*keturunan*) and of racial differences (Gautama, 1997: 33).

Indonesia is just one example of such colonial ethnic policies that have had consequences long after the colonial power has left.[28] In that sense, it seems important for the governments of independent states to realise that such discriminatory policies ultimately serve only to continue colonial economic schemes that disadvantage the majority, as well as the minorities, in a country. Indonesia is finally taking steps to remedy this matter. Important discriminatory decrees have been gradually abolished since the end of the Suharto administration and the subsequent *reformasi* ('reformation') period. Nevertheless, as long as all remnants of the classification system established by the provisions of the colonial Indische Staatsregeling are not clearly abolished, its discriminative effects will remain. Even colonial Dutch lawyers such as Fromberg seemed to understand the recognition of the Chinese at the time that the classification was not primarily meant to categorise the population, but to put them into a position of disadvantage vis-à-vis foreign Asians such as the Japanese and vis-à-vis the 'Europeans' as the dominant race (quoted in Chung Hwa Hui, 1926: 813).[29] In the context of an exploitative colony such as the Netherlands East Indies, such classification policies were hardly surprising. Their continuing relevance in an independent country such as Indonesia, however, is hard to understand. As former Prime Minister of Sweden Olof Palme pointed out of the apartheid system of South Africa, such a system cannot be reformed; it can only be abolished (Tambo, 1988).

Notes

1 Eric Kaufmann (2004: 3) uses the term 'dominant ethnicity' to refer to 'the phenomenon whereby *a particular ethnic group exercises dominance within a nation and/or state*' (emphasis original).

2 *Mardijkers* were emigrants from Malabar, Coromandel, Arakan or Bengal in India, who spoke Portuguese and were baptised members of the Dutch Reformed Church. The term was a Dutch rendition of the Portuguese term *mardekar*, which in turn was based on the Sanskrit term *mahardikka*, meaning 'great man' (Lach and Van Kley, 1993: 1317, fn. 100).

3 *Paranakan* is an old Dutch spelling of *Peranakan*.

4 By Resolution of 26 January 1717, '*De Chineezen werden bij een biljet g'interdiceert buyten haare Natie te trouwen*', and by Resolution of 25 July 1766, '*Geen Chineesche of Mohammedaansche mans of vrouwen zullen zig buiten hare natie in den egt begeeven*' (both quoted in Gautama, 1996: 27). See also van Mastenbroek (1934: 31).

5 Algemeene Bepalingen van Wetgeving voor Nederlandsch-Indië, Staatsblad van Nederlandsch-Indië 1847 No. 23, art. 6: '*De ingezetenen van Nederlandsch-Indië zijn onderscheiden in Europeanen en daarmede gelijkgestelde personen, en Inlanders en met deze gelijkgestelde personen.*'
6 '. . . *Arabieren, Mooren, Chinezen, en alle anderen, die Mahomedanen of Heidenen zijn.*'
7 Bepalingen omtrent de invoering van en den overgang tot de nieuwe wetgeving, Staatsblad van Nederlandsch-Indië 1848 No. 10, art. 3.
8 Reglement op het beleid der regering van Nederlandsch-Indië, Staatsblad van Nederlandsch-Indië 1855 No. 2.
9 Staatsblad van Nederlandsch-Indië 1855 No. 79.
10 The term appears also in art. 73 of the Regerings Reglement.
11 Article 163(4): '. . . *allen, die nit vallen in de termen van het tweede of van het derde lid . . .*'
12 Staatsblad 1910 No. 296; see Gautama (1997: 10).
13 Instruksi Presiden Republik Indonesia Nomor 26 tahun 1998 Tentang Meghentikan Penggunaan Istilah Pribumi dan Non Pribumi dalam semua Perumusan dan Penyelenggaraan Kebijakan, Perencanaan Program, Ataupun Pelaksanaan Kegiatan Penyelenggaraan Permintahan.
14 Instruksi Presiden Republik Indonesia Nomor 4 tahun 1999 Tentang Melaksanakan Ketentuan Keputusan Presiden Nomor 56 Tahun 1996 Tentang Bukti Kewarganegaraan Republik Indonesia dan Instruksi Presiden Nomor 26 Tahun 1998.
15 *Surat Bukti Kewarganegaraan Republik Indonesia*; see Winarta (2008: 65).
16 Instruksi Presiden Republik Indonesia Nomor 14 Tahun 1967 Tentang Agama Kepercayaan dan Adat Istiadat Cina.
17 Translated by the authors.
18 Keputusan Presiden No. 19 Tahun 2002 tentang hari Tahun Baru Imlek.
19 Undang-Undang Republik Indonesia Nomor 12 Tahun 2006 tentang Kewarganegaraan Republik Indonesia.
20 See the definition of 'Indonesian citizen' in s. 2 of the Law.
21 Undang-Undang Republik Indonesia Nomor 23 Tahun 2006 Tentang Administrasi Kependudukan.
22 Staatsblad No. 130 of 1917; see Winarta (2008: 58, 65).
23 Keputusan Presiden Republik Indonesia Nomor 12 Tahun 2014 Tentang Pencabutan Surat Edaran Presidium Kabinet Ampera Nomor SE-06/Pres.Kab/6/1967 Tanggal 28 Juni 1967.
24 Surat Edaran Presidium Kabinet Ampera No. SE-06/Pres.Kab/6/1967 Tentang Masalah Cina
25 Surat Edaran No. SE-06/Pres.Kab/6/1967, art. 2.
26 Undang-Undang Republik Indonesia Nomor 40 Tahun 2008 Tentang Penghapusan Diskriminasi Ras dan Etnis.
27 Winarta (2008: 62) explains that, under Suharto's 'New Order' government, at least sixty-four discriminating regulations against ethnic Chinese were still enforced or newly issued.
28 For other examples, see, e.g., Bethencourt (2013: chs 12 and 13); Premdas (2004); Antons (2001).
29 See also Ong (1943: 238).

References

Antara News (2008) 'Warga Tionghoa Tuding SK Walikota Pontianak Diskriminatif', 12 February, available online at http://www.antaranews.com/berita/93304/warga-tionghoa-tuding-sk-walikota-pontianak-diskriminatif [accessed 23 March 2016].

Antons, C. (2001) 'Ethnicity, Law and Development in Southeast Asia', in F. Hüsken and D. van der Meij (eds) *Reading Asia: New Research in Asian Studies*, London: Curzon Press, 3–28.

Banks, M. (1996) *Ethnicity: Anthropological Constructions*, London/New York: Routledge.

Bethencourt, F. (2013) *Racisms: From the Crusades to the Twentieth Century*, Princeton, NJ/Oxford: Princeton University Press.

Bosma, U., and Raben, R. (2008) *Being 'Dutch' in the Indies: A History of Creolisation and Empire, 1500–1920*, Singapore: NUS Press.

Chung Hwa Hui (ed.) (1926) *Mr P. H. Fromberg's Verspreide Geschriften*, Leiden: Leidse Uitgeversmaatschappij.

Coppel, C. A. (1983) *Indonesian Chinese in Crisis*, Kuala Lumpur/Oxford/New York/Melbourne: Oxford University Press.

Cornell, S. and Hartmann, D. (2007) *Ethnicity and Race: Making Identities in a Changing World*, 2nd edn, Thousand Oaks, CA/London/New Delhi: Pine Forge Press.

Dikötter, F. (1990) 'Group Definition and the Idea of "Race" in Modern China (1793–1949)', *Ethnic and Racial Studies*, 13(3): 420–432.

Doane, A. W. (1997) 'Dominant Group Ethnic Identity in the United States: The Role of "Hidden" Ethnicity in Intergroup Relations', *Sociological Quarterly*, 38(3): 375–397.

Effendy, W. (2004) 'Pembaharuan Hukum Catatan Sipil dan Penghapusan Diskriminasi di Indonesia', *Hukum Online*, 28 June, available online at http://www.hukumonline.com/berita/baca/hol10607/pembaharuan-hukum-catatan-sipil-dan-penghapusan-diskriminasi-di-indonesia [accessed 23 March 2016].

Eller, J. D., and Coughlan, R. M. (1993) 'The Poverty of Primordialism: The Demystification of Ethnic Attachments', *Ethnic and Racial Studies*, 16(2): 183–202.

Fasseur, C. (1995) *De weg naar het paradijs en andere Indische geschiedenissen*, Amsterdam: Uitgeverij Bert Bakker.

Furnivall, J. S. (1948) *Colonial Policy and Practice*, Cambridge: Cambridge University Press.

Gautama, S. (1993) *Hukum Antargolongan: Suatu Pengantar*, Jakarta: PT. Ichtiar Baru Van Hoeve.

Gautama, S. (1996) *Segi-Segi Hukum Peraturan Perkawinan Campuran (Staatsblad 1898 No. 158)*, Bandung: Penerbit PT. Citra Aditya Bakti.

Gautama, S. (1997) *Warga Negara dan Orang Asing: Berikut Peraturan-Peraturan dan Contoh-Contoh*, Bandung: Penerbit Alumni.

Gautama, S., and Hornick, R. N. (1983) *An Introduction to Indonesian Law: Unity in Diversity*, rev'd edn, Bandung: Penerbit Alumni.

Geertz, C. (ed.) (1963a) *Old Societies and New States*, New York: Free Press.

Geertz, C. (1963b) 'The Integrative Revolution', in C. Geertz (ed.) *Old Societies and New States*, New York: Free Press, 108–113; reprinted in J. Hutchinson and A. D. Smith (eds) (1996) *Ethnicity*, Oxford/New York: Oxford University Press, 40–45.

Giddens, A. (1991) *Modernity and Self-identity: Self and Society in the Late Modern Age*, Cambridge: Polity Press.

Glazer, N., and Moynihan, D. P. (1975) 'Introduction', in N. Glazer and D. P. Moynihan (eds) *Ethnicity: Theory and Experience*, Cambridge, MA/London: Harvard University Press, 1–26.

Go, G. T. (1966) *Eenheid in verscheidenheid in een Indonesisch dorp*, Amsterdam: University of Amsterdam.

Hall, D. G. E. (1981) *A History of South-east Asia*, 4th edn, Basingstoke: Macmillan.

Hoetink, B. (1917) 'So Bing Kong: Het Eerste Hoofd der Chineezen te Batavia (1619–1636)', *Bijdragen tot de Taal-, Land- en Volkenkunde van Nederlandsch-Indië*, 's-Gravenhage: M. Nijhoff, 344–417.

Hutchinson, J., and Smith, A. D. (1996) *Ethnicity*, Oxford/New York: Oxford University Press.

Isaacs, H. R. (1975) 'Basic Group Identity: The Idols of the Tribe', in N. Glazer and D. P. Moynihan (eds) *Ethnicity: Theory and Experience*, Cambridge, MA/London: Harvard University Press, 29–52.

Jakarta Post (2014) 'PDI-P Reports Jokowi's Fake Obituary to Police', *Jakarta Post*, 17 May.

Jenkins, R. (1994) 'Rethinking Ethnicity: Identity, Categorization and Power', *Ethnic and Racial Studies*, 17(2): 197–223.

Jenkins, R. (2008) *Rethinking Ethnicity*, London/Thousand Oaks, CA/New Delhi/Singapore: Sage.

Kaufmann, E. P. (2004) 'Introduction: Dominant Ethnicity – From Background to Foreground', in E. P. Kaufmann (ed.) *Rethinking Ethnicity: Majority Groups and Dominant Minorities*, London/New York: Routledge, 1–14.

Kwee, T. H. (1969) *The Origins of the Modern Chinese Movement in Indonesia*, Ithaca, NY: Cornell Southeast Asia Program.

Kwok, Y. (2014) 'Indonesia Reaches Racial Milestone with Chinese Governor of Jakarta', *Time*, 19 November.

Lach, D. F., and Van Kley, E. J. (1993) *Asia in the Making of Europe, Vol. III: A Century of Advance*, Chicago, IL/London: University of Chicago Press.

Lev, D. S. (2000) *Legal Evolution and Political Authority in Indonesia: Selected Essays*, The Hague: Kluwer Law International.

Lindsey, T. (2005) 'Reconstituting the Ethnic Chinese in Post-Soeharto Indonesia: Law, Racial Discrimination, and Reform', in T. Lindsey and H. Pausacker (eds) *Chinese Indonesians: Remembering, Distorting, Forgetting*, Singapore: Institute of Southeast Asian Studies, 41–65.

Lohanda, M. (2002) *Growing Pains: The Chinese and the Dutch in Colonial Java, 1890–1942*, Jakarta: Yayasan Cipta Loka Caraka.

Mackie, J. A. C., and Coppel, C. A. (1976) 'A Preliminary Survey', in J. A. C. Mackie (ed.) *The Chinese in Indonesia*, Honolulu: University Press of Hawai'i, 1–18.

Meilink-Roelofsz, M. A. P. (1962) *Asian Trade and European Influence in the Indonesian Archipelago between 1500 and About 1630*, The Hague: Martinus Nijhoff.

Mertokusumo, S. (2002) *Hukum Acara Perdata Indonesia*, Yogyakarta: Penerbit Liberty.

Miles, R., and Brown, M. (1989) *Racism*, 2nd edn, London/New York: Routledge.

Nagel, J. (1994) 'Constructing Ethnicity: Creating and Recreating Ethnic Identity and Culture', *Social Problems*, 41(1): 152–176.

Ong, E. D. (1943) *Chineezen in Nederlandsh-Indie: Sociografie van een Indonesische Bevolkingsgroep*, Assen: Van Gorcum & Comp.

Ong, H. H. (1991) 'Kapitalisme Cina Di Hindia-Belanda', in Y. Kunio (ed.) *Konglomerat Oei Tiong Ham: Kerajaan Bisnis Pertama di Asia Tenggara*, Jakarta, Grafiti, 80–116.

Ong, H. H. (1995) 'Beberapa Aspek Agama Cina', in A. Wahid (ed.) *Pergulatan Mencari Jati Diri*, Yogyakarta, Interfidei, 141–153.

Ong, H. H. (2005) *Riwayat Tionghoa Peranakan di Jawa*, Depok: Komunitas Bambu.

Phoa, L. G. (1992) 'The Changing Economic Position of the Chinese in Netherlands India', in M. R. Fernando and D. Bulbeck (eds) *Chinese Economic Activity in Netherlands India: Selected Translations from the Dutch*, Singapore: Institute of Southeast Asian Studies, 5–18.

Pompe, S. (2005) *The Indonesian Supreme Court: A Study of Institutional Collapse*, Ithaca, NY: Cornell Southeast Asia Program.

Premdas, R. R. (2004) 'The Dynamics of Ethnic Minority Domination in Fiji', in E. P. Kaufmann (ed.) *Rethinking Ethnicity: Majority Groups and Dominant Minorities*, London/New York: Routledge, 221–241.

Purdey, J. (2006) *Anti-Chinese Violence in Indonesia, 1996–1999*, Singapore: Singapore University Press.

Reid, A. (1996) 'Flows and Seepages in the Long-term Chinese Interaction with Southeast Asia', in A. Reid (ed.) *Sojourners and Settlers: Histories of Southeast Asia and the Chinese*, St Leonards: Allen & Unwin, 15–49.

Reuters (2014) 'Non-Muslim Sworn in as Jakarta Governor', 19 November.

Ricklefs, M. C. (2001) *A History of Modern Indonesia since c. 1200*, 3rd edn, Stanford, CA: Stanford University Press.

Robison, R. (1986) *Indonesia: The Rise of Capital*, North Sydney: Allen & Unwin.

Rush, J. R. (1990) *Opium to Java: Revenue Farming and Chinese Enterprise in Colonial Indonesia, 1860–1910*, Ithaca, NY/London: Cornell University Press.

Salmon, C. (1993) 'Cults Peculiar to the Chinese of Java', in Cheu Hock Tong (ed.) *Chinese Beliefs and Practices in Southeast Asia*, Petaling Jaya: Pelanduk, 279–305.

Setiawan (1992) *Aneka Masalah Hukum dan Hukum Acara Perdata*, Bandung: Penerbit Alumni.

Sochmawardiah, H. A. (2013) *Diskriminasi Rasial dalam Hukum HAM: Studi Tentang Diskriminasi Terhadap Etnis Tionghoa*, Yogyakarta: Genta.

Supomo, R. (1997) *Sistem Hukum di Indonesia*, 15th edn, Jakarta: PT Pradnya Paramita.

Suryadinata, L. (1981) *Pernakan Chinese Politics in Java 1917–1942*, Singapore: Singapore University Press.

Tambo, O. (1988) 'Olof Palme and the Liberation of Southern Africa', 1 March, available online at http://www.anc.org.za/content/olof-palme-and-liberation-southern-africa-oliver-tambo [accessed 27 March 2016].

Tan, M. G. (1995) 'The Ethnic Chinese in Indonesia: Issues and Implications', in L. Suryadinata (ed.) *Southeast Asian Chinese: The Socio-cultural Dimension*, Singapore: Times Academic Press, 13–27.

The, S. G. (1993) 'Islam and Chinese Assimilation in Indonesia and Malaysia', in H. T. Cheu (ed.) *Chinese Beliefs and Practices in Southeast Asia*, Selangor Darul Ehsan: Pelanduk, 59–100.

Tjiook-Liem, P. (2009) *De rechtspositie der Chinezen in Nederlands-Indië 1848–1942*, Leiden: Leiden University Press.

Utrecht, E., and Djindang, M. S. (1983) *Pengantar Dalam Hukum Indonesia*, 10th edn, Jakarta: Penerbit Sinar Harapan.

Van Doorn, J. A. A. (2013) *De laatste eeuw van Indië*, Zutphen: Walburg Pers.

Van Mastenbroek, W. E. (1934) *De Historische Ontwikkeling van de Staatsrechtelijke Indeeling der Bevolking van Nederlandsch-Indië*, Wageningen: H. Veenman & Zonen.

Wahid, A. (1991) 'Beri Jalan Orang Cina', in H. J. Jahja (ed.) *Nonpri di Mata Pribumi*, Jakarta: Yayasan Tunas Bangsa, 224–228.

Wallerstein, I. (1983) *Historical Capitalism with Capitalist Civilisation*, London/New York: Verso.

Wang, G. (1988)'The Study of Chinese Identities in Southeast Asia', in J. W. Cushman and Wang Gungwu (eds) *Changing Identities of the Southeast Asian Chinese since World War II*, Hong Kong: Hong Kong University Press, 1–21.

Weber, M. (1997) 'What Is an Ethnic Group?', in M. Guibernau and J. Rex (eds) *The Ethnicity Reader: Nationalism, Multiculturalism and Migration*, Cambridge/Oxford/Malden, MA: Polity Press, 15–26.

Wertheim, W. F. (1955) 'Changes in Indonesia's Social Stratification', *Pacific Affairs*, 28(1): 41–52.

Wertheim, W. F. (1959) *Indonesian Society in Transition: A Study of Social Change*, The Hague: W. van Hoeve.

Winarta, F. H. (2008) 'No More Discrimination against the Chinese', in L. Suryadinata (ed.) *Ethnic Chinese in Contemporary Indonesia*, Singapore: ISEAS, 57–74.

Wolf, E. R. (1982) *Europe and the People without History*, Berkeley, CA/London: University of California Press.

Yen, C.-H. (1986) *A Social History of the Chinese in Singapore and Malaya 1800–1911*, Singapore: Oxford University Press.

Index

Note: Page numbers in bold refer to tables; those in italic refer to figures and *n* attached to a page number denotes an endnote, with appropriate number.

For Product Safety Concerns and Information please contact our EU representative GPSR@taylorandfrancis.com Taylor & Francis Verlag GmbH, Kaufingerstraße 24, 80331 München, Germany

Batch number: 10726294

Printed by Printforce, the Netherlands